noch 6

CONSUMER CHOICE IN THE AMERICAN ECONOMY

Robert O. Herrmann, Ph.D.
Professor, Department of Agricultural Economics
    and Rural Sociology
The Pennsylvania State University

Published by

HE42   SOUTH-WESTERN PUBLISHING CO.

CINCINNATI   WEST CHICAGO, IL   CARROLLTON, TX   LIVERMORE, CA

Consulting Editor:

Kermeta "Kay" Clayton, Ph.D.
Associate Professor and Chair, Department of Family
    Life Studies and Home Economics Education
University of Southern Mississippi

ISBN: 0-538-32420-1

Library of Congress Catalog Card Number: 86-61341

1 2 3 4 5 6 7 D 3 2 1 0 9 8 7

Printed in the United States of America

FOREWORD

There is widespread agreement that the education of consumers has three major components. Two of these components, the traditional core topics of buying skills and money management, have been part of the consumer education curriculum for decades. In the past decade a new component has been added. This component, consumer citizenship, has to do with the right and the duty of consumers not only to protect their interests and those of other consumers but also to participate in governmental decision-making that affects them. Any program of consumer education which purports to be either comprehensive or contemporary must include all three components. This text, *Consumer Choice in the American Economy,* incorporates all three.

In approaching any unfamiliar discipline, students need to become acquainted with its vocabulary and its basic concepts. With these tools they can begin to master the discipline's fundamental principles. In addition, if students have a framework within which the ideas they are acquiring can be organized, the acquisition of new knowledge becomes easier, as does its application. The concept of evaluative criteria — the characteristics by which products and services can be judged — is used throughout this book. It is essential for thinking clearly about products and services. Students need to learn what criteria are important and why, and how to judge products and services in terms of the appropriate criteria.

The major goal of this text is to provide students with a foundation of vocabulary, concepts, and principles which can serve them in continuing to learn how to function effectively as consumers. With our changing economy and marketplace, there always will be something more to learn. Not only are goods and services changing, the sales techniques and the sellers are changing too. Given a way of thinking systematically about these matters, consumers can analyze and evaluate new circumstances more quickly and effectively.

Education must not only impart knowledge; it must show students how to use the knowledge they have gained. This is particularly important in areas such as consumer economics. Successful application reinforces the learning process and gives students confidence in their ability to use their knowledge and skills in the world outside the classroom. This text works to build student experience and confidence by encouraging them to apply their knowledge in analyzing and evaluating not only marketplace realities but their own behavior as consumers.

The success of consumer education is important not only for individuals and families but for our entire society. Financial stability is so intertwined with family stability that it is sometimes difficult to say what is cause and what is effect.

Consumer education also can contribute to the well-being of our nation. A citizenry that manages its affairs well will have more confidence in itself and its future. Some of the analytical skills citizens must use in managing their own behavior as consumers can be turned to broader purposes. The confidence they gain in managing their personal affairs and in asserting their rights as consumers can give them confidence as citizens. The analytical skills and critical judgment they develop in consumer affairs can serve to protect them from political and social nostrums that are every bit as dangerous as those offered by patent medicine quacks. One of the special features of this text is its emphasis on the analysis of political and social issues affecting consumers. The analytical tools it teaches are not designed solely for consumer controversies. They are, to an important degree, broadly useful citizen skills.

Robert Herrmann, professor of agricultural economics at The Pennsylvania State University, is exceptionally well-qualified to deal with these subjects. He has written extensively on the topics covered and has given attention both to consumer education and consumer behavior—not only to what consumers should do, but to what they actually do.

JOHN W. GARDNER

former Secretary of Health, Education, and Welfare and founder and first chairman of Common Cause

PREFACE

Today's rapidly changing lifestyles and marketplace have created a need for a new kind of consumer economics textbook. It is no longer possible to give students ready-made answers for the problems they will face as consumers. Individual consumers' needs and products and services offered in the marketplace are too varied and quickly changing to make pat answers feasible or useful.

Basic Concepts

While much is new in today's economy, much remains the same. Many basic concepts that served well in the past remain relevant today and will continue to be useful. This text provides basic knowledge from the core areas of consumer economics. In addition to this essential material are new concepts reflecting rapid changes in many fields, including investments, consumer credit, insurance, and taxes.

Analytical and Decision-Making Skills

Along with imparting basic concepts, this text places strong emphasis on the development of analytical and decision-making skills that employ this knowledge. These skills are put into use as the student is asked to make a variety of decisions — individual consumer choices, family and group decisions, and decisions on broad-ranging consumer policy questions.

Identifying Appropriate Evaluative Criteria

A key element in making effective choices is deciding what factors need to be taken into account in a decision. This text indicates the evaluative criteria that are important in particular consumer decisions and how differing weights may be put upon these criteria, depending upon personal values.

Dealing with Varied Consumer Roles

Today's students may find themselves in many different roles in their life careers: young singles, young marrieds, older singles, parents with children, single parents, and older adults living alone. In each role they will have different needs, different resources, different consumer problems, and different money management concerns. This text recognizes this diversity and discusses alternatives that meet differing needs, situations, and resources.

v

Economic and Social Interdependence

Although consumers and sellers need each other, the buyer-seller relationship is, inevitably, one of tension. This text emphasizes that both sellers and consumers have rights and both groups have responsibilities.

The interdependence among consumers is not always well-recognized. The choices of one consumer inevitably affect others. Wasteful consumption choices use up resources and produce pollution, which affects everyone. Careless choices encourage fraud, shoddy products, and exploitative sales techniques. Unthinking use of potentially dangerous products results in injuries that increase insurance costs, again affecting everyone. This text emphasizes that one of the responsibilities of consumers is to each other.

Consumers and Consumer Policy

One of the key responsibilities of consumers is to speak up in behalf of their own interests and those of other consumers. While the specific issues confronting consumers often seem complex and unfamiliar, the basic problems are recurring ones — unsafe products, monopoly power, insufficient information, inadequate redress for problems, and insufficient voice in policy matters affecting consumers. This text focuses on these fundamental consumer problems and on alternative methods of dealing with them.

FEATURES

Consumer Choice in the American Economy begins by setting down a conceptual and analytical base and then demonstrating how these concepts and analytical skills can be used in the familiar problems of purchasing and money management.

Organization of the Text

Part 1 of the text focuses on the knowledge and skills needed to function effectively in the marketplace: effective decision making, evaluation of information, purchasing skills, and remedies for consumer problems. The final chapter in the part considers procedures for analyzing issues that affect consumers.

The second part of the text focuses on purchases of the basic requirements: clothing, food, transportation, shelter, and household equipment. The third part deals with managing personal finances through the use of financial record keeping and budgeting, banking services, credit, and investments. The final part focuses on the use of insurance to manage risk. Auto and household insurance, life insurance, health insurance, social insurance, and employee benefits are considered. The final chapter suggests that an important role of government is to reduce risk, and looks at taxes, government's chief source of revenues.

Supplemental Features

Along with illustrations, figures, and tables, three other types of material supplement the text:

- *Consumer Capsules*—These inserts provide background and how-to information that complements the text. Topics include how to file an insurance claim and how to balance a checking account.
- *Consumer Concerns*—A variety of problems arise out of seller behavior, market performance, and government policies. Others grow out of consumers' own preferences and behavior, as individuals and as groups. Each chapter includes one or more Consumer Concern inserts that examine the origins of consumer problems and possible corrective measures.
- *Consumer Cases*—A number of chapters include real-life cases involving household decision making and violations of consumer protection laws. Each case includes questions to help students identify key elements of the problem.

End-of-Chapter Material

At the end of each chapter are three sections designed to reinforce student learning.

- *Major Chapter Concepts*—To assist students in reviewing key points in each chapter, a list of 12 to 15 key terms and concepts is provided.
- *Consumer Questions*—The questions in this section are designed to help students apply and expand upon what they have learned from the chapter. Included are questions designed to help students recognize which evaluative criteria are most important to them and to employ these criteria in making consumer decisions. Other questions suggest problems for marketplace research and topics for reports.
- *Suggested Readings*—Each chapter also includes a list of 4 to 6 articles and books for additional reading. These titles provide information beyond that included in the chapter and practical how-to information. In addition, there are readings that show the broader social, cultural, and economic implications of chapter material.

Instructor's Manual

In order to assist instructors, the instructor's manual includes the following:

- *Chapter Objectives*—A list of the student goals for each chapter is provided.
- *Answers to Chapter Questions*—Correct answers are provided for the questions raised in each chapter.
- *Test-Bank Questions*—A selection of objective questions designed to test mastery of chapter content is provided.

ACKNOWLEDGMENTS

In years past a major portion of the content of consumer economics texts depended upon the author's personal experiences and research. Today, a far more solid and extensive research base is available. The author is indebted to researchers and educators whose work provides the empirical foundation for *Consumer Choice in the American Economy.*

The author also is deeply indebted to Dr. Kay Clayton of The University of Southern Mississippi, who served as consulting editor. As a result of her suggestions, a number of opaque passages were clarified and gaps in the content were filled.

TO THE STUDENT

Students devote a major portion of their education to preparing for a career. Their future financial well-being depends, however, not only on their ability to make money, but also on their ability to manage it. This book was written to help students become more effective consumers and money managers. The topics considered range from buying clothing, to buying auto insurance, to selecting investments. Despite the diversity of these topics, the analytical skills required are much the same. Once students know the relevant evaluative criteria, the basic concepts involved, and useful sources of information, they are well on their way to making a good decision.

To get the most out of this course, students need to go beyond simply mastering basic concepts and definitions. They need to apply what they learn to the everyday problems and decisions they and their families and friends face as consumers. They also need to consider how they, as individual consumers, relate to the broader national and world economy of which we all, as consumers, are part.

ABOUT THE AUTHOR

Robert O. Herrmann is professor of agricultural economics at The Pennsylvania State University. He previously was a member of the home economics faculty at the University of California, Davis. He received his Ph.D. and Master's degrees from Michigan State University and his Bachelor's degree in economics from the University of Wisconsin.

Over the past 25 years, Dr. Herrmann's research has focused on consumer behavior, consumer education, and the consumer movement. He has published extensively in the *Journal of Consumer Affairs,* the *Journal of Marketing,* the *American Journal of Agricultural Economics,* and the *Journal of the American Dietetic Association.*

Dr. Herrmann is a past president and distinguished fellow of the American Council on Consumer Interests, the national association of consumer educators and researchers. He is a former editor of its *Journal of Consumer Affairs.*

He has served in advisory roles for the U.S. Department of State, the U.S. Department of Agriculture, and the National Research Council. He is a former member of the board of directors of Consumers Union, publisher of *Consumer Reports.* He has also served as a consultant to the Hershey Foods Corporation and the U.S. Office of Consumer Education.

CONTENTS

PART 1

UNDERSTANDING THE MARKETPLACE

CHAPTER 1

TODAY'S CONSUMER

Spending is easy but spending *wisely* is difficult. There has probably never been a time in American history when being a consumer has posed more challenges than it does today. Some of the challenges are familiar ones:

- Deciding what we really need and discovering what product best meets those needs
- Managing our money to best meet present and future needs
- Dealing with problems created by faulty products and misleading advertising claims

Dealing with these challenges always has been difficult, but it has been made extra difficult by the changes occurring in the consumer marketplace, in our economic system, and in American society.

Waves of New Products

Today's consumer is faced with continuing changes in the marketplace, including continuing waves of new and complex products. This newness and complexity make intelligent decisions about these products difficult. A number of new products have been introduced in recent years, including compact-disc players that use laser technology and new applications of computers in automobiles and appliances. More of these types of products are expected in the years to come, including new food and drug products based on applications of biotechnology.

A major incentive to manufacturers for producing new products is the extra profits they provide. In the early years of the life cycle of a new product, innovative producers have the market to themselves. There is little or no competition, and prices and profits are high. As other producers develop similar, or perhaps even better, products, competition increases. Prices fall. It is then time for the manufacturer to look for something new again.

When sellers bring out a new product they hope that it will help them carve out a special niche in the marketplace. They would like their own market segment, one they can have all to themselves. They hope to be able to charge a little extra for what they have to sell because of their special standing with this market segment.

Sellers try to win the loyalty of a distinct segment of the market by meeting that segment's special needs. They may add convenience features; create a unique design; develop a special, handy-to-use package; combine two benefits in one product ("Whiter teeth and a fresher mouth!"); or plan other special features to add value to the product.

While all this change and innovation is exciting, it can also be confusing. Old familiar products and brands disappear, and new ones appear. Not only are the new ones unfamiliar, they often also offer complicated new features that make decision making difficult. Other problems can arise because the complexity of the new product creates the possibility of mistakes in product manufacture and of new safety problems.

Facing these waves of new and unfamiliar products, the consumer is left to decide: Are these things really necessary or useful? How will they perform? Are they fairly priced?

A Changing Retailing Scene

A surge of new stores, new malls, and new, out-of-store retailing outlets is fostering intense competition for customers. Sellers are using a variety of tactics to lure customers: new products, cleverly developed marketing appeals and promotions, and new combinations of services.

The retail market seems to be moving toward one of two extremes. At one end are large stores that put heavy emphasis on competitive pricing. This category includes discounters and stores that feature a succession of sales and promotions. Typically these stores stock large supplies of a limited number of items — the sizes, colors, and styles that sell best. To

Illustration 1-1
Specialty stores secure a place in the market by providing their customers unique merchandise and extra services.

hold down costs, the number of salespeople is kept to a minimum, making product information or advice hard to get. Price-competitive stores vary in their return and refund policies. Some are liberal in allowing returns. Others insist that everything is sold "as is," and all sales are final.

At the opposite end of the retailing continuum is a growing number of specialty stores. These stores specialize in a particular type of clothing, unusual homewares, selected food items, and so on. These boutique-type operations have a limited selection of merchandise chosen to appeal to a particular clientele. Small specialty stores typically charge high prices but often can provide knowledgeable advice and helpful services.

The growth of the large-store retailers and the specialty shops has created a difficult situation for traditional retailers, the department stores and variety stores. Competition for customers is fierce. Sales and promotions leave consumers wondering where the best values are and what combination of product quality, price, and store services is most desirable.

In-store retailers also face challenges from other new forms of retailing. Selling by direct mail from catalogs has been made easier and quicker by credit cards. Purchases from catalogs on computers that can be viewed either at home or in special salesrooms put further pressures on conventional retailers. At the same time, direct in-home selling continues to a be a significant part of the retailing scene. All these changes create exciting, but sometimes unfamiliar, new alternatives for consumers.

Economic Variability

Over a few short years in the 1980s, consumers have seen a shift from double-digit inflation rates to slower rates of price increase. As the United States entered the late 1980s, there began to be signs of an unfamiliar phenomenon — deflation. We had falling agriculture prices, declining oil prices, and low prices for other basic commodities such as minerals and forest products. Whether these declines will be translated into general reductions in consumer prices remains to be seen.

Along with the sharp changes in the inflation rate have come equally sharp changes in interest rates. These changes have affected the availability of credit for car and home purchases and have affected consumers' borrowing costs. Changing interest rates also affected investors' returns and employment opportunities as the home-building industry and business investment in new plants and equipment fluctuated in part in response to borrowing costs.

Changing economic conditions and changing patterns of competition have encouraged some new industries, while others have faded away. These changes have a complex mix of causes — among them, the impact of the business and economic cycle, foreign competition, corporate mergers, and new technology.

Changes in the economy have had their effect on consumers, too. Even small investors have seen some investments collapse in value while others have soared. Stock prices soared in the mid-1980s, but the prices of investment-grade diamonds fell. Opportunities in some old-line occupations have declined while opportunities in others have grown. Assembly-line workers are facing hard times, but opportunities are good for robotics technicians.

Changing Consumer Living Arrangements and Lifestyles

At the same time that these changes have been going on in the retail marketplace and the economy as a whole, there have been other important changes in the lives of consumers. One important change has been in the way consumers live. More and more people live alone. The size of this group has been increased by the growing numbers of young unmarrieds and by divorced and widowed people who live by themselves. Each group faces its own special set of consumer problems, and all face the problem that there is no one else with whom to share consumer chores — buying, managing household finances, and keeping up a household. Members of another growing group, single parents with children, face similar problems plus more. Along with their other problems, many single-parent households face the problem of managing on limited incomes, as do many other one-income households.

In recent years many workers' purchasing power has gone up little, if at all. Income increases in the 1970s and early 1980s seldom kept up with inflation. In the 1980s, though inflation rates have been lower, pay increases have been smaller, too. For many households, increases in purchasing power have been chiefly the result of the wife going to work. While this change has increased spendable income, it has created new pressures on the time available for household management, for child care, and for leisure activities.

Along with being concerned over slowly growing incomes, many workers have had to worry about the security of their jobs. Changing business conditions, corporate mergers, foreign competition, and business relocations all have jeopardized many workers' job security.

Consumers' priorities and lifestyle preferences also have been changing. New emphasis is being given to personal development by individuals who want to realize their fullest potential. They want to be as attractive, healthy, successful, and personable as possible. Linked to these aspirations are a new emphasis on health and well-being. Many people are making an extra effort to eat more nutritiously, exercise more, and adopt other healthful living patterns.

Economic conditions and intense competition for jobs and promotions have made career development a central concern for many. People are working harder to earn more. At the same time, they want to make the most of their earnings by managing better, spending and investing wisely, and limiting tax obligations. While many workers seem more prepared to make sacrifices for job success, others are reluctant to sacrifice family life and personal well-being. Too-long hours, week-end work, and frequent relocations are resisted.

Our discussion suggests that consumers face a variety of concerns and problems arising from a changing marketplace, fluctuating economic conditions, and new lifestyles. Do consumers need help? If so, what kind of help do they need? There are several different perspectives on consumers' needs, as we will see in the next section.

LOOKING AT CONSUMERS

Over the years, several different viewpoints have developed regarding the situation of consumers in the American economic system. Coupled with each of these viewpoints are some distinct ideas concerning what problems consumers have and what should be done about these problems. In the following sections we'll look at three views of consumers: as sovereigns, as dupes, and as information processors.

The Consumer as Sovereign

Some economists and businesspeople are fond of depicting consumers as sovereigns who must be served faithfully by sellers. Some economists in particular are fond of this image, which projects the simplifications of microeconomic theory onto everyday life.

Those who view the consumer as sovereign argue that consumer choices direct the marketplace, determining what will be sold and what will be produced. The assumption is that consumers know what they need and what is available to meet their needs. As a result, making consumer choices is relatively simple. If mistakes in choosing are made, they can be remedied relatively easily with no great cost in either time or money.

This viewpoint is often promoted by people who oppose government regulation. Some see such regulation as unnecessary or too costly. Others feel it interferes with competition and that competition is the best method of correcting problems in the marketplace. Most of those who see the consumer as sovereign agree that some government regulation is needed to protect business competition. Most would favor ensuring that fraudulent claims are controlled so that consumers can have accurate information for making a choice. Additional regulation is not, however, seen as needed because it is felt that consumers will eventually find out which products are effective and reliable, even if not immediately. Their choices will force sellers to provide good quality products at reasonable prices.

Unfortunately, as most people know from experience, this view is oversimplified. Few of us want to learn by trial-and-error which car is best or which doctors are trustworthy. While reliable consumer information is critical, other concerns are important, too. Consumers want safe products, control of abuses by sellers who have more expertise than buyers, and *redress* (the correction of problems) when purchases prove faulty.

The Consumer as Dupe

The views of those who see the consumer as a dupe contrast sharply with those who see the consumer as a fully informed, all-wise sovereign. They see the consumer as someone who is easily deceived—a helpless target of advertising claims and sellers' hyperbole. If a claim is repeated often enough and loudly enough, consumers' resistance will collapse, they believe.

This view is held not only by some business executives who are oversold on the effectiveness of advertising, but also by some whose chief concern is protecting consumers. These consumer protectors seem to see the consumer as totally uninformed about the marketplace and consumer products, incapable of learning much and helpless when things go wrong. Consumers, in their view, need protection not only from unsafe products, but also from inferior ones. In addition, they see consumers as needing assistance in obtaining redress.

While some who view the consumer as a dupe favor more and better information and education, others seem to doubt the effectiveness of that approach. Consumers, they seem to think, are too ignorant or too frivolous to use better information even if it is provided. Besides, they argue, such remedies for consumer problems are often too slow and ineffective.

A third view of consumers has taken shape over the last 30 or 40 years. This viewpoint recognizes that consumers are not always adequately informed, but that they are not stupid either. This view has developed out of the work of consumer behavior researchers in the fields of economics, marketing, home economics, psychology, and sociology.

Those who regard the consumer as an information processor see the consumer as drawing on several sources of information for making decisions. One important source of information is the external environment, including:

- Advertising, other business sources of information, and salespeople
- Media sources such as magazines, newspapers, and television
- Friends and family with relevant experience
- Independent sources of information such as product-testing magazines and government reports

Information is sought out from these sources, and that which is relevant is selected and retained for use. Along with information from the external environment, consumers draw on information from their own experiences.

Information from external and internal sources is reviewed and used in making a decision. In making a decision, individuals draw on decision-making techniques that have been developed through past experience and that may vary in effectiveness. These techniques often rely on one of the following strategies:

- Buy the most expensive brand. It is sure to be the best.
- Buy what is easily and quickly available. Shopping around will not be worth the trouble.
- Buy the brand that rates best on the most important characteristic, such as price, effectiveness, durability, appearance, or perhaps safety.
- Buy the brand that provides the best combination of desired characteristics for the money.

Clearly, some of these strategies are likely to yield better results than others, but each may be appropriate in certain situations.

The information-processor perspective on consumers does not see them as either helpless and ignorant or as all-wise. Consumers, in this view, need correct and relevant information, and they need a decision framework for using this information to make effective choices. They also need reasonable protection from unsafe products and help in obtaining redress.

THE CONSUMER INTEREST

Some people question whether consumers have any special economic interests. "We are all consumers," they point out, "and the interests of consumers are the same as the public interest."

It is important to recognize that consumers are only one of three major elements of our economic system: business firms and investors, workers, and consumers. Each has its separate concerns. No one group can claim that its interests are *the* public interest. The public interest is a fair balance of the different group interests. Sometimes one group will pursue its own interests at the expense of others:

- Consumers as a group may push for lower prices, but it may be possible to lower prices only by underpaying workers or by forcing business investors to accept unreasonably (and uncompetitively) low returns.
- Consumers may urge ceilings on consumer mortgage and loan rates, but ceilings may make loans unappealing to investors, and the supply of consumer credit may dry up.
- Workers may demand unreasonably high wages, thus forcing product prices up, reducing consumers' ability to buy, and reducing business profits.
- Business firms may request controls on imports that compete with their products, but tariffs and reduced supplies may result in higher prices for consumers.

Clearly, consumers, business firms and investors, and workers have different interests and concerns. For the success of our economic system, however, it is important to find some appropriate balance between these three interests — the public interest.

Consumer Rights

The key elements of the consumer interest have been referred to as *consumer rights,* the conditions to which consumers are entitled. The idea of consumer rights was first set forth in a message to Congress from President John F. Kennedy. Other presidents and other groups have proposed additions since that time.

J.F.K. origid uf **The Right to Be Informed.** A critical consumer right is to have the information needed to make an informed choice among alternatives, meaning that sufficient information must be available, it must be correct, and it must be understandable. While a major share of the responsibility for informing consumers falls on manufacturers and sellers, there is a role for others too. Trade associations, including better business bureaus, governmental agencies, and consumer organizations, all have roles to play.

The right to correct information involves protection from misleading information and fraud. Despite the continuing efforts of law enforcement officials, these are chronic problems.

J.F.K. original right **The Right to Safety.** Another critical right is the right to protection from products that are a hazard to life or health. These hazards may arise from the ingredients used, from the way the product works, or from unexpected side effects. When there is a risk of injury from a product, consumers should be given adequate instructions for use and appropriate warnings. When a product involves unreasonable risk of injury, it should be removed from the market.

The Right to a Clean Environment. Consumers have a right to be protected from pollution of the air and the water. According to some, they also have a right to protection from excessive noise. Environmental pollution can be the result of production processes (e.g., factory smoke), by-products from the use or consumption of products (e.g., car exhaust), or the disposal of used items (e.g., solid waste such as empty bottles). Because of the various potential sources of pollution, responsibility for protecting the environment falls on consumers as well as on manufacturers.

J.F.K. original right **The Right to a Choice.** A less well-understood consumer right is the right to a free choice among a variety of products offered by competing sellers at reasonable prices. Free choices cannot be made if the market for a product is controlled by one or a few sellers. Under control by a single seller *(monopoly)* or a few sellers *(oligopoly)*, the supply of products for sale may be limited; prices may be held above competitive levels; or an inferior product may be provided.

Illustration 1-2
Consumers have a right to protection from pollution created by the production and consumption processes and by disposal.

In cases where there is no competition, for example, in the provision of public utilities such as electric power, regulation by government is needed to assure that adequate amounts of products and services are available at reasonable prices and that they are acceptable quality.

The Right to Redress. Not all consumer purchases turn out well. When the problem is the fault of the seller or manufacturer, consumers have a right to fair and prompt action to remedy their problems. The remedy may be repair or replacement of the product or a refund. There also should be fair redress for injuries caused by faulty products and services.

J.F.K. referred to these as the Right to be Heard

The Right to Participate in Government Decision Making. Most lists of consumer rights, including the one offered by President Kennedy, indicate that consumers should have a right to a voice in government decisions affecting them. There are, of course, a wide range of decisions affecting consumers. The Federal Trade Commission, the Food and Drug Administration, and the Consumer Product Safety Commission all have important responsibilities for protecting consumers. The rules and regulations for business activity that these agencies develop and enforce have major impacts on consumers.

Other agencies have responsibilities for protecting consumers that aren't so comprehensive, but their activities have an important impact also. Along with the agencies in the executive branch and the independent regulatory agencies, Congress' decisions on such matters as taxation, education, health and welfare programs, and housing and mass transit subsidies have a major impact on consumers.

Not all the decisions affecting consumers are made at the federal level. State and local governments have important responsibilities for protecting consumers and make significant decisions, too. Consumers need to have a voice in setting program priorities and in suggesting how all these programs will be carried out. They also need a voice in evaluating programs once they are in operation.

Consumer Responsibilities

The list of consumers' rights spells out the elements of the consumer interest in the operation of our economic system, but participants in any system have responsibilities as well as rights. Consumers' responsibilities have not been spelled out in any presidential messages. There is wide agreement, however, that along with their rights, consumers have responsibilities (Stampfl, 1979).

Consumers have a responsibility to help the whole system work better and to act in the interest of other consumers as well as in their own interest. In addition, consumers have a responsibility to help business function more effectively by expressing satisfaction as well as dissatisfaction when appropriate.

The Responsibility to Be Informed. Consumers have a responsibility to seek out and use the best available information to make informed choices. Consumers' purchases are votes, in the form of dollars, for the kinds and quality of products and services they want. If consumers spend carelessly, they can expect the same kind of disappointing outcomes that careless voters can experience: second-rate performance and perhaps dishonesty and fraud.

Consumers also have a responsibility to protect the quality of information available to everyone. When product claims prove to be misleading or seem suspicious, the appropriate authorities should be notified to help protect other consumers from fraud and deception.

The Responsibility to Use Products Safely. Consumers have a responsibility to use commonsense and follow instructions when using potentially dangerous products. As consumers we also have a responsibility to help groups that are particularly at risk. Two groups of people who are especially vulnerable to product-related accidents are children and the aged.

Returning recalled products is part of our responsibility to ourselves and to others. Removal of hazardous products from use permits manufacturers to make needed repairs, provide replacements, or make refunds.

The Responsibility to Protect the Environment. Our right to protection from abuses of the environment carries with it the obligation to protect it ourselves. Our product choices affect the environment both because they involve the use of different resources and because they require different kinds of manufacturing processes. Consumers also have an obligation to use products in a way that will minimize their negative effects. While the actions of individual consumers do not have much effect, their collective actions do. If a few people fail to maintain their car's pollution-control systems or even disconnect them, they will not have much impact on air quality; however, if hundreds and thousands neglect or ignore these obligations, the impact becomes serious.

Consumers' decisions about when and how to dispose of products also affect the environment. The gum wrapper thrown out the car window clearly has a negative impact, even though it is a minor one. Recycling aluminum cans and donating used clothing and furniture to charity so that others may use them help reduce demands on the world's natural resources.

The Responsibility to Encourage Competition. The flip-side of our right to buy in a marketplace free from monopoly or oligopoly power is our duty to encourage competition among sellers. Consumers can encourage competition, as we saw before, by becoming informed about what they buy

Illustration 1-3
When consumers inform sellers of problems they are helping not only themselves but the sellers as well.

and by seeking out the products and services that provide the best value for the money.

The Responsibility to Seek Redress. Consumers who suffer in silence when they have problems with things they have purchased are not being fair to themselves or to the seller. Sellers deserve to be informed when a problem has occurred so that they can correct it. Most firms want to keep customers satisfied and to maintain their patronage.

When consumers let sellers know they are dissatistfied they are not only helping themselves, they are also helping other consumers. Complaints give honest sellers a chance to correct their mistakes and warn dishonest ones that their tactics are not working.

The Responsibility to Participate in Government Decision Making. There are a number of channels consumers can use to influence government decisions that affect them. Often a report of personal experience with a faulty or unsafe product, a misleading ad claim, or another problem has the greatest impact. As reports on a particular problem accumulate, they become evidence that action is needed.

Consumers also may wish to express opinions on laws or regulations that affect them. Consumers' opinions carry more weight when they are based on a careful study of the issues and are directed to the appropriate legislator or federal, state, or local official.

CONSUMER EDUCATION

During a lifetime of work, today's college students can expect to earn well over a million dollars. This substantial cash flow creates the possibility of a comfortable and satisfying lifestyle; however, this possibility will be realized *only* if income is managed wisely and spent carefully. Money cannot buy happiness, but money and careful management can reduce some of the strains that can destroy happiness: unpaid bills, auto accident lawsuits, uninsured medical expenses, an unreliable car, and mismanagement that results in insufficient funds for basic needs.

This book was written to help you achieve your own personal goals as a consumer. (See Figure 1-1.) It provides essential facts about the goods and services consumers buy, about today's marketplace, and about the issues and problems confronting all consumers. As you read the text and work on the suggested projects, you will gain experience in gathering and evaluating information for making effective decisions.

**Figure 1-1
The Three Major Roles
of Today's Consumer**

- *Buyer* — Deciding what we need in a product and making an informed choice among the alternatives available
- *Money manager* — Developing spending goals and preparing a spending plan that directs our income to meet these goals
- *Consumer-citizen* — Becoming informed on issues that affect us as consumers and voicing our opinions through appropriate channels

MAJOR CHAPTER CONCEPTS

1. Consumers have always faced the challenge of deciding among alternatives, managing their money, and obtaining redress for problems. Today these familiar challenges are made more difficult by changes in the marketplace, the economy, and consumer lifestyles.

2. Manufacturers continually introduce new products, seeking extra profits and their own special market segments. These new products often are complex and based on new technologies, making consumer decisions difficult.

3. Retailers seem to be moving toward high-volume, reduced-price selling or toward low-volume, specialty operations. These changes, along with new forms of out-of-store selling, force consumers to rethink the combination of product, price, and services they want.

4. Personal financial planning has become more difficult as economic expectations have fluctuated with changing inflation and interest rates and changing employment opportunities.

5. Many more consumers are living alone or in small households, complicating the sharing of consumer tasks of buying, money management, and household upkeep.

6. For many households, real income increases in recent years have come about only because the wife has gone to work.

7. Consumers are trying to balance a desire for career success with a concern for improved quality of life; that is, realization of their personal potential, good health, physical well-being, and satisying personal relationships.

8. One view of the place of consumers in the American economy is that they are sovereigns whom sellers cannot afford to neglect or ignore. This view holds that consumers are too wise to be deceived for long and that competition among sellers for patronage will solve most marketplace problems.

9. Others see consumers as dupes who know little, are incapable of learning much, and need extensive help. A more contemporary view sees consumers as information processors, drawing information from the external environment and memory to make decisions. They conclude consumers need useful information and some protection.

10. While we are all consumers, the consumer interest is distinct from the public interest. The public interest requires a fair balancing of the concerns of workers, of business and investors, and of consumers.

11. Key elements of the consumer interest include the rights to be informed, to safety, to a clean environment, to a free choice in a marketplace not controlled by sellers, to redress, and to participate in government decision making.

12. Consumers also have an obligation to help the economic system work better. This obligation includes the responsibility to be informed, to use products safely, to protect the environment, to encourage competition, to seek redress, and to participate in government decision making.

13. Today's consumer education includes emphasis on the three roles of consumers: as buyers, money managers, and consumer-citizens.

1. Examine a copy of your local newspaper or of *USA Today*. Identify stories that affect consumers, and list their headlines under the classifications of (a) buymanship, (b) money management, or (c) consumer-citizen. (See Figure 1-1.)
2. What consumer decisions have you made recently as a buyer? A money manager? A consumer-citizen? Where you satisfied with the results? Why or why not? What could have helped you to improve your decision?
3. Have you had any recent problems as a consumer? These problems could include lack of sufficient or accurate information, product safety problems, or redress problems. What did you do about the problem?
4. The problems of concern to consumers change over time. What are some current problems that are causing widespread concern? Check recent issues of consumer-oriented magazines to help you identify significant problems. *Consumer Reports, Changing Times, Money,* and *Sylvia Porter's Personal Finance Magazine* are useful sources.
5. Competition is usually considered to be helpful to consumers. Can you think of forms of competition or competitive tactics that may not benefit consumers or may create problems for them?
6. Some people have argued that the development of special products to meet the needs of only a small segment of the market is wasteful. Do you agree or disagree? Why?
7. Think of a recent major purchase you have made for the first time. How did you decide what to buy? What sources of information did you use? Were these sources of information adequate?

SUGGESTED READINGS

1. Aaker, David A., and George S. Day. *Consumerism: Search for the Consumer Interest.* 4th ed. New York: The Free Press, 1982. This book provides a comprehensive look at consumer problems at different stages of the purchasing process and at government and business responses to these problems.

2. Bloom, Paul N., and Ruth Belk Smith. *The Future of Consumerism.* Lexington, Mass.: Lexington Books, 1986. This is an examination of new issues and trends affecting consumers, including the impact of new technologies, health and safety questions, and the role of government as marketer. The response of business and the use of corporate responsibility programs are examined also.

3. Engel, James F., Roger D. Blackwell, and Paul W. Miniard. *Consumer Behavior.* 5th ed. New York: Dryden Press, 1986. This widely recognized textbook provides an introduction to the consumer as information processor. It examines the use of information in different types of problem solving (pages 21-40). Also included is a useful discussion of the concerns of consumerism and sellers' efforts to deal with these concerns (pages 583-611).

CHAPTER 2

CHOICE
MAKING

Each of us makes dozens of decisions every day — including some consumer choices involving what to buy, what to use, and what to discard. Too often these decisions do not turn out as well as we had hoped. Faulty decision making can lead to several kinds of problems.

- The product you choose turns out to be not worth what you paid for it. The problem here is often a failure to check out the full range of alternatives.
- You spend your money on entertainment when what you really needed is some new clothing. Here the problem seems to be not having your goals clearly in mind.
- You buy a heavy-weight ski sweater when what you really need is a light-weight one you can wear to class. Here the problem is a failure to consider what you need for the specific use you had in mind.

There are many ways people can go wrong in making decisions, but decisions can be improved if you think more clearly about what your goals really are and if you get a clear idea of the alternatives and weigh them carefully. Learning to use these techniques to improve decisions is the focus of this chapter.

FACTORS THAT SHAPE DECISIONS

First, let's look closely at some of the factors that shape decisions:

- *Needs*—Basic human requirements that, if unmet, propel you into action
- *Values*—Criteria that guide the choice of goals and actions as you try to meet your needs
- *Resources*—The assets and abilities you have that determine the alternatives that are open to you

Needs Move You into Action

Basic needs are much the same regardless of a person's race, culture, or geographic location. Over the years, psychologists have developed a number of lists of needs. A list developed by Abraham Maslow is one of the most widely used (Maslow, 1970). Needs Maslow identified are as follows:

1 is most important need

7 is less important

1. *Physiological needs*—Satisfaction of hunger, thirst, need for shelter
2. *Safety needs*—Freedom from fear, security, stability, and order
3. *Belongingness and love needs*—Love of friends and family, affectionate relationships
4. *Esteem needs*—Self-respect and the respect of others
5. *Self-actualization needs*—Satisfaction of the desire for self-fulfillment, realization of one's potential
6. *Desire to know and understand*—Need to learn and satisfy curiosity, acquiring and organizing knowledge, understanding relationships and meanings
7. *Aesthetic needs*—Satisfaction of the desire for beauty, attractive surroundings

Maslow regards his list as a *hierarchy of needs*, with the most pressing needs listed first. He feels that only after these basic needs are met to some minimum extent will you be concerned with satisfying needs that come later on the list. One way to think of the hierarchy is as a pyramid with basic needs at the bottom (Figure 2-1). As you are able, you try to move up the pyramid to satisfy higher level needs. Maslow's hierarchy suggests, for example, that if you are hungry and have difficulty getting enough to eat, you are not likely to worry much about losing your self-esteem or the respect of others by lying, cheating, and stealing to get food.

A particular need comes to your attention when you become aware of a gap between your actual situation and your desired situation. One way this gap can develop is when a product or situation deteriorates: The refrigerator breaks down, the car is wrecked, or the kind of hamburger you used to buy no longer tastes as good as it did. The gap also can occur

Figure 2-1
Maslow's Hierarchy of
Needs

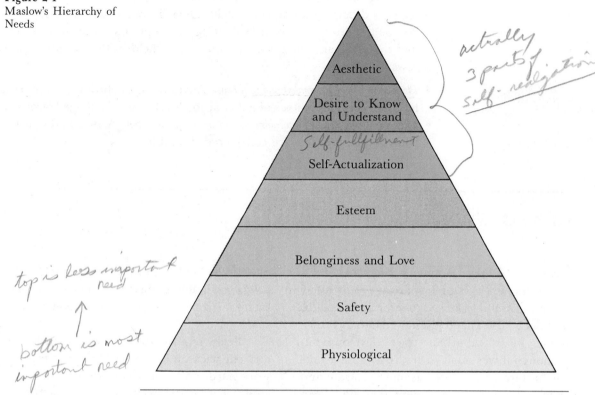

*actually
3 parts of
self-realization*

Aesthetic

Desire to Know
and Understand

Self-fullfillment

Self-Actualization

Esteem

Belonginess and Love

Safety

Physiological

*top is less important
need*

*bottom is most
important need*

when you raise your sights for your desired situation. A new experience can have this result. Once you know your car can get 27 miles to the gallon, you want to do it again. It may also be that new information gives you new expectations and ideas about what is possible. Once you are aware of some new technological breakthrough, it may be hard to regard the old way of doing things quite so favorably.

Values Guide the Way You Meet Your Needs

Even after you become aware of an unmet need, you still have to find some way of satisfying it. _Values_ play an important role in determining the ways you choose to meet your needs. They guide you in selecting a _goal,_ a way of dealing with your unmet needs. Values also guide you in the choice of actions for reaching your goal.

The idea of values is an abstract concept. Values cannot be observed or measured directly in the same way as height and weight. Sociologists and psychologists can, however, make inferences about values by observing an individual's behavior and asking which set of alternative goals or actions are preferred.

There are number of definitions of values; as a result, there are a number of different lists of widely held values. Robin Williams (1967) views values as the criteria used in evaluating different goals and actions. The values that Williams suggests as being widely held in this country are as follows:

- *Physical and material comfort and well-being*. Anything that contributes to physical health or comfort or stock of material goods is likely to be judged favorably.
- *Mastery of the physical environment and one's life situation*. Action and effort to control the situation are considered desirable.

CONSUMER CASE: WHEN VALUES COLLIDE

Tom and Becky Holman's finances are a shambles and so is their marriage. Just a few months ago things looked rosy for Tom, age 25, and Becky, 24. They'd just moved into their own home in a suburban tract development. Although it was small—what real estate agents call "a starter home"—it was more pleasant and spacious than the apartment they had been renting. The Holmans especially liked having a place outside for their one-year-old son, Mark, to play.

The Holmans' marriage has had its ups and downs in the three years they have been married. But Tom was surprised when he came home three weeks ago to find Becky and Mark gone and a note from Becky. Tom admits now that he shouldn't have been surprised. "There were problems. I knew she was upset, but I just didn't pay attention."

Money was one of the Holmans' biggest problems. For the last two years, Tom has been one of the top salespeople at the Oldsmobile dealership where he works. The hours are demanding—fifty- to sixty-hour weeks are common in the big fall and spring seasons. But the pay is good. Tom earned $32,000 a year in base salary last year plus a commission on each car sold.

Becky repeatedly urged Tom to save more and cut back on spending. Tom disagreed. "I work hard, and it just isn't worth it if I can't enjoy what I earn." Becky clearly resented Tom's spending on what she called "Tom's toys," a 30-foot sailboat and an expensive stereo sound and TV system. "When I went out and spent $6,500 on my stereo gear she didn't speak to me for a week," Tom recalls.

Despite Tom's good income and Becky's urging, the Holmans never succeeded in saving much. They had to borrow the $5,000 down payment for their house from their parents. Tom drives a deluxe model Oldsmobile on loan from the dealership, but Becky has had to get along with a 6-year-old car that Tom had taken in as a trade-in at the dealership and bought at a bargain price.

Another focus of disagreement has been Tom's night-owl habits. "I'm a night person," he

- *Conformity to ethical and moral principles.* Choices of behavior and goals are expected to take into account such principles as honesty, fairness, and kindness to others.

Most Americans do not feel that suffering is good for the soul or that you should accept whatever happens as fate. Instead, most of us are convinced that we can and should take action to deal with unmet needs, and we typically are optimistic that our efforts are going to be successful. Most of us consider it unnatural when someone sits back and says that nothing can be done about a bad situation. Most of us are convinced that something

---

says. "I'm all hyped up when I get off work. I really have trouble coming home and just sitting in front of the TV." Instead of staying home, Tom has spent a lot of time at several favorite bars.

Becky resented Tom's night prowlings not only because it left her alone at home with the baby, but also because of what it cost. It wasn't unusual for Tom to spend $20 or $25 in an evening. Tom thought the relaxation was worth the cost. "I don't get much of a thrill sitting home and reading bank books," he says.

Despite these remarks, Tom is embarrassed he and Becky didn't succeed in saving more. In their three years of marriage they accumulated a $500 U.S. Savings Bond (a wedding gift) and $1,000 mutual fund. "I know savings are important to Becky. She wants the security. But we never seemed to have anything left to save," Tom admits.

When Tom looks ahead to the future, he wants his own auto dealership. He realizes he needs more experience but figures that in a few years he will have it and will be able to find a

backer who will help him finance a dealership. "I know I'll need at least $100,000 of my own. But I figure I can find a backer for the rest of what I'll need for seed money."

Tom hopes for a reconciliation with Becky. Becky isn't optimistic that they will ever get together again. "I want a real family life and financial security. I'm not sure Tom will ever settle down. I think he's one of those leopards who can't change their spots," she says wistfully.

QUESTIONS

1. One of the main areas of disagreement between the Holmans seems to have been savings. What values did Tom Holman hold with regard to savings? What values did Becky hold?

2. What importance did Tom Holman put on achievement? What evidence can you cite to support your answer?

3. On what kinds of spending did Tom Holman put high priority? Why did he hold these values? How did Tom' values conflict with Becky's?

more usually can be done (even though there are situations when that is not the case).

Values are reflected in your everyday life. Most of us firmly believe, for example, that we can control our physical environment and that technology and science can provide a solution to our problems. Medical science is expected to provide cures for everyone — if not today, then perhaps next year. Because of our optimism, we are prepared to spend almost unlimited funds seeking new cures. Advertising constantly appeals to these values. If you have a problem — a headache, yellow wax on the kitchen floor, unpleasant breath, or blemished skin — there is a product that is sold to solve it.

Again, values guide you in selecting a goal that satisfies your unmet needs. If you are thirsty, you do not suffer quietly. You look for a solution. Quenching your thirst becomes your goal. Your external environment determines the alternatives that are likely to be available. These alternatives may include water, milk, fruit juice, soft drinks, coffee, tea, wine, and beer.

In evaluating these alternatives a more specific type of values, which we can label *standards,* comes into action. These standards are criteria for evaluating how well a particular alternative will contribute to reaching a goal. Standards include both *evaluative criteria* used in assessing particular goals and *moral and ethical standards* used in evaluating behavior. Moral and ethical standards might lead you to reject some of the beverages available. Your evaluative criteria could help you decide among the other alternatives. In this case, these criteria might include the ability to quench thirst, flavor, calorie content, and cost. Even after all these factors have been taken into account, you still are not in a position to make a decision. You still must take into account the limits your resources place on your decision.

Resources—Limits to Action

Your resources are all the things you can use in reaching a particular goal. These include *physical resources,* such as financial resources and possessions, as well as the community facilities and government services to which you have access. Personal resources also include *human resources,* often referred to as *human capital,* which consist of your knowledge, your time and energy, and your skills and abilities.

Physical Resources. Physical resources are perhaps the most familiar of your resources. You are probably accustomed to thinking about your financial situation, especially when you are making a product choice. Financial resources include not only your cash on hand but also the wages you receive and income from savings and investment. Past savings and the ability to get credit by borrowing against future income are also part of your financial resources. Another type of financial resource is the *transfer payments* from government. These payments are given based on need rather than on the basis of individual efforts. The most familiar type of transfer payment for young people is scholarships but welfare payments and food stamps are also considered transfer payments.

Possessions are also important physical resources. The fact that you have a carton of milk and two bottles of Coke in the refrigerator but no orange juice will probably have a great deal of influence on how you choose to quench your thirst. The tools and equipment you need for sports, hobbies, and home production activities are also important possessions. Availability of these possessions may greatly influence your actions. No matter how much you know about playing tennis, repairing cars, or home sewing, you must have the necessary equipment to put your skills into use.

Community facilities also can help you reach your goals. Public facilities are tax-financed and usually are available free or for a small fee. Schools play a key role in helping people work toward educational and occupational goals. Libraries not only provide assistance in reaching educational and occupational goals, but they also provide information on leisure-time interests and recreational reading. Swimming pools, parks, and playgrounds are resources for achieving recreational goals. Fire and police services help achieve security goals. Privately owned business facilities also make an important contribution to the quality of life and comfort of a community. Life would be dull without theaters, commercial recreation facilities, bookstores, shops, and the whole array of services business provides.

Human Resources. As important as they are, physical resources probably are not as important for reaching goals as human resources. These

Illustration 2-1
One of the substitutions of one resource for another made by consumers is the use of credit instead of cash.

resources, or *human capital,* permit you to use and create new physical resources. An important part of your human capital is your knowledge and your skills. For example, it is the knowledge gained in school that gives you ability to solve math problems and to write business letters. Human capital also includes all the everyday information accumulated over the years: What kind of gas to buy for the car, how to wash jeans, and which local store has the lowest prices on records. Skills such as how to paint a room or repair a broken window can also make an important contribution toward accomplishing goals.

Even a full stock of knowledge and skills is of little help if you are unable to make full use of them. Time and energy are needed to fully utilize human resources. Like other resources, time and energy are limited too. Time spent on a part-time job is not available for studying or for recreation.

In discussing resources so far, we have emphasized how they can widen your opportunities and help you reach your goals. Clearly the more resources you have, the better off you are. Obviously, an absence or lack of resources can seriously limit progress in reaching your goals. Debts, lack of education, poor health, and psychological problems are just a few examples of limited or poor quality resources that may interfere with the pursuit of goals.

The Cost of Resources. Using a portion of a resource to achieve a goal means that it is not available for use in pursuing another goal. Time spent washing the car cannot be used for studying. When you use time or another resource working toward a goal, you lose the opportunity to use it elsewhere. The value of a resource in other possible uses is labeled its *opportunity cost.* The concept of opportunity cost is a reminder that resources are, by their very nature, scarce and that they should be used carefully. Each use of a resource means that other opportunities have been given up.

It is also helpful to recognize that to some extent one resource often can be used as a *substitute* for another. Credit can often be used as a substitute for cash if you are currently short of money. If you lack the skills and time to do auto repairs but have sufficient money, you can pay someone to do the repairs for you. In this case you substitute money for the time and skills you would need to do the repairs yourself.

Often it is necessary to use several resources in combination in achieving a particular goal. For example, you need time, energy, knowledge about automotive operation, and repair skills, as well as tools, to do auto repairs. Economists would say these resources were *complements* because they all must be available and must be used together to produce the desired results. Without tools or without time, the other resources are of little use in making needed repairs.

DECISION MAKING

After you have clearly established your goals and assessed your available resources, a further step is necessary. You must decide which among the identified alternatives will be a priority.

The whole process of decision making undoubtedly is more complicated today than it once was. Most of us have a wider range of goals than our grandparents probably had. We have a greater range of resources as well as more of certain kinds of resources. In addition, we have more alternatives from which to choose. The kinds of clothing, cars, educational opportunities, and recreational possibilities are far wider and more diverse.

The Decision-Making Process

The steps that are most useful in coming to a good decision have not changed over time, however. These steps are the same regardless of whether the decision is a large one or a small one. The amount of time and effort you put into choosing a new raincoat may be greater than the amount of time you put into buying a notebook, but the process is essentially the same. The steps in this process include identifying the goal, identifying the alternatives, gathering information on these alternatives, evaluating them, and making a choice.

Let's use an example to help trace the steps in the decision process. Jerry Fischer is starting his senior year at college and has just gotten an apartment with two friends. He is pleased to have a place of his own, but finds he needs a number of things to equip and furnish it. Jerry has noticed that the light in his bedroom is not very good and after a few days his eyes begin to bother him. Jerry is a serious student and has a strong desire to do well (a need). He also feels that it is important for him to protect his eyes (another need). He concludes that he must obtain an additional source of light (a goal). This judgment is supported by the fact it would contribute to his physical well-being (a value) and would be an action that should resolve his problem (another value).

Identifying a Goal. In solving a problem, it is important first to have your goal clearly defined. This step is sometimes called *goal clarification*. At this stage it is best to think broadly about the problem and the goal that would help you deal with it. After Jerry gave some thought to his problem, he recognized that he did not need better light only at his desk. He also needed a light source so he could read in bed, because he liked to work on his longer reading assignments there. After thinking over his goals, Jerry also realized that he did not necessarily need a lamp. What he needed was what lamps provide—a better light.

Identifying the Alternatives. When setting out to identify the alternative solutions to a problem, you already have some information with which to begin. You have information from your own past experience, information obtained from others, and information gained from seeing what is available in the stores and from contacts with the mass media.

After considering several alternatives, Jerry ended up with two possibilities he wanted to investigate: (1) two lamps—one for his desk and another for his bed—and (2) a single lamp that could be adjusted for reading at his desk or in bed, since they were next to one another.

Gathering Information on the Alternatives. Once you have in mind some alternatives that seem workable, you are ready to begin gathering information. Most of us begin by searching our memories, either consciously or unconsciously, for relevant information. For simple, routine decisions you usually have enough information to proceed without searching for more. In deciding on toothpaste, you seldom seek out all the alternatives and the relevant facts about each. Buying a car or stereo is another matter. For such important and expensive purchases, most people want to go beyond what they already know. Typically they seek new information from friends, magazines, display models, and salespeople.

After thinking a bit more about the alternatives, Jerry recalled seeing lamps that had adjustable arms so that the light could be shifted without moving the lamp itself. Because Jerry's bed and desk were next to one another, he decided to check on lamps with this feature while he was gathering information.

The information you need to gather on the alternatives being considered is of two types. First, you need information about the evaluative criteria or product characteristics important in evaluating a product. In Jerry's case, he had to start by deciding what product characteristics were important to him. Jerry identified the following evaluative criteria that were important to consider in the selection process:

- *Bulb wattage* (size of bulb needed)
- *Amount of area illuminated*
- *Convenience* features (adjustable arm)
- *Styling* (design and color)
- *Construction* (materials used, durability)
- *Price*

The second type of information you need is the rating of each alternative on each of the evaluative criteria used. This rating describes how a particular alternative is measured or scored on a particular characteristic.

When Jerry began to check on what lamps were available in a nearby store, there were three alternatives: a regular table lamp, a gooseneck desk lamp, and a floor lamp. By inspecting the lamps and their labels, he was able to get most of the information he wanted on price, bulb wattage, styl-

Illustration 2-2
Comparing the features of different brands and models is one way consumers can add to their stock of information.

ing, and convenience features. He then turned on the display models to check the size of the area they lighted. Jerry found no specific information of the construction of the lamps and had to judge this on the basis of what he knew. The information he found is summarized in Table 2-1.

4th step

Evaluating the Alternatives. The next step in the decision process is ranking the alternatives. This step helps identify the most promising choices. In selecting the alternative that seems most desirable, you must must answer several questions:

- How do the alternatives compare on the evaluative criteria you are using? In this case, how do the three lamps compare on bulb wattage and the other characteristics? What ratings or scores should each alternative receive on bulb wattage and the other evaluative criteria?
- How important is each of the characteristics? How much weight or importance should each criterion be given? What is most important? Price? Bulb wattage? The area illuminated?

After you rate the alternatives on each of the evaluative criteria and assign a weight to each one, you can combine these ratings and weights into a total score for each alternative. This process is similar to a teacher's calculation of final grades for individual students. Grades (or ratings) on

Table 2-1
Survey of Lamps

Product Characteristic

Product	Bulb Wattage	Area Illuminated	Convenience Features	Styling and Construction	Price
Table lamp	150 watts	Large; 2–3 feet in diameter	No adjustable arm; dimmer switch allows selection of 2 light levels	Contemporary style; black enamel on steel base, white plastic shade	$34.99
Gooseneck desk lamp	60 watts	Small; about 1 foot in diameter	Adjustable arm	Contemporary style; gold painted steel shade and base, brass-plated trim	$18.99
Floor lamp	150 watts	Large; 2–3 feet in diameter	Adjustable arm; dimmer switch allows selection of 2 light levels	Contemporary style; black enamel on steel base, white plastic shade	$49.99

particular evaluation devices (quizzes, exams, and papers) are multiplied by their assigned weights and added together. A total score is the result. Each student is then evaluated on the basis of overall performance as indicated by the total score.

The amount of importance placed on particular product characteristics and the techniques of rating alternatives on these characteristics form the basis of your evaluative criteria. As mentioned earlier, these criteria are used in evaluating products, and they grow out of higher level values. In particular, the amount of importance or weight you put on a particular characteristic is closely linked to your values.

In our example, Jerry began to develop ideas about the relative importance of the different product characteristics while he was shopping. He decided light output was particularly important because that was the basis of his whole problem. He decided that while the amount of area illuminated was important, having an adjustable arm on the lamp was even more important since it would allow him to shift the light to wherever it was needed.

Jerry was not so concerned about styling and construction. He did not feel styling was especially important to him. What he wanted was a good light. While he felt construction was important because it affected durability, he decided he should not put too much emphasis on it because he was not certain exactly how to judge lamps on durability. Price was important too, since he was short on cash, but a little less important than getting a really good light source.

After considering what was important to him, Jerry came up with a set of weights for each of five characteristics he was using in his evaluation. He decided to use numbers between 1 (lowest weight) and 5 (highest weight) to keep the system simple. His weights were as follows:

Evaluative Criterion	Weight
Bulb wattage	5
Area illuminated	2
Convenience features	4
Styling and construction	2
Price	3

Jerry then turned to the problem of rating each of the lamps on the five criteria. He decided to keep his rating system simple, too, and used scores of 1 (lowest) and 5 (highest). The ratings he assigned each of the five evaluative criteria for the three different lamps are set down in Table 2-2.

Once he had decided on the weight of the criteria and each lamp's rating, Jerry was ready to calculate total scores for the three lamps. He made up a worksheet that looked like Table 2-3. On it he multiplied the weights he has assigned a particular characteristic by each lamp's rating. In Table 2-3, you can see that the weight assigned to bulb wattage (4) is multiplied by each lamp's score (5 for table lamp, 1 for the gooseneck lamp, and 5 for the floor lamp). After all the weighted scores are calculated on all five characteristics, they are summed across each row to get the total score for each lamp.

You can see from the total scores that the floor lamp got the highest total score in Jerry's calculations (Table 2-3). After he finished his calculations, Jerry was certain that he needed a flexible lighting arrangement with a high level of light. The floor lamp filled these requirements well, even though it was the most expensive alternative.

Table 2-2
Ratings on Evaluative Criteria

Evaluative Criterion

Product	Bulb Wattage	Area Illuminated	Convenience Features	Styling and Construction	Price
Table lamp	5	5	1	4	3
Gooseneck desk lamp	1	2	4	3	5
Floor lamp	5	5	5	4	2

5th
Step

Making a Choice. After the alternatives have been evaluated, a final choice still must be made. The total scores for each of the altenatives provide a basis for making such a decision. In this case, everything indicated that the floor lamp was the best alternative.

The approach just described to making decisions is called a *decision matrix*. It forces you to break up a complex decision into smaller, related parts. These smaller parts usually are more manageable than the overall decision itself. Some people criticize this approach by charging that it forces people to think about things they have never thought about before, which may be true, but the analysis involved should probably be viewed as an advantage rather than a disadvantage. The decision matrix forces you to think about the product characteristics that are important to you. It also makes you rate alternatives on these characteristics, even if only in a very simple way.

Other Approaches to Decision Making

The decision matrix approach just examined is *multidimensional*; that is, it involves rating the alternatives under consideration on a number of product characteristics (or dimensions) rather than on just one. Traditional economic theory uses a *unidimensional* approach, where alternatives are evaluated on the basis of the total amount of satisfaction (or utility) they are expected to provide.

Another example of the use of a unidimensional approach is the way some people judge a product on the basis of price. They reason, "If it's top-priced, it's sure to be the best."

Table 2-3
Calculation of Weighted Scores (Weights × Ratings) for Evaluative Criteria and Total Scores

Evaluative Criterion

Product	Bulb Wattage	Area Illuminated	Convenience Features	Styling and Construction	Price	Total Score
Table lamp	5 × 5 = 25	2 × 5 = 10	4 × 1 = 4	2 × 4 = 8	3 × 3 = 9	56
Gooseneck desk lamp	5 × 1 = 5	2 × 2 = 4	4 × 4 = 16	2 × 3 = 6	3 × 5 = 15	46
Floor lamp	5 × 5 = 25	2 × 5 = 10	4 × 5 = 20	2 × 4 = 8	3 × 2 = 6	69

Total Score for brand 1 = $W_1 R_{11} + W_2 R_{21} + W_3 R_{31} + W_4 R_{41} + W_5 R_{51}$
where W_i = weight on evaluative criterion i
R_{ij} = rating on evaluative criterion i for brand j

Part 1   Understanding the Marketplace

A multidimensional approach allows you to take several product characteristics into account in making your decision. Consumer behavior research suggests people seldom use more than five to seven evaluative criteria. Apparently dealing with more becomes too complex.

The decision matrix discussed here also has *compensatory* features. If an alternative has a high rating on one characteristic, a low rating on another can be offset. In the final decision, an alternative's good points are weighed against its bad ones. In the lamp example, the floor lamp's high bulb wattage, the wide area illuminated, and its convenient movable arm offset its high price.

Some decision approaches do not attempt to balance an alternative's strengths and weaknesses. They focus strictly on whether an alternative is satisfactory or unsatisfactory on a particular characteristic. Using such *noncompensatory* approaches, the decision maker attempts to search out at least one alternative that meets the minimum standards on all characteristics. Such decision procedures are labeled *satisficing*. The decision maker in these cases is not seeking out the best possible choice, only one that is good enough to be considered acceptable.

An example of satisficing would be the decision rule "Buy any well-known brand that's on sale." In this case two evaluative criteria are used: the familiarity of the brand and the availability of a sale price. Any brand that is not well-known or is not on sale is not acceptable. The decision maker is left to choose among the various brands available if more than one meets both criteria.

From this example of the use of a noncompensatory approach, you can see that a brand with an outstanding reputation that is available at an unusually attractive price would not necessarily be favored over other alternatives. It might end up as only one of a group of alternatives, all of which would be considered equally acceptable. Satisficing can be contrasted with *optimizing* decision procedures. With optimizing, the best available alternative is sought out and chosen.

In sum, the decision matrix used in this chapter is a multidimensional, compensatory decision model. It ranks the alternatives examined and thus permits optimizing.

Types of Decisions

Although researchers who have studied decision making have tended to focus on systematic approaches, they have come to recognize that not all choices are made consciously, nor are they all made systematically. Many choices are governed by custom and social tradition. In most parts of this country it is normally expected that everyone who can possibly afford a car will have one. Few people really consider the possibility of not owning a car, except perhaps residents of very large cities and those with low incomes. Instead, they focus on what kind of a car they should have without ever considering the more basic question of ownership.

Group pressures and behavior patterns also can lead you to a choice without any real decision making. If friends and family smoke, a person may begin to smoke without ever weighing its advantages and disadvantages. If few friends or family members go to college, a person is less likely to give serious consideration to this alternative.

True decisions have been classified into two categories, according to their importance and the amount of deliberation involved.

- *Nonprogrammed decisions* involve establishing new routines or making major new commitments. These often require large amounts of a particular resource. An example is the decision to purchase a new car.
- *Programmed decisions* involve continuing previously established routines or commitments. An example is the decision to make the current month's payment on a car bought on credit.

Decisions also can be classified according to their structural relationships. Major decisions of substantial importance have been called *central decisions*. They often involve a number of related smaller decisions, or *satellite*

CONSUMER CASE: BEN FRANKLIN MAKES A DECISION

In a letter to English clergyman and chemist Joseph Priestley, Franklin described his techniques for making personal decisions:

To get over this (indecision), my way is to divide half a sheet of paper by a line into two columns; writing over the one Pro, and over the other Con. Then, during three or four days consideration, I put down under the different heads short hints of the different motives, that at different times occur to me, for or against the measure. When I have thus got them all together in one view, I endeavor to estimate their respective weights; and where I find two, one on each side, that seem equal, I strike them both out. If I find a reason pro equal to some two reasons con, I strike out the three. If I judge some two reasons con, equal to some three reasons pro, I strike out the five: and thus proceed-

ing I find at length where the balance lies; and if, after a day or two of further consideration nothing new that is of importance occurs on either side, I come to a determination accordingly.

Source: *The Works of Benjamin Franklin,* Vol. V. Edited by Henry Albert Smith. New York: MacMillan Co., 1907, pp. 437-438.

QUESTIONS

1. Did Franklin apply this technique to one alternative at a time or to several alternatives at once?
2. Was Franklin's technique of decision making unidimensional or multidimensional?
3. Did Franklin weigh each "motive" (characteristic) equally or did he give them differing weights?

Part 1   Understanding the Marketplace

decisions, before they can be implemented. For example, the central decision to replace an old car involves satellite decisions about the make and model of the new car, financing for the new car, and whether to trade in the old car or sell it privately.

The alternative chosen in a central decision usually limits the alternatives available for consideration in related satellite decisions. Once you have decided to buy a particular make of car, alternatives for satellite decisions regarding credit terms, body style, engine size, and other equipment become relatively limited. It makes sense to examine the alternatives available for each of these satellite decisions when you are making the central decision. It may be, for example, that the central decision to buy a car involves a choice between the unmanageable alternatives of $280.00 monthly payments on a 24-month loan or $196.00 payments on a 36-month loan. For some people, either amount may be too large and thus mean they should reconsider their choice and think about a cheaper car.

FAMILY DECISION MAKING

Making decisions is often difficult for individuals. Making good decisions requires a clear understanding of your objectives and the alternatives and resources available. It also requires time and effort. The problems of making good decisions can become even more difficult when a group, such as several family members, is involved.

Conflict in Family Decisions

Group decisions necessarily involve differences in viewpoints. As a result of these differences, conflicts over the best course of action often arise. This chapter suggests a number of possible sources of disagreement. To clarify, let's look at some possible disagreements in a family that is making vacation plans.

- *Disagreements about the priority of particular needs*—These disagreements center on how high a priority a particular need should be given relative to other group needs. For example, the husband and children may want to take an expensive trip because they see it as an opportunity for pleasant family interaction and a chance to see new sights. The wife wants instead to build college savings because she puts top priority on family financial security.
- *Disagreements over goals*—These disagreements center on how well a particular choice will meet the group's needs. While father and children agree on a trip to interesting new places, the father favors historic sites because he feels the trip will be educational. The children, however, favor going to an Hawaiian beach because they love to swim.
- *Disagreements on the importance of a particular evaluative criterion*— In these disagreements, conflict arises about how much weight should be put on a particular product characteristic in making a choice. The mother decides

to agree to the idea of a vacation but insists the cost be given a major consideration in making plans. Her attitude reflects the high priority she puts on family financial security. The rest of the family feels, however, that other criteria are more important.

• *Disagreements about how well a particular alternative scores on an evaluative criterion* — In these cases, the disagreement revolves around how an alternative rates on a particular characteristic. The wife feels air travel is too expensive and favors auto travel, which she feels will be more economical. The father calculates the mileage cost for use of the family car and compares it to the cost of an air travel and car rental package deal. When the cost of lodging and meals en route are added in, it becomes clear that the costs of the two alternatives are about the same. This example shows how additional information can help resolve this type of disagreement.

Dealing with Conflicts

To maintain family cohesion and reach shared goals, it is important to control conflicts in family decision making. In general, families rely on persuasion and bargaining to settle their disagreements.

Persuasion. One way disagreements are settled is through persuasion. Efforts to persuade may rely on the exchange of information and logical argument. In conflict situations the information provided may be chosen selectively; that is, information that is favorable to a position may be emphasized and unfavorable information may be withheld. Concealing information may be an effective tactic, but it is not a tactic that inspires trust or goodwill, either in a family or the marketplace.

In some cases, efforts to persuade may rely more on the expertise of one of the parties than on the exchange of information. Arguments may focus on the experience and knowledge of one of the parties: "I know about cars, and I should make the decision about what we buy."

Efforts to persuade can also rely on the authority of one of the parties. Here the emphasis is on status or role: "I'm your father and you'll get the kind of haircut I say." Or the emphasis may be "It's money I earned and I should get first say on how it's spent." Those with limited power may respond to these arguments with an appeal based on affection. In this case, arguments rely on such appeals as "If you really care about how I feel, you'll let me get my hair cut the way I want it."

Bargaining. Conflicts also are frequently settled by trade-offs among family members. Incorporating features that different parties want in a particular purchase may be necessary. For example, in choosing a new car one family member may get to choose the color with the understanding that another gets to choose the sound system. Some bargains are simpler: A purchase of a dozen doughnuts can be split so that each person gets to choose at least two favorite flavors. These compromises usually work well only when a purchase involves a combination of features.

The priority of particular purchases may also be bargained over. A couple may agree that they will get the new car she wants this year and plan the European vacation he wants for next year. This type of solution can be effective, but it may strain family financial resources.

Clarifying. A useful first step in dealing with conflicts is to clarify the situation. What is the basis of the problem? Which one of the four types of disagreements is involved:

- Disagreement about the priority of particular needs?
- Disagreement about goals?
- Disagreement about the importance of a particular evaluative criterion?
- Disagreement about how well a particular alternative rates on an evaluative criterion?

The last type of disagreement can often be resolved with the exchange of information. If the needed facts are available, rating the alternatives on the evaluative criterion is probably the easiest type of conflict to resolve.

The other three types of disagreements grow out of differing individual values. They are likely to be harder to resolve, though discussion of the reasons for individual preferences may help the parties resolve their differences. At least such a discussion will help everyone appreciate the basis for the others' preferences. Conflicts growing out of value differences may have to be solved, however, through persuasive appeals based on expertise, authority, or affection, or through bargaining.

Role Specialization

In most families particular individuals take chief responsibility for a particular job. One person may take care of car maintenance while another does the grocery buying. Sociologists have labeled this allocation of primary responsibility for a particular task *role specialization.* It offers important advantages and time savings. When one person takes responsibility for the car, it means that others are relieved of the burden of keeping track of routine maintenance and arranging for needed repairs. Not only is the job done more efficiently, it is probably done more effectively. The person in charge becomes the household specialist and has the opportunity to become more expert while becoming more experienced.

Like other tasks, decision-making roles tend to become specialized in most families. In traditional societies and in the United States in the past, major financial decisions have been the husband's job or perhaps have been made jointly. Decisions about household operations have been the wife's job. In such families, husbands decide what kind of life insurance to buy and wives decide on the style of furniture.

Illustration 2-3
With role specialization, one family member takes principal responsibility for a task and becomes the household specialist.

This pattern is probably is changing in the United States, though no one is quite sure to what extent. One of the reasons it is difficult to tell is that most of the change seems to be in younger families. Past research has found that younger families make more decisions jointly than do older families, partially because the early years of marriage involve so many important decisions (Deacon & Firebaugh, 1975). Researchers are not sure, however, to what extent today's young adults will allocate decision roles along traditional lines as they get older. Only time will tell.

Single adults who live by themselves as well as single parents face special problems in role specialization because they have to maintain a full-scale household but have no one with whom to share their responsibilities. The single parent is confronted with the problem of finding time to make all household decisions in addition to trying to be an expert on everything from car repairs to the choice of a dentist.

Another advantage of role specialization is that it helps to avoid a problem researchers have observed in group decisions—the *risky shift*. This problem involves the tendency of groups to favor more risky alternatives than would be favored by individuals in the group if they were deciding separately. A possible reason for this shift toward more risky alternatives in group decisions is that responsibility is shared. No one individual must take all the blame if plans do not turn out as expected.

We can see that group decsions may not always be good ones. If responsibility for a decision is shared, it may be made carelessly. A problem of this type may be experienced by a newly wed couple buying a car:

- Husband thinks: "She bought cars on her own before we were married and should be able to judge whether this is a good deal. She seems to think it is."
- Wife thinks: "He knows more about automotive engineering than I do and should be able to decide whether this car will hold up well. He seems to be favorable."

The result may be that the advantages and disadvantages of an alternative never get discussed or examined carefully.

MAJOR CHAPTER CONCEPTS

1. Factors influencing decisions include needs, values, and resources.
2. Unmet needs propel you into action. Needs include physiological needs, safety needs, belongingness and love needs, esteem needs, self-actualization needs, the desire to know and understand, and aesthetic needs. These needs form a hierarchy.
3. Values are the criteria used in evaluating goals and actions. They include physical and material comfort and well-being, mastery of the physical environment and life situation, and conformity to ethical and moral principles.
4. A more specific type of values, standards, guide everyday behavior. These standards include the evaluative criteria used to judge products and services as well as moral and ethical standards.
5. Resources are used to obtain a goal that meets a particular need. These resources include both physical resources and human resources (human capital).
6. Resources are scarce and valuable. You can measure the cost of using them in a particular way by considering their opportunity cost, that is, their value in another use.
7. The decision process includes five steps: identifying a goal, identifying the alternatives, gathering information on the alternatives, evaluating the alternatives, and making a choice.
8. The decision matrix breaks a large decision into smaller parts. It is a multidimensional and compensatory approach to decision making.

9. Decisions can be classified in several ways. Nonprogrammed decisions, in contrast to programmed decisions, involve establishing new routines or making major new commitments and often involve large amounts of resources. Major decisions often consist of a key central decision with many associated, smaller satellite decisions.

10. Group and family decisions frequently may involve conflict because of differing viewpoints, values, or goals. These differences often are resolved through persuasion, bargaining, or clarification. Groups and families can improve the efficiency and quality of decision making through role specialization.

CONSUMER QUESTIONS

1. Each issue of *Money* magazine includes a profile of an individual's or family's finances. A similar article is included in each issue of *Sylvia Porter's Personal Finance Magazine.* After a case is presented, a panel of experts makes suggestions for improving the individual's or family's financial situation. Select a profile that interests you and determine the following: (a) the individual's or family's financial goals; (b) the values that seem to underlie these goals; (c) the plans the subjects have for reaching these goals; (d) the approaches the panel of experts suggest for reaching these goals.

2. List the evaluative criteria that are important to you in an automobile. Assign a weight to each one. Indicate weights of 1 (lowest) to 5 (highest). Explain how these weights reflect your basic values.

3. Study Maslow's hierarchy of needs. For each need, find an ad that suggests the product or service that will meet that need.

4. Suppose you were given an unexpected gift of $1,000. Make a list of what you would do with it. What does your list suggest about your basic values?

5. List your major goals for the next five years.
   a. What does your list suggest about the priority you put on particular needs?
   b. What resources do you have available to use in reaching each of the goals you listed?
   c. How do you plan to obtain the resources you do not have but will need? What substitutions can you make of the resources you have for those you will need?

6. Recall a recent disagreement on a consumer purchase you have had with your roommate, spouse, or parents. What was the topic of disagreement? Which of the four types of disagreements listed in this chapter describes your disagreement? How did you resolve the disagreement?

7. What complex decisions have you made recently?
   a. Identify a central decision and list it along with the satellite decisions it involved.
   b. Was this decision a programmed decision or a nonprogrammed decision? Explain your answer.
8. Think of a major purchase made recently. What was the opportunity cost of your choice? Did you decide not to buy something else or to postpone another purchase?

SUGGESTED READINGS

1. Deacon, Ruth E., and Francile M. Firebaugh. *Home Management: Context and Concepts.* New York: Houghton Mifflin Co., 1975: 105-127. This section gives a comprehensive discussion of the decision process, the types of decisions, and family decision patterns.

2. Maslow, Abraham H. *Motivation and Personality.* 2nd ed. New York: Harper and Row, 1970: 35-38. This section of Maslow's classic work discusses basic and higher level needs and the hierarchy of needs.

3. Vinson, Donald E., Jerome E. Scott, and Lawrence M. Lamont. "The Role of Personal Values in Marketing and Consumer Behavior." *Journal of Marketing* 41, no. 2 (April 1977): 44-50. This article reports research on the link between values and the evaluative criteria used in judging products.

4. Williams, Robin M., Jr. *American Society.* New York: Alfred A. Knopf, Inc., 1964: 397-470. Williams extensively discusses American value orientations (characteristic patterns in making evaluations) and infers a group of more basic values.

5. Wish, John R., Donald G. Steely, and Stephen E. Tritten. *The Consumer: The Art of Buying Wisely.* Englewood Cliffs, N.J.; Prentice-Hall, Inc., 1978: 2-27. This is a useful discussion of the use of a decision matrix for a complex decision involving a large number of product characteristics.

CHAPTER 3

GATHERING
AND EVALUATING
INFORMATION

Every day the American public is subjected to a barrage of information from some 700 television stations, 4,000 radio stations, 9,000 newspapers, and 10,000 magazines and newsletters. Most of the stations and publications include advertising and consumer information as part of their content.

How do we keep from sinking under this bombardment of words? The fact is that we ignore a great deal of it. Subconsciously we screen out most of the information that comes our way and pay attention only to what seems useful and relevant. After we have screened out information that seems irrelevant, we are still left with the challenge of making sense of what we see and hear and using it in making decisions.

When we use information for consumer decisions, we really need two different kinds of information (as we saw in the last chapter). We need to know what evaluative criteria are important in judging a product and how much importance should be given to each one. We also need to know how rate products and services on these criteria — or where to find information about how others have rated them. In this chapter we will look at some of the sources of information available to consumers before they enter the marketplace. In the next chapter, we will look at the information available in the marketplace, such as package labels and advice from store personnel.

We have a wide variety of sources of consumer information. Some, such as relevant personal experiences, are readily available. Other sources may require more effort and have to be sought, but there are certain characteristics we want in information regardless of its source.

EVALUATING
INFORMATION
SOURCES

To be readily usable and reliable, consumer information must have the following characteristics:

- *Objective.* To be reliable, information should be based on observable, measurable evidence rather than personal feelings or opinions. Ratings or judgments based on feelings rather than evidence are said to be *subjective* rather than objective. Scientific tests can provide objective evidence. The judgment of experts and the experience of a group of consumers with a product or service can provide useful subjective evidence.
- *Valid.* Information should be based on evidence that is sound and appropriate. Scientific tests and surveys must be conducted carefully and reported accurately to be valid evidence. Test procedures for a consumer product should simulate the way consumers actually use it.

Illustration 3-1
The most useful information for judging products and services is based on observable, measureable characteristics.

- *Understandable.* Even when information is objective and valid, it may not be readily understandable. Highly technical information is not useful to most of us unless it is interpreted and technical terms are explained.
- *Complete.* Consumer information is most useful when all the relevant evaluative criteria are considered, and all the alternative choices are examined. If some evaluative criteria are omitted and certain brands are not considered, we cannot be confident that we have the full picture. If controversial issues are involved, arguments on both sides should be presented.
- *Up-to-date.* Consumer information is most useful when it is current. New scientific information can change our ideas about the evaluative criteria to use and how important they are. Continuing changes in prices, products, and availability make it important for us to have information on what is currently available, rather than on what was available six months or a year ago.

A variety of information sources is available to consumers. These include consumer-supported product testing organizations, government sources, business sources (including advertising and business-supported sources), and the mass media. In the following sections, we will examine these sources to see what kinds of information each provides and how well it measures up on the characteristics we have identified as important.

CONSUMER-SUPPORTED PRODUCT TESTING

The source of product test information that is most familiar to consumers is *Consumer Reports* magazine, published by Consumers Union. *Consumer Reports* is well known for its test reports on autos, appliances, food products, and other household items as well as for its articles on consumer problems and its stands on issues affecting consumers. Consumers Union (CU) is an independent, not-for-profit organization, supported by the sale of the magazine. *Does not accept advertising*

a source of info that is unbiased or unprejudiced

Consumers Union is an offshoot of the original consumer-supported product-testing organization, Consumers' Research (CR), which was founded in 1929. CU split with CR in 1936 as the result of a labor dispute and has outdistanced CR over the years. By the middle 1980s, CU had a monthly circulation of more than 3 million copies compared to *Consumers' Research Magazine's* monthly circulation of less than 50,000 copies. Because of its small sales, *Consumers' Research Magazine* has only a limited budget and no longer conducts product tests. It does, however, do analyses of products based on information it considers reliable. It also includes news reports of interest to consumers.

Before testing a product, engineers at CU decide which product characteristics are most important. These evaluative criteria include such factors as performance, durability, safety, and convenience. The test engineers

Illustration 3-2
Consumer Reports
magazine is well-known
for its test reports on
automobiles, appliances,
and other consumer
products and services.

then must decide what tests can be used to rate the brands under study on these characteristics. Each brand is then put through standardized sets and rated on its performance.

A brand's rating on each criterion used is multiplied by the weight given the criterion. These values are added up to calculate a total score in much the same way that Jerry Fischer calculated a total score for each of the lamps he was considering in the example in Chapter 2. After the total scores are calculated, brands are ranked on the basis of their overall performance. The procedure of testing and ranking brands is called *comparative testing*. Comparative testing ranks brands in relation to one another rather than evaluating them against some absolute standard.

Product testing works well only when a limited number of brands are available and when their characteristics or specifications are fairly stable over time. If a brand's specifications change frequently, test information goes out-of-date quickly. Information about unbranded products is of little use to consumers because they have no way of identifying similar items without a brand name to guide them.

Testing Procedures   CU uses many standard tests developed for evaluating product performance and materials. Sometimes, however, it is necessary to test characteristics for which there are no recognized test methods. In such cases a special test procedure has to be developed. CU engineers developed one such special technique to test the durability of suitcases. They built a large rotating drum about five feet in diameter that tumbles pieces of luggage in much the same way a clothes dryer tumbles clothes.

Much of CU's testing is done in its own laboratories. CU has elaborate special equipment for testing electronic equipment including an insulated acoustic chamber to test stereo components and a heat chamber to test refrigerators. Some tests are performed in outside laboratories when special equipment or procedures are required. In addition, certain products are subjected to "use" tests. For example, autos are tested by driving them on test tracks and under road conditions. Personal care products, such as shampoos, are typically used by consumer test panels that evaluate them.

To be valid, test results must be based on appropriate tests that have been conducted correctly. It also is important to ensure that the items tested represent the quality typically offered under a particular brand name. Clearly, if manufacturers submitted test samples directly there would be a temptation to prepare them especially carefully. To ensure that its test samples represent the quality of goods actually available in the marketplace, CU uses shoppers located throughout the country to buy samples. The shoppers do not indicate that the item they are purchasing will be used for testing. For some products, only one sample is checked. For others, several may be tested. If test results seem unusual or atypical, the test is usually repeated with a second sample. Brands and models selected for testing are chosen to include those that are leading sellers. Other brands and models of special interest are also sometimes included.

Information Provided

CU does not limit itself to providing product rating reports. Also included in the reports are discussions of the evaluative criteria used in rating a product, along with an explanation of their relative importance. In a report on cassette player/radio systems for cars, for example, *Consumer Reports* rated each brand on nine different performance criteria, including freedom from flutter, frequency response, and dynamic range (*Consumer Reports,* March, 1985). The significance of each of these criteria was explained, and their relative importance was considered. The report indicates that frequency response is the ability to reproduce sounds accurately and notes that it is highly important in determining the quality of an audio system. The report also points out that road noises mask tape hiss, making it a less serious problem for car systems than for home systems.

The test reports also often provide ratings of the brands tested on the individual evaluative criteria used. The brands of car cassette player/radio systems tested by CU were, for example, rated on a five-point scale from best to worst on each of the nine evaluative criteria used.

In developing any kind of overall ratings, it is necessary to put some kind of weight on each of the evaluative criteria considered. Clearly these weights are subjective. How, then, are the weights determined? CU uses weights they feel represent the needs of average consumers. Buyers with special requirements will need to apply their own weights in making a choice.

CU classifies products into three broad categories: Acceptable, Not Acceptable, and Conditionally Acceptable. Products in each category are listed in order of estimated overall quality. Products in the Acceptable category that are clearly superior to other brands tested are "Check-rated." CU does not include price among the evaluative criteria it uses in developing overall ratings. It is, instead, considered and reported separately.

CU's "Best Buy" designation is given to brands that not only rate high in overall quality but also are relatively low-priced. Products occasionally are classified as "Not Acceptable," usually because of safety problems such as electrical shock hazards. The "Conditionally Acceptable" classification is used when a problem exists that can be overcome by special precautions or simple modifications. Consumers Union points out that ratings for a particular brand and model cannot and should not be interpreted as a reliable indication of the quality of other products from the same firm.

Assessing the Impact of Consumer-Supported Product Testing

Since CU is highly conscious of the importance of maintaining its independence from outside influences, it keeps its distance from both business and government. For this reason, *Consumer Reports* does not accept any advertising. In the past it also has tried to prevent use of its test ratings in ads or for other commercial purposes. Overall, the CU organization depends chiefly on the sale of magazines, annual buying guides, and books for income.

Consumer Reports is more heavily used by higher-income, better educated people than by other groups in the population. CU has tried a number of times to provide information to other consumers, but its efforts have never met with much success. Recently, it has been releasing its reports for use on radio and television. This approach may be more successful, because people with less education are heavier users of broadcast media than of print media.

Although *Consumer Reports* is more heavily used by the well educated, its reports have an indirect effect on the rest of the population because of their effect on business practices. Manufacturers are well aware of how their brands rate and sometimes are forced to make needed improvements because of unfavorable publicity about their products.

Manufacturers are also influenced by the effects of ratings on their sales. These effects are especially noticeable for producers of smaller, less well known brands that get wider public attention when they get a favorable rating. The favorable ratings given many foreign compact cars by the two product-testing organizations undoubtedly played an inportant role in increasing their sales during the 1970s. Many consumers probably would not have considered or bought foreign makes without the supporting information provided by *Consumer Reports* and *Consumers' Research Magazine.*

The government is affected by the information the two organizations provide, as well. Test results have sometimes provided evidence of the need for new consumer protection legislation or regulation. CU has actively pushed for improvements in auto safety on the basis of its test results.

LOCAL INFORMATION SYSTEMS

The information provided by Consumers Union falls short of meeting the full range of consumers' information needs. It does not and cannot provide information about the local market for goods and services (Maynes et al., 1977). An information system focused on the local market could provide four kinds of information to consumers:

CONSUMER CONCERN: IS WORLDWIDE CONSUMER PRODUCT TESTING FEASIBLE?

The world has become, in many ways, one marketplace. Electronic equipment, computers, appliances, clothing items, autos, food products, and prescription drugs move out from producing nations to be sold around the globe. The benefits as well as the problems and risks of new technologies are being shared rapidly and widely.

People everywhere have much the same questions about the products they buy. Is separate testing by the consumer product-testing organizations in different countries really necessary? Or is it possible to share the costs and responsibility for testing products sold internationally?

Consumer organizations in different countries have joined together in the International Organization of Consumers Unions (IOCU). IOCU has facilitated sharing of information on test methods and successful consumer programs. There has been, however, relatively little cooperation on joint testing. The most notable examples of cooperation have been joint test programs involving the British Consumers' Association and European testing orgaizations. Consumers Union has been less heavily involved in joint testing, though it did collaborate on tests of 35 mm cameras and Bahamas resorts with the British Consumers' Association some years ago.

International cooperation requires agreement on what evaluative criteria are important and on the appropriate test methods for judging a product on a particular evaluative criterion. Agreement on test methods for electronics equipment is likely to be easiest. Getting agreement on test procedures for food products is likely to be far more difficult, however.

- *Local price information* — Information on the prices charged by local sellers and the range of prices in the market
- *Local availability of products* — Information on local sources of particular brands or services
- *Experience ratings of local service providers* — Summary reports of consumers' ratings of such services as auto and television repair shops
- *Consumer ratings of local retailers* — Summary reports of consumers' evaluation of the services of local retailers, which could include ratings of the quality of personal service, quality of merchandise, and extent of out-of-stock problems

If information on CU's quality ratings could be included in the system, it would be possible to identify the cheapest local source of the brands top-rated by CU.

Not only is there a lack of agreement on how to rate products on particular criteria, there is also a lack of agreement on the weighting of criteria. It seems possible and even likely that the overall ratings of a particular brand could differ between countries. We saw earlier that the weight put on an evaluative criterion depends on culture-linked values. These weights undoubtedly will differ between cultures. For example, the same stove might rate differently in Britain and France. The British rely heavily on the oven for roasting while the French do more stove-top cooking. The British undoubtedly would rate oven performance more heavily than would the French.

Although international cooperation in consumer product testing has been limited, there have been important developments in other areas. Under IOCU sponsorship, an international network has developed for exchanging information on unsafe consumer and drug products that are moving in international commerce. This information has been particularly useful to underdeveloped countries that are able to do little or no testing on their own.

QUESTIONS
1. What are the arguments for international cooperation on consumer product testing?
2. What are the barriers to international cooperation on testing?
3. What kinds of information on consumer products are being widely shared internationally?

One very successful example of a local consumer information system is the operations of Washington Consumers' *Checkbook*. This not-for-profit organization is supported by the sale of its *Checkbook* magazine, which includes major reports on local stores and services. The magazine is supplemented by quarterly newletters. A *Checkbook* organization also operates in the San Francisco Bay area.

The information provided in *Checkbook* and its supplementary newsletters includes the results of surveys of local consumers on their experiences with individual sellers. In addition, information from the files of local consumer agencies, inspections of a firm's past work and its equipment, and reviews of its staff's qualifications are used. In some cases, a firm's performance is checked by giving especially prepared repair problems. In this "blind test" procedure, a piece of equipment with known defects is presented for repair by an apparently ordinary consumer. The accuracy of the repair diagnosis is a check on the repair firm's competence and honesty.

GOVERNMENT AGENCIES

A number of federal government agencies provide consumer information and education materials. These publications range from U.S. Department of Agriculture booklets on food buying to Social Security Administration leaflets on retirement benefits. In addition, the Cooperative Extension Service in each state is an excellent source of materials and information.

Government publications typically identify evaluative criteria and their relative importance. Many also provide information on how to evaluate a product on a particular criterion. Few, however, provide actual ratings of specific products.

Consumer Information Center

Each year the federal government issues hundreds of new publications. Only a few dozen, however, are of interest to most consumers. The Consumer Information Center was created to make available to consumers the government publications that would be of interest to them. The Center is responsible for publicizing and distributing government consumer publications and for encouraging agencies to develop new pamphlets for which there is a need.

The Center publicizes government consumer publications in a catalog issued four times a year. Each issue includes about 250 publications, some of which are free. Others are available for a small charge. The publications included cover such topics as automobiles, housing, health care, and money management. Copies of the current *Consumer Information Catalog* are available free from Consumer Information Center, Pueblo, CO 81009.

Department of Agriculture

The U.S. Department of Agriculture (USDA) publishes pamphlets on a wide variety of subjects. Examples include materials on decision making, buyman-

48   Part 1   Understanding the Marketplace

ship, and product care and use. Topics range from family budgeting to planning nutritious menus; from food buying to selecting shrubbery and landscaping; from removing stains from fabric to selecting life insurance. Buying guides for food focus on key evaluative criteria and their relative importance. They also provide information on how to rate products on particular evaluative criteria. They do not, however, provide ratings of brands or products. The information provided on apple buying is an example of the type of information furnished.

1. The best use of an apple depends on the variety. The familiar Red Delicious apple is good for fresh eating but not for baking.
2. Ripeness affects eating quality. Overripe apples are mealy; one indication of overripeness is skin which yields to pressure.
3. Maturity is related to flavor. Immature apples may lack flavor; immature apples can be identified by their lack of color.

Departmental publications also provide information on the meaning and use of USDA food grades.

USDA also publishes an annual yearbook that provides extensive coverage of a particular topic. Recent volumes have dealt with energy conservation and the food industry.

Cooperative Extension Service

Information and educational programs on family and household management and agricultural topics are provided by the Cooperative Extension Service of each state and the District of Columbia. These efforts are guided by the land-grant universities in each state and are jointly funded by USDA and by individual states and counties.

The Cooperative Extension Service was created initially to improve the welfare of rural families by encouraging agricultural productivity and enhancing the quality of rural family life. It now focuses its efforts on both rural and urban households. As a part of these efforts, extension specialists at land-grant universities have prepared pamphlets on a wide variety of topics. Examples include the following:

- Money Management
  Organizing Family Records (Washington State University)
  Estate Planning for Pennsylvania Families (Pennsylvania State University)
- Buymanship
  A Consumer's Guide to Fabics, Fibers and Finishes (University of California)
  Children and their Clothes — Shopping for Shoes (Iowa State University)
- Home Care and Maintenance
  Better Lighting with Less Energy (North Carolina State University)

- Lawn and Garden Care
  Landscaping the Home Grounds (Utah State University)
- Food Preparation
  Keeping Food Safe to Eat (Michigan State University)

Extension publications focus on good buying practices and money management techniques and discuss evaluative criteria and their relative importance. They do not, however, rate or evaluate brands. A catalog of current state extension publications is available from the Bulletin Room of the College of Agriculture of each land-grant university.

Extension press releases to the mass media also provide useful information on buying skills and money management. These press releases often include information on fresh foods that are currently in plentiful supply and reasonably priced. Others deal with a wide variety of consumer topics, including both buying household goods, such as furniture, and selecting services, such as child care.

Local extension offices are located in the county seat of each county. Extension agents can provide personal help and answers to many consumer questions.

Food and Drug Administration

Protecting the health of the public against impure and unsafe food, drugs, and cosmetics and against unsafe medical devices is the responsibility of the Food and Drug Administration (FDA). The FDA is concerned with educating the public about safe and effective use of prescription and over-the-counter drugs and the hazards of health frauds and quackery.

As part of its education and information efforts, the FDA prepares pamphlets on the treatment of health problems (e.g., *The Common Cold, Insomnia, Back Pain*). Some focus on problems for which ineffective or quack remedies are frequently offered (e.g., *Acne, Arthritis*).

National Highway Traffic Safety Administration

The National Highway Traffic Safety Administration (NHTSA) is the federal government agency responsible for issuing and enforcing regulations on auto safety and fuel economy. As part of its activities it issues a number of booklets on buying practices and on auto operation and maintenance, as well as on such topics as crash protection, tires, brakes, and fuel economy.

The NHTSA booklets dealing with consumer topics discuss the importance of particular evaluative criteria and provide information that can be used in rating auto models and equipment on these criteria. An example is information on the meaning and use of grades for tires. A few NHTSA publications provide ratings of particular auto models on specific criteria. The agency annually issues information on the fuel economy ratings of the different makes available for the new model year. *Gasoline Mileage Guides* are available from the Consumer Information Center, and federal law requires that auto and truck dealers have them available.

Federal Trade Commission

The information and education program of the Federal Trade Commission (FTC) is closely linked to its responsibilities for controlling misleading advertising and other deceptive business practices and for monitoring advertising of credit costs and debt collection practices. The FTC's consumer publications are aimed at educating consumers to avoid problems arising from improper business practices. Some recent publications include *How to Complain and Get Results, Mail Order Rules,* and *Fair Debt Collection.* The information provided by the FTC deals chiefly with evaluating ads and product claims and with purchasing and credit arrangements.

U,S,P,S, (US Postal service) – are responsible for mail fraud,

The FTC provides rating information on only one product—cigarettes. The ratings are only on two evaluative criteria: tar and nicotine content. The FTC tests cigarettes for these two substances to ensure that reliable, standardized information is available. It is included in small print in cigarette ads.

Consumer Product Safety Commission

As part of its efforts to protect consumers from product-related injuries, the Consumer Product Safety Commission (CPSC) produces a variety of booklets and other materials warning about common hazards and describing ways to avoid them. Some recent titles include *Home Fire Safety, What You Should Know About Smoke Detectors,* and *Protect Someone You Love from Burns.*

The materials produced by the CPSC focus chiefly on proper product use to avoid injury. Some, however, also point out safety-related evaluative criteria and provide information about judging products on them. A pamphlet on burn prevention points out, for example, that heavy clothing of tightly woven fabric such as jeans ignites less easily than lighter clothing. It also points out that cotton burns faster and produces a hotter flame than other clothing fabrics. The CPSC does not rate products, but it will move to ban any that it considers excessively dangerous.

MASS MEDIA SOURCES

A wide variety of consumer information is carried in the print media (newspapers and magazines) and to a lesser extent in the broadcast media (television and radio). Media coverage of consumer topics has grown in recent years in response to increasing consumer interest in such topics as wise buying, money management, and consumer issues. This increased interest among consumers seems to be the result of several factors: (1) difficulties in choosing among the wide array of new consumer products available, (2) the need to spend wisely because of economic pressures, and (3) new awareness of consumer problems.

Newspapers

Newspapers traditionally have been an important source of information for consumers, though many newspaper sources are so familiar we may fail to recognize them as consumer information. We do not usually think of newspapers as a source of product and service rating information, but they in fact are. Examples include:

- Reviews of books, movies, and television shows
- Restaurant reviews
- Feature articles discussing travel choices, food, fashion

Because of reader interest some papers have branched into other areas, such as home products, autos, and investments. Many have added more depth and detail to their coverage.

Some of the information carried in newspapers is, however, open to question. Some editors use only material prepared by their own writers and make every effort to ensure that it is reliable. To protect writers against outside influences, some editors forbid their staffs from accepting "freebies"— free meals, free trips, gifts, discounts, or other special treatment.

Newspapers that are concerned about protecting their objectivity also refuse to let advertisers influence the content of their news stories and features. Some papers, however, do not limit gifts and are open to advertiser pressure. A related problem is the practice of using public relations press releases and photos without indicating their source. Readers are allowed to conclude that the material presented was prepared by staff writers when it was, in fact, prepared by a group with a special interest.

Even when newspaper writers are able to maintain their independence, the objectivity of their conclusions must be watched. Newspaper ratings are often given in areas where objective criteria are limited—food, art, drama, literature. It is inevitable that judgments will be highly personal and subjective. There is a validity problem, as well. Should a restaurant be judged on a single meal or a play on the opening night performance? Reports based on a limited sample of a product that can vary over time may be misleading. However, despite the limitations of the consumer information in newspapers, it does have the advantage of usually being understandable and up-to-date.

Magazines

One of the notable changes in the past 20 years in magazine publishing has been the appearance of a wide range of special interest magazines. There are magazines for skiers, golfers, stereo fans, auto buffs, and home owners, to name only a few. An important ingredient in these magazines is information on products and services. As a result, many kinds of specialized consumer information are more readily available than in the past. We may ask, however, just how useful and reliable this information is.

Like newspapers, many magazines work hard to preserve their independence and objectivity. Some, however, provide special coverage of advertisers' products in their editorial columns. The decision to provide this coverage is clearly based more on advertising revenues than on the merits of the product. Magazines also vary in their restrictions on gifts.

In using ratings provided by magazines, you must understand their basis. Magazines do not always provide detailed information on exactly how ratings were developed, which raises questions about their objectivity and validity. Typically magazine ratings are based on personal judgments and limited use tests rather than on comprehensive laboratory testing.

Magazine features can be useful sources of information on the importance of particular evaluative criteria and how to judge them. Their ratings also can be useful if the procedures and evaluative criteria on which they are based are clearly stated. Despite these problems, magazines, like newspapers, do have the advantage of being understandable (some highly specialized magazines may be an exception) and up-to-date.

Three magazines that deal exclusively with consumer topics—*Changing Times, Money,* and *Consumer Digest*—deserve special mention. They include information on consumer buying, money management, and career planning. Typical articles of this type have been "Crooks Are Out to Get Your Credit Cards" and "How Forgiving Is Your Auto Insurance?" Articles usually identify key evaluative criteria and information that can be used in judging alternatives. None of the three magazines conducts any product tests. They do, however, call on their own or outside experts for recommendations. These magazines also provide some coverage of public issues affecting consumers.

A newer magazine, *Sylvia Porter's Personal Finance Magazine,* focuses principally on money management topics: taxes, credit, insurance, investments, house purchase, and career planning. It typically does not provide buyer information or product evaluations.

Indexes of Product Evaluation

It can be difficult to use the consumer information carried in mass-circulation magazines because it can be hard to locate a particular kind of information when you need it. Fortunately, two indexes, *Consumers Index* and the *Magazine Index,* provide a systematic listing of articles evaluating consumer products and services. Article listings are categorized by topics.

Consumers Index covers a wide range of products and services but does not attempt to cover vacations, hobbies, or crafts except for money-saving do-it-yourself projects. Listings by brand name and model describe the type of information provided: descriptive information, results of limited use tests, or results of systematic use tests (e.g., laboratory tests). The articles indexed are drawn from more that 100 leading consumer magazines, including *Better Homes and Gardens, Consumer Reports, Mechanix Illustrated, Motor Trend,* and *Stereo Review.* In addition, new books and pamphlets are also indexed.

The *Magazine Index* provides an index of articles on consumer products, hobby equipment, and computers in more than 400 magazines for a five-year period. The index information is provided on a microfilm installed in its own microfilm reader. The listing information on the film is updated with periodic printed supplements. For each article listed, the index indicates whether evaluative comments are provided. The *Consumer Index* and *Magazine Index* are available in many larger libraries.

Television and Radio

Television and radio provide only limited amounts of consumer information. The most notable contribution of television is in providing how-to-do-it series on such topics as home repair, cooking, and gardening. Television works well for communicating the kinds of skills and manual operations that are important in learning these skills. The how-to-do-it series typically do not pay much attention to consumer questions, but they sometimes do incidentally point out evaluative criteria that should be taken into account.

"Wall Street Week" provides information to investors on the selection of securities and management of their investment portfolios. Service programs on both television and radio sometimes include segments with consumer information such as reports on foods that are in good supply and reasonably priced.

News programs sometimes carry segments on consumer protection topics and issues. Consumer isues that lend themselves to dramatic coverage such as product safety problems seem to get the best coverage. Other, more complex or abstract problems, such as antitrust cases, are likely to be ignored.

BETTER BUSINESS BUREAUS

also know the 3 classification of ads (notes)

Local Better Business Bureaus (BBBs) provide information on the performance of individual retail and service firms in their market areas. They also often can obtain information on firms in other cities that have BBBs.

Information on Local Firms

BBBs do not rate individual firms or tell consumers where to buy. Their reports can, however, be helpful in deciding where not to buy. BBB reports typically include the following types of information:

- The number of years the BBB has maintained files on the firm
- Whether or not the BBB has received complaints about the firm recently and some measure of the number and nature of complaints received
- Whether or not the firm has responded to complaints forwarded by the BBB and what disposition it has made of the complaints

- Recent government actions against the firm, if any
- Information on use of questionable sales practices or misleading advertising statements by the firm

The response to a request for a report on an auto dealer could, for example, include the following:

> This firm has been identified in our files since 1963. In the past three-year period it has been the subject of a large number of complaints. These complaints allege dissatisfaction with auto repair services. In all cases the company has responded to complaints, sometimes providing adjustments or substantiation of their position.

While the report language is a bit complicated, it does seem to indicate that the firm did respond to the complaints forwarded by the BBB (not all do). The report does, however, leave us wondering why the firm had so many complaints and just how satisfied the complainers were, in the end.

BBBs treat complaint cases as closed when a company makes an acceptable response. This response may be that an adjustment such as a reduced bill or additional repair work has been offered to the complainer. Or it may mean that the company has told the BBB that the complaint is not justified, and the BBB has accepted that statement.

BBBs do not follow up to see if consumers who make complaints are satisfied. Therefore, the fact that a BBB regards a case as closed may not constitute valid evidence that the consumer's problems have been solved.

The BBBs do not offer any overall judgments of firms on which they report. Instead, they leave it up to the consumer to make a judgment on the basis of the information provided.

Evaluations of BBB Information

The reports on firms given by a BBB are read in a standard format and often are read quickly. This format, along with their complex language, may make them difficult to understand, especially for people without much education.

The completeness of BBB reports also has been questioned. There is evidence that reports sometimes fail to indicate that complaints have been received and evidence that important government legal actions have been omitted from reports (Munns, 1978). Reports may or may not tell the nature of a complaint.

The objectivity of the BBBs also has been questioned. Critics have suggested that BBBs cannot be completely objective because they are financed by member firms about whom they make reports. Critics also suggest the BBBs are tough on small, nonmember firms but treat large and powerful member firms more gently.

The performance of local BBBs seems to differ a good deal among communities. Some have made outstanding records. Others have been less forceful because of lack of funds or because of fear of the reactions of the business community. BBBs in larger cities often have branches in smaller cities or suburbs nearby. Many smaller cities and town do not, however, have BBBs. In many of these places, local Chambers of Commerce perform functions similar to those of the BBBs. There are more than 170 local BBB organizations in the United States. They are nonprofit and self-governing and operate independently, but they are joined together in the Council of Better Business Bureaus, Inc.

The BBBs also provide pamphlets with consumer information. These pamphlets provide information on evaluative criteria to consider along with information on how to judge individual brands on these criteria. Other pamphlets provide information on warranties, door-to-door sales, frauds, and similar topics. These pamphlets are available through local BBBs. People living in cities and towns that do not have local BBBs may request a list of publications from the national organization: Public Information Division,

Illustration 3-3
Advertising is not only a part of everyday life, it also is part of the cost of almost everything consumers buy.

Council of Better Business Bureaus, Inc., 1515 Wilson Blvd., Arlington, VA 22209. A self-addressed, stamped envelope should be enclosed with any request.

ADVERTISING

In the mid-1980s, American business firms were spending about $80 billion a year to inform and influence consumers. This total amounts to about $350 for every man, woman, and child in the country. As consumers, we are paying for advertising as part of the price of almost every item we buy. Just what are we getting?

A business has several goals when it uses advertising. Making consumers aware of a product and informing them about it is one of these goals. Most consumers probably welcome advertising that makes them aware of new products and provides product information.

Advertisers do not, however, just want to make consumers aware of their product and tell them how their brand rates on key evaluative criteria. Instead, they want to change consumers' opinion of their brand and move them into action to buy it. When advertisers tell consumers about a new evaluative criterion for judging products or about the weight that should be put on a particular criterion, the information they provide is designed to tip consumers' attitudes toward their brand. Most of us do not want to have our attitudes influenced in this way. We say: "Just give me the facts; I'll make up my own mind." The differences in what consumers and business want from advertising have made it the focus of continuing concern and controversy.

Objectivity of Claims

Some researchers who have studied advertising feel that ad claims can be divided into two categories according to whether they are objective or subjective:

- *Objective*. The content of the ad refers to some tangible product characteristic or observable, measurable benefits from using the product. An example is the information that a particular automobile model gets 40 miles per gallon.
- *Subjective*. The ad content refers to a characteristic or a benefit that is not observable or measurable and has no physical reality. An example is the claim that a particular soft drink is "lively" or that a particular shampoo will make your hair feel sexier. There are no widely accepted measures of liveliness for soft drinks, nor are there accepted measures of the sexiness of hair; both are matters of opinion.

A study (Shimp, 1979) that examined a variety of ad claims for objectivity found that a major part were subjective. A total of 293 ads for products ranging from airlines to toothpaste and mouthwash were examined. These ads included 1,450 claims about the characteristics of the product or the benefits of using it. It was found that more than half of these claims focused on opinions or the feelings it would produce in users or their friends (e.g., how it would impress them with the owner's good taste).

There seem to be two reasons why advertisers use subjective claims. Many brands are so similar that there are no objective differences between them. To make their brand seem special and unique, advertisers have to focus on subjective claims. A second reason for the use of subjective claims is that they are not likely to be challenged by regulatory authorities for being untruthful. It can be argued, however, that subjective claims are false because they cannot be fulfilled. No advertiser can provide something that is not actually part of the product.

Validity of Claims

We have seen that a large proportion of the advertising claims made are subjective. Because these claims are not based on observable or measurable evidence, there is no way to devise valid tests to check their accuracy. Objective claims also may have validity problems. Claims that have no valid evidence behind them are, in fact, lies. There are two types of validity problems in advertising:

- *Unsubstantiated claims* — Statements that seem to suggest they are supported by evidence but, in fact, are not. An example is the claim for a pen "sells elsewhere for $12.95, but our price is only $4.95," when the retailer knows nothing about prices in other stores or knows they typically are $5.95. This use of *fictitious pricing* is a widespread deception.
- *Exaggerated claims* — Claims that overstate the attributes of a product or its benefits. These exaggerations are sometimes called *puffery*. Puffery often is regarded as relatively harmless and is frequently ignored by advertising regulators. It is clear, however, that advertisers feel it is effective; and if it is effective, it must mislead consumers (Preston, 1975).

Completeness

Another problem with advertising is that the information provided usually is incomplete. Advertisers typically focus on only one or a few evaluative criteria — ones that are particularly evident in their product. Everything possible is done to make these evaluative criteria seem as important as possible. Other evaluative criteria that may be equally or more important will be ignored.

When it appears likely that essential information may not be provided and that consumers may be deceived without it, its disclosure may be required. Requirements by the FTC and other government agencies that essential facts be provided are called *affirmative disclosure*. Warnings about dangers from the use of products, such as poisonous vapors or shock hazards, are one example. The warning labels on cigarette packages are another example.

Comparative ads that compare several brands on one or more evaluative criteria seem to offer some advantages to consumers. Although the FTC has tried to encourage this type of advertising, advertisers have tended to avoid it. Some feel that mentioning competitors, even unfavorably, helps them. Others dislike taking on competitors so directly and fear lawsuits. In any case, comparative ads are relatively rare. On close examination, those that do appear do not seem particularly useful. Typically only a few brands are compared on a few evaluative criteria.

One characteristic on which advertising cannot be faulted is being up-to-date. However, because much of the information provided by advertising is of limited use, it really does not seem too important whether it is up-to-date or not.

Monitoring Advertising Claims

Many consumers feel they can believe the ad claims because "they wouldn't let them say it if it weren't true." Just who is this vague "they" and just how well do they really protect us? When we begin to look at who is involved in monitoring the truthfulness of ad claims, we find that many different groups are involved—federal, state, and local government as well as business groups and individual firms.

Federal Trade Commission. The FTC plays a leading role in controlling misleading ad claims. Years ago, the FTC relied chiefly on its power to order individual firms to cease and desist from using misleading ads. More recently, it has focused more on getting voluntary cooperation. To outline acceptable procedures and pinpoint the types of claims that are not acceptable, the FTC has issued *trade regulation rules* that apply to entire industries.

The FTC cannot and does not monitor all the ad claims that appear. In some cases when a claim appears suspicious, the FTC will ask the advertiser to supply evidence to prove the validity of the claims as part of its *ad substantiation* program. If the firm cannot provide appropriate evidence, it will be ordered to stop making the claim. A firm also may be ordered, in some cases, to publish *corrective ads* designed to offset the misleading impression created by earlier false claims.

A number of other federal agencies are also involved in monitoring ad claims. The Postal Service monitors claims involving use of the mails, and the Securities Exchange Commission monitors advertising about investments.

State and Local Agencies. The attitudes of local district attorneys and state attorneys general about the importance of policing advertising vary. Many feel they have to give priority to crimes of violence or to other types of crime. As a result, their activities in monitoring misleading advertising differ widely, but most seem to give it relatively low priority.

Self-Regulation by Business. An important part of the policing of ad claims is the result of self-regulation efforts carried on by business-sponsored organizations. Local BBBs can play an important role in monitoring ad claims at the local level. Their influence is, however, limited by their lack of any real enforcement powers and the fact that many communities do not have a local organization. BBBs can ask firms to substantiate their claims but can do little if the firm ignores the request or cannot provide acceptable evidence. At most, they can refer the issue to local law enforcement or consumer protection agencies and expel the firm if it happens to be a member.

The national organization of BBBs, the Council of Better Business Bureaus, handles complaints about advertising at the national level through its National Advertising Division (NAD). If an advertiser cannot satisfactorily substantiate a claim to the NAD and refuses to modify or discontinue it, the problem is referred to the National Advertising Review Board (NARB) for further consideration. The NARB has handled several hundred cases a year in recent years and has had good success in getting compliance from the firms whose ads have been judged negatively.

Trade associations also have played an important role in self-regulation. Many trade groups, such as broadcasters, direct mail, and door-to-door sales firms, have developed codes of good practices to guide their members. Major firms also have developed internal review procedures to ensure that their ads are legally defensible.

PERSONAL EXPERIENCES AND THE EXPERIENCES OF OTHERS

We have talked about a number of sources of information in this chapter, but what about the sources of consumer information that are closest to hand—our own experiences and those of our family and friends? Just how do they rate on the criteria we have used to judge information sources?

Most of us feel we are able to be objective, especially when we are judging such things as products, stores, and services. But there are barriers to objectivity. One such barrier is the tendency to rate things we like high on particular characteristics. This tendency has been labeled the *halo effect*. For example, the halo effect may lead food shoppers to believe a store they like has the best prices.

Is our information and that of our family and friends valid? Do we really know what criteria should be used in judging dentists, for example? Few of us probably have the analytical turn of mind to work out rating procedures for particular goods and services. In addition, few of us have the technical expertise and information to rate goods and services on particular evaluative criteria. Most of us would probably do well to recognize the shaky evidence on which our own preferences and those of others are based. We all have heard people define their judgments by saying, "I'm no expert, but I know what I like." It is important to recognize what this really means: The opinion expressed often has little technical basis.

One of the best things about our own and others' experiences is that they are readily understandable. They are seldom complicated by technical terms or unfamiliar language. The information provided by our own and other people's experiences may, however, suffer from incompleteness. Few people are able to take more than a few evaluative criteria into account in making a judgment. Most of us do not have experience with the full range of brands available or with all the accessible suppliers, but often our experience is limited to one or two. As a result, we are in no position to develop any comparative ratings.

The usefulness of our own experiences and those of others also can be limited by being out-of-date. How useful is a friend's report of an experience with a car bought three years ago in deciding whether to buy this year's model? How relevant is someone's report on an experience with a particular auto repair shop last year to what we are likely to experience there this year?

Overall, our own experiences and those of others may not be quite so useful as they first appear. They may lack objectivity and validity and may be based only on partial or out-of-date information. Unfortunately, poor as they are, personal experiences frequently are the only information available on goods and services in a local market area. For this reason, we may have to use them in making decisions. It is wise, however, to keep their limitations in mind.

IN THE FUTURE: MORE COMPUTER-BASED SYSTEMS?

Information systems that allow users access to computerized data bases have developed rapidly in recent years. A number of kinds of information can be obtained with personal computers equipped with modems that allow phone hook-ups to the data bases. The information that can be accessed includes airline schedules, stock market prices, and business and wire service news. Other systems provide on-line catalog services for brand-name consumer products and on-line hotel and airline reservations. Computerized information services could be used to provide an even wider range of information, including product test information and information on products and services available in local markets.

Information systems have the characteristics of a natural monopoly. The initial investment required for the physical facilities is large, but the cost of serving additional customers is small. The new systems raise several policy questions.

- *Who will have access to the systems?* The costs of access to computer-based systems are relatively high. There are both initial membership fees and user fees, in addition to equipment costs. Historically, public libraries have given all segments of the population access to reading materials. Will there be provisions for low-income people to get similar access to the information in privately operated computer-based systems?
- *Who will regulate the information provided?* If the information is considered news, it will be protected by the First Amendment rights of freedom of speech. If the information is essentially advertising, it will be governed by the rules that apply to other advertising.

The sources of consumer information will continue to change in the coming years. Some are certain to be more useful than others. As consumers use these systems there will be a continuing need to apply the criteria we have discussed to judge them on their reliability and usefulness.

MAJOR CHAPTER CONCEPTS

1. To be reliable and useful, information should be objective, valid, understandable, complete, and up-to-date.
2. Consumers Union (CU), publisher of *Consumer Reports,* is the only consumer-supported product-testing organization. It is an off-shoot of Consumers' Research (CR), which publishes *Consumers' Research Magazine.*
3. Consumers Union engages in comparative testing and ranks brands relative to each other rather than against an absolute standard. Ratings are based on laboratory tests and use tests.
4. Local information systems could serve consumers by providing information on local prices, product availability, and ratings of individual sellers based on consumers' experiences with them.
5. A number of government agencies produce consumer-oriented publications. These publications usually identify important evaluative criteria and, in some cases, provide information on how to judge a product on a particular criterion. Only a few, however, provide actual brand ratings.
6. Newspapers and magazines provide a variety of consumer information including information on judging products and, in many cases, actual evaluations. The bases of these evaluations are not, however, always made clear.
7. Better Business Bureaus can provide reports about the number of consumer complaints against individual firms and the firms' responses to these complaints. BBBs do not rate individual firms or suggest where to buy. They leave the evaluation of the information provided up to the consumer.

8. Current advertising techniques rely heavily on subjective claims about characteristics that are not observable or measurable rather than on objective claims about characteristics that are observable or measurable.

9. Some advertising claims mislead because they are not valid. Their claims are unsubstantiated or exaggerated.

10. Advertising claims are monitored by federal, state, and local government agencies, by business groups, and by individual firms. These groups do not and cannot, however, check all claims.

11. Personal experiences can be an important source of consumer information. We need, however, to judge the information critically, using the same techniques we use to judge other information.

12. Computer-based consumer information systems are in experimental stages. Many questions remain about how they will operate, who will have access to their information, and who will be responsible for the content and accuracy.

CONSUMER QUESTIONS

1. Examine some recent issues of *Consumer Reports* and select a product test report that interests you. What evaluative criteria were used in rating the product? Which ones were given the most weight? What methods were used to test the product? On the basis of the report, which brand do you feel will best meet your own needs? Why?

2. Locate product test reports for the same product (for example, the same or similar makes of automobiles) in *Consumer Reports* and another magazine. Examine the two reports, and use the five characteristics of reliable information to compare them. What tests were used in each report? Do they seem appropriate and valid? Are the reports understandable, complete, and up-to-date?

3. Examine a recent issue of your local newspaper. Prepare a list of the different kinds of consumer information it contains in addition to advertising.

4. Locate an ad for a product in which you are interested. How would you rate it on each of the five characteristics of reliable information? Explain the reasons for your ratings.

5. Compare ads included in a publication aimed at the general public with those in a publication for business people. How do they differ? Which ones seem more informative? Why?

SUGGESTED READINGS

1. *Consumer Reports.* "Advertising in Disguise: How the Hidden Hand of a Corporate Ghostwriter Can Turn a News Report into a Commercial" 51, no. 3 (March 1986): 178-181. This article provides a revealing discussion of the creation of news stories that include plugs for commercial products and the use of these stories on television and in the newspapers.

2. *Consumer Reports.* "Fifty Years Ago" 51, no. 1 (January 1986): 8-10. This article looks at the social and economic forces that led to the idea of consumer-supported product testing. It was written for Consumers Union's fiftieth anniversary.

3. *Consumer Reports.* "Fifty Years Ago: What Happened When Consumerism and Unionism, Two Great Social Movements of the 1930s, Collided?" 51, no. 2 (February 1986): 76-79. This is an historical report on the founding and development of Consumers Union.

4. Preston, Ivan L. *The Great American Blow-Up: Puffery in Advertising and Selling.* Madison: University of Wisconsin Press, 1975. In this look at the use of puffery in advertising and retail selling, Preston asks, "Sellers claim shoppers can recognize puffery and are not mislead by it. If this is true, why do sellers use puffery so frequently?"

5. Silber, Norman Issac. *Test and Protest. The Influence of Consumers Union.* New York: Holmes and Meier, 1983. This book examines the role of Consumers Union as a scientific testing organization and as a voice for the consumer interest. CU's role in studying smoking risks, auto safety, and fallout in food is discussed in detail. Silber argues that over the years CU has shifted from militant activism to put principal emphasis on its role as a scientific organization that can be counted on for accuracy and reliability.

CHAPTER 4

BUYMANSHIP

Consumer decisions were simpler in our great-grandparents' day. Until about a century ago, consumers bought a limited list of relatively simple products from local tradespeople whom they knew well. Country stores stocked only a thousand or so different items — coffee, nails, sugar, and dress fabrics. At most only a few different brands or varieties of each were available.

Today, thousands of different products are available from a whole range of sellers. A typical supermarket offers 10,000 different items, and other retailers offer thousands more. How do we go about selecting what we want from this mountain of alternatives?

Being a wise consumer really involves three different, and important, kinds of decisions:

- Deciding what kind of product best meets our needs
- Deciding which particular brand and model is the best choice
- Deciding where to purchase the brand we have chosen

In Chapters 2 and 3 we began to look at these questions. In this chapter we will look at them in more detail.

We will look first at decisions about the products we need. Next we will look at the types of information we need in order to compare brands. In the final section of the chapter we will look at the considerations we should keep in mind when deciding where to buy.

DECIDING WHAT IS NEEDED

As we saw in Chapter 2, you are moved into action by unmet needs—by gaps between where you are and where you would like to be. For example, you are thirsty, and you want to quench this thirst. You would like to have money to go out this weekend, but you are broke. It is the gap between your desired state and actual state that motivates and spurs you into action.[1]

Determinants of Your Actual State

Gaps between where you would like to be and where you are can come about either from changes in your present situation or from changes in where you would like to be. One of the first steps in dealing with decisions about what you need is finding out what your present situation really is. You can accurately assess your actual state by taking an inventory of what you have on hand. For example, a quick inventory may produce the information that there is nothing cold to drink in the refrigerator. The usual supply of things has run out, and you have an *out-of-stock* problem. Checks of your present situation may, in other cases, produce information that your car will not start, and you have a *breakdown* problem. You may decide that the old jacket you have had for several years looks out-of-date, and you have an *obsolescence* problem.

In this last case, the problem is *psychological obsolescence*—you have decided the style of the jacket is not acceptable any more. Psychological obsolescence is a different problem from having a jacket that is so badly worn it can no longer be repaired (breakdown). Many things become psychologically obsolete long before they wear out. Advertisers, fashion designers, and automobile companies all work hard to convince us the things we own are not the latest or best any more. Creating psychological obsolescence is, in fact, one of the major goals of advertising.

Determinants of Your Desired State

The next step after doing an inventory is determining deficiencies—that is, the size of the gap between the actual and the desired state. To assess deficiencies you need a clear idea of where you would like to be or what you would like your desired state to be. At any particular point in time,

---

1. This section draws on the discussions of the problem recognition process in Carl E. Block and Kenneth J. Roering, *Essentials of Consumer Behavior,* 2d ed. (Hinsdale, Ill.: Dryden Press, 1979), 376-385; and C. Glenn Walters, *Consumer Behavior: Theory and Practice,* rev. ed. (Homewood, Ill.: Richard D. Irwin, 1974), 472-482.

your desired state is the product of a variety of influences both outside and inside yourself. Your ideas about what is appropriate are influenced by your age, gender, family background, religious beliefs, and many other factors. They are also influenced by marketing efforts to create new desires or increase your old ones. Of course, your desired state is also influenced by your own experiences and by the things you gave learned about what you like and enjoy.

New situations may press you into changing your desired states. What you need may change dramatically when you move into your first apartment, get married, or face the arrival of a new baby. In each of these cases, you need things you never needed before. Your actual state has not changed, but your perceived needs have.

Our needs as consumers, in fact, keep changing throughout our lives. Consumer researchers have described these changes in needs at different stages in the *family life cycle*. The family life cycle describes the different stages in the development of the family, beginning with young singles or marriage, continuing through child rearing, and ending with the death of the surviving spouse. These ideas have been adapted to create a *consumer life cycle* that describes the needs, purchases, resources, and consumer problems at different developmental stages from childhood to old age, as well as the consumer knowledge and skills needed to perform successfully at each stage (Stampfl, 1978).

Stampfl notes some typical purchases and services used by young singles:

- First car
- Basic home furnishings
- Home electronic equipment
- Vacations
- Sport equipment
- Education
- Personal care products
- Groceries
- First use of credit

Illustration 4-1
Changes in product design and features are used to make consumers dissatisfied with the things they already own.

In many cases, these items are new additions to the desired state of young singles.

A change in income, up or down, is another factor that can affect your desired state, as can related purchases. If you purchase a new tape player, your ideas about the desired state of your tape collection are certain to be affected.

Setting Priorities for Action

The third and final step in deciding what you need is setting priorities for what you will purchase. Most people have several gaps between what we own and what we would like to have. Because your resources are limited, you have to decide which one of these deficiencies you are going to deal with first. Eliminating certain kinds of deficiencies is usually fairly routine. You make regular trips to the store to keep the kitchen stocked.

Taking care of other deficiencies may take some short-run planning. For instance, it may take a couple of months to accumulate the money for an expensive jacket you want. Other deficiencies may require an even longer planning period. Big purchases such as cars and homes usually require lengthy planning and the use of credit and savings or both.

If your resources are limited, you may never get beyond meeting your most pressing needs; you may never get some of the expensive, but postponable, things you would like to have. You also may miss out if you concentrate on dealing with the deficiencies you can take care of cheaply. You may be well fed and have a good stock of clothes, but you may not be able to buy the car you would like to have.

In thinking about a desired state, your goal is to put together a set of goods and services that will help you create the lifestyle you want. That lifestyle may be simple, or it may be expensive and sophisticated. Either way, it depends in large part on the assortment of goods and services you choose. As your ideas about how you would like to live change, you add to and subtract from this assortment. As some things are used, they are replaced; others may not be if they have proven unnecessary or unsatisfying.

JUDGING BRANDS

After you have decided what you need and established it as a priority, you still are faced with important marketplace decisions about which particular brand you want to purchase. While there are a few consumer products sold unbranded, such as fresh produce and meat, most are labeled with brand names. In fact, some fresh produce and meat products are branded, too. For example, there are Chiquita brand bananas and Dole brand pineapples. Brands are crucial for consumers who are trying to sort through different manufacturers' versions of a particular product.

Brand Name and Label Information

The branding of consumer goods creates both benefits and problems for consumers. Branding helps consumers identify products they have used and liked and ones they would like to buy. At the same time, it allows producers to differentiate their product from others. Branding helps make the product special in consumers' eyes and at least partially insulates it from direct competition with other, similar products. As a result, producers are able to charge extra for their brand.

Consumers who use a favorite brand come to expect that it will provide them the same kind of quality year after year. There is, however, some reason to question brand names as a guide to quality. A look at ratings of particular products in *Consumer Reports* over the years shows that the relative rankings of individual brands often move up and down. Brands that were highly rated one year may not necessarily get top ratings in later years. Clearly, you need to know more about a product than just its brand name.

Types of Brand Names. In using brand names as a guide to product quality you need to be aware that there are three different general kinds of brands:

- *Manufacturers' brands* are usually familiar, heavily advertised names such as Levi's, Ford, and General Electric, which belong to the firm that makes the product. These products usually are labeled "made by ... ."
- *Store brands* (or retailer brands) are products sold only by a particular retailer or chain, such as Sears' brand jeans. These brands may be made by the firm or, more often, made to its specifications by someone else. Store brands can be identified by labels that read "made for..." or "distributed by... ." Store brands often provide good quality at a reasonable price. Lower prices are in part a result of somewhat lower advertising costs.
- *Generic brands* (or no-frill brands) are items that carry no brand name at all. They are most common in grocery stores, where some basic food items, cleaning supplies, and toiletries are offered. While the labels carry no brand name, they do indicate the name of the manufacturer, packer, or distributor. These items usually provide lower quality at a substantial savings. Lower prices are a result of the use of less expensive ingredients, simpler packaging, and savings on advertising and administrative costs. There also are savings on inventory costs because the number of sizes and varieties is limited and sales volume is expected to be high.

Label Information. In addition to brand name, a useful product label should provide:

- Identification of the product by its common or usual name ("weiners," "bologna," "pepperoni," etc.)

- Quantity or size
- Directions for use and care
- Safety warnings about potential hazards in use, storage, or disposal
- Name and address of the manufacturer or distributor

Price and Cost-in-Use

Finding out the price of an item is pretty straightforward; it is easily done by looking at the price or shelf tag. However, you really need to know more than a product's price to make a good choice. For many products you also need to know how much they cost per unit (per ounce, per pound, or per piece). Once you know the package price and the quantity you can calculate unit price. For example, in looking at the prices of two packages of cookies you may find:

19 ounces for $1.79
15 ounces for $1.35

Which package has the lower price, on a per-ounce basis?

$$\frac{\$1.79}{19 \text{ oz.}} = 9.4\text{¢ per ounce}$$

$$\frac{\$1.35}{15 \text{ oz.}} = 9.0\text{¢ per ounce}$$

The answer is sometimes unexpected. The smaller package is cheaper on a per-ounce basis; its unit price is lower.

Although you expect larger package sizes to provide lower unit prices, there is evidence that this is not always the case. Several studies have investigated this problem. One study (Widrick, 1979) checked the prices of 972 brands of grocery products in ten different product categories in major stores in one market area. It found that unit prices were *higher* in the larger packages for about one-third of the brands checked. Surprisingly, the higher costs per unit were most common in stores that provided unit price information to shoppers. Another study of grocery store prices for food, laundry, and personal care products found that larger packages had higher prices for 10 percent of the price comparisons and lower prices in the other 90 percent (Cude & Walker, 1984).

To make the best choice you need to move beyond total price and unit price. You need to know a product's *cost-in-use;* that is, how much it costs per use of per unit of output. You may find a shampoo whose price per ounce is high, but if only a little is required per washing, its cost-in-use may actually be lower than shampoos with lower unit prices. Other examples of cheap products that can turn out to be bad bargains because of high costs-in-use include:

Part 1   Understanding the Marketplace

- Cheap paint that requires two coats, when a more expensive one would do the job with one coat at lower total cost and with less work
- An inexpensive sweater that has to be dry-cleaned frequently and cannot be hand-washed.

Can you think of examples of your own?

Many consumers are convinced that price is a good indicator of product quality. They seem especially likely to rely on price when they are judging an unfamiliar product. These consumers seem convinced of the old saying "you only get what you pay for." Life as a consumer would be a lot simpler if this were always true, but unfortunately it is not.

Several major studies point to the conclusion that price is not a very reliable indicator of product quality. One study compared the brand rankings of 135 different products in *Consumer Reports* (and to a lesser extent *Consumers' Research*) with their price rankings (Sproles, 1977). The 135 products were from five major categories: small appliances, large appliances, sports equipment, tools, and home items. For 51 percent of the 135 products there was a positive relationship between quality rankings and price rankings (i.e., brands with higher quality rankings had higher prices). However, for 35 percent of the products there was no clear relationship between price and quality ranking. For 14 percent of the products studied the relationship apparently was negative (brands with higher quality rankings had lower prices). In evaluating these results, you need to bear in mind that the prices used were list prices, not the prices paid. However, if all the brands in a particular category were discounted by about the same amount, the findings should still hold. Overall, we have to conclude that price is not related to quality often enough to make it a very useful indicator of quality.

A study of the relationship of price and quality rankings for food products suggests the same conclusion (Riesz, 1979). The study examined the relationship of the rankings of forty different food products in *Consumer Reports* tests between 1961 and 1975 and their price rankings. Overall, there was no clear relationship between price and quality ranking.

Another study found that the relationship between price and quality rankings differed with store type (Geistfeld, 1982). The study compared product quality rankings with prices in stores in two Indiana cities. While price and quality rankings were clearly related for appliance and photography stores, the relationship was weak for discount and drug stores. This suggests that price is a better indicator of quality in some types of stores than others.

Overall, the studies of the relationship of price and quality rankings suggest that price cannot be counted on as an indicator of quality. The results also suggest that good quality is not necessarily expensive and that consumers who can recognize quality frequently can make significant savings by checking the alternatives available in the marketplace.

Performance

One key concern in evaluating any product is determining how well it does what it is supposed to do. If you are looking at raincoats, an obvious but crucial question is "How well does it keep off the rain?" One clue to the answer to the question is the material used in making the product. A list of ingredients or materials is required for a number of consumer products: food, drugs, cosmetics, toiletries, and clothing. Ingredients lists can help answer two important questions about the composition of the product:

- Are the materials/ingredients appropriate? Will they do what they are intended to do?
- Are the materials/ingredients of good quality?

Appropriateness and Quality of Materials

The label of a raincoat can tell you which fibers were used. Knowing that the fabric used in a raincoat does not absorb water provides some assurance

---

CONSUMER CONCERN: ARE CENTS-OFF COUPONS AND TRADING STAMPS A GOOD DEAL FOR CONSUMERS?

The use of cents-off coupons has mushroomed in recent years. Manufacturers are using couponing to induce shoppers to try or continue to use their brands. Cents-off coupons offer sizable savings on the purchase price or provide refunds or reductions on the next purchase. The amounts involved can add up to significant totals. Almost every week magazines and newspaper stories report huge savings by devoted coupon clippers.

Not everyone likes coupons, however. Some consumers would prefer to see prices cut and the bother of coupons eliminated. They point out that the use of coupons is expensive and wasteful. When a coupon is used, the manufacturer not only has to reduce the price to consumers, but also has to pay a handling fee to the retailer. Currently retailers are paid eight cents for handling most coupons. In addition, the manufacturer incurs expenses in printing the coupons and processing them when retailers turn them in. Because coupons can be traded for money, they have to be handled carefully all along the line; controls against fraud by both shoppers and retailers are necessary.

Other consumers are concerned because they feel that coupons are not equally accessible to all. They argue that low-income shoppers do not have access to all the newspapers and magazines that carry coupons. The evidence supports this argument, since the major share of coupon-users are middle-income people.

about its ability to keep you dry. (We will talk about the characteristics of different finishes and fibers in more detail in the chapter on clothing.)

A look at a product's label also can provide insights into the quality of the ingredients. You may see, for example, that the leading ingredient in the shampoo you are using is water. Obviously, you have to know something about the appropriateness and quality of different ingredients for label information about them to be very useful in judging performance.

Informative Labeling. Labeling that provides consumers more information on product performance has been urged by consumer advocates over the years. The performance information is referred to as *informative labeling*. Such information can be provided in several different ways. One way is in the form of scores or performance ratings on particular tests. An example of this type of rating is the performance information carried on a light bulb package:

1170 lumens average light output

Having performance information makes comparing different brands quicker and simpler. This information is available for many industrial prod-

In using coupons, shoppers need to bear in mind that they typically are offered by manufacturers of heavily advertised, processed foods. Even at reduced prices these items may not be as good a choice as retailer's brands or generic brands and less heavily processed products.

Defenders of couponing point out that they are a substitute for other forms of promotion and advertising. They argue that, unlike other forms of promotional expenditures, coupons offer clear and immediate benefits to shoppers.

Trading stamps involve some of the same problems for consumers as coupons. They are an alternative form of currency offered by retailers in place of reducing prices. Their big drawback is that they can be spent only at redemption centers and only for selected items. They do, however, offer consumers more direct benefits than other kinds of promotional expenditures by stores.

QUESTIONS
1. Why do manufacturers offer coupons? Why do manufacturers prefer to use them instead of cutting prices?
2. What advantages do coupons offer consumers? What disadvantages?
3. What are the similarities and differences between coupons and trading stamps? Which system has more advantages to consumers?

ucts, but unfortunately it is provided for relatively few consumer products. The usefulness of performance information depends, of course, on the relevance of the information reported and the reliability of the tests used.

Product Standards. The usefulness of performance information is increased if a particular characteristic is measured in the same way by all brands. The need for such measures has given rise to the development of *standards*, agreed-on rules or models against which a product can be judged. The development of a standard requires agreement on both the characteristic to be measured and the measurement technique to be used.

CONSUMER CONCERN: CAN WE MATCH PRODUCT INFORMATION TO INDIVIDUAL CONSUMER PREFERENCES?

Consumers' preferences in consumer information vary as widely as their preferences in other areas. Some like to have large amounts of technical information about the products they plan to buy. Others seem to prefer a smaller quantity of simpler information. Some people, of course, are not really very interested at all. They may prefer to be guided largely by past experiences, their neighbors' choices, or what the store clerk tells them.

Detailed product-testing information of the type carried in *Consumer Reports* seems to appeal to a limited audience. People in this group are well above average in income and education. Most are college graduates, and many have graduate training (Thorelli & Engledow, 1980). They are, for the most part, in managerial and professional occupations. Members of this group are active information seekers and are heavy users of all kinds of print media. Despite repeated efforts, *Consumer Reports* has never had much success in reaching other groups or building up an audience among blue-collar and lower income readers.

Consumers with less education seem to prefer simple types of information in smaller amounts. The range of differences in preferences can be seen in a study of consumer reactions to different types of labels for bread (McCullough & Best, 1980). Respondents from blue-collar families preferred the simplest labels with relatively few items of information. The greater the amount of information provided, the less they liked the label. The other respondents, who were mostly from white-collar families, preferred more complex labels with larger amounts of information. The more information a label provided, the more they liked it.

The differences in consumers' preferences for information seem to arise out of differences in their ability to use information. More educated and experienced consumers seem able to use more information.

Some standards also set minimum acceptable levels of quality that can be specified in two different ways. Probably the most common way is to set *design standards*. Design standards focus on the design and specifications for a product and may also indicate the types of ingredients or manufacturing procedures that must be used. In contrast, instead of focusing on inputs or ingredients, *performance standards* focus on outputs, including nutritional content, strength, and other performance characteristics. If, in buying light bulbs, you accept only brands that on the average produce 800 or more lumens, you would be using a performance standard.

It appears that the needs of consumers would be met best with a variety of types of consumer information. Comparative product testing reports provide a large amount of rather technical information. Understanding this type of information requires both time and some intellectual skill. As a result, it appeals chiefly to more educated consumers. Informative labeling, such as nutritional labels, provides data about a limited number of evaluative criteria. It can help consumers identify key evaluative criteria and can provide information about them quickly and conveniently. This type of information seems well-suited to the needs of the average consumer.

Another approach to providing information about product quality is the use of quality certification, including seals of approval. An example of this approach is the American Dental Association (ADA) seal on fluoride toothpastes. The seal indicates that the ADA has verified the usefulness of flouride toothpaste in preventing tooth decay. Another example is the U.S. Department of Agriculture (USDA) meat inspection seal, which indicates the USDA has verified that the product was processed under sanitary conditions. Quality certification indicates that a product meets minimum standards on one or more evaluative criteria. Although quality certification provides relatively little information, it is easy to understand and convenient. This type of information probably best meets the needs of less well-educated consumers.

QUESTIONS

1. In recent years, consumer protection policy has been to provide more information to consumers. Explain why this policy is not likely to meet the preferences of all consumers.
2. Consumers seem to prefer different types and amounts of information. How can manufacturers deal with these varied preferences?

Some design and performance standards are set by regulation or law and are mandatory. The standards of sanitation for meat-packing plants are an example of mandatory regulations. Others are voluntary. Frequently voluntary standards are the result of agreements by members of industry trade associations.

Grade labeling moves beyond informative labeling and provides an overall performance or quality rating for a particular brand. Grade labels are, perhaps, most familiar for food products, and we all recognize the Choice grade for beef and Grade A for eggs. Grade labels are based on standards of quality that set down the minimum quality level or score a product must have to be given a particular grade.

Durability

Another important concern in judging a brand is how well it stands up in use. How long will it last? How expensive is it to repair? Products that do not stand up well in use create several problems:

- Loss of services of the product, i.e., when a product breaks it cannot perform its basic functions
- Monetary costs of repairs and early replacement
- Time loss and inconvenience of arranging for repairs

Consumers look for ways to protect themselves from this kind of loss. One type of protection is the long-term, comprehensive warranty. The use of extensive warranty coverage is one way that manufacturers can indicate to consumers that their brand is of better quality. The use of warranty provisions (which consumers can observe) to indicate reliability (which consumers cannot observe directly) has been labeled a *market signal* by economists.

There is some evidence that household durables with warranties that provide above-average coverage relative to competing models are, in fact, more reliable (Wiener, 1985). Air conditioners and televisions that *Consumer Reports* judged to provide above average warranty coverage were reported to be more reliable by *Consumer Reports* subscribers than those with below-average warranties. Automobiles with above-average warranty terms also were found to have better reliability records.

The terms *guarantee* and *warranty* can be used interchangeably. Both refer to the written statements given by sellers or manufacturers that set down their obligations to replace or repair a product or to make a refund if the product fails to perform as specified at the time of sale. Warranties are provided with a wide variety of products, but their specific terms differ from brand to brand and manufacturer to manufacturer.

Express Warranties. The familiar written warranty on the side of a package or on a package insert is an *express warranty*. It sets out specific prom-

it can be written or oral

ises about the product. Other promises about a product also become part of a product's express warranty. These include label information ("all wool") and also salespeople's promises. Sellers sometimes use their express warranties to limit their responsibilities to buyers who have problems. The warranty may specify, for example, which specific remedies are available to consumers with problems and what payments for damage will be made.

To make warranty information more readily available and more easily understandable, the FTC has issued several rules concerning warranties for products costing $15 or more. The rules were issued to implement the Magnuson-Moss Warranty-Federal Trade Commission Improvement Act of 1975. The warranty disclosure rules issued by the FTC require that warranties be labeled either a *full warranty* or a *limited warranty.* (See Figure 4-1.) To be designated a full warranty, the warranty provisions must meet several requirements. One is that defects must be corrected in a reasonable time and without charge. The seller must also provide the buyer a replacement or a refund if the original item cannot be repaired after a reasonable number of efforts. Warranties that provide less must be labeled limited warranties.

Regardless of whether the warranty provided is limited or full, the FTC warranty disclosure rules also require that clear, simple language be used to set out warranty terms. Despite efforts to simplify warranties covered by the rules, many are complex and difficult to understand. In fact, many

Figure 4-1
A Sample Warranty. Although the Magnuson-Moss Act of 1975 required the simplification of the language used in warranties, many warranties continue to contain complex language similar to that used in this one.

> ## LIMITED WARRANTY
>
> *North Star Electronics Incorporated* hereby warrants, subject to the conditions hereinbelow set forth, that should this product prove defective by reason of improper workmanship or material during the period of one year from the date of original purchase at retail, *North Star* will repair the same, effecting all necessary parts replacements, without charge for parts or labor.
>
> The unit must be shipped, freight prepaid or delivered to a facility authorized by *North Star* to render services on its products. See the enclosed list for the name of your nearest authorized service facility. Shipment must be effected in the original package or similar package affording an equal degree of protection.
>
> This warranty does not include incidental or consequential damages arising out of product failure, inconvenience or the inability to use the product. Some states do not allow the limitation of consequential damages, so the above limitations or exclusions may not apply in your situation.
>
> This warranty gives you specific legal rights, and you may also have other rights which vary from state to state.

warranties require reading levels beyond the high-school level (Shuptrine & Moore, 1980). The disclosure rule also requires that the warranties include certain key information:

- Whom does the warranty cover? Is it only the original purchaser?
- Who is providing the warranty (name and address)?
- What parts are covered by the warranty and for how long?
- What will the firm providing the warranty do in case of problems covered by the warranty?
- What procedures must the consumer follow in order to get help under the terms of the warranty?

To assist consumers in comparing warranty coverage before they make a purchase, FTC rules require that warranties of products costing $15 or more be made available by sellers for inspection. Stores can meet this requirement by placing them on the outside of the package or on a sign or by providing them on request.

Implied Warranties. Even without a written express warranty, buyers have other types of warranty protection. Manufacturers are responsible for providing a product that works as intended. A tape player, for example, should play and produce sound. When manufacturers offer a product for a particular use, they are guaranteeing its suitability. This type of warranty is called an *implied warranty*. Some firms try to use the express warranty to disclaim some of their responsibilities under the implied warranty. In many cases, however, state laws do not recognize these disclaimers, and manufacturers are still bound by the implied warranty. As a result buyers may still have protection beyond what is indicated in a written guarantee.

Warranty Problems. In some cases sellers try to disclaim responsibility for a product by selling it "as is." Sellers have a responsibility to make such disclaimers fully clear to buyers. Buyers should be aware that a seller's warranty obligations for "as is" items may differ depending on state law.

Disagreements sometimes arise between sellers and consumers over the meaning of "money-back guarantees," "satisfaction guaranteed or your money back," and "free 10-day trial." Under FTC rules, these guarantees should mean just what they say unless special requirements are clearly stated at the time of purchase. A lifetime guarantee for an auto muffler should indicate that the guarantee is for the life of the car, not the buyer's lifetime, if this is what is meant.

Buyers often do not really study product guarantees until they have trouble; therefore, it is important to keep guarantees for reference. Keeping them together in a file folder or file box assures that they can be easily located and checked when necessary. Although many firms provide a registration card with their warranty, consumers are entitled to warranty coverage whether or not they send in the card. Consumers do need evidence of the date of purchase. Either a sales slip or a warranty card can provide this evidence.

Safety

While the federal government tries to control the sale of most products that are unsafe or that involve unreasonable risks of injury, thousands of people are seriously injured every day in accidents involving consumer products, and many are killed. A large proportion of these accidents is the result of the misuse of products (Steeling & Weinstein, 1974). Others, however, are a result of hazards in products usually considered safe, or of product failures and design errors. Table 4-1 lists the relative frequency of accidents associated with different consumer products categories. Some awareness of potential

Table 4-1
Estimated Number of Injuries Associated with Certain Consumer Product Groups: July 1, 1982–June 30, 1983.

Product Group	Number of Injuries*
1. Sports and recreational equipment	3,652,803
2. Home structures and construction materials (e.g., glass doors, stairs, windows)	2,680,065
3. Home furnishings and fixtures	1,336,476
4. Housewares (e.g., cookware, drinking glasses)	712,524
5. Personal use items (e.g., cigarettes, hairdryers, razors)	558,200
6. Home workshops apparatus, tools, and attachments	357,026
7. Packaging and containers for household products	317,325
8. Yard and garden equipment	286,737
9. Miscellaneous (e.g., fireworks, gasoline, business machines)	179,974
10. Space heating, cooling, and ventilating appliances	144,906
11. General household appliances (e.g., irons, kitchen ranges, washers)	142,943
12. Home and family maintenance products	121,223
13. Toys	112,037
14. Home communication, entertainment, and hobby equipment	96,413
15. Child nursery equipment and supplies	88,400

*Estimated from data collected by the Consumer Product Safety Commission's survey of injuries treated in hospital emergency rooms.

Source: U.S. Consumer Product Safety Commission, *1983 Annual Report: 10th Anniversary, Part II* (Washington, D.C.: U.S. Consumer Product Safety Commission, 1984), 5, 7-12.

product hazards is desirable in making brand choices and in using selected items. This knowledge can help consumers protect themselves and others, such as children, who are less aware of product hazards.

Some products carry labels that point out potential hazards. In some cases these warning labels are required by law or regulation. The most useful and effective labels probably are those that provide information about both the hazard and its consequences. An example of this kind of label is the warning on bags of charcoal briquets:

> *Warning: Do not use indoors or without ventilation as fumes may collect and cause death.*

While this label does not spell out all the details about the problem (carbon monoxide), it does make the consequences clear. As a result, it is likely to be more effective than a label that warns only of "dangerous fumes."

Products can be potential hazards for a variety of reasons. Some of the characteristics of products that make them sources of risk include (Thompson, 1974):

- *Energy input and output.* Many products, especially appliances, involve energy inputs and outputs. Many of the inputs are hazardous (gas, electricity, gasoline), and many of the outputs are also dangerous (heat, mechanical power, fumes). Potential dangers from these inputs and outputs need to be controlled.
- *Inadequate insulation or isolation.* Product users need protection from the transfer of energy from products. Insulation reduces the flow of energy such as electricity or heat from one body to another. Isolation removes the product user from the path of an energy flow. An example is a chain guard on a bike, which keeps the rider's clothing out of the chain.
- *Inappropriate materials and construction.* The materials used in making a product should be appropriate for the particular item. For example, flammable materials clearly are inappropriate for children's Halloween costumes. Plastic that shatters into sharp pieces and sharp staples are inappropriate for children's toys.
- *Improper design logic.* Product design should consider potential problems in use or in operation. For example, an auto's brake pedal should be located far enough away from the accelerator that the driver will not stomp on the gas when trying to make a panic stop.
- *Potentially dangerous ingredients.* Manufacturers should, if possible, avoid the use of ingredients that are toxic or may have toxic contaminants. If such materials are used, they should be clearly labeled. They should also avoid use of unsanitary ingredients and should carefully handle those foods in which bacteria can multiply rapidly.

While consumers cannot anticipate all the possible product hazards that may arise, they can be alert for potential problems. They can learn to check for sharp edges and corners and watch for other potential problems such as electrical coffee pots that tip over too easily.

Design Factors

As we saw earlier in the chapter, one of the main reasons that people become dissatisfied with things they own is psychological obsolescence. The items no longer satisfy. They are regarded as out-of-date, out-of-fashion, or perhaps their owners never really liked them in the first place. Discarding things that you no longer like, but which otherwise work satisfactorily, can be expensive. One way you can cut down on this problem is to give more attention to design factors in making your choices.

In evaluating the design of any consumer product, you need to take three factors into consideration:

- How functional is the design?
- How aesthetically pleasing is the design? How attractive is it?
- How well will the product fit in with other things you already have?

In evaluating how functional a design is, you need to look at how easy and convenient it is to use. Are the controls easy to reach and adjust? Are the dials or gauges easy to read? For tools and kitchen equipment, can you see what you are doing when you are using it? Is the item easy to keep clean? Are there crevices and joints to collect dirt?

Evaluating the design aesthetics of a product is a more complex and subjective matter than deciding how functional it is. There are, however, a few key design concepts and principles to use. These principles can be used to evaluate all kinds of design, in consumer products as well as craft work and fine art. Designers manipulate and combine design elements using these principles when creating their designs.

Color. *Color* is a basic design element and can be varied and used in different ways. Colors vary not only in *hue* (e.g., red, orange, yellow, green), but also in *saturation* (dark green to light green) and in *lightness* (gray green to pastel green).

Bright, warm colors (e.g., saturated reds and yellows) are more conspicuous and increase the apparent size of the object in which they are used. They have an active, dynamic feeling. They are particularly popular for use on sports cars and in sports clothing. Darker, cooler colors (e.g., dark blue) are less conspicuous and make a object seem further away. They have a conservative feeling and show up in business suits and limousines.

The combination in which colors are used can also affect the feeling they convey. Sharp contrasts, such as red and white, are dynamic and are popular for team colors and sports clothes. Combinations of related colors such as medium and light blue are less jarring and more relaxing.

Texture. *Texture* provides designers another element. Rough, grainy textures give a weighty solid look and reflect relatively little light. They have an informal feeling. In contrast, smooth textures seem lighter and more formal. They are shiny and reflect more light. Rough and smooth textures not only feel different to the touch; they also convey a very different total feeling. Think how different a wool shirt seems from a cotton one even though they are cut from similar patterns.

Shape. *Shape* is the term used to describe the two-dimensional measure of an object (e.g., circle, square). Designers can use shape to change the psychological effect of an object. Vertical shapes or lines can make it seem taller, stronger, and more dignified. Horizontal lines can make it seem wide and more stable. Diagonal lines, which often are used in sports gear and auto design, convey action and movement.

Form. The three-dimensional measure of an object is called *form* (e.g., cube, sphere, cone). In evaluating an object's form, we often are concerned with its proportions; some combinations of dimensions are more aesthetically pleasing than others.

The four elements of color, texture, shape, and form are key considerations in the design of consumer products. Artists and designers are, however, often also concerned with additional elements such as light, pattern, space, and movement. In manipulating and putting together the elements of design, designers are guided by the goals of appropriateness and variety and unity.

Appropriateness. One factor in considering the appropriateness of a design is whether the design elements used relate well to the item's function. In evaluating the seating in a car you might want to consider:

- Shape. Are the seats comfortable?
- Color. Will the fabric be easy to keep clean?
- Texture. Will the fabric be pleasant to sit on, warm in winter, cool in summer?

Another element of appropriateness is whether the object looks like what it is. A foot stool that looks like a toadstool may seem cute and amusing at first. But over time will it begin to seem too cute and eventually boring? Many designers feel that designs should be appropriate to time, place, and situation. Many would object, for example, to efforts to make a twentieth-floor Manhattan apartment look like a colonial cottage. The same idea applies in clothes. While shorts are acceptable on the tennis court, they are not appropriate for office wear.

Unity and Variety. A second goal in designing is achieving both unity and variety. The elements of a design should combine to make a pleasing whole. At the same time, however, they should provide interesting variety. Too many different colors and textures in a design can be chaotic. On the other hand, if they are too similar, the design will be uninteresting. A bit of the unexpected can make a design more exciting.

Design techniques can contribute to unity or variety. The use of harmony, that is, harmonizing colors and textures, contributes to unity. Contrasting colors and textures create variety. Repetition of colors, textures, lines, and shapes helps unify a design. Movement, or the appearance of movement resulting from slanting lines, diagonals, and wavy lines, provides variety.

The goals of appropriateness and variety and unity are key criteria in evaluating how well something new will fit in with the things you already have. Clearly, it is more aesthetically pleasing to have both variety and unity in your surroundings and in the things you own and use. Too many colors, textures, and shapes can be jarring and make it difficult to relax. Of course, at the same time, few of us really want to live in an all beige world either.

Trade-Offs Among Characteristics

In this section we have looked at a number of desirable product characteristics: economy, performance, durability, safety, and good design. Unfortunately, you may have to sacrifice some of these characteristics in order to obtain others. In order to get good performance and durability in a car, you may have to pay more. In order to increase safety, it may be necessary to add equipment and strengthen the frame. The car will then become more expensive to buy and operate because heavier cars get lower gas mileage.

Which characteristics you will emphasize and which you will sacrifice depend ultimately on your values. If you put a great deal of importance on design and aesthetic factors, you may be willing to sacrifice economy, safety, and durability to get the car whose design appeals to you the most. On the other hand, if your money is tight and you have other interests besides a new car, you are likely to weigh these characteristics in a completely different way.

DECIDING WHERE TO BUY

Even after you have narrowed down your choice to one brand or perhaps a small group of preferred brands, the problem of where to buy remains. Many consumer goods are widely available from different types of retailers. As a result, shoppers are confronted with the problem of deciding on the best combination of brand, store services, and price. The process of collecting and comparing information on the price, brand, and service offerings of different retailers is called *comparison shopping.* Since we have already discussed the problem of comparing brands, this section will focus on problems in comparing services and prices between retailers.

Department and specialty stores traditionally have provided large assortments of the items they carry, with extensive choices of brands, styles, and colors. They have, in addition, emphasized attractive store facilities and services—clerk advice and assistance, delivery, and liberal return policies. To cover the expenses of their large inventories and services, they may charge higher prices than some other types of stores, however.

Discount stores, in contrast, typically do not provide large assortments. They carry only a few brands, colors, and styles, those which have proven to be the best sellers. Discount department and food stores cut expenses by using simpler facilities. Most provide almost no clerk assistance to help shoppers in finding or choosing merchandise. Some have eliminated other services to further reduce costs. Many discount stores do, however, have liberal return policies.

In recent years we have seen a new surge of interest in nonstore retailing, including door-to-door and mail-order sales. One of the major appeals of nonstore retailing is convenience: Shoppers do not have to leave their own homes. Another advantage is that nonstore retailers often can provide access to a more varied or specialized selection of merchandise than can local stores. This variety has particular appeal to the shopper who needs hard-to-find clothing sizes, the hobbyist, and others with special interests that are not well served by the local market. Perhaps because nonstore retailing does not permit easy comparison of prices, nonstore retailers' prices vary a good deal.

Choosing a service provider involves a somewhat different set of problems. Service providers, including professionals such as physicians and attorneys and nonprofessionals such as drycleaners and repair people, often both diagnose the customer's problem and render individualized assistance in resolving it. The choice of service providers is a particularly difficult one for consumers. Key concerns are competence, speed of service, and fair dealing. When something goes wrong it is, unfortunately, often difficult to tell whether the problem is incompetence or dishonesty. Because services are so difficult to compare, prices seem to differ even more widely than those for products.

Prices

Many of the things we buy are offered by the sellers to all prospective customers at a single price. The *one-price policy* developed with the growth of large-scale retailing as increasing store size made it impossible for owner-managers to strike individual bargains with their customers. The prices of some items are still negotiated by bargaining, however. Examples are major durable goods purchases—autos and large appliances. Bargaining also is common in the sale of unique items such as antiques, artwork, and used goods. It also sometimes occurs in the provision of professional services.

Sales Terminology

Retailers have learned the almost magical effect of the word "SALE" on shoppers. If shoppers are unfamiliar with the prevailing prices for an item, they easily can be misled into thinking they are getting a bargain by retailers' claims. Abuse of the term has led some municipalities to pass local ordinances about how and when such terms as "sale" and "clearance" may be used. In an attempt to encourage standard terminology, the Retail Merchants Association has suggested the following use of terms to its members.

- *Sale* should be used when articles are offered at a reduction from the advertiser's own price or from local prices for identical or comparable merchandise. Ads should make clear which basis for comparison is being used. When the term "regularly" or "regular price" is used, it is understood that the merchandise will return to the regular price after the sale period. For merchandise that will not be marked up again after the sale, the terms "formerly" or "originally" should be used.
- *Clearance* or *clearance sale* should be used for sales to clear out leftover items. Prices should be reduced from the previous or original prices. When price comparisons are made, the previous or original price should be indicated. The term "regularly" should not be used because unsold items will not be returned to their previous price, but will be marked down until they sell.
- *Special purchase* or *close-out* is properly used to refer to merchandise purchased from the manufacturer on unusually favorable terms. This merchandise should be offered at prices below those which shoppers would ordinarily expect to pay.

Deceptive Pricing. Deceptive claims about sale prices often confuse shoppers about the fair price of an item. Shoppers can also be confused by the use of inflated claims about list prices or the prices of the same or comparable items elsewhere in the market. The use of such *fictitious prices* can make a discounter's offers appear more attractive than they really are. The use of price comparisons is considered deceptive by the FTC unless a substantial amount of sales actually has occurred at the comparison prices. The use of fictitious comparison prices still, however, appears to be widespread, particularly in catalog showroom discount stores.

Sellers use ads with attractive special prices as a way to lure shoppers to their stores. Such claims are, however, deceptive if the seller does not have the item advertised in stock, does not make it readily available at the advertised price or tries to switch the shopper to some higher priced item. Concern with lack of availability and overpricing of advertised specials in grocery stores lead to a FTC trade regulation rule in the early 1970s. The rule requires retail food stores to have adequate stocks of all items advertised. It also requires that sale items be displayed conspicuously and be readily available at the advertised price or below; however, the availability of specials continues to be a problem. Shoppers appear to be unwilling to ask about out-of-stock or overpriced specials or complain about them, which gives retailers little incentive to conform to the rule (Wilkinson & Mason, 1978).

The use of *bait-and-switch* advertising is another deceptive practice. These ads offer merchandise at unusually attractive prices in order to lure shoppers. Once shoppers are in the store they are told the item is not available or are shown that it is of inferior quality. An attempt is then made to switch them to other higher-priced, more profitable merchandise. This type of violation is of concern to both state agencies and the FTC.

Misrings. Consumers sometimes wonder how accurately sales clerks ring up the prices of their purchases. The results of one small study seem

CONSUMER CONCERN: ARE WE NEGLECTING A BASIC CONSUMER RIGHT—HONEST WEIGHTS AND MEASURES?

A reliable system of weights and measures and its enforcement are fundamental for honest dealings in trade and commerce. The United States has a carefully developed system of weights and measures administered by the National Bureau of Standards; however, it is not clear how thoroughly the use of weights and measures by business is checked.

Years ago the butcher with his thumb on the scales was a common character in the comics, reflecting widespread public concern with honest weights and measures at that time. More recently, however, public interest appears to have declined. One reason for this decline is that it is hard to know just how serious the problem of short weighting really is.

Enforcement of weights and measures regulations is handled chiefly at the state and local levels. State and local agencies are responsible for checking the accuracy of weight and measure devices (including grocery scales, gasoline pumps, and even parking meter timers) and for checking products offered for sale for correct weight and measure. Regulations differ from state to state.

The dispersion of enforcement responsibility among the federal, state, and local governments makes it difficult to get an overview of what is actually happening. Furthermore, there is little information on the extent of the problem. Some of the most recent data date back to the mid-1970s. At that time, a survey of state agencies responsible for food and drug enforcement activities found that 41 states had weights and measures inspection activities in the food area, with a total staff of 280 inspectors (U.S. Department of Health, Education and Welfare, 1978). These inspectors had checked a total of 62.5 million food packages in to suggest the answer: Sales are not rung up very accurately but the effects are relatively minor (Zabriskie & Welch, 1978). Errors seem to be most common in grocery stores. The study found misrings in 21 percent of the grocery store purchases checked. Misrings seem most likely to occur when a large number of items are bought. The total amounts involved in individual transactions were not found to be large. Grocery store overcharges averaged one cent on fifty dollars worth of groceries and undercharges averaged one-half cent on the same size order. Still, the frequency of misrings suggests that shoppers should watch the cash register for the sizable errors that sometimes occur. While the effect of misrings on individual consumers is relatively small, the effect on profits of a store can be sizable.

The use of optical scanners at check-out counters can help eliminate misring errors by store clerks. They may, however, result in another type

the previous year and had found that 7.5 percent were in violation. It also was reported that 7.7 percent of the 2.6 million package lots checked were in violation. (In checking package lots, inspectors will let overweight packages balance off short weight ones.)

While some of the short weight violations are the innocent result of faulty scales, others are deliberate fraud. Short weighting of fresh meat packages seems to be one of the most common violations. Usually these violations involve a failure to deduct the weight of packaging materials from the net weight. Many violations involve trivial amounts—one or two cents per package. While the losses to individual consumers are not large, the gains for retailers and the losses for consumers as a group can be substantial.

While short weighting clearly is a problem, public concern about it is low. Is it really permissible to let sellers continue to cheat consumers as long as they do not cheat them too much?

QUESTIONS
1. Do you think the problem of short weighting and short counts in consumer products is currently a serious one? Why?
2. What are the costs of stiffer weights and measures enforcement? What would be the benefits?
3. Although short weighting and short counts (fewer items in a package than indicated on label) appear to be frequent, few consumers complain. Why?

Illustration 4-2
Optical scanners at check-out counters can eliminate misrings due to errors by clerks.

of error: differences between the posted shelf prices and those included in the scanner–cash register's memory.

The Right Combination of Quality and Price

When a market is competitive, consumers' shopping is expected to reduce the variation in prices over time. If shoppers are able to recognize quality and seek it out, they will shift their patronage to sellers who offer the best combination of price and quality. Such a shift happens in markets where buyers are well informed, the costs of searching out quality and price information are low, and there are no barriers to competition.

In competitive markets in which consumers are fully informed about the price–quality combinations available, we would expect the prices charged to be clearly correlated to product quality. Economists label these markets *informationally perfect markets*. In situations where consumers are not fully informed about the price–quality combinations available (i.e., *informationally imperfect markets*), we would expect a less direct relationship between price and quality.

One way to determine whether a market is informationally perfect or imperfect is to plot the prices charged for products of a given level of quality (Cude, 1985). Suppose, for example, we decided to plot the prices charged for three different brands (Brand A, B, and C) at three different stores. In this case, Brands A, B, and C represent three different levels of quality. In an informationally perfect market, we would expect prices to be higher for the higher quality brands. We would also expect shoppers to seek out the best price for the brand they preferred, eliminating variation between stores in the prices charged. The situation in a hypothetical informationally perfect market is depicted in Figure 4-2. Prices are higher at higher levels of quality, and sellers all charge the same price for a given level of quality.

In informationally imperfect markets, we see a different picture, as illustrated in Figure 4-3. This figure represents a plot of prices for 27 different brands of 35mm single-lens reflex cameras (Brands A to AA) representing different levels of quality (Duncan, 1981). For this example, price quotations were obtained from different stores in the Ann Arbor, Michigan, market. Prices for the same brand are connected by a vertical line. You can see that the prices varied widely between stores for individual brands. The price for Brand N, for example, varied from about $450 to $575. In this study *Consumer Reports* product-rating scores were used to represent quality.

If consumers were perfectly informed, they would seek out the best price–quality combinations available. In Figure 4-3, the points representing the lowest priced camera at a given quality are connected by line segments. This line has been labeled the *perfect information frontier* (Maynes, 1976). It represents the best choices for optimally informed consumers. The defini-

Figure 4-2
The Price–Quality Relationship in a Hypothetical Informationally Perfect Market

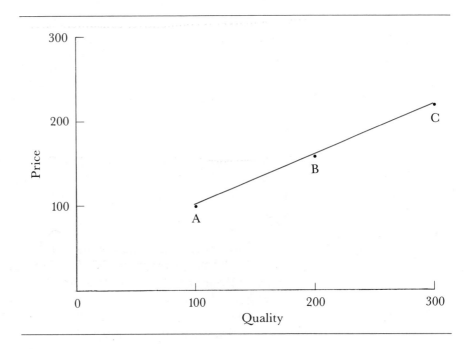

Figure 4-3
The Price–Quality
Relationship in an
Informationally Im-
perfect Market: 35mm
Cameras, Ann Arbor,
Michigan Market

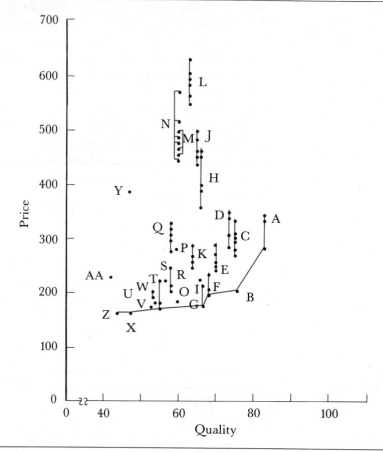

Source: Greg J. Duncan, "The Dynamics of Local Markets: A Case Study of Cameras, *Journal of Consumer Affairs* 15 (1981): 68. Used with permission of University of Wisconsin Press.

tion of the perfect information frontier restricts it to include only positively sloping line segments (i.e., ones that slope upward to the right). Downward sloping or negatively sloping segments would suggest that it was possible to get higher quality for the same or even lower prices.

The slope of the perfect information frontier suggests how much additional quality it is possible to get by paying more. In Figure 4-3 we can see that the marginal cost of additional quality is low. We can move up in quality from Brand Z to Brand G for little additional cost. Even the move to Brand B involves only modest additional expense.

Consumers may ask whether differences in a store's prices represent differences in the quality of its service. If price differences represent differences in services, a particular store should be uniformly high or low on all brands it sells. In the study of prices for 35mm cameras (Duncan, 1981), stores were not found to be uniformly high or low on all brands. This finding suggests that camera prices were not necessarily related to quality of service at that particular time and place.

The Economics of Shopping

Comparison shopping pays off the most when there are large differences among sellers in prices, quality, and additional services. Two types of situations make comparison shopping desirable: when products (or services) are differentiated and when price discrimination is practiced.

Product differentiation occurs when the offerings of sellers include unique features, even minor ones, that make price–quality comparisons between sellers difficult. When consumers become convinced that two similar products are different, it becomes more feasible for sellers to charge different prices for them.

The price–quality offerings for a particular product, such as single-lens reflex cameras, can vary widely in a particular market (as seen earlier). When price quotations in a local market were plotted against quality scores reported in *Consumer Reports,* there was a startling amount of disparity (Duncan, 1981). Several middle-ranked brands were priced at more than twice the best price for the top-rated brand. When prices and quality vary to this extent, it clearly pays to comparison shop.

Prices also vary widely when sellers practice price discrimination. *Price discrimination* occurs when a seller charges different buyers different prices for the same item. This can happen with products on which it is difficult for shoppers to compare the deal they were offered with the deal offered to others. Price discrimination is easy for sellers, for example, in car sales because of differing trade-ins, model choices, and options. Price discrimination also can occur when the nature of a product or service makes it impossible for buyers who got a good deal to resell to others. For example, price discrimination is possible in dental services because one patient cannot sell another a filling. Although comparison shopping is difficult when sellers are trying to practice price discrimination, it can pay off.

Although comparison shopping can pay off when there is product differentiation and price discrimination, it does not always pay off. Clearly, comparison shopping will produce no savings when the same or similar brands are offered everywhere for the same price. This situation can occur when there is only one seller in a local market. This is the situation for utilities — telephones, electricity, and public transportation. There is no advantage to shopping around for the cheapest pay telephone. Prices also can be the same if manufacturers succeed in holding retailers to a suggested retail price. Although the FTC frowns on manufacturers' efforts to prevent discounting, some items, including some well-known clothing brands, are seldom available at a discount as a result of pressure from the manufacturer.

Even when shoppers expect shopping to pay off, it is necessary to balance the savings gained against the time and money costs. One way to save both time and money in shopping is to substitute other methods of obtaining information for store-to-store shopping trips. Information on availability and prices may be obtained from newspaper ads and phone calls. This strategy works best when shoppers are already familiar with the brands available and their characteristics and simply want to locate a desired brand at the cheapest price (Hawkins & McCain, 1979).

Often, however, consumers are not familiar with the alternative brands, prices, and services available. The best strategy would then seem to be to obtain some background information on the product and brands before proceeding into the marketplace. This information should be supplemented with first-hand information from a limited amount of store-to-store search in the stores expected to have the best offerings, plus information from ads and telephone calls.

In this chapter we have discussed some of the ways shoppers can improve the quality of their consumer choices. Unfortunately, even carefully made decisions do not always turn out well. In the next chapter we will discuss the techniques consumers can use in getting help when they run into problems.

MAJOR CHAPTER CONCEPTS

1. Gaps between your actual and desired states motivate you as a consumer.
2. Your actual state can be changed by out-of-stock problems, breakdowns, and psychological obsolescence. Your desired state is a result of many different influences, including family situation, income, and related purchases.
3. The steps in deciding what you need are assessing your actual state (often involving an inventory), determining deficiencies, and setting priorities for dealing with these deficiencies.
4. There are three general kinds of brands: manufacturer's brands, retailer's brands, and generic brands.
5. An understanding of a product's unit price (e.g., price per ounce) and its cost-in-use are necessary in understanding which package and brand are the best buy.
6. Evidence suggests that price is not a very reliable indicator of quality.

7. Information on ingredients and materials provides clues to product performance. Informative and grading labeling provide information on ratings on performance or quality tests.

8. Standards are rules or models used for judging product quality or performance; both design and performance standards are used in judging products.

9. Warranty terms provide an indication of product durability; in addition to the familiar express warranty, consumers are protected by a product's implied warranty.

10. Although many accidents involving consumer products are caused by misuse, consumers should learn to avoid product design and construction features that create hazards.

11. Good product designs use color, texture, shape, and form to achieve the goals of appropriateness, variety, and unity.

12. Comparison shopping is necessary to find the best available combination of brand, price, and store services.

13. Consumers need to know something about prevailing prices to avoid being misled by deceptive price comparisons and sales offers.

14. In informationally perfect markets, product prices are highly correlated to quality, and there is little variation among sellers in the prices charged for a given level of quality. In informationally imperfect markets, there is a lower correlation between price and quality and more variation in the prices charged for a given level of quality.

15. The perfect information frontier is the positively sloping line describing the lowest prices in the market place for different levels of quality.

16. Comparison shopping pays off the most when there are wide variations in prices, brand quality, and store services. These variations occur when there is product differentiation and price discrimination.

17. In comparison shopping it is important to balance expected savings against the time and money costs of shopping. The cost of gathering information can be reduced by checking newspaper ads and making phone calls as a substitute for store-to-store trips.

CONSUMER
QUESTIONS

1. What major article of clothing have you purchased recently? What factors led to your decision? (a) Were there changes in your actual state? What were they? (b) Were there changes in your desired state? What were they? (c) Why did you put a high priority on dealing with the gap between your actual and desired state?

2. Collect labels from three different types of products; for example, a food product, a toiletries or cosmetic product, and a package of notebook paper

or other student supplies. What information does each label provide? What information is not provided? If you were to redesign the label, what information would you provide on each?

3. What store and generic brands are offered in the grocery store or drug store where you usually shop? Make a list of five different product categories in which a store brand or a generic brand is offered alongside a manufacturer's brand. For each product category (a) list the brand name of manufacturer's brand and retailer's brand offered; (b) list the prices, size, and ingredients of the manufacturer's brand, retailer's brand, and generic brand; and (c) indicate information on other evaluative criteria you feel are relevant. Indicate your brand preference in each product category and the reasons for your choice.

4. Identify four grocery-store or drugstore items for which the same brand is offered in several sizes. Record the brand name, package sizes offered, and the prices for each set of items. Calculate the unit prices for each set of items. Which size provides the lowest unit price? Which size would you buy and why?

5. Rewrite the sample warranty in Figure 4-1 to simplify the language used. Try to use language which a ninth grade student could understand easily and keep all the key points set forth in the warranty.

6. Choose a product that you would be interested in buying that is sold in a number of different stores. A toiletries or cosmetics item, a popular record or tape, and a well-known brand of jeans are possible choices. Visit a number of stores in your area and record the item and brand name, the store name, and the price of the item in each store. Also record any special or extra services each store provides. If you were to buy the item, where would you buy it and why?

SUGGESTED
READINGS

1. Casale, Charles A. "Consumerism and Retailing." *Consumerism in the United States.* Edited by Joel R. Evans. New York: Praeger, 1980: 351-390. This is an historical examination of consumers' changing concerns with the retail market and the impact of government regulation on retailers and retailers' responses from the early 1900s to 1980.

2. Maynes, E. Scott. *Decision-Making for Consumers.* New York: MacMillan, 1976, chapter 3: 51-77. This chapter, "Product Quality: Meaning, Measurement and Implications," discusses the concept of product quality. It also explains the concept of the perfect information frontier, the set of prices consumers would choose if they had complete information about product quality and prices in the market.

CHAPTER 5

REMEDIES
FOR CONSUMER
PROBLEMS

Consumers make dozens of purchases each month. Most of them turn out well. But some do not. Just what kinds of problems do consumers have with the products or services they have bought? Some of the most common include (TARP, Inc., 1979, 6-8):

- *Nondelivery of merchandise that was prepaid or failure to perform agreed-upon work.* The nondelivery of merchandise ordered by mail is a leading problem, as is the failure to contractors to perform agreed-upon remodeling and home repairs.
- *Inadequate repair service and warranty problems.* Repairs that are overpriced or difficult to obtain are frequent problems, as are difficulties in getting the repair or replacement of defective products promised by warranties.
- *Poor product quality and performance; defective merchandise.* These problems include errors in manufacture, use of inferior materials, and merchandise in poor condition.

- *Failure of product to live up to expectations or advertising claims.* Sometimes consumers have excessive expectations about how a product will look or perform. Sellers may have fostered these expectations either inadvertently or deliberately; in other cases, the problem may be a result of a poor choice for the intended use.
- *Personal injury or damage from defective product.* Occasionally defective or unsafe products cause injury, result in damage to household items, or result in financial losses.

Consumers are more likely to complain when expensive products or services are involved. New and used autos are a frequent subject of complaints, as are auto repairs, undoubtedly because of the large amounts of money involved. Home repairs and remodeling also are a frequent focus of complaints. Few of us can afford the kind of losses involved when a car purchase goes sour, nor do we want to tolerate careless or dishonest treatment by sellers. Just what can consumers do to protect themselves? A first step is understanding the laws under which consumers can seek help and protection.

THE BASIS OF CONSUMER RIGHTS: CONSUMER LAW

Consumers' rights and responsibilities have been spelled out in detail by the legal system in this country. The laws affecting consumers are part of the whole body of laws society has developed to govern the conduct of its members. These laws come from several different sources:

- *Constitutional law* —The basic laws of the nation and the states
- *Statutory law* — Laws enacted by the legislative bodies of the nation, the states, and local jurisdictions
- *Administrative law* —The regulations developed by governmental agencies such as the FTC, under the authority given them by statutory law
- *Common law* — Law that grows out of the decisions made by courts in deciding disputes between two parties

All these sources have contributed to the development of *contract law,* the body of laws that governs agreements between different parties, such as buyers and sellers. This group of laws plays a key role in determining what protection consumers have when they experience difficulties.

The Law of Contracts

Contracts are agreements between two or more parties that are enforceable by law (Henszey, Myers, & Phalan, 1977). One of the essential elements of a contract is agreement between parties about what each will do (or not do). When the contract is completed, these promises become legal obligations.

Contracts set out the rights and the duties of the parties. A seller of a car, for example, has the duty to deliver the car promised and the right to be paid. Conversely, the buyer has the duty to pay as promised and the right to get the car that was promised. Each party to the contract thus receives some *consideration* (or benefit) and each gives up something. Consideration is a key element of a contract and without it there is no contract. Many promises are not contracts because no consideration is involved. If a friend offers to drive you to class, no contract is involved unless you have promised something in return (a reciprocal agreement).

Contracts do not necessarily have to be in written form to be valid (Henszey et al., 1977). They can be either oral or written. Often only key parts of a contract are put in written form. Examples are sales slips and order forms. Certain kinds of contracts, such as agreements for the sale of real estate, are valid only in written form, however. Consumers should remember that when a written contract is signed, its terms replace all previous oral promises unless there has been mistake or fraud. For example, the promises made by a car dealer are not binding if they do not show up in the written contract.

Enforceability

In enforcing contracts, the legal system is concerned that signers understand the terms of the contract. If the signers do not or cannot understand the terms, the contract may be judged invalid and unenforceable. The belief that people often do not understand the terms of the contracts they sign has led some states to pass "plain-language laws." These laws require that consumer contracts be written in simple, understandable language.

The concern with fairness may also lead courts to set aside contract terms they judge to be *unconscionable* or too one-sided. Examples of unconscionable terms include prices that are unreasonably high compared to the value of the product (Rothschild & Carroll, 1986). The terms of a contract also may be set aside if it appears that one of the parties has been subjected to *undue influence* (unreasonable pressure). Signers should be permitted to make reasonable decisions based on their true preferences.

Freedom from Undue Influence. A desire to protect consumers from making contracts under excessive emotional or time pressure led to the FTC rule providing a *cooling-off period* for contracts in door-to-door sales (Rothschild & Carroll, 1986). Under this rule, individuals are allowed three business days to cancel a contract they have signed if the purchase is more than $25 and is made in their home. Under the rule, sellers are required to inform buyers of this right. Suppose, for example, that you had signed a contract with a door-to-door salesperson for $875 for a set of encyclopedias. Within the cooling-off period, you began to have second thoughts. Under the rule you would have the right to cancel because the purchase was more than $25 and was made in your home. You would, however, have to act promptly, using the information about cancellation procedures the seller is obligated to provide.

The cooling-off rule was designed to provide time for buyers to comparison shop and make careful decisions. The rule may, however, lead some consumers to let their guard down. Some may sign contracts with the idea that they will comparison shop and then fail to do so in the time allowed.

Responsible Parties. The desire to assure that individuals understand the consequences of their actions is also reflected in the laws concerning who is and who is not a legally responsible party to a contract. *Minors* (individuals under legal age) are in a group the legal system seeks to protect. Legal age is set by state law. Traditionally it has been 21 years, but it has been reduced to 20, 19, and 18 years in some states.

The legal system does not limit the power of minors to enter into contracts. It does, however, give them special privileges in cancelling contracts (Henszey et al., 1977). In general, minors can be released from most contracts upon request. Because of this right, a minor can cancel a contract to buy a stereo months after purchasing it, return the stereo in damaged condition, and request the money back. In most states the seller would be obligated to give a full refund. In others, the seller would be permitted to deduct depreciation. The right of minors to cancel contracts makes many businesspeople reluctant to deal with them and is the reason that many sellers insist on dealing with parents or other adults or having adult co-signers on contracts.

Minors have been given special rights to cancel contracts in order to protect them from unwise decisions. The reluctance of businesspeople to deal with minors could, however, create situations in which minors have difficulty buying needed food, clothing, medicine, or other basic essentials. Although minors can get released from contracts for essentials (which lawyers call *necessaries*), they still are obligated to pay their reasonable value. Necessaries include essentials that the minor does not have and that a parent cannot or will not supply. For example, if a minor without adequate shoes bought a pair, she would, under the rule, be obligated to pay their reasonable value. If, however, she already had five pairs at home, they would not be considered necessaries and she would not be obligated to pay.

There are certain kinds of contracts that are felt to be so important that minors are not permitted to cancel them. These include enlistments in the armed services, marriage contracts, and contracts for certain kinds of loans guaranteed by the federal government.

Warranties

One of the important parts of any contract is the *warranty* involved. Warranties are contractual promises the seller makes about the performance or condition of the product sold. As explained in the last chapter, these promises

Illustration 5-1
Although minors can be released from many contracts upon request, contracts for enlistment in the armed services are binding.

always involve implied warranties that arise out of custom or understanding and often also involve express warranties based on the seller's oral or written promises (Henszey et al., 1977).

The implied warranties are created when a seller offers a product for sale. When sellers offer an item for sale, the law holds that they are making certain promises about it. These include the following:

- *Warranty of merchantability* is the implied promise that the product is of the usual quality that is offered for sale and that it is not spoiled, defective, or damaged.
- *Warranty of fitness for particular purpose* is the implied promise that the product is suitable for the purpose intended or for the needs the buyer has indicated to a seller.
- *Warranty of title* is the implied promise that the seller has a right to sell the item.

Sellers often try to limit their obligations under these implied warranties in the written express warranty they provide.

Consumers who are trying to understand their rights under a product's implied warranties often are confused or misled by the express warranty provided. Standard contract forms, leases, and guarantee statements frequently include inequitable terms (Henszey et al., 1977). Sellers, for example, frequently disclaim responsibility for product-related injuries and indicate they will not pay for any losses resulting from product defects except for the cost of repair parts. Courts consider many of these disclaimers unconscionable. The fact that the seller has set them down in writing does not necessarily mean they will be recognized by the courts.

Sellers can make disclaimers about implied warranties in only very specific and very limited ways. Other efforts by sellers to get out of implied warranties are likely to be considered unconscionable. Disclaimers of the warranty of merchantability can be made with a written or oral statement, but it must include the word "merchantability." Implied warranties of fitness for purpose can be disclaimed only with conspicuous statements in writing or if a sale is made "as is."

If a product is unsafe, the seller or manufacturer may be liable under contract law on the basis of the implied warranty of merchantability. Sellers and manufacturers may also be liable under tort law (a body of law covering violation of an individual's noncontractual rights) if they have been negligent.

Remedies

When sellers fail to perform their duties as set by law, regulatory rules, or contract, consumers have a right to seek corrective measures. Lawyers refer to these corrective measures as *remedies*. In the modern marketplace, it is often difficult for consumers to know what remedies are available or how and where to go about seeking them. Consumers should look first to retailers for remedies to most problems. Retailers are legally responsible for the express claims they make to buyers orally or in writing and also for many of the express claims of the manufacturer if they have been involved in relaying them to the buyer (Henszey et al., 1977). Retailers also are responsible for implied warranties about a product.

The responsibilities of manufacturers are less clear-cut. Manufacturers are, of course, responsible for the express warranties they have made. Years ago, however, it was felt that manufacturers did not have any implied warranty responsibility to consumers unless the consumers had purchased directly from them (Henszey et al., 1977). It was argued that if a consumer's purchase was made from a retailer, there was no contract between the manufacturer and the consumer. The only contract involving the consumer was the one with the retailer. Under this line of reasoning, the consumer could seek remedies only from the retailer—not from the manufacturer. Gradually, exceptions to this approach were established on a case-by-case basis and became part of common law. These exceptions were made because the courts felt that it was not socially desirable to excuse manufacturers from responsibility, especially in cases where goods were defective as a result of negligence.

Many states have now accepted the *doctrine of strict liability,* which holds that the manufacturer is liable to the ultimate consumer if (1) a product has a defect that causes injury and (2) the defect was in the product at the time it left the manufacturer's hands. Under this approach, it is not necessary for the injured user to show that the seller was negligent. As a result of this doctrine, manufacturers are more directly responsible to the buyers of their products. One of the results has been a significant increase in the number of product injury suits against manufacturers (see Consumer Concern: "The Product Liability Controversy").

The remedies available to the consumer when a product does not live up to the implied warranties are often limited by the terms of the express warranty (Henszey et al., 1977). Typically, the express warranty promises repairs. It may, in some cases, offer replacement or refund. Express warranties for some expensive items now also provide for arbitration by a third party if there are serious disagreements between the buyer and the seller. Under the Moss-Magnuson Warranty Act, warranties must spell out the procedures consumers should follow in seeking remedies.

If the remedies available to the consumer are not limited by the express warranty, the buyer may (1) keep the goods and sue for damages or (2) return the goods, rescind the contract, and seek to recover the money already paid plus damages (Henszey et al., 1977). It is important to note that if buyers keep goods and continue to use them even though they know they are defective, they may lose their rights to seek remedies. In such cases, if the buyers do not complain promptly, they are considered to be satisfied. Consumers should be aware of the importance of complaining promptly when a problem is discovered in order to protect their legal rights.

EFFECTIVE COMPLAINING

While it is important to understand consumers' legal rights and the available remedies, consumers with problems should not necessarily begin by considering legal action or consulting a lawyer. There are other, less expensive and more appropriate measures that should be tried first.

Deciding When to Complain

A consumer's first problem in seeking remedies is deciding just when to complain. Typically, complaints grow out of breaches of the implied and express warranties for a product (or service). Whenever a product does not live up to these warranties consumers should consider complaining. Specifically, they should consider complaining when:

- *The product does not live up to what reasonably could be expected.* Inferior performance, defects, safety problems, and similar difficulties can all be considered breaches of the implied warranty of merchantability.

**CONSUMER
CONCERN:
THE PRODUCT
LIABILITY
CONTROVERSY**

In the last few years there has been widespread controversy over the growing number of claims against manufacturers for product-related injuries. Some manufacturers and their insurance companies have argued that the growing number of large court awards are threatening the future of many manufacturing companies and workers' jobs and are sharply raising consumer prices.

The number of product-injury liability cases has grown considerably in recent years. The total number of such cases is, however, far smaller than the numbers mentioned in some scare claims. The growth in these cases is, in part, the result of a new awareness by consumers of their rights in product-related injuries. Thirty years ago someone who was injured by an exploding beer bottle had to pay the hospital bills and face many permanent injuries alone. Today, that person is likely to sue the bottler.

Changes in the laws covering product liability probably also have contributed to the increase in cases. The acceptance of the doctrine of strict liability in many states has made it easier for consumers to sue. The willingness of lawyers to accept cases on a contingency fee basis in which their fee depends on the outcome of the case also has made it easier for consumers to sue.

The increased number of product liability cases has led insurance companies to make substantial increases in the premiums they charge manufacturing firms. The premium for the average firm still, however, amounts to less than one percent of total sales — a good deal less than sales and promotion costs. For firms in industries where risks are high, such as sporting equipment, premiums may be as high as 15 percent of sales.

Businesspeople's concern over product liability suits and rising insurance costs has led them to press for changes in state laws covering liability suits (Tochen, 1979). The changes they advocate include:

- *Reductions in the statute of limitations.* State laws typically require injured people to file suit within some limited period after injury. Some states have adopted proposals that also limit the length of time after purchase in which claims can be made. Proponents of this limit argue that it is unfair to hold manufacturers liable for injuries from a product many years after it is sold. Opponents note that these limits are often relatively short. They could leave car owners unprotected after five or six years even though the average car may last for thirteen years. They also point out that these limitations leave consumers no protection when effects take years to show up. Examples are cases of cancer caused by drugs taken or treatment given years earlier.

- *Use of the state-of-the-art as a defense.* Another approach to imiting consumer claims is to release manufacturers from liability if they used the best technology available at the time they made the product. Proponents say it is unfair to hold manufacturers liable for problems discovered years later, if their product was as good as the others being produced. Opponents of this view argue that entire industries sometimes fail to use the best technology available.
- *Compliance with product safety standards as a defense.* An additional limit on claims is the release of manufacturers from liability if their product conformed to the government safety standards at the time it was made. While this seems fair, opponents note that it is well known that safety standards are the result of political compromises and do not necessarily represent the best technology available at a particular time.
- *Alteration or misuse defense.* A further approach to limiting manufacturers' liability is to release them from responsibility if the product has been misused or altered in any way. Opponents note that injuries often are the result of product defects and design errors along with misuse. They argue that in such instances, both the manufacturer and user are at fault and should share the blame.
- *Other limits.* Other proposals have put limits on the size of awards for pain and suffering and on the use of the contingency fee system (*Consumer Reports*, August, 1986a). Opponents point out that it is unfair to limit consumers' legal rights in this way.

The efforts of business interests to change state laws have been only somewhat successful. As a result, efforts in recent years have been focused on getting a federal law that preempts (or overrides) state laws. The proposals offered would limit some of the rights that consumers now have under state law or that they have gained in state court decisions.

Changes are clearly needed in the way product-related injury cases are handled. Manufacturers are facing new uncertainties about claims and rising insurance rates. It does not, however, seem reasonable for them to try to solve their problems by putting new and unreasonable burdens on their customers. There are other possible solutions. One is for manufacturers to give more attention to reducing product risks. Insurance companies should limit premium increases to reflect their losses more fairly. It is also important to remove some of the uncertainties created by the present situation. These uncertainties affect all the parties:

manufacturers, their insurance companies, and consumers. Some of these uncertainties arise from rapid changes in product-liability law and its interpretation and from differences in laws between states. The development of a uniform law, with participation by all parties, to be enacted by all the states could help remove many of these uncertainties.

QUESTIONS
1. Why has the growing number of product-injury-related claims against manufacturers created concern?
2. What changes in product liability law have been proposed? What would be the benefits to consumers of enacting these changes? The costs?

- *The product does not serve the purpose for which it was requested or which it claimed to serve.* Products that are ineffective or inappropriate for the purpose for which they were suggested breach the implied warranty of fitness for purpose.
- *The product fails to live up to advertising and sales personnel's claims or other express claims.* The failure of a product to live up to express claims, either written or oral, is a breach of the express warranties.

Consumers should not hesitate to consider complaining when they have a problem. Reliable businesspeople want their customers to be satisfied and to keep them coming back. If customers who are having problems fail to complain, they lose and so does the business that failed to satisfy them. When consumers complain to less-honest merchants they also are performing a service by helping to convince these merchants they cannot afford to mistreat their customers.

Getting Prepared

There are several important steps to follow before seeking resolution for consumer problems (Rothschild & Carroll, 1986). First, the problem should be reviewed. Were the product instructions followed? Is the problem one that can easily be corrected by following the instructions? Can the problem be described in a concise statement of the facts so that others can understand it?

A second step in preparing a complaint is gathering and reviewing relevant documentation. Sales slips are important for establishing place and date of purchase and purchase price. Warranties, contracts, and documents should also be collected and reviewed. Reviewing the documents related to the problem can help in developing a statement of the problem. The relevant documents are also important for substantiating a claim to the seller or to third parties who may become involved later.

The next step is to decide what remedies seem fair. Do the usual remedies of repair, replacement, or refund seem appropriate? Are there other additional expenses that should be reimbursed? Are damages or physical injuries involved that should be considered?

Consumers often are not familiar with the remedies and channels available to them. Some research may be advisable. The information sources discussed in Chapter 3 may suggest ideas. Local consumer protection agencies can often give advice on appropriate procedures. An attorney may also be consulted. Even though an agency's or an attorney's help may not be needed in dealing with a problem, they may be able to make suggestions about available remedies and appropriate channels for complaints.

Confronting the Seller

Usually the first step in making a complaint is to approach the seller. Other sources of help often refuse to intervene until the seller has been given an opportunity to correct the problem. Complaints and problems should be taken to the service desk or complaint department.

In making a complaint, a consumer should state the problem briefly and politely. Accusations and abusive language will only make the seller's representatives more defensive. In any case, such an approach really is not fair if there is no way the seller could have been aware of your problem. The consumer should be prepared to show relevant documentation, such as receipts, but should not give up the original copies. Store personnel should be allowed copies if necessary.

The consumer should suggest a remedy. Some consumers with problems get so angry that they do not really know what they want. In such cases, it is difficult for sellers to begin to satisfy them. Remedies such as repairs and replacements are usually easier to obtain than refunds. Many stores are reluctant to make cash refunds on returns. While that policy may be reasonable when shoppers have simply changed their minds, it does not seem as appropriate in cases where the product has been found to be defective or unsafe. If an item is left for repair or is returned for credit, the customer should be sure to get a receipt to help avoid future misunderstandings.

Discussions with clerks at the service desk may not produce satisfactory results. An appropriate next step is to contact the service manager or store manager in person or by letter. In discussing the problem, the customer should indicate what further action is planned if the store does not resolve the problem. For future reference, it is important to keep a record of all contacts made, with the names, dates, and results of each contact.

Follow-Up Steps

If the seller of a product is unable or unwilling to help, complaints should be made to the manufacturer. If the product is a retailer's brand, a contact should be made with the firm's headquarters. Contacting the manufacturer is a logical follow-up step in cases of defective products, repair problems, and disagreements over warranty terms. Reliable manufacturers want to know about any problems in getting service from stores that sell their brand.

Finding the Manufacturer's Address. Many consumer products now carry the manufacturer's (or distributor's) address and ZIP code. If the firm's address cannot be located, it may be necessary to do some research at the local library. The reference section probably has one or more directories with the addresses of firms that sell consumer products and services. A particularly useful directory is the *Consumer Complaint Guide* (Rosenbloom, 1981). It identifies the company to which a particular trade name belongs and provides the address of the company.

Complaint letters may be addressed to the "Consumer Service Department," though some consumers prefer to write to the president or to other corporate officers. The names of corporate officers can be found in *Standard & Poor's Register of Corporation Directors and Executives,* which is available in larger libraries.

Preparing Your Letter. A complaint letter should be carefully organized to state the relevant facts. It should include:

- A clear statement of the problem, along with the model and serial numbers and the date and place of purchase
- A clear description of the steps already taken to resolve the problem and their results
- A statement of the suggested remedy (in addition to repair, replacement, or refund, the consumer may wish to ask for reimbursement for shipping costs or other expenses)
- The customer's name and address and a daytime or business phone number

If receipts for other papers are used to substantiate a claim, photocopies should be sent instead of the originals. A sample complaint letter is shown in Figure 5-1.

Letters should be neat and typewritten if possible. Although it is unjust, manufacturers apparently take typewritten letters that appear to be from higher status people more seriously than letters written in pencil on lined paper (Boschung, 1976). A copy of the letter should be kept in case further correspondence is necessary. One advantage of putting a complaint in the form of a letter is that it provides a record for future use.

If an item must be returned, insuring it will provide protection against loss and will also provide a record that it was received. For a small fee, certified mail is available; the postcard receipt can be used as evidence that your letter or package was received.

Figure 5-1

A sample complaint letter

```
1617 Westridge Avenue
College Park, MD 20811
October 30, 19--

Customer Service Department
Northstar Electronics Corp.
1212 Los Gatos Blvd.
Santa Gertrudis, CA 93616

Ladies and Gentlemen

Last week I purchased a Northstar radio/
cassette player Model NS-82X at Old Line
Electronics, College Park, Maryland. I found
when I got it home that the tape deck did
not operate properly and it did not produce
any sound.

I took it to the service department at
Old Line Electronics, since they are your
authorized local service representative.
They attempted to correct the problem but
failed and returned the product to me. They
told me to contact your office directly.

To solve this problem, I am requesting
replacement of the item with one which
operates properly. I am enclosing a copy
of my sales slip as proof of ownership and
date of purchase.

I am looking forward to your resolution
of my problem. You can contact me at my
home address above or by telephone (home:
(202)555-6787; office: (202)555-2300).

Sincerely

Steven G. Smith
```

Statement of problem
with description of
product purchased
and place and date
of purchase

Action taken on
problem

Remedy requested
Copies of relevant
documents

Address and telephone
contact information

Replies usually take two to three weeks. Although large firms have special departments to handle complaint letters, some firms get as many as 1,000 letters a week.

If a problem is a result of misleading ad claims or problems with a local service firm, contacting the local Better Business Bureau or Chamber of Commerce is a logical second step in complaining. If the problem deals with the services of an attorney, physician, dentist, or other professional person, the the local branch of the relevant professional organization is probably the best contact. If you suspect fraud, local law enforcement officials should be contacted at once.

Preparing a Follow-up Letter. If no response is received within a reasonable period of time, a follow-up letter should be written. The fact that no response was received to the first letter should be noted, and the facts must be restated. In addition, any agencies to whom copies are being sent should be identified. The ones selected depend on the problem and can include one or more of the following:

- Federal Trade Commission
- Consumer Product Safety Commission
- Food and Drug Administration
- U.S. Postal Service
- The consumer protection office of the state attorney general's department
- Appropriate business and trade organizations such as the National Automobile Dealers Association, Association of Home Appliance Manufacturers, and the American Apparel Manufacturers Association

These groups and other organizations that can assist consumers will be discussed in the following section.

Complaining can require a good deal of time and effort. Unfortunately, many consumers do not complain about their problems. Those who do are often disappointed by the results. Continuing efforts are needed to encourage consumers to make appropriate complaints and to encourage sellers to offer appropriate remedies (see Consumer Concern: "What Can Be Done to Improve Consumer Redress?").

SOURCES OF ASSISTANCE

If the retailer or manufacturer cannot or will not help with a problem, there are other sources of help to which a consumer can turn. These sources of help are often referred to as *third-party complaint handlers* because they are not one of the two original parties to the transaction.

In choosing which third-party agency to ask for help, consumers must understand the powers and limitations of different agencies. Most agencies have limited geographic coverage. They usually will get involved in problems only if the consumer or the seller (or both) is from their area. Most agencies also have specific rules about the kinds of problems they will handle. These rules may be the result of agency policy or, in the case of government agencies, may be based in the law under which the agency was established.

The powers of agencies also differ. An agency's powers may include one or more of the following:

- *Referral.* Consumers with problems are advised as to whom to contact. In other cases, complaints are received and sent on to the company involved or to the appropriate government agency for action.
- *Mediation.* An effort is made to resolve problems by promoting communication between the two parties involved. Consumer complaints are sent to the seller, who is asked to indicate what action is being taken.

- *Arbitration.* Problems are heard by a person (or panel of people) who is acceptable to both parties and who proposes solutions. If a party to the dispute agrees in advance to accept the decision offered, the decision is said to be binding.
- *Adjudication.* Problems are considered in legal proceedings in which evidence is offered and a decision is made which is enforceable by law.

In using third-party help, persistence may be important. Most third-party agencies have a set routine for handling problems. Once they have gone through these routine steps, they typically do not take any further action unless the consumer asks for it. Agencies that focus on mediation, for example, usually forward complaints to sellers and ask them to respond to the consumer. Sellers are asked to send a copy of this response to the agency. The agency often does not check whether the seller's offer satisfies the consumer. If it does not, the consumer must initiate further action.

Those who have studied consumers' experiences in complaining also suggest that consumers with problems involve only one third-party agency at a time (Rothschild & Carroll, 1986). Sellers may feel harassed and may become more reluctant to help if several different third parties contact them at once.

Better Business Bureaus

The third-party agency consumers often think of first when they have problems is the Better Business Bureau (BBB). We have already discussed (in Chapter 3) the information and education activities of the BBB's and some of the problems that limit their usefulness. The BBBs also play an important role in handling consumer complaints in the communities in which they are located. As we saw earlier, many communities do not have BBBs. In some of these communities, the local Chamber of Commerce provides similar complaint-handling service.

The basic role of the BBBs is to mediate disputes between consumers and sellers. The bureaus handle complaints free. They require that complaints be submitted in writing and usually provide a standard form for this purpose. Consumers should recognize that BBBs focus solely on marketplace problems. One of their chief concerns is controlling misleading advertising and misrepresentation. This is the purpose for which they were founded. BBBs will not become involved in complaints about the price of goods or services unless there is evidence of misrepresentation. BBBs also will not deal with problems involving government agencies and landlord-tenant disputes. The BBBs do not give legal advice and do not deal with problems involving the terms of contracts.

CONSUMER CONCERN: WHAT CAN BE DONE TO IMPROVE CONSUMER REDRESS?

A number of surveys have found that many consumers do not complain about their problems (Andreasen, 1986; Best, 1980). Lower-income and less-educated people in particular seem to be unlikely to complain about problems. There is also evidence that consumers are more likely to complain when the problem is clear-cut than when it is a matter of judgment. For example, consumers are more likely to complain about nondelivery of an item they have purchased than about problems of fading, shrinking, improper operation, or other problems that could be matters of opinion.

Why do consumers so often fail to complain? One explanation is their estimates of the costs and benefits of complaining.

- *Complaining involves time costs.* Returning to the store, writing a letter, or even making a phone call requires valuable time. In addition, complaining often involves unpleasantness and psychological stress that most people would like to avoid.
- *Complaining involves monetary costs that may outweigh monetary gains.* Travel costs, shipping costs, and legal fees may be greater than the money gained from a successful complaint.
- *The outcome of making a complaint is often uncertain.* Consumers with problems are often uncertain about just what the costs and benefits of complaining will be. If they feel the seller is not likely to take corrective action, consumers may be less likely to complain.

These factors help to explain why consumers often fail to complain about problems with inexpensive items such as cosmetics and food. Because the costs of complaining seem to outweigh the gain from even a full refund, consumers often do not do anything except perhaps switch brands. It also explains why most of the complaints received by consumer protection agencies involve expensive items such as cars, appliances, and home repair work. Clearly, anything that can be done to reduce the cost of complaining and to increase the size and likelihood of gains will encourage complaining.

We also can ask why sellers so often fail to help consumers with problems. There seem to be several explanations (Federal Trade Commission, 1980b).

After receiving a complaint in writing, the BBB sends a copy to the seller involved. The BBB asks the seller to investigate the problem and to attempt to solve it. Some companies ignore BBB requests. When this happens,

- *The seller may not know the customer has had a problem.* If the consumer fails to complain, there is no way for the seller to know about it. Some sellers do, however, actively solicit information from their customers about problems.
- *The seller may have no real incentive to help.* If a seller is not really concerned about maintaining goodwill and does not expect return business, there is little reason to help customers with problems. Fly-by-night operators, for example, do not count on repeat business; they simply look for new suckers.
- *The costs of remedying the consumer's problem may outweigh the loss of customer goodwill.* If a customer's problem is small, it costs little to fix it and maintains goodwill; but if the remedy required is costly, the seller may decide that it is cheaper to ignore the problem and risk losing the customer. This may explain the resistance of auto dealers and manufacturers to helping customers who get "lemons."

The costs and benefits of providing remedies help to explain the behavior of different types of sellers. Grocery stores and food processors usually give refunds or replacements quickly. Department stores, which are also interested in repeat business, usually have lenient return policies. Sellers of more expensive items, however, often resist making costly refunds and replacements, though small repairs are usually easy to obtain.

Sellers clearly will be more receptive to helping consumers if the costs of providing a remedy are reduced. Sometimes these costs are reduced by shifting some of them (e.g., labor costs or shipping charges) to the consumer. Sellers will also be encouraged to help if not doing so will result in a significant loss of goodwill. Other forms of encouragement may take the form of publicizing customers' experiences with a seller or making these experiences part of an information bank other shoppers can use in deciding where to buy.

QUESTIONS

1. What measures can be used to reduce the consumer's costs of complaining? What measures can be used to increase the size of likelihood of gains?
2. What measures reduce the costs to sellers of providing remedies? What measures can increase the benefits?

the BBB will suggest other sources of help or legal action. Most companies do respond, however. They may indicate that the complaint is unjustified and may explain why they feel this way. They may also indicate the adjustment they have offered the consumer. It is up to the consumer to decide whether or not to accept the seller's offer. BBBs do not check with consumers to determine whether the adjustment offered is fair.

BBBs have no power to force sellers to take action on complaints. They can expel member firms, of course, but many firms are not members. BBBs also have the power of publicity as a way to control problems. They release information about repeated abuses to the news media, and all provide individual consumers with information about a firm's complaint-handling procedures. The BBBs focus on whether or not a firm makes an acceptable response to the complaints it forwards, not on the fairness of the adjustments offered or their acceptability to consumers.

Many BBBs now also offer free arbitration services (Rothschild & Carroll, 1986). These arbitration decisions are designed to be a substitute for court action. They are legally binding on both parties and are enforceable in court.

Local and State Agencies

Local and state government agencies can often provide assistance to consumers with problems. These agencies have several advantages. They are readily accessible and often can be reached with a local phone call. They are, moreover, familiar with local and state laws and with the local market situation. Local and state government agencies are also in a good position to apply pressure on local business when necessary.

The powers of local and state agencies vary. Some serve mostly a referral function and direct consumers with problems to appropriate sources of help. Local and state government agencies usually insist that consumers first attempt to solve problems on their own before the agency will accept their complaint for action.

State and local agencies serve chiefly as mediators between consumers and sellers. Most receive too many complaints to take legal action on each one and prefer to focus on working out compromises. A few agencies actually have power to investigate problems, render decisions, and order sellers to make restitution when appropriate. Even when an agency has these powers, however, the emphasis usually is on mediation.

The jurisdiction of state and local agencies varies a good deal. Most can handle only certain types of problems, and some will accept complaints only about transactions that took place within their locality. The quality and extent of the services provided by local and state agencies vary as well. Most are swamped by complaints and are short of personnel. As a result, some actually process only some of the complaints they receive.

The types of agencies available differ among localities. Some cities and metropolitan counties have their own consumer protection offices. Some local district attorney offices are active in handling consumer problems, especially complaints that may involve fraud. Other district attorneys, however, feel they must concentrate on violent crimes such as robbery and murder and thus give little attention to "white-collar crimes" such as consumer fraud and deception. Prosecution of sellers who have violated consumer protection laws is likely only when large amounts of money, or large numbers of consumers, are involved.

Every state has some type of consumer protection agency. Usually these agencies are a division of the Office of the State Attorney General. Some states, such as California, have separate Departments of Consumer Affairs. Many state agencies have branches in major cities throughout the state.

In addition to the state-level consumer protection agencies, each state also has a number of boards and departments that regulate business and industry. State departments of insurance, for example, are responsible for overseeing insurance company rates and operations and assisting consumers who have problems with insurance companies. The state department of insurance would, for example, be the place to turn if your auto insurance company cancelled your policy and refused to give any explanation.

Each state also has boards that license members of particular occupations, such as barbers, car dealers, physicians, and dentists. One of the responsibilities of these boards is to ensure that the individuals licensed are competent and to receive complaints about their professional performance. It has been alleged frequently that the state regulatory departments and licensing boards are too close to the groups they are responsible for regulating and are therefore dominated by their viewpoints. State regulatory departments and licensing boards seldom seem inclined to take strong action. Most attempt to settle problems by mediation even if they have stronger powers (Serber, 1980).

Local News Media

Many local newspapers and TV and radio stations have developed consumer complaint centers as a service to their audiences. These centers can help consumers both with their problems with business and with getting service from government agencies. The media-run complaint centers go by a variety of names, including "Call for Action," "Action Line," and "Hot Line."

The centers serve as mediators between sellers and consumers. By opening a new line of communication, they can help to bring about solutions. While they cannot force a seller to take action, they do have the power of publicity.

In addition to helping individuals with problems, the media-run complaint centers also serve an educational function. Selected problems and results are reported in a regular column or broadcast. These reports can help teach consumers how to avoid problems and where they can go for help. Some centers also draw on their experiences to call for needed changes in business practices and consumer protection laws.

Laura Nader has alleged that the media-run complaint centers are most interested in unusual and newsworthy complaints (Nader, 1980). She suggests that they may turn away complaints that are uninteresting, familiar, or too complicated. She also alleges that they tend to be reluctant to name uncooperative firms for fear of upsetting advertisers.

Trade Associations

One of the major roles of business and professional organizations is to preserve and protect the reputation of the group they represent. As part of these efforts many associations develop codes of ethics or good practices to guide their members. Because of their concern with protecting the reputation of their industry or occupation, most trade associations will accept consumer complaints.

The range of complaint-handling services varies widely. Most trade groups seem to limit their action to forwarding complaints and asking the recipient to take action. Acting as a mediator is probably the most that the typical trade association can do. They have only limited power over their members, and the most drastic action they can take is to expel a member. Of course, they have no real power over nonmembers.

A few trade groups have gone a step further by developing consumer action panels to arbitrate problems. The existing panels deal with problems associated with big-ticket items including autos, appliances, and furniture. Some of the panels, such as the Major Appliance Consumer Action Panel (MACAP), operate at a national level. Others, such as Automobile Consumer Action Panels (AUTOCAP), operate at a regional level. The panels typically begin by referring the complaint to the manufacturer or retailer unless they have already have been contacted (Greenburg & Stanton, 1980). In the next step, the CAP serves as a mediator in asking the manufacturer or retailer to investigate the problem and indicate to the CAP what action is being taken. If the manufacturer or retailer fails to take action or if the consumer-complainer indicates dissatisfaction with the adjustment proposed, the case is referred to the panel for arbitration.

Panels typically have a number of members and include business, academic, and consumer representatives. After reviewing the evidence about the complaint, the panel proposes a solution. The proposed solution is not binding on the consumer-complainer. The decisions of some panels are, however, binding on the manufacturer or retailer involved.

Some researchers who have studied them are critical of the CAPs. They feel CAPs cool off consumers who think they are getting action, but often fail to resolve problems. The results may be to increase the time cost of complaining for consumers and lessen pressure for more effective solutions (Nader, 1980). The CAPs do take a good deal of time to complete action on complaints. One reason seems to be the amount of time involved if arbitration is required (TARP, Inc., 1979).

Federal Agencies

The federal government is involved in regulating a wide variety of business activities. Only a few agencies are, however, able or willing to help individual consumers. In most cases, federal agencies check complaint mail to see if patterns of abuse are occurring. If there is evidence of a serious and widespread problem and the agency does take action, only a few agencies have the power to order firms to make restitution to customers with problems. Most agencies focus on preventing future problems rather than remedying past ones. They are, in effect, trying to lock the barn door before more horses are stolen.

Federal agencies concerned with product safety are among those that are interested in problems of individual consumers.

- *National Highway Traffic Safety Administration* (NHTSA). The NHTSA tries to help individual consumers but will investigate only if a problem involves a safety risk on a number of vehicles. When a widespread safety risk is detected, there will be a voluntary or agency-ordered recall, and the defect will be corrected at no charge to the owner.

- *Food and Drug Administration* (FDA). The FDA is interested in individual complaints about safety problems with food (except meat, fish, and poultry products) and with drugs and cosmetics. It does not have authority to order firms to provide restitution to individual consumers. It can, however, ensure that unsafe products are taken off the market.

- *Meat and Poultry Inspection, U.S. Department of Agriculture.* This USDA agency is responsible for the safety and wholesomeness of fresh meat and poultry and processed products. It cannot order refunds or replacements but can ensure that unsafe products are removed from the market.

- *Consumer Product Safety Commission* (CPSC). The CPSC is interested in individual consumer problems with a wide variety of products, including clothing, toys, recreation and power equipment, and household cleaners and chemicals. If a safety problem is detected, the CPSC can ensure repair, replacement, or a refund.

- *U.S. Postal Service.* The Postal Service is concerned with mail fraud, false mail-order advertising, and unsatisfactory mail-order transactions. The Postal Service has had a record of some success in getting refunds for consumers with problems, though it has no power to force companies to make refunds.

Illustration 5-2
To protect consumers from deceptive appeals sent through the mails, the U.S. Postal Service actively pursues mail fraud.

U.S. Postal Service.

Many other federal government agencies accept complaints from individual consumers but will take action only when they detect patterns of abuse. The Federal Trade Commission, for example, has extensive powers to order refunds and other types of restitution to groups of consumers who have been misled by deceptive advertising. (See, for example, Consumer Case: "Manufacturer of Pest Control Device Agrees to End Ad Claims.") Even though a federal agency does not take action on individual problems, consumers should send the agency carbon copies of complaint letters. These letters become "votes" for action on a particular problem.

Small Claims Courts

Many legal problems involve amounts of money that are too large to forget but too small to justify a full-scale lawsuit. The small claims courts were developed for consumers and businesspeople with such problems who need a legal channel that is inexpensive and easy to use.

Small claims courts are readily accessible in most states. They usually are located in the county seat and in the larger cities. Court rules differ slightly from state to state (Rothschild & Carroll, 1986). All have ceilings on the amount that can be claimed, ranging from $150 to $5,000. No attorney is required. Some states permit the parties involved to bring an attorney; others do not.

116   Part 1   Understanding the Marketplace

CONSUMER CASE: MANUFACTURER OF PEST CONTROL DEVICE AGREES TO END AD CLAIMS

The Federal Trade Commission has charged Saga International Inc. with making false and misleading advertising claims about the effectiveness of its Home Free ultrasonic pest-control device. Under a consent agreement settling the charges, the company has agreed to refund the full $19.95 purchase price to consumers who bought the product in 1984 or later.

Saga International, which manufactured and sold Home Free, advertised it in newspapers and on radio and television throughout the country. The company claimed the product effectively repelled insects and rodents from home and business environments and eliminated the need to use traditional pesticides.

According to a complaint issued with the consent agreement, Home Free does not rid homes or businesses of rodents and insects and is not an effective pest-control alternative to traditional products, such as traps, powders, and sprays. In addition, the complaint alleged that Saga International lacked a reasonable basis for making its advertising claims.

The consent agreement requires Saga International to refund Home Free's full purchase price of $19.95 to any consumer who bought the product after December 31, 1983. In addition, Saga must provide signs for retailers to post about the availability of refunds and advertise their availability through newspaper ads. Saga International stopped marketing Home Free in the fall of 1985.

Under the consent agreement, Saga International may not claim that Home Free will:

- Eliminate cockroaches, rats, mice, or other pests from a buyer's home or business;
- Eliminate rodents or insects from a home or business within a specified time period; or
- Serve as an effective alternative to conventional pest-control products, such as sprays or other chemicals.

The order further requires Saga International not to make any performance claims for Home Free or any other ultrasonic pest-control product unless it possesses and relies upon competent and reliable evidence that substantiates its claims.

This consent agreement is the third one that the Commission has issued dealing with effectiveness claims of ultrasonic pest-control devices. It has accepted similar agreements with Sentronic Controls Corp. for claims about its Pest Sentry device and with Wein Products Inc. for claims about its Decimate product.

Consent agreements are for settlement purposes only and do not constitute an admission by a company that it violated the law.

QUESTIONS

1. Why has the FTC required Saga International Inc. to stop claiming its device rids homes of pests?
2. What remedy is the FTC requiring Saga International Inc. to offer to purchasers?
3. Saga International Inc. is the third manufacturer of ultrasonic pest control devices that has entered into a consent agreement with the FTC. What does this suggest about the adequacy of media reviews of ads as a way to protect consumers?

Source: Federal Trade Commission, *FTC News Notes* 86, no. 35/36 (June 16, 1986).

Because the small claims courts are part of the regular court system, the rulings are enforceable by law. A frequent complaint about the small claims courts, however, is that consumers who win their cases still have difficulties forcing the seller-defendant to pay or to take action. They frequently face additional expenses and fees to collect the judgment they have won.

The chief expense in using the small claims courts is the time and money involved in preparing the case as well as a small filing fee. The names of the courts that handle small claims differ among locales. Courts that handle small claims can be found in the state, county, and local listings of the telephone book, through the clerk's office in local courts, and through local consumer protection offices.

Further Legal Action

When an unsolved consumer problem involves a large amount of money, the consumer probably will eventually want to consider full-scale legal action. Because attorney's fees are substantial, court action is usually worthwhile only when a problem involves an expensive item, serious injuries from a product, or major property damage.

A lawsuit is typically a slow, expensive process. Court dockets are crowded in most areas, and there often are months of waiting before a case is heard in court. Many cases are, in fact, settled before they come to court. Seller-defendants often settle cases out of court when consumers with problems press legal action. They are motivated by the desire to save legal costs and the belief that a compromise settlement will be less expensive than the court judgment that might eventually be awarded. Consumer-plaintiffs, in turn, often accept these offers because of the burden of attorney's fees and uncertainty about whether they eventually will win.

Consumers who need legal help but feel they cannot afford a private attorney often can get free or low-cost help from local Legal Aid or Legal Services agencies. These offices can give advice on a variety of consumer problems including landlord–tenant disputes, contract and credit difficulties, and problems in obtaining government services.

Sometimes a large group of consumers will have a problem with a particular seller. While the individual losses involved may be too small to make legal action worthwhile, the total may be substantial. In such situations, a *class action* lawsuit may be feasible. Class action lawsuits involve a large number of plaintiffs with similar problems who band together to bring action against a particular defendant (Rothschild & Carroll, 1986). One well-known example of a class action is the case in the late 1970s which was brought against General Motors by Oldsmobile purchasers who discovered that their cars had engines produced by other GM divisions.

Class action suits can be conducted either in the state or federal courts. Recent changes in the rules surrounding class actions in the federal courts have made federal suits difficult. Bringing action through state courts seems to be somewhat easier.

COMPLAINERS'
PROBLEMS

The previous section of this chapter illustrates the varied sources of help available to consumers. Choosing the best ones is, however, a problem for most consumers. Several considerations enter into the choice.

- Is the seller local, out-of-town, or out-of-state?
- Does the problem involve a product or a service? If it is a service, is the seller licensed? Is the seller a member of a government-regulated industry?
- Is there a trade or professional assocation for the industry or occupation of which the seller is part?
- Do you suspect fraud or misrepresentation?
- Did the problem result in injuries, damages, or other costs beyond the cost of the item?
- Is the amount of money involved small, or is it large?

The answers to these questions can guide the consumer to the appropriate source of help.

Further help is available from other sources. Local consumer protection agencies and consumer groups can often provide useful advice about where and how to complain. The reference department of the local library can also provide help. One or more of the following resources should be available in the local library.

- *Consumer Resource Handbook*, published periodically by the U.S. Office of Consumer Affairs. Free single copies are available from Handbook, Consumer Information Center, Pueblo, CO 81009. This publication includes (1) general information about where and how to complain, (2) addresses of major corporations that sell consumer products and services, and (3) names and addresses of federal, state, and local consumer agencies.
- *Consumer Complaint Guide*, written by Joseph Rosenbloom and published periodically by Macmillan Publishing Company, New York. It provides comprehensive information on complaint procedures; government agencies, trade associations, and media-run complaint centers; and other sources of help. In addition it provides addresses of consumer product manufacturers and the trade names they use.

Once consumers have begun the process of seeking a remedy for a problem, initiative and persistence become very important. After each step of the complaint process is completed, nothing further will happen on the complaint unless the consumers continue their efforts. When one source of help is exhausted, the consumer must seek assistance from others.

MAJOR CHAPTER CONCEPTS

1. Consumers' rights and remedies grow out of the law of contracts. Contracts are agreements between two or more parties that set out the rights and duties of the parties and are enforceable by law.

2. A contract may not be enforceable if its terms are unconscionable (too one-sided), if undue pressure was used, or if a party who is a minor (below legal age) asks to be released.

3. By offering a product for sale, a seller creates several implied warranties: (1) warranty of merchantability (the product is of saleable quality); (2) warranty of fitness for purpose (it is suitable for the purposes intended or the needs the buyer has indicated); (3) warranty of title (the seller has a right to offer the item for sale).

4. Express warranties about a product and its performance may be made orally or in writing. Usually they provide repair, replacement, or refund as a remedy.

5. As legal views have changed in recent years, the original manufacturer has been made more responsible to the consumer-buyer for defective products under the doctrine of strict liability.

6. Consumers should consider complaining when a product's performance does not live up to either the implied or express warranties. When consumers complain they help themselves as well as all other consumers.

7. When a complaint is made, the consumer needs to be thoroughly prepared with a clear statement of the problem and the remedy desired and with supporting documents.

8. Typically, a complaint should be taken first to the seller. If this proves unsuccessful, the manufacturer should be contacted.

9. If these steps fail, a variety of government and business-sponsored sources of help are available. These third-party complaint handlers provide referral, mediation, arbitration, and adjudication of consumers' problems.

10. It is necessary to match the problem to the complaint handler with appropriate jurisdiction and power. The powers of most complaint handlers are limited.

11. When the procedures of a particular complaint handler are completed, consumers who want action will have to be persistent and seek other sources of help.

CONSUMER QUESTIONS

1. Think of a problem you have had recently with a consumer product or service. What would be an appropriate first step in complaining? If the problem is not resolved at this step, what are the appropriate follow-up steps you should take? Would legal action be appropriate for this problem? Why or why not?

2. Draft a complaint letter that would be appropriate for dealing with the problem you described in the activity above. In addition, draft a follow-up letter that could be used if your first letter did not produce the desired results.

3. Check the "Product Recalls" section in a recent issue of *Consumer Reports*. Find recalls involving three different types of products (for example, food products, autos, and household products). For each recall, indicate (a) the product, brand, and model involved, (b) the government agency involved, if indicated, (c) what consumers should do if they own the item, (d) what the manufacturer will provide; that is, repair, replacement, refund, or other services.

4. Study the product warranty in Chapter 4. Answer the following questions. (a) Who is protected under the warranty, the original owner or any owner? (b) How long is the warranty period? (c) How can warranty service be obtained? (d) What services will be provided under the terms of the warranty? (e) Who pays for parts and labor? (f) Why is the warranty labeled a "Limited Warranty"? (g) What changes in the warranty would be necessary for it to be classified as a "Full Warranty"?

5. *Consumer Reports, Changing Times,* and other consumer-oriented magazines sometimes carry feature articles describing consumer problems and experiences in the marketplace. Find an article on a problem that interests you and prepare a report on it. Include the article title and the name and date of the magazine. As part of your report, answer the following questions. (a) What is the nature of the problem? (b) Why has the problem developed? (c) Are any efforts being made to deal with the problem? By whom? What effects are these efforts having? (d) What new methods of dealing with the problem are being proposed?

SUGGESTED READINGS

1. Andreasen, Alan. "Consumer Complaints and Redress: What We Know and What We Don't Know." *Research in the Consumer Interest: The Frontier.* Edited by E. Scott Maynes. Columbia, MO: American Council on Consumer Interests, forthcoming. This chapter is an overview of the extensive research on consumer dissatisfaction and complaining behavior.

2. Best, Arthur. *When Consumers Complain.* New York: Columbia University Press, 1981. This work reports a comprehensive study of consumer complaining ac-

tivity. The relationship of complaining to the consumer's personal characteristics, the product involved, and the specific type of problem were investigated.

3. *Consumer Reports.* "The Manufactured Crisis: Liability-Insurance Companies Have Created a Crisis and Dumped It on You." 51, no. 8 (August 1986): 544-549. This article examines the so-called liability insurance crisis and provides proposals for alleviating it.

4. Dorfman, John. *Consumer Tactics Manual: How to Get Action on Your Complaints.* New York: Atheneum, 1980. The first section of this book provides advice on common consumer problems from Advertising to Workmanship. The second part suggests the most effective techniques for dealing with problems.

5. Nader, Laura, ed. *No Access to Law: Alternatives to the American Judicial System.* New York: Academic Press, 1980. This collection includes studies of various complaint-handling mechanisms ranging from department store complaint departments to a state Department of Insurance, along with suggestions for improving the handling of complaints outside the judicial system.

CHAPTER 6

~~~

ANALYZING CONSUMER ISSUES

Headline: Consumer Advocates Urge Ban of Food Preservative Suspected as Cancer Cause

Headline: Industry Leader Says New Product Safety Regulation Will Cost 300 Local Jobs

Headline: Government Outlines New Deregulation Plan as Way to Cut Prices

Government regulations designed to protect consumers are front-page news and the center of continuing controversy. Regularly consumers are called on to form an opinion on these consumer protection issues. Until this point in the book, we have focused on how to make personal decisions about managing money and choosing the best products. Consumer issues involve a different kind of decision making dealing with how this country should deal with social problems involving consumers.

RECOGNITION OF A PROBLEM

When does a social problem exist? Social scientists suggest that when the consequences of the actions of a group or of an individual affect others, then a potential public problem exists (Cordes, 1976). They also point out that these problems may or may not be recognized as actual social problems.

Factors Affecting Problem Recognition

The public's recognition of a social problem and its feelings about the problem seem to depend on several factors, including the following:

Effects of the Action. Usually there is concern about an action only if the effects are negative. People can also take actions that can affect others positively—such as observing the speed limit, cleaning up their property, and contributing to local charities. The public may want to encourage these actions.

Visibility of the Effects of an Action. If an action produces conspicuous and dramatic effects, it seems more likely to arouse concern than an action with less spectacular effects. For example, people tend to overestimate the number of deaths resulting from such dramatic and sensational causes as accidents, cancer, food poisoning, and homicides. At the same time they tend to underestimate the number of deaths from less spectacular causes such as diabetes, stroke, and asthma (Slovic, Fischoff, & Lichtenstein, 1980).

Concentration of the Effects on a Small Group. The effects of an action may arouse more concern if it seems to put unusual or unfair burdens on a small group or if it seems to give them some unusual or unfair advantages.

Perceived Control over the Problem. People often seem to be less concerned about problems if they feel they have control over them. While kitchen knives are a potential hazard, most people feel they can use them safely and effectively.

Linkage of the Consequences to the Action and Those Who Took It. A person's feelings about a problem are affected by the ease with which the consequences of an action can be linked to the action and to those who took it. Often the consequences of an action are not immediately apparent. Effects may be indirect or a long time in appearing. The results of exposure to dangerous chemicals, for example, may not show up as cancer for many years. When cause-and-effect relationships are not clear, concern may not develop because there is uncertainty about whom or what to blame.

Evaluation of the Consequences of an Action. Awareness of a social problem and feelings about it are also affected by the moral and ethical standards used in evaluating actions and their consequences.

Criteria for Evaluating Economic Behavior

Four criteria are often used in evaluating the effects of economic behavior and the policies of consumers, business firms, and the government itself. These moral and ethical standards, which are derived from widely held values, are:

- *Freedom.* The actions or individuals of groups should not interfere with the freedom of others in making product choices, deciding about jobs, selecting investments, or managing business or personal affairs.
- *Economic efficiency.* The actions of individuals or groups should not interfere with the performance of the market in getting the most out of available resources. Economic efficiency involves technical efficiency, i.e., using the smallest amount of resources to get a given output. Economic efficiency also means that prices reflect the full cost of a product to society. Product prices should reflect not only the cost of labor, materials, and the other resources used, but also such costs as controlling the pollution resulting from the production process. If the price of a product does not include controlling the pollution created, then those affected by the pollution are being forced to subsidize part of the product's cost.
- *Equity.* The actions of individuals or groups should help ensure that each group in the economic system — consumers, workers, managers, and investors — is treated fairly. No one group should benefit at the expense of another. Concern with equity usually goes further. Most Americans believe all members of society should have an adequate level of living, including individuals who currently may not be making any economic contributions such as those on welfare, the unemployed, and the disabled.
- *Security.* The actions of groups and individuals should promote the stability of prices, protect employment opportunities, and ensure the safety of savings and investments. They should also protect consumers from deceptive or misleading information as well as the hazards of unsafe products. Security may also involve ensuring a rate of economic growth sufficient to provide continuing increases in consumers' incomes and investment opportunities.

Why Some Problems Cause More Concern than Others

The following discussion should help to explain why certain kinds of consumer problems cause concern while others do not. Deceptive advertising is a widespread consumer concern and it is not hard to understand why. Deceptive advertising is highly visible and its effects are easily linked to the offending ad and advertiser. The use of deceptive ads falls short on several moral and ethical standards. Deceptive ads interfere with the freedom to make the best possible choice. They promote products that are overpriced and inequitably shift money from the deceived to the advertisers, thereby reducing the economic security of the deceived. Furthermore, they often involve health or safety risks.

The continuing concern with deceptive advertising can be contrasted with the lower level of concern the public seems to feel about the use of corporate power to reduce competition and raise prices. An example of such activities is the continuing effort of some manufacturers of nationally advertised brands of stereo equipment to force retailers to sell their products only at manufacturers' suggested retail prices. Retailers who attempt to discount these suggested prices may find their deliveries are delayed or stopped. The result is that competition in selling the brand is reduced, and prices are higher than they otherwise would be. Such problems are not highly visible. Even the retailer may not be certain exactly what is happening. The gradual disappearance of a particular brand from a stereo store's shelves is not nearly so conspicuous as a deceptive ad.

CONSUMER CONCERN: SHOULD WE ENCOURAGE THE USE OF DIESELS?

Diesel-powered engines offer advantages that have attracted many car and truck buyers. They get more miles per gallon than gasoline-powered vehicles, but the potential savings have to be balanced against the higher price of diesel engines. Many people have decided the advantages of diesels outweigh this extra cost.

The costs and benefits of diesels affect not only individual owners but also the public as a whole. At first glance it appears that a switch to diesels could make a significant contribution to national energy conservation goals. A gallon of diesel fuel provides 25 percent more miles per gallon than a gallon of gasoline. Producing a gallon of diesel fuel, however, takes more crude oil than producing a gallon of gasoline. The net savings in crude oil are estimated to be about 15 percent. The cost advantages of diesel fuel at the fuel pump have declined in recent years. A few years ago diesel fuel was substantially cheaper than gasoline. More recently, the difference has narrowed or disappeared.

Perhaps the greatest concern in any large-scale switchover to diesels would be the health hazards of diesel emissions. The most serious problem with diesel emissions is the large amount of particulate matter, or "soot," given off. Diesel engines without emission control produce many times the particulate matter that a gasoline engine produces. Research has linked airborne particulate matter to an increased risk of respiratory illness.

Concern with the effects of diesel-emitted particles goes beyond their role in increasing the chances of lung infections, bronchitis, and other respiratory illnesses. A more serious hazard arises from the large number of chemical compounds that cling to each soot particle in diesel exhaust. Many of these compounds are known or suspected to be carcinogens (causes of cancer).

The use of corporate power to restrict price competition violates the moral and ethical standards discussed earlier.

- It reduces the freedom to buy a particular brand.
- It interferes with economic efficiency by keeping prices artificially high.
- It is inequitable because it results in unfair gains by the manufacturer at the expense of both retailers and consumers.
- It adversely affects the economic security of retailers by reducing sales and of consumers by increasing prices.

Social problems can be analyzed using much the same process used in making individual decisions. The decision-making process outlined in

Diesel emissions are a concern everywhere but are a particular concern in urban areas, such as New York City, which have a high concentration of diesel-powered trucks and buses. Concern with diesel emissions has led the Environmental Protection Agency (EPA) to issue emissions standards for large trucks, vans, and buses. These standards are to be phased in in three steps over the period 1988 to 1994 to allow time for the development of the necessary pollution control technology (Peterson, 1985).

The EPA also set emission standards for diesel automobiles effective in 1982. Tougher, second-phase standards due to go into effect in 1985 were postponed until 1987 ("Cleaner Diesel Engine Rule Postponed for Two Years by EPA," 1984). This change is expected to have limited effect because sales of diesel-powered autos have declined from the high levels of the late 1970s and early 1980s.

QUESTIONS
1. Why does the EPA regulate emissions from diesel engines? What is the appeal of diesel engines to vehicle buyers?
2. Make a detailed list of the costs and the benefits of diesels without emission controls. On whom would each of these costs and benefits fall? What would be the timing for each cost or benefit?
3. Which of the identified costs and benefits fall directly on car owners? On citizens living and working near roads and highways? Are there other costs and benefits that result from those direct costs? For example, what are the effects on members of the medical professions, those who clean and paint buildings, or those producing and selling automotive fuels?

Chapter 2 can be applied to social issues. The steps in this process are as follows:

- *Identify the goal.* What is the nature of the problem? What are its causes? What is the desired state sought?
- *Identify alternatives.* What alternative solutions are available? Who could take action (business, government, consumers)?
- *Gather information on alternatives.* What facts are available on the effects of the alternatives? What are the costs and the benefits of each alternative?
- *Evaluate the Alternatives.* How well do the benefits of a particular solution offset the costs? How do particular alternatives measure up to the moral and ethical standards that can be used in evaluating economic actions?
- *Select an alternative and implement the decision.* Take action on the decision.

A further step in analyzing public problems is often more explicit and more openly discussed than when making personal decisions; however, it can be used in both kinds of decision making. This step is as follows:

- *Evaluate the results produced by the alternative chosen.* How effective has the selected alternative been in resolving the problem? How effectively was the alternative implemented? What have been its actual costs? Its benefits?

Each of the steps in analyzing social problems will be discussed in more detail in the following sections.

IDENTIFYING THE GOAL

For many consumer problems, the goal often seems rather general. We want to make product X safer, provide better information about product Y, and make the market for product Z more competitive. When goals are stated in such general terms, there seldom is much disagreement about them.

In identifying a goal or a desired state, a standard is set that will be given major weight in evaluating alternative solutions. Suppose, for example, auto safety is a serious problem. An appropriate goal might be to reduce the number of deaths and serious injuries resulting from accidents. Reducing the number of accidents, the number of automobiles in use, or the speed limit may be means towards this goal but are neither the outcomes desired nor ends in themselves.

Although the desired state may be clear, the underlying causes of a problem must be known before remedies can be identified. Disagreements about problems often begin at this stage. Businesspeople often blame consumers for consumer problems. They argue that consumers ignore safety instructions on hazardous products, do not read new label information, and do not show an interest in having a wide choice of brands offered. Consumer advocates, in turn, may suggest that the blame really should be placed on business because it fails to warn consumers about product dangers, it does not provide the information consumers want and can understand, it keeps products and prices so similar that there are no real differences among them, and it fails to include needed safety features.

Clearly the remedies to a consumer problem depend a great deal on the cause. If the cause is consumers' poor choices and poor use of product information, more emphasis is needed on making consumers aware of the information available and educating them to use it. If the cause is the result of poor business practices, then new regulations focused on business may be needed. Once the apparent cause of a problem is decided, the range of solutions is narrowed.

IDENTIFYING THE ALTERNATIVES

In dealing with consumer problems, two related sets of alternatives must be considered. One set deals with *who* will take action; the other, with *what* action will be taken. Because certain actions can only be taken by a particular group, it is difficult to completely separate the two sets of alternatives. For example, laws can be passed and enforced only by government.

Who Should Take Action?

There are four major alternatives as to who should take action.

Free Market. One alternative is to leave the problem to the workings of the marketplace. Many people believe that most consumer problems are only short-run difficulties. They feel that the operation of the free market will correct these problems, given time and freedom from interference. They argue, for example, that the problem of product safety will solve itself in the free market because fear of lawsuits and lost sales will discipline manufacturers. Those who argue for relying on the free market put a high value on keeping the marketplace free of government interference. They seem to feel some risks to individual safety are a small price to protect freedom and limit the activities of government. This group also argues that individual consumers should be free to decide for themselves how much risk they want to take in buying products. They argue that consumers should be free to buy less expensive but more potentially dangerous products.

Government. Others oppose the arguments of the free market advocates and suggest that many problems in the marketplace will not correct themselves. They label situations in which marketplace problems cannot correct themselves as *market failures*. One of the characteristics of market failures is that a transaction affects individuals or groups in addition to the producers and consumers who are parties to it. Economists call these effects *spillovers* (or externalities) because they affect bystanders who neither produce nor use a product. Spillovers can be either positive or negative but most concern is over negative spillovers.

Pollution is one example of a negative spillover. The negative effects of pollution occur when manufacturers reduce their costs by leaving pollution uncontrolled. Because of lower costs, these producers can sell their products for less. These savings are, however, produced at the expense of everyone who is affected by the negative spillovers of the production process. The result of this shift of some costs onto those who live near the plants is that the cost of the product does not really reflect all the costs to society of producing it.

Pollution spillovers violate several of the moral and ethical standards used to judge economic behavior. Pollution results in uncompensated injuries to health and damage to property, thus affecting security and equity. The failure of the product price to reflect the product's true cost to society means that the price does not measure up to standards of economic efficiency.

Economists have suggested the following major reasons why the forces of the market may not correct market failures (Stokey & Zeckhauser, 1978).

- *Information costs and uncertainty.* The corrective forces of the market work best when consumers are well informed. When they are well informed about product quality and prices, they can seek out the best buys and make sellers compete for their business. If consumers cannot get the information they need to evaluate products or cannot understand or use it, the corrective forces of competition will not work.
- *Transaction costs.* Although various kinds of legal and financial arrangements that would make the market work better usually are possible, those arrangements or transactions have costs. We saw earlier that the advocates of the free market feel that product liability lawsuits will control product safety problems. Such suits are, however, costly in terms of both time and money. Because of these costs, not every one with a problem will sue, especially if the loss was a small one. Some sellers of defective products will, therefore, escape the disciplining effects of legal action.
- *The free-rider problem.* When certain kinds of goods and services are produced, there is no way to keep people from benefitting even though they have contributed nothing toward the cost of production. There is, for example, no way to keep everyone in a community from benefitting from flood control efforts whether they contribute money for them or not. Because everyone benefits, whether they pay or not, there is no real motivation for anyone to pay. Everyone will try to be a "free-rider." When there is no way to control who benefits from a good or service, there is no way private enterprise can supply it and make money. One way to ensure that these goods and services are supplied is to have government provide them and finance them with tax revenues. Because such goods

benefit everyone and no one can be excluded from their benefits, economists call them *public goods.*

The free market also may not work well in cases of *natural monopoly.* Natural monopolies occur when it is cheapest to produce a good or service in large volume. In such cases, it is cheapest to let a single producer provide the entire supply of the item and to have government regulate the prices charged to ensure fairness. An example of such an arrangement is the right given utility companies to be the exclusive providers of water, telephone, or electric service. Such arrangements avoid the wasteful duplication of facilities, pipes, and lines. In return for special privileges, the utilities accept regulatory control with the promise they will get a fair return on their investment.

Another situation in which the free market does not work well is in cases of resource scarcity. When a particular resource is scarce, uncontrolled use may create such confusion and disorder that it becomes unusable. For example, the number of radio frequencies available is limited; therefore, some way must be found to control their use. Without such controls, interference will be a continuous problem. One solution is to have government take charge of allocating the available frequencies to different uses and users.

A final reason for government involvement is simply convenience. While it would be possible to leave providing some goods and services to private enterprise, it may be easier and simpler to have government provide them. For example, the provision of roads could be left to private enterprise. In fact, some major roads and bridges were built just this way in the early days in this country; private companies built them and charged tolls for their use. It is, however, much more convenient to have these services provided by government and financed by taxes. Just imagine the inconvenience of shopping for the cheapest route to drive from one city to the next!

Business Self-Regulation. A third possible answer to the question of who should take action on a problem is to have business regulate itself. Business self-regulation is often the result of efforts of trade groups and associations. The role of advertisers in supporting the Better Business Bureaus has already been noted. Many other business groups have codes of ethics and professional review groups to monitor the behavior of their members. Individual firms can also have codes of ethics. Some have consumer affairs officers who examine the effect of company policies on consumers and speak in behalf of consumer interests.

Consumer Action. A fourth and less familiar possibility is to leave the solution of the problem to individual consumers or groups of consumers. Consumer cooperatives, which are businesses owned and operated by and for their member-owners, are sometimes formed to deal with problems such as the provision and regulation of utilities.

What Alternative Actions Should Be Considered?

To reiterate, the first step in identifying alternative solutions to a problem is to identify who can or should take action. The second step is to identify the various policies available for dealing with a problem. Just what kinds of action seem feasible? In determining a policy, the positive approach of taking some particular action or requiring others to take it may be considered. Alternatively, the negative approach of avoiding some particular action or forbidding others to take it may also be considered. It also is possible to consider doing nothing and letting events take their course.

The list of consumer policy tools is a long and varied one. Rules can be used to influence the marketing and consumption process at any number of points and to specify how it should be carried out. Some of these rules are:

- *Controlling who can produce a product or provide a service.* Licensing can be used to ensure that those providing a service have adequate skills (e.g., licensing

Illustration 6-1
Licensing those who provide services is one technique used to protect consumers.

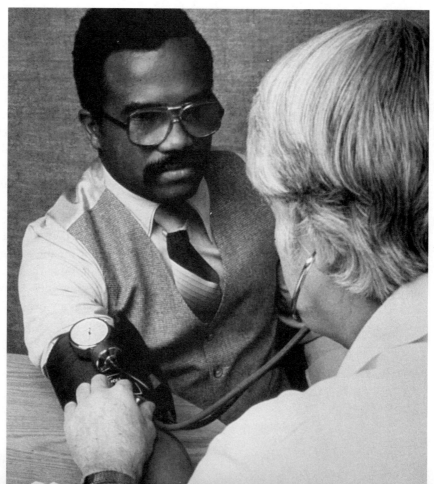

Courtesy of SmithKline Beckman Corporation.

of doctors). It also can be used to control use of a scarce resource such as the available broadcasting frequencies.

- *Specifying the design of a product.* Product standards may specify ingredients that must be used and those that may not be used. They may also specify safety features that must be included.
- *Controlling how a product or service is provided.* Rules may specify where, when, and how a product or service is provided. Information that must be provided to buyers and selling techniques that cannot be used may also be specified. For example, controls may be placed on the retailing of liquor (see Consumer Concern: "Controlling Alcohol Abuse: The Swedish Experience").
- *Specifying the performance a product must provide.* Rules (performance standards) may specify some minimum level at which a product must perform. An example would be rules about cars' performance in crash safety tests or gasoline mileage tests.
- *Controlling who can purchase or use a product or service.* Rules may set down the minimum age for purchase (e.g., for alcoholic beverages) or use (e.g., for driving a car). Drug prescriptions are another example of controls on purchase and use.
- *Influencing the price.* Rules may set maximum prices such as the ceilings put on the interest rates on consumer loans. Action can also be taken to discourage use of a product by making it more expensive (e.g., taxes on liquor and cigarettes). Products and services can be made easier to buy by subsidizing part of the cost so as to lower the prices charged (e.g., government subsidies to reduce fares on mass transit).
- *Controlling usage of product.* Rules may control how a product is used (speed limits) or procedures that must be followed in using it (e.g., wearing of helmets by motorcyclists or wearing of auto seatbelts).
- *Encouraging competition in the marketplace.* A variety of measures can be used to increase business competition or preserve it. Small business can be encouraged, business mergers controlled, and large firms broken up. Barriers to international trade that reduce competition from foreign producers can be eliminated. Anticompetitive behavior (such as price fixing, limits on output, and exclusive sales territories) can be forbidden.
- *Facilitating redress for damages and injuries.* A first step in facilitating redress is ensuring that channels are available for voicing and acting on consumer complaints. The court system can be made more accessible by providing small claims courts for those with problems involving small amounts of money and by providing legal aid for those with limited funds. Permitting class actions in which groups of people with the same problem join to-

gether in a suit may also facilitate redress. Both small claims courts and class action suits help to reduce transaction costs. Consumers' rights can also be limited by restrictions on product liability suits and other types of legal actions.

- *Improving consumer choice.* Consumer problems may also be attacked by providing consumers with better information to guide their choices. This information may be provided on labels or in informational brochures and pamphlets. Consumer education can be used to improve choice by increasing consumers' understanding of what they need and their ability to use information in making decisions.

Not surprisingly, different groups in the economy favor different alternatives (see Table 6-1).

GATHERING
INFORMATION ON
THE ALTERNATIVES
AND EVALUATING
THEM

It is easiest to consider together the next two steps of the decision-making process: gathering information on the alternatives and evaluating them. This section considers both the information which is used to evaluate alternatives and how it is used.

Costs and Benefits
of Alternatives

To evaluate alternatives, each must be measured against the criteria used for evaluating economic policies. Does the alternative maintain freedom? Protect security? Ensure equity? Contribute to economic efficiency?

Economists usually talk of the costs and benefits of alternative solutions to social problems in dollar terms, largely for convenience. It thus becomes easier to compare the total costs and total benefits. Behind these dollar figures are the positive and negative effects we are concerned about. Those that are evaluated positively on the basis of the standards used to judge economic actions are termed the *benefits*. In case of a regulation requiring auto passengers to wear seatbelts, for example, the benefits would include reduced injuries and deaths (improved personal security), reduced losses of earnings, and decreased insurance claims. The effects evaluated negatively are termed the *costs*. The costs of requiring the wearing of seatbelts include the loss of freedom of choice, the costs of the belts, and the costs of enforcement.

Classifying Costs and Benefits. A closer look at the costs and benefits of seatbelts reveals that not all of them fall only on car buyers or the auto industry. Some fall on others. To keep track of where the effects of a policy fall, three different kinds of costs and benefits are identified.

- *Direct costs and benefits* are the effects of a policy that fall directly on the parties involved, usually the buyer and the seller. One form of direct costs is *compliance costs* or the cost to the seller of conforming to a regulation. For example, compliance costs include the design cost for planning the

Table 6-1

Public Views on
Alternative Approaches
to Controlling Product
Hazards

	Top Corporate Executives (n = 402)	Congress (n = 47)	Federal Regulators (n = 47)	Public (n = 1,448)
People tend to not pay attention to warning labels, so stricter controls should be placed on the use of unsafe products	93%	66%	47%	66%
A consumer should be allowed a choice between a very safe product at a higher price and the same product without safety equipment at a lower price—that is, a choice between safety and cost.	59	30	51	51
Making corporations pay large settlements for injuries from defective products is a good way to make them more concerned about safety.	64	72	85	77

Source: Louis Harris and Associates, *Risk in a Complex Society.* New York: Marsh and McLennan, Inc. 1980. Used by permission of Marsh & McLennan, Inc.

installation of seat belts, the cost of the equipment itself, and the extra labor required to install them. Direct benefits to sellers may include increased sales revenues from selling the extra equipment. Costs for consumers in this category include the increase in product prices that may result when new safety equipment is added to a car. Another cost to consumers may be reductions in product performance, efficiency, or convenience. Important direct benefits for consumers include reduced risks of death, disability, or injury.

- *Indirect costs and benefits* are effects that grow out of the direct costs and benefits. Costs in this category include the loss of auto worker jobs if higher prices for cars including safety features reduce sales. Another type of indirect cost is government enforcement costs. Indirect benefits include nationwide reductions in the burden of auto accident-caused deaths, disabilities, and injuries as well as insurance costs. It is evident that indirect effects involve many groups in the economy beyond car buyers and sellers.

- *Induced costs and benefits* are effects that grow out of the indirect costs and benefits. This category includes the effects of the various indirect costs and benefits and the resulting effects on government's tax revenues. For example, if added safety equipment increases car prices and reduces sales, unemployed workers may need welfare benefits and will be paying little or no income tax.

Problems in Measuring Costs and Benefits. The costs and benefits of a particular policy can be discussed in a general way, but measuring them requires more specificity. Conceptualizing costs and benefits in ways that permit their measurement is often difficult. Just what are the benefits

CONSUMER CONCERN: CONTROLLING ALCOHOL ABUSE—THE SWEDISH EXPERIENCE

Alcoholism is the focus of a continuing social debate in Sweden. Posters warn parents not to buy alcoholic drinks for their children. Unions promote efforts to reduce the number of workdays lost through drunkenness, and a whole range of limitations on liquor sales have been under discussion.

In keeping with national concern over the quality of citizens' lives, the alcoholism question has probably been studied more thoroughly in Sweden than in any other country. The problem has attracted new and deeper concern in recent years. One reason may be the 1977 policy change that reduced the number of arrests for drunkenness. Since then the public has seen more public drunkenness, especially among young people (Apple, 1980).

Between 1917 and 1954, Sweden had an alcohol-rationing system. The system was finally abandoned when it was shown that most of those arrested for public drunkenness had gotten their liquor illegally. In recent years, increased prices have been used as one way to limit consumption. Taxes on alcoholic beverages have been increased steadily, with the highest rates on those with the highest alcohol content (Götestam & Röstum, 1984).

The Swedes are not among the world's greatest per capita consumers of alcohol, and Swedish drinking habits have not resulted in an epidemic of alcoholism-related diseases like cirrhosis of the liver. Government studies have concluded, however, that the social costs of alcohol abuse in terms of broken homes, battered children, and shattered careers are high.

of improving product safety? A frequent answer is the prevention of injury and death. Clearly, however, death cannot really be prevented, only delayed. What needs to be measured is the value of the years added to individual life spans.

A variety of approaches to valuing human life have been suggested. The *human capital approach* bases the calculation on an individual's earnings during the years added to the life span. (This calculation is usually discounted to present value.) This approach works well for those who are employed or can be expected to be. It is more difficult in the cases of homemakers or retired workers.

Another approach, the *value of life approach,* is used to determine how much individuals would pay to avoid the risk of death or injury. On the basis of what people will pay, it is possible to estimate the value they put

The campaign against alcohol has strong political support in Sweden. But while the crusade against alcohol is going on, the government is profiting from the liquor trade through its two monopoly organizations, the Swedish Wine and Spirits Corporation, which controls imports and the wholesale trade, and the retail monopoly, which operates retail liquor stores. All profits from these operations go to the government. The retail monopoly does not promote alcoholic beverages. There is no advertising, and there is no pressure from salespeople. The retail monopoly is based on the idea that there should be no private gain from liquor sales. The retail system emphasizes both positive and negative aspects of drinking. Posters warning against excess alcohol use are posted in all its shops.

Government also supports other efforts to reduce alcohol consumption: prevention and information campaigns, leisure activities for young people, alcohol-free restaurants, and temperance organizations. In recent years, higher taxes seem to have begun to cut consumption (Statistics Sweden, 1985). Government leaders, however, feel there is not much more they can do. They feel that the current restrictions are as much as people will accept. Further restrictions, they fear, will only increase illegal home production and lawbreaking.

QUESTIONS

1. Is alcohol abuse regarded as a social problem or an individual problem in Sweden? Why?
2. What policies have been used to control alcohol abuse? Who has implemented these policies? How effective has each been?

on their lives and on avoiding injury. One method of making these estimates has been to look at differences in pay between more and less hazardous occupations. The difference is taken to represent the premium that individuals require to take the extra risks of the more hazardous occupation. This approach is, however, appropriate only if individuals fully understand the risks of different occupations.

Some people are repelled by such attempts to put a value on human life. "Human life is priceless," they argue. In one sense it is, of course; but in another sense it is not. At some point the risks of fatal accidents at intersections do not justify a traffic light. This decision is made knowing that a traffic light could reduce the risk.

The problem of conceptualizing the benefits of consumer information can also be a difficult one. Just what does information do for consumers? It often results in the purchase of more or less of a product. A key benefit of product information can be that consumers buy more or get better quality than might otherwise have been purchased and, as a result, obtain greater satisfaction. Conversely, buying less of a product (or spending less on it) than might result in less dissatisfaction.

Even after deciding what to measure, policy analysts still face the problem of estimating the value of a cost or benefit. In solving social problems, the opportunity to experiment with different approaches to see how they work out is rare. Instead, officials often settle on a single solution without ever really having had an opportunity to try it out and thus base their decision on estimates of its expected costs and benefits. These estimates can err in several ways.

Frequently the benefits of a particular policy are overestimated. Programs expected to help all consumers may help only certain groups. A number of studies, for example, have found that when consumer information is made available, it is used chiefly by people with higher incomes and more education, though use may spread to other groups over time (McElroy & Aaker, 1979).

Errors also may be made in estimating costs. The costs of compliance to new consumer regulations also are often overestimated. Costs are overestimated for several reasons. One is that the development of new technology often makes compliance cheaper than expected. Compliance costs may also be overestimated because, in many cases, businesses comply without being required to do so. Firms are always concerned with protecting their reputations for reliability, safety, and performance. Product changes that help businesses protect their reputations are likely to be adopted even if not required.

Overall, benefits probably are more difficult to estimate than costs. It is more difficult to conceptualize what is being measured with benefits

Illustration 6-2
Product information can guide consumers in adjusting their purchases in order to achieve greater satisfaction.

than with costs. Estimating benefits may involve such problems as assessing the value of information, the preservation of good health, and the avoidance of premature death. Often the problems of estimating benefits are so complex that policy analysts do not even try. When it comes time to use the estimates of costs and benefits to evaluate a policy, the dollar figures for the costs are usually fairly clear, though they often are overestimated. The estimates of the benefits are, however, often only vague guesses. This imbalance tends to work against proposed consumer protection programs.

The Influence of Timing. In choosing between policy alternatives, policy makers and the public are likely to prefer policies whose benefits are large and immediate and whose costs are small and far in the future. The reasons for this preference are easy to understand. Most people are quite willing to pay a small amount now to obtain large payoffs in the near future. In financial terms, the present value of the discounted stream of expected benefits is large, while the present value of the discounted stream of costs is smaller. Most people are not willing to pay much now to obtain a small payoff or avoid a small expense far in the future, however.

Policies that offer large current benefits, but whose costs are far in the future, can create a temptation to live high now at the expense of future generations. Holding the cost of consumer goods down in the present by leaving pollution and hazardous wastes uncontrolled is one way costs can be shifted into the future. Financing high government expenditures by long-term debt is another. Some people rationalize such shifts by arguing that the development of new technology and rising incomes will make it cheaper to deal with these problems in the future than it is now, which may or may not be true. The intergenerational shift of costs could create heavy and unfair burdens for the people of the future.

The Distribution of Costs and Benefits. Another concern in evaluating alternative policies is how benefits and costs are distributed. Questions to be answered include "Just who will benefit from the proposed policy, and who will bear its costs?"

In general, the desire for equity results in favoring policies whose costs fall on those who receive the benefits. For example, because auto owners receive most of the benefits from safety devices, they should not expect the government (and taxpayers) to bear the costs of the equipment. Sometimes, however, a policy whose costs fall on the general public but which chiefly benefits some disadvantaged group (such as the poor, handicapped, or aged) may be favored. In such cases, income is being shifted from taxpayers to the disadvantaged group.

Some opponents of government regulation have argued that instead of shifting income from the affluent to the poor, many regulations do exactly the opposite. They argue that many consumer protection programs focus on the concerns of those with more income and education. The poor, they argue, do not really want to pay higher product prices for more product information, safer products, or a cleaner environment. Government regulations, however, have usually given them no choice.

This argument can be countered by noting that society, as a whole, has an interest in what its members consume and what risks they take. Although individual consumers may want to buy a less safe and less expensive product, society has an interest in protecting innocent bystanders who could be injured. Society also has an interest if product injuries create substantial indirect costs for society as a whole. While drivers of unsafe cars bear some of the costs of accidents (lost earnings, property damage, hospital costs), accidents also create indirect costs that fall on society as a whole. These costs include increased insurance rates for all policy-holders, police and court costs, and the welfare costs of caring for the disabled and surviving family members.

As we noted earlier, there are four different institutions or groups that can be used to implement consumer protection policies: the free market, government, business self-regulation, and consumers. In evaluating each of these alternatives, it is important to remember that each one has certain unique strengths and weaknesses and is especially suited to particular kinds of problems.

The Free Market. We are willing to leave many kinds of questions up to the free market to decide. We are quite content to let market demand control such things as what styles of jeans to produce and the amount of fresh produce to grow. Leaving questions to the free market maintains individual freedom. When the free market works well and there is active competition, its performance may meet other important standards, too. Competition can help ensure equity, and the prices consumers must pay will be fair ones.

Competition and the free market may, however, work against security and stability. They give the individual producer no protection from competitors with new technology that can reduce costs or from economic fluctuations that can increase operating costs or reduce demand. Perhaps this situation explains why businesspeople favor competition for others, especially for the companies from whom they buy; but for themselves, they prefer some shelter from the sometimes violent fluctuations of the free market.

The working of the free market may not ensure economic efficiency either, if spillovers exist. As seen earlier, when spillovers, such as pollution, exist, the free market price does not really represent the full cost to society of producing the product. When this happens the standard of economic efficiency is not met. If spillovers unfairly shift costs from the product's producers and consumers onto innocent bystanders, standards of equity are violated.

As explained earlier, the free market does not work well in cases of natural monopoly. When a natural monopoly exists, it is cheapest to let a single producer supply the entire output. If the free market is allowed to operate, however, there are likely to be multiple producers, and prices will be higher. This situation fails when measured against our standards of economic efficiency, but it does score well on freedom.

We noted another situation in which the free market may not work well: cases of resource scarcity. In such cases uncontrolled use of a scarce resource, such as the radio waves, may create chaos. While imposing controls may reduce freedom, it does help ensure economic efficiency and promote security and stability.

Government Regulation. Government regulation may interfere with individual freedom for some, but it can expand freedom for others. For example, government regulation limits advertisers' freedom to use deceptive

Illustration 6-3
Some marketplace problems must be resolved through the political process and the passage of new legislation.

Photo provided courtesy of Washington Convention and Visitors Association.

claims, but it also frees consumers from the threat of exploitation and fraud.

In some cases, government is called on to intervene in the marketplace because an equitable balance between the various special interests involved is needed. Only government is in the position to find a solution through the political process and to give it the force of law.

The government also has powers to encourage economic efficiency. In the case of natural monopolies, for example, it can limit production to a single regulated firm in order to hold prices down. It can take measures to ensure equity, too. For example, it can require auto owners to carry insurance to help make certain that, as a group, they will meet the costs of the damages and injuries for which they are responsible.

The government has unique powers for ensuring economic stability. Only government is in a position to use economic policy to try to control business fluctuation and inflation. It has special powers over both fiscal policy (tax action and government spending) and monetary policy (the money supply and interest rates). The government has control over other programs that are also used to help ensure economic stability and security as well as equity. Some of these programs include unemployment compensation, social welfare programs for those unable to work, and social security.

Still, government regulation as an alternative does not always work well or produce the desired results. The problem may be too big, too complex, or too difficult, or it may be basically unsolvable. The idea that nothing really can be done about a problem is not acceptable to many Americans, who are committed to action to solve problems. They are convinced that there is always something that will work. When everything else fails, the problem may be given to government, which may not be able to handle the problem very well either.

Business Self-Regulation. Self-regulation by business can offer certain advantages. Business knows the problems of the marketplace first-hand and has ready access to the expertise needed to deal with many of them. Business can be strongly motivated to make self-regulation work. It wants both to preserve its reputation and to ward off government regulation. Business' concerns and emphases in regulating itself may not, however, be the same as the public's. As a result, business' efforts may not really deal with the problems the public feels are most serious.

Because self-regulation minimizes outside interference with business affairs, it measures up well on the criterion of freedom. Self-regulation, however, has a serious weakness. It has proven difficult over the years for most groups to police themselves. Few seem willing to point the finger at members who violate group standards. Even when groups do judge members unfavorably there usually is little they can do to punish them except to expel them. As a result, trade groups have only limited power to control members' behavior.

Some individual firms have tried to police their own activities to ensure better protection for consumer interests. The activities of consumer affairs officers in individual firms seem, however, to have only a limited impact on the company, but they do serve a useful role in handling consumer complaints. Unfortunately it appears that in most firms they have little opportunity to use what they have learned from consumers to influence high-level corporate policy (Fornell, 1976).

Consumers. Consumers as a group have serious handicaps in dealing with marketplace problems. Typically, they do not have the technical expertise to deal with complicated problems. They also have difficulty in getting access to the kinds of funding needed to carry on many kinds of activities. These problems affect all kinds of consumer efforts, from forming consumer cooperatives to organizing groups to influence regulatory decision making in government. Because of their limited resources, consumers have had to focus their efforts on getting government to act in their behalf rather than on acting for themselves.

SELECTING AN ALTERNATIVE

Assessing the seriousness of a problem and evaluating alternative approaches to it is usually left to technical experts. The final decision about the choice of an appropriate policy is, however, a political decision. These policy choices fall on elected officials, government officers, and business leaders who may, of course, decide to take no action at all if the problem seems unsolvable or if the costs of action seem to outweigh the benefits. When they do decide to take action, they must choose both a policy and a way to implement it. Implicit in this choice are decisions about who will bear the costs of the program and who will receive the benefits. Public officials may approach social problems and their solutions in very different ways because of their differing ideological perspectives. (See Consumer Capsule: "Economic Ideology and Consumer Protection Policy.")

No single policy approach ever seems to measure up well on all our standards. Clearly trade-offs have to be made among them. Protecting personal security by ensuring product safety inevitably means more government intervention in the marketplace. It also may mean increased product prices, which adversely affect economic security. Because of the trade-offs that must be made, the approach finally selected to deal with a problem is often a compromise. It frequently is not the most effective way to deal with the problem but may meet other important standards, such as minimizing the role of government and ensuring equitable treatment for all the groups involved. Solutions in other countries in which decision making is highly centralized may be more effective. They may, however, gain in efficiency by sacrificing other goals such as freedom and equity.

EVALUATING THE ALTENATIVE CHOSEN

Even after a particular consumer protection policy has been chosen and implemented, the arguments over it seldom end. Those who feel burdened by the new policy call for modifications. During the 1970s and 1980s there have been many demands for "deregulation" (the removal of governmental regulations designed to protect the public). These demands have been justified by arguing that regulation contributes to inflation by reducing productivity and interfering with competition, that it limits individual freedom and incentives, and that it interferes with efforts to counter foreign competition.

The advocates of deregulation do not, however, entirely agree on what regulations should be removed. Political and economic conservatives argue that all types of regulation should be reduced. Most consumer advocates agree that increased competition in regulated industries such as broadcasting, airlines, trucking, and railroading can be beneficial for consumers. They feel that economic regulation of this type can safely be eased. Few consumer advocates, however, see any potential gains from reducing health and safety regulation.

Evaluating the effects of consumer protection programs often proves more difficult than might be expected. One reason is that it is often difficult

CONSUMER CAPSULE:
ECONOMIC IDEOLOGY AND CONSUMER PROTECTION POLICY

Consumer protection proposals are often controversial because the American public does not completely agree on how our economy works or on how its performance could be improved. We are divided into three or four separate camps, each with its own set of beliefs or economic ideology. Each camp holds certain distinct beliefs about the structure of the economy, about how firms within it conduct themselves, and about the effects of the firms' conduct.

Each ideological camp also has its own beliefs about the kinds of problems consumers may have and the most appropriate ways to remedy these problems. The different camps do not agree on whether or not consumers need more protection. Even those who believe that consumers need more protection disagree on whether it should be provided through marketplace competition, through self-regulation by business, or through government regulation.

ECONOMIC BELIEF SYSTEMS

Before the relationship between economic ideology and consumer protection policy is examined, the most common belief systems will be reviewed.

The Neoclassical Belief System. The oldest and most theoretically developed system is the neoclassical belief system. It holds that our economy is, or should be, characterized by competitive free enterprise. Those who advocate this system see the economy as governed by competition among firms that strive to win new customers by providing the products consumers want. They believe that the power of even very large firms is limited by their current or potential competition.

Consumers in turn are thought to know what they want and to be immune to the manipulation of their basic needs and desires. Their choices determine the fate of the products offered in the market, making consumers the governing force of the economy. Consumers' power over the marketplace is called *consumer sovereignty*. The neoclassical belief system emphasizes freedom for individual consumer choice. Attempts to control consumer spending, such as requirements for safety equipment, are regarded as interference with free choice.

The neoclassicists see little need to regulate advertising claims. Consumers are considered to be able to make informed product choices and to avoid being deceived by inflated advertising claims. Outright deception is seen as a problem, but court action against false claims is felt to be an adequate corrective device. Most neoclassicists favor consumer information as a device to encourage competition. They often, however, resist rules requiring the provision of information and raise questions about whether the benefits of information offset the costs of providing it.

It is argued that, because of concern for their reputations and liability for injuries, most manufacturers produce the safest products they can. Government safety regulation is considered ineffective and an interference with desirable new products. It also is argued that if manufacturers are forced to meet the highest possible safety standards their products will be so expensive that no one can afford them. Strict regulations are seen as denying consumers the chance to assume greater risks and to pay lower prices. The use of the courts is seen as an adequate means of consumer redress for those injured by faulty products.

Competition between firms is seen by the neoclassicists as the best way to ensure that consumers' needs are met and that their welfare is protected. They argue that government regulation of the marketplace should be kept to a minimum because it interferes with the forces of competition. Advocates of the neoclassical belief system include economist Milton Friedman and a number of conservative politicians and businesspeople.

The Managerial Belief System. The managerial belief system emphasizes the central role of the professional manager in the modern corporation. This viewpoint recognizes the many changes that have taken place in the American economy and attempts to update cerain portions of the neoclassical belief system. It recognizes that the economy is dominated by large corporations but nevertheless views the market as highly competitive. Competitive efforts are based on differences in quality, service, design features, and warranties, not just on differences in price.

A basic tenet of the managerial belief system is that the modern corporate executive is a trustee for consumers, employees, and shareholders. The consumer is thought to be protected not only by corporate management's sense of social responsibility but also by its commitment to the idea that the best route to success is to find new ways to serve consumers' needs. This idea has been labeled the *marketing concept.*

The managerial belief system assumes that advertising influences consumers' buying decisions. It argues that such influence is beneficial because it shows consumers new ways to satisfy their needs and also stimulates demand, thereby promoting a high level of economic activity.

The managerial belief system recognizes that the government will have a major role in the economy but focuses its concern on what government does and how effectively it performs. One of government's important roles is felt to be maintaining economic activity at a high level. The need for some regulatory activity to protect consumers is acknowledged, but it is generally believed that consumers are protected by competition and by corporations' sense of responsibility.

In the managerial belief system, consumers and their interests are a key concern. Consumers are not, however, thought to have the degree of sovereignty that they are held to have in the neoclassical belief system. Middle-of-the road businesspeople in both political parties and *Fortune* magazine are advocates of the managerial belief system.

The Liberal-Reform Belief System. Many of the arguments put forth by consumer advocates regarding the problems of consumers and appropriate solutions to them grow out of the liberal-reform belief system. This system has its roots in the reform tradition of the progressive movement of the turn of the century, the New Deal in the 1930s, and the liberal reform movement of the 1960s.

Ralph Nader's perception of the structure of the American economy derives from this tradition. Nader believes the economy is dominated by large corporations that use their size and power to control both the marketplace and the government. He suggests these large corporations operate unchecked by competition, public exposure, or antitrust action by government.

Nader argues for antitrust action. He is a proponent of strict government regulations (1) to control corporations' socially irresponsible activities (such as pollution and fraud) and (2) to force more socially responsible behavior (such as reduction of air and water pollution and the production of safer products). Nader generally has been disappointed in the performance of the regulatory agencies. He has repeatedly urged them to take stronger positions in enforcing existing laws.

Nader and other consumer advocates have argued that consumers also need protection because of the complexity of today's products, contracts, and warranties. Consumers, they feel, must have information that will enable them to perform more effectively in the marketplace.

The Radical Belief System. The fourth system of beliefs — the radical belief system — regards consumers' problems as a result of the flaws of the capitalist system. It is argued that consumers are not provided the full range of goods and services they might desire. Instead, they are offered only those consistent with the capitalistic organization of the economy. It also is argued that the problems of consumers can be remedied only by a complete reorganization of the entire economic system.

To most consumers, such a reorganization seems to involve more danger than the problems it proposes to solve. This belief system seems to have only a few supporters and few visible spokespeople.

SUPPORT FOR CONSUMER PROTECTION PROPOSALS

In view of this variety of economic beliefs, it is not surprising that some kinds of consumer protection proposals have more support than others. Proposals for increasing the availability of product information probably win the widest support. Product information is seen as encouraging competition and the manufacture of better and more reliable products, a goal valued by the three major belief systems. Safety proposals seem to get less general support. While those linked to the managerial and liberal reform belief systems see the need for government involvement in the safety area, the neoclassicists often do not.

Support for antitrust proposals is scattered. Although the neoclassicists value competition, they fear all kinds of government activity, including trust busting. The managerialists see the control of price fixing and other kinds of anticompetitive behavior as desirable, but they see little need for breaking up large corporations just because they control a large share of the market. The liberal-reform tradition puts stronger emphasis on the control of corporate power, which they see as the central problem of the economic system. They advocate antitrust action along with other controls.

QUESTIONS

1. What problems do each of the different belief systems believe consumers have?
2. What remedies does each group believe are appropriate for consumer problems?
3. How would each group feel about consumer education?

to determine what the situation really was before a new law or program was undertaken. Without this baseline information, there is no basis for measuring any changes. For example, because there is no accurate information available on how many consumers really understood consumer credit before the Truth-in-Lending Law was passed, it clearly is impossible to determine the effect the law has had.

The problem of measuring the impact of a new law is complicated by other problems, too. Changes can occur over time for a variety of reasons, and the impact of a new law or program is only one of them. Other factors such as changing economic conditions, purchasing patterns, or population characteristics can also have significant effects. As a result of difficulties in determining the causes of changes, it is often impossible to be certain exactly what effect a particular policy has had.

CYCLES OF CONCERN

The amount of concern with consumer problems and consumer protection varies over time. Historically, there have been three major periods of concern in the United States. The first occurred around the turn of the century, the second in the 1930s, and the third in the 1960s and 1970s. In each period, rising consumer prices and product safety crises focused public attention on consumer issues. Extensive media coverage fed these concerns. In each of these periods, public concern led to new legislation and the organization of new groups to protect consumer interests. After a time, however, concern waned, and consumer issues disappeared from the news.

Several factors seem to contribute to the variation in public concern with consumer issues and with other social issues. One reason for the cyclical fluctuations in concern is the role of the news media. News media coverage of issues is itself cyclical. When an issue first becomes news, it receives extensive coverage. Soon, however, it is no longer "news." Concern also tends to decline if conditions appear to be getting better or to be under control. Once new laws are enacted or new programs begun, public concern is likely to ease. A third factor that contributes to the decline in concern is increasing awareness of the costs or difficulties of really solving a problem.

When a problem first surfaces, there are urgent demands that it receive attention. The problem is often regarded as intolerable, and no cost seems too great to bring it under control. Over time, however, it often becomes clear that the problem is neither simple nor easy to solve.

If resolving a problem involves major sacrifices by large groups of people, public concern may wane. Low-cost technological solutions are usually acceptable, especially if their use is voluntary. Consumer education and information programs are widely favored as solutions because they meet these criteria. Solutions that require significant behavioral changes (e.g., seatbelt interlocks with auto ignition systems) get a less favorable reception, however. Solutions that seem likely to require financial sacrifice (e.g., a $.50 per-gallon tax on gasoline to reduce usage) or that involve major social or institutional rearrangements are even less acceptable.

MAJOR CHAPTER CONCEPTS	1. A potential public problem exists when the actions of a group or individuals affect others.

MAJOR CHAPTER CONCEPTS

1. A potential public problem exists when the actions of a group or individuals affect others.

2. Four standards are often used to evaluate the effects of the economic behavior of consumers, business firms, and government: freedom, economic efficiency, equity, and security.

3. Decisions about alternatives in dealing with consumer problems require consideration as to who should take action and what action should be taken.

4. Action to deal with consumer problems may involve the free market, government, business self-regulation, or consumers.

5. While the free market can deal with many problems, government intervention may be needed in cases of market failures, natural monopoly, resource scarcity, and for convenience.

6. Market failures usually involve spillovers (effects on others besides the buyers and sellers). Market failures cannot correct themselves because of information costs and uncertainty, transaction costs, and the free-rider problem.

7. A wide variety of policies, ranging from controls on the product and its sale to limitations on its use by consumers, may be used to protect consumers.

8. In evaluating alternative policies, we need to assess both the costs and benefits of a policy. These may be direct (affecting buyers and sellers), indirect (affecting third parties besides buyers and sellers), or induced (affecting the overall level of economic activity).

9. In evaluating a policy, we also need to be concerned with the distribution of costs and benefits among different groups and the timing of these costs and benefits.

10. Selection of a policy alternative involves tradeoffs among the standards of freedom, equity, economic efficiency, and security.

11. Evaluating the effects of a policy is complicated both by deciding exactly what its benefits are (e.g., what is the value of reducing risks) and by measuring them (e.g., how should we measure the value of a human life?).

12. Concern with consumer and health and safety problems has varied over time and is influenced by news media coverage, the success of policies to deal with them, and the cost of these policies.

CONSUMER QUESTIONS

1. Have you or someone you know recently experienced a product-related injury? What could have been done to prevent it most effectively? What do you feel would be the costs and benefits of such a measure? Who

150   Part 1   Understanding the Marketplace

would bear the costs and receive the benefits of the measure that you feel would be most effective?

2. Examine recent news reports of controversies concerning product safety. *U.S. News and World Report* and *Consumer Reports* are good sources for such articles. What is the problem? What remedial policies have been proposed? What would be the costs and benefits of the proposed policy? What disagreements are there about these costs and benefits and desirability of the policy?

3. What kinds of product-related risks concern you the most? The least? How do the factors affecting awareness of consumer problems listed early in the chapter help explain your responses?

SUGGESTED READINGS

1. Feldman, Laurence P. *Consumer Protection: Problems and Prospects.* 2d ed. St. Paul: West Publishing Co., 1980. This work extensively examines the major issues of consumer protection and considers regulatory efforts to deal with these problems.

2. Friedman, Milton, and Rose Friedman. *Free to Choose: A Personal Statement.* New York: Harcourt Brace Jovanovich, 1979. The Friedmans make powerful arguments for entrusting the protection of consumers to the operation of the free market. Chapter 7, "Who Protects the Consumer?", focuses specifically on consumer issues.

3. Nadel, Mark V. *The Politics of Consumer Protection.* Indianapolis: Bobbs-Merrill, 1971. This book provides an insightful examination of the development of consumer protection as a political issue and of the involvement of the Congress, executive branch, and consumer advocates.

4. Swagler, Roger M. *Consumers and the Market: An Introductory Analysis.* Lexington, Mass.: D.C. Heath, 1979. Swagler applies basic economic principles to the problems of consumers in the marketplace. Continuing concerns such as the adequacy of consumer information, the impact of advertising, the relative power of consumers in the marketplace, and the appropriate role for government are considered.

PART 2

MANAGING SPENDING

CHAPTER 7

CLOTHING

Most people, if asked, would say they dress to please themselves. In fact, in one survey more than 90 percent of the people questioned said they were more concerned about their own preferences than about what others thought (Roper Organization, 1980, p. 93). Most people are interested in clothes that are comfortable, practical, durable, and easy to care for. These characteristics help us meet the basic need for physical protection from sun, wind, and cold.

However, most people want more from clothes than just protection from the elements. They want clothes in styles and colors that make them look their best. Self-expression through clothing helps meet aesthetic needs as well as enhancing self-esteem. People also want clothing that will make a good impression on others. Despite claims that they dress to suit themselves, most people *are* concerned about what their clothes say to others. They are convinced that it is possible to "dress for success," both on the job and socially. The approval of others is another important need for most people.

Clearly, people want their clothes to meet a variety of needs, and they typically have definite budget limits. Good wardrobe planning and careful buying are therefore very important.

THE FIRST STEP: PLANNING A WARDROBE

Most people cannot get along with just one wardrobe. They really need at least three separate sets of clothing for different kinds of activities:

- *Work clothing* — For the role of employee or student
- *Social clothing* — For informal and formal social occasions, parties, and religious services
- *Casual clothing* — For sports and recreation activities, other leisure activities, and household chores including house cleaning, car care, and home repairs

Some clothing items, of course, can serve several purposes. The sweater worn to class may also be suitable for an informal party or for casual wear. Other items may have more limited use. Black shoes chosen to go with a navy-blue suit probably will not be very useful either for class or casual wear.

An important part of planning is developing a wardrobe that is ready for the kinds of occasions that are likely. Different occasions require different kinds of clothing. Dressing inappropriately may give others a negative impression. For example, wearing jeans and a sweater to an interview for an office job is likely to convince a potential employer either that the applicant is not very interested in the job, or that the applicant is not very businesslike,

Illustration 7-1
Having the right clothing for the occasion can help in making a good impression on others and in building self-confidence.

or both. Casual clothes at a formal wedding may suggest disrespect or disregard for the importance of the occasion.

Dressing to suit the occasion is not just important for the impression it makes on others; it is also important for the effect it has on the wearers themselves. It is much easier to act alert and businesslike when neatly dressed, and it is much easier to enter into the joy and excitement of a wedding if you feel appropriately dressed for the occasion.

Reviewing Your Wardrobe

A wardrobe is most likely to be reviewed when it falls short in some way. Frequently this happens when an important item is no longer usable. Sometimes people tire of an item or become dissatisfied with it even though it may still be wearable. Perhaps the style is dated, the fit is not right, or the color does not harmonize well with other clothes. Involvement in new and different activities can also create a need for different clothing. For instance, taking up tennis may require the purchase of a different type of sportswear. Getting a part-time office or sales job may mean buying a bigger selection of professional clothing.

An important first step in meeting clothing needs is reviewing your activities and deciding what kind of clothes you need for each. The second step is to take an inventory of what is already on hand. Inventory is a good time to double-check the condition of the clothing on hand. A systematic check of the clothing in closets and dresser drawers can reveal any tears or stains. If repairs or alterations are needed, the garment should still be useful enough to warrant the time and money required to put it in good condition. If an item has not been worn in the past year, it should be examined critically. Unless it fits and is still a useful part of the wardrobe, it just may be taking up closet space!

Clothing Combinations. One way to check the usefulness of a wardrobe is to review the possible combinations of clothing that can be put together. An approach used by some women is to write down each skirt, pair of slacks, or dress they own and write below it each sweater or blouse that could be worn with it. Jackets, vests, and other key accessories that can be used in combination should be listed, too. Men can use the same procedure for each pair of trousers they own. This exercise will help identify additional items that would make the clothes already owned more useful. A pair of slacks that is not used because nothing matches them may be worth keeping if other items can be added to make them more useful.

Another check is needed to determine how well the various combinations meet clothing needs for work, social, and casual occasions. After you match each combination with the kinds of occasions for which it is suitable, you can identify the occasions for which you don't have any appropriate clothing. Once you have identified these gaps in your wardrobe, you can set priorities for clothing purchases.

Filling the Gaps. Not everyone can afford to fill all the gaps in a wardrobe right away. A systematic plan is needed. It is possible to build a wardrobe around a basic item such as a blazer, which can be used both for work and for social occasions. Men can then add slacks, shirts, and sweaters to go with it as money becomes available. Women can use a similar strategy, adding skirts, blouses, and sweaters.

Sometimes it is difficult to adhere to priorities for filling the gaps in a wardrobe. It may be difficult to put a high priority on clothes for special occasions if they are not needed immediately; however, last-minute purchases may cost more than purchases planned to take advantage of sales. Students should prepare for job interviews by building a suitable wardrobe.

Buying new clothes is an obvious way to fill the gaps in a wardrobe, but there are other ways. Individuals who have the right skills also have the option of making the clothes they need. The wisdom of this option depends on the opportunity cost of time. The costs of time, fabrics, and supplies have to be balanced against the cost of ready-made items of similar quality.

Renting is another way to fill the gaps in a wardrobe. Men's formal wear is widely available for rent. Bridesmaid's dresses and even wedding gowns are also available. Renting may be a good solution if an expensive item is needed for only a short time. Another approach to filling wardrobe gaps is to buy clothes second-hand. Thrift shops and garage sales in up-scale neighborhoods may include clothing items that are not quite up to the standards of their affluent first owners but are still attractive and wearable.

Another approach to filling wardrobe gaps is to borrow from friends and family. This approach may put a strain on relationships if used too often but can be a solution in an emergency.

What Is Important in Clothes?

Because clothing is expected to provide service over a period of time, there are several important criteria for judging clothing items. How clothing performs for a single wearing is not as important as how it will stand the test of time. The following evaluative criteria are important for key purchases:

- *Design factors.* Is the item attractively designed? Is it flattering to the wearer? Is the item designed so that it is convenient to use?
- *Performance factors.* How well does the item do what it is supposed to do? Will it provide reliable service over time? Is it comfortable?
- *Cost factors.* What is the cost of the item? Is it priced reasonably in terms of its quality? What will be the cost per use or per year of owning it?
- *Care and maintenance.* What upkeep will the item require? How will the costs of using and maintaining it affect the overall cost of ownership?

- *Safety factors*. What risks are involved in using the item? Can these risks be controlled?

Individuals differ in the amount of weight they put on a particular criterion. Chapter 2 noted that the importance placed on a particular evaluative criterion is linked to individual values. The amount of importance put on a criterion also varies with the kind of clothes being purchased. The weight put on a particular evaluative criterion will depend on whether it is to be used for work, social, or casual occasions.

In a recent survey, women were asked which evaluative criteria other than price were most important to them in choosing clothes for different occasions. For social occasions, they mentioned comfort, style, and versatility most often (see Table 7-1). For both casual and work clothes, they mentioned comfort and washability most frequently. In general, the criteria women used for judging casual and work clothes were more "practical" than those used for judging clothing for social occasions. A group of men asked the same questions would probably answer much the same way.

DESIGN FACTORS

Style is an important criterion for many people in choosing clothes, especially clothes for social occasions. When clothing experts use the word *style,* they are referring to a particular combination of line and form in clothing. Every year designers use differing patterns, fabric colors, and textures to create unique styles that retailers offer to the public. Styles that gain widespread acceptance are said to be *fashions.*

Table 7-1
Which Criteria (Other Than Price) Are Most Important to Women in Choosing Clothes?

	Percentage Mentioning A Criterion		
	Clothes for Social Occasions All Women	Casual Clothes All Women	Clothes for Work Working Women
Comfort	60%	85%	76%
Style	55	30	36
Versatility	51	28	23
Washability	38	62	58
Fabric type	26	29	29
Durability	16	31	31
None—Do not purchase	5	1	5
Don't know	1	1	3

Source: Roper Organization, Inc. New York: Phillip Morris U.S.A., 1980. Used by permission.

The Ingredients of Style

One of the distinctive characteristics of a style is the form or silhouette created. As fashions change, the favored styles shift back and forth from fuller to slimmer silhouettes. When the fuller look is in favor, jacket lapels are wide and shoulders are larger and more padded. Men's ties are wider, and collars on shirts and blouses are larger. The fuller look also includes wider skirts and fuller slacks with pleats. Variations in skirt length are an important part of changes in the silhouette of women's clothes. Along with these changes in silhouette come changes in the fabrics used and their colors and patterns.

Associated with the changes in silhouette are changes between more romantic and more functional styles. *Romantic* styles have dramatic, flowing lines: full sleeves, large collars, and full skirts or wide, pleated trousers. The fabrics are soft in texture and often light in color. Peasant and ethnic styles are part of the romantic look.

The other broad category of styles can be labeled *functional* styles. They feature trim lines, with nonworking parts removed, e.g., lapels on coats are deemphasized. Collars are small and men's ties are narrow. Fabric textures are usually crisp. Space-age design features are frequently incorporated. The fashions of the early 1980s ran to more functional styles, but by the mid-1980s preferences were for a more romantic look. Further changes seem certain.

It is hard to combine clothing items in a romantic style with ones that have a more functional emphasis. Jeans are one of the few items that seem to bridge the gap between these two style categories and look good with tops from either.

Clothing designers, manufacturers, and retailers promote new styles as a sales stimulant. Why does the public accept them? Those who adopt new fashions early seem to be motivated by the desire for a change and like the excitement of wearing a new style. Those who accept a new style later seem to be motivated more by the desire for approval of others. Major fashion changes have come less frequently in recent years and have been less extreme, perhaps because of increasing consumer resistance to seeing whole wardrobes go out-of-date. Consumers do have a defense against fashion obsolescence. Classic styles provide a choice that will be attractive and wearable for a number of years. Simpler, less extreme classic styles will never be the height of fashion, but are useful, long-term clothing investments.

The variety of styles, fabrics, and colors available gives consumers a wide range of choices. But consumers are faced with deciding which of all the choices available is best for them.

Communicating with Clothes

Because clothes are an important form of self-expression, it is important to decide what message they should communicate. Clothes can indicate a number of things, including:

- Occupation — Student? Construction worker? Banker?
- Interests — Runner? Hunter? Motorcyclist?
- Personality — Experimental and open to new styles? Conventional?
- Social status

What clothes communicate is especially important when meeting people for the first time. Young adults face many such situations: beginning their studies at college, taking a job interview, moving to a new community, and beginning a new job. It is wise for everyone to give some thought to impressions made by clothing, but it can be expecially important for young adults.

Choosing Colors and Styles

Most people have some general ideas about what impression they want to convey and about what impressions particular styles convey. They know that if they want to look serious and businesslike for a job interview they should wear a suit. There are other subtle considerations that must be taken into account, too. Some of the considerations in choosing clothing for an interview or job are outlined in the Consumer Capsule "Suiting Up for a Job."

Along with style choices, color choices also convey impressions. Bright primary colors suggest activity and vigor. They are popular for sportwear and athletic uniforms. Pastel colors diluted by mixing in white suggest freshness, softness, and innocence. They are popular for children's wear and for summer clothes. Sharper pastel colors have a crispness and freshness that make them popular for summer wear. Darker shades such as navy blue, dark gray, and black suggest authority and status. Combinations of darker shades and white convey a dynamic boldness. Men's formal wear and black dresses with white collars suggest boldness and authority. Many executives wear white shirts or blouses with their dark business suits for this reason. Darker shades are also associated with fall and winter wear. Deep, rich colors, such as garnet red and emerald green, suggest sensuousness and sophistication. Combinations of darker colors, as in a charcoal black and brown tweed, are also sophisticated.

In general, darker colors are favored in cooler climates and cooler weather. Lighter and brighter colors are favored in warmer climates and warmer weather. The linkage of particular colors with particular seasons can limit the versatility of a wardrobe. Versatility can be increased by choosing intermediate colors that can be worn in any season.

In choosing clothing colors, an individual's own natural coloring is another important consideration. Differences in natural coloring have an important influence on what colors look best. Undoubtedly you know

Illustration 7-2
When we meet people for the first time, their clothing plays an important part in the impressions we form.

whether your hair is brown or black or blond. You may, however, be less aware of some of the subtle differences in tone within these broad categories. Brown-haired people can have hair that is light brown, reddish brown, golden brown, or dark brown.

The same subtle differences are present in skin tones, regardless of whether the basic skin color is black, white, red, or yellow. Some individuals, regardless of their racial skin coloring, have subtle golden or orange undertones. Others have blue or combinations of blue and pink undertones.

Fashion color consultants have devised a variety of systems to help people find colors in which they look best (Eiseman, 1983; Jackson, 1980).

These systems typically divide people into those with skins with golden or orange undertones and those with blue or blue and pink undertones. Each of these groups can be divided into those who have stronger and more dramatic natural coloring and those who have lighter coloring. The recommended color choices for each of these groups are as follows.

- *Golden and orange skin undertones.* Warm clothing colors are suggested. For those with brighter coloring, brighter colors including oranges and golds are suggested, along with coffee brown, emerald green, and navy blue. For those with lighter coloring, softer colors are suggested. These include peach, coral, tan, yellow-greens, and light navy.
- *Blue and blue-pink skin undertones.* Cooler clothing colors are suggested. For those with sharper coloring, suggested choices include black and white, red, royal blue, emerald green, burgundy, and navy blue. For those with softer coloring, soft whites, blue-greens, burgundy, cocoa brown, and grayed shades of navy blue are recommended.

Limiting color and style choices to those that go together well can increase the versatility of a wardrobe and reduce wardrobe costs. If a wardrobe is built around a few basic colors, it is easier to put together a variety of combinations that look good together. For example, many colors go together well with such basic colors as navy blue and tan. These two colors combine well with such varied colors as kelly green, light yellow, and burgundy.

Just as there are certain colors that are more flattering to a particular individual, there also are certain styles that are more flattering than others. Few people have perfectly proportioned bodies. Some look too heavy; others look too thin. Some have necks that perhaps look too long; others have necks that look too short. While style choices may be influenced by what is in fashion, some thought also should be given to finding styles that suit bodily proportions. There are some tricks that can be used to deal with proportions that are not quite perfect. Examples of these techniques are outlined in the Consumer Capsule "Dealing with Figure Faults."

PERFORMANCE AND DURABILITY

For many products, comprehensive information on performance and durability is available from *Consumer Reports* and other information sources that report product tests. There is, however, little information available on clothing. Clothing items are too numerous and change too frequently for the publication of product test ratings to be feasible.

Because there is so little test information available on clothing, consumers must learn to judge it on their own. The performance and durability of a clothing item depend in large part on the fabrics used and how they are put together. To judge clothing effectively, consumers have to learn to judge clothing fabrics and clothing construction techniques. They can begin by looking at the fibers and fabrics used in making clothing.

The Building Blocks: Fibers and Fabrics

A basic factor influencing garment performance is the fiber used in making the fabric. *Fibers* are the strands of such materials as cotton and wool that are spun together to make *yarns*. These yarns are then joined together by weaving, knitting, or other methods to make *fabrics*.

The fibers used in clothing include both natural fibers from plants (cotton and linen) and from animals (wool, camel, cashmere, and silk). Manufactured fibers (also called *synthetic fibers* and *man-made fibers*) are made from wood pulp or chemicals derived from coal and oil. Manufactured fibers include such fibers as nylon, polyester, acrylic, and rayon.

Fiber Labeling. The use of synthetic fibers has increased sharply over the past thirty years. When synthetic fibers were first introduced, companies sold the fibers under their own trade names. Increasing confusion resulted because consumers had little idea which products had similar characteristics and care requirements. To overcome this confusion, the 1960 Textile Fiber Products Identification Act requires clothing and many other textile products to be labeled with the generic names of the fibers as well as with the trade names (Corbman, 1983). A label on a T-shirt made of cotton and polyester may, for example, indicate:

Illustration 7-3
Fiber content labels can help consumers form expectations about the performance and care needs of a garment.

Chapter 7   Clothing   163

CONSUMER CAPSULE:
DEALING WITH FIGURE FAULTS

Clothing consultants have developed a number of suggestions for helping people with awkward body proportions present the best possible appearance. These suggestions are based on practical application of some optical tricks.

- *For the short.* The best style choices for those who feel they are too short are ones that keep the viewer's eye moving vertically without stopping. Styles that emphasize vertical lines, those that include fabrics with vertical stripes, and garments with vertical seams and pleats are recommended. Shorter jacket lengths and uncuffed slacks make legs appear longer and also help give the illusion of height. Styles that emphasize horizontal lines should be avoided. Sharp color contrasts above and below the waist should also be avoided because they tend to discourage vertical eye movement. A light blue sweater with navy slacks would be a better choice than a white sweater with navy slacks, for example.

- *For the heavy.* The best choices for those who feel they are too heavy are styles that encourage the viewer's eye to move without stopping. Outfits in a single color or similar colors are a good choice. Sharp color contrasts above and below the waist tend to stop the eye and are best avoided. Large patterns should be avoided. Comfortably loose clothing is a better choice than items that are too loose or too tight. Big or brightly colored belts and large shiny buckles draw the viewer's eye to the waist and are, therefore, an unwise choice. Cardigan sweaters, loose-fitting jackets, and vests all are useful in disguising large waistlines. One way to draw attention away from the waist is to draw it to the face. A colored shirt or blouse, a piece of jewelry, or a bright tie or scarf all can help to do this. Women with large bustlines should avoid turtlenecks and high collars; V-necks and open collars are better choices.

- *For the tall.* The best style choices for a person who feels too tall are clothes that discourage the viewer's eye from moving up and down vertically. Styles with horizontal patterns and stripes or that emphasize horizontal lines help do this. Longer jacket lengths and cuffed slacks help reduce the apparent length of legs. Contrasting colors above and below the waist help discourage vertical eye movement. The contrast should not be too sharp, however.

- *For the thin.* A person who feels too thin should choose clothes cut full and avoid tight-fitting ones. Puffy sleeves and pleated slacks can help give the appearance of bulk. Extra layers that help add bulk are also a good choice. Using a turtleneck under a shirt or blouse is one way to add bulk. Shirts and jackets with patch pockets are another. Textured fabrics also can add bulk, but ones that are too heavy should be avoided.

65% Dacron [trade name of a polyester fiber made by E.I. Dupont de Nemours Co.] polyester [generic or family name]
35% cotton [generic or family name]

Fiber content labeling can help consumers understand fabric composition; however, not all fibers with a particular generic name perform in exactly the same way. Nylon fiber can be used in jeans for strength, but another type of nylon, Qiana, has a silk-like feel and is used in delicate clothing.

Labels must list all fibers that amount to 5 percent by weight or more. Fibers used in smaller amounts can be listed only if they have some specific function. We might see, for example, a label with "4% spandex for elasticity." The limit on listing small amounts of fibers was set to keep consumers from being misled by the addition of small amounts of expensive fibers such as silk or cashmere.

The other major law governing fabric labeling is the Wool Products Labeling Act (Corbman, 1983). It requires an indication of the amount and kind of wool fibers used in making a fabric. Two important types of wool fibers are *wool fibers* (fibers which have not been processed previously, also referred to as *virgin wool* and *new wool*) and *recycled wool fibers* (fibers from remanufactured scraps of unused cloth or from used clothing).

Fiber and Fabric Characteristics. When consumers are buying clothing or other textile items, they may have a number of questions about how long they will last, how they must be cared for, and how they will perform. Key criteria used in judging clothing fabrics include (Corbman, 1983; Joseph, 1977):

- *Resiliency.* Does the fiber or fabric return to its original shape after it is crushed or bent? Is it likely to wrinkle?
- *Absorbency and moisture transmission.* Will the fiber or fabric absorb moisture or allow it to move to the outside surface where it can evaporate? The ability to absorb or transmit perspiration is desirable for undergarments; for outerwear such as a raincoat, nonabsorbent fabrics are preferred.
- *Strength.* Fabrics that resist damage from rubbing or flexing are more durable and will last longer.

- *Dimensional stability.* Another important characteristic is the ability of a fabric to resist undesirable stretching and shrinkage.
- *Transmission of heat and air.* In some clothing, such as that worn in summer, fabrics that allow heat to escape and air to circulate are most comfortable. For winter sportswear, fabrics that hold heat in and limit air movement are desirable.

The fiber used in a piece of fabric has an important effect on its performance. Performance is also affected by the structure of the fibers and the way they are spun into yarns. Some of the fibers used are short, staple fibers. Others, especially manufactured fibers, are long filaments. In general, the longer the fiber, the stronger and more durable the fabric will be. Yarns that are thicker and more tightly twisted will wear better than lighter ones or ones with less twist.

Fabric performance is also affected by how the yarns are joined together to make fabric. Fabrics that are tightly woven of tightly spun, thick yarns will have better strength and durability; however, tightly woven fabrics limit air and moisture movement as well the loss of heat. Tightly woven fabrics that entrap air have good insulating qualities. The tightness of a fabric's weave can be checked by holding it up to the light; the tighter the weave, the less light comes through. Loosely woven fabrics allow more air, heat, and moisture movement, but they are also less likely to wear well. The performance of major textile fibers and the fabrics made from them is summarized in Table 7-2.

Cotton and wool are popular and widely used natural fibers. Cotton is popular because of its absorbency and comfortable feel. Wool is popular because it is absorbent, warm, and comfortable. Silk is seen less often because it is expensive to buy and requires careful cleaning. However, silk's luxurious feel and its distinctive luster make it appreciated by those who can afford it. These characteristics have also motivated synthetic fiber producers to imitate it.

Rayon and acetate are the two oldest manufactured fibers. Both are frequently used to imitate silk. Rayon also is used to imitate other fibers. Of all the manufactured fibers only rayon has a significant amount of absorbency, which can be important for comfort. Fabrics made from other manufactured fibers must rely on *wicking* action and air movement between fibers to carry perspiration from the body surface to the outside of the garment, where it can evaporate.

Nylon is a versatile manufactured fiber used in everything from work clothes to lingerie. Its strength is one of its special characteristics. A frequent use of polyester is in blends with cotton for easy-care fabrics. Polyester is used because of its strength and its resistance to wrinkling. One disadvantage of both nylon and polyester is *pilling*. Pilling occurs over time as a fabric is rubbed and fibers break. Continued abrasion rolls the broken fibers into balls or "pills." Because of the stength of nylon and polyester, pills do not wear off but remain on the fabric surface and mar its appearance. Pilling also occurs in some other fabrics made from manufactured fibers.

Acrylic is another widely used manufactured fiber with wool-like characteristics that make it popular. Modacrylic is a chemically related fiber with many similar characteristics. It is important because of its fire-resistance, which makes it useful for children's sleepwear.

The characteristics of the major textile fibers used in clothing are listed in Table 7-2. Most of the fibers have some disadvantages along with their advantages. One way in which textile manufacturers deal with the disadvantages of an individual fiber is to combine several fibers in a single fabric. The advantages of each can be obtained by creating blends made by spinning two or more different fibers into a single yarn.

Many blends involve the use of a natural fiber such as cotton or wool along with a manufactured fiber. The natural fibers provide absorbency and comfortable feel, while the manufactured fibers provide useful strength and wrinkle resistance.

The popular polyester-cotton blend spins polyester fibers and cotton fibers together into yarns that are then woven into fabrics. The blending of cotton and polyester provides the comfort and absorbency of cotton along with the easy care, strength and wrinkle resistance of polyester. Because the use of permanent press finishes weakens cotton, the strength provided by the addition of the polyester is important.

Fabric Finishes. Textile manufacturers also deal with the disadvantages of particular fibers through the use of special treatments and finishes (Corbman, 1983). Perhaps the best known of the special finishes are the permanent press and durable press finishes. These finishes improve a fabric's ability to return to its original smooth surface and shape after it is laundered. Permanent press finishes, however, tend to weaken cotton and rayon. For this reason, these finishes are usually used in blends in which polyester or nylon is included for strength.

Stain- and soil-resistant finishes are used to increase resistance to water- and oil-borne stains. These finishes retain stains on the fabric's surface and keep them from penetrating into the fabric. Zepel®[1] and Scotchgard® are

[1]Zepel is a registered trademark of E.I. duPont de Nemours and Company; Scotchgard is a registered trademark of Minnesota Mining and Manufacturing Company.

Table 7-2
Textile Fiber Used in
Clothing

Fiber and Selected Trademark Names	Characteristics	Care Recommendations	Uses
Cotton (generic)	Absorbent, dries slowly, stains easily unless special finishes are applied, takes dyes well Low resiliency, wrinkles easily unless permanent finishes are applied Soft and comfortable Medium strength Shrinks easily unless especially treated Easy to launder Burns quickly	Machine wash and tumble dry or dryclean	Jeans, shirts, undergarments, work clothes. In blends with polyester for easy-care fabrics
Wool (generic)	Absorbent, dries slowly, stains easily Resilient, resists wrinkling Warm Relatively weak, especially when wet May shrink unless special finishes have been applied	Dry clean (some garments may be washed by hand with special care)	Suits, dresses, sweaters, outerwear
Silk (generic)	Absorbent, dries slowly, stains easily, takes dyes well Medium resiliency; wrinkles hang out relatively well Strong but weakens over time; weakened by perspiration and many deodorants Luxurious feel ("hand") Good resistance to shrinkage	Dry cleaning preferred (some can be hand-washed with care)	Blouses, shirts, dresses, suits, lingerie
Rayon Avril Coloray Enkaire	Absorbent, dries slowly, stains easily unless especially treated, takes dye well	Machine-wash and dry or dryclean (some require handwashing with special care)	As substitute for cotton or to imitate other fibers. Slacks, women's undergarments, linings

Table 7-2
(cont'd.)

Fiber and Selected Trademark Names	Characteristics	Care Recommendations	Uses
Fibro Zantrel	Low resiliency, wrinkles easily unless especially treated Strength varies with type; some types relatively weak when wet May shrink unless especially treated Inexpensive		
Acetate Ariloft Celanese Acetate Estron Loftura	Low absorbency, resists staining Low resilience, wrinkles easily Luxurious "hand," soft Low strength Resists shrinkage Inexpensive	Dry clean or wash by hand with special care. Iron at low temperatures. (Fabric melts at high temperatures.)	As a substitute for silk. Dresses, blouses, lingerie, shirts, sportswear
Triacetate Arnel	Low absorbency, resists staining Resilient, resists wrinkling Luxurious "hand" Low strength, especially when wet Resists shrinkage	Machine wash and tumble dry	Knitted fabrics, permanently pleated and creased garments
Nylon Antron Cantrece Celanese Nylon Dupont Nylon Enka Enkalure Monsanto Nylon Qiana Zefran	Nonabsorbent, dries quickly, resists stains Resilient, resists wrinkling Strong, broken fibers may pill instead of wearing off Resists shrinkage Easy to launder Special nylons have special characteristics	Machine wash and tumble dry (low temperatures should be used to avoid wrinkling)	Underwear, stockings, blouses, dresses, rainwear, work clothing
Acrylic Acrilan Bi-Loft Creslan	Nonabsorbent, dries quickly, resists stains Resilient, resists wrinkles, creases hang out quickly	Care requirements vary. Some may be machine washed and tumble dried at low temperatures (may	Knitted garments, sportswear, sweaters, fleece and pilelined garments, dresses. Used as substitute for wool

Table 7-2
(cont'd.)

Fiber and Selected Trademark Names	Characteristics	Care Recommendations	Uses
Orlon Zefran	Soft and warm Low strength, broken fibers may pill instead of wearing off May shrink if subjected to excess heat during cleaning	shrink at higher temperatures). Others require careful hand washing.	and blends with wool, cotton, and rayon
Modacrylic Acrilan SEF Verel	Low absorbency, dries quickly, resists staining Resilient, resists wrinkling Medium strength May shrink if subjected to excess heat during cleaning Flame resistant, hard to ignite, does not support combustion	Machine wash (most can be tumble dried)	Children's sleepwear, fake furs, knitted garments, wigs
Polyester Dacron Encron Fiberfill Fortel Hollofil Kodel Trevira	Nonabsorbent, dries quickly, resists most stains but absorbs oily stains Resilient, resists wrinkles Medium to high strength, broken fibers may pill instead of wearing off Resists shrinking Easy to launder	Machine wash and tumble dry (must have cool-down period at end of washing and drying cycles to prevent wrinkling)	Shirts, blouses, lingerie, underwear, ties. In blends with cotton for easy care fabrics. Also in blends with rayon and wool. Hollofil and Fiberfil used in insulated garments

Sources: Drawn from Bernard P. Corbman, *Textile: Fiber to Fabric,* 6th ed. New York: Gregg/McGraw-Hill, 1983; and Marjory L. Joseph, *Introductory Textile Science,* 3d ed. New York: Holt, Rinehart and Winston, 1977.

two familiar brand names of stain-resistant finishes. Oil-borne stains are a particular problem with synthetic fabrics, especially polyester, and fabrics with permanent press finishes. Perspiration and oil-borne stains are the cause of "ring-around-the-collar" on cotton-polyester blend permanent press shirts and blouses. Soil-release finishes such as Scotch-Release®[1] have been developed to make oil-borne stains easier to remove.

[1]Scotch-Release is a registered trademark of Minnesota Mining and Manufacturing Company.

Water-repellent finishes are used for rainwear to provide a fabric that resists wetting but still permits air to move through, thus making the garment more comfortable to wear than a completely waterproof finish. Water-repellent finishes also improve stain-resistance because they prevent stains from penetrating. Familiar brand names include Zepel®[1], Zelon®, and Scotchgard®. Some nonabsorbent fabrics, such as nylon, are water-repellent without special finishes.

Shrinkage is another problem that can be controlled with special finishes. Sanforized®[2] and Rigmel® are used on cotton. The finishes used to get permanent press characteristics also help to reduce shrinkage. Another important concern is the problem of fabric flammability, which is a particular concern for children's wear, especially sleepwear. One method of controlling flammability is the use of flame-retardant finishes.

Putting It All Together: Garment Construction

The fabric used in making a garment is one important indicator of how well it will perform and how it will last. Another important indicator is how well the garment is constructed.

Shape. In making a garment, the manufacturer has to assemble two-dimensional pieces of fabric to cover a three-dimensional figure. Garments get their basic shape from the way the fabric pieces used in making them are cut. Manufacturers of quality clothing are more careful about cutting each piece accurately, which is one reason these clothes fit better. As fabric pieces are sewn together, they are pressed to give shape to the garment. Quality manufacturers use more pressings to shape their garments more carefully. Garments are fitted to the body by using darts, tucks, and pleats to remove excess fabric in some places and provide extra fullness in others (Stamper, Sharp, & Donnell, 1986).

Garments will stay looking good only if they keep their shape over time as they are worn. The fabric used should resist both shrinking and stretching. To help jacket collars and lapels and the waistbands of skirts and slacks keep their shape, *interfacings* are added. Interfacings are extra pieces of fabric sewn inside the garment to give strength and body where it is needed (Stamper et al., 1986). They are also used around arm holes and button holes to provide extra stength. If the interfacings do their job, a garment should fall back into place quickly after it has been rumpled.

Paddings and linings also are used to help smooth the shape of a garment. Padding should be used so that shoulders fit smoothly without any

---

[1]Zepel is a registered trademark of E.I. duPont de Nemours and Company; Zelon is a registered trademark of The Sherwin-Williams Company; Scotchgard is a registered trademark of Minnesota Mining and Manufacturing Company.
[2]Sanforized is a registered trademark of Sanforized Company, a division of Cluett, Peabody, & Company; Rigmel is a registered trademark of Bradford Dyeing Association.

lumpiness. Linings should hang evenly so that the skirts and jackets in which they are used will hang smoothly.

Size. Most garments are constructed assuming certain standard body proportions. Men are assumed to have a waist that is six inches smaller than their chest measurement. Men with different proportions may have trouble finding clothing that fits well, especially suits. Some European styles and designs for slimmer men have a seven-inch difference or "drop" between chest and waist.

Similar assumptions are made about women's proportions in designing their clothes. The general assumption is that women's waist sizes will be seven to nine inches less than their bust size. Fortunately, some account has been taken of women's differing needs by providing different size lines for women.

- *Junior sizes* — Designed for women with small frames and youthful figures
- *Misses' sizes* — Designed for women with an average frame and proportions. Variations are available for different heights such as petites, average, and tall.
- *Women's sizes* — Designed for fuller, more mature figures. This line has less bust-to-waist and waist-to-hips difference than junior or misses sizes.
- *Half sizes* — Designed for fuller, more mature figures and short heights

Despite continuing efforts to standardize clothing sizes, sizes are not standardized in practice (Stamper et al., 1986). Size standards are voluntary, and manufacturers adjust them to what they feel will suit their clientele best. The sizing problem is particularly noticeable in women's clothes. More expensive dresses and suits tend to be cut fuller, so that women who wear a size 8 in a less expensive line may wear a size 6 in a more expensive line. Men's sizes are based on body measurements: chest size for jackets and waist size for trousers. Sizes tend to be fairly standard. There are some differences between lines and manufacturers in proportions, however. Designer lines aimed at younger men may have jackets proportioned for smaller waist and hip measurements than regular lines. Designer trousers and styles for younger men are narrower in the hips for a given waist size than regular lines.

Poor fits may have two different causes: the wrong size or an incorrectly proportioned garment. It may be necessary to try different sizes or different brands until you find one that fits.

Fitting. Because it is difficult to tell whether a garment will fit from the size on the label, it is smart to check the fit on all major purchases and when you are not sure about the correct size.

A properly fitted garment will provide some *ease,* which is the extra fabric that allows for body movements. If there is too little ease, there will be obvious strain marks. Horizontal wrinkles across the front of trousers and skirts indicate that the garment is too tight across the hips. Horizontal wrinkles across the back of a jacket indicate it is too tight across the shoulders. Vertical wrinkles indicate there is too much ease and that the garment probably is too loose.

In a good fit, there are a few key factors to examine. Jackets should fit closely around the neck without gaps. Those who are round-shouldered may need to have their jackets let out across the shoulders for a better fit; those who are unusually square-shouldered may need a bit taken in. For men, the jacket should be just long enough to cover the seat of the trousers. For women, jacket lengths are more variable, and the choice can be based on whatever is most flattering. As pointed out in the Consumer Capsule "Dealing with Figure Faults," a shorter jacket length makes legs appear longer and is a good choice for those who wish to increase their apparent height. Other tips for disguising body proportions are included in that Consumer Capsule.

Jacket sleeves should be short enough to show some cuff—from 1/4 to 3/4 inches. Most people have arms that are different lengths. If you are right-handed, your right arm is likely to be longer than your left one. Jackets should be adjusted so that sleeves come to the same point on the wrist on both arms.

A frequent fitting error among men is to wear their trousers too short. Trousers should just touch the tops of the shoes. The choice of having trousers finished with or without cuffs is a matter of taste. The extra bulk of cuffs does help trouser legs hang straighter, however.

To get the correct lengths on slacks, women who are being fitted should wear the same type of shoes they expect to wear with the slacks. Skirt lengths are dictated by current fashion. In choosing a style, women should bear in mind what length suits their body proportions best.

Workmanship. After checking the fit of a garment, it is smart to examine the workmanship. Begin by inspecting the outside of the garment. Seams should be straight and lie flat without any puckering. Small, neat stitches are a sign of quality. The thread used should match the fabric, and the stitching should be almost invisible. Stitching may be visible at points of strain when extra stitching is used for reinforcement. For example, *bar tacks* (back-and-forth stitching) are often used at the corners of jeans pockets. Patterns should be carefully matched at seams.

Buttonholes should be neatly made and carefully finished, and buttons should be firmly attached. Of course, buttons should button and unbutton easily. Zippers should be smoothly fitted and fully covered by a flap of fabric.

Jacket lapels should spring back into place when wrinkled. In less expensive jackets, lapels are often stiff because of the stiff interfacing fused to the lapel fabric. In more expensive lines, the interfacing is stitched to the lapel fabric and has a softer, more flexible feel.

It is smart to examine the inside of a garment, too. In the past, full lining in a garment was considered a sign of quality. Now it may just be a coverup for sloppy workmanship. The inside of the garment should be well-finished. The edges of seams should be bound with stitching or tape or turned under and sewn in place so seams can not ravel. The finished seam should be pressed carefully so the extra fabric does not make a bulge on the outside of the garment. Pockets should be made of a tightly woven fabric that can withstand use. Pocket linings made of lighter weight fabrics stiffened with starch or sizing that washes out will not wear well.

Clothing Care: Protecting Your Investment

A good wardrobe is a big investment and one that deserves to be protected. Most college students are past the stage of outgrowing clothes and need to think about caring for their clothing to get the most years of use out of it. Well-chosen items of good quality can give a number of years of wear. With the right kind of care, clothing can look good and perform satisfactorily for long periods.

Day-to-day Care. As they are worn, clothes become wrinkled, stretched, and dampened by perspiration. They will resume their shape more quickly if they are hung up promptly after wearing to allow fibers to resume their original shape. To protect their shape, jackets should be hung on padded hangers, not on the wire ones used by dry cleaners. Clothing needs a "break" of several days between wearings to dry out and resume its original shape. To hang out and dry out properly, clothes need adequate space and air circulation. Clothing that is crowded in a closet can not get the ventilation it needs.

It is smart to protect one's clothing investment by doing repairs quickly when they are needed. Minor rips and split seams should be mended before the problem gets bigger and more expensive to repair. It is also smart to remove stains promptly before they set. The recommended procedures for removing stains depend both on the kind of stain and on whether the fabric is washable or nonwashable. Deciding on the best procedure can get complicated. It is best to refer to a guide on stain removal such as the publication prepared by the U.S. Department of Agriculture, *Removing Stains from Fabric.* This guide is available for a small charge from the Consumer Information Center.

Care Labeling. Many fabrics imitate more expensive ones. Rayon and acetate imitate silk, acrylic imitates wool, and rayon imitates cotton. This has created confusion about what cleaning procedures should be used. Even experts at dry cleaning and laundry establishments can be fooled.

Different fibers and fabrics require different cleaning procedures, as can be seen in Table 7-2. Incorrect choices, as some consumers have learned, can ruin garments. To deal with the problems created by look-alike fabrics, permanent care labeling was required by the FTC beginning in 1972. The rules were modified in 1984 to make the label information clearer and more accurate (Federal Trade Commission, 1984).

Permanent care labels are required on most wearing apparel made from textiles. Care information is also required on the end of bolts of fabric for home sewing. The instructions presented should cover cleaning procedures for all parts of the item, including belt, trim, and so on.

Care label instructions emphasize recommended cleaning procedures. Labels for washable items should include instructions on the following:

- *Washing procedures*. Should the article be hand washed or machine washed?
- *Temperature for wash water*. Will the item be harmed by hot water?
- *Drying procedures*. Should the article be machine dried or dried in some other way?
- *Maximum dryer temperature*. Will the item be harmed by high temperatures?

For dry cleaning, the type of solvent used must be indicated unless any type of solvent is acceptable.

Manufacturers are not obliged to warn against cleaning procedures that could injure the garment. They are only responsible for indicating the procedures that *should* be used. For example, if a label provides washing instructions, it does not have to warn against dry cleaning the item. The reverse is also true. If dry cleaning instructions are given, warnings against washing are not required.

Cleaning Procedures. Care labels are a useful guide to cleaning procedures, but there are other procedures that can help get the best possible results in laundering clothing. Experts recommend pretreating stains before washing them. They also suggest sorting clothes into separate loads by the amount of soiling and the water temperature required.

Soiled areas, such as collars and cuffs, should be brushed with liquid detergent or a soap-and-water mixture to help solve the "ring-around-the-collar" problem with cotton-polyester blends and items with a permanent press finish. Heavily soiled items should be presoaked to loosen stains, and they should be washed separately. Dirt from heavily soiled items may be redeposited on other items if they are mixed with ones that are less heavily soiled.

Some common laundry problems can be avoided or controlled if the right steps are taken. Pilling and abrasion can be reduced by turning garments inside out before washing. Shrinking can be controlled by avoiding high temperatures in washing and drying and by not overdrying. Wrinkling of permanent press items can have several causes: washing with water that is too hot, failing to use a cool-down rinse, failing to put damp items into the dryer promptly, or drying at too high a temperature. Permanent press items should be removed from the dryer before completely dry and put on hangers or hand smoothed while still warm for best results. These procedures are necessary because high temperatures soften permanent press finishes, and fabrics pick up wrinkles that remain as the fabric cools. Dinginess and graying can have several causes: hard water, insufficient detergent, improper water temperature, and iron or other impurities in the water.

If items that require dry cleaning are stained, they should be cleaned promptly because warmth and light can set stains over time. Stains should be pointed out to the cleaner and identified if possible. For best results, the cleaner needs to pretreat stains, especially those that will not be removed by the solvent in the cleaning process. Water-soluble stains, such as coffee and soft drinks, for example, are not removed during the cleaning process. It is important to point out all stains even if they do not seem important. Sometimes stains that were not visible previously show up after dry cleaning because inconspicuous stains may be darkened by the heat of the cleaning and drying process.

COST

When buying clothes, it is useful to focus not just on their price but also on how much useful life can be expected from them. Many major items, such as suits and coats, can provide five to seven years of use. They are, therefore, less expensive on a yearly basis than their big price tags may suggest. Useful life is affected not only by how well a garment wears, but also by fashion obsolescence. A garment that is no longer wearable because it is out of fashion is not much more useful than one that is worn out. Buying items in classic styles that stay in fashion is a solution to the problem of fashion obsolescence.

Another factor to consider is the total cost of cleaning over the life of a garment. Cleaning costs will differ with the method required. Silk, for example, requires dry cleaning, which is more expensive than washing. Frequency of cleaning also affects total costs. Some fabrics and colors show spots and soil more quickly, thus requiring more frequent cleaning.

A comparison of all-cotton and cotton-polyester shirts illustrates these cost differences (U.S. Department of Agriculture, 1979). The all-cotton shirt is not only more expensive to buy, but it will also have a shorter useful life. An all-cotton shirt can be expected to last for 50 washings, while a cotton-polyester shirt can be expected to last for 75 washings. In addition, laundering an all-cotton shirt takes twice as much energy as laundering the blend shirt because the all-cotton shirt requires a hot water rinse while the blend shirt requires a cold rinse. All-cotton also dries more slowly and requires more drier time and more ironing. Cotton fans say nothing can beat the softness, luxury, and coolness of all-cotton, but it is smart to recognize that this luxury has its costs.

SAFETY

Most textile fibers will burn if conditions are right. Some, in fact, will burn so rapidly that they almost seem to explode. Brushed and fluffy fabrics in which large amounts of fiber surface are exposed to the air burn especially rapidly. Some fabrics are easily ignited when exposed to flame from stoves, fireplaces, or cigarettes. Over the years many people have been injured in clothing fires. In the 1940s and 1950s, problems with explosively flammable brushed rayon sweaters and negligees led to new legislation. In 1953, Congress passed the Flammable Fabrics Act, prohibiting sale of highly flammable garments and clothing fabrics in interstate commerce (Corbman, 1983). The 1953 legislation, however, did not eliminate the flammable fabrics problem. Injuries to young children were a particular concern. Because of this concern, there was increasing interest in flame-retardant (or flame-resistant) fabrics. Flame-retardant fabrics may burn if exposed to flame but resist ignition and will not continue to burn if the source of flame is removed. There are several ways fabrics can be made flame-retardant, including:

- *Flame-retardant fibers* — Modacrylic, vinyon, and special formulas of other manufactured fibers
- *Modified flame-retardant finishes* — Chemicals added to synthetic fiber solutions before spinning (e.g., special flame-retardant polyesters)
- *Flame-retardant finishes* — Chemicals bonded to the fiber surface to reduce flammability

In the 1970s, the Consumer Product Safety Commission issued regulations requiring children's sleepwear (sizes 0 through 14) to be flame-resistant. Manufacturers moved to comply by using flame-retardant fabrics and finishes. They experienced a temporary setback when Tris, one of the finishes used, was found to be carcinogenic in laboratory animals. Its use was banned in 1977, and the CPSC ordered recall of unsold garments treated with Tris. Most sleepwear is now manufactured without special finishes. The garments available require some special care in washing. Washing with detergents is required to preserve the flame-retardant characteristic, as use of soap will interfere with it. Garments now carry labels detailing their care requirements.

The flame retardance requirements have made children's sleepwear more expensive. They have, however, significantly reduced injuries and deaths, especially among younger children. Concerned citizens continue to ask to have the regulations extended to cover children's clothing as well as sleepwear. Some feel the rules should be extended to clothing for all age groups. There are, however, serious questions about whether the benefits for adolescents and adults would equal the costs of the requirements.

FOOTWEAR

No outfit is really complete without the right kind of shoes. The look of a casual outfit will be spoiled by dress shoes, and the same is true if casual shoes are worn with a dress-up outfit. Every complete wardrobe needs dress shoes for important social and work occasions plus casual and athletic shoes. Activities will determine the number and the types needed. A typical student will probably need more casual and athletic shoes than dressy ones.

Design and Style

Dress shoes for important social and work occasions often have trim lines, smooth leathers, and shiny finishes. Useful styles are lace-up oxford and classic loafer styles for men and pumps and dressy slingback sandals for women. In contrast, informal styles usually feature rougher texture leathers and bulky lines. Casual styles include informal loafers, boots, oxfords, and sandals, as well as moccasins. Athletic shoes are available in a variety of styles and colors. Their comfort, style, and price have made them popular for a variety of casual occasions. The best color choices are the versatile, basic shades.

Performance and Durability

Shoe uppers and soles are made both from leather and from synthetics. Each has its distinct advantages and disadvantages.

Materials. When leather is used for uppers, it should be free of scars and imperfections and evenly colored. Leather has some important advantages. It is porous so air and moisture can move away from the foot. The release of perspiration is important both for comfort and for the life of the shoe.

Several different types of synthethics are used for uppers. Vinyls are the most common. Used in women's and girl's shoes, vinyls are durable, but are inflexible. This characteristic prevents them from molding to the foot and may make them less comfortable than leather. Vinyls also do not allow the movement of air and moisture. Urethanes are more flexible and softer than vinyl, but they also restrict the movement of air and moisture.

The quality of the linings of shoes has an important effect on comfort. Linings should be smooth and free of bumps that can irritate the foot. Leather is a desirable lining because it is flexible and porous. It is, however, used only in more expensive shoes. Synthethics frequently are used in linings but are inflexible and nonporous. Fabric frequently is used along with leather or vinyl.

Soles should be thick enough to cushion the foot from the shock of walking on hard pavements and floors. Leather is porous so it can release moisture and perspiration; however, it has the disadvantage of absorbing moisture in wet weather. Leather soles are also less durable than synthetic ones. Synthetic materials frequently are used for soles, and they have the advantage of not absorbing moisture. Polyurethane is the best-wearing synthetic sole.

In selecting shoes, it is important to check the workmanship along with the materials used. The workmanship can be judged in much the same way as it is in choosing clothing. Seams and edges should be neatly finished and evenly and closely stitched. There should be no loose threads or rough edges.

Fitting. To get the best fit when shopping for shoes, it is wise to shop later in the day. Experts note that people's feet spread as the day goes on. By shopping later in the day, a more accurate fit can be assured. The salesperson should measure both feet because most people's feet are slightly different in size. A size that is comfortable for the larger foot should be selected. If necessary, pads can be used to make the other shoe fit the smaller foot.

It is smart to choose a style that matches the shape of the foot. A good style is one that is longest in the area of the longest toe (which may or may not be the big toe) and that allows enough room for other toes. The shoe size that fits best will vary with the style and the manufacturer. The size decision should be made on the basis of what seems most comfortable, not the size usually worn.

Experts advise against buying uncomfortable shoes with the idea that they can be broken in. Shoes that are too tight can cause discomfort, blisters, corns, and calluses. In purchasing shoes, you should try them on in the store to check for fit. If the heel pulls out at the back as you walk, the heel of the shoe is not shaped properly or the shoe is too large.

Care. Good shoes are a big investment and deserve the right care. It is smart to polish leather shoes before wearing them the first time to protect the new leather from moisture spotting. Experts advise buying enough pairs of shoes so that they can be alternated. Allowing them to dry out between wearings will both increase the shoes' life and improve their comfort. Using shoe trees will help shoes resume their shape as they dry out after wearing.

If shoes get muddy or get salt on them in winter, they should be wiped off promptly. If they need further cleaning, they should be wiped with saddle soap and then polished. Regular polishing not only preserves the appearance of shoes but also increases shoe life by keeping the leather flexible. If shoes get wet, they should be stuffed with paper and allowed to dry slowly away from heat sources. Shoe trees should not be used with wet shoes because they will cause the shoe to stretch too much. When soles and heels need repairs, they should be repaired promptly. Otherwise shoes may be damaged so much that repairs will become expensive or impossible.

CONSUMER CAPSULE: SUITING UP FOR A JOB

In an initial job interview, job applicants have only twenty or thirty minutes to make an impression. How they conduct themselves is an important part of this impression, but their personal appearance is important too.

One fashion consultant advises individuals to dress for an interview as though they already had the job. It is difficult to go wrong with a navy blue or darker gray suit in a traditional style. This look is favored by executives at all levels. High fashion styles for women and European-styled jackets with fitted waists for men generally should be avoided. For men, dark-tone laced oxfords and for women, dark-tone plain pumps are needed to complete the outfit. Choices should convey a feeling of competence and professionalism.

Once on the job, an employee usually has a little more latitude in what is worn. Some companies, especially banks and retailers, have formal dress codes spelling out what their employees are expected to wear. Others typically have unwritten rules and expect "appropriate" choices that are in "good taste."

Most companies expect men to wear ties on the job. Although sports jackets are widely accepted, some companies still expect suits. What is expected differs between companies and locations. Employees in offices in large cities and at corporate headquarters are expected to dress up more than those in more rural areas and branch offices. Expectations are less clear for women. Skirted suits in blue or gray seem to be favored. Slacks are accepted in some offices and under certain conditions, such as bad weather.

Once on the job, it is important to build a working wardrobe systematically. Making a businesslike impression on the job is important to continuing success. Investment in the right clothes can be more important than treating yourself to some luxuries, such as a new car or a better stereo.

MAJOR CHAPTER CONCEPTS

1. Clothes can serve a variety of needs including physical needs, self-expression needs, aesthetic needs, and the need for the approval of others.
2. Each individual needs a wardrobe that includes clothes for various activities: work, social events, casual activities.

3. In planning a wardrobe, an inventory is the first step; next you should decide what else is needed on the basis of your activities.

4. Style is a particular combination of line and form in clothing. A fashion is a style that gains widespread acceptance.

5. Clothing color choices should be guided by the impression you want to convey and by the colors that are most flattering to you.

6. Fabric labels must include the generic or family names of the fibers used as well as the trade names.

7. Each textile fiber has advantages and disadvantages; the disadvantages can be dealt with by creating blends of several fibers and by the use of special finishes.

8. Garments get their shape from the way their fabric pieces are cut, from pressing, and from the use of darts, tucks, and pleats.

9. A poor fit in a garment may be due to the wrong size. It also may result when a garment's proportions do not match the wearer's.

10. In fitting, horizontal strain marks are a sign the garment is too tight; vertical strain marks, a sign it is too loose. In fitting, attention also should be given to the length of both sleeves and trouser legs.

11. Indicators of good workmanship include smooth seams with small, neat stitching, matched patterns, and careful finishing of the interior of the garment.

12. Everyday care, including hanging up clothes when they are taken off, will help protect their appearance.

13. Many fabrics made from different fibers look alike; care labels provide a guide to proper care.

14. Most textile fibers will burn. Fire safety can be increased by the use of flame-retardant fibers and finishes.

15. Different shoe materials perform differently. Leather allows perspiration to move away from the foot and molds well to the foot, but it requires more care than synthetics and is not waterproof.

CONSUMER QUESTIONS

1. Which item in your wardrobe has been the most useful and enjoyable? Which has been the biggest mistake? Rate each on the evaluative criteria discussed in this chapter. Which criteria have been most important in making you satisfied or dissatisfied?

2. Take an inventory of the clothes you have available for the current season. Compare the inventory to what you need for your activities. What gaps do you see? How could you go about filling these gaps?

3. What natural coloring category do you fall in? If you are not sure, ask your friends for help. What clothing colors are recommended for this category? How do the recommended colors compare to what you have?

4. How does clothing quality compare at different price levels? Identify a particular item of clothing that is available at several different price levels. Compare the items available at different prices on the evaluative criteria discussed in this chapter. You can get the information you need by visiting stores or using a major mail-order catalog.

5. If you were buying a raincoat, what evaluative criteria would be important to you? Would you, for example, want to use the coat for cool weather wear? Using the evaluative criteria discussed in this chapter, describe the characteristics you would like. Use store visits or mail-order catalogs to get an idea of the alternatives available.

6. Have you had laundry problems recently? What were they? How does the information in this chapter help you understand the problem? What is the solution for the problem?

SUGGESTED READINGS

1. *Consumer Reports.* "The Good Gray Suit," 51 no. 8 (August 1986): 502-510. Consumers Union occasionally rates basic clothing items such as children's jeans or adults' raincoats. This comprehensive report, with ratings, considers what to look for in men's and women's suits.

2. Lurie, Alison. *The Language of Clothes.* New York: Random House, 1981. Lurie presents a highly literate and sophisticated consideration of the use of clothing as a form of communication.

3. Stamper, Anita A., Sue Humphries Sharp, and Linda B. Donnell. *Evaluating Apparel Quality.* New York; Fairchild Publications, 1986. This is an extensive report on evaluative criteria that can be used in judging clothing.

4. Solomon, Michael R., ed. *The Psychology of Fashion.* Lexington, Mass.: D.C. Heath Co., 1985. This book gives a comprehensive, research-based examination of fashion, its creation by designers, its promotion by advertisers, and its adoption by consumers.

CHAPTER 8

~~~~~~~~~~~

FOOD

Most Americans could eat far more cheaply than they do, but few would find such a diet very appealing. It is possible to put together a nutritionally adequate diet for as little as three dollars a day. Such diets, however, include more bread and inexpensive vegetables, such as cabbage, than most people are used to eating and less meat than many like to eat.

Most people want more-than-adequate nutrition at low cost. They want an interesting variety of foods that taste good and look attractive. Time-saving features are another characteristic consumers often want, one that convenience foods and eating out may provide. They also want foods that are safe and wholesome.

This chapter looks at each of these evaluative criteria in turn and the importance and weight of each. Ways to judge individual food items on these criteria will also be examined. Food eaten away from home has become an important part of both diets and budgets. More than one-third of the money spent for food in the United States goes for food eaten away from home. For this reason, foods eaten away from home will be considered along with the more familiar topic of food for home consumption.

NUTRITION

Basic roles of food are providing materials needed for (1) growth, (2) the continuous process of repairing and rebuilding bones and body tissues, (3) maintaining and regulating body processes, and (4) providing energy (measured in calories) to carry on physical activity.

Nutrition and Health

Good nutritional practices clearly are important for the sizable number of people who are under specific orders from their doctors to change what they eat to control an illness or because they have a high risk of illness. Some common doctor's orders include:

- Reduce intake of salt and other forms of sodium because of its relation to high blood pressure
- Control intake of sugars because of their relation to dental caries
- Reduce intake of cholesterol and saturated fats
- Reduce calorie intake because of its relation to overweight and heart disease

Unfortunately, it is more difficult to create much concern about nutrition in the rest of the population.

Most people are convinced that good nutrition is important, but they also feel that their own deviations from suggested dietary guidelines are not great enough to be of concern. In fact, clear-cut signs of nutritional deficiency diseases are rare in this country. The consequences of the inadequate diets typical in this country are not clear. Many diets provide less than the recommended amounts of nutrients but enough so that deficiency diseases do not develop. One reason may be that the recommended amounts include a margin of safety. However, people eating borderline diets run the risk of not looking as good, feeling as well, or living as long as they could.

In recent years health experts have become convinced that overweight is a serious nutritional problem (Guthrie, 1986). Despite the fact that a large part of the American population has relatively low calorie intake a substantial number of people are overweight. The evidence suggests that many people are so physically inactive that they do not use up even the small amounts of food energy in their diets and that these excess calories end up as weight gain.

Understanding Nutritional Needs

The body is known to need more than 40 different vitamins and minerals, which makes it difficult to keep track of the full range of nutritional needs and the foods which provide them. To help simplify the job, nutrition educators have devised systems of classifying foods. These systems group foods that provide similar nutrients into a particular category. For many years the Basic Four system of groups was used. It was replaced in 1979 with a system that added a fifth group—fats, sweets, and alcohol— to take fuller account of the impact of these foods in the diet. In 1984, fruits and vegetables were split into two separate groups to help emphasize their importance. The revised list has been labeled *The Food Wheel* (Guthrie, 1986).

- *Milk, cheese, and yogurt group*—Whole and skim milk, cottage and cheddar-type cheese, and yogurt. This group is the leading source of calcium needed for bones and teeth. It also provides high-quality protein, riboflavin, vitamin A, and many other nutrients. Two servings each day are recommended for adults and children; three for teenagers, pregnant adult women, and nursing adult women. Pregnant and nursing women under 19 should have four servings.
- *Vegetable group*—All vegetables. Good sources of vitamin A (dark-green and deep-yellow vegetables such as spinach, carrots, broccoli, sweet potatoes, and turnip greens) should be eaten frequently. Unpeeled vegetables and those with edible seeds (such as peas) are an important source of fiber. Three to five servings each day are recommended.
- *Fruit group*—All fruits. Citrus fruits (oranges, orange juice, grapefruit) are good sources of vitamin C, as are strawberries, cherries, and cantaloupe. One good vitamin C source should be consumed each day. Fruits can be a useful source of dietary fiber. A total of two to four servings a day is recommended.
- *Breads, grains, and cereal group*—All products made with whole grain or enriched flour or meal. This group includes bread, cooked or ready-to-eat cereals, spaghetti, and rice. Foods in this group are important sources of protein, iron, and B vitamins (thiamine, riboflavin and niacin). Whole-grain products are a useful source of fiber. Six to eleven servings each day are recommended.
- *Meat, poultry, fish, and eggs group*—Red meats such as beef and pork, chicken, fish, shellfish, dry beans and other legumes, peanuts, and peanut butter. Foods in this group provide protein, iron, thiamine, riboflavin, niacin, and other nutrients. Varied choices from this group are recommended as each food has its own distinct nutritional advantages. Two servings each day are recommended.
- *Fats, sweets, alcohol group*—Fats such as margarine, butter, and salad dressing; sweets such as sugar, jelly, honey, candies, and highly sugared beverages such as soft drinks; and alcoholic beverages including wine, beer, and liquor. Also included are baked goods made from refined but unenriched flour because they provide relatively low levels of vitamins and minerals in relation to their calorie content. Foods in this group provide many calories but few needed nutrients; there are some exceptions such as

vegetable oils that provide vitamin E and essential fatty acids. No specific number of servings is suggested. Items in this group should be limited if calorie intake is being reduced. If alcohol is consumed, it should be used in moderation.

The Food Wheel list does not give much feel for what a day's meals should be like. Table 8-1 shows two different menus for a day, both providing the recommended numbers of servings from each of the food groups. A comparison of these two menus shows that it is possible to get a nutritionally adequate diet at quite different levels of spending. The high-cost menus for a family of four cost almost twice as much as the low-cost menus.

While it is desirable to eat a balanced diet each day, nutritionists are not concerned if the diet for a particular day is not adequately balanced. It is sufficient if diets are kept balanced over a period of several days.

The small amounts many people are eating these days make it difficult for them to get adequate amounts of vitamins and minerals. It is important for people who are not eating much to choose foods that provide significant amounts of needed nutrients along with the calories they provide. The prob-

Table 8-1
A Day's Menu at Different Cost Levels

		Low-Cost Menu	High-Cost Menu
Breakfast		Fruit or Juice (canned)	Strawberries (fresh or frozen)
		Oatmeal with milk	English muffin sandwich with
		Cinnamon toast	cheese, mushrooms, and egg
		Coffee (for adults)	Milk (lowfat) or coffee
Lunch		Peanut butter and jelly	Chicken, lettuce, and tomato
		White enriched bread (in sand-	sandwich
		wich)	Whole wheat bun (in sandwich)
		Banana	Asparagus (frozen)
		Cookies (homemade)	Sherbet
		Milk (nonfat dry)	Milk (fresh)
Snack		Cereal party snack	Cheese and crackers, peanuts
		Beverage (as desired)	Beverage (as desired)
Dinner		Hamburger stroganoff	Beef round roast
		Noodles	Corn on cob (fresh or frozen)
		Carrot and raisin salad (fresh)	Broccoli (frozen)
		Bread (whole wheat)	Dinner roll (bakery)
		Cookies (homemade)	Fresh fruit salad
		Milk (nonfat dry) or coffee	Angel food cake (bakery)
			Milk (lowfat) or coffee

Source: U.S. Department of Agriculture, Human Nutrition Information Service, *Family Food Budgeting...Good Meals and Good Nutrition.* (Home and Garden Bulletin 94). Washington, D.C.: USGPO, 1981, p. 13.

lem of ensuring adequate nutrition while limiting calorie intakes suggests some new rules for good nutrition (see Figure 8-1).

Using Nutritional Labeling

Many packaged foods now carry labels providing nutrition information. Information is included on vitamins, minerals, calories, fat, carbohydrates, and protein. The labels were developed to help shoppers understand the nutritional content of food items and to make it easier to compare them.

For most foods, nutritional labeling is voluntary. However, it is required when nutrients are added. For example, if vitamins A and C are added to a breakfast cereal, the product must have a nutritional label. Labeling is also required if the manufacturer makes any nutritional claims about a product.

Label Content. Nutrition label information is provided in a standard format to make its use easier. Certain information must be included in every label:

- Serving size
- Calories per serving
- Amounts of protein, carbohydrate, and fat (measured in grams)
- Amount of sodium (measured in milligrams)

Figure 8-1
Dietary Guidelines

- Eat a variety of foods. A well-balanced diet can provide the more than 40 different nutrients needed for good health.
- Maintain desirable weight. To lose weight, eat a variety of foods that are low in calories and high in nutrients; increase physical activity.
- Avoid too much fat, saturated fat, and cholesterol. Choose lean meat, fish, poultry, and dry beans and peas as protein sources; use low-fat milk and milk products; limit intake of fats and oils.
- Eat foods with adequate starch and fiber. Good sources are breads and cereals, fruits and vegetables, and dry beans and peas.
- Avoid too much sugar. Use less sugar and high-sugar foods including candy and soft drinks.
- Avoid too much sodium. Learn to enjoy the flavor of unsalted foods; use herbs, spices, and lemon juice to add flavor.
- If you drink alcoholic beverages, do so in moderation. Alcoholic beverages are high in calories and low in nutrients; excessive consumption by pregnant women may cause birth defects.

Source: U.S. Department of Agriculture, U.S. Department of Health and Human Services, *Nutrition and Your Health: Dietary Guidelines for Americans,* 2d ed. (Home and Garden Bulletin No. 232). Washington, D.C.: USGPO, 1985.

- Amounts of protein and of two minerals and five vitamins (measured as a percentage of the U.S. Recommended Daily Allowance [USRDA])

Certain other information items, including information on other vitamins and minerals and on cholesterol, may be included if the manufacturer wishes.

To fully understand the label information, it is necessary to understand the meaning of the USRDA. The USRDA is an amount of a particular vitamin or mineral adequate to meet the nutritional needs of nearly all healthy people. Pregnant women and nursing mothers may require more.

Nutritional labels can provide a variety of information. They can tell us the following:

- There are 90 calories in a glass of lowfat milk (one 8-ounce cup).
- A serving of dry-roasted peanuts (1 ounce or 28.4 grams) contains more fat (14 grams) than protein (7 grams).
- A glass of milk provides 30 percent of the USRDA for calcium.

Nutrient Density. The information provided allows us to determine the amount of particular nutrients a food provides per calorie, which nutritionists refer to as its *nutrient density*. One measure of nutrient density is the *Index of Nutrient Quality* (INQ) (Guthrie, 1986).

$$INQ = \frac{\text{Percentage of a day's requirement for a nutrient provided by a food item}}{\text{Percentage of a day's energy requirement provided by a food item (usually based on 2,000 calories a day)}}$$

It was noted above that a glass of lowfat milk provides 30 percent of the USRDA for calcium. A glass of lowfat milk also provides 90 calories, which is 4.5 percent of 2,000 calories (90/2,000 = .045 or 4.5 percent.) Thus the INQ is:

$$\frac{30}{4.5} = 6.67$$

A glass of lowfat milk, therefore, provides 6.67 percent of the USRDA for calcium for each percentage of the day's calorie needs it provides.

Improving Nutritional Labeling. Some food products do not carry nutritional labels. Fresh foods, meats, fruits, and vegetables typically are not labeled but some people argue they should be. The nutritional contributions of these foods should not be overlooked. Some processed foods are not labeled because their actual nutritional content is negligible or because manufacturers are aware their content is not as good as many people think it is.

Critics of the present system of nutritional labeling have urged that it be required for all foods. Some processors have objected; voluntary programs always seem more acceptable than required ones. Some have asked if fresh foods are to be included and have pointed out the problems of labeling them. Critics have also objected that the present information is too complex for the people who need it most, those who have less education. They suggest the use of symbols or descriptive words. Others have urged the use of the nutrient density concept, arguing that when the concept is understood, it can help people select foods that provide more needed nutrients per calorie.

JUDGING QUALITY

Even though eating is a necessity, there is no reason that is should not be pleasurable, too. Everyone has favorite foods. The amount of enjoyment derived from food can also differ depending on quality of the product. There are good sirloin steaks, and there are bad ones. It makes sense to learn how to recognize the good ones at the meat counter and how to recognize quality in other food items as well.

Product Name

One of the most basic indicators of quality for any food product is its name because the use of many product names is controlled by federal regulation. If an item is labeled with one of these names it must conform to the standard of identity that sets down the characteristics and ingredients for that particular food item. More than 250 basic food items are covered by standards of identity, including such everyday products as bread, jam, macaroni, margarine, and peanut butter.

A standard of identity for a food product is much like a recipe. It identifies key ingredients and the minimum amount of each which must be present. Strawberry jam, for example, must have at least 45 percent strawberries by weight. A jam that includes strawberries but does not include this much would have to be labeled "imitation" strawberry jam. Standards of identity also specify optional ingredients that may or may not be included, such as preservatives, spices, colors, and flavorings.

It is not always easy to tell which products are covered by a standard of identity. One clue is that products covered by standards of identity do not have to list the required ingredients on the label, though optional ingredients must be listed. Some manufacturers of standardized products do list ingredients voluntarily. Products not covered by standards of identity must list ingredients. Standards of identity for most foods are administered by the Food and Drug Administration. Those for meat and poultry products are administered by the Department of Agriculture.

There have been many complaints over the years about the regulations on standards of identity. Many consumers would like ingredient lists on *all* products, whether standardized or not. They feel ingredient information is a useful indicator of quality. The absence of ingredient information can also create serious problems for people with food allergies.

There have been proposals to abolish the present system of food standards. It has been argued that, while they ensure a basic level of quality,

CONSUMER CONCERN: THE PERSISTENCE OF NUTRITION AND HEALTH QUACKERY

Despite our education and sophistication, white-coated quacks posing as nutritional and medical experts are bilking the public with useless and often risky diets, phony and sometimes dangerous medicines, and fake therapeutic devices. What is quackery? Simply defined, it is *misinformation about health*. Quacks peddle their misinformation in a variety of forms—as nutritional supplements, as medicines and miracle drugs, as devices (including copper bracelets and reducing belts), as therapeutic treatments, and in book form. Often these cures are dangerous in themselves. Some nutrition supplements promoted for dietary therapy may result in toxic reactions, not cures. Others are merely harmless and useless. A major danger of all quackery, however, is that competent help will not be sought and effective treatment will be delayed too long.

TELL-TALE SIGNS OF QUACKERY

People sometimes fail to recognize the claims of today's self-styled health experts as quackery. Many have come to believe that no one can get away with that kind of thing any more. Despite the efforts of regulatory officials, quackery persists. One important defense is for consumers to learn to detect quackery on their own. There are some tell-tale signs of quackery:

- Claims about a new or secret ingredient, a special device, or a new technology
- Claims that the "expert" is being persecuted by the medical and scientific establishment because they fear competition or dislike threats to their theories
- Claims of miracle cures for a long list of ailments
- Promises of quick or certain cures
- Use of testimonials and case histories
- Promotion by traveling lecturers, door-to-door salespeople, or ads by unknown book publishers

The quack claims of today frequently pose as breakthroughs in newly developing areas of science. Quacks promote their cures as applications of these new discoveries to the field of health care. As a result, there have been a succession of quack remedies posing as wonder drugs, new dietary discoveries, and new uses of electronic technology.

they also discourage innovation and the development of new food products. For example, because of the regulations, low-calorie margarine with a lower amount of fat must be labeled imitation margarine, a name that might lack appeal to some shoppers.

THE LURE OF QUACKERY

Why do people fall for claims that seem so suspicious? Why are they taken in? Some are simply gullible and cannot tell reliable experts from phonies. Others may distrust experts from the scientific "establishment" on the basis of unfortunate past experiences. Anyone who shares their distrust of physicians and nutrition scientists sounds believable to them. Some may be hoping for miracles because nothing else has worked. They are desperate and willing to try anything.

The victims of the quacks are all too often the poor and the aged. James Harvey Young, author of *The Medical Messiahs* (1967), points out that sometimes even better-educated people fall victim to quacks. They may be attracted by the elaborate systems of logic that explain how a new miracle cure works. Dazzled by the logic, they fail to note a false premise lurking in the background.

The claims of quacks are often difficult to refute. Adequate scientific checks require expensive and lengthy research, which makes it easy for quacks to exploit the public's concerns about their health and diets. Their claims cannot be tested quickly, and they are subject only to limited controls. While label and ad claims are subject to government controls, claims in books and magazine articles and on TV talk shows are protected by the right of freedom of speech and are more difficult to control.

The Food and Drug Administration (FDA) has federal-level responsibility for controlling quackery but seems to have given less attention to the problem in recent years. Some critics charge that the FDA has neglected quackery in recent years because it has shifted its priorities to other areas, such as testing new drugs (*Consumer Reports,* May, 1985).

QUESTIONS

1. What forms can nutritional quackery take?
2. What kinds of nutrition quackery are likely to attract young people? Older people?
3. Are the claims of quacks subject to any controls?

While some food processors would like to see standards of identity abolished, others fear the competition that might result. Many like the present system because it allows them to reformulate their product, within certain limits, as ingredient prices change, without having to print new labels.

Descriptive information linked to the product name can also provide indications of quality. Here are some examples.

- "All beef hot dogs" can contain only beef. No other meats or extenders can be used.
- Canned fruit names usually include information on the type of packing liquid (syrup, juice, or water) and the weight of the syrup. Heavy syrup contains more sugar, has more calories, and is more expensive than lighter syrups.
- Vegetable product names often describe the maturity of the product, such as baby peas. The style of cut may be described. Sliced, diced, or fancy cuts such as French-style (a lengthwise cut for green beans) may be used.

Ingredients

Again, processed foods not covered by a standard of identity must have ingredients listed. Spices, flavorings, and colorings do not have to be listed individually. The product label must, however, indicate if any ingredients in these three categories have been used. The use of preservatives also must be indicated.

Ingredients are listed in order by their relative weight. If a canned stew has more beef, by weight, than any other ingredient, the label will list it first. Clearly, such a product is expected to be of better quality than one in which the leading ingredient is water. Many consumers are not satisfied with the present system of listing ingredients. They would like to have the percentages of major ingredients listed, too. Manufacturers have resisted this proposal for a variety of reasons. A major problem is that it would limit their flexibility in reformulating the product.

Proper identification of ingredients can be a problem for people eating away from home, too. Deceptive or incorrect menu information has attracted increasing attention in recent years and has led to demands for "truth in menus." The substitution of easier to prepare or less expensive products is a common problem For example,

- The menu says "fresh-squeezed orange juice" when frozen concentrate is used.
- The "chopped choice sirloin" is, in fact, neither choice grade nor from the loin.
- The "home-baked apple pie" was baked in a commercial bakery, not on the premises.

Responsibility for detecting violations of this type usually falls on local health officers who inspect food service establishments for sanitation. Enforcement seems to vary widely between communities.

Brand Name

Brand names may also be used as indicators of quality. One of the reasons manufacturers use brand names is to make it easy for satisfied customers to come back for more.

Most larger stores offer a choice of two or three brands of better selling items. The top-priced one is usually a well-known and nationally advertised manufacturer's brand, such as Hunt's, Del Monte, or Campbell's, and is usually of high quality. The next item down the price scale typically is a store brand of equal or slightly lower quality. Store brands are packed to specifications, usually by smaller processors. An example is A & P's Ann Page brand. Many stores also offer another, lower-priced, store brand. It typically is of slightly lower quality. For example, fruits may be slightly blemished and packed in lighter syrup.

More and more stores also offer a line of generic products that are still lower priced. These items carry no brand name; only the name of the product itself, e.g., green beans, appears on the label. The items offered are ones that sell in volume—green beans, golden kernel corn, whole tomatoes. Since these items are often used in mixtures, such as casseroles, color and quality are not so critical. The lower prices of generic items are a result of savings in several areas.

- Generic items are seldom advertised or reduced in price for special promotions.
- Handling and inventory costs are lower because usually only one size is offered and all generic items are grouped in one area of the store.
- Stores add lower markup on generic items than on other brands.

Open-Date Information

Some food processors provide calendar date information on their labels indicating the date by which the product should be sold or used to assure quality and freshness. This practice is called *open-dating* (Murphy & Garrett, 1982). Others use coded dates, which cannot be interpreted without information on the code. Manufacturers provide date information to help stores rotate their stock and make certain older items are sold first.

Four types of open-dating are widely used.

- *Pack date*—The date of final processing or packaging. An example is "packed January 25." Pack dates are sometimes used on fresh meat and poultry. The pack date does not provide shoppers any information on how long they can expect a product to last.

- *Pull date*—The last day a product should be sold at retail, still allowing time for home storage and use. An example is "Sell by August 25," indicating the date the product should be removed from the shelf. The pull date is the most widely used type of open date.
- *Quality assurance date*—The date after which the product is not likely to be at peak quality. Examples are "For maximum enjoyment use by August 14" and "Better when used by December 23."
- *Expiration date*—The last date the product should be used for assured quality. An example is "Do not use after February 1992."

The variety of dating systems used causes confusion. Sometimes dates are used without any explanation of their meaning, adding to the confusion.

CONSUMER CONCERN: IS VARIETY THE SPICE OF LIFE— OR IS IT AN ECONOMIC WASTE?

In recent years, leading food processors have offered an ever-increasing variety of flavors and styles. The soup shelves no longer contain just chicken rice soup and chicken noodle soup. Today's chicken soups include chicken gumbo, chicken barley, chicken noodle O's, curly noodles with chicken, cream of chicken, creamy chicken mushroom, chicken vegetable, chicken alphabet, chicken and stars, chicken 'n dumplings, chicken broth, chicken broth and noodles, chicken broth and rice, and homestyle chicken noodle soup.

These sixteen chicken soups illustrate the array of products that give American food shoppers a range of choices unsurpassed in history or in any other country. Both competitors and supermarket retailers, however, view this proliferation of varieties and product lines with concern. Stores must constantly deal with demands from hundreds of food processors for limited shelf space. At the same time, competitors worry that rivals are trying to tie up supermarket shelf space and crowd them out.

The rivalry on the soup shelves of America's supermarkets is mild compared to the rivalry elsewhere in the store. The same battle is occurring on the breakfast cereal shelves, in the frozen foods display case, on the soft drink shelves, and up and down most other aisles. In each area there is a fierce battle for shelf space and market share among the three or four major food processors that dominate most food product categories.

Rather than trying to undercut each other on price, the big food processors are struggling to turn out new products, advertise and promote them successfully, and win shelf space and sales away from their rivals. Most of the new brands, sizes, colors, and flavors offered to the public

Open dating is not presently required by federal law, though some communities have local laws requiring open dating of some items (such as milk). Many consumers and consumer advocates have argued for open dating on food packages. Industry representatives have countered that how the product has been handled often is more important than how old it is. If a product has not been handled properly, quality may have suffered. Some more uniform system of product dating does seem desirable, however.

Food shoppers should be aware that when food products are exposed to high temperatures, quality is likely to deteriorate. Frozen foods are particularly susceptible if they thaw and are refrozen. Some tell-tale signs are sweating packages and frost-covered packages. Many consumers have ex-

really are minor variations on existing products. The differences are mainly in form, packaging, and advertising appeals.

One reason there are so many new flavors and "natural" and "lite" products is that manufacturers make higher profits from them than from no-frills standard items. As a result, food manufacturers avoid staple items and generic products that provide relatively low profit margins and concentrate their product development efforts on products with differentiating features that can command a premium price.

The cornucopia of new products offers consumers an appealing range of choice but not without significant costs. Whether they want the new products or not, all shoppers have to bear part of the costs of developing, promoting, and distributing new items despite the fact that most fail to catch on with the public. To fend off the new brands and protect their market share, existing brands must be defended with heavy advertising that increases their prices as well. Manufacturers end up fighting harder and harder to protect their market shares, and shoppers end up paying more.

QUESTIONS

1. List characteristics used to differentiate breakfast cereals. Rate these characteristics on their usefulness or importance.
2. Name some foods offered in only a few different forms. What characteristics are used to differentiate each one?
3. Some people argue that the freedom to create and offer new products is a basic right. Do you agree? Why, or why not?

pressed interest in quality indicators on the labels of frozen food products that would show whether the product had ever thawed.

In protecting quality, proper handling of food products at home is important too. Perishable items should be refrigerated. Other items should be stored in cooler spots away from the stove, dishwasher, and other heat sources.

Food Grades

Food grades indicate levels of product quality and can be useful to consumers (Beck, Crosby, & Parris, 1982). They are, however, seen less and less often in retail trade. Food grades are based on a set of evaluative criteria, and an item must meet the specified minimum level on each criterion to make a particular grade. Each quality level is given a name. In the case of beef, *Prime* is the name given the top grade, followed by *Choice, Good,* and so on. Unfortunately grade name systems differ between items, which causes confusion, though some effort is being made to make the system more uniform.

Most food grading is administered by the U.S. Department of Agriculture. USDA grades are most visible on eggs and butter. They are more seldom seen on meat and are seen infrequently on fruits and vegetables. One reason for this may be that quality is more uniform than it used to be. Most meat sold in retail stores would fall in the USDA Choice grade or in the top portion of the Good grade. Prime grade is used principally in fancy restaurants. Although grading is voluntary, any firm that uses it must use the specified system of grade names. USDA grades probably are used more in specifying quality in negotiations between food firms than at retail.

In the absence of grade information, consumers are on their own in judging meat. Meat can be judged on its appearance. Beef cuts should have a high proportion of meat to bone and fat. The lean should be fine-textured and firm, bright red in color with some *marbling* (small flecks of fat). The fat should be white, flaky, and firm. Bones should be red and porous, not whitish (a sign of an older animal).

Some consumer advocates feel there is a need for a grade system more oriented to consumer needs and have called for a major reorganization of the present system. Opponents of this proposal point out that such changes would be costly and that brand names have largely replaced grades for processed items. The present system does, however, give consumers little help in judging the quality of fresh items such as meat, fruits, and vegetables that are sold unbranded.

The FDA is also involved in checking food quality. The FDA sets *standards of quality* for many processed products. These standards should not be confused with USDA grades. They are, in effect, minimum specifications for such evaluative criteria as color and freedom from blemishes. They cover such factors as how "soupy" canned kernel corn can be and how many pits are acceptable in canned pitted cherries. While substandard food may still be sold, it is seldom seen in stores and must be clearly labeled.

Is Price an Indicator of Quality?

Examination of the relationship between food product prices and quality over the years suggests that there is no clear link between the two. Paying a higher price for a food product does not assure better quality.

When the relationship between price and quality was examined for food products rated by *Consumer Reports* between 1961 and 1975, it was concluded that price was not a useful guide to quality. Price was a particularly poor guide to quality in convenience foods and frozen foods. Many of the higher quality brands of these items were less expensive than the lower quality ones (Riesz, 1979).

Quality and Menu Planning

In addition to the quality of individual food items, it is worthwhile to consider the aesthetic factors that contribute to satisfaction in an overall diet. A key factor is dietary variety. Studies of household food spending have found that one of the ways spending differs between income levels is the variety of foods consumed. More affluent households can afford to consume a wider variety of items. Variety helps ensure eating pleasure and also helps to improve the nutritional content of the diet. More varied diets tend to be better balanced nutritionally.

Variety in color, flavor, and texture is also desirable in menus. Picture a dinner of broiled fish, mashed potatoes, cauliflower, and vanilla ice cream. Not only would it lack color, it would also provide little variety in texture. The substitution of a baked potato and broccoli for the mashed potatoes and cauliflower would add both color and texture.

COST

Because food takes a significant share of incomes, careful planning of food spending and careful selection of individual items is important. The cost of an individual item goes beyond the price on the can or on the shelf label. The cost of the item must be computed per serving in consumable form.

Usable Quantity

In determining the cost of a food item per serving an important first step is determining just how much of what is bought will be really usable. How many peaches are actually in the can? How much of the steak will really be edible?

Net and Drained Weight. Processed foods must, under federal law, have their *net weight* on the label. Net weight includes the contents of the packages but not the package itself. Both the weight of the food and the weight of any packing syrup or liquid are included in net weight. Almost all processed products are sold on a net weight basis. Only a few, such as mushrooms and olives, are sold on a *drained weight* basis, in which the weight of packing liquid is not included.

Some canners voluntarily list the weight of the solid product along with the net weight, though this is not required. Many consumers favor use of drained weight labeling for all fruits and vegetables. Tests show that there is a good deal of variation in drained weights between different brands of the same product. Food industry representatives have responded, however, that drained weight labeling would increase costs. Some have argued that because syrups and packing liquids are part of the product and can be eaten there is no reason to measure them separately. In response to this argument, it should be noted that many people do not eat the packing liquids, and some avoid them because they are high in sugar and salt.

Edible Portion. A similar problem occurs in selecting meat because a portion of many cuts is inedible fat and bone. Different cuts vary a good deal in the number of edible portions that can obtained per pound, as can be seen in the following cases:

- Cuts with little or no fat or bone can provide three to four servings per pound. Examples are ground beef, center slices of ham, and fish fillets.
- Cuts with a medium amount of bone can provide two to three servings per pound. Examples include chuck roasts, pork chops, ham, and poultry.
- Cuts with much bone can provide only one to two servings per pound. Examples are spare ribs, porterhouse and T-bone steaks, and chicken wings and backs.

Note that in Table 8-2, sirloin steak provides 2½ servings per pound. The table can also be used to determine cost per serving. For example, if sirloin steak costs $2.00 per pound, then a three-ounce serving costs 85 cents.

Cost per Unit

Another important step in holding food costs down is determining which package size is the best buy. If there are three different package sizes of Cheerios, which costs the least per ounce? The price per unit of measure is the *unit price.* Knowing the unit price facilitates cost comparisons between packages of different sizes. Shoppers should be aware that larger package sizes do not necessarily come at a lower cost per ounce.

Unit pricing is required by law in some states and localities. It is not required by federal law, but some consumer advocates argue it should be. Although unit pricing information was not heavily used when it was first provided, its use appears to be growing as shoppers become more familiar with it. A variety of problems have, however, limited its use in stores that

Table 8-2
Cost of Three-Ounce
Serving of Cooked Lean
Meat

Cost of a Three-Ounce Serving (cents)*

Retail Cut	Approx. Number Servings Per Pound	Price Per Pound of Retail Cuts																	
		$ .60	$ .80	$1.00	$1.20	$1.40	$1.60	$1.80	$2.00	$2.20	$2.40	$2.60	$2.80	$3.00	$3.20	$3.40	$3.60	$3.80	$4.00
Beef																			
Sirloin steak—bone in	2½	26	34	43	51	60	68	77	85	94	102	111	119	128	136	145	153	162	170
Ground beef—lean	4	16	21	26	31	36	42	47	52	57	62	68	73	78	83	88	94	99	104
Chuck roast—bone in	2	27	36	45	54	62	71	80	89	98	107	116	125	134	143	152	160	169	178
Short ribs	1½	35	47	59	70	82	94	105	117	129	141	152	164	176	188	199	211	222	234
Pork																			
Loin roast—bone in	2	30	40	51	61	71	81	91	101	112	122	132	142	152	162	172	182	192	202
Loin chops—bone in	2	27	36	45	54	62	71	80	89	98	107	116	125	134	143	152	160	169	178
Ham slices—bone out	3	19	25	31	37	44	50	56	62	69	75	81	87	93	100	106	112	118	124
Ham roast—bone in	3	21	28	35	42	48	56	62	69	76	83	90	97	104	111	118	124	131	138
Lamb																			
Leg roast—bone in	2½	25	33	42	50	58	67	75	83	92	100	108	117	125	133	142	150	158	166
Loin chops—bone in	2	27	37	46	55	64	73	82	91	100	110	119	128	137	146	155	164	173	182
Poultry																			
Chicken—whole, ready-to-cook	2	33	44	55	66	77	88	99	110	121	132	143	154	165	176	187	198	209	220
Turkey—whole, ready-to-cook	2	24	33	41	49	57	65	73	82	90	98	106	114	122	131	139	147	155	164

* The cost per serving at other price levels can be estimated by multiplying or dividing the figures in this table. For example, if whole chicken is $.50 per pound, divide the $1.00 per pound cost figure (55) by 2. The cost per serving is 27.5¢.

Source: Adapted from Cynthia Cromwell Junker, "Cost Comparison Tools to Stretch Your Food Dollar," *Food—From Farm to Table: 1982 Yearbook of Agriculture*, Jack Hayes (ed.). Washington, DC: USGPO, 1982, pp. 337-339.

do provide it. Labels are often hard to read or difficult to interpret, and labels are sometimes missing from shelves.

Store Choice

Prices do not differ a great deal between supermarkets. Competition in a local area holds the differences to a small percentage. However, because of the substantial amounts most households spend for food, even these small differences can total to a sizable amount.

Although the price differences between supermarkets is small, there are larger differences between supermarkets and other types of food stores. Prices in convenience stores that are open long hours and offer only limited selections are 10 percent or more higher than supermarket prices. The difference is a result of the small-scale operations of convenience stores. The total volume of sales in typical convenience stores is small relative to supermarkets, but long operating hours make costs high. While convenience stores do offer long hours and good locations, it is not economical to purchase these extra services more often than they are really needed.

Other types of food stores offer cost savings and are worth investigating. These alternatives include discount warehouse stores that eliminate extra services and charge lower prices. Some stores cut costs by carrying only a limited assortment of basic foods. Retail food cooperative stores also can offer price advantages, but some require members to put in work-time as a way to reduce costs. Produce markets and farmers' markets may also offer advantages of lower prices and fresher produce. Conditions and prices differ so much between localities and over time that it is difficult to generalize about these alternatives.

Store Specials

Specials are one of the devices supermarkets use to attract new customers and to keep their regular customers coming back. Stores offering specials typically lower the prices of featured items and at the same time raise other prices to make up the difference. Total store revenues stay the same, but the grocery firm is able to project the image of low prices and good values.

Specials offer smart shoppers a chance to stock up at lower prices. Shoppers should be aware, however, that not all the items featured in a store's ads are really on special. Some are included only because the processor is paying part of the advertising costs.

Meat specials are an important part of stores' promotional programs. Unfortunately, it is difficult to compare meat specials between stores because trimming practices and quality differ between stores and may even differ between regular items and specials. The only way to judge the value of store's meat specials is on the basis of experience.

Plentiful Foods

In planning food purchases it is important to take into account the variations in supplies that occur during the year. Prices, especially for fresh items, vary depending on whether or not supplies are plentiful. Many fresh fruits and vegetables are available throughout the year but are more expensive in off-season. When the new crop first comes in, prices are high. Prices decline as supplies become more plentiful and are usually lowest when the local crop comes in.

Changes in supplies of fresh produce follow the same pattern year after year. Apples, as shown in Table 8-3, are available all year long, but prices are lowest in the fall and winter when supplies are largest. As supplies are consumed over the summer, prices will rise. Knowing seasonal patterns enables a shopper to select the fresh items that are the best buys at a particular time.

Meat supplies also follow a cyclical pattern, but these cycles stretch over several years. Beef prices follow a cycle over a period that has averaged about 10 years. These cycles result when cattle breeders cut the size of their herds when prices are low. Eventually market supplies fall and prices begin to rise. Herds are then rebuilt and eventually supplies become too large and prices fall. The cycle then begins again.

Illustration 8-1
The best buys in fresh produce change with seasonal variations in supplies.

Table 8-3
Availability of Fresh Fruit

	January	February	March	April	May	June	July	August	September	October	November	December
Apples	F	F	F	F	F	L	L	L	G	G	G	G
Bananas	G	G	G	G	G	G	G	F	F	G	G	G
Blueberries	L	L	L	L	L	G	G	G	L	L	L	L
Cantaloupes	L	L	L	L	F	G	G	G	G	L	L	L
Cherries	L	L	L	L	F	G	G	F	L	L	L	L
Grapefruit	G	G	G	G	F	F	L	L	L	F	G	G
Grapes	L	L	L	L	L	F	G	G	G	G	G	F
Oranges	G	G	G	G	G	F	L	L	L	L	F	G
Peaches	L	L	L	L	L	G	G	G	G	L	L	L
Strawberries	L	L	F	G	G	G	F	L	L	L	L	L

G = Good to Peak Supply, F = Fair Supply, L = Low Supply to Not Available

Source: U.S Department of Agriculture, Agricultural Marketing Service, *How to Buy Economically: A Food Buyer's Guide.* Washington, D.C.: USGPO, 1981, pp, 26-27.

Keeping track of food supply cycles and plentiful foods may seem a bit complicated. One way to determine which foods currently are in good supply is to check the food pages of the local paper. Home economists and food marketing specialists in the Cooperative Extension Service provide newspapers with information on the foods that currently are in season and, therefore, are good buys.

Economizing on Food

Because meat makes up one-third of the average household's spending for food consumed at home, careful planning and selection is important. There are several ways to economize on meat purchases.

Many nutritionists feel that most Americans eat more meat than they really need. They suggest that many people could get along with fewer or smaller servings. In fact, The Food Wheel calls for two or three servings a day from the meat, poultry, fish, and eggs group. Note that it is possible to use vegetable protein sources such as peanuts and beans to meet part of this requirement. Eggs, cheese, and canned fish also can be economical sources of protein. Another way to cut meat costs is by combining it with extenders such as noodles, spaghetti, macaroni, rice, and potatoes.

There is increasing evidence that large amounts of food are being wasted all along the food distribution chain, from the farmer to the consumer. Some of the most interesting evidence comes from studies of household garbage by anthropologists at the University of Arizona (Fung & Rathje, 1982). After checking households from different neighborhoods, they concluded that households in middle-income neighborhoods were wasting 10 to 15 percent of their food supplies (Rathje, 1984).

The most significant waste they found was of staple items such as fresh fruits and vegetables. A high rate of waste of expensive specialty baked goods was also found. Much of the discards was not table scraps, but rather untouched food, often in unopened or half-used packages. The researchers blamed much of the waste they identified on poor knowledge of when food is no longer safe to eat and on errors in purchasing and menu scheduling. The waste of good food in the amounts found by the Arizona researchers could be a serious drain on a household's food budget. More careful inventory management and purchasing can help reduce such losses.

TIME SAVINGS

Ease of preparation and time savings are an important appeal of convenience foods and eating away from home. They reduce the time requirements for home cooking, allow inexperienced cooks to enjoy better meals with less worry and waste, and may also reduce home energy use by cutting the amount of cooking required.

Convenience Foods

Some convenience foods offering time-saving advantages are actually cheaper than preparing the same item from scratch. The products that offer both time and money savings are typically ones for which processing reduces shipping costs. The production of frozen orange juice concentrate eliminates the costs of shipping rinds and water and also reduces spoilage losses. Similar savings occur for other fruits and vegetables that contain waste portions or have high spoilage losses.

Still, many convenience foods cost more than their fresh or home-prepared forms, it should be noted. Examples are baked goods and main-dish items. The cost gap between convenience items and those prepared from scratch is not so wide, however, when the value of the time saved is taken into account, even if the time is valued at relatively low prices (Odland, Vettel, & Davis, 1986). There may be quality variations, however. Convenience main-dish items, for example, tend to use more low-cost extenders (potatoes or noodles) than do typical home recipes. They also include smaller amounts of the most costly ingredients such as meat, cheese, and vegetables.

A further problem with some convenience foods is their nutritional content. Most are complex combinations of ingredients sold on the basis of their taste appeal. Their pleasing taste often is due to large amounts of fat and sugar. As a result, these foods are often high in calories. They

Illustration 8-2
Convenience foods offer time savings but often cost more than making the same item from scratch.

also often have a high salt content, a problem for those concerned about high blood pressure.

Eating Out

Because of the sizable amount spent for food eaten away from home in many households, spending should be managed with the same care given to selection of food consumed at home. The price of snacks and meals away from home must cover many costs besides that of the food itself. In restaurants and fast-food establishments, about one-third to slightly less than half of the price charged is for the food itself. The remainder covers labor, other operating costs, and profits.

A significant part of the price of food eaten away from home goes to pay for the convenience and pleasure of having food served to you rather than preparing it yourself. The extra costs of eating out should, therefore, be regarded as convenience costs, and perhaps as recreation and entertainment expenses, too.

SAFETY

Most food sold in this country is subject to some type of government inspection to ensure that it is safe. These checks include inspection for contamination resulting from unsanitary conditions, disease, pesticides, and other chemical residues. They also include checks for *adulteration,* the omission of a valuable or important ingredient. Consumers should be aware that not all food items are checked and that most of the inspections are spot checks rather than continuous inspections.

Federal Safety Inspection

Except for meat and poultry products, which are inspected by the USDA, most processed foods are produced under the jurisdiction of the FDA. The FDA monitors food plants through a program of occasional visits. During these visits inspectors check the ingredients and additives being used, key points in the manufacturing process, and the plant's records of its own safety checks.

Recalls of unsafe processed food products are rare, supporting the conclusion that most processed food products are safe. Sanitation in some food plants may not, however, be all it should be. In rating food products, Consumers Union also looks for rodent hair and insect parts, as a check on manufacturing practices; and sometimes it finds them. While the presence of these contaminants is not dangerous, CU does regard them as evidence of poor storage and sanitation practices. It feels their presence indicates lax controls that might permit other, more dangerous contamination.

Inspection of fresh and processed meat and poultry products is under the jurisdiction of the USDA. USDA-supervised checks of these items are a continuous inspection. Every carcass is checked. Inspectors check animals before slaughter to make certain they are healthy. After slaughter, an internal check is made of carcasses for signs of disease. When meat and poultry are made into processed products, both the processing procedures and the ingredients used are checked.

Unlike other types of food inspection, fish inspection is voluntary. It is under the jurisdiction of the U.S. Department of Commerce. The proportion of the fish sold that is inspected has increased in recent years, but legislation is needed to make inspection mandatory for fresh and processed fish from domestic sources and abroad.

Some commonsense rules can help shoppers avoid processed products that may be unsafe. It is risky to buy any package that has been opened. Cans that are bulging or leaking should also be avoided. Dented cans are safe as long as the vacuum seal is intact. Packing liquid that spurts when a can is opened may be a sign of spoilage.

Home Food Safety

Despite improvements in food safety by manufacturers, proper home food-handling practices are still essential to control food-borne disease. Studies of food handling at home suggest that many consumers do not handle food safely. Lack of knowledge of good practices, or failure to use what is known, seems to be a widespread problem.

Frozen and refrigerated foods should be brought home and stored promptly. Refrigerated foods should be kept at approximately 40° F. Refrigerator temperatures should be checked periodically to make certain they are cold enough. Other foods should be stored in a cool, dry place protected from rodents and insects. Experts advise against storing food under the sink because of moisture, warmth, and the proximity of cleaning chemicals. They also advise against storage near the stove and other heat sources.

Frozen meat and poultry should be thawed in the refrigerator or under hot water. Thawing at room temperature aids bacterial growth. After preparing raw meat or poultry, cutting boards and utensils should be cleaned before they are used in preparing other food or serving cooked food. Otherwise, uncleaned equipment may put bacteria back into the cooked product. Meat should be cooked through to be certain that all bacteria are killed.

When serving food, a good rule is to keep hot food hot and cold food cold. If this practice is not followed, bacteria may multiply to unsafe levels in as little as two hours at room temperatures. In hot weather, custard-filled pastry, potato salad, and meat salads can be a particular problem because they are favorable media for bacteria.

Restaurant Food Safety

Restaurant sanitation is under the jurisdiction of local health officers. The extent of enforcement differs a good deal between communities. The experience of some local health officers suggests that sanitation in independent restaurants is more likely to be a problem than in the establishments of large chains. Large chains have set sanitation procedures and police their local outlets. Not all independents are as careful.

A variety of problems may turn up in restaurant inspections. Food storage facilities may be inadequate and permit insect and rodent contamination. Food preparation areas and counters may not be clean. Food may be held at improper temperatures. Dishwashing procedures may be inadequate. Any of these violations can create health hazards. Most municipalities do not publicize restaurant health violations. Probably the best clue consumers have to kitchen sanitation is the cleanliness and general appearance of the eating area and exterior.

MAJOR CHAPTER CONCEPTS

1. The Food Wheel provides guidance for getting needed nutrients: milk group (two servings each day for adults and children; three for teenagers); vegetable group (three to five servings); fruits group (two to four servings); breads, grains, and cereal group (six to eleven servings); meat, poultry, fish, and eggs group (two to three servings); fats, sweets, and alcohol group (no specific number).

2. Because most adults must limit their calorie intakes, it is useful to look for foods with a high nutrient density; that is, more nutrients per calorie.

3. Claims about the special benefits of a particular nutrient or large doses of nutrients often are unsupported by scientific evidence and are a form of quackery.

4. Most food products are sold on the basis of net weight. To know how much is really usable, it is necessary to know the drained weight for canned and frozen items and the proportion of meat cuts that is edible.

5. Unit price, the price per ounce or per unit measure, can be used in comparing the cost of different package sizes.

6. Although prices in different supermarkets are fairly similar, households that spend large amounts for food will find it worthwhile to check prices at several supermarkets and other types of food stores.

7. Specials offer an opportunity for savings; not all items advertised are on special, however.

8. Foods that are in ample supply are usually available at lower prices and are good buys.

9. Waste of usable food is sizable in many households; more careful planning can reduce these losses.

10. Some convenience foods save both time and money; others, including baked goods and main-dish items, are more expensive, but their extra cost is not so large when the value of the cook's time saved is taken into account.

11. Food should be carefully handled at home to keep it safe and sanitary. Care should be used in buying packaged foods, storing, handling, and thawing raw meat and poultry; and serving hot and cold foods.

CONSUMER
QUESTIONS

1. Record the items you have eaten over the past twenty-four hours and classify them by category. What items would need to be added to provide the number of servings suggested by The Food Wheel? What items would you have been better off without?

2. Select a food item with a nutrition label and calculate the Index of Nutritional Quality for each nutrient listed. For what nutrients is the item a good source? A poor source?

3. What other product information is available on the label of the product selected for Activity #2? What information about quality is provided? About cost? Convenience? Safety? What is the unit price for the item?

4. If you were going to buy sirloin steak to serve your family, how much would you need to buy to provide each person with a three-ounce-serving of edible meat? How much ground beef? How much chicken (whole)?

5. Make a list of three to five food items you eat frequently and compare their prices among several food stores in your area. Only well-known brands (e.g., Del Monte, Hunt's, Campbell's) are likely to be available in all stores.

6. Visit a food store in your area that offers processor's brands, store brands, and if possible, generic brands. Buy each brand offered for a particular product (e.g., all the brands offered of cling peach halves). Conduct a "cutting test" of all the brands. Determine how much of the contents were packing liquid. (Drain the contents and weigh them.) How do they rate on appearance? Taste? Which is the best value?

7. Check some recent issues of *Consumer Reports* for ratings of food products and select one report. What product was rated? What evaluative criteria were used? How were the ratings on each criterion determined? What relative weights were given to the criteria used? How do these weights compare to the weights you would use?

SUGGESTED READINGS

1. Deutsch, Ronald M. *The New Nuts Among the Berries.* Palo Alto, Calif.: Bull Publishing Co., 1977. Deutsch, Ronald M. *The Nuts Among the Berries.* New York: Ballantine Books, 1961. These are light-hearted but well-researched studies of the history of food faddism and health foods promoters in the United States.

2. Jones, Evan. *American Food: The Gastronomic Story.* New York: E.P. Dutton, 1975. This book provides an informal account of the historical development of American eating patterns. Earlier eating patterns have changed with refrigeration, processing, and national advertising, Jones suggests. Accompanied by 500 selected recipes.

3. Long, Patricia J., and Barbara Shannon. *Focus on Nutrition.* Englewood Cliffs, N.J.: Prentice-Hall, 1983. This introductory-level text deals not only with basic nutrition principles, but also with nutrition concerns and issues such as the need for dietary fiber, the hazards of sweeteners, the nutritional needs of athletes, and the nutritional impact of junk food and fast food.

4. U.S. Department of Agriculture. *Food—From Farm to Table: 1982 Yearbook of Agriculture.* Jack Hayes, ed. Washington, D.C.: USGPO, 1982. This volume includes more than forty short articles in three areas: the economics of agricultural production, agricultural marketing, and food buying by consumers.

5. U.S. Food and Drug Administration. *FDA Consumer.* Washington, D.C.: USGPO, 10 times yearly. This is a popular-level magazine for consumers with reports on current food and health problems and concerns.

CHAPTER 9

TRANSPORTATION

Traveling can be fun. It means going new places and getting together with friends. But there's another, more serious side to travel. Getting to and from school and work, shopping and doing errands, all require ready access to transportation. The residential and business patterns in this country assume that a major share of our traveling will be done by automobile. As a result, in most parts of the country, a car has become more a necessity than a luxury. In most areas public transportation by train, bus, or taxi is a poor substitute; it may not be available at all in others.

Reliance on cars makes them an important part of a spending plan. In recent years, about 14 percent of the money Americans spent on personal consumption has gone for transportation, most of it for auto transportation. Clearly, owning and operating a car can take a big bite out of a paycheck. With careful planning and good management these costs can be controlled so that transportation for both fun and work will be available.

An important first step in buying transportation is to consider short- and long-range goals carefully. Goal-setting is the first step in the decision-making process outlined in Chapter 2. What type of transportation is needed? What destinations are planned? What passengers and cargo will be carried? A student, an office worker, and a traveling salesperson each will have markedly different answers to these questions and markedly different needs. People who are devoted skiers, gardeners, or campers will also have special needs. Transportation needs will also be influenced by life-cycle stage. Young singles and young marrieds without children are likely to have markedly different needs than families with children.

The second step in dealing with transportation problems involves identifying the alternatives and gathering information on them. Just what are the alternatives? Is public transportation such as buses, subways, or taxis available? Is a car the only alternative? If travel by car seems to be the only feasible means, is it necessary to own the car, or are carpools or vanpools available? What do these different alternatives cost? What are the pluses and minuses of each? Cars are a key part of most solutions to transportation problems. For this reason, they will be the focus of this chapter.

What most people would like in a car probably is not too different from the new cars most Americans have been buying in recent years:

- Four- or six-cylinder engine with automatic transmission
- Power brakes and power steering
- Air conditioning and tinted glass

Most adults have learned the evaluative criteria they feel are important in a car from their past experiences. The following sections systematically examine such key criteria as design, convenience, and comfort; performance; durability; safety; and cost. The reasons these criteria are important and how different cars can be judged against them will be discussed.

DESIGN, CONVENIENCE, AND COMFORT

Many people might be inclined to say that design and styling in cars is a matter of personal taste. The fact is, however, that a car's design has a big effect on convenience and comfort.

Recent styling changes have made cars more aerodynamically efficient. Reductions in wind resistance have improved gas mileage, but at the same time they have had some undesirable effects. Front windshields and rear windows have more slope than in early designs. The new sloped windows increase the sun's penetration into the car, making tinted glass and air conditioning almost a necessity. With sloped windshields, there also are more problems with reflections from the instrument panel lights, which can be a distraction in night driving. Aerodynamic "bubble-shaped" bodies also make it difficult for the driver to know exactly where the ends of the bumpers and fenders are, making it harder to maneuver in tight places.

The design of the instrument panel typically is an important styling feature. Safety and convenience dictate that controls and gauges should be easy to see, to reach, and to use. Too often key controls or gauges are placed behind the steering wheel or placed too low. Even the placement of the radio/tape player can be a serious issue. If it is inconveniently placed, tuning the radio or inserting a new tape can be distracting for the driver.

There are more sizes and body styles from which to choose than ever before: two-doors, four-doors, station wagons, vans, minivans, light trucks, hatchbacks, and convertibles. While styling may influence choices, there are practical considerations, too. How many passengers will be carried? How much and what kinds of cargo will be carried? Will the small rear seat in a fastback two-door sedan be adequate? Will the car be used to transport large amounts of luggage, sports equipment, lumber, or furniture? Many factors are involved in deciding the size and type of vehicle that would be most useful.

PERFORMANCE

One of the key evaluative criteria for cars is performance: How well do they do what they are supposed to do? Are they dependable and economical?

Fuel Economy

Fuel economy became an important criterion in judging cars during the past decade. The Arab oil boycott of 1973 gave many Americans their first taste of high gasoline prices and shortages. Those who did not learn from the experiences of 1973 found the lesson repeated in 1978–79 after the cutoff of Iranian oil. Uncertainty about foreign oil supplies and high prices has continued to make fuel economy an important concern.

Fuel efficiency varies widely among cars and varies even among cars of the same size. For example, some compact cars are estimated to get as much as 37 to 40 miles to the gallon in highway use while others get only 22 to 24, about the same as large cars (Environmental Protection Agency, 1985). For a typical year's driving (15,000 miles), the less economical cars would cost $260 more to drive when gasoline costs $1.00 per gallon.

To encourage the purchase of fuel-efficient cars the federal government requires that estimated mileage per gallon information be included on the price stickers posted on the windows of new cars. The estimated mileage figures presented are developed by the Environmental Protection Agency (EPA) in laboratory tests. The mileage figures are not a completely accurate guide to actual mileage. Actual mileage depends on the car and its condition, the drivers and their driving habits, the speed driven, the accessories in use (especially air conditioning), and the climate (see Table 9-1 for details).

The EPA figures are best used to compare the relative economy of different models. It is a safe assumption that the car rated at 30 miles per

Table 9-1
Factors Reducing Fuel
Mileage

- Automatic transmission
- Tires that are not of radial design
- Underinflated tires
- Use of air conditioning in city traffic (At higher speeds the fuel used by an air conditioner is about equal to the fuel used because of the wind-drag created by driving with open windows.)
- The weight of extra passengers, cargo, or auto accessories
- Driving for short distances
- Fast starts that feed the engine more fuel than it can use efficiently
- Front wheels out of alignment on front-wheel drive cars
- Letting the engine idle for more than a minute when it could be turned off
- Poor engine maintenance (failure to replace spark plugs, air filter, and fuel filters at recommended intervals)

gallon will be more economical in actual use than a car rated at 24 miles per gallon. The EPA requires that fuel efficiency information be provided on the window sticker of new cars and also that dealers make available copies of the EPA guide with ratings for various makes and models. The guide is a useful reference for comparing models.

The high cost of fuel has encouraged the promotion of a variety of fuel-saving devices, such as fuel and oil additives, ignition devices, and devices that change the gas mixture. The EPA has tested dozens of these devices. Their conclusion is that most of them, unfortunately, do not work (Gillis, 1986).

The rising gas prices and shortages of the 1970s made many car buyers interested in the economy advantages of diesels. Diesels get more miles from a gallon of fuel; and until recently, diesel fuel was substantially cheaper than gasoline. Diesel engines also have another advantage; they last longer. There are some offsetting disadvantages to diesels, however. Cars with diesel engines are more expensive than similar gasoline-powered ones. Diesel engines are also more difficult to start in cold weather than gasoline engines and require more warm-up time. In addition, diesel engines are noisier and create more exhaust fumes. There is, in fact, some evidence that diesel fumes are hazardous to health (see the Consumer Concern: "Should We Encourage the Use of Diesels?" in Chapter 6).

Acceleration and Speed

As the cost of gasoline moderated in the 1980s, car buyers, especially younger ones, became interested in higher horsepower cars again. New car and engine designs made it possible to get better performance more efficiently, and new sporty body styles excited the buying public. Power, speed, and acceleration came back into fashion.

More powerful engines can deliver quicker acceleration. Even if the driver is not interested in stop-light drag racing, some extra power is welcome on a highway entry ramp, on a steep hill, or in a tight spot. The kind of power needed for high speeds may be less useful, however, and even downright dangerous.

Extra power has its costs. Optional larger sized engines can add $250 to $500 or more to the cost of a car. At the same time, they deliver lower gasoline mileage. Switching from a four-cylinder to a six-cylinder engine in one popular intermediate size car can, for example, cut gas mileage from 32 miles per gallon to 24 miles per gallon. This drop of 25 percent in gas mileage is accompanied by a 15 percent gain in horsepower.

Turbocharging is another popular way to increase engine power. Turbochargers force air into the engine to increase fuel ignition and produce increased engine power. Turbocharging is available for $200 to $400 extra in some cars. Sports models incorporating turbocharging may, however, cost thousands of dollars extra. Turbocharging has its costs in fuel economy, too.

High performance sport models also have another "hidden" cost—one that does not show up in the sticker price. Most insurance companies charge higher premiums for these models than for other cars of similar price because sports and high performance automobiles have higher than average loss claims.

Handling

The way a car responds in driving is an important part of its performance. A car should be easy to steer and should respond quickly and predictably. Most drivers prefer power steering because it makes controlling and turning the car easier and quicker. However, some power-steering mechanisms operate so easily the driver loses some of the "feel of the road" and may be unaware of how the car is maneuvering and of road conditions. It is also important for a car to be able to respond quickly in accident avoidance maneuvers. In such situations a car must be easily controllable and highly responsive. Power steering or a well-designed steering system that does not need power assistance can provide needed responsiveness.

Reliable braking is important, too. Brakes should be quick and free from fade (the tendency to lose stopping power in long, high speed stops). The tendency of some brakes to lock can cause serious problems. When the brakes lock, a wheel stops turning and begins to skid, often resulting in dangerous loss of control and serious accidents.

Car shoppers can judge for themselves how a car handles by putting a demonstrator through the kinds of situations they typically encounter. How does the car handle in parking lots and the close quarters typical of city driving? How does it do on hills? In high speed driving on interstate highways?

Testing a car in emergency handling and braking situations is, however, beyond the skill of most drivers. Performing such tests so they are truly indicative of the car's emergency performance takes experience. Furthermore, attempts to make these tests could be dangerous. Fortunately, reports of the handling ability of many cars are readily available in *Consumer Reports* and automotive magazines.

Tires

Tires are perhaps the most underappreciated part of a car. Tires serve several critical roles, including:

- Bearing the weight of the car and cushioning the ride,
- Transmitting power to the road,
- Guiding the car as it is steered, and
- Stopping the car when the brakes are applied.

Each of these is important, and all of them must be done well.

There are hundreds of brands of tires, both manufacturer's brands and retailer's brands, but there are only three main types of tire construction.

- *Radials* comprise the major share of all tires sold and are the type installed on most new cars. Radials are a recent development and offer the advantages of good tread life and fuel efficiency.
- *Bias ply* tires have been on the market for the past 60 years. While their design is out-of-date, they are the least expensive.
- *Belted bias* tires are an improvement over bias ply tires. They do not heat up as much as bias ply tires, and they last longer.

These three basic types of tires can come with a variety of tread designs — regular, snow treads, or all-season treads.

Snow treads have wider and deeper grooves than regular tires. While they provide improved traction in snow, they wear out rapidly on dry pavement and must be changed seasonally. To solve this problem, the all-season tread was developed. It provides protection against occasional snow, has good traction on wet roads, and will last longer than snow tires on dry roads.

Retreads are used tires that have been remanufactured to replace worn treads. Their quality depends both on the remanufacturing process and on the quality and condition of the tire used to make them. Retreads provide satisfactory service and are cheaper than new tires.

Tires in the salesroom racks look very similar. Tire grades can help consumers to choose among apparently similar tires. Tires are graded on traction, heat resistance, and treadwear (Gillis, 1986). The standards for traction are based on the ability to stop on wet surfaces. The grades run from A (top) to C (bottom). Tires that heat during use are more likely to experience blow-outs or tread separation. Higher rated tires (A is top) run cooler. Tire makers also are required to indicate the treadwear grade of their tires. The grades measure the relative amount of wear to be expected from a tire. A tire with a grade of 120 should give 20 percent more mileage than one graded 100. The total mileage life of a tire can be estimated by multiplying by 200. A tire graded 120 should last 24,000 miles (120 x 200).

Tires need to be kept properly inflated to insure longer life and good gas mileage. They should be checked periodically with a tire gauge. Recommended pressures are always for a "cold" tire, which is one that has not been driven more than a mile in the last three hours. Pounds-per-square-inch (PSI) readings for "hot" tires will be about 4 PSI over the "cold" reading.

DURABILITY

Another key criterion in judging cars is how well they hold up in use. In judging durability there are several concerns. Just what kinds of routine maintenance are required and how expensive is it? The kinds of repairs that are likely to be needed and their probable cost also are important considerations.

Preventive Maintenance

Preventive maintenance is the periodic service recommended by a car manufacturer to keep a car going satisfactorily. Preventive maintenance includes oil and oil filter changes and lubrication. Owner's manuals indicate service requirements and contain important information on care and use. Unfortunately, few car owners read their manuals carefully.

The recommended preventive maintenance routines for different cars vary widely. Some suggest servicing significantly more frequently than others. As a result, there are sizable differences in total preventive maintenance costs. Calculations for intermediate-sized cars show total maintenance costs ranging from $427 to $1,365 during the first 50,000 miles — a three-fold difference (Gillis, 1986).

In addition to keeping your car running properly there is another motivation for following the prescribed preventive maintenance routine. If the indicated preventive maintenance routine has not been followed, the warranty may not be valid.

Repairs and Repair Costs

Certain relatively costly repairs can be expected if a car is kept 75,000 to 100,000 miles. Certain key parts are likely to fail during this period.

Illustration 9-1
Oil and water levels and tire pressures should be checked regularly between preventive maintenance servicing.

- Brakes probably will require relining.
- Water and fuel pumps are likely to fail.
- Shock absorbers will require replacement.

The total costs (parts and labor) of these repairs for different makes and models vary greatly. Cost estimates show a large difference in the cost of replacing basic parts (Gillis, 1986). There was, for example, a two-fold difference in the cost of replacing front brake pads between the least expensive and the most expensive.

Consumers Union has developed comparative data on the frequency of repair for different automobile makes and models. *Consumer Reports* presents the data in its Annual Auto Issue each April. The data include a frequency-of-repair index showing the number of repairs a particular make and model required compared to others produced that year. Information is presented on the relative frequency of the repairs required for such key parts as the transmission, brakes, exhaust system, and air conditioning, as well as paint and rust problems.

The indices of relative frequency of repairs are based on responses of CU members to its annual questionnaire. In the questionnaire, CU members are asked to indicate their experience over the last year and the cost of repairs. The responses received are adjusted for mileage driven to account for its effect on repair needs.

The *Consumer Reports* indices are a useful comparative indicator of repair problems. They are, however, always behind because information on a new model is not available until after the model year is almost over. The reports can, however, be useful for checking if certain makes and models have any chronic trouble spots. The information can forewarn car shoppers about potential sources of trouble in new models. It also can be very useful to used car shoppers, who can see what type of problems various cars have had.

In addition to frequency of repair information, *Consumer Reports* also presents a trouble index that is an overall measure of the relative frequency of repair problems for a model. A cost index is also available to compare average maintenance and repair costs for a model with others of the same year.

Service Contracts. One of the options new car salespeople promote heavily is service contracts. These contracts provide coverage for repair costs not included in the manufacturer's basic warranty by extending and supplementing it. Service contracts are fairly costly—about $10 per month of coverage. They are available only for new or recently purchased cars.

Car buyers need to look carefully at service contracts to see what is covered and for how long. Are all parts of the car covered or only major mechanical failures? Most warranties exclude such items as replacing spark plugs, which is considered routine maintenance. Another question is how much real protection the service contract provides above and beyond the basic warranty. The regular warranties of some manufacturers provide substantial protection.

Are service contracts a good buy? Most unbiased experts think they probably are not. On the average, the service required will cost less than the contract, which must include some amount to cover administrative costs and profits. Service contracts may be a good buy for car buyers who expect to use their cars a great deal within the time and mileage limits of the contracts. It should be noted that service contracts *do not* provide protection for damage from racing, accidents, misuse, or failure to perform preventive maintenance.

Car buyers have another option instead of buying a service contract. They may protect themselves by building up a reserve fund for repairs. A fund can be built up with monthly deposits to a bank account and can provide repair money when needed.

Dealing with Problems. Needed repairs are likely to be less costly and less troublesome if problems can be spotted before a breakdown occurs. While problems cannot always be diagnosed in advance, there usually are signals that problems are developing. Consumers can also learn to describe the problem to service personnel so that a quicker and more accurate diagnosis can be made. When describing a problem, the following information will be needed:

- *What are the indications of the problem?* Are there unusual sounds, smells, visual signals (including warning lights), or driving sensations?
- *What is the source of the problem?* From what part of the car do the indications of the problem come?
- *At what times does the problem occur?* Does the problem occur on starting? At certain speeds? On certain types of roads? On braking?

Even a brief report on these questions can help service personnel pinpoint a problem.

SAFETY

Safety was not a well-recognized evaluative criterion for automobiles until the 1960s. Until that time, it was felt that auto safety depended chiefly on the driver rather than on automotive design. If drivers could be trained to drive more skillfully and carefully, it was thought, the major cause of auto accidents would be controlled.

The work of Ralph Nader, beginning in the mid-1960s, brought recognition that some cars were poorly designed and engineered and were, as a result, accident-prone. Growing concern with auto safety brought recognition that not only could poor design and engineering cause accidents but that they could make accident results worse. Over the last quarter-century new attention has been given to improving protection for passengers in crashes. There is also more concern with preventing crashes by improving car designs, improving highway design, and educating drivers.

Crash Protection

The real danger to passengers in a car accident does not come from the first collision; that is, when a car hits another car or a telephone pole. Instead, it comes from the *second collision,* which occurs when the passengers hit the inside of the car as a result of the first collision (Gillis, 1986). Most crash injuries come from collisions with the interior of the car: the steering wheel and steering column, instrument panel, and side doors. A restraint system with safety belts or airbags is the best protection against such injuries. A secondary approach is to pad the steering wheel, to make the steering column collapsible, and to eliminate dangerous projections from the dashboard. Head rests also help reduce injuries by limiting the backward movement of the head in crashes, a cause of whiplash injuries to the neck.

Restraint Systems. Unfortunately, most drivers and passengers are not convinced that wearing seat belts is very important and relatively few use them. A variety of complaints have been made: Seat belts are too confining, they are uncomfortable, they are inconvenient, they wrinkle clothing.

One solution to the low level of seat-belt usage is to make seat belts easier to use or to provide an alternative, such as airbags. After more than a decade of controversy, the federal government moved in 1984 to require the provision of passive restraints in new cars.

Passive restraints require no effort from the passenger they protect. They include airbags that automatically and quickly inflate and then deflate in a crash. Automatic seat belts are another type of passive restraint. They wrap around the passenger when the car door is closed and require no effort to buckle up. In experimental tests automatic seat belts have proven that they can reduce injuries. A study of injury claims for 1981 and 1982 Volkswagen Rabbits showed that injury claims were 14 percent lower for cars with automatic seat belts than for those with manual belts (Insurance Institute for Highway Safety, 1985).

Automatic seat belts are only slightly more expensive than the conventional manual belts. Airbags are, however, expensive. They cost several hundred dollars, at a minimum, but they have the advantage of providing protection without any special effort. Airbag devices are hidden in the hub of the steering wheel and on the right side of the dashboard.

Airbags can provide effective protection in frontal crashes for the driver and front-seat passengers. To provide protection in side and rear crashes, seat belts still are needed. Airbags depend on split-second inflation and deflation for their effectiveness. Despite these requirements, there has been no evidence of failure or malfunction in actual accidents.

Another approach to reducing crash injuries is to require the wearing of seat belts. New York state passed such a law in 1984 and it has been followed by a number of other states. These laws have been highly controversial (see Consumer Concern: "Should Wearing Seat Belts be Required by Law?"). There was, however, special pressure put on the states to pass seat belt laws. If enough states passed mandatory seat belt laws, the federal passive restraint requirements were to be dropped. Under U.S. Department of Transportation regulations, if states containing two-thirds of the population pass seat belt laws before April, 1989, the federal passive restraint requirements are to be revoked.

While seat belt laws have been controversial, laws aimed at protecting children from crash injuries have not. Most states now have laws requiring children up to the age of three or four to be in safety seats (if they weigh less than forty pounds) or buckled in seat belts. These laws are defended on the grounds that young children are unable to protect themselves and

CONSUMER CONCERN: SHOULD WEARING SEAT BELTS BE REQUIRED BY LAW?

About 52,000 Americans die and another two million are injured in motor vehicle accidents each year, reports the National Safety Council. Motor vehicle crash injuries produce more new cases of quadriplegia and paraplegia than all other causes combined. They also play a big part in the increased incidence of epilepsy and brain damage, and are the single leading cause of severe facial lacerations and fractures.

One of the leading causes of death, motor vehicle crashes are second only to cancer in their economic burden to society. We pay this huge bill in many ways: increased expenses for insurance, medical services, and law enforcement as well as lost savings, productivity, and human suffering.

Seat belts would help decrease this costly burden, saving lives and preventing injuries. Research shows that one-third of the victims killed in high-speed crashes would survive, and an estimated two-thirds of those who are severely injured would escape with only minor injuries (if any) if seat belts are worn. If every American wore seat belts, says the American Seat Belt Council, 16,300 lives could be saved each year.

Yet even though these benefits have been exhaustingly publicized, less than one in ten Americans buckles up regularly. That figure has been on the decline every year since 1975, a particularly distressing trend since small cars, which offer less crash protection than full-size models, have become increasingly popular at the same time.

LIFESAVING SOLUTION

In this age of increasing hazards and limited resources, with the future of automatic restraints still uncertain, many traffic safety experts now believe that mandatory seat belt laws are the answer. Such laws would require drivers and their front seat passengers to buckle up under penalty of law. Violation is a civil offense, punishable with a modest fine (usually no more than 25 dollars), with no possibility of license penalty points or a jail term. These laws are not meant to harass drivers, but instead to encourage them to buckle up.

Seat belt laws are needed because despite both hard and soft sell campaigns by the government as well as private safety organizations, Americans still do not use belts. A graphic example of the failure of these public information programs occurred in Michigan, a state that has long been a leader in highway safety programs. In 1977, Motorists Information, Inc., an organization formed by the major U.S. automakers, spent some $1.75 million on a media blitz in the Detroit area to promote belt use. When the Department of Transportation (DOT) measured the effectiveness of the 10-week campaign, which used both the electronic media and billboard ads, it concluded that there was "no response" to the effort. In fact, in one of the cities studied, belt use actually declined by one percent. In March 1980, the National Academy of Sciences in a report to the DOT concluded the "past attempts to promote seat belt use have not been particularly successful."

Seat belt laws, on the other hand, have worked in the five Canadian provinces and 24 countries where they have been tried. A study of these laws conducted by the American Seat Belt Council found that, when coupled with enforcement, seat belt laws are highly effective in reducing the deaths, injuries, and societal costs of motor vehicle accidents. The most dramatic reduction was in Sweden, where a seat belt law has been in effect since 1975. Driver deaths there were cut 47 percent and passenger deaths, 67 percent. More than 85 percent of all Swedes use seat belts. Another Swedish study also showed that the country saves between $22 million and $45 million each year in reduced medical and other societal costs.

MAKES ECONOMIC SENSE

"This is a no-cost law," emphasized Thomas O. Reel, executive secretary of the Michigan Coalition for Safety Belt Use. "Police departments won't have to hire new officers to enforce the law," says Reel. He explains that the proposal will work in the same manner as child-restraint legislation: Drivers will generally be fined for violations when they are stopped for other offenses. Nor should there be any personal expense involved (aside from the fines), unless a driver has removed the belt system from his car. Pre-1965 models, which did not come equipped with seat belts, will be exempt from the law, along with buses and trucks.

With laws requiring their use, seat belts begin saving lives "day one," says Thomas Reel. Further, if airbags are eventually required, the double protection couldn't hurt. "You're still better off with a belt on even if you have an airbag-equipped car," Reel explains.

Opponents of seat belt laws argue that this type of legislation infringes on our individual rights. Yet instead of being a right, driving is a privilege, already restricted in many ways. Drivers must pass a test before they can legally drive, obey traffic laws and observe speed limits, and refrain from drinking and driving. Seat belt laws may be one more restriction, but one whose benefits far outweigh the small cost in personal liberty and inconvenience.   *(Consumer Concern questions on next page)*

Source: Abridged from Alliance of American Insurers, "Are Mandatory Seat Belt Laws the Answer?" *Journal of American Insurance* 58, no. 3 (Fall 1982): 23-26. Used by permission.

that auto accidents are the leading cause of death among young children. Seat belts can also help protect unborn children from injury. Pregnant women should wear seat belts, keeping them as low as possible.

Energy-Absorbing Systems. The overall crash safety of a car depends on the car's ability to absorb energy in a crash and its structural integrity, as well as the restraint systems used. The National Highway Traffic Safety Administration (NHTSA) performs crash tests with different models to determine the likelihood of the injury to passengers. The tests are conducted by towing a car into a fixed barrier at 35 miles per hour. The results provide an estimate of the car's performance in a head-on crash.

In the NHTSA tests, the passenger compartments have stayed intact in almost all cases. The cars' bodies did not collapse to the point where they would have caused injury to the car's occupants in an actual crash. It was found, however, that the structural integrity of smaller cars was somewhat worse than that of larger cars.

In car crashes, the crumpling of the body absorbs a portion of the impact, which can reduce the seriousness of the collision between the occupants and the car. In general, the larger the car, the more force absorbed as the body is crushed or crumpled. In small cars, there is less body mass to be crumpled, so less of the force of a crash can be absorbed. As a result, there is greater likelihood of injury in small-car crashes. Insurance companies' experiences confirm these conclusions. Injury claims are much more common for smaller cars than for larger ones (Insurance Institute for Highway Safety, 1985).

The bumpers are an important part of the energy-absorbing system of a car. Requirements on bumper strength were reduced early in the Reagan administration for 1983 and later models. In previous years, federal regulations had required resistance to damage in five mile per hour crashes. In a deregulation move, this requirement was reduced to two and a half miles per hour. It was argued that the lighter bumpers would reduce car prices

Illustration 9-2
Crash-test experiments provide data for evaluating car safety and improving auto construction.

Ford Motor Company.

and increase gas mileage by cutting total weight. Opponents questioned whether these savings would be sufficient to offset increased crash losses.

Some manufacturers have chosen to continue to provide bumpers with five mile per hour crash strength, which makes it possible to study the effects of the change in regulations. Such a study was conducted by the Insurance Institute for Highway Safety. When a 1984 four-door sedan with five mile per hour bumpers was run into a fixed barrier at five miles per hour, it experienced no crash damage. When a similar car from the same company with two and a half mile per hour bumpers was run into the fixed barrier at five miles per hour, the car experienced damages that cost $251 to repair (Insurance Institute for Highway Safety, 1985).

Comparisons of collision claims between 1983 and 1984 models showed a substantial increase in claims for cars in which the bumpers had been weakened. This increase in losses leads to higher insurance premiums for cars with weakened bumpers. It also increases out-of-pocket costs for owners, who must cover the deductible portion of collision insurance claims. The evidence available suggests that the costs of reducing bumper strength outweigh the savings. It is interesting to note that the federal government's purchasing office, the General Services Administration, insists on cars with five mile per hour bumpers for the federal auto fleet.

Reducing the Number of Accidents

Most of the changes in federal auto design standards seek to reduce crash injuries by making cars safer in a crash. Another approach to reducing crash injuries is to try to reduce the number of crashes.

As part of the effort to ensure auto safety, the federal government requires the recall of cars with safety-related defects that could cause accidents or produce injuries. Since the mid-1960s millions of cars have been recalled to remedy such defects. Most of these recalls have been voluntary and have been initiated by the manufacturer. Some, however, have been involuntary and have occurred only as a result of government orders.

If a car is recalled, an owner should remember the following:

- The problem must be corrected at no cost.
- Any authorized dealer can make the repair.
- The vehicle identification number (VIN), which can be seen on the dashboard by looking through the windshield, can be used to identify vehicles involved in a recall.
- The VIN of recalled vehicles can be verified by asking an authorized dealer or calling the National Highway Traffic Safety Administration's toll-free hot-line at (800) 424-9393 or (202) 426-0123 in the District of Columbia.

Predictable handling and reliable braking are important for accident avoidance. Clear visibility also is important for avoiding accidents. To assure clear visibility, the following factors should be considered:

- A clear view out the front windshield is essential. Unfortunately, the tinted glass widely used in windshields reduces vision at night.
- An easy view over the left shoulder is also important for passing maneuvers and lane changes. Some styles have large blind spots. A good outside mirror can reduce the problem but must be easily adjustable to be fully useful.
- A third essential is a clear view out the rear window. A rear-window defroster can be useful in ensuring a clear view. A rear-window wiper and washer can help control the problem of dirt build-up on the rear window.

Having a car that is clearly visible to others can also help reduce the frequency of accidents. Visibility has been improved by the high center-mounted rear brake lights that are now required on new cars. When the lights were used in an experiment with New York City taxicabs, they reduced the rear-end crash rate by 58 percent. Another way to improve car visibility is by using brighter auto paint colors. In general, the lighter the paint color used, the more visible a car is.

COST

Because cars are a major outlay, cost is a key evaluative criterion. Buying a car involves both a sizable initial outlay and continuing operating and up-keep costs. After considering the costs involved in owning a car, we will examine the best techniques for buying a new or used car.

| Ownership Costs | The total cost of auto transportation includes the cost of operation as well as the cost of the car itself. These costs can be divided into two parts: |

- *Fixed costs.* These are the costs of ownership that do not vary with the amount the car is used. Fixed costs occur whether the car is driven or not. They include depreciation, insurance, and licensing fees.
- *Variable costs.* These are costs that depend on the amount a car is driven. They include gasoline, maintenance, and tires.

Fixed Costs. As can be seen in Table 9-2, fixed costs make up a major portion of the costs of ownership. These costs must be borne by owners regardless of how much the car is used. Even the legendary "little old lady from Pasadena," who only drives her car to church on Sunday, has to pay license and registration fees, taxes, and insurance; even an infrequently driven car depreciates.

Table 9-2
Estimated Driving Costs for 15,000 Miles over One Year

	1986 Chevrolet Chevette 4-cylinder (98 in³) 4-door hatchback	1986 Chevrolet Celebrity 6-cylinder (173 in³) 4-door sedan	1986 Chevrolet Impala 6-cylinder (229 in³) 4-door sedan
Fixed Costs			
Depreciation	$1,183	$1,320	$1,522
Insurance	457	509	510
License, registration, and taxes	98	130	134
Total	$1,738	$1,959	$2,166
Variable Costs			
Gasoline and oil	$509	$672	$753
Maintenance	177	206	221
Tires	90	101	114
Total	$776	$979	$1,088
Total Cost for Year	$2,514	$2,938	$3,254
Cost per Mile	16.8¢	19.6¢	21.7¢

Notes: Cost calculations assume a car with standard accessories including automatic transmission but not air conditioning. Gasoline costs of $.971 per gallon were used. Depreciation costs were based on trade-in value at end of 4 years or at 60,000 miles. Insurance costs based on $250 deductible collision coverage, $100 deductible comprehensive coverage, property damage and liability coverage of $100,000/$300,000/$50,000, and personal use of vehicle driven less than 10 miles to or from work, with no youthful drivers.

Source: Adapted from American Automobile Association, *Your Driving Costs, 1986 Edition.* Falls Church, VA: American Automobile Association, 1986. Used by permission.

As shown in Table 9-2, depreciation is the biggest single cost of ownership. *Depreciation* is the decline in value of an item over time. It is the difference between the original cost and the value for resale (or trade) at a particular time. Cars depreciate because of use, damage, and aging. The value of a car declines each year as it ages (the only exceptions are cars that become collector's items). The biggest drop comes in the first year, during which cars lose from 20 to 40 percent of their original value.

A new car immediately becomes "used" once it is driven off the dealer's lot and its value drops accordingly. This is why it is said that the most expensive trip you ever take is home from the dealer's lot. For the Chevette in the example (Table 9-2), depreciation makes up almost half of the total ownership cost for a year. You also can see in Table 9-2 that the more expensive the car, the bigger the depreciation cost per year.

A key determinant of a car's depreciation is how much it is in demand as a used car. Models in high demand have better resale value and thus depreciate less. There is a continuing demand for used sport models, convertibles, and luxury cars. As a result, they typically depreciate more slowly than other models.

Variable Costs. Costs that depend on the mileage a car is driven make up a smaller portion of the total costs of car ownership (see Table 9-2). For a typical annual usage of 15,000 miles, variable costs make up less than half the total annual cost. Gasoline costs constitute the biggest portion of variable costs. When the total operating costs of a large car, such as a Chevrolet Impala, are compared with those for a Chevette, it is apparent that gasoline costs are an important part of the difference. Differences in gasoline costs between the two cars are, however, clearly secondary to differences in depreciation.

Another aspect of costs that is often ignored is the money spent on the car (or other durable goods) that could be spent on other types of investments. In other words, one of the costs of car ownership is the opportunity cost of the money spent on the car. For example, buying a used car for $2,000 results in the loss of the interest that could have been earned if the money had been invested in a savings account, CD, or mutual fund, for instance. If all the money for the car were borrowed, another cost, in the form of finance charges, would then result.

Buying a New Car

Shopping for a car requires a knowledge of your basic needs. The consumer must decide whether a new or used car is needed, what makes and models are desirable, and what options are needed. As information about prices and availability is gathered, needs and wants may be modified or revised. Both needs and financial constraints should be kept in mind while shopping.

One of the confusing parts of shopping for a new car is deciding on the optional equipment. There are dozens of options available, including such basics as automatic transmission, comfort and convenience items such as air conditioning, and less essential additions such as deluxe trim and paint stripes.

The full range of options can add thousands of dollars to the cost of a car. In choosing, it is essential to keep an eye on the total. It is also smart to consider how options will affect resale value. Air conditioning is considered a basic for most cars, and resale may be a problem without it. The same is true for automatic transmission in many models (sports models are the exception). Certain other options are important because of their safety value. These options include a rear-window defroster and power steering and brakes. Options not only add to the initial cost of a car; they also add to operating costs. The extra weight of options reduces gas mileage, and maintenance of optional equipment can add to upkeep costs.

Experts disagree on whether buying a new car off the lot or special ordering will result in the better deal. When a car is bought from the dealer's stock, it may not be exactly what was wanted and the options may not completely match the buyer's preferences. Dealers are, however, pleased to sell from stock because it reduces their inventory and helps keep their operating costs down. They may, therefore, offer a discount. Buyers with special requirements may have to consider a special order. One way to find out which approach is cheaper is to ask for prices on an acceptable model in stock and on a special order for the preferred model and options.

The sticker price posted on a car gives the suggested retail price. This price usually is the starting price for bargaining. Most cars are sold at prices below the sticker price. Models in high demand are, however, sold at sticker price or sometimes more. In recent years the demand for Japanese imports has exceeded the import quota, and they have sold at premium prices. (See Consumer Concern: "Should There Be Quotas on Automobile Imports?" for a discussion of the effect of quotas on prices.)

The amount of discount from the sticker price also depends on the size of the difference between the sticker price and the dealer's cost. For example, a U.S.-made compact with a sticker price of $6,600 may have a dealer's cost of $5,800 — a difference of $800. Clearly, the discount from sticker price is not likely to be bigger than $800. The difference between the sticker price and dealer's price is sometimes referred to as the *margin*. Margins are smaller on inexpensive cars and larger on more expensive ones. For example, a full-size domestic car may have a $1,500 margin, as compared to the $800 for the compact discussed above. Therefore, it may be possible to get a bigger discount on a more expensive car.

Knowing the dealer's costs can be extra ammunition in bargaining. One source of information on dealer costs is *Consumer Reports* Auto Price Service. It can provide a computer print-out with details on list prices and dealer costs for models and options at a minimal cost. Information also is available in car-buying guides sold at newstands and in the *Consumer Reports* April auto issue.

A discount equal to the entire margin cannot reasonably be expected because the margin is not all profit. Part is needed to cover the dealer's operating costs. *Consumer Reports* (April, 1986a) suggests bargaining upward from the invoice price (dealer cost) rather than taking the usual apprach of bargaining downward from sticker price. Suggesting awareness of the dealer cost and offering some reasonable addition to it may be effective in getting the car for a minimum of $150 to $400 above the dealer's cost. Bargaining from dealer cost is not the way dealers are used to operating,

CONSUMER CONCERN: SHOULD THERE BE QUOTAS ON AUTOMOBILE IMPORTS?

In the early 1980s, the American auto industry suffered from the impact of severe recession and competition from Japanese imports. The industry begged for relief, claiming that Japanese imports had an unfair advantage because of lower wages, government assistance, and an unfair exchange rate that priced Japanese goods unreasonably low. Experts noted that not only were Japanese wages lower, but that Japanese auto factories were more efficient and used less labor to produce a car.

American auto makers asked for protection from competition while they retooled their factories for greater efficiency, redesigned their cars, and revised production techniques to improve quality and fuel efficiency. Under pressure from the federal government, the Japanese agreed to limit the number of cars they exported to the United States beginning in 1981.

The effect of these restrictions was to limit the supply of makes in high demand and reduce competition in the whole auto market. Japanese cars sold at full sticker prices without any discount; in some cases, dealers asked for and got premiums over the sticker price. The import restrictions also reduced competition in the market and created a price umbrella for the American makers. As their sales improved beginning in 1983, the American auto makers were able to earn large profits even though they were selling fewer cars than in the 1970s.

The American makers' huge profits led to labor demands for a share of the profits. Workers were no longer willing to settle just for the job and they are likely to argue the shopper's cost figures are wrong. Whether bargaining up from dealer's cost works or not, knowing more about the dealer's cost can increase a shopper's confidence and bargaining position.

Because options are an important source of dealer revenue, salespeople typically push options and extra services such as rust-proofing and protective finishes vigorously. These extra services are usually overpriced and are usually not needed (*Consumer Reports*, April, 1986b). The dealer's margin on any options selected must be taken into account when computing a reasonable discount.

A trade-in makes it more difficult to determine whether or not a deal is a good one. It might be better to sell the car rather than trading it for another one. Asking the salesperson for a price with and without a trade-in is a good way to determine how good a deal is. The dealer's trade-in offer for a car can be compared with the price in used car wholesale price

protection the import quotas gave them. At the same time, consumers began to complain increasingly about the limits on the supply of Japanese-made cars and about the effect of the quotas on all car prices, both foreign and domestic. Despite the promises that quotas would be only a temporary measure, the U.S. industry has begun to count on them and is reluctant to give them up. The industry claims the import quotas really are not costing consumers so much (some expert's estimates are in the range of $400 to $800) and that they still need protection from the Japanese industry's "unfair" advantages. The end of the quota system seems to be nowhere in sight.

QUESTIONS
1. Why did the U.S. auto industry ask for protection from Japanese competition?
2. What kind of protection did the federal government obtain for them?
3. What was the effect of this protection on American automakers? On American auto workers? On American consumers?
4. Why is the American auto industry reluctant to give up its protection?
5. Another proposal designed to protect American auto makers and workers is "domestic content" legislation. It would require a certain percentage of the parts in each car sold in the United States to be made here. What are the effects on car prices of this proposal likely to be?

guides. A bank or credit union loan department will probably have a copy of the guide. In using the guide, any adjustments that must be made for condition of the car and equipment should be noted. Local newpaper ads also can give an idea of asking prices for various cars.

When ready to deal, consumers should be sure they clearly understand the sales agreement that is drawn up. If a deposit is required, the conditions under which it will be returned should be stated in the agreement. (Consumers have been known to change their minds.) The sales manager, as well as the salesperson, should sign the agreement. These signatures can prevent claims at the time of delivery that the salesperson made a mistake and that additional money is needed to complete the deal.

Before the buyer accepts a new car, the salesperson should explain the equipment and let the buyer take it for a test drive. If everything is in order, the final papers can be signed. Bargaining power for getting problems corrected is greatest before the final papers are signed.

Buying a Used Car

New cars are expensive; it is hard to find one for less than $6,000. As a result, used cars are an attractive alternative for less money.

In recent years, new car buyers have been keeping their cars longer. As a result, late model used cars have become scarcer and their prices, higher. The typical used car is older and has more mileage on it than those of only

Illustration 9-3
The prices of used cars are affected by the supply of particular makes and models in the used car market.

a few years ago. Choosing wisely has become more important than ever, but also more difficult.

Used cars are available from a variety of sources. New car dealers sell the best of the trade-ins from their own lots. The rest are sold off in wholesale markets. Not all the used cars sold by new car dealers are ones that they have taken in trade. Sometimes they buy used models of the make they sell from other dealers. New car dealers typically provide good quality used cars at above-average prices. Because new car dealers have garage facilities, buyers can have more confidence about the condition of cars they sell.

Used car dealers buy cars in the wholesale markets and directly from individuals. Their cars are likely to be more variable in quality. Some dealers can service what they sell, but others cannot. In recent years, auto rental companies have also become a major source of used cars. Although the cars they offer are likely to be high mileage, they are likely to have been well maintained. Used cars are also available from private sellers. These cars are also likely to vary in condition and price.

Experts suggest that there are certain types of cars that should be avoided.

- "Orphans" are cars that are no longer in production or are rare. Parts and repairs for these orphan cars may be hard to find.
- High performance, or "muscle cars," may also be a poor bet. They are likely to have been subjected to hard use, and there is an above-average chance that they have been in a wreck.
- "Loaded" models with power windows and other deluxe extras also may be a poor choice. They are likely to be costly and may be expensive to repair.

Checking out the Car. In judging a used car, it is important to distinguish between major problems that will be difficult and expensive to repair and minor problems that are more easily corrected. Cars that need major repairs to the engine, transmission, or body are likely to be poor choices. Major repairs in these areas are expensive, and problems may not even be correctable.

Before test driving a car, a careful visual inspection, inside and out, is a good idea. It is best to do the inspection in daylight rather than at night because problems will show up more easily. The following key points should be checked:

- *Body.* Is there evidence that the car has been in a wreck? Have large areas been repainted? Are there signs of rust? Are there bubbles in the paint that could hide rust underneath?

- *Tires.* Are the tires in reasonable condition for the mileage on the odometer? If not, the odometer may have been rolled back. Do the tires show even wear? If not, the shock absorbers may be worn or the frame bent from a wreck.
- *Underside.* Is the exhaust system in good condition? Are there signs of serious rusting? Is there evidence of repairs to body or frame? Are there oil or transmission leaks?
- *Under the hood.* What is the general appearance of the engine? Remember that cleaning can hide evidence of some problems. Is there evidence of any leaks in the radiator, hoses, or elsewhere?
- *Interior.* Are the seats and rugs clean? Does the car's condition appear right for the indicated mileage?
- *Lights and control panel.* Do all lights, including the emergency blinkers, work? Does all equipment, including the radio and air conditioner, work? Do the wipers and windshield washers work properly?
- *Brakes.* With ignition off, apply steady pressure to the brake pedal for one minute. If the pedal sinks slowly, the brake system should be checked for leaks.

After considering this checklist, it is time for a test drive. It is wise to test a car under a variety of conditions — slow speeds, high speeds, hills, etc. Check the following on the test drive:

- *Engine start.* Does the engine start easily? Does it run smoothly without excessive noise?
- *Transmission.* Does the car move away from stops smoothly? Does it shift smoothly?
- *Handling and steering.* Does the car handle easily? Does the steering respond as expected? Is there vibration in the steering? If so, this may be a sign of problems in alignment of front wheels. In manual transmissions, does the clutch engage smoothly without chattering?
- *Brakes.* Does the car brake smoothly without pulling to one side or the other?
- *Engine operation.* When it is safe, step on the gas. If there is a great deal of white or bluish smoke, an expensive engine overhaul may be needed. Does the car have sufficient power on a hill? If not, the car needs a tune-up or more expensive valve or transmission work.

After the visual check and test drive, there is one further step to take before a final decision is made. A reliable independent mechanic should check the car. It is worth the extra cost for the assurance it provides. If repairs are needed and the car is still appealing, *Consumer Reports* suggests asking the mechanic for a written estimate of the cost. This estimate can be useful in bargaining for a lower price.

Buying a used car has always been a risky business, but a few steps have been taken to control some of the risk. Federal laws have been passed to control tampering with a car's odometer. By law, car dealers must provide used car buyers a signed statement from the original owner with the mileage. This statement should be provided before the title is transferred from the dealer to a new owner. Because the value of used cars depends heavily on their mileage, odometer fraud is a temptation for sellers. Despite the federal law, there are still reports that odometer fraud is common.

Another concern is what the dealer will do if there are problems. As with other contracts, verbal promises that differ from the written terms of the warranty are not worth much. Under FTC regulations, the terms of the warranty must be posted on the car window. After a number of years of controversy, in 1984 the FTC issued a new disclosure rule for used cars requiring clear disclosure of the terms of the warranty provided. Earlier proposals were more comprehensive and would have required disclosure of any known defect.

The asking price for a car should be a fair one. As mentioned earlier, a guide to used car wholesale prices is probably available at the auto loan department of a local bank or credit union.

What to Do About Car Problems

The main sources of help available to consumers who have problems have been discussed earlier, in Chapter 5. There are a few additional, special sources of help for car problems.

When car problems are beyond the ability of dealer to remedy despite repeated efforts, the buyer is likely to conclude the car is a "lemon." Dealers have resented bearing the brunt of consumer complaints about lemons. Along with consumers they have pressed for, and gotten, passage of lemon laws in a number of states.

In the past, it has been almost impossible for consumers to get a refund if a new car proves to be a lemon. The new state laws provide specific rules about when a refund is required. The laws vary slightly from state to state, but in general they have the following provisions:

- They set a period of coverage in which the law applies. Typically this period is one year from delivery or the written warranty period, whichever is longer.
- A definition of a "lemon" is specified. A "lemon" typically is a vehicle that has required four repairs to remedy a particular problem or a vehicle that has been out of service for 30 or more days.

The laws in all states cover passenger vehicles. Some include other types of vehicles as well. Details of the laws are available from each state's Attorney General. To get coverage under the law, it is important to record the repairs required as well as the dates the car was out of service.

All major auto manufacturers now participate in arbitration programs to resolve disputes with consumers. Arbitration of consumer disputes by an impartial third party was discussed earlier. The dealer should provide the details on the appropriate arbitration program and the type of problems that will be arbitrated.

MAJOR CHAPTER CONCEPTS	

1. Transportation is a major expenditure category. Because most people rely chiefly on automobiles for transportation, they account for most transportation spending in the United States.
2. A car's design is not just a matter of aesthetics. It affects convenience and comfort too.
3. Fuel economy has become an important evaluative criterion in recent years. Fuel efficiency information on new cars is provided on the price sticker.
4. Extra engine power increases a car's cost and reduces fuel economy. There are, however, situations in which extra power is useful.
5. A car should handle easily and quickly and respond well in emergency maneuvers.
6. Tires perform a number of key functions: bearing the car's weight, transmitting power to the road, guiding the car as it is steered, and stopping it when it is braked. Radial tires provide the best tread life and fuel efficiency.
7. Preventive maintenance is the periodic service recommended by the auto manufacturer. Costs of preventive maintenance vary widely between different makes and models.
8. The frequency of repairs and the cost of repairs varies widely among different makes and models.
9. Most injuries in crashes occur in the "second collision," when passengers hit the inside of the car. Seat belts and airbags are essential for protection in the second collision.
10. The crushing of a car's body can absorb part of the crash impact. Larger cars can absorb more impact because of their larger size.
11. Automobiles may be recalled if they have safety-related defects. Repairs must be made at no cost to the owner.

12. The cost of owning a car includes both fixed costs (depreciation, insurance, license and other fees) and variable costs (gasoline and oil, maintenance, tires). Depreciation is the largest single cost of owning a new model car.

13. Discounts from sticker price are available for many cars. The size of the discount depends on the demand for the car and the size of the dealer's margin (the difference between sticker price and dealer's cost).

14. In judging used cars, it is important to distinguish between major and minor problems. Engine, transmission, and body defects are likely to be major problems because they are costly to repair.

15. State lemon laws now provide consumers some protection in cases of new cars with continuing problems that cannot be remedied.

CONSUMER QUESTIONS

1. What were your transportation needs in the past year? How did you meet these needs? Were there other solutions you could have used? What were they?

2. What are your particular needs in a car? What style of car is best suited to your needs? What makes and models could meet your particular needs?

3. Identify three different makes of new cars that have models that could meet your needs. Compare the cars on the evaluative criteria identified in this chapter. Use visits to dealers' showrooms, *Consumer Reports,* and other sources to get the information you need. Which of the three cars do you prefer? Explain the reasons for your preference.

4. If you were to buy a used car, what year, make, and model would you prefer? How does your choice rate in the reports of repair frequencies in the *Consumer Reports* April auto-buying guide issue? What are the reasons for your choice? What is the current asking price for this car in your area?

5. Has your car or your family's car been involved in a recall? Use procedures outlined in this chapter to check. Was the car returned to the dealer for the needed repair? Why or why not?

6. Study some recent automobile ads from television, magazines, and newspapers. Record the evaluative criteria emphasized in the ads for particular makes. How well do the criteria emphasized match those you feel are important?

SUGGESTED READINGS

1. *Consumer Reports.* "Annual Auto Issue" 52, no. 4 (April 1987), and succeeding issues. This issue is must reading material for the prospective car buyer. It summarizes test results for current models and provides current information on safety testing and negotiating with dealers.

2. Crandall, Robert, Howard K. Gruenspecht, Theodore E. Keeler, and Lester B. Lave. *Regulating the Automobile.* Washington, D.C.: Brookings Institution, 1986. The effects of federal auto regulations on safety, emissions, and fuel economy are examined and their costs and benefits are assessed in this book. The authors conclude that "of the three programs, only safety regulation appears to be generating benefits at least as great as the regulatory costs."

3. Gillis, Jack. *The Car Book,* 1986 ed. New York: Harper and Row, 1986, and succeeding editions. This wide-ranging book on current car models gives information on operating costs, crash safety, tires, and other key evaluative criteria.

4. Lewis, David L., and Laurence Goldstein, eds. *The Automobile and American Culture.* Ann Arbor, Mich.: University of Michigan Press, 1983. This book comprises a series of articles on the impact of the auto on American life.

5. Stokes, Bruce. "Coping with Glut." *National Journal* 18, no. 44 (November 1, 1986), 2608-2614. By 1990, this article suggests, the world will be able to produce 15 percent more automobiles than can be sold. This overcapacity will create increasing pressures on the U.S. auto industry. Possible solutions include new restrictions on imports and the closing of outdated U.S. production facilities.

6. Sutton, Remar. *Don't Get Taken Every Time: The Insider's Guide to Buying or Leasing Your Next Car or Truck.* Rev. ed. New York: Penguin Books, 1986. A former car dealer informally discusses what car to buy and when, how to deal with auto salespeople, and how to arrange financing. Sutton is full of tips on how to recognize and avoid common sales tactics that put the consumer at a disadvantage.

CHAPTER 10

HOUSING

Part of the American dream is to own a home. Most Americans' dreams are even more specific: They would like to own a single-family detached house with three bedrooms, two baths, and a two-car garage on about a half-acre of land.

The fact is that most Americans do not live in the kind of home they describe as their "dream house." Instead they live in a wide variety of quarters, ranging from one-room efficiency apartments to mobile homes, from town-houses to four-bedroom ranch houses in the suburbs. This range of choices is the result of the need to balance wants against the ability to pay. Fortunately, our housing stock provides a wide variety of alternatives to meet differing needs and abilities to pay.

HOUSING PRIORITIES

Satisfaction with housing or shelter depends on how well specific needs and expectations are met.

Physical Comfort

Housing provides shelter from the wind and weather, but people want more than that. Control of the ambient environment (i.e., the immediate environment surrounding you) means being able to control the temperature, the light and sound levels, and air movements. Being able to manipulate the environment — the airflow, the temperature, the light level, and the music — inside a car makes it a pleasure to drive. A good home provides the same kind of control over the ambient environment. A home in which the ambient environment can be controlled must be both soundly built and have the necessary systems — heating, cooling, electrical, and plumbing systems — all in good working order.

Safety

Physical safety in housing is often taken for granted; people fail to recognize that improper design and construction and inadequate maintenance can create physical hazards. Living quarters are also expected to provide protection from crime and intruders. This protection depends in part on the adequacy of police services in the community, but it also depends on the security provided by locks and doors.

Social Interaction

Homes also provide places for interaction with others. Space is needed for talking and eating; for playing games, watching TV, or engaging in other activities together.

At the same time, private spaces are also needed. People need space to study or to work on an important project, or just to be alone. Ideally, a housing unit should provide for both social interaction and privacy.

Self-Expression

For many people, it is important to make the place where they live or work an expression of their personalities. Many do not feel "at home" until they hang a favorite picture or poster and perhaps add a few plants. They want the place in which they live to show others what they are like and what interests them, whether it is cars, foreign travel, or collecting rocks. (Sometimes they are not so much interested in expressing themselves as in impressing others.)

Aesthetic Factors

The need to manipulate the environment may go beyond a need for self-expression or for impressing others. The chief motivation may be a love of good design as well as interesting colors and textures. An individual's own aesthetic feelings about a dwelling may be more important than what anyone else thinks of it.

HOUSING ALTERNATIVES

The housing alternatives available include both single-family detached houses and units in buildings with a number of units (Meeks, 1980b). Apartment buildings contain a number of housing units all located in a single building. Apartments are available in a wide range of sizes. Efficiency apartments consist of a single room with cooking facilities located in an alcove or a closet. Larger apartments include one or more bedrooms and one or

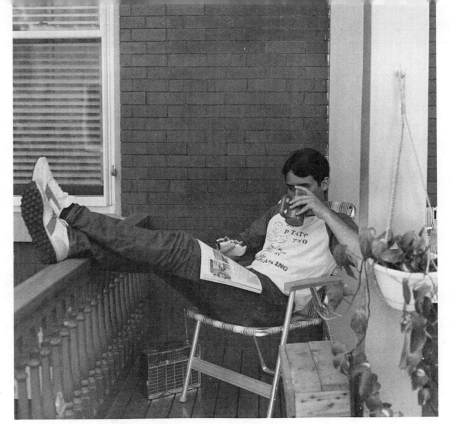

Illustration 10-1
Spaces that provide personal privacy make a housing unit more livable.

more baths. Certain key facilities are shared in an apartment building, often including the outside entrance and hallways. Recreation and laundry facilities are also frequently shared. Sharing these facilities and the proximity to others can lead to problems and friction. Because a number of people are housed close together, noise, cooking odors, scarcity of parking, and lack of consideration in the use of shared facilities can all lead to dissatisfaction. Apartments do, however, provide living space economically. Apartment design permits the construction of more units on a particular piece of land. Construction costs are lowered because walls, roof, and foundation costs are shared between a number of units.

Apartments are popular with both older and younger people because they require less upkeep and maintenance work than a detached house. In an apartment, tenants are responsible for keeping only their own unit clean. The landlord is responsible for repairs throughout the building, for keeping the public areas clean, and for such routine tasks as keeping lawns mowed and shrubbery trimmed.

Attached housing consists of a number of units all in the same building, with shared side walls. Each unit, however, has its own separate front entrance. Attached housing includes townhouses located side-by-side and duplexes, which are two side-by-side units under a single roof. Attached housing can provide many of the advantages of detached houses: privacy and yard or patio space. Attached units are more economical than detached ones because more units can be put on a piece of land and because the shared side walls reduce construction costs. If the shared walls are not adequately soundproofed, however, noise can be an irritating problem.

The detached, single-family house comes in many shapes and sizes. The smallest are about 1,000 square feet in size. Most Americans' dream house is about twice that size. Lot sizes may range from as little as 50 feet by 100 feet for smaller houses to 100 by 200 feet (a half-acre). Detached houses typically provide more privacy and space, both inside and outside. They are also costly and require substantial maintenance work and upkeep expense.

It is possible to own or rent a wide variety of housing types. Renting is popular, especially with young people, because it requires a minimum outlay up front. Still, many people prefer to own the place they live because ownership gives them legal title to the property and more control over it. Buying does require a substantial initial outlay. The down payment and the closing costs associated with arranging the sale and mortgage are usually substantial.

It is now possible to own a wide variety of housing types—apartments, town houses, and vacation property. Ownership of these types of housing usually is a condominium arrangement (Meeks, Ouderkerk, & Bilderback, 1980). In this type of legal arrangement, the owner of the *condominium* gets title to a particular unit and shares in the ownership of common areas such as lobbies, hallways, lawns, parking, and recreational facilities. Condominiums typically have a hired manager who oversees the upkeep of common areas. The costs are allocated among the owners, and a monthly fee is assessed. The opportunity to shift exterior upkeep problems to someone else makes condominiums especially popular with young singles, single parents, and older people.

Cooperatives provide a slightly different legal arrangement for ownership. Under cooperative arrangements, buyers get a share of a nonprofit corporation that holds title to the property. Buyers get the use of a particular unit, and they share the use of common areas with other members.

LOCATION, LOCATION, AND LOCATION!

When real estate agents are asked to name the three most important factors in choosing a place to live, they are likely to reply with a smile, "Location, location, and location!" While this answer has become an old joke, most agents use it to emphasize the critical importance of neighborhood to housing value and satisfaction. Their idea can be expanded to include the community in which a housing unit is located and its immediate site, as well as the neighborhood in which it is situated.

The Community and Government Services

The community in which housing is located has a great deal to do with the quality of government services available. Adequate fire and police services are a basic necessity. Parks and recreation facilities can be important to young adults and families with young children.

The quality of schools is a key criterion in evaluating communities. It is critically important to families with children, and the effects of their judgments can have a major effect on rents and house prices. The quality of schools is difficult to judge; however, experts suggest such measures as class sizes, students' performance on standardized tests, and the adequacy of local support for schools.

The quality of local services is, of course, related to local tax rates and the local tax base. Local governments rely on property taxes, income taxes, and less frequently on sales taxes to finance services. There often are substantial differences in tax levels between communities in a region. Some people are willing to accept fewer services and those of lower quality in return for lower taxes while others are not.

The Neighborhood

The quality of the neighborhood where a unit is located is a second important aspect of location. Is the neighborhood attractive? Are the streets in good condition, shaded by trees, with litter under control? Are the properties well-maintained and occupied? Are noise problems under control? Noise pollution is one of the most frequent complaints in many communities, especially cities. Aircraft noise, traffic noise, and construction noise all contribute to the problem. Streets designed to keep heavy traffic away from residential areas help control noise. Odors are another pollution problem. Fumes from industrial plants, farming operations, and business establishments such as cleaners and restaurants all can be a problem.

One way communities can reduce conflicts between different types of land uses is to develop a zoning plan. *Zoning* sets aside separate areas for residential, commercial, and industrial use. Areas for public facilities such as schools, hospitals, and churches also are provided. Some plans also set aside agricultural areas.

Most people do not like to have commercial and industrial activity in the area where they live. They also may prefer to keep different types of housing separated. Most zoning plans, for example, provide separate areas for single-family detached houses and multiple-unit buildings, such as apartments. Zoning may also set minimum lot sizes and maximum building heights to ensure that development in a particular area is uniform.

There is a great deal of variation between communities in zoning laws and how well they are observed. Zoning is of particular importance if you are looking at a unit next to an undeveloped tract of land. If there is no zoning or it is not strictly observed, you could find a shopping mall next door some day.

Another important consideration in selecting a neighborhood is its distance from work and shopping. Locations that are farther from work and shopping centers may be cheaper because rents, house prices, and taxes may be lower. There are, however, off-setting disadvantages. Distant locations require extra travel costs and time. The extra travel may offset expected savings in housing costs as well as taking valuable time.

In general, people seem to prefer neighborhoods in which they feel the residents are similar in social class, age, race, and ethnic background. Some experts and officials have urged more heterogeneity and argued that the desire for homogeneous neighborhoods is undemocratic (Morris & Winter, 1978). Attempts to make neighborhoods more diverse often risk public resistance. The American idea of fairness suggests, however, that people should be allowed to live where they wish as long as they respect the rights of others. In the past, local laws, deed restrictions, and real estate sales practices kept people of certain racial and religious groups out of some neighborhoods. These discriminatory practices interferred with equal access to available housing.

To end these practices, the Fair Housing Law was included in the Civil Rights Act of 1968. The law promised government assistance in obtaining equal access to housing regardless of race, color, religion, or national origin. In 1974, Congress also prohibited housing discrimination on the basis of sex. Many states and communities have *fair housing laws* similar to the federal law and are committed to equal access for all.

Discrimination in housing can show up in a variety of forms.

- Real estate agents may fail to tell members of certain groups about all the units available or may steer them toward certain areas.
- Real estate agents, landlords, and property owners may refuse to rent or sell to members of certain groups.
- Real estate ads may indicate that a property is available only to certain groups.
- The rental or sales prices quoted to members of certain groups may differ from those quoted to others.

Some of these practices are subtle but can still represent discrimination on the basis of race, color, religion, national origin, or sex.

Real estate operators can, however, discriminate on other bases. They can refuse to rent to students, people with poor credit records, or people with children or pets. Those who feel they have been discriminated against illegally should report their problem to the Office of Fair Housing and Equal Opportunity in the U.S. Department of Housing and Urban Development. In areas with local fair housing laws, state and local agencies also can help.

The Site

The particular site on which a dwelling is located can also affect how satisfactory it is. The site can have a sizable effect on *microclimate*—the temperature, air movements, and weather in an immediate area. A site on the south side of a hill will be sunny, while ones on the north side are likely to be shady, especially in winter when the sun is low in the sky. Ridges are likely to be windy while valleys may be foggy and cold if cold air drains into them from a wide area. Sites are also affected by prevailing wind directions (the directions from which winds typically blow). Good housing and landscaping design can help control both sun and wind problems.

Many housing units have been built in low-lying areas subject to flooding. Although the land is not well suited for housing, it has been developed in many areas because it is flat and inexpensive. Only recently have communities begun to try to keep development out of these areas by zoning. A clue to past flooding is water marks on basement walls.

Swampy, poorly drained areas are not well suited for housing either. The ground usually is unstable and cannot support a foundation. The ground is also likely to be unstable when large amounts of earth have been moved in developing a site. Foundations or water and sewer pipes in buildings on unstable, filled ground may crack.

DESIGN FACTORS

The amount of space in a housing unit and the way it is used can have a major effect on how well residents' needs are met. The relative importance of different space needs and the type of housing chosen to meet them is likely to change with the stage of the *family life cycle* (Meeks, 1980b). The family life cycle is the succession of stages through which a typical family moves, beginning with formation of a new household by young singles. The next stage is the formation of a new family with the marriage of a young couple. Smaller, rented quarters are usually suitable during these first two life-cycle stages.

With the arrival of children, most couples begin thinking about a house. As family size grows during this "full nest" stage, the family may wish for even larger quarters. When children leave home and the family enters the "empty nest" stage, space needs shrink, and a condominium apartment may seem like a good solution. With the death of one of the spouses in old age, the idea of smaller quarters may seem even more attractive.

The variety of household types now common requires the inclusion of other family life-cycle categories. These categories include single parents with children and older singles living alone. This group includes divorced people without children and people who have never married. Another category includes two or more single adults living together.

Stages in the family life cycle affect not only total space needs, but also the most desirable ways of allocating space among different uses, placing rooms in relation to each other, and laying out individual rooms.

Allocation of Space Among Uses

Both the types of rooms needed and the relative room sizes needed typically differ with family life-cycle stage. For example, young singles and young couples might like a large living room for entertaining. They might feel less need for a large, separate dining room with space for seating large numbers of guests. They might also put low priority on a separate family room and see little need for a large kitchen with a table big enough to seat four to six people for meals.

Families with young children typically have a different set of needs. They might want separate bedrooms for their children, even though the rooms may be small. They might also need a play area in or near the kitchen because young children feel most comfortable staying close to their parents and need close supervision. As children grow older, there may be more need for a separate family room so the children can watch television and play without disturbing the activities of other family members.

Other needs can also influence the priority placed on different types of space. Couples concerned about status and impressing others may put particular emphasis on having a large entryway, living room, and dining room for entertaining. In contrast, large, informal families may put their priority on a big eat-in kitchen and a big family room suitable for activities involving the whole family. There are other possibilities, too. Families concerned with encouraging the potential of individual members may feel each one needs a private place for study, reading, and other activities. One solution is extra-large bedrooms.

Placement of Rooms in Relation to Each Other

It is usually desirable to keep different functions in a community separate from each other. Keeping conflicting uses separate inside a home may also be important. The arrangement of different uses to minimize conflict is called *zoning* in home design, too. Zoning is needed to ensure privacy and quiet for individual family members who need to study or sleep. It is also needed to control cooking odors and kitchen noises. Keeping bedrooms located away from the kitchen and family room helps to control potential problems.

It is desirable for rooms with related functions to be close together. The dining room should be next to the kitchen, and the bathroom should

Illustration 10-2
Outdoor play space is a high priority for families with young children.

be in a bedroom area. For families with young children, it is desirable to have the kitchen located close to inside and outside play areas so parents can more easily supervise the children. Parents of young children may also want to have the children's bedrooms close so they can hear them in the night. As the children grow older and develop their own interests (perhaps in rock music), the parents are likely to prefer a bedroom at the opposite end of the house.

While rooms with similar functions should be located close together, it is not desirable to have the entrance of one bedroom be in another. This type of arrangement disrupts privacy and limits the usefulness of both bedrooms.

Layout of Individual Rooms

When looking for a place to live, home shoppers who see model homes and occupied units get the chance to see how furniture can be arranged. Furniture arrangement can be a real problem if the wall space in a room is divided by a number of doors and windows. Another important consideration is a floor plan that permits placement of furniture in areas other than the traffic lanes in a room.

CONDITION AND QUALITY OF STRUCTURE

Renters may believe that the condition and quality of the building in which they are renting is not a major concern for them, which is a mistake. Quality construction helps ensure against the transmission of noise between units, drafty air movements, and rain leaks. A tight, weather-proof building is of particular concern to a prospective renter or owner who will be paying the heating and cooling bills.

In judging a building, it is important to look past such eye-catching features as elaborate entry doors and fancy light fixtures. These trimmings give what real estate people call "curb appeal"— the ability to make a good first impression. What is important is the basic quality of the construction itself.

Foundation

The foundation of a building is a key concern, because it must bear the weight of the structure without breaking or shifting. If a structure has been built on unstable ground or has settled, cracks will develop in the foundation and in basement walls or in the slab of units built on concrete slabs without basements. Hairline cracks are not a cause for concern, but larger ones are.

If the foundation of a unit has settled significantly, the floors will be unlevel. One way to check for this problem is to do the marble test. Place a marble in the middle of a wood or vinyl floor. If the marble rolls, the floor is out of level.

Some people prefer units with basements to those built on slabs. Units on slabs lack the storage space basements can provide, and occupants sometimes complain that slab floors are hard and cold. Slab construction is, however, less costly. In certain regions, basements are prohibitively expensive and thus almost not to be found.

Water leaks and flooding are a particular concern in units with basements. Such leaks are aggravating, as well as difficult and expensive to fix. The basement should be checked for stains from water leaks or flooding when examining a unit. Sometimes a wet basement is caused by the condensation of warm, moist air on cold basement walls. This problem is less serious and can be solved with a dehumidifier.

Frame, Walls, Floors, and Roof

Not only is it important to have a solid foundation but the frame of the structure should be strong and sturdy, too. The frame of the house is the structural skeleton to which exterior and interior walls are fastened. There are several tests for the frame of a building. One is to slam an outside door and listen to hear if the windows rattle. Another is to jump up and down in the middle of a room to see if the floor gives.

Termite damage is a major threat to the frame of a house. Termites are a particular problem in California and the Southeast and can also be a problem in the Middle Atlantic states, Midwest, and Southwest. Before purchasing, a buyer should have a unit inspected and certified free of termites. Termites can move through cracks in concrete slabs and foundations to the wooden portions of a structure, which makes them a problem in all types of homes.

The exterior walls of a structure should be tightly fitted with cracks sealed against the weather with caulking. Interior wall surfaces should be neatly finished. Today most interior walls are surfaced with plasterboard panels. Joints between panels and nailheads should not be visible. The interior walls should be checked for stains from roof and plumbing leaks. Such problems can be a source of continuing trouble and may be expensive to repair. In addition, they may cause costly damage to ceilings, walls, and floors. Repainting walls and woodwork can be a relatively simple and inexpensive do-it-yourself job, but refinishing wood floors and replacing carpeting and vinyl floor covering is costly.

Doors and windows should fit tightly to limit air and weather leaks but should open and close easily. In colder climates, windows should have double insulated glass or storm windows. A unit's roof should be checked for problems when a purchase is considered. Most roofs have to be replaced every fifteen to twenty years — a costly repair job. Buckling, cracks, gaps, patching, and repairs all are evidence of problems and cause for concern. The gutters, as well as the roof, should be in good condition. Good gutters are essential for channeling water away from a structure in most climates.

Insulation and Moisture Control

Energy costs make adequate insulation essential. Insulation in attic floors is especially important for controlling the loss of rising warm air. Eight inches of insulation or more is desirable in attic floors. Insulation also is highly desirable in outside walls (four inches or more) and in floors above unheated spaces (Griffin, 1980). Some superinsulated houses now are being built with six inches of insulation in the exterior walls and twelve inches in the attic floors. For maximum effectiveness, insulation should be evenly and neatly applied and pushed into cracks and corners. You can check the quality of work by looking into the attic.

Improvements in insulation have unfortunately made moisture control a problem. Moisture build-up in outside walls occurs when warm, moist air from inside the home moves into the wall, meets cold outside temperatures, and cools. As moisture condenses inside the wall and accumulates, the insulation's effectiveness is reduced and paint on exterior walls may peel. Continuing problems over a long period can lead to rotting and structural damage.

These moisture problems have to be controlled by the use of a *vapor barrier*. This barrier may be plastic, foil, or another moisture-proof material installed next to the inside wall to keep warm, moist air from getting into the wall (Griffin, 1980). These materials have to be installed during construction.

PERFORMANCE AND QUALITY OF SYSTEMS

Control of the ambient environment in a housing unit depends on the quality and performance of the heating/cooling, electrical, and plumbing systems. These systems are critical not only for comfort but also for health and well-being.

Heating and Cooling

The cost of energy for heating and cooling is a major part of the operating expense of a household. The energy sources used in heating homes differ from region to region and home to home. Gas is the most widely used energy source, followed by fuel oil. The costs of gas and oil have fluctuated in recent years. These fluctuations and differences in prices between regions may make it difficult to generalize about which is more economical. Gas and oil furnaces typically provide about fifteen to twenty years of reliable service, after which they may be candidates for replacement. When considering buying a unit with an oil or gas furnace, the probable remaining life of the furnace must be considered. Oil leaks, soot leaks, and gas odors all are signs of problems.

Electrical heat is also widely used and it is popular because it is inexpensive to install. When electrical ceiling cables or baseboard heat is used, chimney, ducts, and piping are not needed. Furthermore, electric heat is clean. Electricity is, however, an expensive heating source.

Some newer homes have heat pumps, which can provide both heating and cooling. Their initial cost is high, but they operate inexpensively. Heat pumps work best in moderate climates. On extra cold days, electrical heat is needed for backup.

Solar heating created a great deal of excitement in recent years when conventional energy sources were expensive. *Active solar heat systems* use collectors to accumulate heat and then use pumps or blowers to circulate it (Newman, 1980). These systems have proven to be complex, expensive, and trouble-prone. There has been more interest recently in *passive solar systems* which accumulate heat in concrete or masonry walls or floors or in water drums and radiate this heat naturally, without mechanical help. New passive systems often rely on the sunlight coming through south-facing windows to provide heat.

In some areas where wood or coal is plentiful, wood or coal stoves have become popular. The disadvantages of these stoves are that they require a good deal of attention and create a fire danger because of the high temperature they produce.

Electrical System

The growing number of appliances in the typical household has increased the home use of electricity in the last forty years. Both the amount of current available and the number of circuits and outlets for distributing it are likely to be inadequate in older homes. The amount of current available is measured in amperes. Today's home with an electric stove, a large air conditioner, and a large electric clothes dryer needs 200-ampere (200A) service (Watkins, 1972). For lighting and small appliances, 100-ampere service is adequate. Many older homes, however, have only 60-ampere service. The power service can be determined by checking the labels on the fuse or circuit breaker box.

An adequate number of separate electrical circuits is also important. If there is too much use on a particular circuit (for example, two heavy users of power such as a toaster and an electric iron), the wires become overheated. The fuse then blows or the circuit breaker shuts off. In judging the adequacy of circuits, experts suggest there should be an outlet box at least every twelve feet.

If appliances are included in a rental or sale unit, it is important to be certain which ones will remain in the unit and to be sure that they are in good working order. Renters should also be certain they understand which utilities are included in the rent and which will be billed directly to them by the utility company. Since heating and cooling are major expenses, it is smart to check operating costs. A call to the utility or fuel oil company can provide information on past bills or costs for similar units.

Plumbing System

The plumbing system includes both the pipes bringing fresh water and those carrying off waste water. If the plumbing system is improperly installed, leaks can damage walls and ceilings. In cold climates, if pipes are too close to the exterior or are not well insulated, they may freeze and break.

In urban areas waste water is carried off in the public sewer system. In areas without public sewers, individual units rely on septic systems. These disperse waste water through the ground and hold solid wastes until bacterial action can break them down. Septic systems require periodic care and attention.

Inadequate water pressure may be a problem. When pressure is low, the temperature in the shower can change rapidly if the cold water or hot water is turned on elsewhere. This problem can be detected by turning on the shower to the correct temperature and then turning on the hot water and then the cold in the sink.

Some home shoppers are reluctant to trust their own judgment in checking a house. One alternative is to hire an independent housing inspector to check the property. The inspector can identify needed repairs and judge the remaining life of such key items as the furnace and the roof. If an inspector is used, it is wise to make the purchase subject to the inspection. If a serious problem is discovered, the deal can be canceled.

Another source of protection is a home warranty. One widely available warranty for new home buyers is the Home Owner's Warranty provided by the National Association of Home Builders. It provides the buyer with protection for a maximum of ten years. The warranty is provided by the builder and becomes part of the cost. All home warranties should be checked carefully to be certain about what is covered and for how long.

SAFETY

Fire is a serious home safety concern. Young children and the aged are particularly vulnerable to death and injury from fires. Fire prevention is essential, but controlling the spread of a fire is an important back-up measure. One way to prevent the spread of fire is to use fireproof and fire-retardant materials. These materials can be used for the *compartmentalization* of fires; that is, limiting a fire to a particular room or unit in a multiple-unit building. Use of concrete floors and ceilings and cinder-block walls can help prevent the spread of fires. Unfortunately, in most houses and apartment buildings the walls are plasterboard on wood or metal studding.

Smoke detectors are a useful warning device. They are now required in many communities, especially in apartments. If smoke detectors are not required, they are a good investment anyway. Experts say the most important place for a smoke detector is in the bedroom area for warning sleeping occupants.

The safety of new buildings is encouraged by the use of *building codes*. These are local rules governing the design and construction of both residential and commercial buildings. Local codes cover structural strength, the safety of electrical and heating systems, and the adequacy of plumbing and ventilation. When building codes are strictly enforced, renters and buyers can feel more certain about the basic quality and safety of a building.

Safety and sanitation in existing buildings are regulated by local *housing codes*. These codes cover such matters as the adequacy of heat, ventilation and plumbing; the provision of safety exits; maintenance of sanitary conditions; and control of rodents. Housing codes can be a source of protection for renters if landlords are not providing essential services. They also can provide help for homeowners if nearby properties, which are in disrepair, become hazardous.

Burglary and assault are two other safety-related concerns. Break-ins can be reduced by the use of strong doors and door frames. Tightly fitted metal covered doors are most secure. Lightweight, hollow-core doors can be kicked in easily. The most secure door locks are the mortise type. These have the keyhole above the knob rather than in the knob. Mortise type locks can provide extra security when a deadbolt is used (see Figure 10-1). The key-in-the-knob locks used on many apartments can be opened with a plastic credit card. An extra trigger bolt provides some additional security. Doors with key-in-the-knob locks can be opened easily when the knob is damaged or broken off. Renters should press for secure locks and insist that the lock be changed after the previous tenant leaves. When windows can be entered easily by intruders, grilles or other protective devices are needed.

People are especially vulnerable to assault while leaving or entering residential buildings. There are some protective measures available, however. Entry areas should be well lighted and designed so that it is possible to look into the entryway before going into it. In apartment buildings, locked outside doors, well-lighted hallways, and security personnel all can help reduce crime problems.

Figure 10-1
Mortise Locks Provide More Security than the Common Key-in-the-Knob Locks

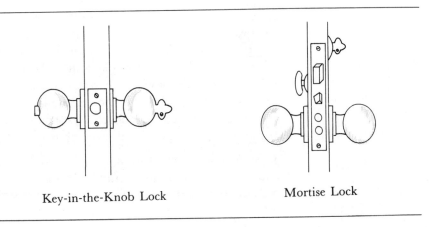

Key-in-the-Knob Lock   Mortise Lock

COSTS

Housing costs are the biggest single item in most people's budgets. The expense makes careful decision making about housing essential. In making this choice you must weigh costs against resources including savings, expected income, and personal skills at home repair and improvement.

How Much Can You Afford to Spend?

Some experts suggest that you should not spend more than 25 percent of your monthly income after taxes for housing, including outlays for mortgage or rental expenses, utilities, home insurance, and other costs. In fact, however, many people spend more than this. A wise approach is to estimate the total costs for a selected home and then decide how it fits into the budget (Meeks, 1980a).

Experts also have offered some rules-of-thumb about how much you can afford to spend when buying a home. The usual suggestion is that you should not spend more than two to two and a half times your annual income. Using this formula, someone with an annual income of $22,000 could afford to spend a maximum of $55,000 for a home. Again, it seems wisest to be guided by estimates of actual expenses and by your budget in deciding how much to spend on housing.

Costs of Owning a Home

Some of the costs of owning a home are obvious. They are out-of-pocket costs that come regularly:

- *Mortgage payment* — Payment of interest and payment to reduce the loan amount (principal)
- *Utility costs* — Heating, cooling, lighting, water, garbage collection
- *Property taxes* — Local taxes based on the valuation of the property
- *Home insurance* — Insurance to provide protection against loss of home through fire, etc.
- *Maintenance costs* — Expenses for maintaining the property, repainting, new rugs, etc.

In addition, there may be other expenses. Condominium and cooperative owners will have monthly bills for the expense of managing the building and maintaining the common areas. Buyers of condominium and cooperative units need to be aware that a significant part of their housing decisions will be made jointly with other owners. Key decisions may include what repairs will be made and who will be hired to manage the building.

There are some less obvious expenses that do not come on a regular basis, but they are costs of ownership nevertheless. They include:

- *Interest forgone on the money invested in the home.* If the owner had not invested in a home, the money could have been used to earn interest elsewhere.
- *Depreciation.* The value of the property declines due to age and wear and tear.

Part 2   Managing Spending

Many people fail to recognize that houses depreciate because some of the effects of depreciation are hidden by the inflationary increases in house prices. One way to see the effect of depreciation is to compare the cost of a twenty-year-old house with the cost of building a new house that is identical. The older house currently selling for $80,000 might cost $100,000 to build new today. The difference is due to the wear and tear on the older house.

Owning vs. Renting

Many people are interested in buying because they feel a home is a wise investment. They hope for the rapid increases in resale prices seen in the 1970s and early 1980s. When looking at a home as an investment, it is wise to recognize that what goes up sometimes comes down. House prices sometimes fall due to national economic conditions, declines in local business activity, and particular neighborhoods going out of favor.

Another problem is that a house is not a very liquid investment. Houses cannot always be sold easily, and selling costs and real estate fees take a sizable bite out of the sale proceeds. The uncertainties about being able to resell quickly and the costs of purchasing and reselling make a house a questionable investment for someone who is likely to be transferred frequently. Some people like ownership because it offers some tax advantages. Mortgage interest and property tax payments are deductible from federal income taxes.

Renting has its advantages, too. It requires a minimum initial outlay, usually a month's rent in advance and a security deposit equal to another month's rent. Renting offers more flexibility than buying. Some rentals are available on a weekly or monthly basis, while others require longer term leases. Because rentals can be arranged for short periods, they are a good choice for those who have to move frequently or whose housing needs are changing.

Another advantage of renting is that housing costs are more predictable. In a rental property, all the major repair and maintenance expenses are the responsibility of the landlord. There will be no unexpected bills for replacing the roof or repairing the plumbing. Renting also has the advantage of shifting many upkeep responsibilities to someone else.

Holding Housing Costs Down

The rising costs of home rents and sale property have caused builders, government officials, and home seekers serious concern in recent years. There has been continuing discussion of how to provide attractive housing at prices people can afford.

One approach has been to increase *housing density,* the number of units per acre of land. Cluster homes and townhouses provide savings by using less land per unit. Another approach has been to reduce house sizes by combining living room, family room, and dining room into one large room and reducing the size of other rooms. At the same time, there has been an effort to give these smaller units a feeling of spaciousness by adding skylights and higher ceilings.

An effort has also been made to reduce material costs. Less expensive materials have been used. Plastic pipe has replaced copper, and wood exterior panelling has replaced brick and stucco. Less expensive kitchen cabinets have been used. Streets and driveways have been made narrower and sidewalks eliminated. More innovative new materials and factory-built modules also are being used. Door frames with prehung doors and preassembled stairs and roof units are examples.

Developers have found, however, that buyers and renters are unwilling to give up certain amenities. They still want outside space — a patio or deck — and adequate bathroom space. They want a place for their car, preferably a garage, and they want their own washer and dryer, even if they are small.

Still another approach to cutting housing costs has been to make it easier for two roommates to share a unit, either as renters or as owners. Units have been developed with two separate master bedrooms and baths but with shared living room, dining, and kitchen areas.

ARRANGING A RENTAL

When looking for a rental, you may find that newspaper ads, real estate offices, local bulletin boards, and friends all can be useful sources of information. Rental services that provide lists of available units may not, however, be so useful. These services often are the subject of consumer complaints about outdated and misleading information. Comparison shopping will give an idea of what is available in various price ranges.

A rental can be arranged with either a verbal or a written agreement. Rentals based on verbal agreements are binding up to one year. They provide for rental on a week-to-week or month-to-month basis. If renters wish to leave, it is usually necessary to give notice one rental period in advance (American Bar Association, 1982).

A lease is a written legal contract setting down the terms of a rental agreement. It commits the lessee (renter) to pay the lessor (owner) a specified amount for the use of the property. The rental terms set down in the lease include:

- The amount of rent to be paid and when and where it should be paid;
- A description of the unit rented, including the address and apartment number;
- The beginning and ending dates of the lease;
- The services to be provided by the landlord, such as utilities and parking.

Many leases also include a list of regulations. This list may include such rules as no pets or no children. Lease terms are often stacked against the tenant, so it is essential to read a lease carefully before signing it (see Consumer Concern: "One-Sided Rental Leases").

Anyone who signs the lease can be held responsible for all the rent. This means that if two roommates sign a lease and one moves out, the landlord legally can press either one, or both, for the rent. There is no good protection in signing a lease with others except to choose roommates wisely.

ARRANGING A PURCHASE

In purchasing a home, a buyer should check local newspaper ads to get a general idea of what is available and price levels. Not all homes for sale are advertised, of course. Usually the help of a real estate agent is needed. Agents handle the sale of most homes in return for a commission (usually a percentage of the sales price) from the sellers. Most real estate agents share lists of the properties they are selling through local multiple listing services; as a result, they know about many other properties. Buyers need to remember that the agents are not working for them; they are working for the seller, who is paying them their commission.

The Sales Agreement

After locating a property to buy, the buyer must negotiate the sales price with the owner. Sellers seldom get or expect to get their asking price. Reduc-

Illustration 10-3
Real estate agents can help home buyers narrow the alternatives to those that are most likely to be suitable.

tions of five percent or more are common. Recent sales prices in a neighborhood can be determined from records in the county office where deeds are recorded. Real estate agents often also have information on recent sale prices. If you are uncertain about whether a price is fair, the advice of an independent appraiser can be obtained. For a fee, the appraiser will check a property, form an opinion of its condition, and indicate a fair price.

CONSUMER CONCERN: ONE-SIDED RENTAL LEASES

Today's leases still follow traditions formed in England centuries ago. While they set down the obligations of tenants in detail, they say little about the obligations of landlords. This tradition reportedly developed because rental agreements were for the land alone. Any house on the land was thrown in "as is," with no promises about its condition or habitability.

This approach is seriously outdated for the rental of housing, but the wording of leases still clings to the old patterns. Many leases still do not spell out the landlord's obligations for repairs, maintenance, heat, or other essentials. Even though the lease does not spell out these obligations, courts now typically rule that in renting a property landlords create an implied warranty of habitability; that is, they have guaranteed that the property is in suitable condition to be lived in by the act of offering it for rent. This means the landlord is responsible for providing basic services even though no promises were made in the lease.

Another problem with many leases is the clauses that put major obligations on tenants but provide little protection for them. For example:

- *Security deposits.* Most leases require a deposit to protect the owner against damage and the failure to pay. Few leases, however, provide any details on how and when this money will be refunded or what deductions can be made. Many states now require the landlord to give an itemized list of deductions. These should be for damages, not ordinary wear and tear (American Bar Association, 1982).
- *Ending the lease.* Most leases spell out how much advance notice must be given to terminate a lease. Sometimes as long as ninety days is required on a one-year lease. If tenants fail to notify the landlord they wish to cancel, the lease is renewed automatically.
- *Rule on subletting.* Since young people often have job transfers, it is important to know whether subletting is allowable (i.e., whether others will be permitted to take over responsibility for the lease). It is important to know of any restrictions that the landlord can place on anyone who takes over the lease.

Purchase offers should be made through the real estate agent handling the property. After a price is agreed on, a written contract or *sales agreement* is prepared. It sets down key terms of the sale, including:

- A description of the property and the equipment included
- The sale price and date the buyer may take possession

- *Repairs and services.* Many leases do not state the landlord's obligations for repairs or services in any detail. Because of the implied warranty of habitability, courts generally hold that landlords are obligated to provide basic services even though they were not promised. Most states now have a provision for withholding rent and diverting it to use for repairs until conditions are satisfactory. Another protection is the concern of local housing code officials with maintaining safe and healthy conditions in rental buildings.
- *Signing away legal rights.* Some leases include clauses in which tenants give up their right to sue if they are injured or suffer financial losses through the fault of the landlord. These clauses may not be regarded as binding by courts (American Bar Association, 1982).
- *Changes to the lease form.* Prospective renters are usually told that the lease is "the standard form." In fact, there are many standard forms that may include provisions that would not be upheld in court. Leases can be changed by crossing out sections and adding new ones. Both parties should initial these changes to indicate acceptance. It is also important to remember that oral agreements about changes to a written lease are not binding. Changes should be put in writing.

QUESTIONS

1. How should the problem of one-sided leases should be solved? Some possibilities include: (a) new laws and regulations concerning leases; (b) education programs for tenants; and (c) development of a new type of court in which landlord–tenant cases can be heard. What are the strengths and weakneses of each of these alternatives?
2. How can leases be made more fair to tenants and still protect landlords? What would you do about security deposits and renewal clauses?
3. If renting becomes an unattractive investment because of controls on the rent landlords can charge, what will happen to the supply of rental housing? Discuss.

- A promise by seller to provide a clear title (i.e., a title free from claims for debts owed others; these debts could be unpaid contractor's bills or unpaid mortgages)
- An agreement on how the property tax bills for the year will be divided

Experts feel the sales agreement is the most risky step in buying a home (American Bar Association, 1980). It is easy to see why. This step is the one at which all the terms of the sale are set. Neither the buyer nor seller can back out easily after the sales agreement is signed. Because this step is so critical, it is wise to get a lawyer to check the sales agreement (Meeks, 1980a). It should cover unexpected problems such as what would happen if the property burned immediately after the sales agreement was signed. To indicate the buyer's commitment, most sales agreements include a deposit (also called a *binder* or *earnest money*). This deposit usually is not refunded if buyers change their minds but may be refunded if they have problems getting mortgage financing.

Getting a Mortgage

Mortgage lenders' willingness to make a mortgage loan depends both on the value of the property offered as security for the loan and their estimate of the buyers' ability to make the mortgage payments. Lenders will appraise the property to be certain it is adequate security for the loan requested. They do not, for example, want to lend $60,000 on a house that might have a resale value of only $50,000. Lenders are also concerned about the credit record and job history of prospective borrowers. Are borrowers in stable jobs that provide enough income to cover the payments?

There are a variety of types of mortgages and mortgage terms available. These mortgages and terms will be discussed in Chapter 14 on credit.

Settlement

The final step in arranging a purchase is *closing* or *settlement*. At this step, the buyer delivers payment to the seller, and the seller gives up title to the property. There are a number of charges buyers must pay at settlement. In the past, buyers were often dismayed at the number and size of these additional charges. To forewarn buyers, lenders are now required to give buyers an estimate of closing costs when they apply for a loan. Lenders also are required to provide a detailed list of costs the day before settlement (U.S. Department of Housing and Urban Development, 1976). Settlement fees include such charges as the following:

- *Fees in connection with the loan.* These charges may include appraisal fees, payments into an *escrow account* used by the lender to accumulate funds to pay taxes, and insurance fees. The fees may also include loan fees. Some lenders charge a small percentage of the loan amount at the time a loan is made, which is essentially an advance payment of interest. The fees are usually called *points,* one point equaling one percent of the loan amount.

- *Title charges.* These charges include the cost of an abstract of the title or a title search, which is a check of official property records to be certain the title is clear. Lenders may require title insurance to protect themselves against loss in case a title is faulty. In some cases, the seller pays the title charges.
- *Government fees.* This charge is for recording the deed and mortgage in the official records. There also may be state and local taxes on the transfer of property.
- *Payments to the seller.* It may be necessary to pay the seller for a portion of the real estate taxes and utility bills that have been paid in advance.
- *Other charges.* These charges may include termite inspection, attorney's fees, appraisal fees, and other fees. Some of these *may* be paid by the seller.

Sellers have expenses, too. They must pay real estate commisions and attorney's fees; and, of course, they have to repay the lender for the balance still due on their mortgage. The number and amount of the payments involved in buying and selling a home are sizable. For this reason, short-term ownership may not make sense financially. Renting may be a better short-term solution.

MAJOR CHAPTER CONCEPTS

1. Basic concerns in choosing a home include (a) physical comfort — shelter and control of ambient environment, (b) safety, (c) social interaction and privacy, (d) self-expression, and (e) aesthetic needs.
2. A variety of housing is available including units in multiple-unit buildings (e.g., apartments, townhouses, and duplexes) and single-family detached houses. With condominiums and cooperatives, it is now possible to own a wide variety of types of housing.
3. In evaluating a home's location, a buyer should consider the community and its taxes and services; the neighborhood, including its condition and possible sources of pollution; and the site and its microclimate.
4. Family life-cycle stage affects the amount of space needed, the types of rooms needed, and their relative sizes.
5. The solidity of the structure, including its foundation, frame, walls, floors, and roof, is important. Adequate insulation holds down heating/cooling costs. Proper moisture control with vapor barriers is needed to prevent moisture build-up in outside walls.

6. The size of heating bills is a consideration in choosing a home, but the changing prices of different energy sources make it difficult to generalize about which is most economical.

7. At least 100-ampere electrical service is needed for small appliances and lighting. More is needed if there are larger appliances.

8. An independent housing inspector can provide useful information about the condition of a house and its systems.

9. Fires can be controlled by limiting their spread through compartmentalization, which is especially desirable in multiple-unit buildings.

10. Metal-covered doors with mortise-type locks plus a deadbolt provide the best protection against break-ins. Well-lighted entryways that can be checked before entering, well-lighted hallways, and locked outside doors provide protection against assault.

11. Although experts offer rules of thumb on how much you can afford to spend for housing, the best approach is to estimate total costs and compare them with available funds and a projected budget.

12. The expense of owning a home includes out-of-pocket expenses and the less visible costs of depreciation and the interest not earned on the money invested in the home.

13. Home ownership can offer investment and tax advantages. Renting offers flexibility and freedom from maintenance obligations.

14. Efforts to hold housing costs down have included designs that reduce land costs per unit, use less expensive and innovative new materials, reduce room sizes, and eliminate certain features.

15. Rentals may be arranged either with or without a lease. Because a lease is a commitment to pay out hundreds of dollars, it should be checked carefully before signing.

16. Experts say that the sales agreement is the most risky step in making a home purchase because it is the stage at which the sale terms are set.

17. Closing or settlement, in which the deed is passed to the new owner, involves a number of expenses and fees for the buyer.

CONSUMER QUESTIONS

1. Study the real estate ads in a local newspaper. Which evaluative criteria do the ads seem to suggest are most important?

2. In deciding on a place to live, what evaluative criteria would be most important to you? How does the place you now live rate on these criteria?

3. Draw a floor plan of your "dream house." It can be a detached house, townhouse, apartment, or whatever you prefer. How do the features of your dream house reflect the evaluative criteria you consider most important in housing?

4. The high cost of housing is a widespread concern. If you had to omit some features from your dream house to cut costs, which ones would you be most willing to drop? Which ones would you be least willing to drop?

5. Study the for rent or for sale ads for housing in a local paper. Find two ads for similar units in different neighborhoods. How do the prices differ? What do you think are the reasons for this difference? Find two ads for different units in the same neighborhood. How do the prices differ? What are the reasons for this difference?

6. Using recent magazine and newspaper articles, prepare a report on one of the following topics:
   (a) Deception and fraud in the sale of vacation home property.
   (b) Discrimination problems in housing and efforts to combat them.
   (c) Housing assistance for low-income people.
   (d) Government programs to assist home buyers.
   (e) Recent changes in housing sales, sales prices, and the affordability of homes.

SUGGESTED READINGS

1. Better Homes and Gardens. *The Decorating Book*. Des Moines: Meredith Corporation, 1981. Along with a useful introduction to interior design, this book provides a good discussion of flooring, lighting, window, and housing design.

2. Kidder, Tracy. *House*. Boston: Houghton Mifflin, 1985. Kidder gives an insightful and engaging report of the construction of a new house. A major focus is the interaction of the key players, the owners, the architect, and the builders, and the ups and downs of the custom-building process.

3. Reader's Digest. *Complete Do-It-Yourself Manual*. Pleasantville, N.Y.: Reader's Digest Association, 1973. This is a basic introduction to do-it-yourself projects including minor repair projects and improvement projects ranging from changing a fuse to installing new plumbing. It includes a useful introduction to tools and construction materials.

4. Rybczynski, Witold. *Home: A Short History of an Idea*. New York: Viking, 1986. This book presents an historical survey of the ideas of home and comfort and their effect on the design of housing.

CHAPTER 11

~

HOUSEHOLD DURABLES

When they furnish the place they live, some people are concerned mostly with impressing others. They want what interior designers call the "drop-dead look"— a set of furnishings so elegant that visitors will "drop dead" from surprise and envy. Others' goals are more modest. What they want is shoes-off, feet-up comfort. For them, it is comfort over style, any time. There are other schools of thought, of course. Some families may want to create a hide-out or nest where they can find shelter from the disturbances and dangers of the outside world. Young professionals, in contrast, may view their homes as a place where they can refresh and restore themselves before setting out to do battle in the work world. Clearly what people want from their homes varies widely. Regardless of how a home is viewed, furnishing it involves substantial expense. Although furniture and appliances are expensive, they can yield useful service over a period of years if they are well chosen.

EVALUATIVE CRITERIA FOR HOUSEHOLD DURABLES

When choosing appliances, furniture, or other home furnishings, you need to consider certain key evaluative criteria. These criteria also are important when considering other kinds of household durables from which years of service are expected. This includes lawn mowers and yard equipment, home repair tools, and personal computers.

Design

Since furniture and appliances are a highly visible part of a home, they must be pleasing to the eye. Colors, the materials used, and style all are factors in the aesthetic appeal of an item. Some of the principles of good design have been discussed earlier.

The shape or form of consumer durables should grow out of the functions they are to perform. In recent years, more and more product designers have been working to design products that are easy and safe to use. They are guided by the principles of *ergonomics,* the study of the relationship between the user and a piece of equipment.

As home electronic equipment and appliances have become more and more complex, designers have paid increasing attention to designs that make it easier to understand how to use the equipment. For example, if starting a piece of equipment involves three settings, it makes sense to have the controls located next to each other, arranged in sequence.

Design should also make equipment convenient, comfortable, and safe to use. For example, it makes no sense to design a vacuum cleaner that is so bulky that it is difficult to manuever and to carry from room to room. A handle that is easy to grip also is desirable. Safety factors should also be taken into account in design. It makes sense, for example, to locate stove controls so that it is not necessary to reach over, or close to, hot pots and pans.

Performance

A second important criterion in judging household durables is performance—how well they do what they are supposed to do. A record player is expected to reproduce sound accurately; a refrigerator, to keep food cold. Upholstered furniture is expected to provide comfortable seating.

If household durables perform well, they can provide several different kinds of services:

- Savings in time and work. Appliances can reduce the amount of time and physical energy required to do some tasks.
- Pleasure and comfort. Household durables, such as stereos, can provide enjoyable music, while air conditioners and sofas can help ensure physical comfort.

Cost

Because household equipment is expected to provide years of service, durability is another key evaluative criterion. The more years of high-quality

Illustration 11-1
When an appliance serves multiple functions, designs which make operation easy to understand are especially important.

service, the lower the cost of ownership per year. *Depreciation,* the decline in value and usefulness of an item over time, is a major cost of ownership for household durables just as it is for cars. The longer an item lasts, the lower the depreciation costs per year.

The selection of durable furnishings not only cuts yearly depreciation costs, it also cuts repair costs, a second major cost of ownership. In addition, operating costs are an important cost factor for appliances. The operating costs of some types of appliances can be sizable and can vary between models.

Safety

Appliances convert energy from electricity or natural gas into light, mechanical power, sound, heating, and cooling. These energy inputs used in appliances can create electrical shock hazards or asphyxiation dangers. Their energy outputs can also cause injuries. These dangers make appliance safety an important consideration. Furniture is not usually thought of in terms of safety hazards. The chief danger, however, comes from its flammability and the toxic fumes that may be produced when it burns.

CHOOSING FURNITURE

Experts who have studied how people buy furniture suggest that the most common mistake is failing to develop an overall plan before they begin buying. Without a plan, consumers run the risk of ending up without some of the pieces they need the most and buying pieces that do not go together well.

A logical first step is to decide what functions the available space must serve. The basics — cooking, eating, and sleeping — must be considered. It is likely a place for entertaining guests will be needed. Additional space may be needed for study or other paperwork done at home. Space may also be needed for games, storage of hobby equipment, and other activities.

A second step is locating these functions in the available space. A useful way to do this is to draw a floor plan of the space available and outline the area that could be devoted to each different function. There will probably be more functions than space; therefore, some areas will have to serve several functions.

The next step is to identify the furniture pieces needed in each functional area. Each piece should be drawn to scale on the floor plan. It is easy to overestimate the space available and to choose pieces that are too large. Oversize pieces are not just a problem in furniture arranging; they are also hard to move. Pieces over seven feet long will not fit in most apartment elevators and create real moving problems.

In recent years, furniture makers have come to recognize that many people are living in limited space. In response, they have begun offering more and more items that can serve several purposes. Examples are sleep sofas, tables that can be adjusted from coffee table height to eating height, and dining tables that also can be used as desks. They have also been offering a wider variety of wall units created with modular pieces that can serve as desks, bookcases, storage units, and space for TV and stereo equipment. Furniture makers also are offering more small-scale pieces that can fit comfortably into limited spaces.

Before buying, some thought should be given to the kind of style preferred. Is a casual and comfortable style preferred? Or are more formal and traditional styles desired? By studying the photos in home magazines and the model rooms in furniture stores, consumers can determine their tastes. While they are visiting furniture stores, consumers should also do some comparison shopping. Furniture differs widely in price and quality, and comparison shopping will provide an idea of what is available and the quality available at different price levels. Many quality differences in furniture are hidden or hard to detect, but knowledgeable sales people can explain the reasons for the differences in prices between pieces that appear similar.

Design

Furniture is available in styles to suit every taste. Some of the styles are *traditional*. They are adaptations of styles of the past. Traditional styles usually incorporate ornamentation such as carvings, moldings, and elaborate hardware. *Contemporary* styles are designs from the present day. They typically are simpler, with little or no ornamentation, and rely on clean lines and attractively grained woods for their appeal.

Some traditional styles are relatively formal, while others are more casual. The same is true for contemporary styles (see Figure 11-1). The formal styles of both traditional and contemporary have a light, graceful look. Finishes are highly polished and upholstery fabrics typically are soft and delicate. In contrast, casual styles have a heavier look. Finishes are rougher and duller, and are often *distressed* to give the appearance of age and wear. Upholstery fabrics are coarser and often have a nubby texture.

Some experts suggest choosing a certain style category and sticking with it throughout the home to give a unified look. This approach makes it easier to shift furniture from room to room as needs change. Shifts also are easier if the color choices are similar.

Style choices obviously should be what is preferred, not what friends or family favor. Many young adults choose contemporary styles for their first apartment. With marriage and children, their taste often shifts to casual, traditional ("country") styles or casual, contemporary styles. These casual styles are both practical and durable and do not show spots, fingerprints, and damage as readily as formal styles.

Some people find a single style category too limiting and prefer to mix several styles. Sometimes they mix two styles from the same general category, for example, two formal or traditional styles. Room designs that combine two or more different styles are labeled *eclectic* designs. A popular and successful eclectic design in recent years has been to combine formal, contemporary styles, such as glass-topped coffee tables with highly polished metal legs, with traditional, formal styles. Attempts to combine formal and casual styles are more tricky and often are not successful (Better Homes and Gardens, 1981). To be successful, combinations should be similar in formality and use unifying colors.

Figure 11-1
Four General Style
Categories of Furniture

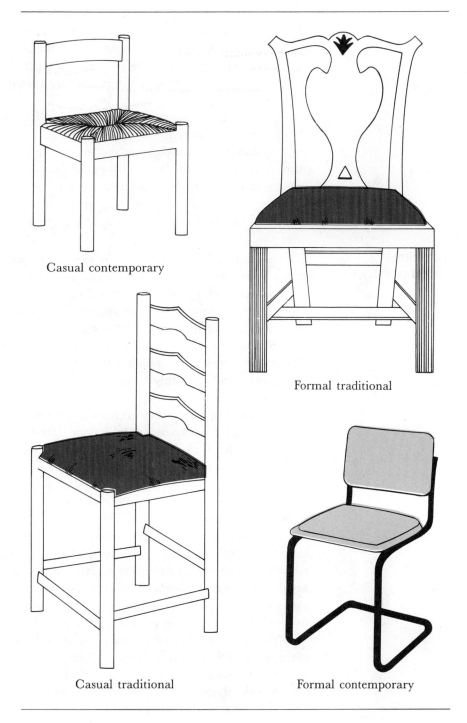

Casual contemporary

Formal traditional

Casual traditional

Formal contemporary

Some style and design choices are especially appropriate for the limited spaces with which young adults often have to deal. Smaller and lighter-scaled furniture is especially appropriate. For example, glass-topped coffee tables seem to have less mass than solid-topped ones. In upholstered pieces, designs without arms and upholstered pieces with exposed legs have a lighter look.

Comfort is an important design consideration for upholstered pieces. People come in different shapes and sizes. As a result, not everyone will be comfortable in the same chair. Shorter people are likely to prefer a chair with a seat closer to the floor and not too deep front-to-back. Taller people will prefer a chair with a higher and deeper seat. These differing seating needs suggest that there should be a variety of seating so family and guests can choose what is most comfortable for them.

Furniture Construction

The way in which furniture is made plays a key role in determining its durability. A first step in evaluating the quality of a piece is a visual inspection. Is the workmanship neat? Is the finish evenly applied to the wood surfaces without drips or runs? Are the upholstery seams neat and straight? Are the upholstery patterns matched at the seams? A check of the less visible parts of a piece can also provide indicators of quality. Are the back panels of all-wood pieces neatly applied and finished? Are drawer sides and bottoms neatly and smoothly finished so they will not snag clothing stored in them?

Another important check is the solidness of a piece. Is the frame rigid, or does the piece sway or sag when one corner is pushed or picked up? A follow-up step is to check moving parts. Do drawers slide easily? Drawer guides or glides help to ensure that drawers will move smoothly without jamming.

Frame. The frame of a piece of furniture serves the same function as the frame of a house. It is the skeleton that supports the exterior finishing materials. A sturdy frame is essential for strength and durability. Experts usually suggest that a frame be made of kiln-dried hardwood. Kiln drying reduces moisture content and ensures against warping. The use of hardwood ensures greater strength. Hardwoods come from trees that drop their leaves each year, such as maple, oak, walnut, and cherry. Softwoods come from evergreens such as pine, fir, spruce, and redwood.

The frame of a piece will be sturdier if the legs are an integral part of the frame. On some less expensive furniture, screw-on legs are used. Screw-on legs are less durable and break off more easily.

Panels. There are two broad categories of furniture: case goods and upholstered goods. Case goods include desks, dressers, and other items made completely from wood. Upholstered goods are for seating and are constructed by placing soft padding over a wooden frame.

In making case goods, flat sheets of wood are fastened together and onto the frame. These sheets are called *panels* by furniture-makers and may be made in several ways, including from solid wood or from *veneer*. Veneer is made by bonding together a number of thin layers of wood (usually five). Years ago, the use of veneer suggested inferior quality, but improved production methods make today's veneers more durable (Better Homes and Gardens, 1981). Veneer panels are considered to be stronger and less subject to warping than an equal thickness of solid wood. They also have the advantage of being less costly than solid wood, since only a thin ply of expensive woods such as walnut or mahogany is used on the exposed surface.

In some moderate- to lower-priced furniture, panels are made of particle board produced by bonding small chips of wood. This bonded material is usually covered by a single ply of a finish wood such as oak or a sheet of plastic or a plastic laminate such as Formica®[1]. These furniture pieces are less costly, but also may be less durable than those made of solid wood or veneer. Hard board or fiber board made from compressed and bonded wood fibers is frequently used for back panels and drawer bottoms in moderate- and low-priced furniture. It can provide durable service if the panels used are thick enough.

There should be a clear indication of the woods used in a piece. If a piece is labeled "solid walnut," all exposed parts should be made from solid walnut wood, and no veneers should be used. If a piece is labeled "walnut solids and veneers," all exposed parts should be made from walnut, but a combination of solid wood and veneers may be used.

Joints. Appropriate frame and panel materials play a key role in durability, and it is critical that they be joined together solidly. A number of different joining methods are used in making furniture. The strongest joints are those in which the two pieces of wood being joined are interlocked, with portions of one piece entering the other (see Figure 11-2). Frequently used interlocking joints include:

- *Double-dowel joints.* Two pieces of wood are butted (or placed) side by side and joined by two short dowels placed in holes drilled in both pieces. This joint is used for dresser and chair frames.
- *Mortise and tenon joints.* The end of one piece of wood is shaped to fit a hole cut in the piece to which it is joined. This joint is used to join chair rungs to legs.

[1]Formica is a registered trademark of Formica Corporation.

Figure 11-2

Furniture Joining Techniques Can Have a Major Effect on the Strength of a Furniture Frame

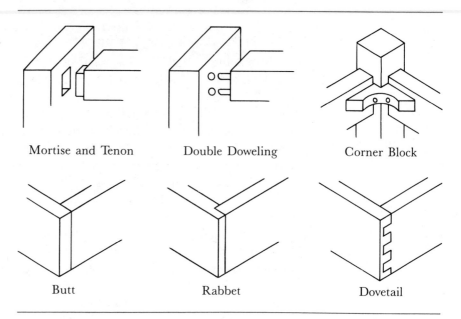

Mortise and Tenon   Double Doweling   Corner Block

Butt   Rabbet   Dovetail

- *Dove-tail joints.* Portions of the ends of two pieces of wood are cut out. The remaining portions of one are fitted into the cut-out portions of the other. This joint is used for joining the sides of drawers.

Noninterlocking joints do not have the strength of those that interlock. They typically are used in less expensive furniture. Two such joints are the butt joint and the rabbet joint (see Figure 11-2).

Frame joints are strengthened with glue in all but the least expensive pieces. Many joints, especially frame joints, need further strengthening. One way of providing this extra strength is to add *corner blocks* (Figure 11-2). These are small blocks of wood glued and screwed into place at a joint. Nails are sometimes added to further strengthen a joint, but screws are considered stronger. Staples are sometimes used but provide relatively little strength.

Padding and Cushions. It is more difficult to judge the quality of upholstered furniture than case goods. Many important quality indicators are hidden. Shoppers can, however, get some useful clues by checking the external appearance of a piece and by asking salespeople for information. Labels and hang-tags also provide useful information about the upholstery and padding materials used.

Upholstered furniture is constructed by fastening springs to the frame and then covering springs and frame with padding materials. Two types of springs are used (Better Homes and Gardens, 1981). Coil springs are used in bulkier furniture, while zig-zag springs are used in lighter-weight furniture. Coil springs should be tied together so they will be more stable and move together. In general, the more springs used in a piece of furniture, the better.

A layer of fabric should be used to separate the padding from the springs. Without it, the springs will eventually cut into the padding. A combination of several types of padding is used in most pieces. Cotton and cellulose are relatively inexpensive and will pack down over time. Fiberfill and foam are more expensive and less likely to pack down. The arms and other sharp corners on a piece should be well-padded. Without good padding, the upholstery on these corners will wear rapidly.

Several materials are used for stuffing cushions. Foam blocks molded to fit the cushion covers are often used in moderately priced furniture. The denser and heavier the foam, the better support it will give. Frequently foam cores are wrapped in fiberfill to give a softer feel and look. Shredded foam also is used. It is, however, likely to pack down in use. Down also is used but is seldom seen except in the most expensive furniture. Although many cushion covers have zippers and could be removed, experts warn against doing this. It is difficult to get the covers back on again.

Labels indicating the padding and cushion materials used are required by law in most states. These labels will provide useful information for shoppers but may be removed after the purchase.

Illustration 11-2
Because people differ in size and cushioning preferences, shoppers should try out a piece of furniture before buying.

Before buying, furniture shoppers should try out the upholstered piece being considered by sitting in it for awhile. Does the cushion compress too much in the middle and pop up around the edges? Some lightweight foam cushions have this problem. When considering a sofa, have several people sit on it together. Do the cushions move independently or do the sitters sag toward each other?

Upholstery Fabric. As mentioned earlier, the quality of workmanship on the upholstery is a useful quality indicator. Seams should be straight and patterns matched. The fiber used in an upholstery fabric will affect both its durability and its cleanability. Frequently used natural fibers are cotton and wool; frequently used synthetic fibers include nylon, olefin, polyester, and acrylic. The characteristics of these fibers were discussed in Chapter 7. Blends of a natural and synthetic fiber are often used to get the best characteristics of each. In general, the synthetic fibers are more resistant to staining and easier to clean. Leather is also used in some expensive furniture. Vinyl upholstery is a less expensive substitute for leather. It is easy to care for and resists stains. Vinyl with a fabric backing is more resistant to tears and is more durable.

Upholstery fabrics are frequently treated to resist staining using such finishes as Scotchgard®[1] and Teflon®. These finishes help control staining by causing moisture to bead up instead of soaking in. Stain-resistant finishes are frequently applied during manufacturing but also are available for application by the retailer or the consumer. Additional finish treatments should not be applied to fabrics that already have been treated.

While some manufacturers put permanent care labels with instructions for cleaning on their furniture, most do not. When purchasing an upholstered piece, buyers should find out what fibers were used in the cover fabric and ask for cleaning advice.

Upholstery fabrics typically are grouped into "grades." These grades should not be interpreted as indicators of quality or durability. They are, instead, groupings by price level (Better Homes and Gardens, 1981). The cost of a particular fabric is related to the complexity of the design, the fibers used, and the amount of yardage required to cover a piece. Patterns that require a lot of yardage for matching are more expensive. The grade level chosen will have a significant effect on the total price of a piece. The same piece upholstered with different grade fabrics may differ in price by hundreds of dollars.

[1]Scotchgard is a registered trademark of Minnesota Mining and Manufacturing Company; Teflon is a registered trademark of E.I. duPont de Nemours and Company.

In selecting an upholstery fabric, it makes sense to buy the most durable fabric you can afford. If upholstery wears out quickly, replacing it by slip covering or reupholstering is expensive.

Finishes. The finish of a furniture piece should both protect and enhance the wood surfaces. Stains should be evenly applied with no noticeably lighter or darker spots. The finish coat should be smooth and even. In better quality pieces the grain is clearly visible. In lower quality pieces, fillers and heavy stains often are used to hide knots and imperfections in the wood.

Many different finishes are used, with lacquer being one of the most frequently applied. The type of finish used is seldom indicated, and salespeople seldom know what was used. While the finishes used today are tougher and resist water spots better than those used years ago, they are still susceptible to damage. Lacquer and most other finishes will be softened and damaged by alcohol, nail polish, nail polish remover, and other solvents.

Vinyl and plastic laminates with a woodgrain finish are frequently used in lower-priced furniture. While these finishes have the appearance of wood, many are just photographs of real wood. Some of these finishes wear well and resist water damage well. Others scratch easily. Unfortunately, it is difficult to hide or repair dents and scratches in these finishes. The hardware used in a piece should be examined, too. Drawer pulls receive a good deal of stress and should be well-made from heavyweight metal.

Buyers frequently discover damage or faulty workmanship after a piece is delivered. It is important to report such complaints to the retailer at once. Written warranties are uncommon for furniture, but retailers still have legal obligations to protect buyers against defects in materials and workmanship. Most are readily willing to do this. Retailers are not, however, willing to cover the cost of repairing abused furniture. Before they decide whether they will make adjustments on a piece, retailers typically insist on checking the piece for abuse.

Because furniture is expensive, it is the focus of many consumer problems and complaints. These include late deliveries as well as damage in delivery and defects in materials and workmanship. Consumers with problems should first turn to the retailer, then to the manufacturer. If they are still dissatisfied, they should contact the Furniture Industry Consumer Advisory Panel, P.O. Box 951, High Point, NC 27261. The Panel will help when retailers and manufacturers cannot or will not resolve a complaint.

Cost

As with other durables, depreciation is a major cost in owning furniture. The longer furniture lasts, the lower its cost per year. Good quality furniture should provide years of service. Case goods, such as dressers, should last a lifetime or more. In moderate use, upholstered furniture should give seven to ten years of service before showing signs of wear. Similar to other durables such as cars, furniture depreciates sharply the first year. This depreciation makes used furniture worth considering (see Consumer Concern: "Psychological Obsolescence"). Because of the rapid depreciation of new furniture, renting or leasing instead of buying may make sense when pieces are needed for only a short period. Antiques can be an interesting alternative to new furniture. They are available in a variety of price ranges and, if well chosen, may appreciate rather than depreciating.

Money spent on furniture is tied up for years and is not available for investment or other uses. This makes it appropriate to consider the interest forgone as a cost of ownership along with depreciation.

Routine care and upkeep costs for furniture are relatively minor. The slipcovers and reupholstering needed to continue the useful life of upholstered pieces are, however, major expenses unless they can be done by the consumer.

CONSUMER CONCERN: PSYCHOLOGICAL OBSOLESCENCE

Consumers often discard things they own long before they are really worn out. Although appliances, furniture, and clothes still have a useful life, their owners may become tired of them. This phenomenon has been labeled *psychological obsolescence*. Discarding things that still can provide useful service can be a costly behavior pattern.

Consumers can decide to discard things for several reasons. It may be that they no longer meet their needs very well. Or it may be that the items' newness and novelty simply has worn off. They just are not quite so interesting or exciting anymore. In other cases, it may be that newer models seem more desirable, even though the new features they offer represent only minor improvements. Marketing and product development executives, of course, count on these new features to make their new models attractive to both first-time and replacement buyers.

Those who decide to discard used items usually find they have little or no salvage or resale value. One reason is that there often are no organized markets where buyers and sellers can get together easily. Some communities have dealers who will buy used furniture and appliances for resale to others. Garage sales and flea markets are ideas that have developed in the last fifteen to twenty years to bring buyers and sellers of used household goods together.

The fact that the salvage value of used durables is well below the

Other kinds of do-it-yourself projects may provide savings. Unfinished furniture can be finished to suit individual preferences. It should be checked for quality, since unfinished furniture often is not well made. In estimating the savings with unfinished furniture, do not forget to include the cost of sandpaper, stain, and other finishing materials. Of course, the opportunity cost of the time also should be taken into account. The same considerations are important in deciding whether or not to buy used furniture and refinish it.

Knocked-down (KD) furniture can also provide savings. It comes disassembled and packaged in cartons, reducing shipping costs; because the customer usually can carry it home, delivery costs are eliminated.

Many retailers offer seasonal furniture sales several times a year. It is smart to plan ahead to take advantage of them. Some manufacturers feature special promotional pieces during these sales. Before buying, be certain to understand why they are less expensive. Sometimes the quality is not exactly the same as the manufacturer's regular line.

value of their useful remaining life can make them a good bargain for astute shoppers. It is, however, not always easy to judge the useful life remaining in some appliances and furniture. It is hard to judge in a few minutes how well an appliance such as a refrigerator is working. A used stereo or TV may be easier to judge. Upholstered furniture also may be hard to judge because damage to the frame may be hidden. Case goods are easier to examine and judge.

Prices in the used market usually take the risks involved into account. The buyer of used items may make an occasional mistake, but if the price is low enough, the loss will not be great. Some appliances, especially gas appliances, may involve safety risks. It is wise to get them checked by experts before they are used.

QUESTIONS

1. Why do consumers discard items that still can provide useful service?
2. Have you recently discarded anything that still could have provided useful service? What was it and why did you discard it?
3. What are the arguments for buying used items? What are the arguments against such purchases?
4. What used items involve the most risk to buyers? Why? Is there anything that can be done to reduce these risks?

Safety

Years ago, mattress fires caused by cigarette smokers who fell asleep while smoking in bed were a serious problem. The resulting fires often were fatal to the smokers and to others. There were, in addition, serious property losses. Concern with the problem led to the issuance of a mandatory federal standard aimed at reducing the risk of ignition when a cigarette is dropped on a mattress. The standard, which became effective in 1973, requires materials and designs that will not burst into flame and will char only to a limited extent.

Concern with cigarette fires in upholstered furniture led to demand for a similar standard there. The industry resisted the proposal with several arguments:

- The choices of upholstery fabrics would be reduced, with cotton, silk, linen, and rayon fabrics virtually eliminated.
- The cost of upholstered furniture to consumers would be increased.
- Taxpayers would have to bear the cost of administering the program.
- The existence of the large number of small manufacturers without laboratory test facilities would be threatened.

The upholstered furniture makers also argued that most upholstery fires were due to careless smokers but that the proposal should create increased furniture costs for all.

As an alternative, the upholstered furniture industry proposed a voluntary standard to the Consumer Product Safety Commission (CPSC). The industry organized the Upholstered Furniture Action Council (UFAC) to develop a voluntary standard and to organize industry efforts to promote compliance with it. The CPSC has agreed to this approach and is monitoring its effectiveness.

Compliance with the voluntary standard is indicated by a UFAC hang-tag attached to individual pieces. Most upholstered furniture (but not all) now conforms to the standard. The hang-tag notes that the materials and methods used reduce the likelihood of fires from cigarettes. It also points out that some furniture materials burn rapidly if ignited and emit toxic gases. Because of these continuing dangers, careful smoking and smoke detectors are essential preventive measures.

CHOOSING APPLIANCES

Most people acquire appliances in the same order. If a range and refrigerator are not furnished in the place they live, these appliances have first priority. Next comes a TV set and then perhaps a stereo. A series of small appliances are added: a vacuum cleaner, toaster, electric iron, and so on. At some point, a washer and dryer are purchased. Over the last sixty years these appliances have become so widely owned that they are more likely to be considered necessities than luxuries. Periodically, new appliances come on the scene and work their way onto the list of necessities. Microwave ovens are becoming so widely owned that they are well on their way to becoming neccessities. Video cassette recorders (VCRs) are another example of an appliance that may be moving from the luxury to the necessity category. As with furniture, years of service are expected from appliances. As a result, careful choices as well as careful use and maintenance are important.

Design and Convenience

Appliance manufacturers devote a good deal of effort to making their products aesthetically pleasing, but more is expected from an appliance than just good looks. Convenience and ease-of-use also are very important.

A basic requirement for an appliance is controls that are easy to set and adjust. Dials and controls should be easily read and easily reached and adjusted. More and more appliances have replaced traditional dials with digital read-outs that can provide greater accuracy in setting. In designing controls, there is a conflict between flexibility of operation and simplicity. A large number of controls facilitate operation at a variety of levels and make it possible to fine-tune performance. At the same time, this makes operation more and more complex.

Clearly, some balance between flexibility and simplicity is needed. A hair dryer should have more than just one heat and speed, but there is no need for a large number. Appliance manufacturers are receiving more and more complaints about equipment that is so complicated it is hard to understand and use. Because there are more and more working women, it is important for appliances to be simple enough that the whole family can operate them easily.

A feature appearing on more appliances is automatic controls that monitor performance and make adjustments as needed. For example, sensors can check the dryness of clothes in a dryer and then stop the cycle when they are dry (*Consumer Reports,* May, 1986). Other features, such as the self-cleaning abilities of some stove ovens, save time and work. The self-cleaning feature, it should be noted, costs extra and requires extra electricity to operate. An increasing number of appliances incorporate microcomputers into the control system. These can provide convenience and improve performance. For example, the FM receivers in today's stereo amplifiers usually incorporate a microcomputer to tune in a station accurately which will minimize noise and distortion (*Consumer Reports*, July, 1984). Microprocessors are also found in some microwave ovens, washing machines, and dryers.

Providing special features is one way manufacturers differentiate their products. Some of these features are desirable and well worth their cost, while others are merely gimmicks of little real use.

Performance

A key consideration in judging different brands and models is how well they perform the job they are supposed to do. For example, how well does Brand Y cassette player record and reproduce sound? How well does a Brand X washing machine clean clothes?

Performance has several different dimensions, each of which may be of concern. *Consumer Reports* and other magazines that rate appliances typically point out aspects of performance they consider critical. These discussions can provide useful guidance on what to look for in an appliance. One evaluative criterion is the potential work the appliance is able to perform — its *capacity.*

In deciding on an appliance, it is important to choose the right capacity. One with too little capacity will not do the job, but excess capacity is unnecessary and a waste of money. Stereo buyers, for example, frequently purchase more capacity than they really need. For stereo amplifiers, capacity is the ability to drive speakers and is measured in watts of power. Amplifiers with twenty to forty watts of power are satisfactory for most purposes. Stereos with fifty watts or more of power are needed only for playing music loudly in very large rooms and are more expensive.

Stability of operation is another dimension of performance that is important in some appliances. An appliance that will perform without distortions and fluctuations is desirable. Sometimes these distortions are due to the design of the equipment itself. In other cases they are due to outside interference. Improperly designed stereo equipment, for example, may fluctuate in speed as tapes or records are played, with the result that sound is reproduced inaccurately. Outside interference from aircraft flying overhead can distort TV signals. Some TVs and VCRs have been found to resist this interference better than others.

Quietness of operation can also be a valued dimension of performance. Operating noises from kitchen appliances can be annoying, and background noises in stereos and radios are distracting. Some equipment controls unwanted noise better than others.

The best performance can be achieved if the user understands what equipment can do and becomes fully familiar with proper operating procedures. It is wise to read and save the instructions when a new appliance is acquired. Instructions, warranty information, and purchase receipts should be kept together in a file.

Durability

Unsatisfactory appliance repair service is a frequent headache for consumers. In some cases, the repairs do not solve the problem, or they may seem too expensive. In other cases there is disagreement over whether they should be covered under the terms of the warranty. These types of problems make trouble-free appliances especially valued by consumers.

It is wise to check out appliances as soon as possible after they are purchased and to make complaints promptly. This will make it easier to get the appliance repaired, or to get a replacement or refund quickly. Appliances sometimes fail during the initial break-in period. Electronic equipment is especially susceptible to this type of problem. Other problems may occur as a result of wear-and-tear over time. Mechanical parts and motors are susceptible to wear-and-tear.

As part of its ratings, *Consumer Reports* provides information on the frequency of repairs its subscribers have experienced with some major appliances. This information unfortunately is not available for smaller appliances and may not be applicable to new models.

Warranties. Since appliance repairs can be expensive and complicated, warranty coverage of new appliances is an important evaluative criterion. Warranties differ between brands on coverage. The parts covered and the length of coverage both differ. Coverage of labor costs may also differ. Warranties for some appliances, such as refrigerators and freezers, may provide for *consequential damages,* losses that result from the failure of an appliance. Warranties that do provide this coverage will reimburse the loss of spoiled food, but the amount of coverage is limited and typically the warranty runs for only a short period early in the life of the appliance. Again, because warranties do differ, it is wise to compare them systematically.

Because repair problems are almost inevitable, it is useful to find out, before purchasing, by whom repairs can be made. Just how accessible is the repair service organization that repairs equipment under warranty? How long does it typically take to get repairs? Local service usually is available for major appliances, but smaller appliances often have to be mailed to another location for servicing.

Consumers often ask if the registration cards enclosed with new appliances have to be mailed in to get warranty service. The answer is "no, but... ." Registration cards are used as evidence of date of purchase for determining the period of coverage for warranty repairs. Other evidence, such as a receipt indicating the item purchased and date, is also acceptable (Electronic Industries Association, 1984).

Repair Services. When appliances are no longer under warranty, experts recommend using factory-run or independent factory-authorized repair shops. While this service may be relatively expensive, there is greater assurance of competent work. Service for small appliances may be slow, especially if they have to be mailed away for service. Repairs to small appliances can also be costly in relation to the purchase price. Sometimes it is cheaper to replace a small appliance than to repair it, if the appliance is no longer under warranty.

When an appliance is not functioning properly, it is wise to make some preliminary checks before taking it for repairs or calling a repair shop. Many service calls are unnecessary and often the problems are simple ones. Common reasons for problems include:

- The appliance is unplugged.
- The circuit breaker or fuse is blown.
- The controls are not set properly.

Check the instruction book to determine if the appliance is being used correctly. Many instruction books have useful sections on diagnosing problems.

In choosing a repair shop, it is best to deal with an established firm that provides both an address and phone number. Some consumers who have called firms whose ads listed only phone numbers have allowed their appliances to be taken away for repair, only to find later that both their appliances and the repair company have disappeared.

Before requesting repairs, appliance owners should make certain they understand how charges are determined. Most firms make a charge for home service calls or in-shop diagnoses of a problem. This fee usually covers a description of the problem and an estimate of the cost of repairs. The charges for the actual repairs will be in addition to the diagnostic charges.

When turning in an appliance for repair, it is wise to get a claim check with the company's name, the date, a description of the appliance, and the technician's initials. The technician should be given clear instructions about what is to be done. If an estimate is desired before repairs are undertaken, this should be indicated.

When servicing is completed, the owner should insist on a service invoice with a description of the problem and what was done to solve it. There should be a list of parts replaced and their prices as well as a description of labor charges. This information will provide a basis for claims if a problem has not been fully corrected.

Complaints. Problems with an appliance or with repairs should be reported first to the retailer or repair shop and next to the manufacturer, as we discussed earlier. If problems are not resolved, two industry trade associations may be able to provide assistance:

- For electronic equipment including TVs, radios, stereos, and computers, contact:

    Electronic Industries Association
    Consumer Electronics Group
    2001 "Eye" Street, N.W.
    Washington, DC 20006

- For major appliances such as ranges, refrigerators, freezers, and home laundry equipment, contact:

Major Appliance Consumer Action Panel
20 N. Wacker Drive
Chicago, Il 60606

Cost

As noted, a key part of the cost of owning a consumer durable is its annual depreciation (the decline in value from one year to the next). Annual depreciation depends both on the initial cost of an item and its expected life. The lower the initial cost and the longer an appliance's life, the lower the annual depreciation costs will be.

Most appliances are available at discounts from list prices. In some cases, these list prices may be inflated to make the store's price appear more attractive. In addition to these discounts, most appliances are on sale periodically. It is smart to anticipate these sales if possible.

During sale periods, retailers typically feature promotional models provided by the manufacturer. These are low-priced models that are advertised heavily to draw shoppers into the store. Salespeople may try to convince interested shoppers to trade up to more expensive models. Typically promotional models are stripped and have a minimum of special features. Before buying, the shopper should understand exactly how the sale items differ from regular models.

The purchase of an appliance provides a flow of services over a number of years. It does, however, tie up the money invested so it cannot be devoted to other uses. As a result, the interest forgone has to be regarded as a cost. Operating costs also must be considered.

Energy Usage

As can be seen from Table 11-1, the annual operating costs of different appliances differ widely. Small appliances such as electric clocks cost little to operate. Appliances that involve heating and cooling (water heaters, refrigerators, and clothes dryers, for example) are, in contrast, heavy energy users.

Different brands and models use differing amounts of energy to do the same work. These differences in energy efficiency become particularly important for the appliances that are heavy energy users. To provide consumers comparable information on energy use, the federal government requires that appliances that use large amounts of energy carry energy efficiency labels. These labels indicate how efficient a particular model is compared to other models of similar capacity. The labels appear on refrigerators, air conditioners, clothes dryers, water heaters, and several other heavy energy users.

Some manufacturers are now offering new high-energy-efficiency models. These models typically are more costly because they include extra insulation, more efficient motors, and other special features. They do, however, offer

Table 11-1
Annual Energy Use of
Some Electrical
Appliances

Appliance	Estimated Kilowatt Hours Consumed Annually	Estimated Annual Operating Cost*
Water heater (quick recovery)	4,811	$367.08
Refrigerator (17.5 cubic feet, automatic defrost)	1,591	171.68
Clothes dryer	993	75.77
Air conditioner (room size −1000 hours of operation)	860	65.62
Electric range (with self-cleaning oven)	626	55.70
Electric range (with regular oven)	596	53.71
Dishwasher	165	27.70
Television (color, solid state)	100	24.42
Radio/record player	109	8.32
Hair dryer	25	1.91
Electric clock	17	1.30
Mixer	2	.15
Shaver	.5	.04

*Based on electric costs of 7.63 cents per kilowatt hour.
Source: From Edison Electric Institute, *Annual Energy Requirements of Electric Household Appliances.*
Washington, DC: Edison Electric Institute, 1984. Used by permission.

energy savings that can be significant. The extra cost of the more efficient appliance will be paid back in a relatively short time. Suppose, for example, that a more energy-efficient air conditioner costs $45 more, but saves $15 a year in operating costs. The payback period on the extra $45 spent for the energy-efficient model is only three years. The formula for computing the payback period is:

$$\frac{\text{extra cost of energy-efficient model } \$45}{\text{savings per year in operating costs } \$15} = 3.0 \text{ years}$$

The return on the extra investment is quick enough in relation to the projected life of the appliance that the higher-cost energy-efficient model seems a wise choice.

Heating and cooling costs constitute about half of total household energy costs. These costs make energy conservation efforts for heating and cooling especially worthwhile. Some general methods for reducing operating costs include:

Illustration 11-3
To encourage attention to energy usage as an evaluative criterion, the federal government requires energy efficiency labels on appliances that are heavy energy users.

- Choosing efficient equipment
- Keeping equipment in good operating condition
- Controlling waste and leakage
- Keeping unnecessary use to a minimum

Replacement Reserves. The young household that is fortunate enough to buy all new appliances does not have to deal with the problem of replacement right away. After five or six years, however, some small appliances will have to be replaced; after ten to twelve years, major appliances will begin to need replacement (see Table 11-2). The cost of these replacements can be sizable

Table 11-2
Estimated Service Life of New Home Appliances

Appliance	Estimated Service Life (years)
Electric range	12.1
Gas range	13.5
Refrigerator	15.2
Dishwasher	11.1
Washing machine	10.8
Electric clothes dryer	13.7
Gas clothes dryer	12.8

Source: From Katherine S. Tippett, "Service Life of Appliances by Selected Household Characteristics," *Family Economics Review* (Summer 1978): 7-13.

and often comes unexpectedly. The best way to prepare for replacing appliances is to build up a financial reserve as they depreciate. Accumulating a replacement fund has the double advantage of earning interest as it grows and eliminating the need to use credit when it is time to make a purchase.

Safety

Because of the energy sources used (electricity and gas), there are inherent safety hazards in appliances. Electrical shock hazards are particularly dangerous because they are not recognized until there is an accident.

Shock hazards are created by the leakage of electrical current from an appliance or electric cord (Reader's Digest, 1977). The leakage can be the result of worn insulation, poor design, or the absence of safety devices. Users can touch appliances with current leakage and be unaware of it. They will receive a shock only if they are in contact with a *ground*. A ground is a material that conducts electricity and is in contact with the earth. Both cold water pipes and puddles on a damp basement floor can be grounds.

When current is leaking from an appliance it seeks the shortest and easiest path to the earth. It will move through grounds. A person in contact with both an appliance with current leakage and a ground becomes part of the electric current's path to the earth and receives a shock. The danger of a shock is eliminated if the appliance is linked directly to the earth with a grounding wire. Grounding wires are built into some appliances with three-wire cords. The extra wire is connected to a ground with a three-prong plug or a "pig-tail" from the plug to the outlet box (see Figure 11-3). It also is possible to control shock hazards by insulating an appliance, such as an electric drill, against current leakage.

Shock hazards are a particular problem with electric hair dryers because they are often used near tubs and basins full of water and near cold water pipes that can serve as grounds. Safety experts advise against using hair dryers while in the tub or near a sink full of water because of the danger of electrocution (*Consumer Reports,* June, 1984). The danger of electric shock from hair dryers is not widely recognized, and each year there are a number of deaths from their misuse. Young children are particularly frequent victims. While hair dryers are plugged in, there is a danger of electric shock, even when the dryer is turned off, because the cord is "live" from the outlet box to the switch. If there are breaks in the insulation of the cord, there is a shock hazard. The best solution is prevention — keeping hair dryers away from water and water pipes.

MAJOR CHAPTER CONCEPTS

1. Important considerations in choosing household durables include design, performance, cost, and safety.

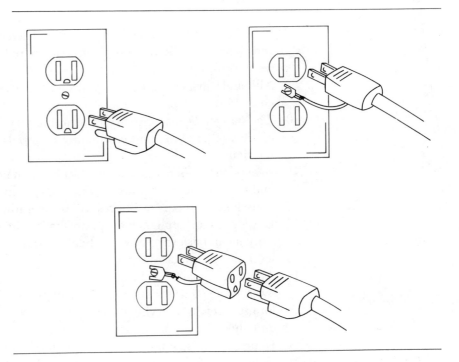

2. A frequent error among furniture shoppers is the failure to make an over-all plan before they begin to buy. The plan should account for the functions needed, the space available for each, and the furniture needed.

3. Furniture styles should be chosen with lifestyle preferences in mind. Styles can be divided into traditional and contemporary. Each of these categories includes formal and casual designs.

4. The frame of a furniture piece provides support for the panels used in case goods and the upholstery materials used in upholstered furniture. Frames of kiln-dried hardwood are recommended.

5. Veneers and solid wood are both widely used panel materials. Veneers are less expensive and less subject to warping.

6. Interlocking joints such as double-dowel joints, mortise and tenon joints, and dove-tail joints provide greater strength, especially when reinforced with corner blocks, than noninterlocking joints.

7. Upholstered furniture is constructed by placing padding and cushions over springs. Padding and cushion materials differ in performance. These materials used can be identified from the labels attached to the piece.

8. The fiber used in an upholstery fabric will determine both its durability and cleanability. Staining problems can be reduced by the use of stain-resistant finishes.

9. Although furniture pieces may last a lifetime, depreciation is a major cost of ownership.

10. The danger of mattress fires and upholstery fires has led to the use of fabrics, padding, and cushioning materials that reduce the risk of ignition.

11. In appliances, there often is a conflict between flexibility in performance and the simplicity of controls. Simplicity is important if a number of household members of all ages will be operating a piece of equipment.

12. In judging an appliance on performance, its capacity (the potential work it can perform), its stability of operation, and its operating noise level all are important.

13. Appliance repairs can be a major headache. Problems can be reduced by choosing models with lower frequency of repair, checking instructions for use carefully, knowing the protection provided by warranty coverage, and choosing a repair shop carefully.

14. Depreciation is a major cost of appliance ownership, but annual depreciation costs can be reduced by choosing less expensive appliances with long expected lives.

15. Appliances that provide heating and cooling are heavy energy-users. Energy efficiency labels can help to identify those that are most efficient.

16. A shock hazard may exist if there is current leakage in an electric appliance. Users will receive a shock, however, only when they are using the appliance and are in contact with a ground.

CONSUMER QUESTIONS

1. Suppose you needed to furnish a one-bedroom apartment with a living-room 12' by 18' and a bedroom 12' by 12'. (a) What functions would you want to include? (b) Where would you locate each function? (c) What furniture and appliances would you want for each area? Assume a refrigerator and range are furnished. (d) Develop low-cost and high-cost plans for equipping your apartment with furniture and appliances using price information from catalogs and visits to retail stores, used furniture and appliance stores, and unfinished furniture stores.

2. Suppose you bought a new two-bedroom condominium equipped with only a range and refrigerator. (a) List all of the appliances you would like to have, in the order you would acquire them. Explain the reasons for your priorities. (b) List all the furniture you would like to have in the order you would acquire it. Explain the reasons for your priorities.

3. Select an appliance item you would like to buy (for example, a stereo set). Read *Consumer Reports* and other information sources and visit stores and then report on the following questions. (a) What evaluative criteria do experts consider most important in judging this item? How would you rate these criteria on importance? (b) How do quality or the features offered differ at different price levels? (c) Of the different brands and models you've seen, which one would you prefer, and why?

4. Select an item of furniture you would like to own (for example, a desk or a lounge chair for reading). Visit stores and prepare a report on quality differences between two different price levels. (a) How do the materials used differ? (b) How do construction methods, including joining methods, differ? (c) How do the finish, hardware, and quality of workmanship differ? (d) Which piece do you think will give better service? Why?

5. Look around the place you live, the student lounge at school, and other furnished rooms. What signs of wear-and-tear do you see on the furniture? What is the cause of these problems? How could different furniture choices have helped to avoid some of these problems?

6. What conservation measures have you and your family taken to save energy around home? What other measures could you take? Since heating and cooling are the biggest energy users, which measures do you feel deserve first consideration? Rate each conservation measure you propose on how costly you feel it would be.

SUGGESTED READINGS

1. Better Homes and Gardens. *New Decorating Book*. Des Moines, Iowa: Meredith Corp., 1981. This popular and widely used guide to home design provides basic principles on color and style and applies them in actual rooms.

2. Gilliat, Mary. *The Complete Book of Home Design*. Boston: Little, Brown and Co., 1984. This extensive guide to home design and furnishing begins at the beginning with a consideration of what is needed and the development of a design plan and continues with a discussion of the selection of furniture and fabrics.

3. Kron, Joan. *Home-Psych: The Social Psychology of Home and Decoration*. New York: Clarkson N. Potter, 1983. Kron examines the influences on home and interior decoration choices. These influences include a desire to express one's individuality, the desire for status, an concern with family comfort, and a need to express group membership.

4. Reader's Digest. *Fix-It-Yourself Manual*. Pleasantville. N.Y.: Reader's Digest Association, 1977. This comprehensive guide for the repair of appliances, furniture, other household equipment, and automobiles provides information on dozens of simple repair jobs.

PART 3

MANAGING PERSONAL FINANCES

CHAPTER 12

PLANNING
SPENDING
AND SAVING

A few years ago an article entitled "Getting By On $100,000 a Year" appeared in a leading magazine. It detailed the financial problems of a young bachelor investment banker living in Manhattan. The unfortunate fellow, whose name was Stanley, was having serious difficulty making ends meet on his $105,000-a-year income. Stanley's sizable tax bill, vacation and entertainment expenses, and auto expenses were overwhelming him. In fact, Stanley had a deficit of $3,600 the previous year, according to the article.

The article provoked a storm of comment, largely unsympathetic. Most readers felt they would welcome a chance to try to manage on a similar income. Stanley's problems show that even a big income does not guarantee freedom from money difficulties. Expenses can exceed income and lead to financial strains at any income level.

Most people must manage with incomes far more modest than Stanley's. Fortunately, with good management, most people can achieve an acceptable level of satisfaction and even save some money.

This chapter will examine the basics of money management. The last section of the book looked at ways to get the best values on individual purchases. In this section, the whole range of personal financial decisions and how to handle them will be the focus of the discussion.

PERSONAL FINANCIAL MANAGEMENT

Management is a process of setting goals, making plans to reach those goals, and implementing the plans. Management makes sense only if the planner has clear goals in mind. Without goals, planning is pointless. Business firms set profit goals and sales and market share goals for their management efforts. What are appropriate goals for individuals and households?

Personal Financial Goals

The goal of personal financial management is to use personal and financial resources to produce a satisfactory level of daily living and to build financial reserves to meet future needs and emergencies. Management, thus, has both present goals and future goals. Of course, these two general categories of goals must be balanced against each other. Money spent now cannot be saved for the future, and borrowing for today's purchases creates an obligation that will reduce the money available for daily living in the future.

Planning for the future involves setting both short-term and long-term goals. Short-term goals may include building savings for some planned expenditure such as a vacation or a new car. Longer term goals may be more

Illustration 12-1
Accumulating money for a special vacation is a frequent short-term planning goal.

Virginia State Travel Service

CONSUMER CASE: AS AMERICANS SPEND, WARY JAPANESE SAVE

The 10 Americans at the table in Florham Park, N.J., are swapping stories about home buying. They talk of borrowing down payments, of "trading up" to bigger houses, of buying houses they can't really afford.

Halfway around the world in Tokyo, a group of Japanese consumers are telling radically different home-buying stories. They speak of saving for 10 or 15 years, of making big down payments, of buying their first and perhaps only housing when they are on the brink of middle age.

The two groups have been assembled by the Gallup Organization and the Nippon Research Center on behalf of this newspaper to explore the saving and spending habits of middle-class American and Japanese consumers. Both groups include men and women, married and single people, the young, the middle-aged and the elderly. But as the two conversations flow their separate ways, the differences grow wider and deeper.

The Americans are generally optimistic about the future and willing to take risks. They like to spend, so they have trouble saving. On the average they save only 7% of their after-tax income, slightly more than the U.S. average of 6%, the lowest in the developed world. By contrast, the Japanese are generally worried about the future and wary of risk. They are cautious about spending and save like crazy, giving Japan prolific savings rates, averaging more than 17% of after-tax income.

Why the enormous disparity? Radically different tax policies are certainly part of the reason. Interest income on savings of up to $58,000 is tax-free in Japan, but such income is taxable in the U.S. Capital-gains taxes in Japan are nonexistent in many cases, inconsequential in others. Interest payments on home mortgages aren't tax-deductible in Japan, so Japanese have far less incentive than Americans to look for the biggest house, the biggest mortgage, and the biggest tax shelter they can possibly find.

"I think everybody we know buys more house than they can really afford," says William McCormick, 31, a dairy-company salesman and member of the group gathered in New Jersey. (He recently bought a bigger house.) Those who have small mortgage payments seem almost ashamed. Andrew Bruner, a retired schoolteacher whose mortgage is only $200 a month, says, "We could have bought more house, and we should have. I wish we had."

The mentality is different in Japan, where richer and poorer are more likely to live side by side, and where being conspicuous is unforgivable. "I'm the managing director of a bank," explains Hiroshi Takeuchi, chief economist of the Long-Term Credit Bank of Japan. "You might expect that I'd wear a fancy tiepin or something. Not in Japan. If I wore a diamond tiepin or diamond cuff links, people would despise me. That's why even most rich people don't build grand homes."

Other cultural constraints may also keep Japanese savings rates high. Pensions are relatively low by Western standards. Many Japanese still work six days a week, with correspondingly small amounts of leisure time. Some economists believe that the economic hardships of World War II and its aftermath have left today's adult Japanese with an ineradicable strain of frugality.

The tradition of semiannual bonuses, which account for nearly 20% of the average worker's annual salary, also appears to encourage the Japanese propensity for thrift: Surveys show that the overall savings rate leaps to more than 40% during the June and December bonus seasons.

More important, perhaps, land in Japan is expensive, house and apartment prices are high, and down payments average 32% of the purchase price. As a result, the Japanese spend many years saving the down payments.

Some of the New Jerseyans say they plunge fearlessly into debt because of a basic optimism about the future. Mr. Ash, the man who bought his house while unemployed, came out a winner. He says he was offered a chance to sell his house at a profit, just two weeks after he bought it. He didn't sell. Today, nine years later, the house has tripled in value.

Members of the Tokyo group are much less confident of rising values. Condominiums, particularly small ones, are seen as risky purchases.

The Americans were far more tolerant of building up credit-card debt than their Japanese counterparts. Asked what they would do if $5,000 fell out of the sky, several of the Americans said they would use the money to reduce their credit-card balances. None of the Japanese said they would use $5,000 that way. The ones who use credit cards normally wipe the slate clean after the end of each month.

Of the eight people gathered around the table in Tokyo, Dr. Amari and Kozo Kirata, a 51-year-old accountant, are the only ones who use credit cards very much. The younger members of the group generally shun cards. They buy electronic goods and appliances through friends who work in such companies and who get them discounts. Or they head for a Tokyo neighborhood called Akihabara, where everything is routinely sold at 20% discount. "There are advantages to credit cards," says Masatoski Takahashi, 26, an employee in the marketing department of the J. Osawa trading company. "But there are a lot of other ways to get things cheaply."

Source: Taken from Bernard Wysocki, Jr., and Christopher J. Chipello, "As Americans Spend, Wary Japanese Save, and Taxes Are a Cause," *Wall Street Journal* 25 July 1985: 1ff. Reprinted by permission of *Wall Street Journal*, © Dow Jones & Company, Inc. 1985. All Rights Reserved.

QUESTIONS

1. Why do the Japanese consumers see their financial situation as more risky than the Americans see theirs?
2. How can we explain the differences in savings rates between Americans and Japanese?
3. What factors are identified as influencing the home-purchasing decisions of Americans? Of Japanese?

general. They may involve saving for purchasing a home, for educating children, or for meeting living expenses after retirement.

Excuses for Failing to Manage

Most people recognize the need to develop and carry out plans for managing their money, but somehow many of them never really get around to taking action. Some people make the excuse that there isn't really any point in trying to manage their finances. Because they do not have any money to spare, there is no way they can save anything, and it is all going to be spent.

Others give the excuse that even if they could save, they could not save enough for it to be worthwhile. Then there are some who say that they simply do not have enough time to manage their finances. There are just too many other demands on their daily schedule.

All these excuses ignore the importance of management as a way of avoiding financial difficulties. They also ignore the importance of forming good management habits when incomes are small as a way of preparing to manage larger future incomes.

Excuses for not trying to manage personal finances may hide psychological problems. Some people are reluctant to take charge of their own lives. The prospect of being responsible for what happens to them seems frightening. Can they trust their own judgment? What if they make a mistake?

Others may be unable to manage because their life is dominated by the need to impress others, though no amount of money, however large, is completely adequate to do this. And some people are unable to control their spending because it is a way to escape boredom and find excitement. Then there are those who are reluctant to make financial plans because they feel that planning shows a level of concern with money that is materialistic and somehow immoral.

For a few people, these psychological excuses are linked to problems so serious they require treatment, but most people can move beyond these excuses once they recognize them for what they are. They can then use financial planning to move toward their personal goals.

DIMENSIONS OF FINANCIAL MANAGEMENT

A successful financial plan has a number of parts. For most people, all or most of these parts must be present for the plan to be useful and effective.

Record Keeping

The starting place for financial planning is a good set of financial records, including bank statements, copies of insurance policies, investment records, and other key papers. (See Consumer Capsule, "Keeping Personal Records.") Along with these records, a spending record is needed. It should record income received and expenditures. Spending records for one or two past months provide a basis for other aspects of planning, particularly budgeting.

Budgeting

A spending record is a summary of what has been received and spent, but it is not a budget. A *budget* (or spending plan) is a plan for spending that reflects personal goals. A budget looks ahead and sets down a spending plan for future months. A spending record sets down only what has been spent in the past.

Savings and Investment Planning

One of the chief goals of a budget is to allot savings for building financial reserves to meet future needs. *Savings* are possible when income is greater than money spent. Most of us put our savings to work to earn a return by investing them. *Investments* can provide returns in the form of interest and dividends, increases in resale value, or tax advantages.

Tax Planning

The development of a plan to limit one's tax obligations often is clearly linked to investment choices. Certain kinds of investments offer tax advantages because the interest earned is tax-free or because the investment allows deductions from taxable income.

Tax-sheltered retirement plans permit workers to invest a portion of their earnings in special accounts and pay taxes on this income and what it has earned only after it is withdrawn. Tax law changes, such as those in federal tax laws for income earned in 1987 and after, may make periodic changes in strategies to reduce taxes necessary.

Managing Risk

Individual consumers face a number of kinds of unexpected events that can disrupt their financial well-being. *Risks* include the range of possible situations facing the consumer. An auto accident, for example, can have several outcomes: (1) the car is totally destroyed, or (2) it is just a fender-bender, or (3) there is no damage or injuries. Generally, consumers are concerned with downside risks, situations with negative effects. Individuals can manage risks by purchasing insurance to protect against financial loss, by building financial reserves for use in case of a loss, or a combination of both.

Estate and Retirement Planning

Individual workers also need to plan for income for the time when they no longer wish to work or are unable to. Pension plans, Social Security, and personal savings are the basic tools for retirement planning. Workers with family responsibilities also need to develop plans to provide incomes for their families in the event they die or are disabled. Combinations of life and disability insurance, Social Security, and savings can be developed to meet those needs.

Career Planning

The aspects of financial management that have been discussed so far deal chiefly with how earned income is used. A broad-scale financial plan con-

CONSUMER CAPSULE: KEEPING PERSONAL RECORDS

Types of Records	Suggested Location	Uses	How Long to Keep
Financial			
Cancelled checks; bank statements; check registers	Home files	Proof of payment; establish tax deductions	Cancelled checks — as needed for as long as needed for tax purposes
Savings account passbooks and statements	Home files; record of account number in safety deposit box	Deposits and withdrawals; determining interest earned and net worth	For duration of account
Savings certificates	Safety deposit box	Determining interest earned and net worth	Until maturity
Credit card numbers and office addresses	Home files	Reporting lost cards	For duration of account
Stocks; bonds; other securities	Safety deposit box or deposit with broker; description in home file	Determining earnings and net worth; making buy and sell decisions	For duration of ownership; keep description as long as needed for tax purposes
Net worth records	Home files	Determining financial progress from year to year	Indefinitely
Property			
Real estate deeds; title papers; mortgages	Safety deposit box	Establishing proof of ownership; documenting insurance claims; preparing tax returns	For duration of ownership or long as needed for tax purposes
Evidence of cost of home purchase and home improvement expenditures	Safety deposit box and home files	Establishing cost of residences and improvements for income tax	Indefinitely

Inventory of household possessions	Safety deposit box; copy in home file	Documenting insurance claims	Indefinitely; up-date regularly
Motor vehicle titles and service records	Title in safety deposit box; records in home file	Establishing proof of ownership; documenting warranty claims	For duration of ownership
Other warranties and proofs of date purchase	Home files	Documenting warranty claims; proof of ownership	For duration of ownership
Taxes			
Tax returns (copies) with receipts; records of tax payments	Home files	Establishing proof of deductions; figuring taxes	Minimum of six years
Insurance			
Policies	Home files with record of policy numbers in safety deposit box	Settling estate; filing claims	For duration of policies
Personal and Family			
Will	Original copy with attorney or in safety deposit box; copy in home file	Settling estate	Indefinitely
Birth, marriage and death certificates, divorce papers, military service papers	Safety deposit box	Settling estate; obtaining insurance, Social Security, and other benefits	Indefinitely
Social Security card	Carry card in wallet, stub in home files	Providing identification number to employers; establishing eligibility for benefits	Indefinitely

Source: "Personal Record Keeping" Consumer Information Report 21 (San Francisco: Bank of America, 1978); Sylvia Porter, *Sylvia Porter's New Money Book for the 80s* (Garden City, NY: Doubleday and Co., 1979).

siders not only earned income but also the succession of jobs used to earn it. Career choices are closely linked to other parts of a financial plan. If money is borrowed for college expenses, plans will have to provide for repaying it in the future; but at the same time, what has been earned should make it possible to earn more after graduation. College, therefore, can be looked at as a type of investment.

From this discussion it is evident that the different aspects of financial planning are related. It is impossible to develop a budget without accurate records. It is also impossible to build savings or pay for a car insurance policy without finding money to pay for it in the budget.

This discussion makes financial planning sound like a great deal of work, but it does have significant payoffs. As plans take shape, reaching set goals and knowing that financial resources have been used wisely are positive, rewarding experiences. Peace of mind comes from knowing your obligations are met and creditors are paid. Successes build self-esteem, an asset that is invaluable to us as workers, family members, and friends.

Because the subject of financial management is complex, a whole section of this book is devoted to its major parts. The remainder of this chapter is devoted to record keeping and budgeting. Following chapters are devoted to savings, investments, consumer credit, insurance, and taxes.

BUILDING A BUDGET

As noted, a budget is a plan for managing money in order to achieve financial goals. Budgets have several purposes:

- Planning the allocation of money among spending categories in order to achieve selected goals
- Providing a mechanism for balancing spending with income
- Monitoring changes in spending and in the level of savings and debts

A Comprehensive Approach to Budgeting

Many approaches to budgeting focus chiefly on spending. They emphasize setting spending limits for individual categories and keeping actual spending within these limits. A more comprehensive approach seems needed, one which takes full account of income and changes in the level of debts and savings.

Years ago, households seldom had debts other than a mortgage and a car loan. It was unusual to carry debts over from month to month on a credit card or charge account. Now the widespread availability of lines of credit has made it easy for consumers to carry debts for months and even years. A comprehensive picture of your financial situation has to include additions to savings and debts and reductions in savings and debts.

A cash-flow budget of the type shown in Figure 12-1 provides the needed detail. It provides six types of essential information:

Figure 12-1
Cash Flow Budget

	January	February
Cash Balance		

At beginning of month
  (cash on hand, checking account balance)

Add: Cash inflows

  Wages, salary
  Interest earnings
  Investment gains
  Gifts
  Other (bonuses, scholarships, etc.)
  Miscellaneous _____

    Total inflows
    Total cash available

Less: Cash outflows

  Food
  Rent
  Utilities and household supplies
  Household equipment and furniture
  Clothing (including laundry and cleaning)
  Auto expenses
  Other transportation
  Medical and dental care
  Education expenses (tuition, books, fees)
  Contributions (donations, gifts, etc.)
  Dues (clubs, etc.)
  Recreation
  Reading materials (newspapers and
    magazines)
  Taxes
  Miscellaneous _____

    Total outflows
    Surplus (deficit)

Transfer to savings

Transfer from savings

Additional borrowing

Repayment of borrowing

Interest payments

Cash balance
At end of month
  (cash on hand, checking account balance)

- Beginning and ending cash
- Cash inflows
- Cash outflows
- Changes in savings (increases and decreases)
- Changes in debt (increases and decreases)
- Interest payments

Preparing a Spending Plan

Before spending patterns can be adjusted, you need a clear picture of your past spending. A record of spending for one or two recent months can provide this information. A spending record can be developed by reconstructing what has been spent in recent months from check stubs, receipts, and memory. Detailed records can also be kept for a month or two to accumulate the needed information.

With a spending record in hand, planning for the future can begin. Experts suggest that beginners plan a budget only one or two months ahead (Porter, 1979). They know that as budgeters gain experience they recognize the need for changes and adjustments.

The categories used in a spending plan should be adapted to your personal needs. Students may wish to have separate categories for tuition and fees, books, supplies, and so on. If they live in a dorm or rent an apartment, they will not need the detailed categories home owners might need for expenditures such as home repairs and upkeep; heating; electricity; water, sewage, and trash removal; cleaning supplies; and so forth.

The length of time covered by a budget estimate has to be adapted to personal needs too. If income is received on a monthly basis and most bills come monthly, planning a budget one month at a time makes sense. If most income is received on a weekly basis and rent and other major expenses are paid weekly, planning spending for a week may be appropriate.

Estimates of future spending should be based on past experiences and bills that will be coming. It is important to include major expenses that are coming up in future months—car insurance bills, tax bills, tuition charges, etc. These expenses arise only periodically, but because of their size it is important to plan ahead for them. One way to deal with large periodic expenses is to build savings reserves so as to have money on hand to meet them. Another approach, of course, is to borrow in months when expenses are heavy and then repay later.

The spending plan and the amount allocated to individual categories should reflect personal goals and values as well as your personal situation. If you want an expensive car, you might spend less on clothing and housing. If your rent is high, other expenses may have to be reduced, but that is your choice. Average spending patterns frequently are offered as guides to planning spending, but it is smart to remember that they are averages — a blend of a number of different people's spending plans. Averages cannot and do not take account of individual preferences and unusual situations. The averages in Table 12-1, for example, probably do not match the spending of any individual household.

A frequent budget problem is dealing with a sizable debt load. Monthly payments have to be met to protect credit standings and meet contractual obligations. Some financial experts suggest that it is unwise to let debts build beyond a point where monthly payments (not including mortgage payments) exceed 20 percent of take-home pay.

Table 12-1
Average Annual
Expenditures of Urban
Consumer Units,
1982-83

Food, at home	$2,204
Food, away from home	933
Alcoholic beverages	285
Housing (rental or ownership costs)	3,262
Utilities, heating	1,489
Household operations	271
Furnishings and household equipment	762
Apparel and care services	1,030
Auto expenses	3,484
Public transportation	228
Health care	822
Entertainment	870
Personal care services	176
Reading	127
Education	274
Tobacco	205
Miscellaneous	270
Cash contributions	576
Life insurance, other insurance	258
Retirement, pensions, Social Security	1,367
Total expenditures	$18,892
Income before taxes	$22,702

Consumer Unit Characteristics

Number of persons	2.6
Number of earners	1.3
Number of children under 18	.7
Percentage of homeowners	60.0
Number of vehicles	1.8

Source: Bureau of Labor Statistics, *Consumer Expenditure Survey Results from 1982-83,* Press release, September 1985.

It is possible to accumulate large, and perhaps excessive, debts using this rule. The minimum monthly payments required on bank credit cards are small. These payments typically cover the monthly finance charge and make a modest reduction in the amount owed. A $60 to $75 monthly payment may be all that is needed to stay current on a $2,000 debt. Even though borrowers may be able to meet the required payments, they may find it difficult to pay off the underlying debt.

Making Revisions

As you accumulate experience, you can make further adjustments in your budget. For example, if drycleaning and laundry costs have not been included in the budget, money to pay for them must be found.

Discussions of budgeting often speak of fixed and variable expenses. They suggest that expenses such as food and clothing are *variable* because they can be adjusted. Others, such as rent and car payments, are called *fixed* because they have been set by contract. It should be recognized that, over time, fixed budget items can be adjusted. If the rent is too high, moving somewhere cheaper can be the solution. A car can be sold and replaced with something cheaper if the payments prove unmanageable.

Strategies for Making a Budget Work

For many people, the only money available for savings is what is left at the end of the month. Too often nothing is left. To insure that high-priority savings goals are met, savings should be taken out at the *beginning of the month*, rather than being treated as a month-end residual (Porter, 1979). Budgeting experts suggest the rule of "pay yourself first"; that is, put aside savings before beginning to pay others for purchases.

There are several approaches to making saving easier. One technique is to arrange a payroll deduction at work. A variety of savings vehicles may be available, such as U.S. savings bonds, stock purchase plans, and tax-sheltered savings (accounts on which income taxes are postponed until withdrawal). Another technique is to arrange an automatic transfer each month from a checking account into a savings account. Banks are happy to make this arrangement. A third approach is to enter into a contractual agreement that requires regular payments. A variety of insurance, savings, and investment plans are based on this type of arrangement.

A workable record-keeping plan also is essential for keeping a budget working. If the records required are too complex and keeping them is too time consuming, the budgeting process is likely to be abandoned.

Some people feel most comfortable with very simple budgeting approaches. One popular and widely used budget technique is what has been called the envelope or sugar bowl method. This technique requires a minimum of written records. On payday, the amount of money available for each budget category is put into the appropriate envelope or container. As bills arise, money is taken out to pay them. As the month progresses, money may have to be shuffled between categories, but it is easy to see where the money goes and what obligations are left.

The envelope method does have its disadvantages. Keeping large amounts of cash on hand creates a risk of loss, and there is always a temptation to shuffle cash from one category to another without a real plan. Money may be taken from the grocery account even though it is clear there will be grocery bills to be met later in the month. The envelope method does have the advantage that it is concrete and easily understood and no complicated record keeping is involved. For this reason, this method is especially appropriate for people who are not comfortable with complex record-keeping techniques.

Comprehensive written records work well for people who are comfortable with more abstract budgeting techniques. They do not need to handle cash to understand what is going on. They can see what is happening simply by looking at their written records. For this group, records such as the one shown in Figure 12-1 may work well.

MEASURING FINANCIAL PROGRESS

The management process really is not complete without a method to measure progress toward the goals that have been set. The most widely used method of measuring financial progress is changes in net worth. *Net worth* is the difference between what you own and what you owe. Year-to-year increases in net worth are an indication of financial growth. Net worth is calculated by determining the difference between *assets* (the value of cash on hand, investments, and possessions) and *liabilities* (debts, loans, and other obligations).

A systematic listing of assets and liabilities is called a *balance sheet*. After all assets and liabilities are listed, net worth can be determined and indicated on the balance sheet. Net worth can, of course, be positive or negative. If liabilities are less than assets, net worth will be positive. If liabilities exceed assets, the balance will be negative. Figure 12-2 shows a sample balance sheet.

Determining Assets

To prepare a personal balance sheet, it is usually necessary to do some preliminary research. The same records discussed earlier in this chapter will be needed. Current balances can be determined from your checking and savings account records.

Other assets that can easily be converted to cash can also be included in the "cash" category. These include certificates of deposit and government savings bonds. Another, less visible asset is the cash value of life insurance,

Figure 12-2
Personal Balance Sheet

Assets		Liabilities	
<u>Cash</u>		<u>Current Obligations</u>	
Cash on hand	_____	Charge account debt	_____
Checking account	_____	Bank and travel credit card debt	_____
Savings account	_____	Other major personal bills due	_____
Money market account	_____	Taxes due	_____
Certificates of deposit	_____	<u>Mortgage Debt</u>	
Government savings bonds	_____	Balance owed on mortgage	_____
Life insurance cash value	_____	<u>Loan Debt</u>	
<u>Marketable Securities</u>		Auto loans	_____
Stocks	_____	Educational loans	_____
Bonds	_____	Life insurance loans (loans against cash value)	_____
Mutual funds	_____		
Other investments	_____	<u>Personal Debts</u>	
<u>Personal Property</u>		Debts owed to others	_____
Automobiles	_____		
Collectibles, jewelry	_____		
<u>Real Estate</u>			
Home	_____		
Other real estate	_____		
<u>Employee Benefits</u>			
Refundable contributions to retirement fund	_____		
<u>Other</u>	_____		
Debts owed you by others	_____		
Security deposits (on apartments, etc.)	_____		
Business interests	_____		
Tax-sheltered investments (e.g., IRA and Keogh accounts)	_____		
Total Assets	_____	Total Liabilities	_____
		Net Worth (assets minus liabilities)	_____

which is the amount that could be borrowed from the insurance company against the policy or the amount that would be received if the policy were cancelled. Cash values are sometimes listed in the policy. If not, an insurance agent can provide information on cash value.

Another important group of assets, for some people, is investments in marketable securities. These investments include stocks, bonds, mutual fund holdings, and other similar investments. The value of stocks and bonds can be determined by checking financial market quotations in the newspaper. A stock broker can also provide this information.

The appropriate value to list for a car is the wholesale value (what a dealer would pay), not the retail value (what a retailer would charge). An approximate value can be determined from the wholesale "blue book." Most car dealers and bank auto loan departments have a current copy.

Other important personal property should be included among assets. This property may include valuable collections (e.g., stamp and coin collections) and expensive jewelry that could be sold in an emergency. For an estimate of the value of these items, the help of an expert appraiser may be needed. In deciding on a value of such items, the emphasis should be their value for resale, not their sentimental value.

Illustration 12-2
Homeowners' share of the resale value of their home is an asset that typically increases from year to year.

Some people include the value of household furniture, appliances, and clothing among their assets. While these items are valuable to their owners and their replacement would be costly, their resale value often is neglible. Including them in a balance sheet may be more trouble than it is worth.

A home is probably most people's most important asset. It should be listed at current market value, less sales commissions and costs. Those who are employed may want to include the value of their retirement contributions. This amount is what would be received upon leaving the company. Workers who have earned guaranteed pension rights sometimes include the value of future pension payments as an asset. Other assets that should be listed include amounts owed by others, any refundable security deposits, business interests not listed earlier, and tax-sheltered investments.

Determining Liabilities

The next step in determining net worth is putting together a complete listing of all debts and financial obligations. This list should include current obligations such as debts on bank, department store, and gasoline credit cards. It should include other major personal bills and taxes that are due, as well.

Liabilities also include the amount still owed on real estate mortgages and car loans. Educational loans should be listed. Loans against the cash value of life insurance, if any, should be included. Debts owed to others (e.g., debts you owe friends and family) should also be included.

Determining Net Worth

The difference between total assets and total liabilities is *net worth*. The balance is often negative for young adults because they borrow to buy cars and household items and to purchase a home but have had little time to accumulate assets. Young people many also have a negative net worth because they have outstanding educational loans. Prevailing financial practice does not permit showing the human capital created by an education as an asset.

A household's net worth typically grows over the family life cycle. The "empty nest stage," after children have left home, is often a period of rapid asset accumulation (Engel, Blackwell, & Miniard, 1986). As a result, household net worth usually peaks about the time of retirement. It then may be gradually drawn down to meet retirement needs.

HOW CONSUMERS GET INTO FINANCIAL DIFFICULTY

Every year hundreds of thousands of consumers get into serious financial difficulty. The result is a continuing flood of repossessions of cars and appliances bought on credit, personal bankruptcies, and defaults on home mortgages. Just how do so many people get into such serious financial difficulties?

Those who are familiar with the consumer credit scene say that in a major share of cases the cause is poor money management: Incomes that would be adequate if handled properly have been mismanaged. In some cases, consumers are overwhelmed by an accumulation of consumer debts. One credit account after another is added and used to its limit. Eventually the total becomes unmanageable. Part of the responsibility here is the banks' and retailers'. They often are too casual in granting credit and frequently are unaware of an applicant's existing debts. A major share of the responsibility is, however, the consumer's. New obligations are taken on without any clear idea of how they will be met.

Other money management problems are a result of what has been called the "money illusion," the failure to adjust ideas about what a given income will buy for inflationary price increases. Victims of the "money illusion" may get the idea that a $25,000 income is big money, the kind of income that will finance a large house and two new cars with ease. It could have done that 25 years ago! Inflation has seriously eroded buying power in the years since.

Those in consumer finance indicate that young people frequently suffer from another kind of illusion: the idea that they can start off with a lifestyle similar to the one it has taken their parents two or three decades to achieve. Young people with this illusion need to lower their expectations a bit. They overspend and overborrow and may realize how deep they are in debt only after it is too late.

Another major cause of financial distress is inadequate reserves for emergencies and insufficient insurance. Too many households are vulnerable to car accidents in which losses exceed their insurance coverage. These losses may include heavy medical expenses and costly lawsuits. Other families find themselves unprepared for unemployment and layoffs (Herrmann, 1966).

A smaller number of consumers get themselves into difficulty with unwise investments. They borrow money to pursue a highly promoted "opportunity" without checking it out thoroughly. When the opportunity fades, they are left with a heavy debt and nothing with which to repay impatient lenders.

Financial problems frequently appear together with marital problems. As a marriage fails, communications usually break down. Whatever financial coordination existed previously disappears. At the same time, a desire for revenge, a wish to "get a fair share," and a need to repair battered feelings may take over. Each spouse begins indulging what had been controlled. The result is a spending surge just as the marriage goes on the rocks, further complicating an already difficult situation.

CONSUMER CASE: SAVING AND SPENDING IN THREE GENERATIONS

This case is abridged from an article published in the *Wall Street Journal* a few years ago. The values described remain important despite the passage of time.

The three generations of the Heldman family are all middle-class Americans, born and raised here. They all still live here, too, although their feelings about money suggest they inhabit different worlds.

In many ways they do. Each came of age in a different economic era. And each occupies a different stage of the family's own economic evolution. The Heldmans have been neither destitute nor extremely rich. Like thousands of other American families, they knew hard times in the 1930s, growing prosperity in the 1950s and 1960s, and taken-for-granted comfort in the 1970s.

Figuring out how people like the Heldmans view money is the chief preoccupation of the country's most-powerful financial institutions, which are warring among themselves for bigger shares of the $5 trillion of personal assets held in the U.S. Increasingly, these institutions find themselves in the unfamiliar position of psychologists, trying to fathom the different attitudes that guide each generation. What they're discovering is that each age group seems to have sharply different assumptions about saving, spending, and investing.

"People who came of age in the 1970s take certain material advantages for granted," says Sandra Shaber, a senior economist with Chase Econometrics, the economic research unit of Chase Manhattan Corp. Their forebears, she says, were taught by the Depression that both income and assets could disappear quickly. As a result, the older generations are more inclined to save than spend, and they put a premium on safety.

While every family is different, the Heldmans represent many of the attitudes that financial institutions are trying to decipher and cash in on. Mrs. Heldman, who worked for 45 years in a dress shop just to get by, remains fearful of falling behind in her obligations, even though she is now financially secure. Today, she still refuses to carry credit cards or incur any form of debt. Her main concern is holding on to what she has.

Her grandson Tim carries eight credit cards and prizes their convenience and the easy access to his money. He is wary of the stock market, but earlier this year he had no qualms about buying a house even though he had to borrow $8,000 from his father to cover the down payment. Because he has a hard time saving, Tim Heldman, who is single, views his $480-a-month mortgage payments as a form of forced saving. He bought a $50,000 whole-life insurance policy for the same reason.

In the middle is Tom Heldman, who has spent three decades building his assets and who strongly believes in the stock market. His chief financial worry these days is that inflation will reignite and plague his retirement years by gnawing away at all he has stored up.

The way people handle money as adults often depends on how much of it they had while they were growing up. Tom Heldman, the chief financial officer of Southwestern Ohio Steel Inc., still remembers a childhood of doing without. He has one brother, William, now an Aspen, Colo., real-estate man. Their father pursued a hit-and-miss career that mostly missed. In 1944, the two boys' parents were divorced, but long before that their mother had to work to make ends meet at a time when middle-class working mothers were still uncommon. As a result, "I have always had this compelling desire to succeed," says Tom Heldman, a compact man with thick, curly gray hair and a ready smile.

His success in his present job and earlier in the accounting profession has been largely of his own making. He decided on accounting after being "mind-boggled" by the $7-an-hour salary described by a visiting accountant at a high-school career day in 1941—a time when many people were working for 40 cents an hour. After serving in the Army during World War II, he studied accounting at Northwestern University on the GI Bill.

The late 1940s for Tom Heldman and millions of other Americans marked the end of a sobering era of Depression and war. It seemed that only opportunity lay ahead. In 1947, 23-year-old Tom Heldman joined a predecessor of the accounting firm of Deloitte, Haskins & Sells in Cincinnati. Believing that America would blossom again, he decided to buy a piece of that future. His early strategy: the purchase every week of one share of American Telephone & Telegraph common stock.

STARTING FROM SCRATCH

Investing in the stock market was central to Tom Heldman's plan for building a financial base. While fundamentally cautious, he wasn't scared off by the vicissitudes of the market. "I never had the feeling that anything disastrous could happen to me," he says. "I was starting from a base of zero."

The times were with him and with many others who shared his optimistic outlook. The Dow Jones industrial average ran from 235.40 at the end of 1950 to a high of 985.21 in late 1968, while the inflation rate was inching up only about 2.4% a year during those two decades. Tom Heldman's share of the market surge enabled him to finance his first house, which cost $25,000, in 1956, when Tim, his first child, was three months old. Today, the Heldmans occupy a $175,000 house, and Tom's stock portfolio, heavy with old favorites such as IBM and Procter & Gamble, is "in excess" of $500,000, he says.

Tim Heldman's childhood was the inverse of his father's. As Tom Heldman prospered, his three sons enjoyed summer camps, travel in Europe and membership in the Loganwood Country Club. Still, Tim absorbed a heavy dose of his father's work ethic and generally conservative outlook. As a teen-ager, he picked up summer jobs; later, he followed his father into the accounting profession, and he now works at Price Waterhouse & Co.

LEGACY OF THE SEVENTIES

But Tim Heldman was also influenced by the turbulent economic times that shaped the rest of his generation. His attitude toward money sometimes makes his father wince. While Tom Heldman saved and built, Tim mostly spends. "I was never concerned about where my next dollar was coming from," he says. "If I spent all the money in my checking account, it wouldn't be the end of the world." His two brothers, Andy, 24, a medical technologist, and Kenny, 19, a college student, share the same viewpoint, "only more so," their father says with a laugh.

The Hudson Institute, a New York research organization, recently concluded in a study that the postwar generation enjoys "real purchasing power (that) is much higher than that of their parents at the same age." The study notes: "They have more income and credit to manage and higher material expectations."

Tim Heldman already has bought his own country-club membership. He recently purchased a 280-Z Datsun sports car for $11,000. (Says his father, who drives a 1978 Buick: "I wouldn't have minded if he bought a Chevy sedan, but he buys a 280-Z!") In appearance, Tim Heldman is a younger, more expensive version of his father. "He buys his clothers at Brooks Brothers," sighs Tom Heldman with a grin. "I didn't and still don't."

Tim acknowledges he likes the good life, but adds that his expensive tastes aren't purely sybaritic. The Brooks Brothers suits and country-club membership are ways to enhance his career at Price Waterhouse, he says. He is trying to enhance that career in less flashy ways, too, such as taking accounting courses at night for a tax specialty. "Everything I do is pretty much career oriented," he says.

BUYING A DIAMOND
Whereas young Tom Heldman gradually built a portfolio of blue-chip stocks, his son's first investment was a diamond, bought for $500 from a dealer who went bankrupt shortly afterward. Again, his son's behavior baffled the father. "I'm not averse to risk," says Tom Heldman. "I'm averse to foolishness, like buying a diamond or buying a fancy car."

In fairness, Tim Heldman, like thousands of other investors, was drawn to unorthodox investments like diamonds, gold, and silver in the late 1970s and 1980s because they had appreciated hugely in those inflationary years. And, despite his usually good-natured criticisms of his son's financial habits, Tom Heldman recognizes the surrounding economic forces that helped shape his son's attitudes. He admits to a glimmer of envy, too. "I think Timmy is having a lot more fun that I did when I was his age," he says.

For Tim's grandmother, the magnitude of changes spanning the generations is flabbergasting. "Our grandchildren are like everybody's grandchildren," says Jean Heldman, a tiny attractive woman. "When they want anything, they get it."

Mrs. Heldman didn't feel financially secure until she was in her 60s, when she received

A POSSIBLE SOURCE OF HELP— FINANCIAL PLANNERS

Managing personal finances can be tricky. Many of the problems are complex and interrelated, and decision making is further complicated by continuing changes in tax laws and in the kinds of investment opportunities available. Many people find identifying their goals and considering their alternatives bewildering. Where can you find help? And who can be trusted?

The need for comprehensive financial advice has given rise in the last decade to a new profession—the financial planner. A qualified planner can provide the kind of advice needed by those who want to manage and invest an inheritance from two elderly aunts. That inheritance enabled her 20 years ago to move into the comfortable suburban apartment building where she still lives in an efficiency apartment. She leaves management of her money to advisers chosen by her son, Tom. Occasionally, she voices a concern for safety, so recently her son transferred funds held in a money-market fund to an insured bank account offering money-market rates.

A NO-FRILLS EXISTENCE

Other than the purchase of a $300 black-seal fur coat shortly after her marriage in 1919, Mrs. Heldman remembers no frills in a life that revolved around paying for necessities. She managed her family's limited budget before and after her divorce, when Tom was 21, but, she says, "I don't remember ever, ever talking about money." As for investing in those days, she shakes her head and looks mildly indignant. "Why, there was nothing to invest," she says.

In Mrs. Heldman's day, there were far fewer options for how people saved or invested money, largely because for most people there wasn't any money to invest, says Irving Leveson, director of economic studies for the Hudson In-

stitute. "In the earlier generations, financial management was a question of dealing with problems day to day." Like her mother-in-law, Tom's wife, Carol, doesn't get involved much in the financial world. She doesn't even balance her checkbook, partly because her husband is an accountant. "If I was married to a plumber and the toilet was broken, I'd let him fix it," she laughs.

Source: Taken from Tim Carrington and Julie Salamon, "Attitudes on Saving Vary Widely in Family of Ohio Businessman," *Wall Street Journal*, 23 May, 1983: 1ff. Reprinted by permission of *Wall Street Journal*, © Dow Jones & Compnay, Inc. 1985. All Rights Reserved.

QUESTIONS

1. What life experiences have influenced Mrs. Heldman's financial decisions? What factors have influenced her son Tom and her grandson Tim?
2. What is Mrs. Heldman's general approach to managing her finances? What are the approaches of her son Tom and her grandson Tim?
3. How have the different experiences and management approaches of the three generations of the Heldman family affected their financial decisions?

more wisely. Young singles and young couples with sizable incomes and sizable tax bills may find their advice especially beneficial.

Services Provided   Competent financial planners can provide advice on a full range of questions: tax, retirement, estate, and investment planning. Unfortunately, anyone can call himself or herself a "financial planner" because there are no licensing requirements or controls. Several organizations are, however, certifying financial planners who meet their qualifications. Abuses in the financial planning field have led to legal investigations and calls for regulatory action, but there are, as yet, no government controls. This makes it important to be certain about the objectivity, competence, and honesty of individuals claiming to be financial planners.

The services provided by financial planners vary widely in detail and complexity and in cost. Planners typically begin by assessing the individual's or family's financial situation in an initial interview. If the prospective client needs and can afford the service, the planner will gather information on the client's financial situation using a list of questions or a written questionnaire. Questions are asked about income, assets, liabilities (including mortgages and other contractual obligations), life insurance holdings, company benefits, and so on.

Planners also ask prospective clients to detail their major financial goals and to estimate the amounts needed to reach those goals. They often also ask about prospective clients' willingness to accept risk: Do the clients prefer a conservative strategy or are they willing to take more risks? Some planners favor high-risk strategies such as borrowing against one's home to get investment money. Consumers should look for a planner who has investment strategies with which they feel comfortable. Most planners do not charge for the initial interview.

Data from the initial interview and questionnaire are set down in a standard form. These data become the basis for the completed plan, which may range in length from a dozen pages to 30 or 40 pages. The completed plan, which is frequently a computer print-out, will assess the adequacy of present resources to meet the goals established. It also may identify insurance and investment needs. In considering the qualifications of a planner, it is useful to ask to see a sample completed report. Some planners give very detailed advice and recommend specific courses of action. Others make only very general recommendations. It is useful to know the detail in which advice will be given.

Cost of Services

As a part of their recommendations, many planners suggest investments and life insurance programs that they sell. Most planners depend heavily on commissions on these sales for their income. This procedure raises questions about how objective they can be when they depend on the sale of particular investment and insurance programs for their livelihood. Some so-called financial planners are merely thinly disguised salespeople pushing life insurance, mutual funds, tax shelters, and other types of investments. What they have for sale may be offered as the solution to almost every problem, whether or not it is the best choice. Because commissions differ for different types of sales, it is legitimate to ask a planner about the percentage sales commission he or she will receive to determine whether it may have influenced the recommendations.

A smaller proportion of planners work on a fee for service basis. They sell no financial programs and receive no commissions. They usually charge on a hourly basis. Typical fees range from $60 to $100 an hour. Some planners work on a combination of hourly fees and commissions.

It is useful to determine early how a planner is paid: commissions, hourly fees, or a combination of the two. It is also useful to know whether or not the client will get the completed plan even though no purchase is made through the planner.

Selecting a Planner

If financial planning help is needed, it is advisable to investigate and interview several planners before settling on one. Friends and acquaintances who have had successful experiences can help identify planners to consider. Professionals such as lawyers and accountants whose advice can be trusted can also help identify prospects.

Consumers' needs probably will be best served by a planner with a broad perspective who can help them construct the framework of a financial plan and begin to implement it. The planner should draw on experts in such areas as tax law, accounting, and investments, and on the client's own accountant and attorney, as appropriate. It will be useful if the planner has specialized knowledge in some area (such as insurance or investments) that is likely to be central to the plan.

At a minimum, the planner should have a degree from a four-year college in a financial field such as finance, accounting, or economics. Additional college training, such as an M.B.A., is desirable. Planners are likely to be more effective if they also have work experience in some segment of the financial services industry, for example, as a bank trust officer, stock broker, or insurance salesperson.

A small proportion of financial planners have become certified by several private, professional organizations. These organizations accredit planners following completion of a curriculum of study and fulfillment of field experience requirements. One such organization for training personal financial planners is the College for Financial Planning. Those who pass its examinations are permitted to label themselves as Certified Financial Planners (CFPs). Because there are several certifying organizations operating, with varying requirements, planners who indicate they have an organizational certification should be asked to explain the requirements they have fulfilled. While certification is evidence of some degree of competence, it cannot, of course, guarantee objectivity or honesty.

As shown in this chapter, some overall plan for managing money is essential. Without a clearly specified set of goals and a plan to reach them, success is unlikely. There are a number of components in a financial plan. Each chapter in this section of the book deals with one of these components.

MAJOR CHAPTER CONCEPTS

1. A large income cannot guarantee freedom from financial strain. Income, no matter how large, has to be managed to produce the maximum satisfaction.

2. Personal financial management is the process of setting personal financial goals, making plans to reach these goals, and implementing these plans. The goal is to allow a satisfactory level of daily living and to build financial reserves to meet future needs and emergencies.

3. Personal financial management includes a number of related and interdependent parts: record keeping, budgeting, savings and investment planning, tax planning, managing risk, estate and retirement planning, and career planning.

4. A cash-flow budget provides a comprehensive picture of personal finances by taking account of cash inflows and outflows, changes in savings and debt, changes in cash balances, and interest payments.

5. The spending plan included in a budget should be based on personal goals and preferences. The budget categories and time periods used should be based on one's personal situation.

6. A frequently recommended strategy for ensuring that a budget provides money for savings is to deduct money for savings when you receive income.

7. Personal financial progress can be measured by changes in net worth on a personal balance sheet that includes a detailed listing of assets and liabilities.

8. Poor money management is the most frequent cause of financial difficulties. Too often, incomes that would be adequate if handled properly are mismanaged.

9. Other major causes of financial difficulty include inadequate reserves for emergencies, insufficient insurance, and unwise investments. Financial problems are often linked to marital problems.

10. The profession of personal financial planner has arisen because of consumers' need for a comprehensive financial plan that takes into account varied and complex investment opportunities and changing tax laws.

11. Competence, objectivity, and cost are important considerations in choosing a financial planner. Charges may be based on commissions, hourly fees, or a combination of both.

12. Several private, professional organizations certify financial planners. In judging planners, consumers should ask planners to explain the qualifications required for certification.

CONSUMER
QUESTIONS

1. Make a list of short-term goals and long-term goals. What financial resources will be needed to reach these goals? What methods can be used to obtain these resources?

2. Prepare a spending record/spending plan form adapted to your individual needs and situation. Use the form in Figure 12-1 as a model, adjusting it as appropriate.

3. Using the budget form prepared, develop a spending record for the past month. Reconstruct spending as well as possible. How does actual spending compare to planned spending? In what ways could spending be adjusted?

4. Prepare a spending plan or budget for the month ahead. What adjustments have been made in the way money was spent in the past as indicated in the spending record?

5. Each issue of *Money* magazine and Sylvia Porter's *Personal Finance Magazine* includes a profile of an individual's or family's finances. After discussing personal goals and financial situation and reviewing a spending record and balance sheet, financial experts recommend financial management strategies. Review a profile that interests you and determine the following: (a) What goals did the individual or family indicate? (b) How was spending influenced by personal or family goals and situation? (c) What changes in spending and saving were suggested by the experts? (d) What changes in investment strategy were suggested? (e) What other changes were suggested in career planning, estate and retirement planning, tax planning and risk management?

6. Prepare a research report on personal financial planners. Include a discussion of the services they provide, the costs of these services, and their qualifications. What criticisms have been made of financial planners? What attempts are being made to meet these criticisms? Use footnotes to indicate the sources of information you have used. The *Readers' Guide to Periodical Literature* and the *Magazine Index* are useful sources of references on this topic.

7. Check the local telephone book's yellow pages for listings of "Financial Planning Consultants" and "Financial Planners—Certified." (a) How many individuals or firms are listed? (b) How many individuals indi-

cate they are Certified Financial Planners (CFPs) or have other certification? (c) In what other business activities do the individuals/firms listed engage? (Check the listings in the white pages for clues about other business activities.)

SUGGESTED
READINGS

1. *Consumer Reports.* "Financial Planners: What Are They Really Selling?" and "Looking for Mr. Good Plan" 51, no. 1 (January 1986): 37-44. These articles look first at the types of people who are providing financial plans and their qualifications. Next, there is a report of a "test" of the advice of seven major financial firms, all of whom were given the same financial information about a hypothetical couple.

2. *Consumer Reports.* "Where Does All the Money Go?" 51, no. 9 (September 1986): 581-592. This article discusses how to keep track of your money and how to control its use. It is of particular interest because it is based on responses of readers to a special questionnaire.

3. Morgan, James N., and Greg J. Duncan. *The Economics of Personal Choice.* Ann Arbor, Mich.: University of Michigan Press, 1980. Chapter 5 provides an economist's approach to long-term financial planning and its implementation through day-to-day budgeting. The chapter includes a useful figure that depicts the relationship between income, consumption, and household stocks of financial, physical, and human capital.

4. Porter, Sylvia. *Sylvia Porter's New Money Book for the 80s.* Garden City, NY: Doubleday and Co., 1979. Chapter 2 provides a useful, in-depth discussion of how to construct and use a budget. Especially interesting is the consideration of six different possible systems for keeping budgeted funds.

CHAPTER 13

CHECKING AND SAVINGS ACCOUNTS

An essential part of effective money management is the ability to store money safely until it is needed and to transfer it quickly and cheaply. Most Americans use checking and savings accounts to meet these needs. Unfortunately, choosing a checking or savings account is no longer as simple as it used to be. Before banking deregulation in the late 1970s, checking account services were available solely from banks, at minimal expense. Now there are a variety of types of accounts, with some paying interest and with differing fee schedules. Checking accounts are now available not only at commercial banks but also at savings and loan associations and at some credit unions. (See Consumer Concern, "The Aftermath of Banking Deregulation.")

Savings accounts have changed too. Limits on interest payments [have] been removed, and new types of accounts have appeared. This ch[apter fo]cuses on two of the most basic financial assets for consumers: [checking ac]counts and savings accounts. These are among the first fi[nancial assets a] typical household acquires (see Table 13-1). Checking [accounts are ex]amined first. Then electronic methods of transfe[r...]

Table 13-1
In What Order Do
Consumers Acquire
Financial Assets?

1. Checking account
2. Husband's life insurance
3. Savings accounts
4. Wife's life insurance
5. Stocks
6. Bonds
7. Trusts
8. Mutual funds

Source: Reprinted by permission of publisher from "Consumer Behavior in Accumulating Household Financial Assets," by Edward F. Stafford, Jr., Jack J. Kasulis, and Robert F. Lusch, *Journal of Business Research* 10, no. 4 (1982): 409. Copyright 1982 by Elsevier Science Publishing Company.

rely on written checks will be studied. Finally savings accounts and other savings instruments will be discussed.

CHECKING ACCOUNTS

While some financial institutions are competing vigorously for all kinds of checking account customers, others are focusing their attention on higher income customers who will maintain large balances. The variety of accounts available, differing fee schedules, and the range of financial institutions make shopping for a checking account more important and more complex than ever before.

Basically, three types of checking accounts are available:

- *Regular accounts.* No interest is paid on the deposit.
- *NOW (negotiable order of withdrawal) accounts.* Interest is paid at a fixed rate, based on the balance maintained in the account.
- *Super NOW accounts.* These often are referred to as "Money Market Checking Accounts." A split interest rate is paid on balances in these accounts. ~~T~~, a set interest rate is paid on balances up to a certain level. Above ~~ ~~el a higher variable rate is paid, based on rates in the money

for use of a checking account depend on two factors: the balance
~~a~~nd the level of use of the accounts. Prospective account holders
~~a~~re prices on types of accounts that match their use patterns.
~~ho~~lder with a low income may write only 10 checks a month
~~min~~imum balance of $600. Higher income account holders typ-
~~~~e checks and also maintain higher minimum balances (*Con-*
~~~~ptember, 1985).
~~~~*nce fees* are calculated one of two different ways. They may
~~~~west daily balance during the accounting period or on

the average daily balance. If the minimum balance dips below the bank's specified minimum, service charges will be imposed. These charges may be in the form of per-check charges or a monthly maintenance fee. There may be other charges, such as a charge for printing personalized checks.

Banks also levy fees when an account requires special services. Charges for *returned checks* (bounced checks) may be $15 to $20 or more. Similar charges may be made for *overdrafts* (checks paid by the bank even though there are insufficient funds in the account). There also are charges for stopping payment on a check.

Some banks offer basic, no-frills accounts. For a flat monthly fee, the account holder is allowed to write a limited number of checks and to make a limited number of deposits and withdrawals. There typically are sizable charges for exceeding these limits. Some banks also offer free accounts for young adults and senior citizens.

Convenience

A critical factor for many people in choosing a place to bank is its convenience. People prefer a bank that is handy to their home or their place of work so that it is easily accessible. The hours of operation are important too. Evening hours and Saturday hours may be essential for working people. Today most banks provide automatic teller machines (ATMs) outside their branches and in other convenient locations to provide a limited range of services around-the-clock.

Credit unions typically provide a more limited range of services than banks and savings and loans, and these services are available only to those who are eligible to join. Credit union membership is usually limited to those associated with the sponsoring organization, which may be a business firm, a government agency, or another group such as a church. Hours are often more limited than those of banks and savings and loans, and few credit unions provide ATM services.

Automatic Payments. Banks can make preauthorized deposits and withdrawals from checking accounts. Payroll and Social Security checks may be sent to the bank and deposited directly, saving a trip to the bank. Transfers within the bank to cover mortgage and car loan payments can be arranged, as can transfers to savings accounts. Other direct payments, such as regular payments to insurance companies, can also be arranged.

Overdrafts. Instead of rejecting checks for which there are not sufficient funds, some banks will make payment on the check and create an overdraft on the account. The bank then notifies the account holder to deposit funds in the account and charges a service fee for handling the overdraft.

It is possible to get protection from overdrafts in two ways. One way is to arrange for automatic transfers from a savings account to a checking

CONSUMER CONCERN: THE AFTERMATH OF BANKING DEREGULATION

The economic upheavals of the Great Depression of the 1930s put severe strains on the American financial system. Unbridled competition and speculation in the 1920s had weakened many institutions and these weaknesses became obvious in the 1930s. To facilitate economic recovery, the federal government imposed a set of regulations designed to limit competition among financial institutions and promote their stability (King & Whitehead, 1984).

From the consumer's standpoint the most important of these regulations were those limiting interest payments. No interest could be paid on checking accounts, and maximums were set for savings accounts.

There were also restrictions on the services an institution could offer. Banks were prohibited from giving financial advice and selling insurance or securities. Savings and loan associations were restricted to making home mortgage loans. They could not provide auto loans or personal loans, nor could they provide checking account services. Although credit unions were permitted to provide a range of savings and lending services, they were not permitted to offer checking account services. In addition to the restrictions on interest rates and services, there were also limitations on the geographic spread of financial institutions. (These regulations are still partially in effect.)

Under the regulations, the offerings of different banks were relatively similar. Checking services were available at little or no cost and the stated interest rates on savings accounts usually were identical. There were, however, some small differences in effective yields between banks because of differing methods of calculating the interest to be paid. As a result, there was only limited pay-off to consumers who shopped around for checking and savings services.

During the late 1970s and early 1980s, banks and savings and loans found it increasingly difficult to compete for consumers' savings. Concerns about inflation and the availability of new kinds of outlets for savings encouraged consumers to shop around. The deregulation law passed by Congress in 1980 permitted the banks to compete more effectively by gradually removing restrictions on interest paid. By 1986, all limitations on the interest payable on savings accounts were removed. As the interest rates paid by banks and savings and loans rose, their costs rose also; they became increasingly conscious of the costs of providing particular services (*Consumer Reports*, September, 1985).

The banks concluded that many small accounts were not paying their way. They required a full range of administrative services but were so small that earnings on the money deposited did not equal the costs of the services provided. To deal with the problem, banks began to institute a variety of new rules and fees. Many banks specified minimum balance requirements. For savings accounts with balances below this amount, no interest would be paid. For checking accounts, service fees would be charged. Accounts with large balances escaped these fees; but for small accounts, the charges often seemed exorbitant. Many people with lower incomes began to feel they no longer could afford checking and savings accounts. At the same time that these people were dropping their accounts, the banks and S and Ls competed vigorously for the more profitable business of higher income customers.

The financial services scene has changed markedly since the early 1980s. There is more competition for the business of middle and higher income customers. Higher income people are sought because their checking and savings account business is profitable. Middle income customers are sought because they are good customers for consumer credit, which also has been profitable. There also are new combinations of services available, such as checking accounts with interest and savings accounts with check writing privileges. Services are available from new sources — institutions that previously were prohibited from providing them. Savings and loans associations are now providing consumer loans as well as mortgage loans and credit unions are providing checking accounts.

The squeeze on lower income customers has concerned both bank executives and consumer advocates. There have been calls for stripped-down, "no-frills" services at a minimum cost for people who need them. Some banks are providing these "lifeline" services for students, those over 65, and others. Another alternative for small account customers are savings and loans and credit unions that have limited their fees and charges to attract customers.

QUESTIONS

1. What were the purposes of the financial regulations of the 1930s?
2. One of the effects of banking regulations was to subsidize services to small account holders at the expense of large account holders. Was this fair? Why or why not?
3. What are the advantages of the current competitive situation? The disadvantages?

account whenever an overdraft would be necessary. The other way is to sign an agreement with the bank authorizing it to create a loan whenever a checking account is overdrawn.

Special Purpose Checks. Personal checks may not meet all your needs for transferring funds. Banks can also provide special purpose checks that are accepted more readily because they indicate that the funds are actually on deposit with the issuer of the check.

- *Cashier's check.* These are checks drawn on the bank and signed by a bank officer. The payee is indicated on the check. These checks can be purchased for a fee at any bank. They are especially suited for large payments, such as payment for a car or a down payment on a house.

- *Money orders.* Banks selling money orders guarantee payment of the amount indicated to the payee designated by the purchaser. The fee for money orders varies with the amount of the order. The U.S. Postal Service provides a similar service at post offices.

- *Traveler's checks.* These are available in $20, $50, $100, and some larger denominations from such issuers as American Express, Visa, and Bank of America, which guarantee payment. The purchaser signs each check immediately when it is purchased and then signs it again and fills in the date and payee when it is cashed. Traveler's checks provide extra security to the purchaser, because the issuer will replace them when they are lost or stolen. To get replacements, the serial numbers of the lost or stolen checks must be indicated. The fee for travelers' checks usually is one percent of their face value.

- *Wire transfers.* A less familiar way of shifting money between cities is the wire transfer. Upon payment, the sender's bank arranges electronic transfer of funds to the receiver's bank. The receiver can pick up the funds immediately. Funds can be transferred in the United States within a day or less; overseas transfer may take longer. Fees for wire transfers are significantly higher than those for cashier's checks, money orders, and traveler's checks. Western Union provides a similar rapid transfer service between its offices.

Availability of Funds. There are significant differences between banks in how quickly they will credit deposits to an account. Some banks will allow checks to be drawn on an account as soon as the deposit is made. Others will insist on delayed availability of funds. Banks argue that the delays are necessary to protect against fraud: They should not be expected to pay until they are certain the deposited check is good.

Critics have argued that banks that insist on delayed availability impose too long a wait before they allow payments against deposited checks. Waits are most common on out-of-town checks and often involve a week-long delay. Some banks even impose waits of several days on in-town checks. Critics say that such waits seem excessive in an age of electronic funds transfer. Bankers respond that bad checks that are being returned move back through the system slowly.

Consumers have become increasingly upset with delayed availability problems, especially when they recognize that banks that impose delays get several days' free use of their money. Consumer irritation with the problem may lead to new laws or regulations. In the meantime, it is wise to find out bank policies before opening a checking account.

Not all banks insist on delayed availability of funds from deposited checks. Some banks, especially smaller ones, make funds available at once. Policies also may be eased for steady customers and those with savings accounts.

Delayed availability of funds may be a particular problem for people who are moving to a new community. They should inquire in advance about the rules of the bank they plan to use in their new community. One way to avoid problems may be to wire funds to the new bank before moving. Unfortunately, even wire transfers are subject to delayed availability at some banks. Another way to avoid problems is to carry some funds in the form of traveler's checks.

Funds in the form of checks in process of collection often are referred to as *float* in financial circles. Banks gain from float when they delay the availability of funds from a deposited check that is drawn on another bank. Because they usually have the funds before they make them available, the banks have use of the money for a short period.

Some consumers take advantage of float, too. Some consumers mail checks to pay bills before the funds are actually in their accounts. They know it will be several days before the check is presented to their bank for payment. This gives them time to deposit funds to cover the check before it is processed by their bank. Although using float this way is improper, the practice is not uncommon.

Services

One criterion for judging checking accounts is the services provided with the account. The return of cancelled checks is a service that some banks are eliminating as a cost-saving measure. Instead of returning checks, the banks store them or keep photocopies. This procedure is called *truncation* in financial circles. When describing the procedure to customers, banks use such terms as *check safe-keeping*.

Critics of truncation note that cancelled checks often are important for straightening out checkbook errors and are useful as legal evidence of

CONSUMER CAPSULE: HOW TO USE A CHECKING ACCOUNT

INFORMATION ON THE CHECK

Checks are a request by an account holder (the drawer) to a financial institution (the drawee) to pay a specified amount to another party (the payee). At savings and loan associations and credit unions, checks are referred to as *share drafts*. To ensure that checks move smoothly, certain rules for properly drawn checks should be followed.

Date. The current date should be entered on the face of the check. If it is omitted, the bank can consider the check current and cash it. Postdated checks are those bearing some future date. Payees often refuse postdated checks because banks may refuse to cash them or hold them until the date indicated. Checks dated several months in the past also may be a problem. Stale-dated checks (for example, checks more than six months old) may be refused by banks.

Amount. The amount to be paid is written both in numbers and in words. If the amounts indicated disagree, the amount written out in words is paid.

Endorsements. Endorsements are entered on the back of the check when they are cashed or deposited. They are used to control the transfer of ownership of the check and to assure those who accept the check that it is good (Bank of America, 1977). Three types of endorsements are commonly used.

- *Blank endorsement*—An endorsement with the signature of the payee. It means that anyone holding the check may cash it. A blank endorsement can create problems if the check is lost or stolen.
- *Special endorsement*—An endorsement that restricts payment to some particular person or firm. Checks endorsed "Pay to the order of [name]" may be cashed only by the party indicated.
- *Restrictive endorsement*—One that limits what can be done with a check. "For deposit only" with the signature of the payee indicates that the check may only be deposited to the payee's account. This endorsement is useful when checks are deposited by mail.

BALANCING A CHECKBOOK

Keeping an accurate record of checks written and other transactions and an accurate balance will help you avoid the embarrassment and the expense of returned checks (Bank of America, 1975). Each check should be listed in a check register before it is written. Other transactions should be recorded as they occur.

Reconciling checkbook balances with balances on their account statements is a recurring problem for many consumers. To help their customers, banks often include a form on the back of the statement indicating the steps to follow in balancing a checkbook. These steps should be followed.

1. Identify the date of the last check paid, or the last other transaction in your statement. All or most of the activity in your account before this cut-off date can be verified.
2. In your check register, check off all cancelled checks listed on the statement. At the same time, check the amounts entered in your checkbook register against the statement for errors.
3. Identify all checks with dates before the cut-off date that have not been listed as paid on the bank statement. List these checks by number and amount and then total the amounts.
4. Compare your checkbook and bank statement information on the other transactions made before the cut-off date. These include withdrawals at automatic teller machines and transfers to savings and to pay off loans. Be certain they have been deducted from your checkbook balance. Interest payments on NOW accounts should be entered in the checkbook and added to the balance. Service fees for transactions, printed checks, and so on should also be listed in the checkbook and subtracted.
5. Compare the deposits listed on the statement and in the checkbook. Note amounts of deposits made just before the cut-off date that do not appear on the statemtent.
6. Calculate the adjusted statement balance by adjusting the new or final balance on the statement for deposits the bank had not credited and checks written that had not been paid yet.
   a. To the new balance, add the amount of deposits made before the cut-off date that are not shown on the bank statement. (These deposits already are entered in the checkbook, so they must also be added to the statement balance to make the two totals comparable.)
   b. Next, subtract the total of unpaid checks (This amount already has been deducted from your checkbook balance, so it must also be subtracted from the statement balance to make the two balances comparable).
   c. The resulting amount is your adjusted bank statement balance. It should match your checkbook balance. If it does not, these

steps must be repeated. Omitted items, errors in entering amounts, and arithmetic errors are common.

QUESTIONS

1. Why should you refuse to accept a postdated check?
2. Some stores immediately stamp customers' checks with a "For deposit only" endorsement. Why do they do this?
3. Because withdrawals from automatic teller machines do not require a check should they be entered in your checkbook register any way? Why?

payment. Banks that use truncation will provide photocopies of checks if needed, but they may make substantial charges from them.

Safety

The safety of bank deposits was taken for granted for may years, but the wave of savings and loan and bank failures in the 1980s has made consumers more aware of the importance of being certain their deposits are safe. Deposits in most (but not all) banks, savings and loans, and credit unions are insured up to $100,000 by federal deposit insurance agencies. Deposits in most commercial banks are insured by the Federal Deposit Insurance Corporation (FDIC). Similar insurance on savings and loan accounts

Illustration 13-1
Bank service charges and fees should be entered in the check register along with checks written, to ensure that the recorded balance is accurate.

is provided by the Federal Savings and Loan Insurance Corporation (FSLIC) and by the National Credit Union Administration (NCUA) for credit unions.

All national banks have FDIC insurance, while federally chartered savings and loan associations and credit unions have FSLIC and NCUA insurance. State-chartered banks, savings and loan associations, and credit unions that can meet the eligibility standards of the federal deposit insurance agencies can obtain deposit insurance from them.

Not all financial insitutions have federally sponsored deposit insurance, however. Some state-chartered banks and savings and loan associations are members of state-sponsored insurance programs. Some savings and loan associations in states such as Ohio and Maryland have been members of privately operated insurance funds. The difficulties experienced by these private funds in handling failures in the mid-1980s suggest they do not provide adequate protection for depositors (Bowyer, Thompson, & Srinivasan, 1986). Some credit unions rely on private insurance funds.

ELECTRONIC FUNDS TRANSFER

An increasing proportion of transfers of funds is made electronically without the use of checks or other documents. This procedure, *electronic funds transfer* (EFT), allows rapid transfer of funds and eliminates the need for checks. EFT services are expanding because they offer convenience to customers and reduce costs for handling checks and delays in check processing.

Automatic Teller Machines (ATMs)

The most familiar use of EFT is at automatic teller machines (ATMs). These machines permit withdrawals, deposits, and transfers between a customer's accounts. Since they are in operation 24 hours a day they provide around-the-clock banking services, quick service when tellers' lines are long, and service in locations away from bank branches.

ATMs are operated with *debit cards* that look like plastic credit cards. After the debit card is inserted in the ATM, the customer punches in a secret personal identification number (PIN). Then the type of transaction desired and the amount involved are punched in.

ATMs first appeared at bank branches. More and more are appearing in or outside convenience stores and supermarkets, at airports, and in other high traffic locations.

Other EFT Transfers. Another type of EFT system is making slower headway. This system uses point-of-sale (POS) terminals. POS terminals are installed in stores and permit electronic payment of the store's charges with a debit card. Funds are transferred from the card holder's account into the merchant's account without use of a check. POS installations are expected to become common first in gas stations and supermarkets.

Another type of electronic transfer made without a check is the *preauthor-*

ized transfer. Authority for such transfers is given to the bank and to a third party, if one is involved. This permits automatic deposit of paychecks, Social Security checks, and other recurring deposits. Automatic withdrawals for mortgage and car payments, insurance premiums, utility bills, and other recurring obligations also can be authorized.

Telephone transfers are yet another type of EFT transfer. Transfers can be made by phone between checking and savings accounts and to some local merchants, doctors, and others.

Using a Debit Card

Some people who have studied EFT procedures have asked why anyone would want a debit card. They note that debit card users lose the advantages of checks and credit cards. There is no float with debit cards because payments are deducted immediately. The float advantages that credit cards have offered may, however, be eliminated if banks eliminate the grace periods before a finance charge is imposed on purchases. Some financial experts see this as a growing trend. Debit card payment also eliminates some of the protections available when paying by check (e.g., the opportunity to stop payment on the check) or by credit card (rights to delay payment if merchandise is faulty). There also is the serious problem of liability for unauthorized use of lost debit cards (Federal Trade Commission, 1980a).

Illustration 13-2
An automatic teller machine not only permits withdrawals from checking accounts, it also permits deposits and other types of transactions.

Liability limits for debit cards are not the same as for credit cards; the same protections do not apply.

- Account holders' liability is limited to $50 if the bank is notified within two business days after learning of the loss or theft of a debit card.
- Liability is limited to $500 if the loss is not reported within two days after it is detected.
- There is no set limit on the loss if the account holder fails to report unauthorized transfers within 60 days after the bank statement reporting them is mailed. In these cases, losses could include all deposits and the entire line of credit available to the account holder.

These rules make it essential to keep track of debit cards at all times. Debit cards and personal identification numbers should always be kept separate. Some account holders write their PIN numbers on the back of their cards in case they forget them. This is asking for trouble!

Because of the possibility of errors, the printed receipts issued by ATM and POS terminals should be saved and checked against checking account statements. Statements listing EFT transfers are legal proof of payment and can also be used as records for tax purposes.

The rules about unauthorized use of debit cards are different from those for credit cards, and the rules for correcting errors are different, too. When an error is spotted, the account holder should notify the bank by letter or phone at once. After 60 days, the bank is no longer obligated to correct the error. The bank is required to investigate the error and notify the account holder within 45 days.

Debit cards have become increasingly popular because of the convenience of ATMs. Point-of-sale use has grown more slowly partly because it offers consumers fewer conveniences. POS use may begin to grow more rapidly in the future if gas stations and supermarkets begin to insist on payment by debit card.

Some debit cards are issued by individual banks, and Visa and Master-Card also issue debit cards. A growing number of interlinked systems permit the use of one bank's debit card at another bank's ATMs.

SAVINGS ACCOUNTS

Managers often find that they need to shift money over time. They may need more money now than they have immediately available — so they borrow. They may wish to build up reserves for future needs through saving. Income above what is needed for current needs provides the basis for building these savings reserves.

Checking accounts provide a place for keeping short-term savings: money needed for expenses a few weeks hence. You also need a place to keep longer term savings, savings for needs farther in the future. Savers have five general types of goals.

- *Meeting anticipated expenses.* These savings may be for a variety of needs, such as an auto insurance bill that will come due in two months or a reserve for replacing a car that is wearing out.
- *Meeting unanticipated expenses.* Savings may also be needed for some less predictable expenses, such as auto repair bills, medical bills not covered by insurance, and so on.
- *Reaching special goals or targets.* Some people save for some special purpose, such as a special vacation trip or a down payment on a first home.
- *Replacing lost or reduced income.* Another need is for supplemental retirement income or replacement of earnings if one is disabled.
- *Providing a bequest for heirs.* People with families often are concerned about the future economic security of their children and grandchildren and try to ensure it by building financial assets that can be willed to them.

Even though the need for savings is seen, most people would prefer to enjoy money by spending it now. To be induced to save, some people have to be paid to postpone consumption. One way savers are paid to postpone consumption is with interest payments. Three major factors influence the supply of and the demand for savings.

- Savers' and borrowers' *time preference* for money. How much must savers be paid to postpone consumption? How much are borrowers willing to pay to consume now rather than at some future time?
- Savers' and borrowers' assessment of the safety of the money loaned. If savers feel there are significant risks involved, they will insist on some extra return, a *risk premium*.
- Savers' and borrowers' inflationary expectations. If savers expect the real value of their money (its purchasing power) to decline, they will want a bigger return. If borrowers expect to be able to repay with "cheaper" dollars, they will be willing to pay a higher return.

Evaluative Criteria

In the first part of this chapter we discussed checking accounts. These often are labeled *demand deposits* in financial circles because money in such accounts must be paid to depositors on demand without delay. Savings accounts often are labeled *time deposits*. Money deposited in savings accounts is accepted with the stipulation that it may be released only after prior notice (e.g., 15 days' advance notice) or only after some specified time period. Banks and other financial institutions seldom actually refuse to release time deposits on request. They often do, however, impose some financial penalty such as a reduction in the interest paid if a deposit is withdrawn early.

When money is deposited in savings accounts or other savings instruments, the depositor expects to get the deposit (or principal) back plus a return in the form of an interest payment. This section looks at three major types of savings instruments: savings accounts, certificates of deposit, and government savings bonds. When alternative places for savings are considered, the amount of earnings (i.e., the yield on the account) influences the choice, as do the financial risks involved and convenience factors. Each of these evaluative criteria will be examined below.

Yield. A major concern when saving money is earning a fair return for postponing consumption until some future time. The largest return without unreasonable risk is the desired combination.

Savers are paid for the use of money in the form of interest. In some cases interest payments are calculated using the *simple interest* method. The actual interest paid is the nominal, or stated, interest rate multiplied by the number of years the money is on deposit. The interest earnings are not added to the account. For example, suppose a nominal interest rate of six percent is to be paid on a $1,000 deposit for two years.

$$\$1,000 \times .06 \times 2 \text{ years} = \$120 \text{ simple interest earned}$$

Another approach to paying interest, *compound interest*, pays interest periodically during the deposit period and adds these interest earnings to the principal (or amount) on deposit. The addition of interest earnings to an account and payment of interest on them is called *compounding*. The effect of compounding is to make interest earnings grow significantly faster (see Table 13-2).

The example shows that the simple interest on $1,000 deposited for two years at 6% is $120. Table 13-2 shows that the same amount would

Table 13-2
Interest Earnings on $1,000 for Simple and Compound Interest (Interest Paid Quarterly, 6% Nominal Annual Rate)

Number of Quarters Elapsed	Total Interest Earned	
	Simple Interest (Interest Withdrawn as Paid)	Compound Interest (Interest Left on Deposit)
1	$ 15.00	$ 15.00
2	30.00	30.23
3	45.00	45.68
4	60.00	61.36
5	75.00	77.28
6	90.00	93.44
7	105.00	109.84
8	120.00	126.49

earn $126.49 over two years if the 6% interest was paid and compounded quarterly. Money left at compound interest can grow quickly, as can be seen from Table 13-3.

Another factor affecting the yield on a savings deposit is the stated or *nominal interest rate* in use. The nominal interest rate typically is given on a simple interest basis, without the reinvestment of the interest earnings. There is thus no compounding.

As Table 13-4 shows, the level of the nominal rate has a significant effect on the amount of interest earned. Table 13-4 shows growth of $1,000 at different nominal rates with quarterly compounding.

How long does it take money left at compound interest to double? A simple rule-of-thumb that is widely used is the *rule of 72.* The number of years required for doubling is obtained by dividing the nominal interest rate into 72. For example, if you want to know the number of years for

Table 13-3
The Effects of Compounding on Interest Earnings for $1.000 at a Nominal Annual Interest Rate of 6%, Paid and Credited Quarterly

Quarter	Interest Earned for Quarter	Balance on Deposit at End of Quarter
1	$15.00	$1015.00
2	15.23	1030.23
3	15.45	1045.68
4	15.68	1061.36
5	15.92	1077.28
6	16.16	1093.44
7	16.40	1109.84
8	16.65	1126.49

The formula for calculating the effect of compounding interest on a deposit is:

$$B = P(1 + \frac{i}{t})^n$$

where B = balance on deposit after compounding principal
   P = total amount of deposit
   i = nominal annual interest rate
   t = number of times interest is compounded per year
   n = number of periods in which compounding occurs

In the example above, for the end of the fourth quarter:

$$B = \$1000(1 + \frac{.06}{4})^4$$
$$B = \$1000(1.015)^4$$
$$B = \$1000(1.06136)$$
$$B = \$1061.36$$

Table 13-4
Effect of Differing
Interest Rates on the
Growth of $1,000,
Interest Compounded
and Paid Quarterly for
One Year

Nominal Interest Rate	Amount on Deposit at End of One Year (Principal plus Interest Paid)
4%	$1040.60
5	1050.95
6	1061.36
7	1071.86
8	1082.43
9	1093.08
10	1103.81
11	1114.62
12	1125.51

money to double at 6% compound interest, you divide 6 into 72. The answer is 12 years.

In the two examples of interest rates calculated using simple interest and compound interest, the nominal rate was the same (6%), but the results for a two-year period were different.

- Simple interest = Interest paid at the end of period without compounding
- Compound interest = Interest credited and compounded quarterly (or on some other regular basis)

You can see from Table 13-5 that the interest rate on an account earning compound interest will vary depending on how long the money is left on deposit. For example, at the end of one year (four quarters), $61.36 has been earned on a $1,000 deposit, which is the same as a simple interest rate of 6.14% for one year. When interest is compounded, the interest earned on a deposit increases each successive period. Because of the effects of compounding, the actual yield, or *effective rate*, is not the same for each period. The effective rate for two years (eight quarters) can be calculated as follows:

Table 13-5
Effective Interest
Earnings on $1,000
when Interest is
Compounded Quarterly

Quarters Elapsed	Total Interest Earned	Effective Rate
1	$ 15.00	6.00%
2	30.23	6.05
3	45.68	6.09
4	61.36	6.14
5	77.28	6.18
6	93.44	6.23
7	109.84	6.28
8	126.49	6.32

$$\text{Effective rate} = \frac{\text{Interest earnings for period}}{\begin{array}{cc} \text{Amount on deposit} & \text{Number} \\ \text{for period} \quad \times & \text{of years} \end{array}}$$

$$\begin{aligned} \text{Effective rate} &= \frac{\$126.49}{\$1,000 \; \times \; 2 \text{ years}} \\ &= .0632 \\ &= 6.32\% \end{aligned}$$

The effective rate takes the effects of compounding into account. (The example assumes that there were no fees or charges.)

Some banks, as a promotional device, publicize the fact that they pay compound interest daily or even more frequently. Those who are aware of the beneficial effects of compounding may find such procedures attractive. The amount of benefit from more frequent compounding should not be overestimated, however. Table 13-6 shows earnings in one year of $1,000 at six percent interest with compounding at various periods. Frequency of compounding is a greater concern when large amounts are to be left on deposit for an extended period.

The balance on which the bank calculates interest earnings can also have a major effect on the yield of a savings account. Not all banks calculate the amount on which they pay interest in the same way. Several different procedures are used. The easiest to understand and the fairest to depositors is the day-of-deposit to day-of-withdrawal method (or DIDO—day in, day out). Under this method, interest is earned on the amount on deposit each day. This procedure produces the highest returns of any method used.

Another procedure is to pay interest only on the minimum balance in the account during a period. This *low balance method* results in a lower rate of return. The other approaches produce returns that fall between the DIDO and low balance methods.

Other bank bookkeeping procedures also can affect returns. Grace periods permit account holders to make deposits during an interest period and earn interest for the entire period. For example, some banks treat

Table 13-6
Earnings on $1,000
Deposited for One Year
at Six Percent Interest
with Compounding

Annual compounding	$60.00
Semiannual compounding	$60.90
Quarterly compounding	$61.36
Monthly compounding	$61.68
Weekly compounding	$61.80
Daily compounding	$61.83

deposits made before the tenth day of the month as if the deposit had been made on the first day. Some banks also have *dead days*. These are days at the end of an interest period, after interest for the period has been calculated and paid, in which withdrawals can be made without loss of interest.

As account records are further computerized and banks shift to keeping daily records of balances, grace periods and dead days are likely to disappear. Another issue that is sometimes of concern is the delayed availability of funds deposited by check. Banks may impose waiting periods before deposits made by check begin to earn interest. These delays are similar to delays on the availability of funds deposited by check into checking accounts.

Another factor to consider is extra fees and penalties, which may reduce the yield on small accounts. In fact, the fees and penalties on small accounts at some banks are so large they can quickly eat away the balance on deposit.

Minimum balance requirements are widely used. If the balance falls below this limit, no interest is paid on the account. A number of banks charge monthly or quarterly fees ($1 or $2 a month is typical) if the balance is below a specified level. Some banks make extra charges if more than a specified number of withdrawals are made.

Early withdrawal of money in certificates of deposit or other fixed time deposits also can result in penalties. Usually this is a reduction in or loss of interest earned.

It is obvious from the variety of procedures discussed here that banks and savings and loans calculate interest in a number of different ways. There are, in fact, dozens of different methods in use. The result for consumers is that it is difficult to impossible to compare yields at different institutions. Clearly, some method of stating yields on a comparable basis is needed.

A few states now require financial institutions to provide statements that make comparisons easier. One method is to provide the effective rate (or annual yield percentage) based on the assumption that principal and interest are left on deposit for the full stated term. Another is to indicate the number of cents earned per day on a $100 deposit (Morse, 1986). Consumer advocates argue that a federal *truth-in-saving law* is needed to provide better information to consumers in all states and to ensure that this information is provided in a uniform way.

Convenience. The chief convenience issue for savings accounts is how easy it is to make deposits and withdrawals. Most banks and savings and loans provide bank-by-mail services for deposits. Both deposits and withdrawals may be made through automatic teller machines.

It was noted earlier that savings accounts and certificates of deposit are time deposits, meaning that there are some limitations on access to the funds on deposit. In financial circles, ease and speed of access to funds is referred to as *liquidity*. Funds in checking accounts are highly liquid. Those in savings accounts are somewhat less so. At the other end of the liquidity spectrum is money in antiques, real estate, and jewelry. These funds are usually considered illiquid because there may be a long wait to find a buyer and sales costs may be substantial.

Financial institutions can impose delays in paying out withdrawals against time deposits. Although they seldom insist on enforcing these delays, there may be some interest penalties for early withdrawals.

CONSUMER CONCERN: DOES ONE-STOP FINANCIAL SHOPPING MAKE SENSE?

Freed of past restrictions by deregulation, financial institutions are turning themselves into financial supermarkets. Their goal is to draw — and hold — customers using a wide range of financial services. Banks are only one group of institutions to enter this marketing battle. Stock-brokerage firms (e.g., Merrill Lynch) and major retailers (Sears, J.C. Penney), like many in the financial industry, are also convinced that one-stop financial shopping is the wave of the future.

Although many past restrictions have been removed, these corporations still cannot offer a complete range of services. They can, however, move into a number of new areas barred to them in the past: lending services, insurance, brokerage services, real estate sales, and financial planning advice. Just what do these new financial supermarkets have to offer consumers?

One major benefit is convenience. A range of services is available in one place, and transfers from one account (e.g., from savings to stock purchasing) can be arranged easily and quickly. Financial supermarkets can also offer customers other "relationship" advantages. When they handle the full range of a customer's financial affairs, an organization often is willing to provide better interest rates on loans and lower service charges. These reduced charges are justified on the basis of service costs and the security provided by holding some of the customer's assets. The result may be lower rates on mortgages, credit-card financing, and other personal loans, and reduced credit card fees and checking account service charges.

Doing financial business in one place should make it easier for consumers to get comprehensive financial advice. The firm with one-stop services might be expected to have a fuller picture of the customer's financial situation. It should be easier for a financial adviser to develop recommendations, and the firm's range of services should make the appropriate

Safety. Money deposited in savings accounts, certificates of deposit, and savings bonds is subject to two kinds of risks:

- Loss of balance on deposit
- Loss of earnings on the deposit

As discussed earlier, most financial institutions are insured by the Federal Deposit Insurance Corporation, the Federal Savings and Loan Insurance Corporation, or the National Credit Union Administration. A smaller number of banks and savings and loans, all of them state-chartered, have state-

combination of solutions easier to obtain. Unfortunately, few firms actually provide comprehensive financial planning services. Providing such services is time-consuming and expensive. Few firms can afford to provide these services free to middle income customers. Banks cannot provide these services because they are still prohibited from providing financial advice.

Critics of the financial supermarket idea suggest that consumers still need to shop around to get the best deals. The institution that provides the best mortgage rates may not be the best place to buy stocks or get a credit card. Sellers hope to discourage comparison shopping by providing a full range of services, but shopping around is still to the consumer's advantage.

An advantage to maintaining relations with several financial firms is a degree of safety because not all of one's financial "eggs" are in one basket. It also provides the consumer an alternative source of loans or services if the relationship with a particular firm becomes unsatisfactory.

The one-stop financial center seems to have its biggest appeal to the less knowledgeable and less self-confident. More knowledgeable and more affluent consumers seem to prefer to seek out the detailed advice and expertise available only from specialists. They want to deal with specialists, not generalists (Bennett, 1984).

QUESTIONS

1. What factors have encouraged the development of "financial supermarkets"?
2. What are the advantages of one-stop financial shopping? The disadvantages?
3. Do such services appeal to you? Why or why not?

sponsored deposit insurance. A limited number of savings and loans and credit unions have relied on privately operated insurance corporations, which in some cases have proved inadequate to deal with problems.

Some financial experts have questioned whether the federally sponsored insurance programs would be adequate in a major financial crisis. Although they probably would not be, it seems certain that the federal government would intervene to provide additional help and guarantees. State governments could be expected to offer similar help, to the extent they were able.

The amount of insurance coverage provided by the federal deposit insurance corporations is more than adequate to meet the needs of most consumers. In the mid-1980s, individual accounts were insured up to a maximum of $100,000. Couples can obtain this amount plus even more coverage. They can, for example, each have individual insured accounts, plus a joint account that also will be covered to $100,000.

The goal of deposit insurance is to provide insured institutions and their depositors with security by assuring the liquidity of deposits. The insurance allows the institutions to meet demands for withdrawals and helps head off runs by panicked depositors who fear they will be unable to get their money out.

The amount of interest to be paid on savings accounts and certificates of deposit is guaranteed when the money is deposited. The exceptions are savings accounts that pay money-market-based interest rates. Interest paid on these accounts will fluctuate with changes in the money market. The interest paid on U.S. Government Savings Bonds varies with interest rates on government-issued securities but is guaranteed not to fall below some specified minimum.

From this discussion it can be concluded that insurance on deposits is an important evaluative criterion. Federal deposit insurance offers by far the most protection. Prospective depositors can check for deposit insurance by looking for the identification plaques displayed by federally insured institutions or by asking specifically about it.

Savings Instruments There are three major categories of saving instruments available: savings accounts, certificates of deposit, and savings bonds. There are some important differences among them in yield, risk, and convenience. In the following sections, each category will be examined more closely.

Savings Accounts. The oldest and most familiar form of savings account is the passbook account. Deposits, withdrawals, and interest payments are all noted in the account holder's passbook by a teller. While the procedure is simple from the customer's point of view, it is time-consuming and costly for the bank. While banks would like to phase out this type of account, it continues to be popular. Perhaps customers like the feel of a passbook in hand. Regular passbook accounts provide a high degree of liquidity. The specified limitations on withdrawals are almost never actually imposed. The accounts, however, provide relatively low yields. Rates were uncapped in 1986, so consumers should begin to see more variation in rates among banks. Special passbook accounts require a higher minimum deposit but pay a higher rate of interest. They do impose more limitations on withdrawal. Thirty days' advance notice is required to avoid loss of interest earned.

Club accounts, including Christmas club and vacation club accounts, have been popular with lower income consumers for many years. They provide a systematic way to save for a specific goal and help some savers develop the discipline they need to save. These accounts typically involve only small amounts and are relatively expensive to administer. As a result, they pay relatively low rates of interest.

Banks have tried to shift customers into a newer type of account, *statement savings accounts.* These accounts operate in much the same way as a checking account. There is no passbook. Instead, account holders are given receipts for savings and withdrawals and are sent periodic statements (monthly or quarterly) that provide a record of transactions and interest earnings.

One advantage of statement savings accounts is that they are linked to banks' EFT systems. Funds may be deposited and withdrawn at automatic teller machines as well as in person. It is also possible to arrange automatic deposits into these accounts from a checking account or payroll deposit.

More and more banks are offering *money market deposit accounts.* These accounts are the banks' effort to hold depositors with large accounts who have been attracted to the money market funds offered by some large brokerage firms. Money market deposit accounts provide a multitier interest system. A lower, fixed rate typically is offered on a basic amount, with a higher, variable rate paid on amounts above the minimum. The variable rate is linked to money market rates but typically is slightly lower.

Money market deposit accounts offer limited check-writing privileges. A limited number of checks may be written each month, but a minimum amount (such as $500) may be specified. These accounts should not be confused with super NOW accounts (money market checking accounts), which pay lower, money-market-linked rates but put no limits on check writing.

Prospective depositors should choose a savings account on the basis of their expected use. Smaller depositors will have to choose accounts with lower minimum deposit requirements. They will have to be content with lower interest yields or perhaps no earnings at all. In fact, they may face significant fees if their minimum balance is low or if they make frequent deposits and withdrawals.

Certificates of Deposit. *Certificates of deposit* (CDs) are receipts issued to account holders for deposits that are repayable at some specified date. The certificates set down the interest rate to be paid and the limitations on withdrawal of the money. The length of the deposit period typically is specified at the time of deposit. The periods may run from one week to many years. Some common periods are three and six months and one, three, and five years. The rates offered typically are higher for longer term commitments.

Some banks are now offering variable rate CDs, though their advantage is not completely clear. These deposits do not have any guaranteed yield, and withdrawal privileges are limited. Depositors who want money-market-linked rates but more liquidity should consider money market deposit accounts.

Money held in a certificate of deposit cannot be withdrawn prior to maturity without an interest penalty. Advance notice also may be required for withdrawal.

Savings Bonds. During the 1970s and early 1980s, when inflation and interest rates were high, savings bonds were considered to be a bad joke by financial experts. The bonds offered no protection against inflation and the interest rate provided was low, far below the rate of inflation and rates available elsewhere.

In 1982, Series EE bonds replaced earlier versions. They provide more competitive returns and are a more attractive alternative for savers. The bonds are available in a number of denominations, beginning at $25. Bonds held five years or more carry a variable interest rate that is 85 percent of the average for U.S. Treasury securities with a 5-year maturity. A minimum rate is guaranteed. This guaranteed rate is adjusted periodically. In late 1986 the minimum rate was reduced to six percent per year. Interest earnings are compounded semiannually. There are interest rate penalties for bonds cashed before they are held five years.

In addition to providing a guaranteed minimum return with an opportunity for higher returns, the bonds offer security because they are a U.S. government issue. The bonds have the further advantage that interest earnings are exempt from state and local taxes. Bond holders have the option of paying federal taxes on the interest either as it is earned or when the bond matures. Savings bonds are available at banks, savings and loans, and other financial institutions and through payroll deduction plans.

OTHER BANK SERVICES

With deregulation, banks are providing a number of services they did not provide previously. One is discount brokerage services. Banks will buy and sell stocks and other securities at reduced rates, below those charged by full-service brokerage houses. Investment advice is not provided as part of this service. Banks can also provide account services for their customers. They can hold securities for them, collect and deposit dividends and interest, and send out statements summarizing account activity.

Banks have been traditional providers of trust services, which involve taking legal title of property and holding and managing it for the benefit of an individual, a group of individuals, or some legal entity. Trusts are used for a variety of purposes: to gain financial management assistance, to reduce income and estate taxes, and to help assure income security.

MAJOR CHAPTER CONCEPTS

1. The three types of checking accounts are (1) regular, (2) NOW accounts (a fixed rate of interest is paid), and (3) super NOW accounts (a fixed interest rate is paid on a basic amount and a higher variable rate is paid on additional amounts).
2. The parties to a check are the drawer (account holder), the drawee (financial institution), and the payee (the party to be paid).
3. Endorsements are used to guarantee the payment of a check and to control the transfer of ownership. The signature of the payee is a blank endorsement: Anyone holding the check may cash it. Special endorsements indicate the person to whom ownership is transferred. Restrictive endorsements limit what can be done with the check.
4. The charges for having a checking account depend on the balance maintained and the level of use of the account.
5. In addition to personal checks, cashier's checks, money orders, traveler's checks, and wire transfers can be used to transfer funds.
6. Delays in crediting deposited checks to an account (delayed availability) have created problems for many consumers.
7. Federal deposit insurance agencies (FDIC, FSLIC, and NCUA) provide deposit insurance in many, but not all, financial institutions.
8. Electronic funds transfer permits transfers at automatic teller machines, at point-of-sale terminals, by telephone, and by preauthorized arrangements.
9. Savings may be accumulated for anticipated expenses, unanticipated expenses, special goals, replacing lost or reduced income, and providing bequests.

10. The supply of savings and the demand for savings is influenced by the borrowers' and the savers' time preference for money, their assessment of the safety of the funds, and their inflationary expectations.

11. Savings instruments often are referred to as *time deposits* because advance notice may be required to withdraw them.

12. Compounding of interest adds interest earnings to the principal on deposit and makes the effective rate of interest greater than the nominal rate.

13. Interest earnings are affected by the interest rate, frequency of compounding, calculation of the balance, and any fees and penalties.

14. The risks to savings may involve loss of principal and loss of earnings.

15. Savings instruments available to savers include savings accounts, certificates of deposit, and savings bonds; they differ in yield, liquidity, and safety.

CONSUMER QUESTIONS

1. Do you have any savings goals? What are they? Are they short- or long-run goals? How would you rank your goals in order of importance?

2. In this chapter, some evaluative criteria for checking accounts (cost, convenience, and safety) and for savings accounts (yield, convenience, and safety) have been identified. Are there other evaluative criteria that are important? How would you rank the evaluative criteria? Why?

3. Do you have a checking account? A savings account? What fees or charges are involved? What is the yield on your savings account?

4. How well does your checking (or savings) account perform on the evaluative criteria you feel are important?

5. Make a comparison chart showing the advantages and disadvantages of the different types of checking accounts and the different types of savings instruments.

6. Prepare a report on recent developments in one of the following areas:
   a. Deposit insurance and the safety of the banking system
   b. The interstate spread of financial institutions
   c. The impact of deregulation on financial institutions and their customers
   d. Banking services for low-income consumers (e.g., "lifeline banking")
   e. Electronic funds transfer
   f. Movement of other types of corporations, such as retailers (e.g., Sears), brokerage houses (e.g., Merrill Lynch), and others (e.g., American Express) into the banking services market

7. What credit unions operate in your area? (One source of information is the yellow pages in the phone book.) Who is eligible to join?

SUGGESTED READINGS

1. *Consumer Reports.* "Shopping for Savings" 50, no. 11 (November 1985): 669-675. In this article, evaluative criteria for selecting a savings accounts, certificates of deposit, and money market savings accounts are discussed. With deregulation, increasing variations in returns to savers were found after a survey of 100 banks.

2. *Consumer Reports.* "To Tell the Truth" 50, no. 11 (November 1985): 676-677. A wide variety of methods of calculating interest paid on savings accounts is used. A uniform method of stating interest is needed so consumers can make easy comparisons.

3. *Consumer Reports.* "You and the Banks" 50, no. 9 (September 1985): 508-516. This article discusses the evaluative criteria that should be considered in choosing a checking account. A survey of fees and services from 100 banks in ten cities found substantial differences among banks in the same city and among banks in different cities.

4. Cook, John A., and Robert Wool. *All You Need to Know about Banks.* New York: Bantam Books, 1983, Chapters 1 to 6, 13 to 15. This book provides an insightful discussion of how to get the best service from a bank. The senior author is a former vice president of the Bank of New York.

5. Mayer, Martin. *The Money Bazaars: Understanding the Banking Revolution Around Us.* New York: E.P. Dutton, Inc., 1984. Martin Mayer, a well-known author on business topics, examines recent changes in the banking industry resulting from the growth of electronic funds transfer, deregulation, and the appearance new sources of competition.

CHAPTER 14

CONSUMER CREDIT

In the middle 1980s, consumer borrowing in the United States went over two trillion dollars for an average of $8,000 per person. This figure indicates how important credit has become to American consumers.

Consumer debt has grown rapidly in the past two or three decades. Growth has been fed by the appearance of new sources of consumer credit and vigorous competition among credit grantors to win a share of this lucrative market. Consumers, for their part, have seized the opportunity to borrow. They have been eager for new homes, new cars, and new appliances and they have chosen to buy them on credit — spending now and repaying later. They have also been encouraged by optimism about their own financial situations and by the growth of the American economy. While recessions periodically have slowed the growth of consumer credit, the slowdown has been only temporary.

MOTIVES FOR BORROWING

Just why do consumers borrow? A simple answer is that they prefer to shift the time period in which they consume. Instead of gradually building savings to pay cash for a purchase, they buy on credit and gradually repay the loan

344

plus finance charges. The finance charges (or interest) are the cost they pay for borrowing. Finance charges represent what is called the *time value of money*, that is, the cost to borrowers of borrowing so that they can consume sooner rather than later. Finance charges also represent the payment to savers for postponing use of their money for consumption until some later time.

Paying savers to postpone their consumption is only part of the cost of a loan. Borrowers also may have to pay a premium because of savers' concern about the risk of loss and their expectations of inflation. That is, if savers expect price increases to reduce the purchasing power of the money they are lending, they will try to ensure that the amount of money repaid will have the same real value as the amount they lent. The interest payment they demand will reflect their estimates of the future rate of inflation.

Borrowers, of course, do not usually deal directly with savers. Instead, savers' funds are administered by banks, savings and loan associations, insurance companies, credit unions, finance companies, and other financial institutions. These financial institutions must be paid for their efforts as intermediaries between borrowers and savers. They must cover the costs of administering funds, including the cost of opening accounts, keeping records, and covering losses from defaults when borrowers fail to repay.

All these cost factors — savers' time value of money, premiums to cover the risk of loss and possible declines in purchasing power due to inflation plus lenders' administrative costs and credit losses — help to determine the cost of credit.

ESTABLISHING CREDIT

A lenders' assessment of an applicant's creditworthiness is often said to depend on three C's:

- *Capacity.* The applicant's ability to repay a loan is a key consideration for lenders. The applicant's earnings, the stability of these earnings, and the applicant's financial obligations (including other loan obligations, living expenses, and dependents) are all important factors affecting ability to repay.
- *Character.* The applicant's responsible handling of financial matters, honesty, and demonstrated willingness to repay are all evidence of good character.
- *Capital.* The applicant's financial resources that can be used to repay the loan or as security for the loan are important, too. Capital may include savings, property, and other financial resources.

Application Information

Credit application forms are designed to gather evidence concerning the applicant's three C's. They include four general categories of information:

- *Personal information* — Name, address, and dependents (Marital status may be asked only in certain instances, such as for an application for a joint account.)
- *Employment information* — Occupation, place of employment, length of employment, annual income
- *Financial information* — Savings and checking accounts and name of bank, owner/renter status, amount of monthly mortgage or rental payment
- *Credit information* — Credit cards held and amounts currently owed, other loans outstanding.

It is important for credit applicants to be both complete and truthful in filling out an application form. Lenders become suspicious if they discover that major debts or information that could reflect unfavorably on the applicant has been omitted.

Credit grantors frequently verify at least some of the information provided. The applicant's employer may be called to verify employment and income information. Checking and savings account information also may be verified. Some credit grantors want a more thorough check on an applicant. Rather than doing this check themselves they usually turn to their local credit bureau.

Credit Bureau Information

Credit bureaus are agencies that serve as clearinghouses for information on local credit users. They collect information from participating firms and maintain files on individual borrowers. This information is provided to credit grantors for a fee.

Files include basic personal and employment information along with a record of accounts opened, information on current credit balances (though not all credit grantors provide the bureau this information), and payment record. Files also include information on legal actions that could affect ability or willingness to repay. Arrests, divorce actions, law suits, and bankruptcy petitions are of particular concern.

Most credit bureaus are locally owned and independently operated, though some large city bureaus are part of corporate networks. Regardless of their status, local bureaus have links to those in other areas. Applicants who have recently moved can expect the credit bureau covering their new area to check the bureau where they lived previously. These checks make it difficult to escape a bad credit history, but they make it easier for those with a good credit history to obtain credit when they move to a new area.

If credit applicants are to be judged fairly, it is critical that a credit bureau's information be complete and accurate. Unfortunately, errors do occur. Credit bureaus maintain files on thousands of people, and errors

Illustration 14-1
Although credit bureaus keep records only on local residents, they also exchange information; as a result, borrowers' credit history can follow them from place to place.

and omissions are possible. Records for people with similar or identical names may become confused, information may be misfiled, and other information may become out-dated. The fact that several credit bureaus serve the area in which the applicant lives may create further confusion.

Because the accuracy of the information on file can have an important effect on individual consumers, federal law (Fair Credit Reporting Act of 1971) gives consumers the right to review the information in their files. This same federal law also requires that applicants be informed if they are denied credit on the basis of information supplied by a credit bureau. In these cases, the credit bureau must allow people the right to review the information in the bureau's files. If erroneous information is found, credit grantors who have received the information from the bureau must be informed of the error. If the bureau does not agree that a report is in error, the individual has the right to put a statement in the files.

Until a few years ago, credit record procedures made it difficult for married women to establish their own independent credit histories. Accounts and credit reports were carried in the husband's name in a joint file. In cases of divorce or the husband's death, the wife had difficulty establishing credit in her own name because she had no credit history independent of her husband. To remedy this problem, federal law (Equal Credit Opportunity Act) has required since 1977 that joint accounts be reported under both names and that information on joint accounts be carried in both files.

Credit Rating Decisions	Credit grantors make an overall judgment about whom they will grant credit to, based on the information they have gathered. A basic source of information is the application form. Some firms base their decision solely on the information presented. Others will analyze this information using *credit-scoring* techniques (see Consumer Concern, "Is Credit Scoring Fair?"), awarding positive and negative points for characteristics that have been found to be related to borrowers' credit performances in the past.

The information on the application may or may not be supplemented with information from the local credit bureau and other sources. Regardless of whether credit bureau information is used or not, it is important to recognize that the final decisions are made by individual credit grantors, not by the credit bureau. As a result, it is possible for different lenders to reach different decisions using the same information.

Equal Opportunity in Obtaining Credit

As noted, credit grantors look for evidence of good character and personal and occupational stability, a good payment record on past debts, and financial capacity to repay future debts. Certain personal characteristics cannot be used as a basis for decisions on granting credit under federal law (Equal Credit Opportunity Act of 1975). Lenders are not permitted to discriminate on the basis of sex, marital status, religion, color, race, national origin, or because an individual receives public assistance.

The equal credit opportunity rules essentially mean that people cannot be refused credit solely on the basis of any of the specified characteristics. Decisions must be made on other bases. Age also cannot be used as a basis for refusing or reducing the credit granted to older people. Applicants under legal age who cannot sign legally binding contracts can, however, be refused.

Equal credit opportunity rules prohibit credit grantors from several types of discriminatory activity:

- Discouraging applications for loans
- Refusing loans
- Offering different loan terms than those offered others with similar qualifications

As mentioned above, one important result of the act is that women no longer can be denied credit on the basis of their sex or their marital status. In the past, married women were often required to have their husbands *co-sign* (or provide a guarantee) when they applied for credit in their own names, even when the wife had adequate income to make repayment. Single women were asked to have their parents co-sign or were refused credit because single women were considered unreliable. Now women can apply for their own separate credit accounts and are entitled to be judged solely on the basis of their characteristics without regard to sex.

Rights of Those Denied Credit

After people apply for credit, federal law requires that lenders inform them of their decisions within 30 days. If they are refused, the reason for denying credit must be indicated. This rule makes it easier to recognize instances in which a refusal is based on incorrect or out-dated information or on misunderstandings or misinterpretations of information in a credit record. Those who are denied credit should make an effort to correct the errors in their records. If the errors are allowed to remain, they will continue to cause problems.

Establishing a Credit History

Young people often wonder about how they should go about establishing their creditworthiness. "If you can't get credit," they ask, "how can you establish a reputation for repaying promptly?" What they need to do is to attack the problem one step at a time.

An important first step is to establish financial credibility by opening a checking account. Maintaining a reasonable balance and avoiding overdrafts (bounced checks) is evidence of the ability to manage money. A savings account with a solid balance is also useful because it is evidence of emergency funds that can be used for repayments if necessary.

Once bank accounts have been established, the easiest places to obtain credit are usually local retailers and department stores. Credit experts suggest applying for only one account at a time. Applying for several at once may raise concerns. Once local retail accounts have been established, it is important to use them carefully and pay promptly. A next step may be an application for a gasoline credit card.

An application for a bank credit card (a Visa or MasterCard, for example) should then be made. If the application is accepted, a limited credit line with a charge limit of $500 or less is usually approved. This limit will allow the bank to see how credit is handled. If all goes well, a higher limit can be requested later. There is some evidence that it is easier to get a bank card when the bank invites the individual to apply than when individuals initiate the applications on their own.

These steps provide a basis for applying for larger loans, including small personal loans and auto loans. In establishing creditworthiness, it is important to continue to demonstrate capability as a financial and credit manager. As this credibility is established, lenders will be willing to increase credit limits.

In earlier and simpler days, the corner grocer and other credit grantors were able to make credit decisions on the basis of knowing their customers personally. Neighborhood shopkeepers knew a great deal about a family's financial situation and about how promptly they paid their bills. The anonymity of big cities and a mobile population have made granting credit on the basis of personal acquaintance a thing of the past. New methods of evaluating creditworthiness have had to be found.

An alternative method of determining credit eligibility has been the use of credit-scoring systems based on the applicant's personal characteristics. These systems look at such factors as age and number of credit cards held and assign positive or negative points to each characteristic. The points assigned are then added up and a total score determined. On the basis of the score an applicant may be accepted or rejected or perhaps classed in a gray area and investigated further.

Scoring systems help credit grantors identify the best prospects quickly and also help them eliminate poor loan prospects. A good system helps to avoid the errors of turning down good risks or accepting poor ones.

Credit-scoring systems are based on identifying the characteristics that distinguish those who are good credit prospects and those who are likely to perform poorly. The records of past credit recipients are analyzed to identify the personal characteristics of those who performed well and those who performed poorly. Point values are estimated for each of a dozen or more characteristics. For example, score values can be estimated for being in particular age categories or for having a car of a certain age.

The factors considered are similar to those used in determining any credit rating. Characteristics that can't be considered because of laws on credit discrimination (e.g., sex or race) cannot, of course, be used.

It is possible to achieve an acceptable total score in a number of different ways. A low income may be offset by good scores for evidence of personal and financial stability. Many firms make their credit decisions solely on the basis of the score a credit applicant receives. Some also use credit bureau information. Others use credit bureau information only if the score is near their cut-off point. An applicant's credit score is not always the final word on whether a loan will be made. Some firms allow loan officers to override poor scores to grant credit, but others do not.

Credit-scoring systems have frequently been criticized as too impersonal. Some people feel they do not take the full range of personal factors into consideration. Those familiar with credit-scoring systems respond that they help prevent discrimination by emphasizing only those factors that have been shown to be relevant for credit-granting decisions. Factors such as sex and race, which were often the bases for discrimination in the past, cannot be considered. While credit scoring is mechanical, it takes many characteristics into account. The number of factors considered is undoubtedly far larger than loan officers typically would consider.

Individual firms develop their own scoring systems. As a result, systems differ between firms and, in some cases, between a store's branches. The systems are only as good as the data and the analytical procedures used. The methods used in developing a credit-scoring system and in scoring usually are not disclosed, which raises concerns that a system may omit variables that could indicate good credit potential. Some critics of credit scoring say too much attention is paid to personal characteristics and not enough is given to such obviously important factors as an applicant's debt-to-income ratio. Only a few models include such information.

Other critics are concerned that applicants are rejected on the basis of probabilities. If an applicant's score is low, estimates based on information from the firm's credit accounts may, for example, indicate there is a 30 percent chance of failure to pay. If the credit grantor rejects all those with similar low scores, 70 good risks will be rejected to avoid 30 bad ones. What are those who have been judged unfairly to do?

QUESTIONS

1. Why were credit-scoring systems developed?
2. How are the points assigned to different personal characteristics estimated?
3. Why do some people feel credit scoring is unfair? What are the responses to those arguments?
4. If you are turned down by one firm that uses credit scoring, will you be turned down by others too?

The sources of consumer credit have multiplied in recent years with the deregulation of the banking industry. Each of these lending sources has designed loan arrangements to help compete for loan customers. The costs and terms of the loans offered vary widely. Some of the differences make comparisons difficult and limit competition between lenders and different types of credit.

Cost

The federal Truth-in-Lending Law requires lenders to provide information that makes it easier to compare loan costs. By law, lenders must provide information on the *annual percentage rate* (APR), which is the cost of a loan stated on a yearly basis (see Consumer Case, "Two Boston Auto Dealers Pay Penalties"). Lenders must also indicate the finance charge, or the total dollar amount the loan will cost. The finance charge includes interest charges plus required fees and service charges such as premiums for credit insurance if it is required.

Truth-in-Lending. The provision of the APR and finance-charge information overcomes past problems in comparing the rates of different lenders. Prior to Truth-in-Lending, loan rates were calculated many different ways and the costs of what one lender called a 10 percent interest rate could be twice that of another's.

The APR and finance charge are cost information that can be compared easily. For example, consider these two loans:

- $1,000 borrowed for one year and repaid at the end of the year along with a finance charge of $100. In this case the APR is 10 percent.
- $1,000 loan and $100 finance charge to be repaid over one year in 12 equal monthly installments. In this case the APR is 18 percent.

The finance charges are the same for both loans, but why are the APRs so different? For the second loan, the borrower doesn't have full use of the money for the whole year. The amount of money still owed declines each month as payments are made, so the borrower, on the average, has use of only about half the money.

The loan in the second example is calculated the same way as many auto loans and installment loans. This method of calculating interest is called the *add-on method*. Before Truth-in-Lending, lenders said such loans had a 10 percent interest rate, based on the relation of the finance charge to the amount of the loan. You can see that in no way was this 10 percent rate comparable to the 10 percent rate in the first example, which was based on *simple interest*. The confusion that resulted in consumers' minds and their difficulties in comparing rates from different lenders were what made Truth-in-Lending so necessary.

Adjustable Interest Rates. In the late 1970s and the early 1980s, interest rates rose rapidly in response to high rates of inflation. Lenders who had made long-term loans for mortgages and car purchases were faced with a serious problem. They had to pay savers high rates to get the funds needed to continue their long-term loans. Some institutions found they had to pay savers more than they were charging long-term borrowers who had arranged loans at the lower interest rates of earlier years. The gap between the interest rates being paid to savers and the rates charged borrowers on old loans was a particular problem for mortgage lenders, especially savings and loan associations.

To protect themselves from fluctuations in interest rates, mortgage lenders began offering adjustable rate mortgages. More recently this idea has spread to other types of loans. Rates on *adjustable rate loans* are linked to one of several different indexes describing the cost of funds in financial

---

CONSUMER CASE: TWO BOSTON AUTO DEALERS PAY PENALTIES

Two Boston automobile dealerships will pay a total of $70,000 in civil penalties under proposed consent decrees settling Federal Trade Commission charges they violated federal laws by giving consumers incomplete credit information in their advertisements. The FTC complaints name Boch Oldsmobile Inc. and Boch Toyota Inc., and their president, Ernest J. Boch.

The complaints and proposed consent decrees were filed in federal court by the Department of Justice at the request of the FTC. The decrees are subject to the court's approval.

The complaints charge the dealers failed to bring their advertising into compliance with the Truth in Lending Act, even after FTC staff notified the companies that their ads did not comply with the law. According to the Commission's complaints, the companies advertised certain credit information, such as low down payments, without also stating other information the law requires, including the annual percentage rate and monthly payments. Under the proposed consent decrees, Boch Oldsmobile and Boch Toyota and their president are prohibited from violating the Truth in Lending Act in the future.

In March 1983, the FTC began a comprehensive ad monitoring and industry education program to improve automobile credit advertisers' compliance with the act.

Source: Federal Trade Commission, "Boston Auto Dealers," *FTC News Notes* 86, no. 30 (28 April 1986): 1.

QUESTIONS
1. What law did the FTC charge the dealers had violated?
2. What credit information did the dealers provide? What information did the FTC charge should have been included?
3. What effects do the violations have on shoppers?

---

markets. Adjustable rate loans are also referred to as *variable rate loans* and *flexible rate loans*.

As the interest rates in the financial market go up, the rate for adjustable rate loans will rise too. Loan arrangements differ on how frequently rates are adjusted. As the interest rate on a loan is adjusted upward, the finance charge will increase.

The uncertainties of an adjustable interest loan make it important for borrowers to understand the adjustment procedure before entering into a loan agreement. Understanding is especially important for long-term agreements such as mortgages, which involve large finance charges.

Given the uncertainties involved in an adjustable rate loan, why do borrowers agree to them? One reason is that those loan terms may be the only ones available. Another reason borrowers accept adjustable rate loans is that the rates charged typically are lower, at least initially, than the available fixed loan rates. Lenders offer lower rates on adjustable rate loans than on fixed rate loans because they involve less risk. The adjustable rate helps protect lenders against losses if loan rates should rise.

Shopping for Loan Rates. Studies of loan terms in different localities usually find substantial variations in the APRs being charged in a particular market. APRs from different lenders in a market often differ by several percentage points. This variation can make a sizable difference in the total finance charges for longer term loans. For auto loans the difference may amount to $300 to $500. For mortgages, the differences in finance charges may be as much as $50,000 on a 30-year $80,000 mortgage (*Consumer Reports*, October, 1985). When such large amounts are involved, it is clearly worthwhile to shop around.

Overall, the APRs charged on retailers' and bank credit cards make them one of the most expensive ways to get credit. A substantial proportion of credit card holders carry over balances from month to month and pay finance charges on them. They would be better off if they could arrange to obtain credit in other ways.

Some banks and credit unions make unsecured personal loans to customers at lower rates than those charged on balances carried on bank credit cards. *Unsecured personal loans* do not require any property (e.g., a car) to be pledged as security. These loans require special arrangements but do offer a cheaper way to finance sizable purchases than credit cards.

Rates for *secured personal loans* are even lower than those for unsecured loans. The security provided by the use of a car or an appliance as collateral, or the use of financial assets such as stocks or bonds as collateral, reduces the lender's risk and makes a lower APR feasible. Banks, credit unions, and auto finance companies such as General Motors Acceptance Corporation all are potential sources of secured loans.

Under the 1986 tax law, deductions for consumer loan interest were phased out. Only mortgage interest remained deductible under the new law. This change has led to a surge in offers of loans secured by the borrowers' home equity. Such loans should be approached with caution. They may involve substantial fees and the interest on home equity loans is not always fully deductible.

Some banks offer lower APRs to customers who make their loan payments with automatic transfers from their checking account. Banks like this arrangement because they reduce paperwork, eliminate late payments, and increase the certainty of getting paid.

Convenience

Often when you want to borrow money, you need to do it quickly. Speed and a minimum of hassle have a high priority. Getting credit by charging a purchase on a credit card is easy and quick. Unfortunately, it is a relatively expensive way to get credit because credit card APRs are higher than those for most other forms of credit. Unsecured personal loans or secured personal loans may take more time to arrange, but they almost always will be cheaper.

TYPES OF CREDIT

Credit comes in a number of forms. Some of them are familiar—the credit card that lets you charge now—but other forms aren't always recognized as credit. When doctors provide service and bill you later, that's credit; when the electric company provides power and bills you later, that is credit, too.

Forms of Credit

Credit is provided in two basic forms. *Sales credit* is credit for the purchase of goods or services. Sales credit includes department store charge accounts, bank and gasoline credit card purchases, and other purchases for which you promise to pay at some later time. *Cash credit* is credit provided in the form of money that can be spent as desired. Cash credit includes personal loans in the form of cash from a bank, credit union, or finance company.

Repayment Arrangements

Credit is often classified according to how it is to be repaid. *Installment credit* is provided for a specific amount and is repaid in a series of payments over a specified period. Installment credit is typically used for large purchases such as cars, with the loan terms set down in a written agreement. For installment purchases, the lender often keeps title to the item financed as security for the loan.

The other major category of credit is *noninstallment credit*. The amounts involved and duration for this type of credit vary. Noninstallment credit may be paid off in a single payment or in a continuing series of payments:

- *Single payment credit.* The amount owed is due in full within a specified period, typically a month. Examples include doctors' and dentists' bills and utility bills. Regular 30-day charge accounts also fall in this category. Usually there is no finance charge for credit extended in this way.
- *Open-ended credit* (also called *revolving credit*). The amount owed will vary as the account is paid off or new purchases are added. Department store and bank credit cards are both forms of open-ended credit. Some open-ended accounts provide for charges to be paid off within 30 days with no finance charge; others impose a finance charge that begins at the time of the purchase. Balances that are carried to future months are subject to a finance charge.

THREE COMMON TYPES OF CREDIT

There are so many types of loan arrangements that it is difficult to describe them all in detail, but it is useful to look at some frequently used types to see how they work. The following three sections take a close-up look at mortgage loans, installment loans for cars, and credit card loans.

Mortgage Loans

Conventional mortgage loans, even though they involve large amounts of money, are one of the simplest types of loan agreements. They are a closed-end installment loan, with a fixed interest rate, calling for equal payments over a specified number of years. The property purchased is pledged as security for the loan. Other types of mortgages have appeared in the last decade. The operation of those with adjustable interest rates is somewhat more complex and will be considered later.

Conventional Mortgage Loans. The conventional mortgage loan provides for the reduction of the debt with periodic payments (usually monthly) of equal size. The payments cover the interest on the loan and also pay off part of the principal. This repayment procedure is called *amortization*. At first most of each payment goes for interest; but as the loan is paid off, the portion going to interest decreases, and the portion going to pay off the loan principal increases.

The size of the monthly payments is determined by three factors:

- The amount borrowed (the loan principal)
- The annual percentage rate (APR)
- The length of the loan period

The amount borrowed has a major effect on the finance charge for a mortgage loan. Most home buyers use mortgage loans, making a *down payment* (or initial payment) from their savings and borrowing the remainder. Down-payment requirements vary among lenders.

A larger down payment reduces monthly payments in several ways. First, it will reduce the amount of debt that has to be amortized and the finance charge on it. A larger down payment also reduces the risk to the lender and sometimes results in a slightly lower interest rate, or the elimination of mortgage insurance. Two examples show the effect of the down payment on the purchase of a $80,000 home with a 20-year, 12 percent APR mortgage:

	20 percent down payment	10 percent down payment
Amount financed	$64,000	$72,000
Monthly payment	$704.71	$792.80 + mortgage insurance premium

In cases where mortgage loans are arranged with only small down payments, the lender usually is protected against loss by *mortgage insurance*. One of the major sources of mortgage insurance is the Federal Housing Administration (FHA). FHA mortgage insurance was developed to make it easier for low- and middle-income people to purchase homes. Because lenders are protected against financial loss on the loan, they are willing to accept a lower down payment and a lower interest rate. The cost of providing the insurance is covered by a small monthly fee added to the mortgage payment. Several private firms also provide mortgage insurance.

The annual percentage rate (APR) is the second factor affecting the finance charge on a mortgage loan. For long-term loans, such as home mortgages, small changes in the APR can have a big effect on total finance charges. The effects of such changes can be seen in Table 14-1. Monthly payments and total finance charges increase rapidly with increasing interest rates. The reason for the negative effects of high interest rates on housing sales also become clearer.

Many lenders make additional charges to increase their return on the loan when the interest rate charged is below current market rates. The addi-

Table 14-1
The Effect of APR on Monthly Payments for a $60,000 Mortgage Loan for 30 Years

Interest Rate	Monthly Payment (principal and interest)	Total Finance Charge for 30-year Loan Period
8%	$440.26	$ 98,493.60
10	526.55	129,558.00
12	617.17	162,181.20
14	710.93	195,934.80
16	806.86	230,469.60
18	904.26	265,533.60

tional charges are referred to as *points*. One point equals one percent of the amount loaned. A one-point charge on a $50,000 mortgage would be $500; a three-point charge would be $1,500. Point charges are really prepaid interest charges. Some lenders offer a reduced interest rate in return for points. Basically they are offering to sell a lower interest rate in return for part of the interest up front. These offers should be examined carefully. If a home will be lived in only a short time, the offer is not likely to be a good deal because the savings from a reduced interest rate come only if the mortgage is held over a long period.

Lenders may also insist on other fees to increase the total finance charge. A common fee is an *origination fee*, a charge for the administrative costs of preparing a loan. Interest charges, points, and origination fees all become part of the finance charge and must be disclosed to prospective borrowers.

The length of the loan period is the third factor affecting the finance charge on a mortgage loan. Longer loan periods offer borrowers the opportunity to reduce their monthly payments, as can be seen in Table 14-2. While a smaller monthly payment seems desirable, it comes at a substantial price. Lengthening the period of a loan substantially increases the finance charge (see Table 14-2).

For a $60,000 mortgage loan at 12 percent (APR), going from a 20-year loan to a 30-year loan reduces the monthly payment from $660.66 to $617.17. You can see also that the total finance charge increases from $98,558.40 to $162,181.20, however. Lenders frequently offer lower interest rates for shorter loan periods because they involve somewhat less risk, which helps to reduce the higher monthly payments of a shorter term mortgage.

There are a number of variations of the fixed rate mortgage but two deserve special mention. *Balloon mortgages* are short-term mortgages, usually for a period of three to five years. The principal is not fully amortized over this brief period, and there is a large final payment. The large final payment

Table 14-2
The Effect of Length of Loan Period on the Finance Charge for a $60,000 Mortgage Loan at 12 Percent APR

Length of Loan Period	Monthly Payment (principal and interest)	Total Finance Charge over Loan Period
5 years	$1,334.67	$ 20,080.20
10	860.83	43,299.60
15	720.11	69,619.80
20	660.66	98,558.40
25	631.94	129,582.00
30	617.17	162,181.20
35	609.33	195,918.60

Part 3   Managing Personal Finances

is what gives these mortgages their name. If borrowers cannot meet the final payment, they have to refinance the mortgage or sell the property. Some lenders will agree to refinance, but will not guarantee the rate.

Another variation of the fixed rate mortgage is the *graduated payment mortgage.* These mortgages are designed to meet the needs of young people who expect to have increasing incomes. Graduated payment mortgages provide for monthly payments to rise gradually over a period of five to ten years. They then become constant for the remainder of the mortgage.

Consumers with fixed rate mortgages always know exactly what their monthly payments will be. Payments will never change over the life of the mortgage, nor will the total finance charge. They may have to pay extra for this peace of mind, however. In recent years, fixed rate mortgage interest rates have been two to three percentage points higher than those for adjustable rate mortages.

Adjustable Rate Mortgages. Interest rates on *adjustable rate mortgages,* like other adjustable rate loans, are adjusted periodically on the basis of indexes of the cost of funds. These indexes include Treasury Bill rates, the Federal Home Loan Bank Board's national average mortgage rate, and the average cost of funds for federally chartered savings and loan associations.

Adjustable rate mortgages (ARMs), which also are referred to as *flexible* and *variable* rate mortgages, may be adjusted each year, every three years, or at other times. The more frequent the adjustment the lower the interest rate demanded because the risk to the lender is less. In comparison shopping for a mortgage, borrowers should note that while all ARMs provide for upward adjustments, not all of them provide for downward adjustments.

To reassure borrowers who are concerned about knowing how much their interest rate or monthly payments may go up, some lenders put limits or caps on the amount of change allowed. Some ARMs include *rate caps* that limit the amount the interest rate can be increased at any one adjustment. The rate caps may include limits on the total increase in the interest rate that can occur over the life of the mortgage.

Some ARMs include *payment caps* that limit the amount the monthly payment will increase even though the interest rate on the mortgage has increased. With payment caps, the amount of principal paid off each month will be reduced if the interest rate goes up. Payment caps had unexpected effects in the mid-1980s when the interest payments due on some ARMs exceeded the payments. On these mortgages the principal actually increased each month as unpaid interest was added to the amount owed. This phenomenon has been labeled *negative amortization* and has lead to some serious criticism of ARMs with payment caps. Because of the negative amortization problem, financial experts recommend that consumers seek ARMs with rate caps rather than with payment caps.

There are many different combinations of features in ARMs, which makes it important for consumers to work through the worst-case scenario. Could you live with the greatest changes possible under the terms of the mortgage?

One of the variations of the ARM is the *renegotiated mortgage* (or rollover mortgage). It has a specified rate for the first three to five years. At the end of the period, the rate is renegotiated. Another variation is the *buydown*. This technique lowers the monthly payments in the early years of a mortgage. Rates can be bought down when someone pays the difference between the rate charged the borrower and market rates. This payment, which may be made by the builder, relatives of the buyer, or others, subsidizes the lower rate. Interest rates and monthly payments gradually increase over several years, at which time the mortgage becomes an adjustable rate mortgage. Buydowns, especially those paid for by builders and developers, do not come free because their costs become imbedded in higher housing prices.

The mortgage types we have discussed are only a few leading examples of current mortgage arrangements. There are hundreds of different types of fixed and adjustable rate mortgages with different combinations of features, making careful study of the features of each mortgage essential.

Automobile Loans

Continuing price increases for automobiles have kept consumers dependent on credit to help finance their purchases. The typical auto loan is an installment loan. The purchase price (less trade-in) plus finance charge is repaid in equal payments over a specified period, with the car serving as collateral for the loan.

Cost. As with home mortgages, the finance charge on car loans depends on (1) the amount financed, (2) the annual percentage rate interest charged, and (3) the length of the loan.

In the mid-1980s, APRs for new cars were in the 12 to 14 percent range. Rates for used cars were slightly higher, reflecting lenders' belief that those loans are somewhat riskier and their attempts to cover the fixed costs of arranging a loan, which are much the same regardless of the amount financed.

Studies comparing APRs on auto loans within a market area find significant variation — as much as two or three percentage points. This difference can have a sizable effect on finance charges when a major loan is financed for three, four, or five years.

The length of the average car loan has increased along with car prices. In the mid-1970s, 36-month loans were typical. By the mid-1980s, the typical loan was for 48 months and 60-month loans were not uncommon. The effects of long length on the cost of a loan of $8,000 at 13 percent can be seen in this example:

	Monthly Payment	Finance Charge
24-month loan	$380.34	$1,128.16
36-month loan	269.56	1,704.16
48-month loan	214.62	2,301.76
60-month loan	182.03	2,921.80

Lengthening the loan period does lower the monthly payment, but you can see its effect on the finance charge.

Sources. Many car buyers arrange their loans through the dealer. Dealers serve as agents for both local banks and sales finance companies (such as General Motors Acceptance Corporation and Chrysler Credit). For handling these loans, dealers receive a portion of the finance charge.

Car buyers usually can get a better deal by arranging their own financing directly with a bank or credit union and eliminating the dealer's commission. Consumer finance companies also provide auto loans, but their rates typically are higher.

In the mid-1980s, car manufacturers offered reduced financing rates as a sales incentive. There rates were subsidized by the car manufacturers and were so attractive that the sales finance companies were, at least temporarily, the chief source of auto loans.

Credit Cards

The American public has found that "plastic money" is almost as useful as cash and is accepted almost everywhere. In a publicity stunt a few years ago, a woman who was sent off across the United States with only a credit card and no cash reported encountering few problems. Her biggest difficulties, she noted, were dealing with parking meters and pay toilets. There are, however, still a few holdouts who refuse credit cards: some small stores and restaurants, plus some discount stores with a cash-only policy.

Credit cards are issued by several types of firms.

- *Retailer's credit cards* provide sales credit, permitting credit purchases in the firm's stores. These accounts typically provide open-ended credit.
- *Bank credit cards* are issued by individual banks or by banks participating in the Visa, MasterCard, or other systems. Banks that are members of Visa and MasterCard set their own terms and select their own account holders. The national organizations advertise and promote the cards and supervise the movement of charge slips between banks. Billings are handled by the individual member banks. Bank cards provide open-ended credit. The new Discover card issued by Sears Roebuck and Company operates like a bank card.
- *Travel and entertainment cards* are issued by American Express, Carte Blanche, and Diners Club. They provide single payment credit. Amounts charged are due within 30 days. Balances may be carried over only if special arrangements are made.

Cost. Bank and travel and entertainment card issuers levy annual fees of $18 or more on cardholders. Only a few banks have no annual fees.

Interest rates for balances carried on retailers' and bank cards vary widely between card issuers. In 1985, *Consumer Reports* (January, 1985) noted that rates from different issuers range between 12 and 22 percent. Despite the fact that a large proportion of card holders carry balances from month to month, most are not aware of these differences in rates. Bank promotions for credit cards do little to inform them. Rates appear to be rather "sticky"; that is, they do not respond much either to competition or to declining interest rates in the financial markets.

CONSUMER CONCERN: CREDIT LIFE INSURANCE—DO YOU REALLY NEED IT?

Credit life insurance is often linked to consumer loan arrangements to pay the balance due if the borrower dies. Credit life insurance policies are offered and frequently pushed by lenders. In some cases, lenders insist on coverage.

CRITICISMS

Those interested in protecting consumers have several concerns about credit life insurance (Williams, 1977). A major concern is that it is overpriced (Rubin, 1978). Few consumers pay much attention to the costs of coverage, because it usually is only a few dollars a month for car loans. Consumer experts point out, however, that credit life coverage is often far more costly than an equal amount of regular life insurance.

Critics also charge that there is no real competition on price and that borrowers are offered no alternatives. They also note that the sale of credit life coverage is highly profitable for both lenders and the insurance companies, and perhaps unreasonably so.

Concern has also been expressed frequently about lenders' tactics in selling credit life insurance. Sales procedures often leave consumers uncertain about whether coverage is required or voluntary and uninformed about its cost. Some consumers, in fact, are unaware they even have coverage and fail to make appropriate claims.

RESPONSES TO CRITICISMS

Members of the credit industry have responded that credit life policies serve a real need for lower income consumers who lack regular life insurance coverage. They note that a large proportion of those with coverage think it is a good thing to have. Those with less education and

Competition between bank card issuers usually has not focused on the annual percentage rates charged. Instead, card issuers offer "enhancements"—extra services available free or for a small fee. These extras may include discounts on hotel rooms and rental cars or other purchases, rebates based on credit use, or registration services that will notify issuers of lost or stolen cards.

Not only do banks differ in the rate of interest they charge, they also differ in the *grace period* they allow. (This period is the amount of time before finance charges are imposed on a purchase.) More and more banks have begun making finance charges at once. Others may wait for as long

lower incomes have especially favorable attitudes toward coverage (Eisenbeis & Schweitzer, 1978).

WHO NEEDS IT?

Questions frequently are raised about who, if anyone, should buy credit life insurance. Some financial experts argue that if life insurance coverage is needed, it is needed all the time, not just in connection with a loan. They suggest buying permanent coverage and taking advantage of its lower cost for most people.

Credit life insurance may, however, be a good deal for a few people: those who are unable to get regular life insurance coverage or for whom it is very costly. Credit life insurance premiums are the same for all regardless of age, sex, or health; no physical examination is required. The attractiveness of credit life insurance for borrowers with problems in getting regular life insurance is, however, limited by the provisions in some policies. Policies may have exclusions that eliminate coverage in case death was due to pre-existing conditions (i.e., health problems that existed at the time coverage was arranged).

QUESTIONS

1. What are the criticisms of credit life insurance and the way it is sold? What responses have been made to criticisms?
2. For what types of people may credit life insurance be useful? Why?
3. Those who like credit life insurance best are groups who often are less informed on consumer questions. Do you think their favorable attitudes reflect a lack of information or an informed preference? Explain your answer.

as 30 days before beginning to make charges. The result is a big difference in the cost of credit to card holders.

There is a hidden cost to all consumers for bank and travel and entertainment credit cards. This cost is the charge made to merchants who present sales draft slips for payment. Charges range from one to six percent of the amount charged. The expense becomes part of the merchant's cost of doing business and is included in the price of goods and serices. Retailers with their own credit cards also have costs when they provide credit, though these costs are not quite so explicit.

Some critics of the present system argue that credit card users should pay extra to cover the costs of providing credit. This approach is not feasible. Charging higher prices for credit purchases would amount to a higher interest rate, a rate far beyond legal limits. Discounts for cash are permissible, however. They have not been widely offered, except at gasoline stations.

Convenience. The most useful kind of credit card is the one accepted at the places where a consumer wants to buy. Visa and MasterCard are widely accepted both in this country and abroad. Of the travel and entertainment cards, American Express is the most widely accepted. The others are, however, accepted at many deluxe hotels and restaurants.

Credit limits will also affect how useful a card is. Bank cards often initially have a $500 or a $1,000 limit that can be adjusted upward later after the issuer sees how they are handled by the consumer. Credit limits are higher on special cards (e.g., gold and platinum cards), and there are extra annual fees. Travel and entertainment cards seem to have no set limits. Instead, charges and payments are monitored as new requests for credit are made.

Bank credit cards also can be used at bank offices and at many automatic teller machines to obtain cash advances. Some travel and entertainment cards can be used to obtain traveler's checks or cash advances if prior arrangements have been made with the issuer.

Does a person really need a bank or travel and entertainment credit card? The answer is probably yes. Cards are useful in emergencies when it is difficult to obtain cash or get a check accepted. They are especially handy for out-of-town travel, and they are almost essential for renting a car.

When applying for a bank credit card, it is useful to remember that each bank selects its own cardholders. If a consumer is turned down by one bank, another may still grant the request for a card.

Credit Card Fraud. One of the advantages of having a credit card is that it is almost as useful as cash. This ease of use can be a problem, too, if the card or card number falls into the wrong hands.

Lost and stolen cards are a major problem for both card issuers and card holders. Card holders can protect themselves from responsibility for illegal charges by notifying the card issuer *immediately* when a card is lost, misplaced, or stolen.

Problems not only arise from stolen cards, but may also arise from fraudulent use by employees working for merchants who accept cards. One trick of dishonest employees is to use a card to make impressions on two sales drafts. One is presented with the bill for the customer to sign. The employee then can fill in the other, forge the customer's signature, and pocket the amount filled-in from the cash register. Experts suggest never letting a card be taken out of sight, but this is easier said than done. Another practice used by dishonest employees is to change the amount written in on the sales draft and then pocket the extra amount from the cash register.

Credit card fraud artists do not always need the card itself; just the number may be enough. With the number they can place phone orders for expensive merchandise. Experts suggest protecting yourself by destroying the carbons from sales drafts. They also warn against giving a card number to unknown callers on the phone.

CONSUMER CAPSULE: CUTTING THE COST OF BORROWING

- Keep the duration of the loan as short as possible to reduce total finance charges and reduce the risk of rate increases if the interest rate is adjustable.
- Offer security or collateral if possible as a way to reduce the annual percentage rate on a loan. Savings accounts, stocks, life insurance, and home equity all can be used as collateral.
- Shop for the best loan terms. A bank may offer an advantageous rate, especially if the loan payments are made with an automatic transfer from a personal checking account. A credit union may also offer a good rate because they have the security of being repaid by a deduction from your pay check.
- Pay bills on time. Most creditors levy late fees and penalties when a payment is late. There are no regulations limiting the amount charged. A consumer may have the unpleasant surprise of being charged $10 for being late with a $10 payment. Read the details of the agreement on how an account works to avoid such surprises.

CREDIT PROBLEMS AND BILLING ERRORS

People with charge accounts and credit cards sometimes face a dilemma. They know they need to pay on time, but they are not willing to pay charges that seem to be in error, that aren't adequately identified, or that are for defective merchandise. What can you do to protect yourself? The appropriate steps differ depending on whether the problem is basically a billing error, a problem with defective merchandise, or related to a lost or stolen credit card.

Billing Errors

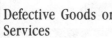

Errors in credit bills may be of several different types:

- Errors in the indicated cost of an item
- Problems because an item is not adequately identified. This is a common difficulty because most charge account statements indicate only the date of purchase, the store or store department where the purchase was made, and the purchase total.
- Billing for something that was not purchased or for unauthorized use of an account
- Billing for something that was never delivered or an item on which delivery was not accepted
- Errors in the calculation of the amounts due, the interest charges, or other errors in the administration of the account

One protection is to save copies of sales drafts so that the account statement can be checked when it arrives. Another important step is checking each monthly statement to be certain the charges listed are correct.

If there are problems or errors, there are steps that can be taken. Inform the creditor of the error in writing within 60 days after the bill was mailed. The report can take the same form as any other complaint letter. Provide identification of the account (i.e., name on the account and the account number). Indicate the nature of the problem and the reasons why the item is wrong or needs explanation.

Pay all portions of the statement that are not in dispute while waiting for an answer. Under federal regulations, neither the amount in dispute nor the finance charges on it need to be paid. Creditors are obligated to respond to letters about credit problems within 30 days. They must correct the error or explain the reasons for their action within 90 days. If there is no error, the creditor will indicate what is owed and the finance charges owed on it. If you are still not satisfied, notify the creditor within the time allowed to pay the bill.

Defective Goods or Services

Sometimes consumers have problems with purchases that they are unable to return. Are they still obligated to pay? The answer is both yes and maybe.

Consumers do have *some* rights to withhold payment on damaged or shoddy goods and poor quality services. Consumers have full rights to withhold payments on store charge cards. Consumers' rights to withhold payment on bank credit cards and travel and entertainment cards are, however, more limited.

Billing and Crediting of Payments

Under federal regulations consumers must be notified promptly of amounts due on credit accounts if finance charges can be made to give the account holder time to pay the bill so as to avoid the finance charge. Bills must be sent at least 14 days before they are due. Payments must be credited the day they are received by the card issuer.

Lost or Stolen Credit Cards

Because of problems with credit card fraud, card holders need protection from unauthorized charges. Present regulations provide card holders a good deal of protection, but this protection depends on *prompt* notification of the card issuer. It is crucial to have a record of account numbers and notification addresses in a safe place in case cards are lost or stolen so that creditors can be notified immediately.

Any unauthorized charges made *after* creditors are notified do not have to be paid. Consumers are obligated to pay only up to $50 per card for unauthorized purchases made *before* creditors are notified.

Illustration 14-2
When a purchase on a store credit card proves unsatisfactory, customers have a right to withhold payment.

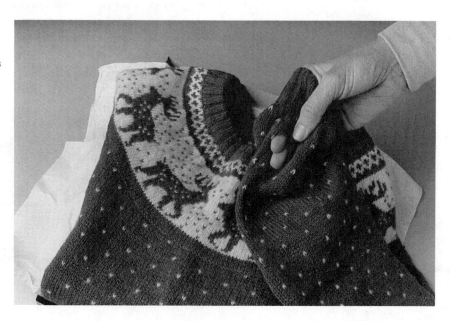

CONSUMER CAPSULE: CREDIT DANGER SIGNALS

- Charging more each month than the amount made in payments on credit accounts
- Juggling payments on credit accounts; stalling one creditor in order to pay another
- Using cash advances on credit to cover payments on other credit accounts
- Receiving past-due notices on credit account statements
- Adding new credit accounts when near the credit limits on the accounts currently held

It is illegal for card issuers to send out unrequested credit cards. They can, however, send out replacements for expiring cards without the card holder's permission.

If credit problems cannot be resolved and a bank is involved, a consumer can get advice from the Federal Reserve System offices in Washington or the nearest district office. The Federal Reserve System handles complaints concerning national- and state-chartered banks that are members of the system. They will refer complaints about other banks to the appropriate authorities.

As seen in this chapter, there are many different types of credit available from a number of different sources. In fact, credit is so widely available that it is easy to get overcommitted. One protection is to set one's own credit limits. Consumers should decide how much credit they can handle on their own and not depend on the bank and the department stores to decide for them.

Credit is a useful tool, but like other tools it can cause injuries if it is not handled wisely. It is useful to be able to shift the timing of consumption to spend now and pay later, but paying for consumption this way decreases flexibility in managing finances. When next month's paycheck arrives, there already are bills waiting to be paid.

MAJOR CHAPTER CONCEPTS

1. The time value of money is the cost of borrowing to consume now, with repayment later.
2. Credit grantors' criteria for judging creditworthiness include capacity (ability to repay), character (willingness to repay), and capital (resources that can be used to repay).

3. To provide a basis for evaluating creditworthiness, credit applications gather personal information, employment information, financial information, and credit information.

4. Credit bureaus collect information on local credit users and sell it, for a fee, to credit grantors.

5. Credit-granting decisions may be based on information on the credit application, credit bureau information, or a combination of both.

6. Under equal credit opportunity rules, credit-granting decisions cannot be based on sex, marital status, religion, race, or age (if applicant is of legal age).

7. Individuals who are denied credit must be informed of the reasons within 30 days.

8. To build a credit record, an individual should begin by establishing a checking and a savings account and then applying for credit at local stores. Good management of these accounts will be evidence of creditworthiness.

9. Under federal regulations, lenders must indicate both the annual percentage rate of interest (APR) and the total finance charge on loans.

10. Adjustable interest rates are linked to one of several different indexes of the cost of funds in financial markets. Lenders like adjustable interest rates because they reduce the risk of losses from rising interest rates.

11. Credit can be classified as either sales credit or cash credit (money is provided). Credit also can be classified as installment credit and non-installment credit, which includes single payment credit and open-ended credit.

12. The size of the payments required to amortize a mortgage depends on the amount borrowed, the annual percentage rate interest, and the length of the loan period.

13. "Points" on a mortgage are a one-time finance charge, with one point equal to one percent of the mortgage loan.

14. Changes in payments on adjustable rate mortgages may be limited by rate or payment caps or limits.

15. Studies have found that auto loan rates, like other loan rates, vary a good deal between lenders.

16. Bank credit cards provide open-ended credit. Travel and entertainment cards provide single payment credit.

17. To protect against unauthorized charges on a credit card, the card holder should notify the issuer at once if a card is lost. If this is done, the card holder is obligated to pay only up to $50 per card for unauthorized charges.

18. In case of suspected billing errors, consumers should notify the credit grantor within 60 days and pay portions of the bill that are not disputed. The credit grantor should respond in 30 days to the inquiry.

CONSUMER QUESTIONS

1. For what purposes are you using credit currently? For what other purposes do you expect to use credit in the near future? What are some purposes for which you would not use credit?
2. If you are using credit currently, what interest rates are you paying? What are the terms of the loan? For example, are you providing security?
3. Which of the following types of loans have the lower interest rates? Why is this?
    a. Secured or unsecured loans
    b. Adjustable or fixed rate
    c. Shorter term loans or longer term loans
4. Prepare a report on a consumer issue involving credit. Some possible topics include:
    a. Discrimination in granting credit
    b. Usury laws (i.e., laws setting limits on the interest rate charged) and their effects
    c. Unfair credit collection procedures
    d. Consumer bankruptcy
    e. Discounts for cash
    f. Recent trends in the use of consumer credit
    g. Credit problems of the poor
5. Check the yellow pages of your local phone book under "Credit Reporting Agencies" for listings of credit bureaus in your area. What agencies are listed and where are they located? What services does each provide? What other information do the ads provide?
6. Check the yellow pages of your local phone book for the "Loans" section. What organizations are listed? What information is provided about the types of loans each makes?
7. Check local newspapers for ads indicating APRs for loans (e.g., mortgage loans, auto loans). Make a list of loan sources and APRs.
8. What kinds of credit are available in the retail establishments where you usually shop? List the establishments and the kinds of credit each provides. Do any provide discounts for cash? If not, find out why.
9. Collect some recent magazine ads for credit cards or watch for TV ads. What evaluative criteria are emphasized? What important information is not provided in the ads?

SUGGESTED READINGS

1. *Consumer Reports.* "Playing Your Cards Right" 50, no. 1 (January 1985): 47-51. *Consumer Reports* looked at the credit card terms for the three major travel and entertainment cards and for the two major bank cards. (The offerings of 133 banks were checked.) Considerable variation in annual fees and interest rates was found.

2. *Consumer Reports.* "Shopping Smart for Loans" 50, no. 10 (October 1985): 581-586. This article considers evaluative criteria for choosing mortgage and car loans and unsecured personal loans. The results of a survey of loan rates at 100 banks round the country are reported.

3. *Consumer Reports.* "What Makes You a Good Credit Risk?" 48, no. 5 (May 1983): 254-259. This article examines lenders' credit-granting procedures, including the use of credit scoring. The hypothetical scoring scheme presented is of particular interest. What consumers can do if they are turned down for credit also is considered.

4. Cook, John A., and Robert Wool. *All You Need to Know About Banks.* New York: Bantam Books, 1983. Chapters 7 to 10. Four chapters of this book provide an extensive discussion of how to get the best credit arrangements from a bank. The senior author is a former vice president of the Bank of New York.

CHAPTER 15

INVESTMENTS

Athletes frequently repeat the saying "No pain, no gain!" They are convinced that if you do not push yourself, you won't achieve the gains you want. The saying applies in the investment world, too. If your goal is big financial gains, you have to take some risks—perhaps some painful ones that cause worry.

Chapter 13 pointed out the advantages of savings accounts and CDs, including safety of principal, a guaranteed return, and high liquidity. The returns are, however, lower than those usually available from stocks, bonds, and other investments. Those who want higher returns have to take some risks. Each individual has to decide which evaluative criteria are most important and then decide what combination of investments—including stocks, bonds, and other alternatives—is the best.

This chapter will examine some popular types of investments including bonds, stocks, real estate, and also gold, jewelry, and collectibles. Matching investment strategies to personal situations will also be considered.

Chapter 13 noted that bank deposits provide a guaranteed interest and return of the amount deposited. Deposits can be easily and quickly withdrawn. *Investments,* in contrast, provide an opportunity both for income (e.g., dividends from stocks and interest payments from bonds) and for gains as they increase in value. Unlike savings accounts and CDs, investments such as stocks and bonds are transferrable and can be bought and sold.

There are two general types of investments:

- *Debt investments.* The most common investment of this type is bonds, which essentially are loans to a corporation or government body by investors. Debt investments provide an opportunity for income in the form of interest payments and also from *capital gains* (i.e., profits from an increase in value).
- *Equity investments.* These investments represent ownership of a share of a corporation (stocks) or the ownership of real estate, gold, or collectibles. Stock and real estate ownership provide an opportunity for income in the form of dividends or rent and also for capital gains. Gold and collectibles produce no income but may provide an opportunity for capital gains.

CRITERIA FOR EVALUATING INVESTMENTS

Individual investors have different objectives in investing. To meet these needs, the securities business has developed a wide range of investment alternatives. The array is, in fact, bewildering. There are thousands of different stocks, mutual funds, bonds, and other investment vehicles available. In considering them, investors need to bear in mind how they serve three key objectives:

- *Growth or capital appreciation.* Some people whose income is more than sufficient for their current needs use the excess to build assets for future use. These individuals seek out investments that will gain in value over the years from price appreciation or the compounding of earnings.
- *Income.* Other people may need current income to cover their daily living expenses and feel they cannot afford to wait for future returns or capital gains. They seek investments that provide high current yields and safety of the principal invested.
- *Tax management.* Some individuals seek out investments that will provide them tax-free current income. Others look for investments that provide tax advantages of other kinds.

These different objectives give rise to a number of criteria that are important in evaluating investments. Virtually no investment, however, scores well on all points. The investments that provide the greatest safety typically have lower yields. High liquidity often is matched with lower yields. Investors must decide which combination of characteristics will suit them best and expect to make some trade-offs.

- *Yield.* An important goal is the size of the return (or yield) on an investment. This yield may be in the form of interest payments, dividends, or perhaps income from a real estate investment.
- *Safety of yield.* A second critical goal is the safety of the yield from an investment. Are the dividends paid stable (or growing) or is there risk they may decline? Will the corporation issuing a bond be able to maintain the interest payments it has promised?
- *Potential for capital gains.* An important objective for some investors is to make capital gains by selling investments they have made for more than they paid for them. The value of investments fluctuates with changing interest rates, inflationary pressures, and business conditions. These changes in value provide an opportunity for gains — and for losses, too.
- *Liquidity and marketability.* We noted earlier that *liquidity,* the ease and speed with which financial assets can be converted into cash without loss of principal, is important in judging places for savings. It is important in considering investments, too. A related criterion is *marketability,* which is the speed with which an asset can be converted into cash. Some assets, such as stocks and bonds, have high marketability because there are readily available financial markets where they can be sold. Such a sale may result in a loss, but a speedy sale is possible. Ready markets are harder to find for such assets as jewelry and antiques.
- *Tax advantages.* Federal, state and local governments tax different types of investment income differently. Some types of investment income (e.g., interest from Treasury bonds) are exempt from state and local taxes; interest from municipal bonds is exempt from federal income taxes. For individuals in higher tax brackets, these exemptions from taxation may be an important consideration.

APPROACHES TO INVESTING

Individual investors settle on differing combinations of risk and returns that suit them. Because of their differing preferences, their choices of investments and their strategies in the market may differ markedly. Three groups with differing approaches to financial markets can be identified (Merrill Lynch, 1985):

- *Investors.* The people who seek conservative investments, such as high quality stocks and bonds and other high quality assets, have been labeled *investors.* Those in this category are looking for current income or capital gains without significant risk.
- *Speculators.* Those who make short-term investments looking for quick growth in value have been labeled *speculators.* This group seeks out situations in which firms are in temporary difficulty and their securities are

depressed in price along with other high-risk situations that provide an opportunity for profit.

- *Traders.* Those who make short-term investments they may keep for only a few days are labeled *traders.* This group looks for temporary situations in financial markets that offer an opportunity for quick capital gains. Typically they do not hold an asset long enough to receive any earnings. Traders accept significant risks but usually have experience in the market and understand the behavior of prices.

BONDS

Bonds are interest-paying IOU's or promissory notes issued by corporations and governments. The issuer promises to repay the loan principal at some specified future date and to pay interest on the debt. Interest usually is paid periodically, typically semiannually, over the loan period. Some bonds, however, pay out interest only at the end of the loan period.

Just as consumers borrow to buy a new car, business and government may need to borrow to finance major projects such as a new factory, a new bridge, or a new hospital. The loan can then be repaid from future income as the completed project is used. Governments also need to borrow when taxes and other revenues fall short of expenditures. While some of these

Illustration 15-1
Even though bonds and stocks are registered in individual names, they can easily be traded through financial markets.

U.S. Government Securities

The federal government is a major borrower of funds to finance long-term debts. To raise the money it needs, the federal government and government-sponsored agencies issue a wide variety of debt securities. These securities are backed by the "full faith and credit" of the federal government, probably the strongest guarantee available. Because of the government's commitment to repayment and its unbroken record of meeting its commitments, federal government securities have strong appeal to investors concerned about the safety of yields and principal.

U.S. Treasury Bonds. *Treasury bonds* are long-term bonds issued by the federal Treasury Department. They are issued in denominations of $1,000 and up. This is the *face value* (or maturity value), the amount the government promises to pay at the end of the loan period. The maturity of Treasury bonds is 10 years and up, with 20 to 30 year maturities typical. (*Maturity* is the date on which a bond, or other loan, becomes payable.) Interest is paid to bond holders every six months.

While investors are assured of getting their principal back in full at maturity, they should recognize that the *market price* of bonds, the price at which they are sold on financial markets, will fluctuate as interest rates change. Market prices of bonds change because the flow of interest payments and return of principal they promise become more (or less) valuable as interest rates change.

Consider a $1,000 20-year bond, promising an 8 percent interest rate. Each year interest payable totals $80. Now suppose that after a year the interest rates available on new bonds had risen to 10 percent. Investors buying these new bonds would be earning $100 a year on their $1,000 investments. Clearly an investment earning $80 a year is not as valuable as one earning $100 a year. The market price of the bond paying 8 percent would fall to reflect its lower earning power.

Beginning investors often have trouble remembering how changing interest rates affect the price of bonds. The relationship is simple: *Bond prices move in the opposite direction from interest rates.* As interest rates rise, bond prices fall; as interest rates fall, bond prices rise.

Because of the effect of changing interest rates on market prices, loss of principal is possible if Treasury bonds are not held to maturity. Changing interest rates may reduce (or increase) market prices in the period prior to maturity. Government securities provide full security of principal only if they are held to maturity.

Treasury Notes. Treasury notes are used to finance the intermediate-term debt of the federal government. They are issued with face values of $1,000 and up, with maturities of one to ten years. Interest is paid twice yearly.

Treasury Bills. Every Monday, the U.S. takes competitive bids on a new issue of Treasury bills (or T-bills), which the government uses to finance its short-term debt. T-bills are issued with maturities of 13, 26, and 52 weeks, making them ideal for short-term holding. T-bills are issued with a $10,000 minimum face (or maturity) value and are sold at a discount from face value. The discount reflects the interest that will be paid along with the principal at maturity.

Federal Government Agency Securities. A large number of federal agencies and government-chartered corporations issue securities backed by the federal government. These securities are *not* direct obligations of the U.S. Treasury, and not all are backed by the full faith and credit of the federal government. The federal government has, however, never allowed any of these agencies or corporations to default on debt repayments. One well-known goverment-sponsored corporation is the Government National Mortgage Association (GNMA or "Ginnie Mae"), which buys up federally insured mortages from lenders and issues certificates backed by a pool of mortgages. Investors are repaid as mortgage borrowers repay principal and interest on their loans. The interest earned on GNMA certificates is not exempt from state and local taxes.

The Student Loan Marketing Association (SLMA or "Sallie Mae") is another government-sponsored corporation that issues short-term notes backed by federally guaranteed student loans. Other government-backed issuers include the Federal Home Loan Banks and the Farm Credit System.

Interest on all Treasury-issued securities is exempt from state and local taxes. Interest earnings from some, but not all, federal agency securities is also exempt from state and local taxes.

Newly issued Treasury securities may be purchased directly from the U.S. Treasury or a Federal Reserve Bank or through securities dealers. Some securities dealers create a *secondary market* in Treasury securities. They buy the securities when issued for later resale to investors. Federal agency securities are not available directly from the issuing agency, but must be purchased through securities dealers.

Municipal Bonds

Bonds issued by state and local governments are lumped together under the label *municipal bonds*. Also included are bonds issued by state and local agencies and authorities, including bridge and toll-road authorities and hospital authorities. It has been estimated that there are more than 30,000 different issuers of municipal bonds and more than a million separate issues (Merrill Lynch, 1981).

There are several major categories of municipal bonds.

- *General obligation bonds.* Bonds in this category are backed by the full faith and credit and the taxing power of the issuer. Because of the scope of this backing, general obligation bonds are considered the safest category of municipal bonds.
- *Revenue bonds.* Bonds in this category are backed by income from the project financed by the bond issue, e.g., bridge and highway tolls, hospital patient fees. Because that income depends on the success of the project, revenue bonds typically are considered less secure than general obligation bonds.
- *Other categories.* There is a variety of other municipal bonds: bonds for hospital and public housing construction, bonds backed by special taxes, and bonds for financing local industrial development.

One of the major attractions of municipal bonds is the exemption of interest earnings from federal income tax. Earnings also may be exempt from state and local taxes, particularly if the investor lives in the issuing locality. Because of their exemptions from taxation, municipal bonds typically provide lower interest yields than other securities.

Investments in municipal bonds usually are ranked as second in safety only to U.S. government securities. Although investments in municipal bonds generally are secure, some caution is needed. In the 1970s both New York City and Cleveland had financial difficulties that created a temporary threat of loss for creditors. The most spectacular disaster in the municipal bond market was the 1983 default by the Washington Public Power Supply System (WPPSS). The system's problems came as a result of difficulties completing new nuclear reactors and may result in a $2 billion-plus loss for investors. This potential loss has brought the wry comment that the WPPSS bonds, which are referred to in financial markets as WHOOPS bonds, have lived up to their nickname.

Not all municipal issues are rated by the bond rating services (see below). In judging municipal bonds, the issuer's tax (or revenue) and outstanding debt, as well as the area's population statistics and economic climate, should be checked.

Investors can purchase individual bonds from securities brokers. They can also purchase municipal bonds by buying shares in *bond funds* that specialize in municipal issues. Funds pool the purchase money of a large number of investors to buy a diversified portfolio of bonds. The bond funds pay a variable rate of interest because their composition is continually changing.

Investors also have the option of purchasing *unit investment trusts*. Investors in these trusts purchase a portion of a fixed portfolio of bonds that typically are held to maturity. Unit investment bond trusts usually pay a fixed return because their holdings do not change over time. In addition to the bond funds and unit investment bond trusts specializing in municipal issues, there also are bond funds and bond trusts specializing in corporate and federal government issues.

Corporate Bonds

Along with stocks, bonds are a major source of long-term financing for corporations. Bond purchasers become creditors of the corporation, providing money for new equipment and factories, research and development, and other long-run projects. Bond holders are not, however, part-owners of the corporation as stockholders are; they have no voice in running the corporation.

Corporate bonds typically are issued with a face value of $5,000 with maturities running from 4 to 40 years. Most bonds pay interest twice yearly. As is the case with other bonds, corporate bonds seldom sell at their face (or maturity) value. Instead, the market price either represents a discount from face value (if market interest rates are higher than those paid by the bond) or a premium (if market rates are lower than the bond's).

The safety of a bond's yield is affected by whether it is *callable* or not. Callable bonds can be called in and repaid before their specified maturity. Bonds are especially likely to be called if they are paying an interest rate substantially above current market rates. While there is no loss of principal to investors when bonds are called, the expected stream of earnings is cut short. Most new bonds include a promise that they will not be called any earlier than five or perhaps ten years after issue.

Investors who purchase *convertible bonds* have the privilege of exchanging their bonds for common stock. Conversion of a bond to stock becomes attractive when a corporation's stock rises sharply in price.

Another type of bond provides *stock purchase warrants*. These warrants allow investors to purchase stock at a specified price. Stock purchase warrants are issued with both bonds and preferred stocks. They can prove profitable if a corporation's stock rises above the sale price specified in the warrant. Because bonds with convertibility and stock purchase warrants offer extra possibilities for profits, they typically provide somewhat lower interest returns than other bonds.

There are two classifications of bonds based on the security provided to guarantee interest payments and return of principal:

- *Mortgage bonds* (or secured bonds) are backed by a guaranteed right to the property of the issuing corporation. Mortgage bonds are generally issued by large utility companies and make up a major share of the bond market.

- *Unsecured bonds* (or *debentures*) are backed by the full faith and credit of the issuer but not by a mortgage claim. Debentures typically are issued by manufacturing corporations.

It is difficult for the the average investor to assess the safety of yield and principal for the hundreds of different bond issues available. Two investment services, Moody's Investors Services and Standard & Poor's, provide ratings of major corporate and municipal bond issues. Each service grades bonds into a number of different categories based on their judgment of the safety of yield and principal. Although their grading systems differ, the two services clearly differentiate bonds they feel are acceptable investments from those they regard as speculative.

Bonds that sell at large discounts from their maturity value because of the low credit rating of the issuer sometimes are referred to as *junk bonds*. Because of their large discounts, these bonds can provide high yields but are very risky. Junk bonds were used frequently in financing the surge of corporate mergers in the mid-1980s.

Bonds pay interest in two slightly different ways.

- *Registered bonds* are registered in the name of the owner with the issuers. Interest payment checks are sent periodically to the owner. All bonds being issued currently are of this type.
- *Bearer bonds* are not registered, and interest is payable to the holder. Bearer bonds include *coupons*, which are detachable certificates of interest due on a specified date. These coupons must be clipped and presented for payment when due. Since the holder of a bearer bond is presumed to be the owner, there is risk of loss if bearer bonds are stolen or misplaced.

In recent years, an increasing number of bonds have been issued as *zero coupon bonds*. On these bonds, no interest is paid until maturity. Instead, interest payments are compounded and both interest and principal are paid at maturity. Zero coupon bonds sell at deep discounts for a fraction of their face (or maturity) value. The prices of zero coupon bonds are highly susceptible to interest rate changes.

Zero coupon bonds are issued by corporations and state and local government bodies. The federal government issues some zero coupon bonds, and several investment houses have created zero coupon issues by selling investors shares in special accounts backed by Treasury bonds. These shares are sold at a substantial discount from the bonds' face value, with both interest and face value paid at maturity.

CONSUMER CAPSULE: READING BOND QUOTATIONS

Bonds			Cur Yld	Vol	High		Low	Close	Net Chg
Alamo	8¾	05	9.4	12	93		92¼	92¾	+¼
	(1)	(2)	(3)	(4)		(5)		(6)	(7)
Alpha	14 s	95	13	20	105¾		105¾	105¾	...
									(8)

Key:

(1) The name of the corporation and the interest rate stated on the bond are listed first. The Alamo Corporation bond was issued at an 8¾ percent rate.

(2) The bond's maturity date is indicated by the last two digits of the year. This bond will mature in 2005.

(3) The Cur Yld (current yield) on the bond is not 8¾ (or 8.75) but 9.4% because the bond is selling at a discount from its face value. Current yield is calculated to one decimal place to provide useful detail.

(4) The Vol (or volume) figure indicates that 12 of the bonds were traded during the day.

(5) The columns labeled High and Low give the bond's highest and lowest prices for the day. The last zero is dropped so the market prices of Alamo were a high of $930 and a low of $922.50.

(6) The Close column reflects the last price of the day's trading, which is $927.50.

(7) The net change figure indicates that the bond closed at a price $2.50 above the previous day's close (.25 × 10 = $2.50).

(8) Dots in the change column indicate there was no change from the previous day.

STOCKS

Stock ownership is no longer just for the wealthy. Today's average stockholder is about 44 years old with some college education, income in the $25,000 to $50,000 a year range, and about equally likely to be a male or a female. About one-fourth of the American people own stock.

Common and Preferred Stocks

Stocks represent an ownership interest in a corporation, sold to raise capital for the corporation's operations. A corporation that needed to raise $100,000,000 to build a new plant might decide, for example, to sell a million shares of stock at $100 each. Each share would be represented by a *stock certificate* as evidence of ownership. All corporations issue *common stock*, which typically gives shareholders one vote for each share in electing the board of directors of the corporation. The directors, in turn, select the corporation's officers and set corporate policy.

Many corporations also issue *preferred stock* in addition to common stock. Preferred stock represents a claim on the earnings of the corporation, for example, a claim for payment of $3 each year. Preferred stockholders usually have no votes for the board of directors or only limited voting privileges. In many ways preferred stocks are similar to bonds.

When corporate activities are profitable, the claims of bondholders are paid first. Next the claims of preferred stockholders are paid out. This payment, like the payment to the bondholders, is always a fixed amount. The directors then decide how to allocate the remainder of the profits. Part of the remainder may be retained for reinvestment in the corporation. The rest is available for payment of *dividends* to common stockholders. Dividends are allocated to shareholders in proportion to the number of shares they own.

Common stocks do not pay a fixed rate of return. Instead, dividends may move up and down as a corporation's financial situation varies. If profits are poor, dividends may be eliminated by the board of directors; or the directors may decide to pay dividends using retained earnings from previous periods. Dividends are usually paid in cash. Sometimes, however, stockholders are given *stock dividends* of additional shares of the corporation. This action allows the corporation to keep earnings for reinvestment and leaves the stockholders free to keep the stock dividend shares or to sell them.

The prices of individual common stocks fluctuate with the earnings prospects of the corporation and with the interest rates available in financial markets. If the dividends of a stock go from $5 to $10, it clearly becomes a more attractive investment, and its price will rise accordingly. Falling interest rates also can increase the price of a stock.

For example, suppose a stock costs $50 and pays dividends of $5 a year — a 10 percent yield. As interest rates in financial markets fall farther and farther below 10 percent, this yield will look increasingly attractive and the price of the stock will be bid up. Worsening earnings prospects and rising interests rates can be expected to have negative effects on the prices of common stock. The prices of preferred stock will fluctuate with interest rates in the same way the prices of bonds do.

Stock Market Funds

Many investors have stayed out of the stock market because they felt they lacked the necessary expertise or because they could afford to buy the stock of only one company and were hesitant to put all their financial eggs in one basket. *Stock market funds* are designed to appeal to investors seeking management expertise and diversification. Stock market funds are created by investment companies or trusts that pool the funds of a number of investors and use the capital to invest in other companies. The investment choices differ with the goals of the fund. The fund managers may seek favorable returns from dividends and interest earnings and from capital gains.

There are two general types of stock market funds. One type is the *closed-end fund.* Closed-end funds have a fixed number of shares, which remains the same over time. Closed-end fund shares are readily transferrable in the open market; some are traded on the New York Stock Exchange in the same way shares of common and preferred stock are traded.

The second type of stock market fund is the *open-end fund* or *mutual fund.* Mutual funds continuously sell new shares to investors based on the current value of the funds' assets. They also buy back shares. The total number of shares is not fixed; more are issued as purchases require. Mutual finds are not traded on stock exchanges; instead, buying and selling is handled by the fund organization. Some investment companies direct a family of funds among which free or low-cost switching is permitted.

Some funds charge an amount in excess of the value of a proportional share of their assets. This extra charge, or *loading charge,* is used to cover sales commissions and marketing costs. The loading charge for mutual funds varies widely. Many make no charge. These funds are called *no-load funds.* Charges on others run as high as 8½ percent. A fund's management is paid for services with a management fee that is deducted from earnings before they are distributed. These fees take a continuing bite out of earnings. No-load and lower-load funds also frequently deduct marketing fees. Most funds make no charge for repurchasing shares, but some do make charges if shares have been held for only a short time.

There are a variety of common stock-based funds:

- *Growth funds* emphasize capital gains
- *Income funds* emphasize high dividend yields
- *Combination funds* seek both growth and income
- *Index funds* buy all the stocks in a major stock index such as Standard & Poor's 500 to provide diversification
- *Gold funds* buy gold-mining stocks as an inflation hedge
- Other fund types emphasize stocks from a particular industry, such as high technology stocks, or other special categories of stocks

In addition to the common stock funds, there are other funds that specialize in corporate bonds, U.S. Treasury issues, municipal bonds, money market issues, and other categories of investments.

Market for Stocks

Trading in securities began in the United States almost 200 years ago under a buttonwood tree in lower Manhattan. The trading that went on there gradually evolved into today's New York Stock Exchange (NYSE). The NYSE, along with other *stock exchanges*, provides an organized marketplace for securities, especially common stocks. The members of the stock exchanges buy and sell for their own accounts and for institutional investors (such as banks and pension funds) and for individual investors. Not all stock trading is handled through exchanges. A significant share of sales are arranged directly between securities dealers or between dealers and investors. This market is called the *over-the-counter market*.

Listed Stocks. A major share of the buying and selling of stocks in this country is on the NYSE. The American Stock Exchange (AMEX) also handles a significant, but much smaller, volume of trade. There are, in addition, other smaller, regional exchanges in major cities throughout the country. They specialize chiefly in stocks of local and regional interest.

For a stock to be traded on an exchange it must be accepted or *listed* by the exchange. Listing involves providing essential information to the exchange and to the federal agency that regulates securities markets, the Securities Exchange Commission. To be listed on the NYSE, a firm must have a large number of shares outstanding and these shares must be widely held. This requirement helps ensure that trading in the stock will be active. The company also must conform to the exchange's rules governing information disclosure and protection of stockholders' interests.

At the New York Stock Exchange trading in a particular stock is centralized at one location on the exchange floor. The members buy and sell from each other. If sellers find no buyer or buyers find no seller, a *specialist* may buy or sell the needed shares. Specialists are members of the exchange who make a market in a particular stock and carry an inventory of the stock to help even out fluctuations in demand for it. Trading is in lots of 100 shares. Trades in multiples of 100 shares are called *round lots;* trades for fewer than 100 shares are *odd lots.*

Individual investors' purchase or sale orders are made through brokers. The broker's order is carried electronically or by telephone from the broker's office to a member of the exchange, who carries out the purchase or sale. Suppose, for example, that a typical investor, Ms. Jay, is considering buying 100 shares of General Motors.

- Ms. Jay calls or visits the account executive handling her account at a local brokerage office and inquires about the stock. The account executive checks the stock's current price for her.
- Ms. Jay decides the current price is acceptable and asks the account executive to buy the shares for her "at the market"—the best current price.
- The account executive sends an order to the firm's broker on the exchange floor. The broker goes to the post on the floor where GM stock is traded and matches Ms. Jay's buy order with a sale order for 100 shares.
- Information on the purchase is sent back to Ms. Jay's account executive, and she is notified of the purchase price and the commission due.

Over-the-Counter Stocks. A large proportion of the corporate stocks in this country are not traded on exchanges. These *unlisted stocks* are the stocks of smaller corporations, many of which are not well known outside their own localities.

Over-the-counter stocks are traded through a network of brokers and dealers. When brokers are given a purchase order for stock, they will either arrange a sale out of their own firm's inventory of the stock or contact another broker who makes a market in that particular stock. The investor's broker then tries to arrange a purchase at the best possible price. Not only are many common stocks traded over the counter but most bonds are also sold this way, including U.S. Treasury issues and municipal and corporate bonds.

The most visible part of the over-the-counter market is the National Association of Securities Dealers Automated Quotations (NASDAQ) market. The *NASDAQ market* is an electronic system that stores and transmits price quotations on hundreds of domestic and foreign securities. For each security listed, there are two or more dealers (the average is seven) ready to buy and sell. Their judgments of a stock are reflected in the prices at which they indicate they are willing to buy or to sell. These prices are quoted in the NASDAQ system. Sales are arranged through an associated electronic system or by telephone.

The NASDAQ market is the second largest stock market in the United States and has been growing rapidly. Some financial experts believe that a national, or international, electronic market such as the NASDAQ market is the wave of the future and that the familiar exchange system is outdated (Macklin, 1984).

Brokerage Firms

Consumers who wish to buy or sell stocks or other securities usually arrange the transaction with the help of a *stock brokerage firm*. At most firms, customers apply for an account in much the same way they would apply for a checking account. Purchases and sales handled through this account.

Firm Services. In full-service brokerage firms, customers are assisted by an *account executive* (or more technically, a registered representative) who not only arranges transactions but also provides investment advice. The cost of these services is covered by the brokerage commissions the firm charges. Some investors who feel confident about making their own decisions prefer *discount brokers* who provide fewer services, but charge lower commission fees. The fees are advantageous for large or frequent traders. For smaller traders, discount brokers' fees are about the same as full-service brokers'. Many banks also arrange securities purchases at discount rates.

The job of an account executive is a demanding one. An effective account executive shound be informed about hundreds of different investment alternatives and be prepared to suggest the ones best suited to the needs of a particular customer. A good account executive will spend the time needed to determine a customer's objectives, financial situation, and willingness to accept risk before suggesting an investment possibility. Account executives in large brokerage firms receive extensive formal training from the firm; smaller firms typically rely more on on-the-job training.

Consumers should shop for brokerage services in the same way they shop for other professional services. Financially knowledgeable friends and acquaintances often can provide helpful suggestions. The prospective investor should talk to several different account executives to see how appropriate the advice given is to a particular situation before making a final decision.

In dealing with account executives and brokerage firms, customers have a right to expect that transactions will be handled promptly and accurately. Because account executives' income depends on commissions for transactions, consumers sometimes worry about the *churning* of an account — excessive trading designed chiefly to earn commissions rather than to benefit the customer. This is rarely a problem, but is a concern of which consumers need to be aware.

Stocks purchased can be credited to the customer's account. In this case, they are held by the brokerage firm in a pool of stocks and are said to be held in a *street name.* Consumers sometimes are concerned about the safety of stocks held in a street name and the safety of cash in their account. Most firms have insurance to protect their customers against such losses (see Consumer Capsule: "What Protections Do Stock Investors Have?"). When stocks are held in a street name, the broker acts as agent for the customer, receives dividends, and credits them to the customer's account. Stock purchasers can also have stocks registered in their own name. In this case, they will receive stock certificates from the corporation and will be sent their dividends directly.

Cash and Margin Purchases. Stock purchasers may pay for their purchases in one of two different ways. If they have a *cash account,* they must pay for the purchase within a specified number of business days, usually five. Many investors have *margin accounts,* which permit then to pay only part of the cost of a purchase and to borrow the rest from the broker, using the stock as security. Margin accounts permit the account holder to use financial *leverage,* the purchase of an asset with a minimal amount of cash. Leverage makes the purchase of stocks on margin a popular tool for speculators.

In the late 1920s, speculators were able to buy stock on margin with only small amounts of cash. This policy encouraged the run-up of stock prices and helped pave the way for the Great Stock Market Crash in 1929. To control excessive speculation using margin accounts, the Federal Reserve sets margin requirements. These requirements have varied from 40 percent to 100 percent of the purchase price. The greater the Federal Reserve's concern about speculation, the higher they will set the margin requirement. In the mid-1980s the margin requirement was set at 50 percent.

Other Ways to Participate in the Market

Most people buy stocks they expect to rise in value and hold them to sell later when the price has risen. Is it also possible to make a profit if a decline is expected in a stock's price? Yes, by making a *short sale.* A short sale involves the sale of a borrowed stock with the expectation that it will be possible to buy shares later at a lower price to repay the loan.

Short sales are popular with speculators who expect a decline in the market. They require special arrangements with a broker who lends the stock sold, and they are open only to larger investors.

Options provide another way to participate in the stock market. *Options* are rights to buy or sell a particular stock such as General Motors at some specified price within a limited period of time. If the market price of the stock goes up and rises to a level higher than the cost of the contract to buy, the option buyer makes a profit. If a stock falls below the agreed sale price, the option seller makes a profit. Losses are, of course, also possible. The purchase of rights to buy (a *call*) or rights to sell (a *put*) can be a complex process and requires special study from investors who want to use the technique successfully.

In addition to the purchase of options on individual stocks, it is also possible to buy options on all the stocks in the major stock market indexes. The purchaser can take a position on what will happen to the entire market, rather than to just a single stock. Index options are available for the NYSE

Index, for the Standard and Poor's Index and for several other market indexes.

Options magnify the effects of a small change in an individual stock or in the market. Small changes can result in large gains or large losses.

CONSUMER CONCERN: WHAT PROTECTIONS DO STOCK INVESTORS HAVE?

Many investors leave their stocks and cash on deposit with their brokers. While this is convenient, it creates the potential for loss from mismanagement or fraud. What happens if the firm fails? If the stock certificates are lost in a fire? If there is dishonesty?

The first line of defense for investors is the receipts they receive when a purchase or sale is made. The brokerage firm should send these out promptly and the investor should check them for accuracy. Monthly statements should be checked carefully too. Have all the transactions been entered? Has the cash been credited correctly?

The second line of defense is the Securities Investors Protection Corporation (SIPC). SIPC is a nonprofit corporation that provides protections to investors similar to those FDIC provides to bank depositors. It is not, however, a government agency but is chartered by Congress. Most brokerage firms are members of SIPC.

SIPC members contribute to a customer protection fund. In the mid-1980s the agency provided protection of up to $500,000 per customer for securities and up to $100,000 for cash claims, to a total of $500,000. Many firms carry insurance above and beyond SIPC coverage. If a brokerage firm fails, accounts may be frozen temporarily if another firm does not take over the failed firm. This situation can create problems for investors in a rapidly changing market.

The performance of brokerage firms is an important concern for investors. An equally important concern is the performance of the stock market itself. Among the factors that contributed to the Great Crash in 1929 were the stock market abuses of the 1920s. There were no checks on the quality of the stocks being traded and no controls on manipulation of the market. The Securities Exchange Commission (SEC) was created in 1934 to oversee the financial market. The SEC is an independent regulatory agency with its main offices in Washington, D.C., and field offices in the major financial centers of the country.

The three main purposes of the SEC are:

- Ensuring that securities industry professionals deal fairly and justly with customers

Keeping Up With the Market

Around the turn of the century, financial wizard J.P. Morgan was stopped on the street and asked what was going to happen in the stock market. "It will fluctuate," he answered and walked on briskly. In the decades since, the market has continued to fluctuate. Careful investors need to monitor

- Keeping financial markets operating in a fair and orderly manner
- Ensuring that corporations make public all the information investors need to make intelligent decisions

The SEC cannot guarantee the value of any security, but it does work to ensure that consumers can obtain the information they need to assess its value. Before securities are offered for sale, the corporation must file a registration certificate with the SEC. Prospective investors must be provided a *prospectus* detailing the operations and financial situation of the firm. Larger companies must provide the SEC periodic reports that update their financial situation.

The SEC also works to make sure that markets are free of fraud and manipulation and that brokers do not violate their responsibilities. In the mid-1980s the SEC became heavily involved in pursuing cases of *insider trading*, purchases and sales of securities by business and financial executives based on information not available to the general public. Because such transactions are a threat to fair and orderly markets, the SEC prosecutes these cases vigorously. Brokers who wish to buy and sell on an exchange must register with the SEC and meet exchange requirements. They usually also have to meet the requirements of the brokers' trade association, the National Association of Securities Dealers (NASD).

Much of the responsibility for the regulation of the market is left to the exchanges themselves and to the NASD (Rothman & Fischetti, 1984). These organizations set rules on many key issues:

- Establishment of rules governing trading
- Decisions on the qualifications required of professionals
- Regulation of the conduct of members.

QUESTIONS

1. How does leaving securities in a street name create a risk of loss for investors?
2. How much protection does the SIPC provide investors?
3. What are the major purposes of the SEC?
4. What roles do the exchanges and NASD play in regulating the securities market?

the changes in the value of their stock investments and to get some perspective on how their investments are performing relative to the rest of the stock market. To gather and interpret this information, they need an understanding of how stock market information is reported.

Market Quotations. Stock market *quotations* (or quotes) provide records of changes in market prices and are carried in many newspapers. The *Wall Street Journal* carries a complete set of quotations on stocks listed on the New York Stock Exchange and the American Stock Exchange. Local papers usually carry shortened lists, with emphasis on major companies and stocks of local interest.

The information for each stock provided falls into two general categories. There is *trading information* on the previous day's transactions:

- High and low prices of the day
- Closing price for the day

CONSUMER CAPSULE: READING STOCK MARKET QUOTATIONS

52 Weeks High	Low	Stock	Div.	Yld %	P-E Ratio	Sales 100s	High	Low	Close	Net Chg.
37⅜	15	Alpha Prod	2.05	6.1	7	2435	33¾	33⅝	33⅝	+1⅜
(1)			(2)	(3)	(4)	(5)	(6)		(7)	(8)

(1) These two figures represent the highest and lowest prices for Alpha Products over the previous two 52 weeks. The highest price per share was $37.375 and lowest was $15.

(2) The current annual dividend Alpha Products is paying. Alpha Products is expected to pay $2.05 in dividends based on its most recent dividend.

(3) Yld % is the yield on an annual percentage basis. It is calculated by dividing dividends ($2.05) by the closing price of the day ($33.625).

(4) P-E Ratio is the price-earnings ratio. It is calculated by dividing the closing price for the day ($17.25) by the earnings per share for the most recent 12-month period.

(5) This figure indicates the day's sales in hundreds of shares. For the day indicated, 243,500 shares were sold.

(6) These two figures indicate the high and low prices for the day's trading.

(7) When trading closed, this was the last price paid ($33.625) per share.

(8) This figure is the change in this day's closing price from the previous day's closing price. The stock gained $1.375 per share.

- The number of shares of the stock traded
- The net change of the day's closing price from the previous day's close

Prices are quoted in eighths of a dollar (or 12.5¢ units). A quote of "3⅛" is equivalent to $3.125.

The quotation listings also include *yield information* that can be used to evaluate the investment potential of a stock:

- Annual dividends (plus footnotes on special or extra dividends)
- Yield percentage (the current annual dividends divided by the closing price)
- Price-earnings ratio (the closing price per share divided by the earnings per share for the previous year)

In interpreting the price-earnings ratio it is useful to recall that the current price reflects expectations about what the corporation will do in the *future*. The earnings portion of the ratio represents what the corporation has done in the *recent past*. Stocks with high price-earnings ratios sometimes are considered overvalued, but they can be good buys if earnings are rising rapidly.

Indexes and Averages. Stock market indexes and averages are used as statistical indicators of fluctuations in the market. The oldest and most

CONSUMER CAPSULE: READING MUTUAL FUND QUOTATIONS

	Sell	Buy	Chg
American Eagle	2.45	N.L.	+ .03
	(1)	(2)	(3)
Atherton Growth	11.60	12.53	+ .14
	(4)	(5)	

(1) American Eagle Fund had a net asset value (NAV) of $2.45 per share. This is the value of the fund's holdings divided by the total shares outstanding. This is the price a purchaser would be charged and is the amount the Fund would pay investors for shares redeemed, less possible fees.
(2) American Eagle Fund is a no-load (N.L.) fund. The price to investors buying shares is the same as the net asset value ($2.45).
(3) This figure is the change in net asset value from the previous day. American Eagle increased in value by 3 cents.
(4) Atherton Growth is a load fund. This figure is the net asset value and is the price at which shares would be bought back, less possible fees.
(5) This figure is the price Atherton Growth investors would be charged to buy a share. The difference between the net asset value and this figure is the sales commission ($12.53 − $11.60 = $ .93). This represents an 8 percent load ($ .93/$11.60 = .08 = 8%).

widely cited of the market indicators are the Dow Jones averages (Stabler, 1984). These include:

- *30 Industrials.* This group consists of major corporations such as General Electric, AT&T, and Exxon. This average is considered a *blue chip* indicator because the stocks are all nationally known companies with sound reputations and long records of earnings and paying dividends.
- *20 Transportation Stocks.* This group includes transportation companies such as TWA, Federal Express, and Norfolk and Southern Railroad.
- *15 Utilities.* This group includes utility companies such as Pacific Gas and Electric, Consolidated Edison, and Consolidated Natural Gas.
- *65 Stock Composite.* This average includes all the stocks in the three groups above.

The Dow Jones averages are based on the sum of the prices of the individual stocks included.

The Dow Jones averages have been criticized for failing to reflect the whole economy. It is alleged they put too much emphasis on older manufacturing firms and neglect the high technology and service industries. It should be noted, however, that the averages include International Business Machines (IBM) and American Express and that McDonalds has been added recently.

Others have argued that the Dow Jones averages focus on too few stocks and are too heavily affected by changes in the prices of only one or a few stocks. These critics suggest that broader based indexes such as the Standard & Poor's Index and the New York Stock Exchange Index are more useful.

The Standard & Poor's 500 Stock Price Index measures changes in the aggregate market value of 500 major stocks (Hosbach, 1984). Both the value of a particular stock and the total number of shares outstanding are taken into account in calculating the index. As a result, each stock influences the index in proportion to its importance in the market. The index includes a large number of industrial companies from almost 100 subgroups and also includes smaller numbers of public utilities, transportation, and financial firms. Most are listed on the NYSE, while some are listed on the AMEX.

The New York Stock Exchange Index measures changes in the aggregate value of all the common stocks listed on the NYSE. It is broad-based, including every stock listed on the exchange. Because of its scope, it is closely watched by Wall Street professionals. The index has four subgroups: industrials, transportation, utilities, and financial. As with Standard & Poor's Index, the effects of changes in a stock's price are proportional to its importance in the market.

The American Stock Exchange Market Value Index measures changes in the aggregate value of common stocks and some other listings on the AMEX. The National Association of Securities Dealers has an index that includes a large number of over-the-counter common stocks. The National Association of Securities Dealers Automated Quotations (NASDAQ) Index is a measure of the aggregate value of the stocks it includes, as are the NYSE Index, the Standard & Poor's 500 Index, and the American Stock Exchange Market Value Index.

References and Periodicals. Several available reference series can help investors to keep informed abut recent market activity in the stocks in which they are interested. In addition, the reports include firms' recent financial results. Three widely used references are:

Illustration 15-2
Some stock indexes, such as the New York Stock Exchange Index, include all stocks listed on the exchange; others include only selected stocks.

Edward C. Topple, New York Stock Exchange

- *Moody's Handbook of Common Stocks* (issued quarterly). New York: Moody's Investor Service. Financial and business information on 900 major stocks with a one-page summary on each
- *Value Line Investment Survey* (issued weekly). New York: Value Line Inc. Discussions of firms within major industry groups; updated periodically
- *Security Owner's Stock Guide* (issued monthly). New York: Standard and Poor's Inc. Information on the financial and business performance of 5,300 common and preferred stocks.

These references provide information to track changes in earnings over the years, changes in stock prices, and changes in the volume of stock traded.

A number of magazines regularly feature articles on various aspects of the securities market. *Changing Times, Money,* and *Sylvia Porter's Personal Finance Magazine* are useful sources for less experienced investors. *Forbes* is a highly regarded source for more experienced investors.

Annual Reports. A corporation's *annual report* is a formal statement of the firm's financial condition at the close of the reporting year and a report of its business activities for that year. Firms have made continuing efforts to make their reports more interesting and readable. At the same time, changing stock exchange and SEC regulations have required the inclusion of increased amounts of information.

A good place to begin reading in an annual report is the management's letter to shareholders. This letter provides an overview of the firm's condition, its operating results, and its current prospects. A comparison with previous years' reports will show whether management's projects have paid off (*Money,* 1985).

Annual reports also include a *balance sheet,* which is a condensed statement of the firm's assets, liabilities, and capital. If the ratio of assets to liabilities approaches one or less, the firm may be overburdened with debt.

The other major portion of the report is the *income statement.* This section reports on sales revenues and on the cost of producing what was sold. After deductions for taxes and interests, the balance is net income. Net income information can be compared to the dividends paid per share. If dividends per share exceed earnings per share, the company is using up capital. If earnings per share exceed dividends, the company has chosen to retain a portion of earnings to get new capital.

Another important section of an annual report is the auditor's report. This is usually brief unless the firm faces some special problems. If this is the case, the auditor's concerns bear careful reading.

COMMODITIES

The commodities markets offer speculators a chance to forecast the future prices of about 50 key commodities and make (or lose) money, depending on the accuracy of their forecasts. The commodities traded cover a wide range:

- Agricultural products—including wheat, soybeans, hogs, and beef cattle
- Minerals—including silver, gold, copper, aluminum, and platinum
- Petroleum products—including gasoline and heating oil
- Currencies—including Japanese yen and British pounds
- Securities—such as U.S. Treasury bonds and notes
- Composite stock indexes—such as the NYSE Composite Index

Futures traders buy and sell *futures contracts,* which are legally binding promises to deliver or receive some specified quantity and grade of a commodity at some specified place at the price agreed on. Prices are set by negotiations between buyers and sellers in a *futures market.* There are a number of futures markets in the U.S. The Chicago Board of Trade and the Chicago Mercantile Exchange are two of the most active in terms of dollar volume (Zachowski, 1984).

Few actual deliveries are ever made on futures contracts. Instead, most contracts are *closed out* before their expiration by an offsetting purchase. If the contract holder has promised to sell, an identical offsetting purchase is made. The opportunity for profit arises when prices move in the expected direction. If speculators have agreed to sell, there are profits if they can buy an offsetting amount for less than their sales price. If they have a futures contract to buy, there are profits if they can sell at a higher price.

Transactions in the futures exchanges help set world prices on the commodities traded. Prices on the exchanges are fluctuating constantly with news of crop failures and changes in industrial needs. The volatile nature of prices makes the changes attractive to speculators and dishonest operators who try to manipulate prices. Activity on the U.S.-based exchanges is monitored by the Commodity Futures Trading Commission, which seeks to prevent price distortions and manipulations and to protect customer rights.

REAL ESTATE

Real estate appeals to some investors because they feel it provides something tangible for their money, not just a piece of paper. Owning something physical gives them a sense of security. Real estate, like other real assets, also is popular as a haven from inflation. Property prices are expected to rise along with increases in the general price level.

Another appeal of real estate has been the tax advantages it provides. The tax advantages of real estate depend on several factors:

- *Depreciation rate permitted.* How quickly can the property be depreciated? In general, higher annual depreciation rates over a shorter time are more desirable for reducing taxes.

- *Capital gains taxation.* Gains from long-term increases in the value of assets were taxed at a lower rate than regular income until 1988. This tax treatment made capital gains more desirable than regular income.
- *Tax treatment of losses.* Some real estate investments have been attractive from a tax standpoint because they generated large operating losses (due to high depreciation and other costs) that could be deducted from other income. The 1986 tax law tightened the rules on the extent to which losses could be deducted.

Rental Property

Buying a small house or condominium has been a popular investment for many smaller investors. One advantage has been that these investments provide substantial leverage. A valuable property sometimes can be acquired with only a 10 percent down payment. However, real estate investors do need to bear in mind that real estate can decline in value as well as gain.

In addition, managing a rental property is a demanding job. Someone has to pay the bills, collect the rent, and make certain that repairs are made. Investors may choose to manage a property themselves or hire a real estate management firm to do it for them.

Real estate can provide an inflation hedge; but it is not always easily marketable. Selling a property may take months. There is also no assurance that investors wil get their money out without losses.

Real Estate Investment Trusts

Real estate investment trusts (REITs) provide the same type of advantages to investors in the real estate market that mutual funds provide in the financial market. REITs are corporations that pool investors' money to finance or to purchase real estate projects. The projects may include apartment and office buildings, shopping centers, industrial buildings, and even sports stadiums. Along with capital from investors, borrowed funds are also used.

- *Equity REITs* — Purchase and hold properties and generate income from rents and sales of properties.
- *Mortgage REITs* — Finance properties and generate income from interest earnings
- *Hybrid REITs* — Both purchase and finance properties

Many REIT shares are sold on stock exchanges and are readily marketable. As a result, they fluctuate in price over time. REITs usually are *diversified;* that is, they own several different types of properties. This approach is used to reduce the effects of losses. REIT shares usually sell for less than $20, so investors can easily buy shares of several different REITs to diversify on their own.

REIT earnings and capital gains are passed to investors untaxed. Investors then pay taxes on them according to their own tax rate.

Real Estate Limited Partnerships

Real estate limited partnerships pool investors' money to buy properties and also use borrowed money. Projects are initiated by a general partner who builds or buys a property. The general partner then sells portions of the project to limited partners.

General partners charge both an initial fee for developing the project and an annual fee for managing it. These fees can be substantial. Limited partners are financially liable only to the extent of their ownership share. In some projects this may be as small as $2,000.

Some real estate syndications were, in the past, designed with emphasis on income tax advantages. The new tax laws limit the extent to which losses can be deducted from other income. Income-producing investments will, in the future, be more attractive than earlier (Eisenberg, 1986).

GOLD, GEMSTONES, AND COLLECTIBLES

Gold, gemstones, and collectible items often are promoted as investments. We hear amazing tales of profits from gold speculation, big price increases in investment-grade diamonds, and handsome offers on restored 1957 Chevrolets. Gold, gems, and collectibles are exciting, but are they really investments?

Gold

Gold's almost magical qualities have made it the subject of fairy tales, daydreams, and nightmares. Because of the mythology surrounding gold, consumers looking for an investment alternative have not always used good sense in buying it. Viewed rationally, gold has three potential uses:

- For jewelry, ornaments, and dental work
- As a medium of exchange, in coins, and as backing for paper currency
- As a store of value, i.e., as a physical asset, and as a way to get protection from inflationary losses as the purchasing power of money declines

Gold's appeal as an inflation hedge made it a focus of heavy speculative activity in the late 1970s and early 1980s. Then, as inflation eased and demand from oil-rich middle Eastern countries fell, prices plunged. Gold hit a high of $875 an ounce in January 1980. By the mid-1980s, it was in the $300 range.

It is possible to invest in gold in two different ways: in actual physical form and through the purchase of financial instruments. Gold is available in physical form as bullion coins including the American Eagle, the Canadian Maple Leaf coin, and others, and as bars of various sizes. Gold coins that have been used as money usually have a value that exceeds their gold content and are of interest chiefly to coin collecters.

Although gold markets have become more developed in recent years, buyers of bullion coins and bars may still have marketability problems. Places to sell gold holdings may be difficult to locate. The fluctuating prices of gold coins and bars as well as purchase and sales charges make gold an illiquid investment (i.e., an investment which cannot be easily converted into cash without a loss of principal). Investors who hold gold in physical form are also confronted with storage charges and insurance costs. In addition, because bars and coins produce no earnings, investors have to consider the opportunity cost of holding gold. In periods of high interest rates, these opportunity costs can be substantial.

Several forms of financial instruments are available for investing in gold. *Gold futures* provide a contract to buy or sell a specified amount of gold at an agreed-on price at some future date. They operate in the same way as other futures contracts. *Options* provide the right, but not the obligation, to buy (or sell) a specified amount of gold at an agreed-on price before some future date. If prices move in the direction the option purchase anticipated, the option can be executed for a profit. Stock in gold-mining companies provides another vehicle for investing in gold. There are also investment funds specializing in gold-mining shares.

The speculative fever of the early 1980s attracted a number of con artists. Phone and mail solicitations promised handsome profits with no risk. Investors who became involved without checking references often ended up not with profits but with sizable losses from fraud and mismanagement. Gold futures are regulated by the Commodity Futures Trading Commission. However, because gold is not considered a security, the SEC has no jurisdiction over sales of gold in physical form. When misleading advertising is involved, state attorney general offices and the Federal Trade Commission have jurisdiction.

Gemstones

Jewelry buyers are often told that their purchases will have investment value. But gemstones and jewelry, in fact, have serious drawbacks as investments.

- *Poor marketability.* There are no organized markets in which small individual investors can sell. When they decide to sell, those who have bought at retail find that offers will be at wholesale levels or lower. While some sellers may promise to rebuy, such firms often come and go quickly.
- *Cost of holding and storage.* Investments in gems and jewelry may produce enjoyment, but they do not produce any income. The opportunity cost of the money invested has to be considered, as do safety deposit and insurance costs.
- *Problems in determining quality.* All natural gems and many jewelry pieces are unique. Because they are nonstandard, it is difficult to place a value on them, which makes it difficult for inexperienced investors to know whether the price is fair when they buy and whether an offer is reasonable when they decide to sell.

While independent appraisals can provide information on valuation, they may not be fully reliable. Appraisals are only an opinion. Some appraisers may be tempted to inflate their estimates if they are paid a percentage of the estimate, so percentage commission arrangements are frowned upon by trade groups. Or they may be tempted to understate an estimate if they expect an item to be offered to them for purchase. A further problem is determining whether the appraisal price is based on retail value, wholesale value, replacement value (the amount to be paid by an insurance company in case of loss or theft), or value in a sale to a dealer by a private individual.

Speculative excesses and fraud have been common in the gemstone market in recent years. A frequent problem has been claims that stones were "investment grade" when they were not. To protect themselves, gemstone buyers need to learn more about the bases of value. The key evaluative criteria used are often referred to in the jewelry trade as "the 4 C's":

- *Carats* — size of the stone by weight
- *Color* and brilliance
- *Clarity* — including the number of bubbles and other flaws
- *Cut* — the shape of a stone and the quality of the work in cutting

Very few stones are truly flawless. While a flawless stone may be desirable for investment purposes, a stone with good color and brilliance and with flaws invisible to the naked eye should be acceptable for use in jewelry.

Collectibles

The search for inflation hedges in the late 1970s and early 1980s created a surge of interest in old baseball cards, classic cars, art work, ceramic plates, antique furniture, and other collectibles. As inflation eased later in the early 1980s, prices declined, in some cases sharply. Interest revived in the mid-1980s, however, as new concerns about inflation arose.

Collectibles have many of the same drawbacks as investments as gemstones. There is no organized market for resale, valuation is difficult, and storage and insurance may be costly. As with gemstones, collectibles produce no earnings but do involve opportunity costs.

Those who have fared best in making profits on collectibles have been buyers of rare, top quality items. Prices of medium- and lower-grade items typically have been hardest hit when prices decline (Hershman & Knecht, 1982).

The collectibles market, like the jewelry and gemstones market, is influenced by the amount of disposable income consumers have, concerns about finding havens from inflation, and fads. In the late 1970s, a new demand for Tiffany glass developed as recording stars became interested in it. Elton John, Barbra Streisand, and Rod Stewart were reported to be big collectors, and others copied them. But as inflation eased and recording industry profits fell off in the early 1980s, prices dropped by as much as half. The moral on investing in collectibles seems to be: Collect what you like, but do not count too much on making a big profit out of it.

BUILDING A PORTFOLIO

Investors ususaly prefer to put together a diversified set of investment holdings. These holdings, their *portfolio,* should first provide for liquidity and safety (see Figure 15-1). Cash, savings accounts, and highly liquid money market accounts and funds can be used to provide these needs. A second goal after basic security and liquidity needs are met is current income or long-term growth. High quality stocks and bonds and other high-quality assets can be used toward this goal.

Once these more basic needs are met, the individual investor is in a position to consider speculation and high-risk investments. A number of factors influence investment goals. These include:

- Personal situation — Age (younger people are considered to have more time to replace assets if they are lost), family obligations to children, aged parents, handicapped members
- Temperament — Willingness to accept risk, tendency to worry over risky investments, willingness to make changes if investments are not performing well
- Financial situation — Adequacy of current income to provide necessities, adequacy of net worth to provide for emergencies, ability to replace assets if they should be lost

Figure 15-1
The Hierarchy of Investments

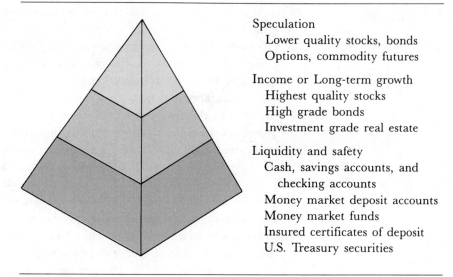

Speculation
    Lower quality stocks, bonds
    Options, commodity futures

Income or Long-term growth
    Highest quality stocks
    High grade bonds
    Investment grade real estate

Liquidity and safety
    Cash, savings accounts, and
      checking accounts
    Money market deposit accounts
    Money market funds
    Insured certificates of deposit
    U.S. Treasury securities

Part 3   Managing Personal Finances

These factors suggest very differ investment objectives for young singles, young couples with children, comfortably well-off middle-aged couples, and retirees. As you go through life, the most appropriate investments change. For this reason, it is important for investors to continue to review their investment objectives and make certain their holdings match what they are trying to achieve.

MAJOR CHAPTER CONCEPTS	1. Investments, including both debt investments and equity investments, provide an opportunity for earnings and for capital gains.
	2. The objectives of investors include growth or capital appreciation as well as income and tax management opportunities. Growing out of these objectives are the key evaluative criteria: yield, safety of yield, potential for capital gains, liquidity and marketability, and tax advantages.
	3. Bonds are interest-paying promissory notes issued by corporations and governments. Their prices will rise if interest rates fall, or they will fall if interest rates rise.
	4. U.S. Treasury securities include long-term bonds, intermediate-term notes, and short-term bills. These securities are considered highly secure and are backed by the full faith and credit of the government. Not all securities issued by other federal agencies carry this assurance. All, however, are backed by government promises.
	5. Bonds issued by state and local governments and by state and local government agencies are called municipal bonds.
	6. Corporate bonds may be either registered bonds or bearer bonds with coupons. Some are secured by property (mortgage bonds); others are backed by the firm's full faith and credit (debentures).
	7. Zero coupon bonds pay interest upon maturity and are sold at deep discounts from maturity value.
	8. Common stocks represent a share of ownership in the issuing corporation. In contrast, preferred stocks represent a claim on corporation earnings.
	9. Stock market funds permit investors to obtain a diversified portfolio and management expertise. Closed-end funds have a fixed number of shares and are traded on stock exchanges. Open-end funds issue shares as needed and are sold directly. Funds may invest in common stocks, bonds, or other securities with a variety of objectives.
	10. Purchases of stocks listed on exchanges are arranged through brokers and executed on the exchange. Over-the-counter stocks are not traded on exchanges, but can be purchased from brokers' inventories.
	11. Account executives working for full-service brokerage firms can both provide investment advice and arrange securities purchases. Discount

brokers provide more limited services. Purchases may be on a cash basis or on margin (on credit).

12. Investors can keep up with the market by checking quotations, using basic references, and reading periodicals that feature financial news and annual reports.

13. Commodity futures provide an opportunity for speculators to forecast the future price of traded commodities and make money if their predictions are correct.

14. Real estate has been a popular investment because of its tangibility and its advantage as an inflation hedge. Investors may own property directly, as limited partners in partnerships or syndicates, or as share owners in real estate investment trusts.

15. Gold investments can be made by buying gold coins or bars or by buying financial securities, including options, futures, and gold-mining shares. Gold in physical form is regarded as a good inflation hedge but has drawbacks. It may have poor marketability and may involve significant holding, storage, and opportunity costs. Investments in gemstones and collectibles have the same problems as gold plus the further problem of determining quality.

16. An individual portfolio should first provide safety and liquidity. It is then feasible to seek income or long-term growth. Once these basic needs are met, speculation and high-risk investments are feasible.

CONSUMER QUESTIONS

1. Choose two stocks from different corporations which might be a good investment and investigate them.
   a. Check stock market quotations for recent yield and trading information and interpret this information.
   b. Check business periodicals for recent stories on the performance and prospects of the two companies.
   c. What are the strong points of each stock? The weak points? Which would you buy if you were investing? Why?

2. Check recent bond market quotations in the *Wall Street Journal* and find bonds from two different companies that mature in about the same year.
   a. What is the current yield of each?
   b. Investigate the companies and bonds to determine the reasons for the difference in yields.

3. The investments market has a continuing crop of get-rich-quick schemes and fraudulent operators. Check recent issues of *Changing Times, Sylvia Porter's Personal Finance Magazine,* and *Money* for stories on dubious schemes.

a. What appeals were used to lure investors?

b. Evaluate the information given investors using the criteria discussed in Chapter 3: objective, valid, understandable, complete, and up-to-date.

4. Each year *Money* magazine publishes a guide to mutual funds. Study this guide in a recent issue.

a. What information is provided on each fund?

b. How are funds evaluated? Why is performance evaluated for different periods of time?

5. Check the stock market indexes and averages reported on the next to the last page of the *Wall Street Journal*.

a. What percentage changes occurred in the Dow Jones Average? The NYSE Index? The Standard and Poor's 500 Index?

b. Which index gives the best picture of what happened on the NYSE? Explain.

6. What are the advantages of using financial leverage? What are the potential disadvantages?

7. Gold, gemstones, and collectibles fluctuate in popularity as investments. Investigate recent and price changes in a particular market of this type. Using the evaluative criteria for investments discussed in this chapter, how would you rate the item you investigated?

SUGGESTED READINGS

1. *Consumer Reports.* "A Guide to Mutual Funds — In the 289 Stock Funds We Rated, You Could Have More Than Doubled Your Money — or Lost Half of It." 50, no. 12 (July 1985): 390-397. This article discusses evaluative criteria for judging common stock mutual funds. *Consumer Reports* also published reports on money-market funds in January 1983 and on bond funds in October 1984. Each article also provides a rating of the performance of funds. *Money* magazine annually publishes rankings of mutual funds, as does *Changing Times. Forbes* also periodically publishes rankings of mutual funds.

2. Engel, Louis, and Brendan Boyd. *How to Buy Stocks.* 7th rev. ed. Boston: Little, Brown and Co., 1982. This book provides a clear and easy-to-read introduction to the securities markets. Engel's classic was first published more than 30 years ago and has been updated again for this edition. It is also available in paperback.

3. Galbraith, John Kenneth. *The Great Crash, 1929.* Boston: Houghton Mifflin, 1961. Galbraith, who is widely known for his readable examinations of economic issues, considers the factors that led up to the stock market crash of 1929.

4. Schwab, Charles. *How to Be Your Own Stockbroker.* New York: Dell Publishing Co., 1984. This book gives suggestions on operating effectively in the stock market by the man who pioneered in developing the discount brokerage business.

5. Tobias, Andrew. *Money Angles.* New York: Linden Press, 1984. The first four chapters provide useful insights for choosing investment objectives. Later chapters provide interesting insights into the operations of financial markets.

6. Tobias, Andrew. *The Only Investment Guide You'll Ever Need.* Rev. ed. New York: Bantam Books, 1983. This is a lively and easily read introduction to investing, with emphasis on the stock market. The book suggests investment philosophies and strategies for beginners.

PART 4

MANAGING
RISK

CHAPTER 16

~~~~~

INTRODUCTION
TO INSURANCE

On a typical day, the following things happen in this country:

- 2,800 cars are stolen.
- 85,000 motor vehicle accidents occur, with losses averaging $2,000 each.
- 1,700 home fires occur.
- 250 people die in accidents.
- 107,000 people are admitted to hospitals, where they run up bills averaging $3,000 each.

Most of these losses and expenses are unexpected. All involve major emotional shocks along with substantial financial expense. How can people deal with the unexpected extra expenses that could shatter their financial well-being? One way, of course, is through the use of insurance, the subject of this chapter.

INSURANCE FUNDAMENTALS

In the course of a day, consumers are exposed to a number of _risks_ that create the possibility of a financial loss. The risks of concern to most consumers are *pure risks,* ones in which losses are unexpected or accidental and there is no possibility of gain. These risks are not like those in gambling, where there is at least some possibility of gain. Insurance can provide protection against three categories of losses:

- *Property losses* — Damage to or loss of autos, housing, and other personal property caused by fire, collision, flood, or other perils
- *Personal losses* — Loss of income due to sickness, death, disability, or unemployment, plus extra expenses due to sickness or injury
- *Legal liability losses* — Financial losses growing out of legal responsibility for injury to others, or damage to their property. These losses are due to *negligence,* that is, failure to use proper care to prevent injuries to others and damage to their property.

The losses covered by insurance involve unexpected reduction or disappearance in value, e.g., collision damage or loss of earning power due to death or disability. Insurance does not cover expected losses such as those from wear and tear or depreciation, nor does it cover the sentimental value of losses.

Managing Risks

Insurance is only one of the ways consumers deal with the risk of losses. We do not buy insurance for every possible type of loss. In some cases, we deal with losses in other ways.

Risk Prevention and Reduction. One method of managing risks is to reduce the frequency or the severity of losses. There are a number of ways to control the likelihood of loss.

- Installing smoke alarms to provide early warnings of fires and to help reduce the severity of loss
- Using seat belts can help to reduce the severity of injury in an auto accident
- Being careful to never leave the keys in a car's ignition when it is unattended to prevent theft losses

Risk Avoidance. Another way to manage risk is simply to avoid a hazard, which may mean giving up hobbies that can be dangerous — skydiving, motorcycling, auto-racing, piloting a private plane. Flood losses can be avoided by selecting real estate that is not located in a flood plain.

Risk Retention. Sometimes, people take no special steps to deal with risks because they are not aware of the risk. Many consumers, for example, are unaware of their legal responsibility to people injured on their property. Risk also may be retained because consumers underestimate the likelihood of loss. They mistakenly think, "It won't happen to me." Most young adults seriously underestimate the likelihood that they will suffer a loss of income

Illustration 16-1
One approach to
reducing risks is to use
safety devices such as
seat belts.

due to disability or illness. Consumers may also retain risks because the expected losses are so small that they do not feel the need to take special steps to deal with them. Consumers do not, for example, insure their everyday glassware against breakage. Such losses are relatively small and can be covered out of household expenses.

Risk Transfer. Another method of managing risk is to transfer it to someone else. The usual way to transfer risk is to buy insurance. Insurance providers are able to pool the risks of large numbers of people. Each insurance buyer contributes a small amount to a pool so that the insurance provider can pay those who experience losses. Insurance protection may be provided by profit-making insurance companies, customer-owned companies, and government agencies such as the Social Security system.

Using Insurance to Limit Losses

The operations of insurance companies are based on the *law of large numbers.* This mathematical principle, when applied to insurance, states that as the number of possible loss situations increases, the number of actual losses comes closer to the expected results. Suppose, for example, that police records reveal that an average of 80 cars out 1,000 in a town have been damaged in crashes in each of several past years. Or, stated differently, 8 percent of the cars are damaged in a given year. It is difficult to predict accurately whether the cars belonging to a particular household will be damaged in a given year, or even what percentage of the cars in a given neighborhood will be damaged. As the group of cars considered gets larger and larger, however, the number damaged is likely to get closer and closer to 8 percent.

The possibility of accurately predicting losses for large groups makes it possible to offer insurance to those facing the risk of losses. The insurer is able to predict the likely number of losses and spread this cost over the entire group at risk. Suppose, for example, that an insurer sold insurance contracts covering 1,000 cars in the town discussed above. If, in a typical year, 80 had accident damage averaging $1,500, the total loss would be $120,000. An insurer could spread this loss across the group, along with administrative costs, with each car owner sharing equally.

$120,000	total damages
+ 30,000	administrative costs
$150,000	total costs

$$\frac{\$150,000 \text{ total costs}}{1,000 \text{ insured cars}} = \$150 \text{ per car}$$

Insurance against crash damage in this case could be provided for $150 per car.

When insurance is purchased, the *policy holder* (or *insured*) becomes a party to a contract with the insurance company (the *insurer*). The contract, referred to as a *policy,* sets down the terms under which the company will pay the policyholder for losses. In return for this insurance coverage, the policyholder agrees to pay a specified *premium.* The premium is set to cover the insurer's expected losses, plus the costs of doing business.

What Is Important in Selecting Insurance?

There are thousands of insurance companies in this country. Each one is free to decide the premium charges,[1] specify the policy coverage and provide the customer services it thinks are appropriate, within the broad guidelines set by the state agency that regulates insurance. Insurance shoppers must

---

[1] In a very few states, all companies charge identical premiums for auto and property insurance, as required by state law.

sort these alternatives to find the combination that suits them best. Three useful evaluative criteria—the coverage provided, cost, and company service—are discussed in the following sections.

Coverage Provided. Insurance policies set down the terms of the coverage provided. These terms determine to what policyholders are entitled in return for their premiums.

- *Basic contract terms.* The first page of most policies, the *declarations* page, provides basic details about the policy. The insurer and the insured are identified, the property covered is indicated (in cases of property and auto insurance), the beginning and ending dates of coverage are indicated, and the type or types of coverage provided are listed along with the premium for each.

- *Perils covered.* A critical portion of any policy is the details on the particular causes of losses (*perils*) covered. These perils may include losses of property due to fire, theft, or collision. Life insurance, of course, covers loss of life. Medical insurance policies may specify particular perils such as cancer or appendicitis or provide more general coverage. It is essential to consider not only what perils are included but also important ones that are omitted.

- *Types of losses covered.* Several different types of financial losses can occur in connection with an insured loss. Basic coverage provides for reimbursement for the value of property, the medical expenses incurred, or the insured value of a life. More comprehensive coverage may also provide coverage for other losses, including (1) loss of income in cases of illness or injury in an accident and (2) other related expenses, such as travel costs to obtain medical treatment, or car rental expenses while an insured car is under repair.

- *Payments for losses.* The amounts payable under the terms of the policy and the limits on these amounts are set down in detail. The higher the limits, the more protection the policy provides the insured, and the higher the premium charged. A particular auto policy may, for example, set a limit of $10,000 for collision damage to the insured's car, with losses covered only up to that amount. Homeowner's policies also set limits on certain types of coverage. Losses due to the theft or disappearance of jewelry typically are covered only up to $500. *Deductible clauses* reduce the payments to policyholders by deducting a specified amount from the payment for a covered loss. With $100 deductible auto collision coverage, a policyholder who had a $600 loss would receive only a $500 payment. By requiring policyholders to retain some risk, insurers are able to reduce premium charges.

- *Exclusions.* The *exclusions* portion of a policy sets out specific limits on the coverage provided. Auto insurance policies, for example, will not provide liability coverage if the vehicle has been used deliberately to cause bodily harm or damage to property. Auto and property policies also exclude liability for injuries if a vehicle has been used to carry people for a fee. This exclusion typically does not, however, apply to shared-expense car pools. Homeowner's policies typically exclude losses due to injury of pets or damage to autos or other motor vehicles.

- *Conditions.* The *conditions* portion of a policy sets down the obligations of both the insurer and the policyholder. For example, the obligations of a policyholder after a loss and procedures for making a claim are indicated (see Consumer Capsule: "How to File an Insurance Claim"). The insurer's obligations in settling claims are also spelled out. The conditions section of a policy also sets down the procedures each party must follow for cancellation or nonrenewal of the policy.
- *Amendments.* Sometimes it is necessary to add to or change the provisions of a policy. This is done with an amendment to the policy. An amendment to an auto or homeowner's policy is referred to as an *endorsement.* An amendment to life insurance policies is referred to as a *rider.* Many auto insurance policies do not cover losses of tape player or tapes. Policyholders who want protection against these losses can obtain an endorsement that covers them for an extra premium.

Cost. The typical auto, homeowner's, medical, and life insurance policies are a bundle including several different types of coverage. A typical auto policy will include collision coverage for damage to the insured's car, liability coverage for injuries to people in other cars, and medical payments coverage for injuries to passengers in the insured's car, along with other coverages. Premiums for each coverage are determined separately, but they are typically bought as a package. Consumers who are making price comparisons should focus on the total premium for a policy, rather than the prices for specific coverages.

Insurers try to identify factors related to the likelihood and severity of losses so that they can charge appropriate premiums to different groups in the population. They have found that the likelihood and severity of a loss are affected both by the characteristics of the insured and, in the case of property or auto insurance, the characteristics of the property or the car insured. Each insurer develops a *classification system,* or *rating system,* based on the factors they have found affect losses. This classification system then is used to determine premiums. In the case of auto insurance, premiums will be affected by the characteristics of the insured, by the type of car insured, and by how it is used.

Studies of insurance costs have found a surprising amount of variation in premiums. Identical coverage may cost twice as much from one

CONSUMER CAPSULE: HOW TO FILE AN INSURANCE CLAIM

In auto accidents, these steps should be followed:

- *Call the police immediately, if appropriate.* If anyone is injured in an accident or if damages are serious, most states require that the police be notified. It also may be necessary to file a written report. If medical help is required, ask the police to obtain it; they can arrange it quickly and efficiently.

- *Exchange information with other drivers involved.* Drivers involved in an accident should exchange information including their names, addresses, phone numbers, driver's license numbers, license plate numbers, and names and addresses of passengers. Drivers also should indicate the name of their insurance company and their policy number. If an unattended car or other unattended property is damaged, a note should be left with the necessary information.

- *Record accident information.* The names, addresses, and phone numbers of witnesses should be recorded, as should the names and badge numbers of police officers. A pad and pencil should be kept in the glove compartment for these emergencies. A photo of the accident should be obtained, if feasible, or alternatively a sketch should be made.

- *Do not admit guilt or responsibility.* Drivers involved in accidents are not obligated to admit responsibility. They are required only to state the facts. To protect their own interests and those of their insurer, drivers should not admit responsibility. Offers of money for injuries or damage from a driver who is at fault should be considered carefully; there could be after-effects from the accident or concealed damage to the car.

The following steps are appropriate in cases of auto accidents and losses covered by homeowner's policies:

- *Protect property from further damage.* In cases of auto accidents the car should be moved off the road and flares lit. If the car is disabled, it should be towed to a safe storage place. Repairs should not, however, be begun without permission of the insurance company. The adjuster may wish to see the car in its damaged state. In cases of home fires, steps should be taken to prevent weather damage and entry by thieves. When locks or doors are damaged in a break-in, repairs or other security measures should be taken immediately.

- *Contact insurance agent immediately.* Agents can assist in determining whether a loss is covered and give advice on necessary steps for filing a claim. In cases of theft, insurance companies typically insist that losses be reported to the police.
- *Obtain estimates of repair costs.* Claimants are expected to obtain one or more estimates of the cost of repairing covered damages. In cases of theft, it is necessary to prepare an inventory of stolen items along with their estimated present value or replacement cost. Bills, receipts, and photos can provide helpful documentation. Receipts for related costs should be saved; these costs can include towing charges, motel bills if a residence is no longer habitable, and medical bills for injuries.
- *Cooperate in the verification of the claim.* If damages are large, an adjuster will have to inspect the property, and claimants should cooperate in making it available. Claimants also are obligated to cooperate with the insurance company in court cases or other legal action related to the accident.
- *If a proposed settlement is not satisfactory, take further action.* If the amount offered in settlement is not satisfactory, the next step is to contact the adjuster's or agent's supervisor. If it is still impossible to reach agreement, arbitration is a possible further step. State departments of insurance also may be able to render assistance. Going to court is a last resort.

company as it does from a competitor (Maynes, 1975). Clearly comparison shopping can pay off.

Service. It is possible, with some study, to evaluate the coverage and cost of an insurance policy before purchase. It is harder, however, to evaluate the insurer's service. Only the individual policyholders are in a position to judge how well an insurer serves them, and accumulating such information may be difficult. Fortunately, *Consumer Reports* periodically queries its subscribers about their experience with their auto and homeowner's policies.

A basic element of service is how billing for premiums is handled. Are charges explained clearly? Are bills free from errors or corrected quickly? A common complaint among policyholders is that premium increases are not explained.

Because policyholders buy insurance for the financial protection it provides, the speed with which an insurer settles claims is an essential part of service. Delays in handling claims seem to result from two sorts of problems:

- *Delays in handling claims.* These delays may be the result of difficulty in getting an adjuster to inspect damaged property or difficulty in getting paperwork for a claim completed.
- *Delays in settlement.* These delays occur when a company is slow in issuing the settlement check after the claims paperwork is completed.

Dissatisfaction with the settlement offered is a frequent problem for auto and homeowner's policyholders. When repairs are needed, the policyholder and the insured may disagree about just what should be done to restore damaged property to its original condition. Policyholders who are not satisfied with a settlement offer should next consult the supervisor of the person making the offer. If this does not produce an agreement, the state Department of Insurance can be consulted. They can provide assistance on such problems as unreasonable denials of claims and delays, unfair cancellations of coverage, refusals to renew coverage,and similar problems. If these steps fail, a lawyer should be consulted.

AUTOMOBILE INSURANCE

Every year American drivers roll up more than one trillion miles. Most of these miles are travelled uneventfully, but accidents happen; when they do, those involved begin to wonder about their own and the other driver's insurance coverage. The smart driver, of course, already has auto insurance and has given some thought to the coverages needed, to cost, and to insurer service.

Coverage

A variety of coverages are available to protect drivers from claims by others based on negligence, property losses, and medical expenses. Just who is protected by this coverage? The insured and other family members are insured while driving a covered car and also while driving other cars, including rented cars. In addition, others using a covered car with permission are usually covered. In case of accident, people who have borrowed cars are expected to take care of accident losses on their own policy, if they have one.

Liability Coverage. *Liability insurance* protects policyholders against claims caused by negligent operation of a car. Some liability claims are for *bodily injury* (personal injury) to others. Liability insurance will pay not only medical expenses, but also rehabilitation expenses, claims for loss of income, loss of future earning potential, and compensation for pain and suffering. The other category of liability claims is those for *property damage* caused by negligence, including damage to others' cars, fences, and property.

Liability coverage also provides insureds with legal services to defend them against others' claims and to cover court costs. This protection is a valuable part of liability insurance coverage. Suits for small amounts are not permitted in states with no-fault insurance laws, as will be discussed below, but suits for large amounts are permitted, and liability insurance protection is essential in all states.

In serious accidents, claims often run into the thousands of dollars. Claims of more than a million dollars are no longer unusual. Without the protection of liability insurance, drivers held negligent could lose their property and even part of their future income.

All policies specify a limit on the liability protection that will be provided for bodily injury and property damage claims. Some policies specify one *overall limit*, such as $50,000, for payments for injuries and property damage in an accident. Other policies specify a *split limit*. Those policies are often referred to by the limits set for different portions of the coverage. "25/50/10" coverage can be interpreted as follows:

- 25 means maximum coverage of $25,000 for injuries to one individual
- 50 means maximum coverage of $50,000 for injuries to two or more people
- 10 means maximum coverage of $10,000 for property damage liability

Every state has laws that require drivers to be able to pay for injuries or damages they cause in accidents. The requirements are usually low and not adequate to provide real protection either for the injured or the insured. Limits such as 10/20/5 and 25/50/10 are common. Most drivers carry liability insurance because it is required by law or because it is the easiest way to meet financial responsibility requirements. Some drivers, however, ignore these laws either because they are unable to obtain regular liability coverage or because they consider the cost too high.

Because of the size of accident settlements in recent years, drivers should have coverage well beyond the minimums required by state laws. For a split coverage policy, 100/300/25 is probably a safe minimum. For a single limit policy, $300,000 coverage is a minimum. Because large claims are less likely than smaller ones, the cost of raising the limits on a policy diminishes with each additional increment purchased.

Medical Payments. When injuries occur to riders in an insured's car, it is medical payments coverage that covers their expenses. This coverage includes the driver, family members, and guests (paying passengers typically are excluded) when riding in a covered car or in others' cars. Medical payments coverage also will cover car-caused injuries to insureds and their families as pedestrians. When a covered person is killed, reasonable funeral expenses are provided rather than medical expense payments.

In many states, drivers and car owners can make their own decision about whether they want medical payments coverage or not. Coverage may not be necessary if the insured already has good medical and hospitalization insurance. However, medical payments coverage still would be needed to protect guests. In states with no-fault insurance, a certain amount of medical payments coverage is required by law. Coverage beyond the usual minimums is available and it may be desirable to get at least $10,000 of coverage.

Wage Loss Coverage. When an insured or family member is injured and earnings are lost, wage loss coverage can reimburse all or part of these losses. Payments do not run indefinitely, however. There are limits on the total amount of money that can be collected and the number of weeks of payments. Wage loss coverage is required in states with no-fault insurance and is optional elsewhere. Wage loss insurance is not an adequate substitute for disability insurance. Individuals can be disabled in many ways. Wage loss coverage in an auto insurance policy deals with only one of them.

Uninsured Motorist Coverage. Under the liability system (which also has been called the *tort* system and the *fault* system), drivers are liable if they injure others. There are, however, some drivers who do not have insurance to cover their obligations: hit-and-run drivers, drivers of stolen cars, and drivers who have not bought insurance or have let their policies lapse. Uninsured motorist coverage provides protection to aid policyholders, their families, and nonpaying passengers for accidents in which uninsured motorists are at fault.

Uninsured motorist coverage provides for payment of medical expenses a driver and passengers would be entitled to collect from another driver. This coverage also may reimburse car damages if the insured can prove that the damage was caused by a hit-and-run driver. If it cannot be proved, the repairs will be reimbursed under the insured's collision coverage and will be subject to the applicable deductible. If insurance companies did not require proof that damage was hit-and-run, a *moral hazard* would be created. Insureds would be tempted to lie in order to collect repair costs under their uninsured motorist coverage rather than under their collision coverage with its deductible.

In addition to the uninsured motorists on the road, there are others who are underinsured. While they have coverage, it may not be sufficient to provide adequate liability payments. Some insurers provide separate underinsured motorists coverage to provide protection against this problem. Others include that coverage in their uninsured motorist coverage.

Collision Coverage. Damage to an insured's car is reimbursed by collision coverage, regardless of who is at fault. Payments under this coverage are limited to the current market value of the car before the accident. If repair charges exceed the value of the car, the insurer will pay only the value of the car. In general, it does not pay to get collision insurance for low-priced, older cars because the payments are limited to the car's market value. Owners of classic Corvettes or other cars whose value is unusual for their age should arrange special coverage.

Collision insurance typically is sold with deductibles of $100, $200, $250, or $500. The deductible reduces the insurer's payout by requiring the insured to retain part of the risk of loss. The bigger the deductible, the lower the premium payment, so insurance buyers should select the biggest deductible they can afford.

When an accident is the other driver's fault, an insured who has difficulty collecting from the other driver's insurer can request payment from his or her own insurer. The insurer will then attempt to collect from the other driver's insurer. Most companies expect drivers to first attempt to collect on their own before asking for help.

Comprehensive Coverage. Collision coverage provides protection only against crash damage. There are many other perils that can cause a loss: hailstones, fire, theft, vandalism, flood, falling rocks, and unexpected perils such as running into a deer. Comprehensive coverage also provides some limited coverage of losses of luggage and personal effects.

Tape players and tapes are a frequent target of thieves, and they also have been the subject of many fake claims. To protect themselves, some

Illustration 16-2
Premiums for collision and comprehensive coverage are affected by a car's value and by the costs of repairs.

insurers do not cover these losses as part of comprehensive coverage. Instead, they require a special endorsement to the policy and an extra premium to obtain coverage.

Miscellaneous Coverages. In addition to these coverages, insurers offer several others. Towing and labor coverage reimburses towing expenses (typically limited to a specific amount, such as $25) and on-the-road repairs. Rental reimbursement coverage covers car rental expenses when an insured car is under repair for an extended period.

No-fault Insurance. In many accidents it is not clear who was at fault. Often both drivers are partially at fault. In these cases, legal action may be necessary to settle who is at fault and financial responsibility. Over the years legal action in auto accidents has grown increasingly costly and has been subject to long delays. It has, moreover, dealt with claims erratically. Some people with less serious injuries have been paid too much while others with more serious injuries have been paid too little. A further problem has been that legal fees take a big bite out of the settlements paid, typically as much as one-third.

One solution to these problems has been *no-fault insurance,* which provides payments to an insured regardless of who was at fault. The injured get the help they need at once and insurers settle who was at fault out of court between themselves later. State laws that have created no-fault systems have provided this kind of protection for those injured in auto accidents. At the same time, they have limited the injureds' right to sue for damages. Because of this limitation, trial lawyers who argue injury cases have opposed no-fault laws, as have others who believe that suing for injuries is a fundamental legal right.

While about half of the states have enacted some form of no-fault law, none has enacted a pure no-fault law under which an insurance company pays all for injuries and damages for those that company covers and no law suits are permitted. Most of the state laws enacted are *modified no-fault laws,* because all permit suits for injuries under certain circumstances, when a specified *threshold* is exceeded. A few states permit suits only if injuries are very serious (e.g., death or disfigurement). A number permit suits when medical expenses for injuries exceed some dollar threshold. These laws have, however, been criticized because they encourage inflated medical bills and lying.

Another group of states have *pseudo-no-fault laws,* which do not limit the right to sue. They do, however, require insurers to offer no-fault insurance; in some of these states, drivers are required to buy it.

All state no-fault laws require purchase of medical payments coverage and wage loss coverage. State no-fault laws do, however, differ in two major ways:

- The limits placed on benefit payments vary.
- The thresholds beyond which a lawsuit is permitted differ.

Some states require no-fault policies to cover the cost of providing the personal services injured persons can no longer provide for themselves. This coverage provides payments for housekeeping and child-care services with some specified limit. Under no-fault (in all states except Michigan), damage to the insured's car is covered by her or his collision insurance and is subject to a deductible. If the other driver is at fault, an insured can recover the deductible.

The different states that have enacted no-fault laws have had varying experiences with them. Some have made improvements to make no-fault work better while others have moved away from the no-fault principle. In some states, no-fault has not reduced premiums as much as hoped—perhaps because the right to sue was not limited to any significant degree. One important benefit of no-fault laws has been to facilitate the rehabilitation of the injured. Rehabilitation services, though costly, can speed recovery, reduce disabilities, and help the injured person return to the workforce. No-fault insurance also has provided better help for those seriously injured in one-car accidents.

Cost

Insurers know from experience that accidents are more likely to happen to certain people and to certain cars than others. They also know that they are more likely to happen in certain places than in others. Insurers use this experience information to set rates. The factors used in determining premiums can be grouped into three general categories: where and how the car is used, the type of car, and the characteristics of the driver. These factors along with the coverage limits selected all affect the cost of coverage.

Where and How the Car Is Used. Insurers divide states into *rating territories* on the basis of population density, traffic congestion, and other factors. Accident rates are calculated for each of these territories, and the premiums charged are affected by the number and the severity of losses in a particular territory. Rates typically are lower in rural areas than in congested city areas because insurers have found their losses are lower there. The rating territory to which a car is assigned is based on where it is kept rather than on where it is driven.

The number of miles a car is driven annually and whether or not it is driven to work also affect premiums. The more a car is used, especially at peak traffic times, the greater the possibility of accident, so premiums are set accordingly.

Type of Car. Differences in the value and model of a car affect the premiums for several different coverages. Insurers know, for example, that expensive luxury cars such as Mercedes-Benzes and popular sports models such as the Toyota Celica Supra are favorite targets for thieves. To offset the likelihood that these cars will be stolen, the premiums for comprehensive coverage are set higher than for other cars.

Insurers also have learned that some cars are more likely to be involved in accidents than others. Four-door sedans and station wagons are less likely to be involved in accidents than sports models, perhaps because of differences in the people who typically drive them and in the ways they are driven. Car design and construction also can affect the probability of damage and the cost of repairs. For a few years prior to 1983, federal standards required auto bumpers to be resistant to crash-damage for speeds up to five miles per hour. For 1983 models and those since, the standard was reduced to 2.5 mph. Some manufacturers reduced the strength of the bumpers, while others did not. Experience has shown that cars with the weaker bumpers are more vulnerable to expensive crash damage.

Some companies provide premium discounts when certain equipment has been installed. Discounts from the costs of comprehensive insurance are widely available when antitheft devices have been installed. Discounts from no-fault and medical payments coverage often are available for cars with airbags or passive restraints (wrap-around seat-belt system).

Characteristics of the Driver. Insurers have found that past driving records are a good way to predict future accidents. People who have been responsible for accidents or who have had serious driving violations are especially likely to have an accident in the future. For this reason, many companies levy a surcharge on operators who have had serious accidents or have been convicted of a serious violation in the previous three years.

Young drivers as a group have a notorious reputation, not without some reason. Drivers under 25 constitute only about 20 percent of all licensed drivers but were, in one recent year, involved in 36 percent of the fatal accidents and in 42 percent of the alcohol-related fatal accidents (U.S. Department of Commerce, 1986).

Young male drivers who own or operate their own cars have been found to have particulary high accident rates. The accident rate for young women is lower than for young men, though the gap between them is narrowing. In states where sex is taken into account in ratemaking, premiums for young women are correspondingly lower. Premiums for young drivers usually are scaled down as they grow older and as they marry. Apparently age brings driving experience and marriage brings stability, both of which improve driving records.

The impact of extra-high premiums can be lessened by taking advantage of some of the discounts available. Many insurers offer discounts when a young driver has completed a state-approved driver training course. Many also provide good student discounts to high school and college students with superior grades or high class rank. Discounts also are available on family policies when students are attending college more than 100 miles from home and are not using the family car regularly. Policyholders should ask their insurer about what discounts are available. Insurers do not and cannot always know which ones may be applicable.

Rates for coverage vary between insurers in most states. In slightly less than half the states, insurers can set rates at whatever level they wish without interference from state regulators. Price competition in these states

CONSUMER CONCERN: COULD LYING ON AN INSURANCE APPLICATION AFFECT MY COVERAGE?

One of the concerns of insurers is that they will accumulate too many below-average risks in their pool of policyholders, a problem which is called *adverse selection* by insurance professionals. Adverse selection can occur when a company is too lenient or careless in accepting applicants. It also can occur when applicants deceive the company about their appropriate risk classification.

Insurance applicants may be tempted to lie on their applications in order to get into a classification for which the premium is lower. A young auto insurance applicant might, for example, be tempted to indicate an older age in order to avoid the high premium for young drivers. Other drivers might try to conceal information about past accidents.

Insurance policies are a form of contract and are subject to the laws governing contracts. Under contract law, the applicant is obligated to supply correct information in response to both verbal and written questions. If an insurance applicant conceals information or provides false information, the policy can be declared void by the company, and it may refuse to cover claims.

Insurance companies do not refuse coverage in every case where they could do so. In some cases, policyholders have successfully sued insurers to demand coverage. Honest consumers will not take the risk of losing their coverage even though they could reduce their premiums through deception.

QUESTIONS

1. Why do insurance applicants sometimes conceal or misrepresent facts about themselves and their situation?
2. What can insurance companies do to protect themselves against policyholders who have misrepresented or concealed information?

tends to be vigorous, and premiums for coverage vary a good deal. In most of the other states, insurers must get approval before changing rates and price differences between companies are smaller. In three states, all companies are required to charge the same rate, so there is no price competition (Gillis, 1986).

Comparision shopping for coverage will pay off in many areas. One 1984 study by an industry group compared policies for a hypothetical couple with clean driving records and two cars, living in a small city in New York state. The prices quoted ranged from $793 to $1,262 for the same coverage (*Consumer Reports,* September, 1984). There may be even more variation in prices in some other states because New York is one of the states that requires prior approval of rate change and may, as a result, have more limited price variation.

Another possible way to cut insurance costs is to purchase group auto insurance. Group auto policies, available through employers and membership groups, are becoming increasingly popular.

Service

Some of the criteria on which policyholders evaluate any insurer were discussed earlier. Settlements on auto insurance claims and other property damage claims involve extra problems growing out of how the extent of loss will be determined and its amount. Problems with cancellations and the refusal of renewals are also a problem because they are more frequent for auto insurance than for other types of policies.

Estimating the Repairs Needed. Insurers develop estimates of the cost of crash repairs in several different ways. Some use adjusters who prepare the estimates themselves, while others let claimants get estimates from the repair shops they prefer. After surveying policyholders' experience with claims, *Consumer Reports* found that those who were allowed to select the shops providing estimates were more likely to be satisfied with their settlement than those for whom an adjuster set the settlement (*Consumer Reports,* September, 1984).

Claimants and insurers often disagree on the amount of repairs needed. A claimant may insist on replacing a damaged bumper with a new one, while the company argues for straightening the old one. Claimants have a right to hold out for the repairs needed to get a satisfactory job. Continuing disagreements may, however, delay a needed settlement. Beyond some point, claimants may decide they cannot afford to hold out any longer. In these cases, they can accept the settlement offered, but only as partial payment on their claim.

Disagreements over the type of repair parts to be used may also arise between insurers and claimants. The high cost of repair parts provided by

Illustration 16-3
When a car is damaged, insurers sometimes disagree with claimants on how it should be repaired.

auto manufacturers has led some insurers to push for use of parts from cheaper, alternative sources. These parts often are of variable quality but are lower priced than the "genuine" parts supplied by the auto manufacturers.

Nonrenewals and Cancellations. Policyholders may have their coverage cancelled or be refused renewals because of claims for accidents in which they were at fault or because of a record of serious traffic violations. Some companies are more inclined to drop policyholders than others. Dropped policyholders should insist on the reason for the company decision and check to be certain the decision is within the conditions set down in their policy. Policyholders who feel they have been treated unfairly may appeal to their state's Department of Insurance.

Policyholders who have been dropped often have difficulty finding another company which will take them on. Young drivers, inexperienced drivers, and others who have not previously had insurance also may have trouble in finding a company to accept them.

The problems of drivers who have difficulty getting insurance create conflicting public interests. While it is in the public interest that all drivers have insurance, policyholders and company executives want their companies to hold down costs by refusing undesirable risks. To deal with this problem, every state and the District of Columbia has made special arrangements to ensure that auto insurance is available to everyone. In every state but Maryland, this insurance is provided by private insurers through arrangements commonly referred to as *assigned risk plans.* In Maryland, the insurance is provided by a state-operated fund (Insurance Information Institute, 1985).

The most common arrangement is *auto insurance plans* that assign insurance applicants to insurers in proportion to the insurers' shares of the total market. Insureds have no choice in where they are assigned and insurers generally cannot refuse an assignment. In other states, insurers are required to accept all applicants but can be reimbursed for excessive losses for a certain number of poor risks from a pool created by assessing all insurers. In other states, a group of companies accepts all assigned business but shares the losses on these policies with all other insurers.

Assigned risk drivers constitute only about 8 percent of all drivers. They have, however, created continuing losses for insurers despite the extra premiums charged. These losses have been passed along by insurers in the premiums of all policyholders.

Another alternative to assigned risk plans is the nonstandard market. This consists of insurers that provide coverage to drivers who are considered above-average risks because of their past driving records or because they drive high-performance or expensive sports cars. Nonstandard insurers also serve the needs of applicants who want more coverage than they can obtain through assigned risk plans. In return for accepting these special risks, nonstandard insurers charge higher premiums than insurers serving the regular market.

HOUSEHOLD INSURANCE

Americans spend about $15 billion a year for home insurance. What motivates householders to pay out this kind of money to protect against things that may never happen—fires, tornadoes, and explosions? The answer is that their homes are many homeowners' most valuable assets. They recognize that they cannot afford to take any risks, however remote, on their loss. They also recognize that the loss of personal property could be a severe financial blow and want protection against those losses too. In addition, they are aware that liability claims arising out of negligence could threaten their financial independence and want protection from them. While renters do not need to protect against loss of a dwelling because it belongs to someone else, they do need protection against personal liability claims and may wish to insure against losses of personal property.

In the following sections, the coverages available to protect against property loss and liability claims will be examined, along with certain related coverage. Next, the cost of this protection and insurer services, two other important evaluative criteria, will be considered.

Coverage

Home insurance is today sold in package form. Typical policies provide protection against property losses from such perils as fire, windstorm, and theft, and from personal liability claims. Years ago such coverage had to be purchased in three separate policies, one for property losses from fire and other perils, a second for theft losses, and a third for liability claims. Today a variety of combinations of coverages are available to meet the needs of house-owners, condominium and apartment owners, mobile home owners, and renters.

Property Insurance. *Property insurance coverage* provides protection against losses from damages to a dwelling or to other structures on the property such as garages and toolsheds. This coverage also provides protection of personal property including furniture, clothing, appliances, and jewelry. The protection to personal property applies both at home and away. For example, theft losses on a vacation trip would be covered. Coverage of some valuables such as antiques, silverware, jewelry, and guns is, however, subject to limits that may be relatively low compared to the value of the items. Additional insurance is often necessary to protect these items to their full value.

In addition, this coverage provides protection against losses due to unauthorized credit card use, check forgery, and acceptance of counterfeit money. Some insurers are adding protection against unauthorized use of EFT cards. Household policies exclude losses from damage to autos or injury to pets. They also exclude losses to any extensive business operations conducted at home.

Protection is provided for related losses when damage to a dwelling is so extensive it is no longer habitable. Additional living expenses are provided for staying in a hotel, when necessary, as are expenses for removing personal effects and storing them.

The coverages available differ in the perils covered (see Figure 16-1). The Basic Policy (HO-1) provides protection against damage to the home and contents from ten common perils. Coverage against these ten perils plus seven additional ones is provided in the Broad Form Policy (HO-2). Even more extensive protection is provided by the Special Policy (HO-3), which provides so-called "all-risks" protection for the dwelling. The HO-3 policy does not, in fact, cover all risks. It covers all except those specifically excluded in the policy. The perils typically excluded include flood, earthquake, and war and nuclear accidents. HO-3 policies provide protection for personal property only for the seventeen named perils.

Full all-risk coverage of both the dwelling personal property is available with a Comprehensive Policy (HO-5). Some insurers are phasing HO-5

Figure 16-1
Perils Against Which Properties are Insured Under the Various Homeowner Policies

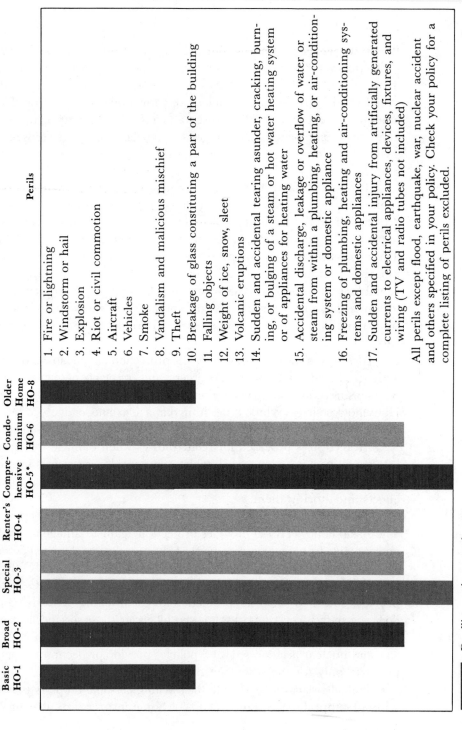

	Basic HO-1	Broad HO-2	Special HO-3	Renter's HO-4	Comprehensive HO-5*	Condominium HO-6	Older Home HO-8	Perils
								1. Fire or lightning
								2. Windstorm or hail
								3. Explosion
								4. Riot or civil commotion
								5. Aircraft
								6. Vehicles
								7. Smoke
								8. Vandalism and malicious mischief
								9. Theft
								10. Breakage of glass constituting a part of the building
								11. Falling objects
								12. Weight of ice, snow, sleet
								13. Volcanic eruptions
								14. Sudden and accidental tearing asunder, cracking, burning, or bulging of a steam or hot water heating system or of appliances for heating water
								15. Accidental discharge, leakage or overflow of water or steam from within a plumbing, heating, or air-conditioning system or domestic appliance
								16. Freezing of plumbing, heating and air-conditioning systems and domestic appliances
								17. Sudden and accidental injury from artificially generated currents to electrical appliances, devices, fixtures, and wiring (TV and radio tubes not included)
								All perils except flood, earthquake, war, nuclear accident and others specified in your policy. Check your policy for a complete listing of perils excluded.

■ — Dwelling and personal property
■ — Dwelling only
■ — Personal property only

*Under the new homeowners program, comprehensive coverage is available by endorsement to the HO-3 special policy instead of the traditional HO-5 comprehensive policy.

Source: Insurance Information Institute. Used by permission.

426

policies out and replacing them with HO-3 policies plus an endorsement for all-risk coverage on personal property. A variety of losses fall outside the seventeen named perils, but are protected by all-risk coverage:

- The family dog chews a hole in the carpet.
- A can of paint is spilled and stains a pair of draperies and a bedspread.
- A valuable piece of silverware is destroyed in the garbage disposal.

Because none of these perils is specifically excluded in an all-risk coverage, all are covered.

Renters do not need coverage on their dwelling because it is owned by someone else. Coverage of their personal property against seventeen named perils is provided by a Renter's Policy (HO-4). Condominium owners usually are protected from losses to their dwelling by a policy purchased by their condominium association. A Condominium Unit-Owner's Policy (HO-6) covers their personal property and any modifications they have made that are not insured by the association's policy.

The homeowner's policies discusssed (HO-1, HO-2, HO-3, and HO-5) provide for replacement of damage without depreciation if a dwelling is insured to at least 80 percent of its value. Replacement of many older homes with custom woodwork, stained-glass windows, and other special features could be prohibitively expensive. Premiums for insurance to provide for repairs also would have to be high. The Older Home Policy Policy (HO-8) provides for coverage for market value rather than replacement cost, at a lower premium than would otherwise be required. A Mobile Home Owner's Policy also is available with coverage similar to HO-2. Because of the susceptibility of mobile homes to damage in high winds, the premiums are relatively high.

Although floods and earthquakes are specifically excluded in all-risk coverage, coverage for these perils is available. Insurers are reluctant to offer flood insurance coverage separately because of the problem of adverse selection, since only property owners who expected water damage problems would buy the coverage. Flood insurance is available in many areas through a federal government-assisted program from regular insurance agents. Earthquake coverage can be added to homeowners' policies by endorsement.

To receive full payment for replacement cost, the policyholder must insure a property to at least 80 percent of its replacement cost. If this rule were not in effect, policyholders might be tempted to insure a property for less than its full replacement cost, gambling that a total loss is unlikely, in order to save on premiums. For a home insured to 80 percent or more of replacement cost, full replacement costs for damages are paid. For example, if a $100,000 home was insured to $80,000 or more and $10,000 damage occurred in a kitchen fire, the full repair costs would be paid (less the deductible). However, if the home is insured for less than 80 percent of replacement cost, only a partial payment for the loss would be made. The payment would be calculated in two different ways and the owner would receive the greater amount. If the $100,000 house was insured for only $50,000 instead of the minimum of $80,000 the owner should have (80 percent of replacement cost), one calculation would be as follows:

$$\frac{\$50,000 \text{ actual coverage}}{\$80,000 \text{ minimum required coverage}} \times \$10,000 \text{ loss} = \$6,250$$

The other calculation is based on replacement cost adjusted for depreciation of the property. If the kitchen appliances and kitchen area had served about one-half their useful life, this would be deducted from the loss:

$$\$10,000 \text{ loss} - \$5,000 \text{ depreciation} = \$5,000$$

In this case, the homeowner would receive the larger of the two amounts, which still is far below actual replacement cost.

Homeowners who do not insure to 80 percent or more of replacement cost retain part of the risk of loss, though they may not be fully aware of this. Policyholders who want full protection clearly need to insure for more than 80 percent of replacement. Unfortunately it is not always easy to determine replacement cost. Market value often is not an adequate guide. Market value represents the depreciated value of a dwelling, while replacement cost is based on the cost of repairs with new materials. Repairing a seriously damaged home may cost more than its market value.

Property prices and replacement costs in many areas have risen sharply with inflation in the 1970s and 1980s. As a result, many homes have become seriously underinsured. Insurers recommend a regular review of coverage and appropriate increases. Some companies provide an *inflation guard endorsement* that provides for regular increases in coverage. To protect their policyholders, some insurers have raised the policy limits provided without waiting for a request from the policyholder, but they will adjust it downward if the policyholder objects.

While standard homeowners' policies pay replacement cost for damage to the dwelling if it is insured to 80 percent of its replacement cost, they pay only actual cash value for lost or damaged personal property. The settlement is based on depreciated value of the items, not their replacement cost. If a TV set that cost $350 three years ago is stolen, the settlement might be only $250 (less $100 deductible), despite the fact that the set might cost $400 to replace. Many insurers now are offering replacement cost coverage for personal property by endorsement to their regular policies or as part of special new packages.

Personal property coverage is usually limited to half the coverage on the dwelling. If a dwelling is covered for $100,000, personal property is covered up to $50,000. New, revised policies are raising this limit to the same level as the coverage on the dwelling. Limits on losses away from home are set relatively low and probably would not provide full protection for a major loss.

Individuals who own jewelry, antiques, musical equipment, guns, and collections whose value exceeds the limits in personal property coverage often want more protection. This protection is available with a *personal property floater*. Coverage applies to items specifically listed (or scheduled) in the policy and "floats" with the scheduled item, providing coverage anywhere, at home or away. Personal property floaters are available as endorsements or as separate policies.

Moving and storing personal property creates extra risks of loss. These losses may be covered under a homeowner's policy if it kept in force, but it is wise to check. Movers carry liability insurance, but it is for their protection and is not designed to meet the property owner's needs. Movers' coverage may provide only limited protection because it is subject to relatively low limits.

Personal Liability Coverage. Homeowners need protection from claims for bodily injury and property damage arising from their negligence just as drivers do. This *personal liability coverage* is available as part of homeowner's packages. It covers a variety of possible claims:

- Due to a homeowner's carelessness in cutting down a tree, it falls on a neighbor's house and damages it.
- A golfer forgets to yell "fore" after driving a ball and injures a fellow golfer.
- A delivery person stumbles on a loose entry rug and breaks an arm.

Personal liability coverage applies both on and off the insured premises.

Liability coverage also provides some limited protection for accidental damage to the property of others. It covers the damage done by the baseball that breaks a neighbor's window and also intentional damage and vandalism caused by children under 13.

Homeowners' policies typically include $25,000 to $100,000 personal liability coverage, and more coverage is available by endorsement. A minimum of $300,000 coverage is advisable. Some people may decide they need coverage beyond this limit because they have substantial assets and believe they are vulnerable to lawsuits. Personal liability coverage beyond the usual auto and homeowner's policy limits is available with an *umbrella liability policy*. This coverage is available with limits of $1 million or more and pays claims that exceed the limits of auto or homeowner's coverage. Umbrella policies also cover liability from other perils, including claims arising from libel and slander suits.

Medical Payments to Others. Payment for the treatment of nonfamily members injured on the insured premises is provided by *medical payments coverage,* regardless of who is at fault. In addition, injuries caused by the policyholder, family, and pets elsewhere are also covered. This coverage provides protection in cases of minor injuries to visitors and in cases where the insured feels some moral obligation. This coverage does not apply to the insured and family members, only to others (unlike medical payments coverage in auto policies). The coverage provided is relatively low with limits of $500 or $1,000 in most policies. Again, larger amounts can be obtained.

Several states require homeowners and renters who regularly employ household help, either full-time or part-time, to carry *workers' compensation* coverage as part of their personal liability coverage. Workers' compensation often is thought of as protection for industrial workers injured in factory jobs. In fact, it provides medical, disability, and survivor's insurance coverage for any type of worker.

CONSUMER CONCERN: WHAT'S BEHIND THE INCREASING COST OF INSURANCE?	In the mid-1980s the daily mail carried unexpected jolts for many Americans: "Your car insurance policy will not be renewed"; "The premium on your homeowner's policy is being increased by 20 percent." The daily news had its share of jolts too: "The town's July 4th fireworks have been cancelled because liability insurance is unavailable"; "Two local physicians are giving up the obstetric portion of their practices because they feel malpractice insurance for delivering babies has gotten too high."

Just what has been behind these problems of rising costs and unavailability? While the problems are clear, the causes have been the subject of controversy. Some analysts have argued that rising premiums really are a result of unreasonably low premiums in previous years. They suggest that when interest rates were high, insurers competed for business and cut rates to unreasonably low levels to get customers. They made up for their low premium incomes by investing their assets at the high interest rates then available. When interest rates fell, the insurers' investment earnings dropped sharply and some found themselves with too many high-risk clients. "The industry literally competed itself into the ground," one state insurance commissioner has suggested (Wayne, 1986, p. D1). The insurers took the obvious corrective steps of raising premiums, dropping the worst risks, and refusing coverage for new applications that involved uncertain risks. |

Cost

The cost of property insurance is affected by three major factors:

- *Replacement cost of the dwelling.* This cost depends on the square footage and materials used, along with local materials and labor costs.
- *Location.* Some dwellings are more vulnerable than others because they are located long distances from a fire station or a fire hydrant, or they are in high-crime areas or areas with high arson loss rates.
- *Construction.* Certain types of dwellings are more susceptible to damage than others. Newer homes and homes of brick construction are considered less susceptible.

The cost of coverage is, of course, also affected by the limits requested. Premiums can be reduced if the policyholder retains some of the risk by accepting a higher deductible. Some discounts are available, including discounts for fire and burglar alarms and for smoke detectors.

The insurance industry has tended to put much of the blame elsewhere. Industry leaders have argued that the culprit is unreasonable court awards in liability cases of all kinds: auto accidents, product liability cases, and medical malpractice suits. Another factor has been the continuing increase in the cost of things for which insurance must pay: auto repair parts, doctors' fees, and construction materials for home repairs.

Not only is there a lack of agreement about the cause of rising insurance costs and unavailability of coverage, there also is disagreement about what should be done about these problems. Some insurers, along with business and professional liability policyholders, have argued for caps on the amounts that will be paid on liability claims. Consumer groups and trial lawyers who specialize in liability suits argue that this is an unfair limit on the injured's rights.

QUESTIONS

1. Some of the causes of the insurance industry's problems appear to be the result of excessive competition for customers. What are the arguments for and against more control on competition?
2. Should Congress or state legislators put limits on the awards in liability cases, or should the injured be allowed to take whatever they can get?

Service

Because the sales commissions for property insurance are relatively low, it is not sold aggressively in the same way life insurance is. One result is that many people, especially renters, do not have the coverage they need. Another result is that policyholders do not always get much advice about the most appropriate coverage for their particular situation. To get the best possible service, applicants and policyholders may have to raise questions about any special needs they have.

Some individuals have difficulty getting an insurer to accept them or to renew their policy because their neighborhood is considered to be high-risk. Discrimination against applicants from particular neighborhoods is called *red-lining* because of the red lines insurers are alleged to draw around the areas on their rating territory maps. Red-lining is illegal, and insurance applicants who suspect they have been refused insurance because of it should complain to their state Department of Insurance.

About half of the states have programs to ensure that property insurance is available to everyone who wants it. The state FAIR (Fair Access to Insurance Requirements) Plans are supported by insurers who sell insurance in the state and policies are sold through regular agents. These plans accept applicants from high-risk areas, many of which are blighted and distressed, but charge higher premiums for doing so. Similar plans are offered in many Atlantic and Gulf Coast states to provide hurricane and windstorm protection to property owners in coastal areas.

Federal government-assisted flood insurance is available to property owners in many communities through regular insurance agents. As was noted earlier, flood damage is specifically excluded, even in all-risk homeowner's policies. Federal government-assisted insurance against theft and burglary is available in many high-crime areas where coverage from regular insurers is not available. This coverage is also available through regular agents.

BUYING INSURANCE

There are thousands of corporations, organizations, and associations that provide insurance in this country. The prospective purchaser has to sort through these different sellers because an insurer's legal structure affects the way the insurer operates and the premiums charged. The system for marketing insurance also has taken several different forms and these too can have implications for consumers.

Types of Insurers

Insurers can be classified in several different ways: (1) according to the types of insurance they write, including property and casualty or life and health insurance; (2) according to the marketing system they use to sell insurance; and (3) according to the legal organization of the firm. This section considers the different legal forms under which insurers are organized and their effects.

Mutual Insurance Companies. The oldest form of insurance company in this country is the *mutual insurance company.* The oldest surviving mutual company was organized by Benjamin Franklin to provide fire insurance for its members. Mutual companies are owned by their policyholders, who elect the board of directors. The directors, in turn, select the officers who run the company. There are no stockholders. Any profits are returned to the policyholders, usually in the form of policyholder's dividends. Some of the leading mutual life insurance companies include Prudential, Metropolitan, Equitable, John Hancock, and Northwestern Mutual. Leading mutual property insurance companies include State Farm, Nationwide, and Liberty Mutual.

Stock Insurance Companies. Insurers organized as profit-making corporations, *stock insurance companies,* are owned by stockholders and operated for their gain. When the company's operations are profitable, the stockholders are paid dividends as in any other corporation. Stock insurance companies usually issue *nonparticipating policies.* No policyholder dividends are paid on these policies in the way dividends are paid to policyholders with mutual insurance companies. Some stock insurance companies do, however, issue participating policies because many consumers find the idea of policyholder dividends appealing.

Aside from these differences, the stock companies and mutual insurance companies operate in much the same way. The leading stock property insurance companies include Allstate, Travelers, Hartford Fire, and Aetna Life and Casualty. Among the leading life insurers are Connecticut General and Aetna Life.

Reciprocal Exchanges. Another type of insurer is a nonprofit organization of people who pool risks and share losses proportionally. This type of organization is labeled a *reciprocal exchange.* In their original form, each member-subscriber's premium is kept in a separate account and a proportionate share of losses is deducted from each account. Some reciprocal exchanges now operate much like stock and mutual companies and charge regular premiums.

Reciprocal exchanges are unincorporated and are managed by an attorney-in-fact, either an individual or a corporation, which receives a share of the premiums for their services. Major reciprocal exchanges include Farmers Insurance Exchange and United Services Auto Association.

Health Associations. The Blue Cross and Blue Shield insurance organizations specialize solely in health insurance. These organizations are nonprofit and nontaxable but are not policyholder-owned. They are directed by boards that include physicians, hospitals, and the general public. The "Blues" are organized to provide medical services to their subscribers rather than to reimburse them for their expenses. Services are provided to subscribers and the doctor and hospital providers are reimbursed directly. This system allows subscribers to prepay medical services, in anticipation of need, rather than to wait for reimbursement after an expense has been incurred.

Government. The federal and state governments provide insurance to individual citizens. An important federal government program is the Social Security system, which provides life insurance, disability insurance, and health insurance (Medicare and Medicaid). The federal government also assists the operation of the FAIR program, a flood insurance program, and a robbery and burglary insurance program. A number of states operate insurance programs. The most important are the state's workers' compensation programs.

Insurance Marketing Systems

Marketing is a key part of the insurance system because insurers need a way to promote their products to consumers. Consumers, for their part, need advice on what policy best meets their needs and on arranging coverage. These services are provided through insurance agents and by direct selling.

Independent Agents. A significant portion of property insurance is sold through *independent agents,* who are independent business people representing more than one company. They are paid commissions by companies on the basis of the premiums generated. In selling insurance to consumers, they emphasize their role as independent advisers who can arrange coverage with the company they feel is most appropriate. When necessary, they can arrange the shift of a policyholder from one company to another. Aetna Life and Casualty, Travelers, and Kemper are leading insurers selling through independent agents.

Exclusive Agents. Most life insurance companies and a number of major property insurance companies rely on *exclusive agents.* Exclusive agents represent one company and sell only its policies. Exclusive agents are closely associated with the company and are trained by the company on the variety of coverages it offers. Sales promotion is a major part of their job. Agents may be paid commissions, receive a salary, or get some combination of salary and commission.

The exclusive agent system can provide efficiencies in operations. Billing and most paperwork are handled in the insurer's corporate offices, while agents concentrate on selling. Because of these services, exclusive agents have some advantages in pricing. To counter these advantages, many companies selling through independent agents now bill policyholders directly rather through the agent.

Sales promotion is particularly important in marketing life insurance. Few people seek out an agent and ask to buy. Instead, most have to be convinced. Selling reluctant customers is difficult and agents' incomes depend on their commissions on what they sell. Turnover rates among salespeople are high. As a result, many agents are relatively inexperienced and may give uninformed advice. They also may be tempted to emphasize alternatives that produce the best commissions.

Direct Sales. A few insurers arrange sales through their own employees who receive salaries and commissions rather than through commissioned representatives. Liberty Mutual sells coverage in this way. A few others sell policies by mail. These include GEICO (Government Employees Insurance Company), a company which sells policies to government employees, and USAA (United Services Auto Association), which sells policies to Armed Forces officers, former officers, and their families. While selling by mail is economical, it can be difficult for policyholders to get needed advice on the most appropriate coverage.

Because insurance costs take a significant part of household budgets, consumers need to allocate their premium dollars to get the most protection for their money. Consumers should focus on protecting themselves against major catastrophes, rather than trying to get back their premium dollars with claims for minor losses such as stolen hubcaps and broken windows. Many consumers would benefit by raising their deductibles and retaining some risk and using the dollars saved to buy higher coverage limits.

Whenever a major life change occurs, consumers need to consider its implications for their insurance coverage. Do they need a new kind of coverage? Higher limits of coverage? To add new individuals to their coverage? To notify insurers of a change of address? Remember, as your life changes, your coverage needs change.

MAJOR CHAPTER CONCEPTS

1. Consumers can use insurance to protect themselves against three major categories of losses: property losses, personal losses (including loss of income and medical expenses), and legal liability losses.
2. Consumers can manage risks by risk prevention and reduction, by risk avoidance, by risk retention, and by risk transfer through the purchase of insurance.
3. An insurance policy is a legal contract between the policyholder and insurer. The policy sets down the perils covered, the terms of coverage, and the obligations of both parties.
4. Costs vary among insurers, and comparison shopping is advisable.

5. Auto liability coverage protects against claims arising from negligence that has resulted in bodily injury or damage of the property of others.

6. Collision coverage reimburses insureds for crash damage to their own car less some deductible. Comprehensive coverage protects against other perils including fire, hail, flood, and theft, and also has a deductible.

7. No-fault automobile insurance is available in about half the states. It provides protection for insureds regardless of who is at fault and can help to avoid the long delays of court cases and unpredictable settlements. No-fault laws require insured to carry medical payment coverage protecting themselves and their passengers and wage loss insurance.

8. Auto insurance premiums are affected by where and how the car is used, the type of car insured, the characteristics of the driver, and the limits of the coverage.

9. Drivers who have trouble getting insurance or experience cancellation or nonrenewal of policies can seek insurance from assigned-risk plans or from insurers who handle nonstandard risks.

10. Homeowners and renters need protection against property losses from fire, theft, and other perils and against personal liability claims arising out of negligence. Coverage is available in a variety of homeowners' policies designed to meet various needs.

11. Property insurance coverage protects against varying numbers of named perils, either ten perils, seventeen perils, or "all" perils. So-called all-risk coverage usually excludes flood and earthquake coverage, which must be obtained separately.

12. The cost of property insurance is affected by the limits and deductibles selected, the replacement cost of the dwelling, its location, and its construction.

13. To ensure that they will be paid full replacement costs for damages, homeowners' policyholders must insure to at least 80 percent of replacement cost for the proerty. Those who insure lower proportions will not receive full payment for replacement costs.

14. Insurance buyers should allocate their premium dollars so as to get the best protection for catastrophic losses. Higher deductibles can reduce premiums so that higher coverage limits can be purchased. Coverage should be reviewed regularly and when major life changes occur.

CONSUMER QUESTIONS

1. What type of auto insurance system do you have in your state? What criticisms have been made of the way it operates and what proposals for change have been made? What groups favor and oppose change?

2. Get a copy of your own (or your family's) auto insurance policy. What coverages do you have? What are the limits and deductibles for each?

What discounts, if any, are in effect? Are there any changes needed? Explain what they are and why they are needed. (If you or your family do not have a car, explain the coverages you would want if you had one.)

3. Get a copy of your own (or your family's) homeowner's insurance. What coverages are included? What are the limits and deductibles? Do any changes in the coverage seem needed? Explain. (If you or your family do not have a homeowner's policy, what coverage would be appropriate?)

4. Auto insurance is the subject of continuing controversy. Check recent periodicals for discussions of a current issue and prepare a report on it. Topics could include (a) no-fault auto insurance, (b) auto insurance costs, (c) auto insurance claims settlement procedures, (d) the susceptibility of different models to crash damage, and (e) adequacy of state regulation procedures.

5. Jack de Haas wonders if he really needs any insurance because he is renting a furnished apartment. He does have a large color TV set, a VCR, and a large sound system, plus two pieces of art worth $500 each. In addition, he has two antique guns valued at $2,000 and a stamp collection he estimates is worth $3,500. He also has a large number of clothes, which cost $6,500 new. Jack is away a good deal on his job as a traveling sales representative, which earns him $35,000 a year in salary and commissions. What insurance recommendations would be appropriate for Jack?

6. Sally Hampton feels the best way to get her money's worth with car insurance is to choose low deductibles. She believes she can get more of her premium money back that way. "Why, I got back $295 of the $400 I spent on my 10/20/5 car insurance policy last year," she reports. Evaluate Sally's approach to car insurance.

SUGGESTED
READINGS

1. *Changing Times.* "Crash Course: It Takes a Shop Experienced with Unibody Frames to Fix Today's Cars." 40, no. 7 (July 1986): 53-56. New unibody auto construction makes crash repairs a complicated job, requiring special equipment.

2. *Consumer Reports.* "What Ever Happened to No-Fault." 49, no. 9 (September 1984): 511-513, 546. This article reviews the rationale for no-fault auto insurance and experience with its operation in various forms in particular states.

3. Eldred, Gary W. "How Wisely Do Consumers Select Their Property and Liability Insurance Coverages?" *Journal of Consumer Affairs* 14, no. 2 (Winter 1980): 288-306. After a survey of North Carolina households, this study concluded that many households had gotten little help from their insurance agents and had allocated their premium dollars unwisely.

4. Golonka, Nancy. *How to Protect What's Yours.* Washington, D.C.: Acropolis Books Ltd., 1983. This is a detailed guide to the purchase and use of property, auto,

life, and medical insurance. It includes useful chapters on what to do if you are turned down for auto insurance and on holding down auto insurance cost.

5. Tobias, Andrew. *The Invisible Banks: Everything the Insurance Industry Never Wanted You to Know.* New York: Linden Press/Simon and Schuster, 1982. This is a highly readable and highly critical examination of the insurance industry.

6. Worthy, Ford S. "A War Over Parts for Wrecked Cars." *Fortune* 113, no. 6 (March 12, 1986): 71-73. A battle has developed between automakers who want to sell their "genuine" replacement parts for crash repairs and auto insurance companies who like the lower cost of imported substitute parts and argue that the auto makers have exploited their monopoly position to charge excessive prices.

CHAPTER 17

LIFE INSURANCE

There's a saying in the insurance industry: "People don't *buy* life insurance; it's sold to them." Few consumers seek out a life insurance salesperson and ask to buy a policy. Instead, most adults push the subject into a back corner of their minds. For some, the idea of death seems too remote to worry about. Others avoid the subject because it seems so complicated and so many questions seem to be involved:

- How much life insurance do I really need?
- What kind of policy would best suit my situation?
- Which company offers the best policy of the type I need?

Only a few consumers set out to answer these questions on their own. Too often they are easy targets for the first insurance salesperson who comes along and supplies a version of the answers.

The purchase of a life insurance policy is a commitment to spend substantial amounts of money over a number of years, and poor choices can be costly. Uninformed consumers may buy the wrong kind of coverage or spend more than necessary for what they do buy. Consumers who want to manage their financial affairs successfully need to learn how to assess their life insurance needs and shop for coverage effectively.

LIFE INSURANCE NEEDS

Life insurance is used to fulfill several needs. Its most important role is to protect against the financial risks created by premature death (see Figure 17-1). When a family is counting on a continuing stream of earnings and services from a household member, his or her death can create a financial crisis for the survivors. Some way to replace that expected income is needed, and it may also be necessary to hire outside help for housekeeping, child care, and household maintenance services. Building up the amount of savings required to meet these needs would take years. One of the appeals of life insurance is that an *estate*, or an accumulation of assets to be passed to heirs, can be created quickly and easily with the purchase of a life insurance policy.

A second use for life insurance is to provide for final expenses. At death, there may be an accumulation of medical bills, funeral expenses, and other bills left behind. Life insurance can help to meet these obligations. Life insurance proceeds can also provide the money for family members to make needed adjustments: to get training to prepare for employment, to look for a job, to move to a new location, or to make other changes.

Another use of life insurance is to build needed savings and, at the same time, insure that the savings program will be completed. In years past, endowment life insurance policies were promoted widely as a way to build savings for the college education of children. Policies were available that matured when children were ready for college and provided life insurance protection until that time. Although few people are buying endowment policies today, life insurance can provide a way to build savings. One of its special attractions is that the interest on these savings accumulates tax-free.

Life insurance can also be used to build savings for retirement. Policies can be used to accumulate savings that can be used at retirement to provide periodic income payments.

Life insurance is only one of the ways to meet these financial needs (see Figure 17-1). Social Security will meet part of these needs for most workers' families (as will be discussed in Chapter 19). Personal savings and investments along with employee pension and retirement benefits can also serve to meet a significant portion of these needs. After analyzing their financial needs, single people and married couples with no children may find they have only limited life insurance needs. Married couples with young children are, however, likely to find they have substantial needs. The amount of money required to provide for a child until that child can be financially

Figure 17-1
Estimating Life
Insurance Needs

Financial Assets

  Cash and savings
  Investments
  Equity in home
  Pension fund contributions refund
  Life insurance already owned
  Other assets

Needs

  Funeral expenses
  Uninsured final medical expenses
  Probate costs, attorney's fees, estate taxes
  Repayment of debts
  Emergency fund
  Education fund
  Household services expenses (replacement of homemaking and
    home maintenance services)
  Family income needs of children (expenses less incomes less
    Social Security) × number of years of dependency for each
    child
  Annual income needs of adults (expenses less incomes less Social
    Security less pensions) × number of years

Life Insurance Needs

 Total Assets   _____

 Minus Total Needs   _____

 Additional Insurance Needed   _____

independent is large (see Consumer Capsule: "The Cost of Raising a Child").
For most couples, life insurance is the only feasible way of meeting these
obligations.

  Many adults have life insurance coverage under employee group policies
where they work. This coverage can be an important element in providing
needed protection. In many cases, however, the protection provided will
not be adequate and the purchase of individually owned policies will be
necessary.

  The evaluative criteria that are important in choosing life insurance
are the same as those for other types of insurance: coverage, costs, and service.

To meet different customer needs and to create marketing excitement, the life insurance industry has created a variety of policy types. The provisions of these policies differ significantly, as do their costs, making both coverage and costs important criteria in choosing a policy and an insurer or carrier. Service also is an important evaluative criterion, though the services of a life insurance provider are somewhat different from those of an auto or home insurer. Most insurance buyers require advice on the types of policies available to meet their varying needs. In addition, they may require assistance in updating coverage as their needs change.

This chapter will first examine some of the major types of life insurance policies available and their provisions and will then consider some of the alternative sources of life insurance coverage.

TYPES OF LIFE INSURANCE

While there are many types of life insurance policies, they are all variations of two basic categories:

- *Term life insurance* provides only basic protection during some specified period, such as 5 or 10 years or up to a specified age.
- *Permanent life insurance* includes basic protection plus a savings component.

Illustration 17-1
Life insurance can help young couples to be certain that their children will be provided for financially if the couple dies.

This section will discuss term insurance. The next sections discuss various types of life insurance that build cash value.[1]

[1]The terminology suggested by the American Council of Life Insurance (1984) has been used throughout this section.

CONSUMER CAPSULE: THE COST OF RAISING A CHILD

Probably the biggest financial decision a couple can make is the decision to have a child. The birth of a child creates sizable financial responsibilities for parents, ones for which they are both morally and legally obligated. The total costs of raising a child to the age of financial independence approach $100,000. This amount does not include the cost of a college education, something which many families would regard as a necessity.

The cost of raising a child from birth to age 18 varies somewhat by locale. Recent estimates by the U.S. Department of Agriculture ranged from a low of $85,556 for rural nonfarm families in the Midwest region to a high of $106,725 for rural nonfarm families in the West. The figures below, for urban households in the Northeast, represent the midrange between the two cost extremes:

Food at home	$21,138
Food away from home	2,548
Clothing	6,432
Housing (shelter and utilities)	33,140
Medical care	5,778
Education	2,232
Transportation	13,042
All other (personal care, reading and miscellaneous)	12,624
Total	$96,934

Annual costs differ with age. They peak at ages 16 and 17, when food and clothing costs are particularly high.

Cost figures such as these make the need for life insurance clear. Parents are obligated to provide for their children, and life insurance is one way of assuring that they can do this even if they are no longer alive and producing an income.

Source: "Updated Estimates of the Cost of Raising a Child," *Family Economics Review* no. 4 (1986): 28-29.

Term Insurance

Term insurance is the no-frills product of the life insurance industry. It provides coverage for a specified number of years (such as one, five, or ten years) or to some specified age. If the insured dies during the period, the face value of the policy is paid. If the insured survives until the end of the policy term, he or she receives nothing because no cash value has accrued. The premiums paid have been used up covering the risk of death during the term of the policy.

Coverage. Because the probability of death increases with age, premiums for term insurance increase with age. Some term policies provide the same *face amount* or death benefit for each year of the policy's term. These policies are *level term policies*. Premiums remain the same over the one- or five-year term of the policy. If the policy is renewed for another term, the premiums will be higher to take account of the increasing likelihood of death. Another type of term policy, *decreasing term insurance,* also has the same premiums but the face amount payable decreases periodically. The declining face amount offsets the increasing risk of death over the life of the policy. Decreasing term insurance often is sold for terms of fifteen or twenty years in the form of mortgage insurance, with the decreasing face amount matched to the declining mortgage balance owed. It may also be offered for shorter terms as credit life insurance for auto loans and other shorter-term consumer loans.

Several variations of level term insurance are offered. *Renewable level term* policies can be renewed for one or more additional terms beyond the initial one if desired. Because of the renewability feature, the insured is not required to take another physical examination or present other evidence of insurability. Term policies may also be convertible to whole life insurance, which can be continued indefinitely. Convertibility provisions permit an insured to make this switch without presenting new evidence of insurability.

Because term insurance provides only basic protection against the risk of death and has no savings component, it is less expensive than other types of life insurance. This feature is attractive to consumers who want the most protection for the lowest outlay. The cost of coverage does, however, increase each year for new coverage or with each renewal. At older ages, when the mortality risk is high, the cost of term coverage is relatively high, and it becomes harder and harder to afford. Fortunately, the insurance needs of older consumers are often lower than those of consumers with young families. The higher cost of coverage may be offset by reducing the amount of coverage. Another problem with renewable term insurance is that there may be limits to the number of terms for which it may be renewed or it may not be renewable beyond a certain age.

Cost. Although term insurance buyers typically plan to keep their coverage for a limited number of years or until a certain age, they still need to pay attention to the long-run costs of different policies. Differences in the premiums at different ages and in dividends (if the policy is a participating policy) can both affect long-run costs.

The cost analysis should, however, be carried one step further. The cost of owning a policy is not simply the net premiums (the premiums paid less the dividends, if any). The interest forgone on the premiums paid also needs to be taken into account. Money saved in the early years of a policy will be worth more to a policyholder than savings 20 years in the future because of the time value of money. One way to take account of the time value of money is to adjust for the timing of the net premiums. To permit comparison of policies, an *interest-adjusted net cost* is used in the insurance industry to compare the costs of owning policies for different periods of time. The value frequently is computed for 5-, 10- and 20-year periods. A 5 percent interest rate is currently being used to estimate interest forgone.

The interest-adjusted net cost is often converted to index form for simplicity. The index shows what a policy costs as compared to depositing the premiums in a savings account at compound interest.

Interest-adjusted net premiums for the period	÷	The amount to which $1 deposited annually at interest will grow over the period	=	Interest adjusted net cost index

For example, for one relatively low-cost policy, the 10-year index value is calculated as follows:

Interest-adjusted net premiums for for 10-year period	÷	The amount to which $1 deposited annually at 5 percent interest will percent interest will grow over 10 years	=	
		$23,773 ÷ $13,207	= 1.80	

Index values can be used to compare similar policies. The lower the index value, the better buy the policy is. The index can also be used as a guide to cost. The policy in the example above costs $1.80 per $1,000 coverage per year.

The cost of owning different term policies can vary widely. When *Consumer Reports* compared the costs a 25-year-old male could expect for owning a $50,000 policy for 10 years, it found that the most-expensive choice would cost more than twice as much as the least-expensive choice. For females, the most expensive policy costs almost three times what the least-expensive one would cost (*Consumer Reports,* June, 1986).

Whole Life Insurance

Permanent life insurance provides lifetime insurance protection. The premiums on permanent life policies typically are greater than the amount needed to cover the risk of mortality in the early years of the policy. The excess builds up to create savings. This amount is used to offset the high premiums that would be required at older ages. Figure 17-2 shows the increasing risk of mortality with age. Instead of increasing premiums with age, most types of policy have a level premium, building a savings component in the early years that is sufficient to meet the high risk of mortality at older ages. Because of its savings components, permanent life insurance also is referred to as *cash-value life insurance.* The category of permanent life insurance includes all types of life insurance except term insurance. The category includes whole life insurance, universal life insurance, and other types of policies that are discussed in the following sections.

Coverage. *Whole life insurance* is payable to the beneficiary named in the policy on the death of the insured, whenever that occurs. Whole life

Figure 17-2
Accumulation of the Savings Component of Whole Life Policies

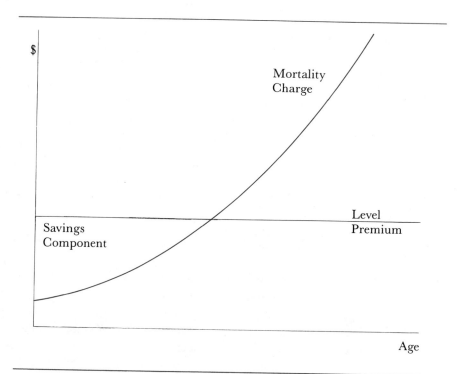

Part 4   Managing Risk

policies differ in the number of years over which premiums must be paid. For a *straight life insurance policy,* premiums are payable either as long as the policyholder lives or until the policyholder reaches a specified age, such as 90, 95, or 100. At this age the cash value accrued in the savings component of the policy equals the face amount of the policy. As can be seen in Figure 17-2, the cash value of a policy accrues gradually from the date it is issued until the specified age. In the early years, the death benefit is a result of the protection component of the policy. As cash value builds, the money paid to a beneficiary is, increasingly, the accumulated savings in the savings component.

Because straight life policies require payments over many years, the premiums charged for a given face amount of coverage are lower than the premiums for policies that are paid up more quickly. *Limited payment policies* provide for payment for some specified period or to some specified age. One common form, popularly referred to as "20-year pay," calls for premium payments for 20 years from the date of issue. Another common form of limited payment life insurance is paid up at age 65.

Variations of straight life insurance are available and are promoted to meet special needs. *Modified life policies* are straight life policies on which the premiums are reduced for the first few years. These policies are designed to appeal to young people who are expecting income increases in future years. After the initial period, in which premiums are lower than on conventional straight life policies, the premiums rise to a level somewhat above those on conventional policies.

Many companies offer combinations of term and straight life policies. *Family income policies* combine a straight life insurance policy with a term policy that may run for 10, 15, or 20 years from the date of purchase. With a 20-year family income policy, if the insured dies during the 20-year period, the beneficiary is paid a monthly income for the remainder of the 20-year period. Because the total amount of income that would be paid out declines over the 20-year term, the term coverage is, in effect, decreasing term insurance. The proceeds of the whole life portion of the policy are payable either on the death of the insured or at the end of the 20-year payment period, depending on the terms of the policy. If the insured outlives the 20-year period, the straight life portion of the policy continues at a reduced premium. This policy is promoted as a way for families with young children to meet their need for extra coverage while the children are growing up.

Family maintenance policies also combine straight life insurance with term coverage. On the death of the insured, payments from the term portion of the policy continue for some specified number of years. For example, if 20-year term coverage is chosen and the insured dies within 20 years of the date the policy was issued, payments continue for a full 20 years after the death of the insured. This term coverage is, in effect, a level term policy. Payments from the straight life portion are made when specified in the policy. Twenty years after the policy was issued, the term coverage expires; but the straight life portion of the policy continues in force. Similar coverage may be created by adding a term insurance rider to a whole life policy.

Family plan policies combine straight life coverage on the income-earner(s) and smaller amounts of term coverage on dependents. While insuring the whole family seems appealing, insurance experts usually suggest the need for insurance on a nonworking spouse or on children be considered carefully (Belth, 1985). Nonworking spouses make important contributions to family well-being and provide household services that would be costly to replace. The economic loss from the death of a nonworking spouse would be a serious one but usually should not be so serious as the death of the sole or primary income-earner. If insurance dollars are short, coverage should be concentrated on the individual whose death would represent the greatest economic loss.

Children usually contribute little or no income to the household. The death of a child, while emotionally shattering, usually does not represent an economic loss to the household. Except perhaps for providing for final expenses, life insurance coverage of children does not need to be given high priority. For families that can afford them, policies for children that permit the purchase of additional coverage at later dates do have advantages. They ensure that a child will be able to obtain coverage even though medical problems arise that could affect future insurability.

Cost. The growth of cash value in a whole life policy is often a key part of the sales argument of life insurance agents. Tables are presented to show that eventually the cash value of the policy exceeds or approaches the premiums paid in. This evidence is used to suggest that the insurance protection that the policyholder gets is "free" or costs very little.

Years ago this approach to calculating the cost of life insurance was generally accepted. The premiums paid were totaled and their cash value and any dividends paid were deducted. The result was the net cost of the policy. This *net cost method* ignores the opportunity cost of the premiums that are paid in year after year. If the policyholder had invested these funds instead of using them to pay insurance premiums, they would have earned interest over time.

The newer approach to comparing the cost of owning different policies is the interest-adjusted net cost method discussed earlier. For whole life policies, the interest-adjusted net cost shows the cost of owning a policy if it is surrendered after some specified period such as 5, 10, or 20 years. For whole life policies, the interest-adjusted net cost is calculated by deducting the cash value and the dividends paid (if any) from the premiums paid. This net cost is then adjusted for interest forgone. Currently a 5 percent rate is used.

Again, the interest-adjusted net cost is usually converted to an index value. Because the index for whole life policies measures the cost of owning a policy until it is given up or surrendered, it also is referred to as a *surrender index*.

Index values for whole life policies unfortunately cannot be compared with those for term policies. For term policies, the index does not take into account the investment alternatives open to policyholders who invest the savings from their lower premiums.

When *Consumer Reports* compared the cost of owning $50,000 whole life policies for 20 years it found wide differences in cost. The least expensive policies had negative index values, indicating that the accumulated dividends plus the cash values were greater than the net premiums (*Consumer Reports,* July, 1986).

The costs of owning policies differ over time. In the early years of a policy, the cash values grow slowly because agent's commissions and administrative expenses are deducted. After the first several years, cash values grow more rapidly. Because cash values grow at differing rates over time, the cost of owning a policy also changes. A policy that is not a particularly good buy if held only five years may be a better buy over a longer period.

Agents are required by law in many states to disclose the interest-adjusted net cost index value but only after the policy is purchased. In these states, agents must disclose the index values before the policy is purchased if the customer asks for it, but it frequently is difficult to obtain (*Consumer Reports,* July, 1986). The index can be a useful tool for comparing costs between policies and companies.

In showing prospective customers what a policy is likely to cost, agents usually show a print-out that includes annual premium figures along with dividends if it is a participating policy. It is important to understand the basis for these dividend figures as they are an important element in the cost of a policy. The dividends shown are not guaranteed. They may be based on the company's recent experience or what it hopes or expects to achieve. In either case, the figures should be ones that seem reasonable in light of economic circumstances.

Universal Life

In the 1980s a new type of life insurance, universal life policies, appeared and won a sizable share of the market. *Universal life policies* were designed to meet the criticisms leveled at whole life insurance over the years. One of the major appeals of universal life is its two-way flexibility:

- Premiums may be increased or decreased by the policyholder within limits. This slows down or speeds up the growth of cash value and may even decrease it.
- The death benefits provided may be raised or lowered by the policyholder within limits. These changes may affect growth of cash value. If the increase in face amount is substantial, new evidence of insurability may be required.

A second appeal of universal life policies is that they are "transparent," meaning that the investment component, the protection component, and expense charges are indicated separately so that policyholders can see what part of their premiums is going into each category. The interest rate being paid on the cash value is also clearly indicated. When a premium is paid, it goes into the cash value account. Each month the *mortality charge,* which is the cost of insurance protection, is deducted from this account. *Expense charges,* which cover administrative expenses, are also deducted from the cash value account. The balance remaining in the cash value account grows at interest.

The mortality charge deduction in universal life policies is used to cover expected death claims. The charge increases with the insured's age and is not guaranteed in the policy as it is with whole life and term life policies. Expense charges may be levied when a premium is paid, when a cash value withdrawal is made, or at both times. On "front-loaded" policies (on which expense charges are made initially), a company typically deducts 5 to 9 percent of each premium for its expenses before it credits the premium to the policyholder's cash value (*Consumer Reports,* August, 1986). On "back-loaded" policies, substantial charges are made at withdrawal. Withdrawal charges are often so large that no cash value is available for the first year or so.

The interest rate paid on the cash value of universal life policies is variable and is adjusted by the insurer with changes in the financial markets. A minimum rate of 4 or 4½ percent is, however, guaranteed in most policies. The variable interest rate on universal life policies is another major difference from traditional whole life policies. Interest rates on traditional whole life policies are fixed for the life of the policy.

One of the major appeals of universal life has been the opportunity it provides to invest in the money market without immediate taxation of earnings. Increases in cash value are not taxed when they are paid, only when they are withdrawn. When the full cash value is withdrawn, the excess of cash value over premiums paid is taxable. The taxation of partial withdrawals has been the focus of disagreement between the Internal Revenue Service and the insurance companies. Insurance company literature suggests policyholders consult their tax adviser on the question.

As was noted, one of the chief appeals of universal life insurance is its flexibility. It can be adjusted, within limits, to changing life situations and changing income and financial obligations. To maintain the appeal of universal life, insurers continue to offer policies with newer features. One of the new variations on universal life is policies that allow policyholders to chose among different investment portfolios including money market instruments, bonds and preferred stocks, and common stocks. These policies have been labeled *variable universal life insurance.*

Cost. The special features of universal life insurance make it difficult to evaluate alternative policy choices. Prospective purchasers must keep their eyes on three key variables:

- Mortality charges, which will change with the insured's age and the insurer's loss experience
- Expense charges, which can be changed as the insurer's administrative expenses change
- Interest rate paid on the cash value, which is variable, though a minimum rate may be guaranteed

In creating new policy offerings, insurers try to find new combinations of these variables that will appeal to buyers. Some insurers have featured high interest rates but have also set their mortality and expense charges relatively high. The result may be that cash value grows more slowly than in policies with lower interest rates. Shoppers need to be aware that the interest rates paid will change, and in some cases they may be set so high initially that they cannot be maintained. Another problem in comparing universal life policies is that interest rates are not cited uniformly. Some insurers quote a nominal rate while others quote an effective rate based on compounding.

One way to look at the purchase of universal life policies is to regard it as the purchase of renewable term insurance with the option of paying excess premiums so that cash value that can be invested is accumulated. The return on this investment is variable rather than guaranteed as it is with whole life. This variability makes the interest paid on universal life insurance accounts of special concern to prospective customers. In general, universal life policies performed much better as investments than did whole life policies in recent years. However, prospective buyers should consider carefully whether they want to combine their life insurance coverage with their investments.

Universal life insurance can be made to function in much the same way as a whole life policy. The policyholder can pay the *target premium,* which will build cash value sufficient to keep the policy in force for the insured's lifetime. The level target premium builds up cash value necessary to meet the higher mortality charges at later ages.

It is possible, however, for policyholders to pay either more or less than the target premium. Policyholders who pay less have a policy that is more like term insurance. The cash value built up may not be sufficient to meet the higher premiums that will be required to cover rising mortality charges at older ages. The cash value build-up may also be insufficient if the interest rates actually paid fall short of those expected when the policy was bought.

Adjustable Life Insurance

The appeal of *adjustable life insurance* is that it offers greater flexibility than traditional cash value policies. Policies are adjustable in two ways:

- It is possible to switch back and forth between cash value and term coverage as the policyholder's ability to pay the necessary premiums changes.
- Policy face value amounts can be increased or decreased within limits without providing evidence of insurability.

These features are designed to appeal to people in changing financial circumstances, and to deal with the need to increase policy face amounts as inflation erodes the purchasing power of coverage.

Variable Life Insurance

The special characteristic of *variable life insurance* is that its cash value fluctuates with the investment performace of the cash value account. Cash values usually are invested in equity assets such as common stocks or other financial instruments, making the investment performance similar to that of a mutual fund. Because of the investment aspects of these policies, the Securities Exchange Commission has been monitoring their sale and performance.

Because investment performances can vary, cash values and death benefits on variable life policies fluctuate. Policies do, however, carry a minimum guaranteed death benefit. Above that minimum, benefits will depend on the state of the financial market when the insured dies. While variable life policies may provide greater cash value increases than conventional whole life policies, policyholders need to be certain the minimum guaranteed coverage will be adequate to meet their basic protection needs.

Single Premium Whole Life Insurance

Single premium whole life insurance policies are one of the newest products of the life insurance industry. They offer the same tax advantages as other life insurance policies in a highly flexible form. Single premium policies are sold principally as an investment device and secondarily as a life insurance policy (Duncan, 1986). A major appeal of these policies is the relatively high interest rates paid. Interest rates are typically guaranteed for only one year and could drop. Companies must, however, strive to keep their rates competitive, because purchasers are free to withdraw their money. Withdrawals are discouraged by the withdrawal fees levied during the first eight years of the policy. As with other life insurance policies, interest earnings accumulate tax-free. Another appeal of single premium policies as investments is the safety of the policy principal, which is guaranteed by the insurance company.

Loans against the policy principal and interest earned are easily arranged. Interest earnings may be borrowed after the first year. A major portion of the policy principal also may be borrowed without tax consequences. Policies are available in face values from $5,000 and up. Because of taxes on withdrawals, single premium policies are best-suited for long-term investments. Rollovers into new policies without taxes are permitted.

Endowment Insurance

Endowment policies are designed to provide insurance coverage if the insured dies during a specified period and to pay out the face amount to the insured if he or she is alive at the end of the period. The cash value of an endowment policy grows over its life until it equals the face amount at the end of the endowment period. A $50,000 20-year policy, for example, provides $50,000 death benefits during its 20-year duration and pays $50,000 at the end of the 20-year period if the insured survives.

Endowment policies are, in effect, a combination of decreasing term insurance with an increasing savings fund. Because these policies build cash values rapidly, premiums are relatively high for the face amount of protection provided. The high cost of endowment policies per dollar of coverage provided make them a poor choice for consumers who are short of funds but need extensive coverage.

Endowment policies are sold with durations of 20, 25, and 30 years, or are sold to endow (pay off) at a specified age such as 65. In the past, endowment policies were promoted as devices to build education funds for children or retirement nest eggs, along with providing insurance coverage. The appeal of other investment possibilities has reduced the sales of endowment policies in recent years. They now constitute only a small proportion of the policies sold.

The insurance industry is constantly developing new products to appeal to consumers. Most of these new types are combinations of the basic policy types discussed here (see Table 17-1).

RIDERS AND OTHER POLICY PROVISIONS

The provisions of the life insurance contract set out how the contract will be administered. Special provisions may be added to life insurance policies through the use of *riders*, which are endorsements to a policy. Riders typically are used to provide an increase in benefits for an increase in premium. Other provisions set out payment and loan procedures and rules restricting the payment of policy proceeds to beneficiaries.

Table 17-1
Major Features of
Different Types of
Life Insurance

Type	Face Amount	Cash Value	Premiums
Term	Fixed for term of policy	None	Relatively low at younger ages, but increase progressively with age
Whole Life	Fixed for life of policy	Increases according to guaranteed schedule in policy	Relatively high; builds savings component to offset mortality risk at older ages
Universal	Can be adjusted within limits by policyholder	Grows at variable rate depending on interest paid by insurer and on fees and mortality charges	Relatively high but policies can be adjusted to perform like term insurance or similar to a whole life policy
Adjustable	Can be adjusted within limits by policyholder	Depends on whether policyholder chooses term or cash value coverage	Vary depending on coverage selected
Variable	Varies with investment performance with a minimum benefit guranteed	Varies with investment performance	Relatively high because of savings component
Single Premium Whole Life	Fixed for life of policy	Increases at rate set by insurer, which may change over time	One time initial premium purchases whole life coverage
Endowment	Fixed for life of policy	Increases at schedule guaranteed in policy to equal face amount of policy at maturity	Relatively high because cash value is built up rapidly

Accidental Death

A popular feature of murder mysteries is greedy husbands or wives who are unable to resist the lure of collecting double the face amount of an insurance policy on their spouse if the death is accidental or can be made to appear so. The policy provision that provides this increase in benefits is an *accidental death rider*. These riders increase the benefit provided in the policy if the insured dies in an accident prior to the age of 65 or 70. The typical rider provides *double indemnity* or double the face amount of the policy, though higher multiples are sometimes sold.

The premiums required for accidental death coverage are small, but the coverage is of questionable usefulness. Dependents' needs for funds are much the same regardless of how a breadwinner dies and most premature deaths are not accidental (U.S. Department of Commerce, 1985). If extra coverage is needed, it should not depend on the cause of death. A similar argument can be made against buying trip life insurance. The economic loss from the death of a breadwinner will be much the same regardless of where or how he or she dies.

Guaranteed Insurability

Another type of rider, the *guaranteed insurability rider*, permits an insured to buy additional coverage at specified future dates without new physical examinations. A typical rider of this type permits purchase of additional coverage every three years beginning at the issuance of the policy. This is a useful option if the policyholder expects to need more coverage in the future but does not want to purchase it at the present time. Guaranteed insurability can be a useful option for young people who have little need for life insurance but want to be certain that they can buy it at some future date, regardless of their medical condition.

Waiver of Premium

Another form of rider provides for waiver of the premium if the insured is totally disabled before some specified age. The typical *waiver of premium rider* provides that the policyholder will not have to pay policy premiums if the insured becomes totally disabled before age 65 or 70. Total disability is usually defined as a disability that lasts for more than six months. For those who are disabled for more than six months, premiums paid during the six-month eligibility period are refunded.

The waiver of premium can be viewed as a form of disability insurance. In case of extended disability, it provides a supplement to income. This coverage is free from some companies and available for a small premium from others. While some consumer experts view the waiver of premium as a useful, but limited, form of disability insurance (Belth, 1985), others disagree. They suggest that because a person who is permanently and totally disabled no longer has any earning potential, there is little point to continuing to insure that person's life (Morgan & Duncan, 1980).

Payment of Dividends

The dividends on participating policies may be used by policyholders in four different ways:

- Taken in the form of cash as they become payable
- Used to reduce the amounts of the premiums payable

- Left with the company to earn interest
- Used to buy paid-up additions to the coverage provided by the policy

The first two options are appropriate if insurance coverage is already adequate. Leaving dividends with the company to earn interest may be desirable if the company is paying a competitive interest rate. The paid-up additions to a policy that can be purchased with dividends will be small, but they do offer a way to increase coverage for those who have problems obtaining new policies.

Grace Period

The premium amounts due and the dates they are due are stated in the policy. Policies allow a *grace period* of 30 or 31 days after this date in which an overdue premium may be paid without penalty. After the grace period the policy may lapse or late penalties may be imposed.

Nonforfeiture Options

Insurance applicants and policyholders sometimes wonder what would happen if they were to stop paying premiums. Years ago they would have lost claim to the policy and to any accumulated cash value. Companies now are required to return any accumulated cash value. Policyholders have four alternatives, or *nonforfeiture options,* for using the proceeds of cash-value policies:

- They may be paid in cash.
- They may take a loan against cash value to pay the premium due; some policies provide for *automatic premium loan* if a premium is not received.
- They may purchase a reduced amount of paid-up insurance, on which no further premium payment will be required
- They may purchase extended term coverage. The policy is converted to a level term policy of the same face amount for whatever term the cash value will cover.

Policy Loans

Policyholders in need of a loan can borrow the cash value of their policy from the insurance company. These loans can be easily arranged through the agent and make the cash values of policies a convenient source of funds. The interest rate on such loans is stated in the policy. Recent policies specify rates up to eight percent. Loans may be paid back at any time, in full or in part. If they are not paid back before the death of the insured, the loan principal and any interest due will be deducted from the face amount of the policy when settlement is made with the beneficiary.

Policyholders often wonder why they have to pay the insurance company interest to borrow what they consider to be their own money. Interest is charged because the performance of cash value policies is based on the assumption that the savings component of the policy will be invested at interest.

For the policy to perform as stated, this interest must be obtained from borrowers, regardless of whether the borrowers are policyholders, real estate developers, or other borrowers.

Insurance companies and agents often argue that policy loans are unwise because they reduce the proceeds payable to beneficiaries. While this argument is true, the loans have the same effect on the estate of an insured as any other type of loan. Life insurance policies with cash value can also be used as collateral with other lenders, such as banks.

Suicide Clause

If people considering suicide could obtain benefits for their beneficiaries without any restriction, serious problems of adverse selection could arise. To control this problem, companies put some restrictions on the payments to beneficiaries in cases of suicide. Under the *suicide clause,* if a policyholder dies by his or her own hand within two years of the issuance of a policy the beneficiary receives only the premiums paid. After two years, death by suicide is treated the same as any other cause of death.

Incontestability Clause

Life insurance policies are contracts, and both parties are expected to enter into these contracts in good faith and to supply full and accurate information to one another. The *incontestability clause* in policies limits the ability of the insurer to deny policy benefits if the information provided by an applicant was inaccurate or false. Usually the clause gives the company two years within which it can cancel a policy or deny death benefits if applicaton statements were inaccurate. This gives companies some additional time to investigate policyholders after a policy is issued; however it limits the ability of companies to quibble about application statements or deny benefits many years after a policy is issued.

The incontestability clause does not apply to misstatements of age. Applicants may be tempted to understate their age to obtain reduced premiums. If such a misstatement is discovered, the insurer may reduce the face amount to the amount that could have been purchased with the premiums paid if age had been stated correctly.

SETTLEMENT

On the death of the policyholder, the eligible beneficiary receives the proceeds of the policy. The proceeds include the following:

- The face amount of the policy
- Benefits from any riders, such as an accidental death rider
- Any dividends left with the company plus interest earned
- Any portion of the premiums paid covering the period after the date of death
- Less any loans against the cash value of the policy

The proceeds are payable on submission of an application for payment and submission of evidence of death. The insurance agent can render assistance in this simple procedure.

Beneficiaries may receive policy proceeds in several different forms. The choice is usually left to the beneficiary, though the policyholder can specify the arrangements in advance. Usually policyholders are advised to leave the choice to the beneficiary to ensure flexibility. Policyholders sometimes fear that a spendthrift beneficiary will use up all the proceeds too quickly. In these cases, arrangements can be made to pay the proceeds to a trustee, such as the trust department of a bank. The trustee can then control the release of the funds.

The settlement options available include following:

- Acceptance of a lump sum payment, permitting investment elsewhere
- Deposit of all or part of the proceeds with the insurance company to earn interest
- Arrangement to take the proceeds in the form of installment payments
- Purchase of a *life annuity* from the insurance company to provide income at regular intervals for some specified period (such as for life or for some specified number of years)

PURCHASING LIFE INSURANCE

There are hundreds of companies represented by thousands of agents selling life insurance in this country. Consumers need to learn how to sort through all these alternatives to find the best company and best agent.

Deciding on a Company

One of the first problems in choosing a company is being certain about who is who. Insurance companies seem to favor names that suggest that they are old and long established or that they are financially stable or fair and honest or friendly or that they have far-flung operations. As a result, the names of many companies are similar (Belth, 1985). There are, for example, nine life insurance companies with the word "Lincoln" in their names. There are many others with confusingly similar names. For example, the Northwestern Mutual Life Insurance Company is headquartered in Milwaukee and the Northwestern National Life Insurance Company is headquartered in Minneapolis. When checking on a company, it is wise to determine both its full name and home office.

Life insurance policyholders, and especially the purchasers of cash value policies, are entrusting large amounts of money to the companies from which they buy. This makes the financial stability of the company of critical importance. The most widely recommended source of information on the financial strength of companies is *Best's Insurance Reports,* published by the A.M. Best Company (A.M. Best Co., 1985). The *Reports* rate companies on a scale from A+ down to C. From more than 2,000 companies that write life insurance policies, there are hundreds of companies with A+ and A ratings, both of which are considered excellent. Careful consumers should confine their choice to this group of firms.

Insurance companies must be licensed by the states in which they sell insurance. The regulation of companies is, however, stricter in some states than others. Unfortuantely, the state departments of insurance may not be very good sources of information about the financial stability of insurers because they typically do not release any judgments of companies in distress until their investigations have been completed (Belth, 1985). One of the reasons is that disclosure that a company may be in difficulty would only further aggravate its problems.

Consumer Reports rates life insurance policies periodically. Their attention is focused on a price comparison of policies from companies with top financial ratings. While these ratings can be helpful in identifying low-priced policies from top companies, they have limitations. Comparisons are based on a limited number of age–sex categories and face amounts. The ratings may not be a fully reliable guide to the premiums for other age–sex categories or for other types of policies. Like other industries, the life insurance industry is constantly bringing out new products. As a result, *Consumer Reports* ratings have a limited useful life.

Classes of Policies

One of the ways of classifying life insurance is according to how it is sold. Policies are marketed in two different ways: (1) *Individual policies* are sold by agents to individual policyholders; (2) *group policies* are sold to groups and provide coverage for a number of people under a single policy.

Individual Policies. The most familiar form of individual policy is *ordinary life insurance*. It is typically sold in multiples of $1,000. Premiums are sent directly to the company annually, semiannually, quarterly, or monthly. Ordinary life makes up a major share of all policies sold and of all coverage.

Industrial life insurance policies were developed to serve the needs of low-income consumers who were unable to save up the amounts needed for periodic ordinary life premiums. Industrial life insurance is sold in small face amounts, usually $1,000 or less. Premiums are collected weekly or monthly by an agent who calls in person. For this reason, industrial life insurance is also referred to as *home service life*. The policies generally provide whole life or endowment insurance. While this type of policy was popular in the early years of this century, its use has declined with the spread of group insurance and Social Security coverage.

Group Policies. There are two forms of policies sold to groups. One is *group life insurance*, which typically is arranged by employers and also by unions, associations, and other groups. Premiums for coverage may be paid wholly or in part by the employer, with the employee paying the rest. In other types of groups, the members pay for the coverage they select. Group coverage typically is term insurance with no cash value. It is a widespread employee benefit.

The other type of insurance purchased by groups is *credit life insurance.* It covers the lives of borrowers with installment debt. Credit life insurance is arranged by lenders and usually is in the form of declining term insurance covering the balance owed. Credit insurance is frequently sold by lenders at the time an installment purchase is arranged. Although premiums are small, they are excessive in relation to the benefits insurers pay out. Credit life insurance is highly profitable for the insurance companies that provide it and is also highly profitable for the retailers who sell it because of the generous commissions provided by insurers. Lenders sometimes insist on credit insurance. It usually is not legal for them to require that the policy be purchased from them, however. Other sources may be substituted. Many credit unions provide credit life insurance with their loans without an additional charge.

Choosing an Agent

Along with choosing a company, choosing an agent is an important part of a life insurance decision. Although life insurance is available in other ways, most of the life insurance purchased is sold through an agent.

Life insurance agents play a central role at several steps in the decision-making process. Few people decide they need life insurance on their own. Instead, most are made aware of their needs and are motivated to consider the purchase of insurance by an agent. A knowledgeable agent can be particularly helpful in matching what clients need with what is available and what they can afford. Prospective buyers may be less appreciative of agents' role in pressing for action, but this can be helpful, too. Once an appropriate decision is made, it has little meaning unless it is acted on. In addition to helping consumers purchase policies, agents can serve an important function in helping clients to review their life insurance needs periodically. Reviews are important because of the effect of changing family and financial situations on insurance needs.

Agents vary widely in knowledge, experience, and ability. Selling life insurance is a demanding job, and the turnover among new agents is high. Full-time agents with at least several years' experience are likely to be knowledgeable and professional in their approach. Insurance expert Joseph Belth (1985) has suggested that the best agents gravitate to the best companies because their policies are easier to sell.

One of the criteria for judging an agent is involvement in professional development and continuing education programs. There is a wide variety of certificates and recognitions awarded to life insurance agents. The most rigorous certification is Chartered Life Underwriter (Belth, 1985). This certification is indicated by the letters *C.L.U.* after an agent's name. The requirements include the mastery of technical information on life insurance and the related areas of taxation, law, and finance. To be certified, candidates must pass a series of examinations and have three years' experience. While a C.L.U. is not an assurance of reliability, it is an indication that an agent has made a commitment to life insurance as a career.

In selecting an agent, the advice of respected members of the local business community can be helpful, as can the advice of trusted friends. Some agents will provide references. The references' standing in the community and what they say and do not say about an agent can provide useful information about an agent's ability to assess insurance needs, knowledge of alternative policies, and overall professionalism.

Life Insurance Without An Agent

Several types of life insurance coverage are available without the use of an agent. *Savings bank life insurance* is available from many thrift institutions in Connecticut, New York, and Massachusetts. Purchasers must be residents of the state or employed there. Because of pressure from life insurance agents, the face amounts available from an individual bank are limited. Buyers do, however, have the option of purchasing from several different banks. Savings bank policies are comparatively low in cost and are frequently recommended as a bargain.

Life insurance may also be purchased through the mail in response to television ads and direct mail solicitations. While the ads sound appealing and the celebrity testimonials convincing, these policies frequently have serious limitations. The face amounts of coverage typically are small, often only a few thousand dollars. The policies often are described as "supplemental," recognizing their limited ability to meet the full-range of insurance needs. While the premiums are small, the death benefits are too. Advertising typically emphasizes that no medical examination is needed, which can be an advantage for those with medical problems. The premiums are, however, relatively high for those in good health because of the problem of adverse selection.

Life insurance is also available by mail to the members of many groups, including professional associations, military officers, college teachers, ministers, and members of fraternal organizations. These groups use no agents and often are able to hold administrative expenses to a minimum, making their policies good buys.

Other forms of life insurance are available from the federal government. They include policies available to military personnel and to veterans. Social Security coverage is required of employees in most occupations. It can provide substantial death benefits for survivors, especially for families with children. Social Security will be discussed in more detail in Chapter 19.

ESTATES AND WILLS

A great deal of hard work is required to build up an estate to provide financial security for dependents. Accumulating assets to create an estate that can be passed to heirs is only half the job, however. Planning for orderly transfer of these assets to heirs is also of critical importance. Without planning, assets may pass in ways or to individuals other than what was intended; and taxes and fees may consume a significant part of the estate.

Transferring Property at Death

An individual's estate includes only property he or she owns separately. This property passes, at the owner's death, to heirs named in a valid will, or according to state inheritance law if there is no will. Some property that

CONSUMER CONCERN: CONTRACT READABILITY

One of the concerns voiced by consumer advocates in recent years has been that contracts and warranties are often too difficult to read. Because of their complex wording, consumers may have difficulty understanding their rights and exercising them. The life and health insurance industry provides a useful example of how contracts can be simplified and demonstrates what other industries could do.

The task of rewriting a contract is not an easy one. Because a contract is a legal document, it must set out the rights and duties of each of the parties in a way that will be acceptable in court. Most life and health insurers have, however, taken the effort to rewrite their policies into simpler language. This effort has been motivated by laws requiring contract simplification that have been passed in more than half of all the states. Many companies have gone beyond the requirements of law and have rewritten other documents and information policyholders receive.

To increase readability, the following techniques have been used:

- Sentences are put in the active voice, e.g., "you will be paid" not "payment will be made."
- Verbs are used, rather than nouns made out of verbs, e.g., "the company will determine the cash value" not "determination of the cash value will be made by the company."
- Personal pronouns or names for each party are used, e.g., "you may borrow" not "the policy holder may borrow."

One interesting outcome from the rewriting efforts is that the simplified policies are often not only easier to understand, but they are also shorter. The results of one rewriting effort may be seen below.

is jointly owned will pass to survivors even without a will. The rules for the passage of jointly owned property have developed out of common law practice, though some states have statutory law that modifies common law. Overall, there are four types of joint ownership:

- *Tenancy by entireties.* This type of joint ownership is restricted to the ownership of real estate by spouses. The property cannot be transferred without mutual agreement. On death of one of the spouses, the title passes to the survivor, unaffected by any will.
- *Joint tenancy.* Two or more people, related or unrelated, may be joint tenants for any kind of property, real estate, business, or bank account. Any party may dispose of his or her share without permission of the others. This type of title provides rights of survivorship. On the death of one owner, that person's share passes to the surviving joint tenants.

BEFORE

Grace Period. Thirty-one days of grace are allowed for payment of every premium after the first, during which time the policy shall remain in full force. If death occurs within the grace period, any premium then due and unpaid will be deducted from the amount otherwise payable hereunder. Except as otherwise provided herein, the policy shall be cancelled and forfeited at the end of the grace period if such premium has not been paid.

AFTER

Grace Period. We allow each premium after the first one to be paid within 31 days after its due date. These 31 days are called the grace period. The policy remains in effect during the grace period. If the insured dies during this period, the unpaid premium will be deducted from the amount we would otherwise pay.

QUESTIONS

1. What is an appropriate goal in simplifying policies and contracts? How simple should they be?
2. State legislation on policy readability applies, in most cases, to life and health policies. Is there evidence auto insurers also are simplifying their policies?
3. Can you find other financial areas in which legal language aimed at consumers needs simplification? Check bank documents, the backs of credit cards, and other sources for examples.

Source for contract examples: "Consumerism: Contract Readability," *Teaching Topics 33,* no. 2 (Fall 1985): 3-5. Used by permission of American Council of Life Insurance and Health Insurance Association of America.

Illustration 17-2
Recent changes in the wording of insurance policies demonstrate how consumer contracts can be simplified.

- *Tenants in common.* This type of joint ownership is common in cases where the owners are not husband and wife. There is no right of survivorship, and the property is included in a deceased's estate.
- *Community property.* This type of ownership has been created by statutory law in some western states. Under community property laws, property acquired after marriage is assumed to be jointly owned regardless of who paid for it. The state laws vary on the disposition of property upon the death of a spouse. In California, if there is no will, the deceased's share of community property passes to the surviving spouse. If a will has been prepared, community property can be willed to a spouse, children, or others (the same as separately owned property).

As a result of the laws governing property ownership, individuals can bequeath (i.e., pass to their heirs) only property that they own separately, or their share of property held as tenants in common, or (in some states) their share of community property. There are some limits on this right under common law. To protect surviving spouses from unfair wills, widows and widowers can claim a portion of an estate if the share provided in a will is unreasonably small.

Wills. The laws of the individual state control how property is passed to heirs at the death of the owner (Henszey, Myers, & Phalan, 1977). The goal of these laws is to set up workable systems to handle the distribution of property to heirs according to the wishes of the deceased as expressed in a will or as a deceased would have desired if intentions had been indicated. When an individual makes a will, wishes usually are fairly clear.

The *will* provides written instructions from the owner of property about how any property is to be distributed upon death (see Figure 17-3). People who fail to make a will are said to be *intestate*.

Anyone who is of sound mind and meets a state's age requirements (age 18 in most states) can make a valid will. When the person dies, the will is submitted to judicial officials with evidence it is genuine and valid. Usually the signatures of witnesses to the deceased's signature are all that is necessary as evidence. Wills are sometimes challenged at this stage; but if the judicial officials are satisfied, a decree recognizing the will is issued. The will is then said to have been *probated*. Along with recognizing the will, the court also recognizes the person the deceased has designated to administer the estate, if one is named.

Most wills name an *executor*, an individual or an institution such as a bank trust department, to administer the estate and distribute it to the heirs. The executor is responsible for assembling and protecting the deceased's assets, for determining debts and paying them, and for distributing the balance of the estate to the heirs.

When a person dies intestate the estate must be distributed according to the rules set down by state law. In many states the rules are as follows:

Figure 17-3
The Parts of a Will

- *Introduction*—Identifies the testator (maker of the will), indicates that the document is last will and testament, and revokes previous wills if appropriate
- *Special Instructions*—Instructions on payment of taxes, other debts, and funeral expenses out of the estate
- *Appointment Clauses*—Names the person to be appointed to administer the estate; names guardian for minor children and the trustee for any trusts to be established; usually the executor is the spouse or a close relative
- *General Gifts*—Gifts out of the general assets of the estate in the form of money, stocks, or other items that cannot be distinguished from each other
- *Specific Gifts*—Gifts of specific items of personal property such as jewelry, automobiles, antiques, and collections
- *Allocation of Residual*—Provides for the distribution of any remaining portion of the estate among the heirs
- *Execution Clause*—Signature of testator with date to establish the validity of the will
- *Attestation Clause*—Signatures attest that the witnesses saw the testator sign the will on the date indicated

- If the deceased was unmarried and without children, the parents or parent receive the estate. If no parents survive, then the estate is distributed among the parent's children.
- If the deceased was married with no children, the surviving spouse receives the full estate.
- If the deceased was married and leaves one child, the spouse receives some amount specified by state law ($50,000 in many states) plus one-half the remaining estate. The child receives the other half.
- If the deceased was married and has two or more children, the spouse receives some specified amount ($50,000 in many states) plus one-third of the remainder. The children split two-thirds of the remainder equally.

This distribution may not conform to a deceased's real wishes, and it may create legal complications. If minor children are heirs, a guardian must be appointed for each one. If the guardian is someone other than a surviving parent, administrative fees may be charged, reducing the inheritance.

When a person dies intestate leaving a sizable and complex estate, interested parties may ask the court to administer the estate. The court-appointed *administrator* serves the same function as an executor and receives a fee for services. Appointment of an administrator usually is not necessary for smaller, simpler estates. For such estates, distribution usually is handled by agreement among the family.

While people may draft their own wills, they need to be thoroughly familiar with relevant state laws to ensure that their will is valid. Most states, for example, require only two witnesses, but a few require three. The assistance of a lawyer is generally a good idea. For a simple will, the preparation and fees are modest. For a more complex will, the assistance of an attorney is probably a necessity, even though the fees will be higher.

Wills should be reviewed and updated periodically. Changes clearly are in order in the following instances:

- When marital status changes
- When children are born
- On moving to a new state

Minor changes can be made by adding a *codicil* to the will. A codicil is a legal instrument prepared after a will is drawn that modifies it. If more extensive changes are needed, it may be necessary to draw up a new will.

A *letter* of *last instructions* is often written to accompany a will. It provides instructions to the executor on handling the estate. Burial instructions, information on the location of bank accounts and safety-deposit boxes, and other appropriate information can be included. Letters of last instructions are not legally part of the will and do not require an attorney's assistance.

Transfers without a Will. As noted above, certain jointly owned property passes to the surviving joint owners without being included in an estate. Some other transfers are arranged by contract. Life insurance companies transfer the proceeds of policies to the beneficiaries named in the policy. These transfers are made separately from the court-supervised probate process for settling an estate. Certain other transfers also can be made by contract, including savings bonds and pension plan benefits. Social Security benefits are also paid separately from any probated estate.

The creation of a trust prior to death can also be used to create financial benefits for heirs outside the probate process. A *trust* is a legal arrangement that puts control of assets in the hands of a trustee, who administers them for the benefit of the trust's beneficiaries. The beneficiaries of a trust can be the individual(s) creating it, relatives, or others. The operation of trusts is governed both by state law and by the terms of the agreement creating the trust. One of the uses of trusts is to avoid federal and state estate taxes. Because of changes in federal law, federal estate taxation is a concern now only for relatively large estates, those involving $700,000 dollars or more.

MAJOR CHAPTER CONCEPTS

1. Life insurance may be used to build an estate for heirs, to provide for final expenses, to build needed savings, and to build savings for retirement.
2. The two major categories of life insurance are term insurance, which provides protection for some specified period, and permanent life insurance, which provides lifetime protection and also has a savings component (cash value).
3. The premium for term life insurance increases with age because of the increasing risk of mortality.
4. Permanent life insurance policies typically have premiums that are greater than the amount needed to cover the risk of mortality in the early years of the policy. The excess value accrues to offset the higher risk of mortality at older ages.
5. Whole life policies require payment of premiums for varying periods. Straight life policy premiums are payable up to death of the insured. Limited payment policies require payment up to a specified age or for some specified number of years.

6. Straight life policies may be modified in various ways to suit the needs of particular groups. Some policies combine term and straight life features.

7. Universal life policies include both a protection component and an investment component on which a variable interest rate is paid.

8. Adjustable life insurance permits shifts back and forth between cash value and term coverage and also changes in face value amounts.

9. The cash value and death benefits of variable life insurance fluctuate with the investment performance of a policy's cash value account.

10. Endowment policies provide insurance coverage if the insured dies before the end of a specified period and pay the face amount if the insured survives.

11. Riders are endorsements to life insurance policies that expand or limit policy benefits. Common riders cover accidental death, guaranteed insurability, and waiver of premiums.

12. Policy proceeds may be paid out in a lump sum, left with the company to earn interest, taken in installments, or taken as a paid-up life annuity.

13. Industrial life (or home service life) policies were developed for lower income people who could pay only small premiums.

14. Two forms of policies are sold to groups: group life insurance, which usually is an employee benefit, and credit life insurance.

15. If an individual dies without a will, his or her estate will be divided according to the provisions of state law.

16. Wills provide for the division of an estate among heirs. The administration of this division is the responsibility of the executor.

CONSUMER
QUESTIONS

1. What financial obligations do you have which might create a need for life insurance? How much coverage and what type or types of policy would be appropriate?

2. Describe the financial situation and the insurance needs of a family you know with young children. How much coverage and what type or types of policies would be appropriate for this family?

3. Choose insurance policies from two different companies that would be appropriate alternatives for the family in Question 2 above. Obtain cost information using *Consumer Reports'* ratings or the help of an insurance agent, if available. What criteria are appropriate for judging cost in this case? Which policy would you recommend and why?

4. The increasing occurrence of divorce has created some new kinds of insurance questions. Should a divorced parent be required to carry life insurance for the benefit of a child who is not in his or her custody? Why or why not?

5. Investigate the financial stability of the two companies whose policies you investigated in Question 3 above. Use *Best's Insurance Reports* or other sources to obtain information on their financial situation.

6. Find a magazine or newspaper ad for life insurance sold by mail. What type of policy is being offered? What face amount of coverage is available? What are the eligibility requirements for acceptance as a policyholder? Using the information available, what advantages and disadvantages do you see in the coverage being offered? What other information about the policy would you like to have to make an informed decision about it?

SUGGESTED READINGS

1. Belth, Joseph M. *Life Insurance: A Consumer's Handbook.* 2d ed. Bloomington: University of Indiana Press, 1985. Belth gives a readable report of what consumers need to know in purchasing life insurance, including how to assess needs, how to determine the cost of policies, and how to evaluate companies and agents.

2. *Consumer Reports.* "Isn't It Time You Wrote a Will?" 50, No. 2 (February 1985): 103-108. Seven out of ten Americans don't have wills. This article tells then how to go about getting one.

3. Editors of Consumer Reports Books. *The Consumers Union Report on Life Insurance: A Guide to Planning and Buying the Protection You Need.* 4th ed. Mount Vernon, N.Y.: Consumers Union, 1980, and succeeding editions. This introduction to life insurance presents information on how to assess needs, read policies, and compare prices. Also included are *Consumer Reports'* ratings of policies.

4. Tobias, Andrew. *The Invisible Bankers: Everything the Insurance Industry Never Wanted You to Know.* New York: Linden Press/Simon and Schuster, 1982. This is a highly readable examination of how life insurance companies handle the savings component of cash value policies and other investment funds.

CHAPTER 18

~~~

HEALTH INSURANCE

Going without health insurance is a gamble. No one can be certain just what card may turn up next. Most consumers can still stay in the game if they are dealt a $75 trip to the emergency room. A $3,000 emergency appendectomy could, however, be a real wild card; and $35,000 in bills for cosmetic surgery after an auto accident would break the bank for most consumers. Consumers need protection from large, unexpected medical bills, and a major portion of the American population has at least partial protection through health insurance. More than 80 percent of the American population has some kind of health insurance coverage, though the coverage is often far from complete. Most people are insured through a group policy arranged by an employer or an organization such as a union or fraternal group.

As with household, auto, and life insurance coverage, cost and service are key evaluative criteria. Health insurance is, however, more complex than most other kinds of insurance, and understanding it requires careful study.

LIMITATIONS ON COVERAGE

The complexity of health insurance policies arises from provisions used to control costs. A number of factors, if left uncontrolled, would push up health care costs. These factors include the following:

- *Large numbers of small claims.* Many medical expenses, such as those for many prescriptions, are relatively small, but processing claims for these expenses is costly.
- *Lack of incentives to hold down costs.* Patients want the best possible care, and doctors want to provide it. Providing this care may involve the use of expensive new equipment, complex and lengthy treatments, hospital stays that may be longer than really necessary, excessive use of laboratory tests, and other possibly unnecessary expenses.
- *Adverse selection.* The inclination of people with serious health problems to seek insurance could create serious problems for insurers if not controlled. This same problem affects both life and health insurers. Concealment of existing physical conditions that are likely to result in claims creates a *moral hazard* for insurers. Such hazards arising from dishonesty increase the likelihood of loss for an insurer (Vaughan, 1986).
- *The lack of competition in the provision of health services.* The number of health service providers in any local market is limited by licensing requirements for hospitals, physcans, and dentists. The limited number of health service providers restricts the supply of services and tends to increase prices. In some areas, however, the number of health service providers has grown rapidly, creating the competition for patients (see Consumer Concern: "Should Medical Service Providers Advertise?"). Competitive efforts have tended to emphasize nonprice factors (e.g., extra services) rather than reduced prices.

To control these upward cost pressures, health insurers use some of the same devices, such as deductibles, used by providers of other types of insurance, plus other devices. These limitations on benefits are discussed in the following sections.

Exclusions

One of the major cost control techniques used by health insurers is to refuse coverage of certain types of expenses. These *exclusions* include both medical conditions and circumstances for which benefit payments are not made. These exclusions are listed in the policy and fall into several general categories:

- *Preventive care expenses.* Some insurers require policyholders to bear the cost of physical examinations. They also insist that other relatively minor routine preventive expenses should be borne by the insured.

- *Particular categories of illness.* Expenses for the treatment of *pre-existing conditions* (i.e., physical or mental conditions that appeared prior to the issuance of the policy) are typically excluded or are subject to some waiting period before they will be covered. Many policies exclude treatment costs for mental illness or place limits on the benefits payable. Medical policies exclude dental care services. Occupational injuries and diseases for which benefits may be available from some other source also may be excluded.
- *Injuries received as a member of the Armed Forces or in time of war.* Members of the Armed Forces are expected to seek treatment from military facilities. Wartime injuries are judged so unpredictable insurers avoid providing any coverage for them at all.
- *Particular types of services.* Most policies do not include coverage of such "extras" as the cost of a bedside phone for hospital patients or the use of a television set. Services from institutions that do not meet the policy's definition

CONSUMER CONCERN: SHOULD MEDICAL SERVICE PROVIDERS ADVERTISE?

In the last few years American consumers have begun to see more ads from doctors, dentists, and hospitals, groups that have never advertised before. This new advertising effort is motivated by a scramble for patients. In many areas, an excess of doctors and dentists and a growing number of unused hospital beds have convinced medical service providers that they not only need to use advertising, but also need other marketing tactics, too (Tyndall, 1986). Another factor underlying this change of heart is a desire to win back more control of the provider–patient relationship. In recent years, payers (including insurers and employers providing group coverage) have insisted on more control over the services given as a way of holding down costs, though providers have resisted.

Advertising by medical service providers violates old traditions and professional regulations. Most providers were content, in years past, to let others sing their praises. Medical ethics forbade self-promotion, and professional rules even controlled such details as the size of lettering on office signs. All this changed after 1977, when the U.S. Supreme Court ruled the restrictions of professional organizations on advertising to be a violation of freedom of speech (Shapiro & Majewski, 1983). Advertising by physicians, as well as by dentists and attorneys, now is commonplace. In fact, the American Medical Association itself is providing one-day seminars on marketing strategies that are consistent with medical ethics (Tyndall, 1986).

Traditionalists have viewed these changes with concern. They suggest that ads may raise patients' expectations to unrealistic heights. Ads that of a "hospital" or from individuals who are not licensed physicians are also usually excluded.

Deductibles

Most health insurance policies require policyholders to pay some initial amount of the expenses incurred before benefits are paid for expenses covered by the policy. A policy may, for example, require the policyholder to pay the first $100 of covered expenses incurred in a calendar year before any benefits are payable. In some family policies, the deductible is waived once one person has paid it. Other insurers may waive the deductible after two or three family members have paid it.

Coinsurance

Policyholders are encouraged to hold down unnecessary costs by the *coinsurance provisions* included in many policies. These provisions specify the ratio that will be used in sharing covered expenses between the insurer and the insured.

report high success rates for complicated medical procedures are particularly suspect, they suggest. Some puffery and exaggeration seems likely, but are there any benefits for consumers from medical advertising?

Advertising does provide consumers with more information about the medical services available in their community. It can also help to sharpen consumers' ideas about what evaluative criteria are important in selecting a provider. The new emphasis on marketing has other benefits. It serves to focus suppliers' attention on patients' needs and concerns and makes suppliers more patient-oriented. With this new emphasis, providers begin to look at their practices and hospitals through the patient's eyes.

Most of the marketing tactics used to date have been forms of non-price competition: newsletters for patients and extra services, such as a special dinner at the hospital for parents of newborns. Some price competition has appeared too. A few advertisers publicize their prices for particular services, and there even are reports of discount coupons for trips to the dentist.

QUESTIONS

1. What forces have pushed medical service providers into increased use of advertising and other marketing devices?
2. What are the benefits and possible drawbacks of this new emphasis on marketing?
3. What forms have the marketing efforts of providers taken?

A frequently used arrangement is for the insurer to pay 80 percent of covered expenses and the insured 20 percent. The inclusion of coinsurance provisions not only motivates policyholders to hold down expenses, but also reduces insurers' costs by reducing the total benefits paid out.

Scheduled Fees

Many policies specify a maximum amount to be paid for covered expenses. For example, the policy may specify that the *scheduled fee* for performing an appendectomy is $500. This amount is the maximum that will be paid to a surgeon for the operation. Maximums may also be specified for hospital room charges, laboratory tests, and other services.

Limitations on Benefit Payments

In order to prevent people from profiting from their medical claims, most policies include *coordination of benefits* provisions. These provisions limit the amount that will be paid in cases where a person has overlapping coverage from two or more policies. Coordination of benefits provisions limit the total benefits payable to 100 percent of the covered expenses. They also specify the order in which insurers will be responsible for payments in cases of overlapping coverage.

Most policies also include some limit on the amount of benefits that will be paid in a calendar year, for a specific illness, or over the lifetime of the insured. A policy might, for example, specify that benefits will be paid up to a lifetime maximum of $50,000. In some cases, the limits are specified for a particular illness. These limits may be a dollar amount or a limit on the number of days of hospitalization covered.

Waiting Periods

Another way that benefits are restricted is by imposing waiting periods before an insured is eligible for benefits. Frequently health insurance policies will not pay maternity benefits until coverage has been in effect for nine or ten months. This restriction is designed to control adverse selection. If newly pregnant women aware of their condition and without coverage could obtain it easily, they would be tempted to do so. To allow them to purchase coverage would raise insurers' costs. Waiting periods may also be imposed for coverage of pre-existing conditions.

Eligibility Rules

Insurers also limit claims by restricting the number of family members eligible for coverage. Unmarried children living under the family roof typically are covered to age 19 or 21. Those that remain in school and are financially dependent may be covered to age 23 or older. Eligibility for coverage is usually lost if a child enters the Armed Forces, takes a regular job, or gets married. Children who are handicapped usually continue to be eligible for coverage as long as they remain financially dependent (American Council of Life Insurance and Health Insurance Institute, 1979).

Overall, benefits are calculated in a series of steps (see Figure 18-1). At each step, different factors limiting benefits are taken into account.

TYPES OF HEALTH INSURANCE COVERAGE

Insurers may provide benefits in three different ways:

- *Reimbursement benefit contracts.* These policies provide payments for covered expenses. Payments are based on scheduled fees listed in the policy. Payment may be made to the policyholder or may be sent to the service provider as partial or full payment when the insured so indicates.
- *Service benefit contracts.* These policies provide actual services from third parties rather than cash payments. Hospitals, physicians, and other providers are paid directly at previously agreed-on rates. Blue Cross organizations are the major source of hospital service benefits. Blue Shield organizations are the major provider of surgical service benefits.
- *Valued benefit contracts.* These policies pay some specified amount per day when the insured is hospitalized, regardless of the actual expenses incurred. Such a policy might, for example, pay $100 a day, which an insured can spend as needed.

Basic Protection

Some health insurance policies are designed to provide protection for routine, but still relatively costly, expenses such as prenatal care and the delivery of a child, tonsillectomies, and appendectomies.

Reimbursement Benefit Policies. More than 800 private insurance companies in the United States write policies that provide partial or full

Figure 18-1
Calculation of Health Insurance Benefits

TOTAL MEDICAL EXPENSES
|
LESS EXCLUDED EXPENSES
(e.g., routine physical examinations, custodial nursing home care, dental services)
|
LESS ANY PORTION OF ALLOWABLE CHARGES ABOVE SCHEDULED LIMITS
|
LESS DEDUCTIBLE
(e.g., first $50 of allowable expenses for calender year)
|
LESS COINSURANCE OBLIGATIONS OF INSURED
(e.g., 20% of allowable expenses)
|
BENEFITS PAYABLE
(up to maximum benefit limit for calendar year illness duration, or lifetime)

reimbursement for covered expenses. *Hospital reimbursement policies* pay a specified maximum, such as $100 or $200 a day, for hospital room and board charges. These policies also provide coverage for charges for other hospital services to some specified limit. The maximum stay allowed may range from 31 to 365 days.

Surgical expense policies written on a reimbursement basis provide for payments to some scheduled maximum for particular services. The scheduled fee for a tonsillectomy may, for example, be $400. If a surgeon charges more, the insured must make up the difference. The scheduled fees for particular surgical services are usually listed in the policy.

Hospital and surgical expense coverage may include reimbursement for office visits to a physician and services performed there. This *physician's expense insurance* (formerly referred to as *regular medical insurance*) usually is not written separately but may be available as part of a hospital or surgical expense policy.

Payments under reimbursement policies are made to the insured unless the insured indicates on the claim form that the payment is to be sent directly to the service provider. This arrangement, under which benefit payments are sent to a third party, is called *assignment* of the benefits. If the assigned benefits fall short of the total bill, the insured is responsible for paying the difference.

Service Benefit Policies. A group of about 70 different not-for-profit Blue Cross and Blue Shield organizations across the nation and some commercial insurers offer service benefit policies. These policies provide those insured with actual services rather than cash payments. These services are provided through member hospitals and participating physicians who are paid directly. Most participating providers agree to accept the negotiated fees as payment in full for the services they provide.

Hospital expense policies written on a service basis provide a semi-private room for some specified maximum number of days (usually 70 to 365 days). Necessary services are also provided as needed. Not all hospitals are members of a Blue Cross Plan. If an insured is admitted to a nonmember hospital, the insured is paid on the same basis as a member hospital would have been paid.

Surgical expense policies offered by Blue Cross Plans and commercial policies with service benefits provide surgeon's and physician's services to insured patients. In some plans, participating physicians and surgeons agree to accept the scheduled fee as full payment for services, provided the subscriber-member's income is not above some specified level. Other plans developed more recently pay for services in full as long as the fees do not exceed what is customary and reasonable.

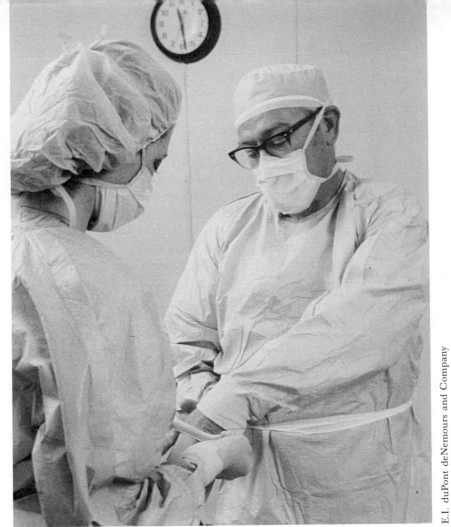

Illustration 18-1
Surgical expense policies
provide a specific
scheduled payment for a
particular type of
operation.

E.I. duPont deNemours and Company

Hospital Indemnity Policies. Policies are also available that provide benefits, such as $100 a day, when the insured is hospitalized. The value of these benefits is based on the contractual amount, not on the expenses incurred. *Hospital indemnity* (or cash payment) *policies* are sold by agents, by mail and through newspaper and magazine ads. While the ads sound appealing, the coverage provided is often reduced by exclusions, waiting periods, maximum benefit restrictions, and other limitations and pay only while the insured is hospitalized. The amount of coverage, such as $1,000 a month, sounds generous, but only amounts to $33.33 a day. Since the average hospital stay is only seven days (Health Insurance Association of America, 1985), the benefits paid are likely to be small, even without the typical restrictions.

Limited Policies. Certain policies provide benefits only for specified diseases or in case of accident. The *limited policies* may be written to cover travel accidents or some dread disease such as cancer. Limited policies cover only a small part of all the potential risks to health. Because of the restricted coverage they provide, they are not considered a good buy (Vaughan, 1986).

Dental Expense Insurance. The Blue Cross/Blue Shield organizations, commercial insurers, and dental group plans all offer insurance to cover the costs of dental care. The expenses covered include preventive care, fillings, and major services such as crowns and dentures. Many plans also include orthodontic services. Coverage is available on a service benefit basis or on a reimbursement basis. Reimbursement benefit policies typically include deductibles, coinsurance, scheduled fee limits, maximum benefits limits, and the other restrictions seen in medical policies.

Major Medical Protection

The expenses of a long-term illness or a serious accident usually exceed the limits on basic protection policies. *Major medical policies* provide a second level of protection and take over where basic policies leave off. Major medical policies are based on the insurance principle that coverage should be concentrated on protecting against large losses, rather than used to cover small, routine expenses.

Major medical coverage is a more recent creation than basic coverage and is provided by private insurers, Blue Cross/Blue Shield Plans, and other independent plans. Coverage is available either with or without basic coverage. Two types of major medical policies are available. One supplements basic hospital-surgical-physicians' expense policies. The other, *comprehensive major medical insurance,* provides both basic and major medical benefits in one policy. Comprehensive major medical coverage is usually available only to groups.

Major medical coverage typically includes a relatively high deductible because it is designed to cover major expenses. Required deductibles may be $500, $1,000, or $2,000. The high deductible eliminates small claims that are expensive to process and reduces the cost of coverage. When an insured has basic health insurance coverage, it often covers much of the deductible. When basic and major medical coverage are included in one comprehensive major medical policy, there typically is a *corridor deductible* between the basic and the major medical coverage. This deductible is whatever is paid by the basic coverage, plus another $50, $100, or $200.

Major medical coverage also includes coinsurance provisions. Usually 75 to 85 percent of covered expenses is provided. Many policies have a *stop-loss provision* that limits the insured's coinsurance expense to some specified amount, such as $1,500. After the insured's coinsurance share exceeds this amount, the policy covers all further expenses fully, and the co-insurance requirement ceases.

Policies also include maximum benefit limits. These may be limits on the benefits payable for one injury or illness; $25,000 or $50,000 limits are common. Other policies have lifetime benefit maximums, while some are unlimited.

Medicare and Medicare Supplement Policies

Medicare is a federal health insurance program for which almost everyone 65 or over is eligible. In addition, individuals suffering from kidney failure and certain disabled people also are eligible (U.S. Department of Health and Human Services, 1986a). Medicare coverage is separated into two parts:

- *Hospital insurance* (Medicare Part A) covers hospital care and, under certain conditions, care in skilled nursing and rehabilitation facilities, home health care, and hospice care. In-hospital tests, x-rays, and many other services are also covered.
- *Medical insurance* (Medicare Part B) covers physicians' services and many other services not included in the hospital insurance coverage, including tests, x-rays, and outpatient services. Under certain conditions home health visits are also covered.

Hospital coverage provided by Medicare is financed with Social Security taxes. The medical coverage is, however, voluntary and is financed by monthly premiums paid by those enrolled and by federal tax revenues. Despite the small fee, the medical insurance is generally considered a bargain (in 1986, it cost $15.50 per month) and is widely recommended.

The benefits provided by the hospital coverage are limited by deductibles and restrictions on the length of stay covered. The medical coverage is limited by an annual deductible, coinsurance provision, and government rules that limit fees to a "reasonable charge." Under these provisions the insured must pay 20 percent of any covered charge up to the fee limit the government considers reasonable. The insured must also pay all of the portion of any charge above the level considered reasonable. Often this difference is substantial. Physician's fees are often twice what the government considers reasonable (Rankin, 1985).

Medicare does not cover dental care or dentures, eyeglasses, hearing aids, prescription drugs, or routine annual checkups. It also does not cover long-term custodial care (care involving feeding, bathing, and supervising daily activities). Because of these restrictions on eligible expenses, the other limitations on Medicare benefits from deductibles and coinsurance, and the differences between the government-approved physician's fees and actual fees, many older people have purchased health insurance policies to supplement their Medicare coverage. Such extra coverage clearly is needed; the available evidence suggests that Medicare is, at most, paying less than half of older people's medical expenses.

Most supplemental policies (often labeled *Medigap* policies) focus on the gaps left by the deductible and coinsurance. They seem to do a good job of covering these gaps. *Consumer Reports* (June, 1984b) found, however, that typical policies provided little protection on physicians' fees and very little coverage on drug bills or nursing home charges.

COVERAGE OUTSIDE GROUP PLANS

A major share of the population has health insurance through employee group plans. What about coverage for those who do not have access to group plan coverage? (See Consumer Concern: "Who's Without Health Insurance?") Those who are not a member of a group at work may have access to coverage through other groups, including professional or fraternal groups.

CONSUMER CONCERN: WHO'S WITHOUT HEALTH INSURANCE?

For much of the population, the financing of health care has come to be dominated by commercial health insurers and the Blue Cross/Blue Shield Plans. Their policies provide a way for many Americans to deal with large, unexpected health expenses. In developing health insurance coverage, commercial insurers have used some of the same approaches employed in other insurance areas, including experience rating. Using this approach, insurers identify groups that have differing loss patterns and develop rates based on these patterns. Initially, the Blue Cross/Blue Shield Plans based their rates on average costs for the entire community, thus sharing costs among the entire community. It became easy for commercial insurers to pick off groups with superior experience ratings and to offer them lower rates. The Blue Cross/Blue Shield Plans have had to make greater use of experience rating in order to remain competitive (Starr, 1982, p. 330).

The health insurance system that has evolved has made it possible for 75 percent of Americans to have private health insurance (U.S. Department of Commerce, 1985). However, as the private health insurance system has evolved some categories of the population have been left out, especially those who are less likely to be members of group plans. Some 80 percent of those with private health insurance are group plan members. Those left out include the unemployed, the irregularly employed, the self-employed, and those employed by small companies that do not provide extensive benefits.

Some other population categories are especially likely to be without coverage. While only 14 percent of whites are without any coverage from

Policies can also be purchased on an individual basis. The premiums on these policies are, however, higher than on group plan policies, and the coverage offered may be more limited. Temporary policies, which are non-renewable, are available for three months to a year. They are especially appropriate for new college graduates who need coverage while looking for a job and individuals between jobs. Employees who are leaving a job in which they have had group coverage may be able to convert their group policy to an individual basis. In many states, group insurers are required to make individual policies available. These conversion privileges may be especially useful to individuals who have been laid-off or who are between jobs.

Another possibility is obtaining protection through a prepaid health plan or health maintenance organization. This type of protection from medical expenses will be discussed in the next section.

private insurers or government, 22 percent of Blacks have no coverage. Among individuals of Hispanic origin, 29 percent are without coverage. Young adults also are frequently without coverage: 23 percent have none (this group includes those who have lost coverage because they are no longer at home but do not have a job that provides health insurance benefits). Relatively few of the aged population are without any health insurance coverage because of the Medicare and Medicaid programs. Their coverage, like that of other groups in the population, may, of course, not always be adequate.

While there has been periodic support for a national health insurance program run and financed by the federal government, these proposals have made little headway. One reason apparently is that the groups that often are most vocal politically, including the middle class and union members, have fairly adequate coverage. As a result, any program of national health insurance seems unlikely as long as our present system of health insurance/health care continues to function in a fashion the public considers acceptable (Starr, 1982).

QUESTIONS

1. Why do health insurance providers charge higher rates for certain groups than for others?
2. Why are certain groups in the populations less likely to have health insurance coverage than others?
3. Why is there little political support for national health insurance?

AN ALTERNATIVE TO HEALTH INSURANCE: PREPAID HEALTH PLANS

More and more Americans are relying on *health maintenance organizations* (HMOs) to provide health care and protection against large and unforeseen medical bills. HMOs provide comprehensive health services, including hospitalization and surgery, for a fixed annual or monthly fee. Because members pay their fees, which are referred to as *premiums,* in anticipation of later need, HMOs also are labeled *prepaid health plans.* With traditional health insurance plans, policyholders are free to select the physician of their choice and the insurer pays the provider or insured when services are provided. In contrast, HMO members have a restricted choice of physicians, with the selection limited to those on the staff of the HMO or under contract with it.

HMOs had their origins in the West in the 1930s when physician groups began providing prepaid medical services to employee groups. Today there are more than 300 HMOs serving more than 15 million members (U.S. Department of Commerce, 1985). Their growth was encouraged by federal legislation in 1973, which overrode state laws restricting HMOs and required employers with more than 25 employees to offer them HMO participation as an alternative to health insurance benefits, if a federally qualified HMO operated in their area (Mackie, 1981). HMOs may be operated on a non-profit or for-profit basis. Several major insurance companies are operating for-profit HMOs.

Illustration 18-2
Health maintenance organizations provide members with prepaid medical services including surgery and hospitalization.

Types of HMOs	There are two broad categories of HMOs (Rosenberg & Mackie, 1981). *Group practice HMOs* provide services at central locations. The doctors may be salaried employees of the HMO (referred to as the *staff model*), or they may be working in a group practice that contracts with an HMO to supply services. The second form is referred to as the *group model*. Members use doctors who are employed by or under contract to the HMO, or they go to outside specialists when they are referred. If members choose on their own to go the doctors outside the plan, their expenses are not covered except in clear cases of emergency.

Members of group practice HMOs pick a primary physician or are assigned to one. This physician coordinates all care and treatment. HMOs can provide a wide range of services because their staffs include family practitioners and a variety of specialists. The services of other, outside specialists are obtained on a contract basis.

The second major form of HMO is the *individual practice association* (IPA) in which care is provided by individual physicians, under contract to the HMO, in their own offices. The participating physicians may continue to see fee-for-service patients along with HMO member patients. The HMO has no central facility and may or may not maintain centralized records. Members can choose a physician from a list of those who have contracted with the HMO. IPAs typically provide their members with a wider choice of physicians than do the group practice HMOs, and members are more likely to be able to retain their present physicians (Friedland, 1981). While having a choice of physicians at different locations can be a convenience for members, the absence of a centralized facility may be inconvenient when a variety of tests or other services are needed. In addition to the group practice HMOs and individual practice association HMOs, there are a number of variants representing combinations of the characteristics of these two major forms.

Costs and Coverage

HMOs have a record of containing costs better than other insurance plans. The major source of savings is their more limited use of hospitalization. Surgery is more often done on an outpatient basis, and other techniques are used to reduce hospitalization and shorten stays (Friedland, 1981). HMOs' cost savings often are attributed to their emphasis on preventive medicine. HMOs frequently provide fitness programs, health seminars, and programs aimed at alcohol abuse and smoking. Such programs can contribute to members' quality of life, but do not seem to be a key factor in reducing HMOs' costs. Another cost-reducing device used by HMOs is the use of physician assistants, nurse practitioners (registered nurses with advanced education in a specialty), and registered nurses to handle many routine matters.

While the costs of belonging to an HMO may be higher than the costs of a health insurance policy, the coverage provided typically is more complete and the benefits greater. HMOs have very limited or no deductibles and no coinsurance provisions. Many do, however, make a small charge for office visits to discourage excessive use. In addition to medical services, some HMOs offer dental care and physical and occupational therapy. Few HMOs, however, cover eyeglasses or contact lenses or provide long-term psychiatric treatment or extensive nursing home care.

Service

Critics have suggested that HMOs put too much emphasis on cost control and that, as a result, quality suffers. In 1982 Consumers Union found no research evidence to support these allegations (*Consumer Reports,* May 1982). Some HMO members complain of impersonal service. Another concern is long waits for appointments for routine problems. HMOs do make provisions to handle emergencies and have urgent care centers to handle relatively minor medical emergencies such as cuts and burns.

One special feature of some HMOs is a clear-cut complaints procedure for handling and resolving member problems. The mechanism provides a channel for complaints that is not available in most other medical organizations.

Competition from HMOs has led physicians in some areas to form another type of organization designed to reduce health care costs. These *preferred provider organizations* (PPOs) agree to provide services to employee groups and other groups at discounted fees that in many cases cover the entire charge. Plan members who choose to go to nonparticipating physicians or hospitals may do so, but payments are limited to the amounts paid to participating providers. In return for accepting services from a restricted list of participating providers, members are usually offered improved terms on deductibles, coinsurance, and maximum limits (Vaughan, 1986). Providers benefit from increased volumes of patients and prompt payment of bills.

While PPOs, like HMOs, offer advantages in cost control, they are fundamentally different. Employees are not required to use only PPO providers. They may go elsewhere if they are willing to pay the extra charges. Providers are paid on the traditional fee-for-service basis (which most prefer) but are forced to control costs because their fees are discounted.

WHAT'S IMPORTANT
IN HEALTH
SERVICES?

Continuing increases in health-care costs have had significant effects on the provision of health insurance and the organization of the health services industry. The industry has faced increasing pressure to control costs from groups that foot the bill—the general public, insurers, employers with group plans, and the federal government. Health services providers have resisted these pressures because of an understandable desire for independence and their concern about interference in the provider–patient relationship. They argue that the role of third parties in this special relationship should be held to a minimum.

The provision of health services has been a persistent national issue in the last four decades. A variety of reforms has been proposed, including *national health insurance* — a government-run and financed system of health insurance coverage.

Concerns about our health system fall into five general categories. Any analysis of the performance of health services should deal with all five of these evaluative criteria. These criteria are applicable not only to our national system of health care but also to the performance of individual physicians and hospitals (Hirschhorn, 1979).

Availability

This criterion is concerned with the existence of needed services. It suggests that any proposed program should take account of the proposal's effects on the demand for services. Can present personnel and facilities handle the likely patient loads? If not, what changes or increases will be necessary? Will the services be available to all members of the population who need it?

Accessibility

This evaluative criterion deals with how easy it is to use services. Even though services are available, it may not be easy for people to use them. Inability to pay may restrict some people's access. Problems in obtaining transportation, inconvenient operating hours, long waiting times to get an appointment, or time spent in the waiting room can also interfere with access. Language barriers and discrimination sometimes also limit access to care.

Acceptability

This evaluative criterion deals with the sense of trust and confidence generated in the patient. When patients are trusting and confident, they are more willing to accept care and follow prescribed routines, thus increasing the likelihood of successful treatment. The "art of caring" is an important aspect of the acceptability of services. The emotional concern and compassion conveyed to a patient can play a significant role in the healing process.

One evidence of concern with the acceptability of services is a clear-cut routine for handling complaints. Complaints should be accepted readily and investigated and dealt with quickly to ensure the continued acceptability of services.

Quality of Services

Another key evaluative criterion is the quality of the health services provided. Do they meet accepted medical standards and public expectations? Four different approaches are used to ensure the quality of medical services.

- *Controls on who can provide services.* These controls include training and licensing requirements for physicians and other health personnel.
- *Regulation of the procedures used.* Treatment procedures may be monitored to ensure that accepted practices have been followed. For example, medical charts can be monitored to ensure that the tests and drugs prescribed and care and treament procedures used were appropriate.
- *Control of inputs.* These controls include regulations on the drugs and equipment that can be used to provide treatment. These regulations should focus both on safety and on effectiveness.
- *Monitoring of performance and outcomes.* Another method of ensuring the quality of care provided is to monitor the success rate for treatment. High success rates and high recovery rates suggest that high quality care is being delivered.

Cost

The fifth criterion deals with the costs of health care services. Rapid increases in medical-care costs have created three concerns. (1) Are excessive resources being devoted to medical care? (2) Are the resources devoted to a particular medical care goal being used effectively? (3) Are individual programs being operated efficiently?

The first question is one of costs and benefits (Owen, Riddick, & Cordes, 1979). The costs of providing medical care are fairly clear-cut. As noted in Chapter 6, however, it is often difficult to express the benefits of health care because of the problems in putting a value on human life. Sometimes it is difficult to decide whether too much is being spent on health care as compared to other services, such as education or highway construction. The problem of putting a value on human life also makes it difficult to decide whether an infant's life is more valuable than that of an ailing 65-year-old retiree.

Whether the resources being allocated to a particular health-care goal are being used effectively is also an important question. There are often several ways a particular goal can be pursued, and it is possible to compare the costs of these alternative approaches to determine their effectiveness. Suppose, for example, that the goal is reducing automobile-accident deaths. A number of approaches seem possible:

- Requiring the installation and use of seatbelts
- Reducing highway speed limits and enforcing these limits strictly
- Improving drivers' car-handling skills through driver education
- Restricting driving by drivers with a record of drunken driving or frequent accidents
- Improving care services for accident victims by adding more ambulances and emergency room facilities

A comparison of the costs and effectiveness can provide a basis for deciding which approach is most effective in relation to its cost.

Once a particular type of service is decided upon, it is important that it be operated as efficiently as possible. The program should be managed so that the least possible amount of resources is used to provide the service. For example, costly equipment that is used infrequently shoud be shared, if feasible.

All five of these evaluative criteria should be borne in mind while reading the following section on controlling health care costs. Unfortunately, programs that score well on one criterion often rate poorly on others. Efforts to reduce costs, for example, may interfere with quality. Programs that attempt to increase availability and accessibility may at the same time strain existing facilities, increase costs, and reduce quality.

CONTROLLING THE COST OF HEALTH SERVICES[1]

In addition to the cost of production, demand is the other determinant of the amount of health services purchased and the price of those services. Demand is, in turn, heavily influenced by the health status of the population and people's ability and willingness to purchase health services. In particular, demand tends to increase with an increase in the number of health problems or in the ability and willingness to purchase health services. As demand increases, so do total expenditures because an increase in demand generally causes both price and the amount of services purchased to increase.

Factors Affecting the Demand for Health Services

A number of factors other than health services affect the health status of the population. Among the more significant factors are age, environment, heredity, and lifestyle. For example, a greater number of health problems is typically found among the elderly; as the percentage of elderly in our population increases, so does the demand for health services. In general, improvements in health status lead to a reduction in the demand for health services, and a deterioration in health status leads to an increase in demand.

Even if the health status of the population remains unchanged, there can still be a significant change in the demand for health services. For example, an increase in income might allow some people to purchase the physical examination they had been postponing. Or more pregnant women might seek prenatal care if they could afford it.

When demand changes without a change in health status, there has been a change in the ability and willingness to purchase health services. This demand is determined jointly by the consumer and provider. This prominent role of the provider or producer is not found when purchasing most other goods and services in our society. Because of this phenomenon,

1. This section is adapted from Cordes (1981). Used by permission.

the following discussion distinguishes the influence of the provider from that of the consumer.

Consumer-Induced Demand. Two major influences on consumer-induced demand are the consumer's income and the extent of health insurance coverage. Both have increased significantly during the past quarter-century, which led to an increased demand for health services.

The growth in consumer income is simply a reflection of the historical growth in the nation's economy. The increase in insurance coverage also follows because consumers have more income with which to buy health insurance; however, several other reasons are behind the growth in third-party insurance coverage. One reason is that consumers find themselves in a vicious circle. As the price of health services rises, the risk of financial hardship due to illness increases, and more insurance is purchased. This causes demand to increase and prices are driven up even further. The upward spiral continues when consumers respond to rising prices by purchasing even more insurance protection.

Another important reason behind the growth in insurance is its favorable tax treatment by the Internal Revenue Service. This favorable treatment ocurs at two levels. First, when an individual purchases a health insurance plan, a portion of the premiums is a tax-deductible expense if the person itemizes deductions. [Only those premiums and expenses that exceed a specified percentage of taxable income are deductible, and they are deductible only if all deductions are itemized.] Second, if the premiums are paid by an employer—which is the more typical situation—this fringe benefit is not taxed. Because of these two aspects of the tax structure, more health insurance is purchased than would otherwise be the case.

Provider-Induced Demand. The existence of provider-induced demand is apparent in a number of ways. For example, the provider has a major say in when and how often the patient should be admitted to a hospital and where (depending, in part, on the hospital at which the provider has privileges), and when the hospitalized patient should be discharged. This is not to say the consumer has no choice in the decision-making process. The consumer makes the initial decision to seek care and has the option of changing to another provider or refusing to follow the provider's orders. However, the consumer's role is definitely more limited than when purchasing most other goods and services.

The ability of the provider to heavily influence the decision of what, when, and where to purchase services invariably leads to a fundamental question:

Will the provider's influence reflect only his or her concern for the patient, or will it also reflect at least some concern for the provider's self-interest?

Two aspects of the current health system increase the probability that self-interest will play at least some role. One aspect is the rapid growth in malpractice suits. The increased probability of being sued has likely led to the practice of "defensive medicine" in which certain nonessential laboratory tests and other procedures are performed. Having performed these tests and procedures, the provider is better protected in the courtroom against charges of negligence. In short, the increase in malpractice suits has increased provider-induced demand for certain health services.

The fee-for-service method of paying the provider is the second aspect of the current system that increases the probability that self-interest will come into play. Under this method of payment, more income is generated as more patients are seen and as more procedures are performed. While this payment method may serve as an incentive to overprescribe. The provider may strongly recommend tests, other procedures, and follow-up visits that are really discretionary.

The Rationale for Controlling Health Care Spending

There is nothing necessarily wrong when the amount of resources going into particular industry increases. In the last several decades, our nation has dramatically increased the amount of spending on recreation, and these expenditures are applauded as symbols of the "good life." Why then all the concern over health care expenditures? The concern reflects a general skepticism that the increased amount of spending on health care is not generating an equal increase in benefits. This skepticism is, in turn, based on the fact that the health services industry *does not* meet the following conditions of a competitive economic system.

- Consumers are well-informed and able to determine what quantity and quality of goods and services best meet their needs. This means that providers will be at the mercy of the consumers and those who respond will profit. Those who do not are forced from the industry by their more responsive and efficient competitors.
- Providers openly and actively compete with each other on the basis of economics.
- The single most important motive of providers is that of maximum profits.

The fact that the characteristics of the health services industry are not consistent with the conditions of a competitive economic system is not entirely bad. For example, if hospitals were run only for profit, services that are greatly needed in a community, but happen to be unprofitable (as is often true with emergency room services), would probably be unavailable. Nevertheless, the fact that the health services industry does not meet the basic conditions of a competitive system is one reason for being concerned about its economic performance. The result of this concern has been a variety of proposals designed to control the nation's health care expenditures. Some proposals emphasize increased regulation of the health services industry, and others emphasize nonregulatory mechanisms for bringing about change.

The Regulatory Approach to Control

Throughout most of this century, the health services industry has been subject to considerable regulation. For example, 50 years ago many states had laws and regulations that prohibited physicians from practicing in groups and from receiving payment on any basis other than fee-for-service. The licensure of facilities and personnel and laws that prevented providers from advertising are more recent examples of regulation in the health services industry. However, only very recently has the regulatory approach been directed toward controlling health care expenditures. Although an attempt can be made to control expenditures directly, there are also three indirect regulatory strategies available: regulating the price of services, regulating the amount of services used, and regulating the availability of inputs [e.g., hospital bed space, equipment, and services].

Regulating Total Expenditures. Regulating total expenditures for health care requires some governmental or public authority to determine the amount of money that will be allocated to health services. This type of funding is a fairly common practice for a number of other public services. At the national level, for example, Congress sets so much money aside each year for national defense. In other cases, such as with secondary education, the budgetary authority is decentralized, and local school districts detemine the amount that will be spent.

The potential benefits and problems of placing a budgetary lid on total expenditures were recenly summarized as follows.

> There is a fair amount of evidence from England and from public education here that this lid-type of public utility approach can make expenditures controllable...we might not always make wise decisions on what the budgetary lid should be; we might under-invest or over-invest. But at least we will be able to make the decision. In the present system, we can't decide; the medical care system now does whatever it will and we run after it shoveling out the money. (McClure, 1979, p. 22)

Regulating the Prices Charged for Services. *Prospective rate setting* is the term used when fee schedules are determined prior to the year in which they would apply. In some cases, prospective rate setting involves a fixed statewide or regional fee schedule, and in other cases negotiations are conducted with each provider. Other variations exist in the way prospective rate setting is conducted. However, the basic goal of all such programs is to reduce the price of services by avoiding the undesirable incentives associated with reimbursing providers retrospectively on the basis of their cost.

Approximately one-half of the states now have some type of prospective rate-setting program. Most of these programs have been in place for only a few years, but preliminary evidence suggest that they may be having some success in containing hospital costs (Biles, Schramm, & Atkinson, 1980; U.S. General Accounting Office, 1980).

Regulating the Amount of Services Used. The major regulatory effort aimed directly at service use is the Professional Standards Review Organizations, which are federally mandated organizations operated by local physicians and designed to ensure that inpatient care for Medicare and Medicaid patients is necessary. For example, suppose a Professional Standards Review Organization determines that a patient insured by Medicare was hospitalized needlessly or was allowed to stay in the hospital longer than necessary. In that case, payment will be denied. Only a limited amount of high quality research has been undertaken on this program. The evidence that does exist indicates that Professional Standards Review Organizations have reduced the number of days of hospital care by about 2 percent. However, the evidence is mixed as to whether the monetary savings associated with this reduced hospitalization were greater than the costs of operating the program (Congressional Budget Office, 1979).

Regulating the Availability of Inputs. The main regulatory mechanisms for preventing the inefficient use of inputs [e.g., hospital bed space] are the Certificate of Need legislation and the national network of Health Systems Agencies. In general terms, both are in a position to prevent the development or expansion of health services if the services are unlikely to be used efficiently. In other words, it must be demonstrated that the services are "needed" and will be used. One well-designed study has shown that the early Certificate of Need programs were *not* effective in reducing hospital investment (Salkever & Bice, 1977). However, additional research is needed before definitive conclusions can be drawn.

Recently, much discussion has also focused on regulating new medical technology. Considerable concern has developed that at least some of this new technology is often of questionable value. In response to this problem, there is considerable support for a regulatory mechanism or agency akin to the federal Food and Drug Administration. The purpose of such a mechanism would be to determine which medical procedures and equipment should be allowed on the market. A modest beginning of such an approach was the establishment in 1978 of the National Center for Health Care Technology. The Center evaluates new and existing equipment and procedures in an attempt to answer questions such as:

- Is the device or procedure safe?
- What are its ethical implications?
- Is it cost effective?

Answers to these questions are made available to various organizations and agencies, including the Health Care Financing Administration (HCFA). HCFA administers Medicare and is, therefore, in a position to withhold reimbursement to providers who use technology that is of questionable value. It is too early to gauge whether such efforts are having an impact on the diffusion of medical technology.

The Nonregulatory Approach to Control

Attempts to control expenditures via the regulatory approach require providers and consumers to change certain practices or behaviors. In contrast, the nonregulatory approach tries to encourage changes in practices or behaviors using more positive tactics — incentives, education, and the like. Most of the nonregulatory efforts have been directed at:

- Changing the way providers are paid
- Restructuring the insurance system
- Promoting competition

Changing the Way Providers are Paid. Most physicians are paid on a fee-for-service basis. This system provides physicians with a strong incentive to increase the amount of service provided (Gabel & Redisch, 1979). As a result, it has been proposed that physicians should be reimbursed on a prepaid or salaried basis or on the basis of how many clients they have (in contrast to the number of client visits). This is the type of reimbursement typically found in health maintenance organizations (HMOs), and hospital admission rates for HMO enrollees are significantly lower than for persons receiving care on a fee-for-service basis. Moreover, one estimate suggests that the yearly health care expenditures for HMO enrollees were 10 to 40 percent below those of a comparable group of persons not enrolled in HMOs (Luft, 1978).

Restructuring the Insurance System. In addition to cost-based reimbursement, two other concerns exist with the present system of health insurance. First, in many cases, insurance coverage is provided only for inpatient care. This creates an incentive to hospitalize patients even when their needs could be handled without hospitalization. Hence, it is frequently argued that insurance coverage for certain services or procedures should always include the option of outpatient provision. The potential effect of that change can be gauged by comparing the health care received by persons with different kinds of health insurance coverage. One such study analyzed the surgical workloads of surgeons working in an HMO and compared their workloads to those of non-HMO surgeons. The HMO plan encouraged outpatient surgery. Results of the study showed that non-HMO surgeons performed very few outpatient procedures, and the types of patients treated on an outpatient basis in the HMO tended to be admitted as inpatients by the non-HMO surgeons (Hughes et al., 1973).

Another problem with the current insurance system is that people may be overinsured. Because of this, it has been suggested that the tax system be restructured by (1) no longer allowing individuals to count health insurance premiums as deductible expenses and (2) treating the employer's health insurance payments as income to the employee. The presumed effect of these changes would be to reduce insurance coverage, thereby reducing the demand for health care. Even greater attention has been given to "reforming" health insurance plans by increasing the consumer's out-of-pocket expenditure at the time of purchasing service. The most common way of doing this is through copayment in the form of deductibles and coinsurance. As might be expected, a number of objections range from practical matters related to administrative efficiency, to the major equity concern that copayment may create a substantial financial barrier for the poor.

Promoting Competition. The most recent nonregulatory proposal for controlling rising health care expenditures is to foster competition in the health services industry. One aspect of this approach has been a series of specific actions to deregulate the health services industry by challenging laws and procedures that appear to hinder competitive economic behavior. Most of this work is being undertaken by the Federal Trade Commission and the Justice Department's Antitrust Division. Recent and current targets include laws that restrict advertising, medical fee-setting practices, domination of Blue Shield boards by providers, procedures for accrediting health professionals, and laws that inhibit midlevel practitioners from practicing their trade.

The second aspect of the competitive approach is to develop an environment where consumers have alternative types of delivery systems from which to choose and a financial incentive to choose the one which is most efficient. Currently in most areas of the country there are no alternatives to the fee-for-service system. An exception is the Twin Cities of Minneapolis–St. Paul. In the early 1970s, General Mills and several other large Twin Cities corporations began giving their employees a choice between an HMO and the traditional fee-for-service mode of delivery. As more and more employees opted for the HMO approach, it forced more and more of the nonorganized physicians into forming their own HMOs and other types of organized delivery systems. Currently, there are seven organized delivery systems in the Twin Cities, and they are actively competing with each other for clients. The competition for clients is apparently placing pressure on the provider to be efficiency minded. For example, the number of days of hospital care in the seven organized systems averaged 496 per 1,000 members. This compares to 860 days per 1,000 persons for those enrolled in Minnesota's Blue Cross/Blue Shield Plans (Christianson & McClure, 1979). It is unlikely that this huge difference can be attributed to other factors, such as differences in the age structure between the two groups (Blumberg, 1980).

Source: Adapted from Sam Cordes, *The Economics of Health Services.* Community Affairs Pamphlet Series No. 1. University Park: Cooperative Extension Service, The Pennsylvania State University, 1981.

PUBLIC PREFERENCES ON COST CONTROLS

The public seems to find measures that put controls on health providers more acceptable than those that limit benefits (see Table 18-1). Proposals that would fix providers' fees or put price controls on medical services get a favorable response from a significant portion of the public. HMOs also seem to get a favorable reaction. In contrast, proposals to increase deductibles or coinsurance requirements find less favor. Overall, the public seems to favor restrictions on providers, not themselves.

Table 18-1
Acceptability of Different Methods of Controlling Health Care Costs

	Acceptable	Not Acceptable	Not Sure
Encouraging uniform, preset fees based on the treatment required	70%	26%	4%
Joining a prepaid health maintenance organization	69	28	3
Establishing government price controls on doctors and hospitals	60	40	—
Increasing the patient's deductible	50	48	2
Making the patient pay a higher percentage of the cost of treatment	37	61	2

Source: *Business Week/Harris Poll.* (New York: McGraw Hill.) October 15, 1984: 148. Used by permission.

MAJOR CHAPTER CONCEPTS

1. The complexity of health insurance policies is due to the provisions used to control costs.

2. Restrictions on health insurance benefits are necessary because of the large number of small claims, the problem of adverse selection, the lack of incentives to control costs, and the lack of competition in the provision of health services.

3. Certain types of expenses are refused coverage by exclusions written into policy provisions. Deductibles are another cost control device, requiring payment of some portion of covered expenses by the policyholder.

4. Other methods of limiting benefits include coinsurance, the use of scheduled fees, limitations on total benefits payable, waiting periods, and eligibility rules.

5. There are three ways in which insurers can provide benefits: reimbursing expenses, providing actual services, or providing some specified amount per day when an insured is hospitalized.

6. Basic protection policies provide protection for routine, but relatively costly, expenses. Major medical policies provide coverage beyond that provided in basic protection policies.

7. Medicare hospital coverage is financed with Social Security taxes. Medicare coverage of medical expenses (e.g., physicians' services) is voluntary and is financed by a small premium for those enrolled and federal tax revenues.

8. Prepaid health plans such as health maintenance organizations (HMOs) provide comprehensive health services for a fixed annual or monthly fee and are an alternative to health insurance.

9. Group practice HMOs provide services at central locations using salaried employees. Individual practice associations provide care through individual physicians who maintain their own offices and may continue to see fee-for-service patients.

10. Preferred provider organizations (PPOs) are an alternative to HMOs. They provide services to employee groups and other groups for discounted fees in return for the group's patronage.

11. In judging health services, important evaluative criteria include availability, accessibility, acceptability, quality of services, and cost.

12. Demand for health services is affected by the cost of health services, the health status of the population, consumers' incomes, and consumers' health insurance coverage.

13. The principal rationale for controlling health care charges is that consumers are not well-informed about the quality of services or able to judge them, that providers do not compete vigorously, and that providers do not always strive for maximum efficiency.
14. Regulatory approaches to controlling health services costs include regulating total governmental expenditures, regulating the prices charged for services, regulating the amount of services used for individual patients, and regulating the availability of inputs.
15. Nonregulatory approaches to controlling costs include restructuring the health insurance system and promoting increased competition.

CONSUMER
QUESTIONS

1. If you or your family have a health insurance policy, examine it to determine the extent of the coverage provided. What expenses are excluded? What are the deductibles? The coinsurance provisions? Are scheduled fees indicated? If so, what are some of those specified? Are there limitations on payments?
2. Have you had experience with services provided by an HMO? (Many colleges and universities provide student health services that operate similarly to staff model HMOs.) How would you compare your experiences to those with physicians who operate on the traditional fee-for-service basis? What is the experience of other students you know?
3. Consumers often confront serious problems in choosing a physician. Use the five evaluative criteria for health care services to frame a set of questions that could be used to guide the choice of a physician.
4. Identify a current proposal for reducing or controlling health care costs. (Check *U.S. News and World Report* and other periodicals for information.) How would the proposed plan work? How would you rate the proposal on the five evaluative criteria discussed in this chapter?
5. A variety of proposals for controlling health care costs have been made, including those in the last section of the chapter. What types of proposals are most acceptable to you? What types are least acceptable? Explain the reasons for your preferences.

SUGGESTED
READINGS

1. Anderson, Odin W. *Health Services in the United States: A Growth Enterprise Since 1875.* Ann Arbor, Mich: Health Administration Press, 1985. Anderson gives an historical analysis of the development of the American health services system. The author divides the study into three parts: the emergence of basic services (1875-1930); the era of the third-party payment system (1940-1965); and the era of management and control (1965 to present).
2. *Columbia University College of Physicians and Surgeons Complete Home Medical Guide.* New York: Crown Publications, 1985. This is a comprehensive home reference on illness.

3. "The HMO Approach to Health Care: Are Health Maintenance Organizations Finally Taking Hold?" *Consumer Reports* 47, no. 5 (May 1982): 246-250. *Consumer Reports* provides a useful overview of the advantages and disadvantages of HMOs.

4. Roemer, Milton I. *An Introduction to the U.S. Health Care System.* 2d ed. New York: Springer Publishing Company, 1986. This brief overview of the U.S. health services system includes discussions of the role of public health, ambulatory care, national health insurance, medical ethics, and other areas of continuing concern.

5. Starr, Paul. *The Social Transformation of American Medicine.* New York: Basic Books, Inc., 1982. This comprehensive Pulitzer prize-winning study examines the development of medicine as an honored and powerful profession and the growth of medicine as an industry so powerful that health insurers, employer-sponsors of group health insurance plans, and government are unable to control it. In the closing section, the author examines the rise of large-scale, corporate health conglomerates.

CHAPTER 19

SOCIAL
SECURITY
AND EMPLOYEE
BENEFITS

An important part of what American workers are paid never shows up in their salaries or hourly wages. This "hidden pay" is the compensation they receive in the form of fringe benefits including employer's contributions for health and life insurance, pensions, and Social Security taxes. These benefits are valuable and do not come cheap. They cost employers another 20 percent on top of the salaries and wages paid (Munnell, 1984).

Fringe benefits play an important role in the physical and financial well-being of today's workers. They often replace or supplement financial arrangements employees would otherwise have to make on their own. As noted in the last chapter, most employees rely chiefly on the group policy they get at work for their health insurance coverage. Employer contributions to pension funds and Social Security replace funds workers might otherwise have to put into life insurance to protect their families or save for retirement. Other fringe benefits such as employee discounts, subsidized meals, and free parking reduce workers' out-of-pocket costs.

In recent years, employee benefits have become more generous and more diverse. They have also become increasingly connected with other aspects of workers' financial affairs. These changes make them more important than ever before.

SOCIAL SECURITY

Social Security is a national program for assuring continuing income to workers and their families when earnings stop or are reduced by retirement, disability, or death. Social Security payments are not intended to replace all of the earnings lost. Instead, the payments are expected to supplement personal savings, pensions, investments, or other insurance. Social Security has become a significant factor in the financial security of most Americans (U.S. Department of Health and Human Services, 1986d):

- Nine out of 10 U.S. workers are earning protection under Social Security.

Illustration 19-1
The variety of fringe benefits provided to workers are an important part of their pay.

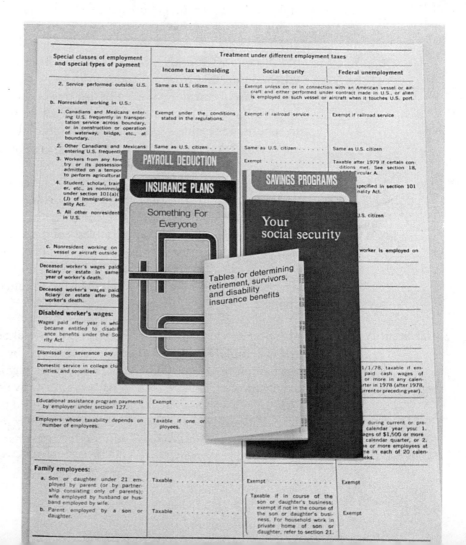

- About one out of every six people in the country receives monthly Social Security checks.
- In addition, nearly all of the nation's older population (more than 28 million people 65 and over) have health insurance under Medicare.

Social Security payments are made to workers and their dependents when the worker retires, becomes severely disabled, or dies. Medicare hospitalization insurance, which is financed by Social Security, helps pay the cost of care for eligible people who are 65 or older or disabled. Coverage under Social Security includes three types of benefits.

- *Retirement benefits* are payable to covered workers on retirement, as early as age 62. Payments are made to retired workers and to other family members, including spouses age 62 or older, unmarried children under 18 (or under 19 if they are full-time high school students), and disabled children under certain circumstances. Payments are also made to spouses caring for children who are under age 16 and therefore eligible for benefits.
- *Disability benefits* are payable to workers who become severely disabled before 65. Workers are considered disabled if they have a severe physical or mental condition that prevents them from working and is expected to last (or has lasted) for at least 12 months, or is expected to result in death. In addition to the payments to disabled workers, payments also are made to spouses 62 or older, to unmarried children under 18, and to disabled children. Payments are also made to a spouse caring for a child who is under age 16 and who receives benefits.
- *Survivor's benefits* are payable to certain survivors of a covered worker. In addition, a lump sum payment (in 1986 it was $255) can also be paid when a covered worker dies. Survivor's benefits are payable to unmarried children under 18, to certain disabled children, to widows or widowers if they are caring for a child under 16 who is getting benefits, and to widows and widowers age 60 and older. Certain other dependents of the deceased worker may also be eligible for benefits, including divorced spouses.

Social Security Taxes Social Security funding is obtained from the Social Security tax payments made by employees during their working years, by their employers, and by self-employed people. This money is used to pay benefits to the people currently getting benefits and to pay administrative costs of the program. When today's workers' earnings stop or are reduced because of retirement, death, or disability, benefits will be paid to them from taxes paid by people who have covered jobs or are self-employed at that time.

Tax Rates. Employees and their employers each pay an equal share of Social Security taxes. Self-employed workers pay taxes for retirement, survivors and disability insurance, and hospital insurance at a rate twice the employee rate. Individuals who have earnings that are covered by the law must continue to pay Social Security taxes regardless of their age, even though they are receiving Social Security benefits. Present and future Social Security *tax rates* now scheduled in the law are shown in Table 19-1.

Self-employed people receive a credit against the self-employment Social Security tax. The credit amounts to 2.0 percent of self-employment income for 1986–89. After 1989, this credit will be replaced with deductions designed to treat the self-employed in much the same manner as employees and employers are treated for Social Security and income tax purposes under present law.

The Earnings Base on Which Taxes are Collected. The maximum amount of annual earnings subject to Social Security taxes (the *earnings base*) rises automatically as earnings levels rise. (In 1986, a maximum of $42,000 was subject to taxes.) Every year the increase in the average covered wages will be computed. If wage levels have increased since the earnings base was last set, the base will be raised, but only if there is a benefit increase the same year due to an increase in the Consumer Price Index.

Table 19-1
Social Security Tax Rates

Tax Rates for Employees and Employers			
	Percentage of Covered Earnings		
Years	For Cash Benefits	For Hospital Insurance	Total
1986-87	5.70	1.45	7.15
1988-89	6.06	1.45	7.51
1990 and after	6.20	1.45	7.65

Tax Rates for Self-employed People			
	Percentage of Covered Earnings		
Years	For Cash Benefits	For Hospital Insurance	Total
1986-87	11.40	2.90	14.30
1988-89	12.12	2.90	15.02
1990 and after	12.40	2.90	15.30

Source: U.S. Department of Health and Human Services, Social Security Administration, *Your Social Security* (Washington, D.C.: U.S. Department of Health and Human Services, 1986): 31.

Payment of Taxes. Social Security tax is deducted from each employee's wages each payday. Employers match the payment and send the combined amount to the Internal Revenue Service. Workers who are self-employed with net earnings of $400 or more in a year must report their earnings and pay self-employment tax when they file their income tax return. This tax must be paid even if they owe no income tax.

Workers' wages and self-employment income are entered on their Social Security *earnings record* throughout their working years. This record of earnings is used to determine eligibility for benefits and the amount of cash benefits workers and their dependents receive. Social Security account records are maintained by the Social Security Administration.

Individuals who work for more than one employer in a year and pay Social Security taxes on wages over the maximum amount may claim a refund of the excess amount on their income tax return for that year. Individuals who work for only one employer who deducts too much in taxes should apply to the employer for a refund. A refund is made only when more than the required amount has been paid. Questions about taxes or refunds should be directed to the Internal Revenue Service.

Employers are required to give workers a statement of the Social Security taxes deducted from their pay at the end of each year. These records, such as Form W-2, can be used to check on a Social Security record. Records should be checked every three years to make certain earnings are being reported correctly to a record. A postcard form is available at Social Security offices for this purpose.

Determination of Benefits

To obtain protection under Social Security, workers must first establish their eligibility for benefits from the system. The credit they obtain for covered work establishes their eligibility, but the size of the benefits paid will depend on their earnings over a period of years.

Eligibility for Benefits. Before a worker or the family can get monthly cash benefits, the worker must accumulate credit for a certain amount of work under Social Security. The exact amount of work credit required depends on the worker's age. Social Security credit is measured in *quarters of coverage.* In 1986 employees and self-employed people received one quarter of coverage for each $440 of covered annual earnings. No more than four quarters of coverage can be credited for a year. The amount of earnings needed to get a quarter of coverage is increased periodically, based on changes in average wages.

Those who stop working under Social Security before they have earned enough credit to get benefits are not eligible to receive them. The credit they have earned will, however, stay on their record and can be added to future work under Social Security.

To receive most types of benefits, a worker must be *fully insured*. In general, to be fully insured most workers need to have accumulated as many quarters of coverage as the number of years that have elapsed between age 21 and 62 and their death or disability. Table 19-2 shows the amount of credit needed to be eligible for retirement benefits.

Requirements for work credit to obtain disability benefits differ from those for retirement benefits. Workers disabled before age 24 need credit for 1½ years of work in the 3 years before they were disabled. At older ages, increasing amounts of work credits are needed for eligibility. The years of work credits required for survivors and disability benefits for workers who become disabled is shown in Table 19-3. Individuals disabled by blindness do not have to meet the recent work requirement in order to obtain benefits.

Under a special rule, survivor's benefits can be paid to a worker's young widow or widower with children if the deceased worker worked under Social Security 1½ years in the 3 years before death. Such workers are considered *currently insured* even though they are not considered fully insured.

Special eligibility rules apply to some workers:

- Individuals who are self-employed
- Household workers
- Farm owners, operators, and workers
- Students employed by their school or college
- Waiters, waitresses, and others who receive cash tips
- Individuals who work outside the United States (United States Department of Health and Human Services, 1986d).

The Size of Benefit Payments. Benefits for workers who are currently retiring are based on past earnings adjusted to take account of changes in average wage levels in the economy. This *indexing method* is used for cal-

Table 19-2
Work Credit Required to Establish Eligibility for Retirement Benefits

For Those Reaching 62 in	Years of Work Needed
1983	8
1984	8¼
1985	8½
1986	8¾
1987	9
1988	9¼
1989	9½
1991 or later	10

Source: U.S. Department of Health and Human Services, *Your Social Security* (Washington, D.C.: U.S. Department of Health and Human Services, 1986): 18.

Table 19-3
Work Credit Required for
Survivors and Disability
Benefits

Born after 1929 die or become disabled at	Born before 1930, die or become disabled before age 62 in	Years of work credit needed
28 or younger		1½
30		2
32		2½
34		3
36		3½
38		4
40		4½
42		5
44		5½
46		6
48		6½
50		7
52		7½
54		8
56	1985	8½
58	1987	9
60	1989	9½
62 or older	1991 or later	10

Source: U.S. Department of Health and Human Services, Social Security Administration, *Your Social Security* (Washington, D.C.: U.S. Department of Health and Human Services, 1986): 20.

culating benefits for all workers who reached age 62, died, or were disabled in 1979 or since. This method insures that benefits paid will reflect changes in wage levels over a covered worker's 30- or 40-year working lifetime. After a worker's average indexed monthly earnings have been determined, they are inserted into a benefit formula that determines the worker's *primary insurance amount* (PIA). All Social Security benefits payable are based on this primary insurance amount (U.S. Department of Health and Human Services, 1986b). The relationship of benefits payable to PIA is indicated in Table 19-4.

An idea of the benefits being paid can be obtained from the following examples (U.S. Department of Health and Human Services 1986d):

- Individuals who reached 65 in 1986 can be paid maximum retirement benefits of $760 per month.
- Individuals who became disabled in 1986 can be paid a maximum benefit of $960 per month, depending on age and past earnings. For workers with eligible dependents, the total monthly family benefit can be as much as $1,440.
- Survivors of a worker who died in 1986 can receive as much as $1,727 a month for a family of three or more.

Part 4   Managing Risk

Table 19-4
Insured Status
Requirements to Receive
OASDI Benefits

Benefits	Worker Must be
Retirement Insurance Benefits	
Monthly payments equal to 100 percent of the primary insurance amount (PIA) are payable to a retired worker age 65 or over (reduced benefits are payable at age 62)	Fully insured
Monthly payments equal to 50 percent of the PIA are payable to:	
A divorced spouse age 65 or older (reduced benefits are payable at age 62)	Fully insured
A dependent child or grandchild under age 18, or 19 if in school	Fully insured
Wife of any age caring for an entitled child under age 16	Fully insured
Survivor Insurance Benefits	
Monthly payments equal to 100 percent* of the PIA are payable to:	
A surviving widow(er) age 65 or older (reduced benefits payable at age 60)	Fully insured
Monthly payments equal to 75 percent of the PIA are payable to:	
Widow(er) or surviving divorced spouse under age if caring for an entitled child under age 16	Fully or currently insured
Dependent child or grandchild under age 18, or age 19 if in school	Fully or currently insured
Dependent parent or parents age 62 or older	Fully insured
Disability Insurance Benefits	

Monthly payments equal to the amount payable in retirement cases are payable to:
    A disabled worker under age 65
    His or her spouse
    His or her children
	Fully insured and has 20 quarters of coverage in the 40 calendar quarters ending in the quarter in which he or she becomes disabled

*Where retired worker was already receiving reduced retirement benefits, this amount will be adjusted.

Source: U.S. Department of Health and Human Services, Social Security Administration, "Social Security Programs in the United States," *Social Security Bulletin, 49,* no. 1 (January, 1986): 12.

No fixed minimum benefit has been set for workers who reach 62, become disabled, or die after 1981. The benefit rates for these workers and their dependents and survivors are based entirely on the worker's earnings covered by Social Security.

After a worker's initial Social Security benefit has been determined, the amount paid is increased each January to reflect increases in the cost-of-living. These upward adjustments are made if the Consumer Price Index (CPI) increased by more than 3 percent in the previous year. After this *automatic increase* provision was put into effect in 1975, there were increases each year through 1987. The largest of these increases was 14.3 percent in 1980. The 1987 increase (effective January 1987) was the lowest during this period at 1.3 percent. If Social Security trust fund reserves fall below specified levels, increases are limited to the increase in average wages or increase in the CPI, whichever is smaller (Bondar, 1986).

Retired and disabled workers who become eligible for a pension based in whole or in part on work not covered by Social Security will receive reduced Social Security benefits. These benefits will be calculated using a different formula from that for other covered workers and will result in a lower Social Security benefit. This procedure is designed to take account of the years in which they worked but did not contribute to the Social Security system. The rule will not generally apply to employees of the federal government and nonprofit organization employees who were mandatorily covered in 1984.

Individuals who qualify for checks on the account of more than one worker are permitted to receive payments only from one account. Frequently, retired workers would qualify to receive payments based on their own account and on their spouse's. They are, however, only permitted to receive payments from one account. Most people elect to receive the larger of the two amounts.

Benefits are not paid automatically. An application including the Social Security account number must be filed and proper identification presented. Workers applying for benefits must present proof of their age. Applicants for wife's, widow's, and widower's benefits must present a marriage certificate. Children's birth certificates must be presented if benefits are requested for them.

Retirement benefits can be paid as early as age 62. Those who begin receiving benefits prior to age 65 are given permanently *reduced benefits* because they can be expected to receive benefits over a longer period. Retirement benefits for those who began receiving benefits at age 62 are 20 percent lower than those paid at age 65 (U.S. Department of Health and Human Services, 1986c). Starting in the year 2000, the retirement age for receiving full benefits will be increased gradually, until it reaches 67 in 2027. Those who work past the *full benefit retirement age* (currently age 65) will have their benefits increased by 3 percent for each year in which they do not receive benefits. Beginning in 1990 the credit will be increased until it reaches 8 percent in 2008.

Factors That Reduce or Stop Payments. Benefits may be reduced or stopped for individuals who return to work and are not yet 70. No reductions are made if earnings are below the *annual exempt amount*. Income from savings, investments, and insurance is not counted as earnings in determining benefits. The annual exempt amount is increased automatically as the average wage level rises. In 1986 the exempt amount was $7,800 for people 65 or over and $5,760 for people under 65.

If earnings are greater than the annual exempt amount, benefits are reduced by $1 for each $2 of earnings above the limit. Starting in 1990, benefits will be reduced by $1 for each $3 in earnings above the limit for those 65 and over. Beginning in the year 2000, the age at which the reduction rate applies will increase as the retirement age for full benefits increases.

Social Security benefits are, in some cases, reduced when recipients are receiving other government benefits. Individuals who receive social Security benefits as a survivor or dependent and also receive a pension based on work in federal, state, or local government jobs not covered by Social Security may have their Social Security benefits reduced. Benefits to disabled workers and their families may be reduced when they also receive a disability benefit paid by federal, state, or local government programs.

A maximum of one-half of the benefits paid may be subject to federal income tax for any year in which a recipient's income exceeds a base amount. The amount of benefits subject to tax will be the smaller of:

- One-half the benefits, or
- One-half the amount of combined income (adjusted gross income plus nontaxable interest plus one-half of total benefits) in excess of the base amount.

Benefits are taxable when the smaller of these two amounts exceeds $32,000 for a couple filing jointly, $25,000 for an individual, and $0 for a couple filing separately if they lived together any part of the year.

Establishing a Social Security Account

Workers need a Social Security number if their work is covered by Social Security or if they have certain kinds of taxable income. Social Security numbers are also used for federal income tax record-keeping. Application should be made at least 2 weeks before the card is needed. Evidence of age, identity, and U.S. citizenship or immigrant status is required when an application is made. Application for a Social Security card can be made at any of the 1,300 Social Security offices throughout the country. People who are age 18 or older and have never had a Social Security number card must apply in person. Others can apply by mail or telephone.

Workers should show their employer their identification card when starting a new job. The number will be used to keep a record of their earnings. Covered workers should have only one Social Security number during their lifetimes. Individuals who receive more than one number should notify their nearest Social Security office. Duplicates of lost cards can be obtained through local Social Security offices. Individuals who change their names should apply for a new card showing their new name. Identification must be presented when applying for a duplicate or corrected card. Individuals who are changing their names must present identification with both their old and new names.

CONSUMER CONCERN: HOW SECURE IS THE SOCIAL SECURITY SYSTEM?

Many younger Americans fear that when the time comes for them to retire there will not be adequate funding to finance their Social Security payments. Their concerns grow out of the knowledge that the Social Security system is largely dependent on current tax payments for funds to pay current benefits. With the aging of the American population, there will be fewer active workers for each retiree in the future. Currently there are about 3.3 workers paying Social Security taxes for each beneficiary. By 2030, when today's college students are retiring, there will be only 1.6 to 2.5 (depending on the projection used) workers in covered jobs per beneficiary (Ballantyne, 1986). Can the system continue to function with fewer workers per beneficiary?

Concern over the effects of declining birth rates and longer life expectancies on the long-run status of the system already has led to a series of changes. These include several important amendments to the Social Security Act in 1983 (U.S. Department of Health and Human Services, 1986b). These changes include the following:

- Speeding up planned increases in tax rates so they become effective sooner
- Making a portion of Social Security benefits subject to income tax for some higher income beneficiaries (with the resulting revenues returned to the Social Security trust funds)
- Adding new civilian employees of the federal government to the system along with employees of nonprofit organizations
- Providing for advancing the age of eligibility for full benefits from 65 to 66 by 2009 and to 67 by 2027.
- Increasing the reduction in benefits for those who retire at 62

The status of the system is assessed annually, and 75-year projections of its financial operations are prepared. These projections represent a

OTHER SOCIAL INSURANCE PROGRAMS

While the OASDI program is the best known social insurance program, there are several other programs that are important to the financial security of American workers and their dependents. These programs are designed to protect against financial losses resulting from job-related injuries, temporary disability, and involuntary unemployment.

Workers' Compensation

Workers' compensation provides cash benefits and medical services to workers who are injured in connection with their jobs and provides benefits to their

reasonable range of possible future experiences. Actual income and outgo depend on economic growth, inflation, unemployment, and birth and death rates. While most of those who will receive benefits over the next 75 years have already been born, making their numbers fairly predictable, the number of individuals who will be working is harder to predict because many have not been born yet.

Present projections for the Old Age and Survivors Insurance (OASI) revenues and benefits that fall between those based on more optimistic and pessimistic expectations suggest that the trust fund reserve will increase until 2020 (Ballantyne, 1986). About that time, the reserves in the fund will begin to be drawn down. The reserves built up before 2020 plus interest earnings are expected to come close to meeting the system's obligations until 2060. However, to keep the OASI system adequately funded beyond 2060, future changes designed to increase revenues or reduce payments will be necessary. While the prospect of future changes may seem frightening, the fact is that both benefit and tax provisions have been adjusted repeatedly since the original Social Security Act was passed in 1935. Further adjustments in OASI taxes and benefits will be needed as we approach the year 2020.

QUESTIONS

1. Why is there concern about future funding for Social Security benefits?
2. What steps have been taken to ensure the soundness of the system?
3. What is expected to happen to reserves in the Old Age and Survivors Insurance trust funds between now and the year 2020? After 2020?
4. What steps should be taken to ensure the soundness of the system beyond 2020? When should these steps be undertaken, at once or at some later time?

Illustration 19-2
The federal program of benefits for miners with black lung disease supplements the workers' compensation program.

Ibid

survivors. Currently there are 55 workers' compensation programs covering the 50 states, the District of Columbia, Puerto Rico, and the Virgin Islands; and federal programs for civilian employees and another for longshoremen and harbor workers throughout the country (United States Department of Health and Human Services, 1986b). Another federal program protects coal miners who suffer from pneumoconiosis (or "black lung" disease). These programs cover most but not all American workers.

Before workers' compensation laws were enacted, workers who were injured on the job could receive damages only if they sued their employer and could prove negligence. Workers' compensation established the principle that workers who suffered occupational injuries would be compensated regardless of who was at fault and provided payment with a minimum of delay and legal formalities. At the same time, the laws limited employers' legal liability, making workers' compensation benefits the only remedy for work-related injuries.

Financing. Workers' compensation programs are financed chiefly by employers, but operate in several different ways. Most programs permit employers to carry commercial insurance to insure their liability for injury or to insure themselves if they can establish their financial ability to insure their own risk. A few states require employers to insure with a state insurance fund. Some state laws permit employers to insure with a state fund or to self-insure. In a number of states, employers have a choice between the state fund and commercial insurers. Federal employees are protected by a federally financed and operated system.

Coverage. Only those who suffer injuries that "arise out of and in the course of employment" are entitled to workers' compensation benefits. Employees who are injured as a result of their own intoxication, willful misconduct, or gross negligence are excluded from benefits in most programs. Workers' compensation benefits originally were designed to provide protection for those injured in industrial accidents. Over time, however, coverage has been broadened to include benefits for those suffering from occupational diseases. This coverage does not apply, unfortunately, for diseases that take a long time to develop.

Benefits. The benefits provided include periodic cash payments to injured workers or their survivors, medical services for the period of disablement, and funeral expenses. Most workers' compensation cases involve total disability for a temporary period. Workers are eligible for payments during the healing period. They are regarded as having *temporary total disability* up to the point where no further improvement can be expected from medical treatment.

When the healing period ends, most workers return to work. Some, however, may be classified as having a *permanent total disability*. In these cases, most of the programs make periodic payments for the lifetime of the disabled worker or for the entire period of disability. Some programs, however, have limits on the length of time for which payments will be paid. Payments to workers with temporary or permanent total disability are based on past earnings and commonly are two thirds of weekly earnings up to some maximum amount.

Some injured workers may suffer a *permanent partial disability* that may, or may not, lessen their working ability. These workers receive benefits that are compensation for their injury, resulting suffering, and handicap and for possible reduction in their earning ability. Benefits may be scheduled (i.e., be specific set amounts) for such injuries as the loss of a hand or a leg, or they may be nonscheduled if the injuries involve the head, back, or nervous system.

The death benefits payable to survivors of injured workers are based on the worker's earnings. Payments may be made both to a surviving spouse and to children under specified ages. The majority of programs pay lifetime benefits but some limit the duration or the maximum amount payable. Payments for funeral expenses also are made.

Virtually all medical expenses of injured workers are payable, including first aid, hospital and physicians' services, drugs, artificial limbs, and rehabilitation care. Most programs have provisions requiring the review and approval of expenses by the administering agency.

Disabled workers may be eligible for benefits under both a workers' compensation program and Social Security. In such cases, Social Security benefits may be reduced by an *offset provision* so total benefits under both programs do not exceed 80 percent of the workers' former earnings. Under federal law the offset provision is not applied in cases where state law provides a workers' compensation offset, which reduces benefits because an injured worker is receiving Social Security disability insurance payments.

Temporary Disability Insurance

Workers' compensation provides no protection for wage loss as a result of off-job injuries or maternity leave. Protection against loss of income because of short-term disability is provided by temporary disability insurance programs in five states (Rhode Island, New York, California, New Jersey, and Hawaii), in Puerto Rico, and in the railroad industry (U.S. Department of Health and Human Services, 1986b). These programs cover most workers in private industry. Domestic workers, government employees, and the self-employed are typically not covered. Overall, about one-fourth of the nation's labor force in private industry is covered by the seven programs.

The programs are financed by employee contributions (except in Puerto Rico) and by employer contributions for five of the seven programs. The methods of providing coverage differ among programs. A program may use state-operated funds, a commercial insurer, or an employer's self-insurance plan.

The programs have been designed to provide income replacement for those who are actively working in the labor force. To be eligible for benefits, disabled workers must fulfill the requirements for earnings and employment. They must also meet the disability requirements and be certified by a physician.

Benefits are related to previous earnings in covered employment. In general, these benefits are designed to replace at least half of worker's wage loss for a limited time. In early 1985 the maximum weekly benefit payable ranged from $224 in California to $104 in Puerto Rico. Benefits are payable up to 26 weeks (39 in California).

Unemployment Insurance

Unemployment, like disability, can create serious disruption in the stream of earnings from employment. *Unemployment insurance* has been developed to replace the earnings of those who are willing and able to work when their earning power is interrupted by involuntary unemployment. The first unemployment compensation program was enacted in Wisconsin in 1932. It became the model for provisions included in the Social Security Act of 1935 (U.S. Department of Health and Human Services, 1986b). Unlike the old age and survivor's insurance program, which is operated by the federal government alone, the unemployment insurance program is a joint federal/state program.

Financing. Unemployment insurance programs are operated by all 50 states, the District of Columbia, Puerto Rico, and the Virgin Islands. These programs are financed by state and federal payroll taxes levied on employers.

In general, each state decides the amount and duration of benefits to be paid, who will be covered, and the eligibility rules for benefits. Each state also decides its contribution rates (within limits), collects contributions, and pays benefits. States finance benefits almost entirely through employer contributions. Only three require contributions from employees. In most states, a standard flat tax rate of 5.4 percent is levied on taxable payroll; however, the taxes actually payable may be adjusted downward depending on an employer's record of employment stability. Most programs adjust taxes based on an employer's experience rating. Contribution rates may also be modified according to the current balance in the state's unemployment insurance trust fund.

Employers also must pay a uniform national tax. The federal tax rate was 6.2 percent of the first $7,000 of each worker's covered wages in 1985. Credit is, however, given to employers for contributions to state programs that meet federal standards. Employers in states with an approved state unemployment insurance can use a maximum of 90 percent of their state tax payments to offset their federal tax obligations. Credit is also given based on the experience rating of particular employers.

Coverage. About 97 percent of all wage and salary workers are covered by unemployment insurance. Originally coverage was primarily for industrial and commercial workers in private industry. In the 1970s coverage was expanded; it now includes many farm workers, domestic workers, state and local government employees, and federal civilian employees.

Benefits are available to unemployed workers who have a record of recent work or earnings in covered employment. To be eligible for benefits a worker must be ready, willing, and able to work and must register for work at a state public employment office. Most states also require that a worker make a job-seeking effort independent of the agency's effort in order to qualify for benefits.

Workers who have voluntarily left a job, who have been discharged for misconduct or fraud, who have refused to apply for suitable work, or who are unemployed due to a labor dispute may be entirely or temporarily disqualified from receiving benefits.

Benefits. The amount payable to workers varies with past wages within certain maximum and minimum limits. In most states the benefit formula is designed to pay a worker about 50 percent of the usual weekly wage, subject to specified dollar limits. In 1984, the average weekly benefit paid was $123 (U.S. Department of Health and Human Services, 1986b).

Most states have a waiting period of one week before benefit payments begin and limit the payment of benefits to a maximum of 26 weeks. The payment period may, however, be shorter in a number of states depending on past earnings or total benefits paid.

A federal–state program of extended benefits may supplement regular state benefits. The extension of benefits is triggered by high unemployment in a particular state. Extended benefits continue for at least 13 weeks and are jointly financed from state and federal funds.

EMPLOYEE BENEFITS

Type of Benefits

Studies of the benefits provided workers by their employers have identified hundreds of different kinds of nonwage compensation, ranging from free beer to free child care (Greenlaw & Kohl, 1986). These benefits can be classified into three broad categories:

- *Employee services*—Including social and recreational activities, free legal services, and merchandise discounts
- *Compensation for time not worked*—Including paid vacation time, excused absences (e.g., time for jury duty and funerals of family members), sick pay (paid time off for illness), and other paid nonwork time such as paid lunch and rest periods
- *Employee security and health benefits*—Including health, life, and disability insurance; company-sponsored pension plans; as well as legislatively mandated programs such as Social Security, worker's compensation, and unemployment insurance

A variety of forces have promoted the growth of employee benefit programs. Employee benefits are an allowable business expense for tax purposes along with wages and salaries. For firms subject to relatively high tax rates, the after-tax cost of providing benefits is relatively low. Employers also find that, because of the economics of size, group benefit programs, such as health insurance, can be provided to workers for far less than it would cost workers individually.

Employees, for their part, have welcomed fringe benefits because, unlike an increase in wages, many are untaxed or receive advantageous tax treatment. As a result, nonwage compensation has been an important focus of union and labor contract negotiations in the past four decades. Social and humanitarian concerns and management's concern with employee morale have made management receptive to such demands. Both management and workers have also found that increased nonwage benefits are a way around the government controls on wages that have been imposed several times since the beginning of World War II as a means of controlling inflation.

Only a few kinds of employee benefits are mandated by state and federal law. These benefits are part of the broad Social Security program in this country, which provides not only retirement income, but also disability income, worker's compensation, unemployment insurance benefits, and payments to survivors. These benefits were discussed earlier in this chapter. Most other benefits are set at the discretion of the individual employer. As a result there are significant differences between firms in the benefits offered and in their provisions. (See Table 19-5.)

Because of the differences in the benefits provided in the rules concerning employee contributions, it is important for prospective employees to understand not only what benefits are available but also how they are financed and the key provisions of any programs. (See Figure 19-1.)

Table 19-5
Employees in Medium and Large Firms Receiving Employee Benefits, 1984

Percentage of Employees Receiving Benefit*

	Professional and Administrative Employees	Technical and Clerical Employees	Production Employees
Paid vacations	99	100	98
Paid sick leave	92	92	42
Paid personal leave	29	34	15
Health insurance	98	95	97
Noncontributory	57	48	71
Life insurance	97	95	96
Noncontributory	80	78	83
Pension	83	84	80
Noncontributory	74	78	72
Long-term disability insurance	67	58	30
Noncontributory	47	42	26
Accident–sickness insurance	29	37	70
Noncontributory	20	27	61

*Covers only benefits for which employer pays part or all of premium or cost involved.

Source: U.S. Department of Commerce, Bureau of the Census, *Statistical Abstract of the United States: 1986* (106th ed.). Washington, D.C.: 1985, p. 421.

CONSUMER CONCERN: IS OUR SYSTEM OF EMPLOYEE BENEFITS FAIR?

Employee benefits have grown more rapidly since 1950 than wages and salaries (Hefferan, 1985). While these benefits have increased workers' welfare, they have created several concerns:

- Are employee benefits fairly distributed? Are there age, sex, or occupational groups that are being slighted?
- Many benefits are not subject to income tax, and others receive favored tax treatment. Is this fair and reasonable?
- Is the link of key benefits to employment having an adverse effect on the unemployed, the retired, or those who are changing employers?

The available evidence indicates that fringe benefits are not equally distributed across the working population. Full-time workers are, for example, much more likely to have health insurance coverage and pension benefits than part-time workers (Hefferan, 1985). Workers who work a full year rather than part of a year also are much more likely to have these benefits. This finding suggests that full-time workers are far more likely to have benefits than workers employed part-time or seasonally. As many women and minorities are in part-time or seasonal work, they are inevitably disadvantaged in access to fringe benefits. How can these groups be given benefits based on brief or limited employment without putting an unreasonable burden on their employers?

As more and more of workers' compensation is provided in the form of untaxed benefits, potential sources of tax revenue are reduced. Both income taxes and Social Security taxes are based on wage and salary income. When compensation is shifted into untaxed fringe benefits, the tax base is reduced and tax rates must be higher than they would otherwise be. If benefits are distributed unequally, the result is a shift of the tax burden from those who receive more benefits onto the rest of the population.

The favored tax treatment of fringe benefits appears to have a significant effect on tax revenues. One estimate was that the exclusion of nonwage compensation from taxes cut tax receipts for 1983 by $64 billion. If these benefits had been taxed, tax rates could have been reduced 18 percent without affecting revenues (Munnell, 1984).

The case for taxing benefits may be exaggerated. While some benefits are untaxed, many others are tax-deferred. For many benefits, such as pensions, taxes must still be paid at a later time, though presumably at a lower rate because total income will be lower. In addition, many key benefits are widely distributed. Such costly benefits as health insurance are, for example, generally available to workers at all income levels. However, because of the continuing pressure to increase tax revenues, it seems inevitable that the taxation of nonwage benefits will continue to be discussed.

The current system of benefits has linked many key services (e.g., health insurance) to employment. This link makes unemployment, retirement, or a change of employers a far more serious problem than it would otherwise be. When unemployment rates run at 8 to 10 percent or more (as they have in the 1980s), a significant proportion of the population clearly is going to be affected. A growing number of workers and their families are depending on employer-provided pensions as a major source of retirement income. Their dependence on these pensions makes pension rights and the financial integrity of these funds a more critical issue than ever before.

Another concern about our present system of providing job benefits is the restrictions it imposes on individual choice. Many employers provide a similar package of benefits for all their workers, even though the needs of two-earner households, childless couples, single workers, and workers with families are clearly different. The differences in family obligations among workers make standardized benefit packages obsolete and often unfair. For example, providing the medical insurance coverage for a worker with a family of five is far more costly than covering a single worker. Workers with covered dependents thus are, in effect, being paid more than those with no dependents.

Two-worker households often find that they have overlapping insurance coverage in some areas but gaps in others. A more flexible system would give workers more control over their benefits. One approach has been to offer *cafeteria benefit plans* (or flexible benefit plans) that permit employees some discretion in selecting the benefits they want up to some limit.

Under these cafeteria benefit programs, employers would provide a basic core of benefits, including an insurance coverage, a retirement plan, and time off with pay. Based on their salary, years of service, and other factors, workers would be allocated a certain number of credits that can be used to "buy" additional benefits such as more vacation time, better medical insurance, or day-care privileges. One consequence of cafeteria benefit plans is that the line between wage and nonwage compensation would become blurred, increasing the likelihood that benefits would be taxed. *(Consumer Concern questions on next page)*

QUESTIONS

1. What are the arguments for taxing employee benefits? Against taxing them?
2. What are the arguments for cafeteria employee benefit plans? Are there any arguments against them?

Pension Plans

Social Security can provide a modest income for retiring workers and can be used as one of the bases for retirement income planning. For many workers, an employer or union-sponsored pension plan is another important part of retirement planning. In 1983, 43 percent of the civilian labor force had some coverage in such plans (U.S. Department of Commerce, 1985).

Financing. Most pension plans are *contributory,* i.e., they require contributions from the employee as well as the employer (see Table 19-5). A small proportion are *noncontributory* and are funded solely by the employers.

In years past some companies financed their retirement benefits on a pay-as-you-go basis. Benefits were paid out of current income or general reserves (Russo, 1984). No systematic attempt was made to build a separate reserve to meet pension obligations. As a result, some firms found they were unable to meet their obligations in years when business was poor.

Figure 19-1
Some Questions Employers Should Be Asked About Employee Benefits

What?	What employee benefits are provided to employees?
Who and When?	Are all employees eligible to receive benefits? How soon are they eligible to participate in particular benefits programs?
How Much?	How are the costs of particular programs financed? What employee contributions are required? For health insurance policies, are there significant exclusions, deductibles, or coinsurance requirements?
How Flexible?	Are employees permitted to enter or leave certain programs at later dates? Can terms of participation be changed at later dates? (For example, if a spouse now has health insurance coverage at work, could he or she be added to an employee's policy at a later date?)
How Long?	If an employee leaves, can health and life insurance coverage be continued temporarily? Is an employee paid for unused vacation time upon retiring or resigning? If an employee takes a leave of absence (for example, to return to college full-time to get a Master's degree), is benefit coverage still available?

The more responsible approach has been to create a *funded plan* in which funds are set aside each year as new obligations are incurred. The accumulation of these funds and their growth through investment helps ensure that funds will be available when needed. Not all funded plans have, however, taken full account of obligations incurred before the funding program began. Those funds that are receiving adequate contributions to meet obligations as they currently are being incurred and have adequate funds to meet obligations incurred in the past are said to be *fully funded*.

Full funding is now required by federal law. This requirement was imposed by the Employee Retirement Income Security Act of 1974 (ERISA). While employers are not required by law to have pension plans, the law requires pension plans that promise specifically defined future benefits to become fully funded. Under ERISA, existing plans were allowed a period of years to become fully funded.

The ERISA legislation also defined the fiduciary responsibilities of fund managers. That is, their obligation is to act as responsible trustees for the funds under their control and management.

Coverage. Under ERISA rules employees become eligible to participate in a pension program relatively quickly. They must be allowed to participate after one year of service or upon reaching age 21 (Greenlaw & Kohl, 1986).

Under most plans, if employees leave before a specified number of years they lose all their retirement benefits. Employee contributions are, however, returned. After a certain number of years employee pension rights become vested and are not lost even if employees leave their jobs. *Vesting* is the nonforfeitable interest of participants in their accrued benefits or retirement account balances.

Some plans provide for full and immediate vesting. They allow participants full claim on their pension benefits as soon as they begin participation. Most plans base vesting on years of service. Prior to the passage of ERISA there was no requirement that pension benefits be vested. Employees with many years of service who had anticipated pensions found themselves without benefits when they changed jobs or lost their jobs because of changing economic conditions. To correct these injustices, ERISA required the use of one of three minimum vesting options:

- 10-year vesting. Under this option, there is no vesting before 10 years, but full (100 percent) vesting afterward.
- 5- to 15-year vesting. Under this option, there is 25 percent vesting after 5 years, increasing to 100 percent after 15 years.
- Rule of 45. This option provides for 50 percent vesting at 10 years of service or when the participant's age and years of service (with a minimum

of 5 years service) equals 45, whichever is earlier; this is upgraded to 100 percent vesting 5 years later.

Another variant is widely used. It is acceptable to the federal authorities because it is more liberal than the 5- to 15-years option or the Rule of 45 (Russo, 1984). The requirements of this plan are as follows:

- 4-40 plan. This plan provides 40 percent vesting after four years, increasing 5 percent each year to reach 100 percent after 11 years.

Under this plan, someone whose full pension rights would be $200 a month would have a nonforfeitable right to $80 a month after four years.

Benefits. Pension plans are based on one of two different approaches. *Defined benefit plans* pay benefits on the basis on some defined formula. At any given time an employee can tell exactly what the pension would be if he or she were to retire. The other general category of plans is *defined contribution plans*. For these plans an employer pays in some specified amount each year. For example, an employer may promise to pay in 5 percent of an employee's annual salary to the retirement account. No fixed level of benefits is established, however. Instead, the funds paid in are invested and their growth depends on the investment success of the fund manager.

Defined benefit plans provide some unit of benefit for each year of service. Benefits frequently are calculated with a formula. A formula might, for example, provide the following:

Average annual salary for five highest years		Pension multiplier		Years of service		Annual retirement benefit
$42,000	×	.015 (or 1½%)	×	36 Years	=	$22,680

A variety of ways of determining the salary base are used. Some plans use the average salary over the entire period of service. Some use an average of highest paid years (e.g., highest three years or highest five years). With inflation it is usually advantageous to have benefits based on the most recent or highest paid service rather than the average salary for the entire period of service.

Benefits sometimes are integrated with Social Security benefits. In such cases, the benefits payable may be reduced by the amount of Social Security benefits received. Benefits may also be reduced depending on the retirement pay-out option selected. The basic method of payment usually provides for lifetime payments to the participant with some guaranteed minimum number of payments to the participant or a designated beneficiary (Russo, 1984). Other payment options also are usually available.

- Life annuity. Payments are made to the participant for his or her lifetime. Upon death, no further payments are made to anyone.
- Joint and survivor option. Payments are made to both the participant and beneficiary while both are living. Upon the death of either the participant or beneficiary, a reduced amount is paid to the survivor for as long as that person lives. Payments end at the survivor's death.
- Lump-sum option. A cash payment equal to the present value of the payouts expected under the basic method is made to the participant.

The benefits provided by the defined benefit plans of larger employers are insured by the Pension Benefit Guarantee Corporation (PBGC). The PBGC was created by ERISA in 1974 as a self-financing government corporation (Jones, 1984). It insures the benefits of about one-third of the nation's workers and an increasing number of retirees (Kilborn, 1986). Coverage is financed by a per-worker premium levied on employers with participating defined benefit plans.

The PBGC insurance premium has been raised several times as increasing demands have been put on the PBGC. In early 1986 the annual premium was raised from $2.60 to $8.50. The termination of the pension funds of several large employers, including two major steel producers, has strained the PBGC's resources. It was clear by late 1986 that the new premium would be inadequate to meet the demands on PBGC's funds. The legislation creating the PBGC provided for protection of workers and retirees in single-employer and multi-employer plans (typically these are union-sponsored plans) through two separate funds. PBGC coverage does not provide for protection of all pension benefits. Payments are guaranteed only to some monthly maximum.

In addition to regular pension programs, several other programs have been developed that allow workers to put a portion of their earnings into special tax-deferred accounts to build savings for retirement. These earnings become taxable only on withdrawal. These programs will be discussed in Chapter 20, on taxes.

MAJOR CHAPTER CONCEPTS

1. The Social Security program provides retirement benefits to covered workers, benefits to their survivors, and disability benefits to covered workers.
2. Social Security benefits are financed with taxes on workers and their employers and on self-employed individuals.
3. Social Security taxes are levied on a worker's annual earnings to some maximum amount. These earnings in covered employment are recorded in their earnings account.

4. To be eligible for benefits a worker must have certain amount of work credit, which is measured in quarters of coverage.
5. The size of retirement benefits is affected by both a worker's past earnings and retirement age.
6. Retirement benefits may be reduced for individuals who return to work and are under age 70.
7. Worker's compensation provides cash benefits and medical services to workers injured in connection with their jobs and provides benefits to their survivors.
8. Temporary disability insurance available to workers in five states covers loss of income due to temporary disability whether on the job or off.
9. Unemployment insurance replaces the earnings of those who are willing and able to work but whose earnings are interrupted by involuntary unemployment.
10. Employee benefits fall into three broad categories: employee services, compensation for time not worked, and employee security and health benefits.
11. Pension programs may be contributory or noncontributory. Under ERISA, the defined benefit retirement plans of larger employers must move toward full funding.
12. Upon vesting, workers have nonforfeitable pension rights.
13. Defined benefit plans promise future benefits based on a defined formula that typically includes a salary base, a pension multiplier, and years of service. Defined contribution plans require the employer to contribute some specified amount each year; this amount is invested and may grow at varying rates.
14. The Pension Benefit Guarantee Corporation, a self-financing government corporation, guarantees the pensions of about one-third of the nation's workers and retirees.

CONSUMER QUESTIONS

1. If your were to begin a job next week, what employee benefits would be most important to you? Which benefits would be relatively unimportant? Explain the reasons for your answer.
2. In what year will you be 62? To be eligible to receive Social Security retirement benefits, what provisions (based on current laws) will you have to meet concerning years of work credit? Retirement age for full benefits?
3. Prepare a report on changes over the past 10 years in the Social Security system's Old Age, Survivors, and Disability Insurance program. What were the reasons for the changes made?

4. Are you or any adult members of your family participating in a pension program? What are the rules for vesting? How are benefits determined? If the plan is contributory, what contributions are required?
5. Do you have a Social Security account? If so, what work credit have you accumulated? If you are not sure, check. If not, apply for an account and discuss the application procedure.

SUGGESTED READINGS

1. Boskin, Michael J. *Too Many Promises: The Uncertain Future of Social Security.* Homewood, IL: Dow-Jones-Irwin, 1986. Boskin, a Stanford economist, argues for reforming Social Security to make it fairer, more efficient, and financially sound. He suggests raising the retirement age and linking benefits more exactly to taxes paid while providing a supplement for the low-income elderly.

2. Kosterlitz, Julie, "Getting Out Early." *National Journal 18,* no. 4 (October 4, 1986): 2374-2378. American workers are retiring earlier, but the trend is not without problems. It creates financial pressures on the rest of society and reduces the pool of available labor.

3. Levering, Robert, Milton Moskowitz, and Michael Katz, *The 100 Best Companies to Work for in America.* Reading, MA: Addison-Wesley, 1984. Plunkett, Jack W. *The Almanac of American Employers: A Guide to America's 500 Most Successful Large Corporations.* Chicago: Contemporary Books, 1985. These two volumes rate corporate employers on a number of evaluative criteria including pay, benefits, job security, opportunities to move up, and ambience.

CHAPTER 20

TAXES

Although people seldom think of them this way, taxes are a payment for reducing risk. "Taxes are," Supreme Court Justice Oliver Wendell Holmes, Jr., observed, "what we pay for civilized society." With their tax payments, citizens support government efforts to protect them from physical harm, ensure their financial security, and promote the stability and growth of the economy. Individual citizens are not allowed, however, to decide on their own whether or not they wish to pay taxes. Instead, *taxes* are compulsory charges levied by government to support its programs.

Taxes may be used for a variety of purposes (Watters, 1984):

- Providing revenue for government operations. Revenue generation is the major purpose of taxation.
- Promoting economic stability. Stabilization programs can use tax cuts when extra spending power is needed to stimulate the economy and can raise taxes when it appears desirable to slow down economic activity.
- Encouraging economic growth and development. Such encouragement can be provided by allowing new industry lower property taxes or other tax breaks.

- Redistributing income to the poor. The government, in effect, shifts resources to lower income people and provides them substantial benefits by holding down their taxes.
- Facilitating social goals. Socially desirable goals can be encouraged by favorable tax treatment. For example, home ownership is encouraged by allowing mortgage interest and property taxes to be deducted in calculating income taxes. Taxes can also be used to discourage behavior that is considered harmful. Taxes on cigarettes and alcoholic beverages raise prices and discourage consumption.

EVALUATING TAX SYSTEMS

Taxes were collected even before money existed. In ancient times taxes were paid in kind; taxpayers paid with the resources they had—their labor and a portion of their crops. Tax systems have always been a focus of controversy. In 1776, as war loomed over the issue of taxing the colonies, British economist Adam Smith set down what he felt were the characteristics of a fair tax system. He suggested that a fair system should fall equitably on those taxed, be certain as to amount and time of payment, be convenient to pay, and be economical to administer. These principles are the basis for the evaluative criteria that have been suggested for judging contemporary tax systems (Watters, 1984).

Fairness and Equity

A tax system should be based on the *principle of neutrality* and should not favor one group over another. In fact, however, this principle is often violated. Home owners, for example, are given different tax treatment from renters because they are allowed to deduct real estate taxes and mortgage interest from their taxable income.

In discussing equity, two different types of equity can be identified. One important characteristic of an equitable tax system is *horizontal equity*, the treatment of equals in the same way. With horizontal equity those with the same income and similar circumstances would pay the same taxes. The implementation of horizontal equity is complex because not all people are in similar circumstances. Family sizes differ, and the burden of medical expenses may differ. Another aspect of equity is *vertical equity*, fairness to those with differing ability to pay. Vertical equity provides a rationale for taxing those with higher incomes at a higher rate than those with lower incomes. While there is general agreement that it is fair to base taxes on the ability to pay, there is less agreement on exactly what constitutes vertical equity. Just exactly how much more is it fair to compel the rich to pay?

Ease of Calculation

A tax should be easily understood and calculated. The taxpayer should be able to determine the amount due easily.

Convenience of Payment	A tax is easier to pay if it is collected in small amounts. Sales taxes would be burdensome if we had to pay the tax on our purchases in a lump sum at the end of each year. Paying small amounts with purchases is far less burdensome. To make income taxes easier to pay, the federal government requires *withholding* of tax payments from salaries and wages by employers. Withholding taxes are remitted to the Treasury by the employer and credited against the taxes due from the employee.

The pay-as-you-go method of paying taxes is less burdensome than a single large annual payment. Some people, however, argue that it is undesirable to make it easy to pay taxes because people become less aware of how much they are paying and less concerned about how their money is used. |
| Ease of Administration | A good tax system requires a minimum of administrative expenses for collecting taxes. The collection machinery should be efficient and require a minimum number of people. |
| Minimal Economic Distortion | A tax system should affect economic activities as little as possible. Taxes can have the effect of raising prices and reducing consuption and of discouraging certain kinds of business activity. Because of these possible effects, taxes may distort business activity in undesirable ways. Sometimes, however, taxes are used to encourage certain kinds of social behavior or economic activity, as was noted earlier. |
| CLASSIFICATIONS OF TAXES | Over the years, several classifications have evolved for describing taxes. One of the oldest classifications focuses on the *incidence* of taxes, i.e., on who actually pays them in the end (Watters, 1984). *Direct taxes* are those that cannot be shifted to others. Familiar examples include personal income taxes and property taxes on owner-occupied homes. *Indirect taxes* are those that can be shifted to others. One example is the federal excise tax on tobacco products. These taxes are levied on manufacturers but are passed on to consumers as part of the price of the product. When a tax is levied on business, it is not always clear on whom it ultimately falls. For example, if there is a tax on employee payrolls, such as the employer's share of Social Security, an employer may hire fewer workers or pay those hired somewhat less. A portion of the tax may also come out of profits, and part may be passed on to consumers.

Another classification focuses on the issue of equity and ability to pay. A *progressive tax* is one that taxes those who are well off at a higher rate than those who are less well off. The federal income tax is usually regarded as progressive because increments to income are taxed at an increasing rate. A *regressive tax* is one which performs in the opposite way and takes proportionally more from those who are less well-off. Because lower-income people |

spend a larger percentage of their income on food than the wealthy, a tax on food would be regarded as regressive. For this reason most state sales taxes exempt food or at least food for home consumption. A *proportional tax* is neither progressive nor regressive. One example is an income tax that applies the same tax rate to all levels of income. Some state and city income taxes use a single tax rate. Proposals for a flat-rate federal income tax incorporate the same feature.

Taxes also may be classified according to how they are calculated. An *ad valorem tax* is based on the value of the taxed item. A state sales tax of 6 percent is an ad valorem tax because it is based on the price of the item taxed. Property taxes that are a percentage of the assessed value of the property also are ad valorem taxes. In contrast, a *specific tax* is a given amount per unit. For example, the state highway tax of 10 cents per gallon on gasoline is a specific tax.

Taxes also can be classified by the base on which they are levied. *Income taxes* are taxes against income, including wages and salaries, interest earned, and business profits. *Consumption taxes* are paid for the purchase and use of particular goods and services. Sales taxes are the most familiar example of a consumption tax. Others include local amusement taxes levied on movie and show tickets, and local guest taxes added to hotel room bills. *Wealth taxes* are levied on the basis of property, which may include real property such as a home, an office building, or a factory. Taxes also are sometimes levied on intangible property such as stocks and bonds owned. Income, consumption, and wealth taxes are based on the ability to pay, but each measures this ability in a different way.

Taxes may also be based on benefits received or the use of a service provided. Taxes on gasoline and diesel fuel used to fund highway construction and maintenance link taxation fairly directly to use. The use of hunting and fishing license fees for wildlife protection programs makes those who benefit from these government programs bear part of their cost.

In general, the public seems to feel it is fairer to focus additional taxes on consumption through the use of sales taxes rather than focusing on income (Advisory Commission on Intergovernmental Relations, 1986). The federal income tax, in particular, finds little favor. (See Table 20-1.)

CALCULATING INCOME TAXES

The first United States federal income tax law was passed in 1862 to raise revenue for fighting the Civil War. According to the first commercially published taxpayer's advice book, the procedures for determining tax obligations under the law were relatively simple:

> A party is permitted to swear as to the amount of his income liable to assessment, and the amount thus sworn to is received as the sum on which duties are to be assessed and collected...[or, he] may be permitted to declare under oath

Table 20-1
Public Opinions on
Taxes and Government
Services

Which do you think is the worst tax, the least fair?	
Federal income tax	37%
State income tax	8%
State sales tax	17%
Local property tax	28%
Don't know	10%

Source: Advisory Commission on Intergovernmental Relations, *1986 Changing Public Attitudes on Governments and Taxes*. (Washington, D.C.: U.S. Government Printing Office, 1986): p. 1.

CONSUMER CONCERN: SHOULD WE TAX CONSUMPTION MORE HEAVILY?

Over the past decade, a number of critics of our present tax system have argued for more taxes on consumption to replace existing taxes and to provide the tax revenues needed to reduce federal budget deficits. Spending, they suggest, is clear evidence of ability to pay and can be a fair basis for taxation. They also point out that our present tax system encourages spending at the expense of saving. This argument lost some of its force when the 1986 tax law ended the deduction of sales taxes and began to phase out the deduction for consumer interest costs. Another advantage of taxing consumption, it is argued, is that these taxes are more difficult to evade than income taxes. The growth of tax evasion and the so-called "underground economy" have made enforcement a more critical issue than before.

Various roles have been proposed for consumption taxes. Some proponents would like to see them replace a portion of the federal income tax or supplement Social Security taxes. Others argue they are needed to reduce federal budget deficits.

Different types of consumption taxes have been proposed. One proposal puts forward a national sales tax that would operate in much the same way as state sales taxes. Others have suggested a value-added tax. These taxes are widely used and successful in Western Europe and could work well here too, their backers claim. A value-added tax (VAT) levies tax at each level of production on the value added at the stage. A wholesaler who pays $100,000 for a shipment of clothing and sells it for $130,000 would pay tax on the $30,000 gain in value (Lekachman, 1980). The VAT becomes embedded in the price of a good or service as it is produced. The tax thus differs from a sales tax, which is levied only on the final sales price.

Under the European system, VATs are self-administered and enforced by business people who pay tax on their total sales but get credits for taxes paid at earlier stages. While VATs raise prices for domestic con-

or affirmation, that he is not possessed of an income of $600 liable to assessment. ... He is then exempt. (Axelrod, 1984, p. 318)

Despite the simplicity of the system, the Internal Revenue Service (IRS), which was also created in 1862, was still there to verify the individual's tax liability.

Calculating today's federal income tax is a far more complex process. The amount subject to tax is adjusted downward at several stages to take account of ability to pay. These adjustments take account of such factors

sumers, they can be rebated on exports to minimize their impact on foreign trade. Imports have a VAT added to prevent them from gaining an unfair advantage (U.S. News and World Report, 1979).

A number of arguments have been offered against national sales taxes and a VAT. One is that both types of tax raise prices and boost inflation. They are, it is argued, unfair to poor people, who must spend a high percentage of their income and can save little. It is, of course, possible to exempt food, medicine, and other necessities—or grant the poor extra credits on their income tax. Another criticism is that a national sales tax or a VAT would cut into a tax area that until now has been reserved mostly for state and local government.

A third type of consumption tax has also been proposed, a spending tax. Taxpayers would add up their annual income and any withdrawals from saving and subtract any additions to saving. The result, their total spending, would be taxable. While such a tax would not affect prices as would a national sales tax or VAT, it would put lower-income taxpayers, who spend most of their incomes, at a disadvantage.

Some of the criticisms focused on consumption taxes reflect concerns over any new tax. Fear is expressed that new revenues will simply facilitate more government spending. Opponents also suggest that the inconspicuousness of a new sales tax or VAT would make it of less concern to taxpayers than it should be.

While a consumption tax has its good points and its bad ones, some form of consumption tax is expected to come eventually. Its backers feel that once it is explained to the public, its advantages will become clear.

QUESTIONS

1. How do the three types of consumption-based taxes rate on the evaluative criteria for taxes?
2. Which advantages and criticisms of a consumption-based tax are most significant to you? Why?

as household size and the special needs of the aged and blind. Adjustments also are made to encourage certain social goals. Gifts to charity may, for example, be deducted from the income subject to tax. Home ownership is facilitated by permitting deduction of mortgage interest and property taxes. Expenses for improving one's job performance through membership in professional organizations and enrollment in job-related education courses also are encouraged through special tax treatment.

The federal income tax system is still based on self-assessment, as it was in 1862. Individual tax payers, by themselves or with professional help, calculate their tax obligations and remit the tax due. This system of self-assessment and voluntary compliance is backed up by IRS monitoring. It can be contrasted with other tax systems, such as local property taxes that are based on an assessment by a government-paid assessor and are calculated at the tax office and then billed to the property owner.

Since the present income tax system was instituted in 1913, it has grown increasingly complex. Special features have been written into the law to encourage business and personal investment, to shift income to the poor, and to serve various other economic and social goals. At the same time, more and more *tax loopholes,* special tax advantages for particular groups, have been added to the law. As these changes occurred, the public increasingly came to believe that the tax system benefitted the rich and was unfair to the ordinary tax payer (Price Waterhouse, 1986). There was also increasing concern among the general public and government officials that large amounts of income were being illegally concealed and were escaping taxation. Studies suggested that the underground economy, business activities

Illustration 20-1
A knowledge of tax regulations, accurate records, and careful calculations are all essential in preparing a tax return.

being conducted so as to avoid official notice and taxation, was increasing in size.

Concerns with the existing tax laws found expression in the Tax Reform Act of 1986. It somewhat reduced the complexity of calculating taxes and attempted to increase horizontal equity by eliminating some tax loopholes. The dividend exclusion, which permitted a reduction in the amount of dividends subject to tax, was eliminated. The deduction of interest paid on consumer credit was also phased out. The new law also reduced the use of tax incentives for social purposes. These special treatments were, in effect, *tax subsidies.* Tax rules on the deferral of taxes on income set aside for retirement were tightened; such deferrals were retained for lower income tax payers but reduced for those with high incomes.

Determining Total Income

Individuals receive money from a variety of sources: wages and salaries, interest payments, Social Security, gifts, and reimbursements from insurers for damage to cars or property. Not all these items are subject to tax, however. In general, receipts that are the results of personal efforts or business and investment activity are taxed, while those that are not the result of personal efforts (e.g., gifts, insurance proceeds, and welfare benefits) are not taxable.

Some people have the mistaken belief that if no cash changes hands in a transaction, the transaction is not subject to tax. This is not correct. Many individuals barter services in the mistaken belief that the benefits they receive are not taxable. The exchange of an attorney's services in handling a lawsuit for a painter's services in repainting a house are taxable income for both in the eyes of the IRS, even though no money changed hands. People may also receive taxable fringe benefits from their employers. Even though the employee receives no cash, such benefits as unusual amounts of group life insurance coverage and personal use of a company car are taxable benefits.

Items Subject to Tax. A wide variety of items are subject to taxation and are included in *gross income:*

- Payment for personal services
  - Wages and salaries
  - Tips and commissions
  - Awards and bonuses
- Withholding
  - Amounts withheld from pay for federal or local income taxes, Social Security taxes, savings bonds purchases, etc.
- Certain fringe benefits
  - Group life insurance coverage above specified limit
  - Personal use of company car

- Retirement and disability income
  - Employee pensions (the portion over and above the employee's contribution)
  - Disability retirement income
  - Disability pensions (if disability insurance cost was paid by employer)
- Interest income
  - Savings accounts
  - Certificates of deposit
  - U.S. Savings Bonds
  - Corporate bonds
- Dividends and other corporate distributions
  - Dividends on capital stock
  - Capital gains distributions paid by mutual funds
- Alimony received
- Taxable refunds of state and local income taxes
- Rental income (less expenses)
- Social Security income
  - Benefit payments (if income exceeds specified limits)
- Unemployment compensation
- Miscellaneous income
  - Cancelled debts
  - Gambling winnings. (Losses may be deducted, up to amount of winings, if deductions are itemized.)
  - Prizes in contests, lotteries, etc.
  - Property or services received as barter for goods or services provided
  - Income from business partnerships
  - Royalties from books; patents; oil, gas, and mineral properties
- Gains on sales or exchange of property. (Under the Tax Reform Act of 1986, any capital gains are taxed at the same rates as other types of income. Under previous law, gains on assets held over six months were taxed at a lower rate.)
- Gains on sale of real estate. Gain, or loss, equals original cost plus allowable expenses such as improvements and sales commission less sales price.
- Gains from sales of stocks, bonds, and other securities.
- Losses on sales or exchanges may be deducted up to a maximum of $3,000.

For individuals who are married and live in a community property state, half of any income described by state law as community income is considered to be part of gross income.

Items Not Subject to Tax. While the list of items subject to tax is a long one, there are certain items that are not subject to tax. These nontaxable items include the following:

- Accident and health insurance proceeds
- Casualty insurance proceeds (e.g., reimbursement for auto crash repair costs)
- Child support payments received
- Gifts and inheritances
- Interest on state or local obligations (bonds, notes, etc.)
- Life insurance proceeds
- Scholarship and fellowship grants. The portion required to pay tuition and course-related expenses is nontaxable; the portion above this amount is taxable under Tax Reform Act of 1986.
- Social Security benefits (if total income is below specified level)
- Welfare benefits
- Worker's compensation

Determining Adjusted Gross Income

When the total income subject to tax has been determined, taxpayers are permitted to make adjustments to this figure for certain types of expenses involved in producing income. They are, for example, allowed to deduct expenses of moving to a new job or a new job location. The deductible moving expenses include the cost of shipping household goods, travel, and temporary living arrangements. Business travel and entertainment expenses are also deductible at this stage, subject to some restriction. Under the Tax Reform Act of 1986, other business expenses such as professional dues and subscriptions must be included among miscellaneous itemized deductions at a later stage in the tax calculation process.

Contributions to *Individual Retirement Accounts* (IRAs) are also deducted at this stage. IRAs are retirement saving plans financed by contributions to a separate investment account. Under the Tax Reform Act of 1986, working tax payers with adjusted gross incomes of less than $25,000 a year ($40,000 for couples filing jointly) are permitted to deduct their full IRA contribution up to a maximum of $2,000 per tax payer. Working tax payers who are not covered by an employer-provided retirement plan also are permitted to deduct their full contributions. Working tax payers with incomes between $25,000 and $35,000 (or couples filing jointly with incomes between $40,000 and $50,000 a year) who are covered by another retirement plan are allowed a partial deduction. Those with higher incomes who participate in an employer-provided retirement plan are not allowed any deduction but are permitted to make a nondeductible contribution. Earnings in an IRA are not taxed until withdrawn. IRA contributions that were not taxed at the time they were contributed are taxed at the time they are withdrawn.

Alimony paid to a former spouse is deductible at this stage. As noted earlier, alimony income is subject to tax for the individual who receives it. After deducting moving expenses, business travel and entertainment expenses, eligible IRA contributions, and alimony from total income, the resulting amount is *adjusted gross income.*

Determining Taxable Income

Individual taxpayers have certain personal expenses that affect their ability to pay. These expenses are taken into account in calculating *taxable income.*

Deductions. Taxpayers are permitted to take a *standard deduction* that varies with household type to take account of the expenses typical households face. The size of the standard deduction allowed varies with the *filing status* of the taxpayer. Five filing status categories are identified:

- Married and filing a joint return
- Surviving spouse of a recently deceased individual
- Head of a household with a dependent child or other eligible dependents
- Single
- Married couple filing separate returns

Married couples filing jointly are allowed the largest standard deduction. For 1988, it is $5,000; starting in 1989, this amount will be adjusted upward for inflation (Price Waterhouse, 1986). Single individuals are allowed slightly more than half this amount. Married couples who file separate tax returns are allowed half the standard deduction for couples who file jointly. Elderly people age 65 or over and blind people are allowed extra amounts for standard deductions.

The inflation adjustment in the standard deduction starting in 1989 will help to reduce the problem of *bracket creep.* This problem arises as inflation increases incomes, pushing taxpayers into higher tax brackets without any increase in their real incomes or in their ability to pay. Adjusting the standard deduction upward with inflation will help keep the amount of real income taxed constant from year to year.

Some taxpayers may have tax deductible expenses that exceed the standard deduction. In such cases, the taxpayer is allowed to *itemize deductions,* listing them by categories, and to deduct them from adjusted gross income instead of taking the standard deduction. The following expenses may be included as itemized deductions:

- Interest on mortgages for first and second homes.
- Interest on consumer debts. (This deduction is phased out starting in 1987 and ends with the 1990 tax year.)
- Interest on investment debts — Such as purchase of stocks on margin. Rules were tightened by the Tax Reform Act of 1986. After 1990, investment interest expense is deductible only to the extent it exceeds investment income.
- Charitable gifts — Gifts of cash or noncash contributions to qualified organizations. Gifts are deductible up to a limit of 20 percent of adjusted gross income.
- Miscellaneous itemized deductions — Including subscriptions to investment publications, job-hunting expenses, unreimbursed business expenses, work-related educational expenses, and work uniforms. The deduction is limited to the amount in excess of 2 percent of adjusted gross income.
- Casualty losses from fire, accident, theft. Only losses not covered by insurance are deductible. Losses are deductible only when total amount lost in any year (reduced by $100 per casualty incident) exceeds 10 percent of adjusted gross income.
- State and local taxes — Including state and local income and property taxes. Although previously deductible, sales taxes are not deductible under the Tax Reform Act of 1986.
- Medical expenses — Such as dental expenses, physician's fees, hospital fees, and prescription drugs. Only that portion of total expenses that exceeds 7.5 percent of adjusted gross income is deductible.

Exemptions. To take account of differences in family size and their effect on ability to pay, an amount set by Congress may be deducted from adjusted gross income for the tax payer(s) and each dependent. The size of this *exemption* for each family member was adjusted upward for the 1987 to 1989 tax years and will be adjusted for inflation from 1990 on. Prior to 1987, extra exemptions were allowed for the elderly and blind. Under the Tax Reform Act of 1986, these extra exemptions were repealed and the elderly and blind were given larger standard deductions.

The issue of who is or is not a dependent for tax purposes is a complex one. To be claimed as a dependent for an exemption, an individual must meet all five of the following requirements:

- Must be either a relative of the tax payer or a full-time member of the household
- Must be a U.S. citizen or a resident of U.S. or a resident of Canada or Mexico

- Must receive more than one-half of support from the tax payer
- Must have an income that does not exceed the personal exemption amount unless he or she is the tax payer's child and is under age 19 or is a full-time student
- Must not file a joint return with another person (Bernstein, 1986)

The way in which these rules work can be seen in the case of a 20-year-old full-time college student who earns $4,000 in a tax year and is provided $4,500 for support by his parents. In this case the child receives more than half his support from his parents and can be claimed by them as a dependent. However, if the child also files a tax return, he cannot claim a personal exemption.

The subtraction of the standard deduction (or itemized deductions) and exemptions from adjusted gross income produces *taxable income,* the amount of income on which tax liability is calculated.

Determining Tax Liability

The federal income tax has, in the past, had highly progressive rates. Prior to the Tax Reform Act of 1986, there were 15 *tax brackets* with progressively higher rates for successive increments to income. The top bracket was 50 percent. At this level, 50 cents of each additional dollar was taken for federal income tax. The high *marginal rates* on successive increments to income were of concern because they were felt to penalize financial initiative and to encourage tax shelters and tax avoidance schemes that had limited benefit

Table 20-2
Tax Brackets for 1988 and Beyond

Single Individuals	
Taxable Income	
Up to $17,850	15%
$17,850 to $43,150	28%
$43,150 to $89,560*	28% +5% surtax
Above $89,560	28%**
Married Couples Filing Jointly	
Taxable Income	
Up to $29,750	15%
$29,750 to $71,900	28%
$71,900 to $149,250*	28% + 5% surtax
Above $149,250	28%**

* The income range subject to surtax will be adjusted for inflation after 1988.

** Income in this bracket is subject to the 5% surcharge until the benefit of personal exemptions is exhausted.

Sources: "Playing to Win by the New Tax Rules," *U.S. News and World Report 101,* no. 9 (September 1, 1986): 49; Price Waterhouse, *The Price Waterhouse Guide to the New Tax Law* (New York: Bantam Books, 1986): 6-8.

to the economy beyond their tax advantage. A further concern was that high marginal tax rates encouraged tax evasion, illegal concealment of business activity and the resulting income.

The Tax Reform Act of 1986 both reduced the number of tax brackets and lowered marginal tax rates. The 1986 law provided for two tax rates, 15 and 28 percent. It also instituted a *surtax* or extra tax. The result was that four tax brackets were created. (See Table 20-2.) The initial portion of income is taxed at 15 percent. The second increment is taxed at 28 percent. The third bracket is taxed at 28 percent but is subject to a 5 percent surtax. Tax payers in the top bracket pay at a 28 percent marginal rate. Because of the effect of the surtax in the third bracket, tax payers who have a portion of their income in the top bracket have an overall *average tax rate* of 28 percent. In effect, they are subject to a flat-rate tax of 28 percent.

For example, for a single person with a taxable income of $50,000, the calculation is as follows:

		Tax due
Up to $17,850	15%	$2,677.50
$17,850 to $43,150	28%	$7.084.00
$43,150 to $50,000	28% + 5%	$2,260.50
	Total tax due	$12,022.00

$$\text{Average tax rate} = \frac{\text{Total tax due}}{\text{Taxable income}} = .24 \text{ or } 24 \text{ percent}$$

Determining Tax Owed

Even after a tax payer's tax liability is determined, there are further calculations required because there are offsets that can be used to reduce tax liability. These *tax credits* may be subtracted directly from the tax liability calculated.

Tax credit is allowed for the following items:

- Child and dependent care credit — Including babysitting expenses while working or looking for work. If care arrangements are necessary to permit working, expenses for care of children under 15 or other disabled dependents may be used as a credit to specified limits.
- Credit for the elderly and the permanently and totally disabled. This credit is available for lower-income people over age 65 and lower-income people under 65 who are totally and permanently disabled.
- Earned income credit. This credit is designed to reduce taxes on earnings of low-income taxpayers who care for a dependent child in their household. It is also available as cash payment to those who pay no income tax at all.

When the applicable tax credits have been subtracted from the tax liability, the result is the tax owed for the year.

Determining the Payment Due

By the time they calculate the taxes they owe for the previous tax year, most people will already have paid the government a substantial portion of the amount owed. These payments are of two types. One is the taxes withheld from wage and salary income by employers on the basis of expected tax liability. The amount withheld is calculated using the *W-4 form* filed by the employee, detailing information that affects tax liability.

At the end of the calendar year, the employee is obligated to give the employee a *W-2 form* that reports taxable earnings and the amount of tax withheld and forwarded to the Treasury Department. A copy of the W-2 form is included with a completed income tax return to indicate the portion of tax owed that has already been paid.

Self-employed people not subject to withholding and others with substantial amounts of income not subject to withholding (e.g., investment income) are required to make *estimated tax payments*. Payments are made quarterly and under the 1986 Tax Reform Act should equal 90 percent of the tax owed for the current year or 100 percent of the tax owed for the previous year. Taxpayers whose payments fall below those amounts are subject to penalty.

The payment due with a completed tax return is determined by subtracting federal income tax withheld and estimated tax payments from the tax owed for the year. The resulting figure is the payment due with the return. If the total of withholding and estimated tax payments exceeds the tax due, the taxpayer is entitled to a refund. Refunds may either be taken in cash or applied to the following year's estimated taxes.

PREPARING TAX RETURNS

The previous section has outlined the general principles behind the calculation of income taxes. Individual tax payers are, however, faced with concrete problems of deciding whether or not it is necessary to file returns, determining how to prepare their returns, and finding assistance if they feel it is necessary.

Who Must File a Return?

Citizens of the U.S. and Puerto Rico and resident aliens must file a federal income tax return if their income is over some specified minimum amount. This minimum differs with marital status, filing status, and age. It changes from year to year as the amount allowed for exemptions and for the standard deduction are adjusted for inflation. Parents with dependent children with incomes below this amount should file, in many cases, to receive the benefits of the earned income credit. Low-income parents may be eligible to receive a cash payment from the federal government even though they are liable for no taxes.

Self-employed individuals, even those with relatively low net earnings, must file a return. Individuals with low earnings are required to pay self-employment Social Security taxes even though they have no income tax liability.

People also should file if they had tax withheld from wages or salaries but did not have enough income to be required to file a return. These people should file and request a refund.

Selecting a Tax Form

The IRS provides three different tax forms for use in preparing a return. They vary in complexity. The use of the simpler forms is, however, restricted (U.S. Department of the Treasury, 1986).

1040EZ form. The use of this form is restricted to single people with no dependents. Income must be only from wages, salaries, and tips; interest earnings must be under $400. Taxable income must be under $50,000. Because of the simplicity of the 1040EZ form it does not provide for itemizing deductions or for claiming tax credits.

1040A Form. This form may be used only if income is solely from wages, salaries, tips, interest and dividends, and unemployment compensation. Taxable income must be under $50,000. The only deduction permitted is an IRA contribution. There is no provision for itemizing deductions on this form. Certain credits to offset tax liability may be used, including

Illustration 20-2
Taxpayers' sources of income and their claims for exemptions and deductions determine which federal income tax form they should use.

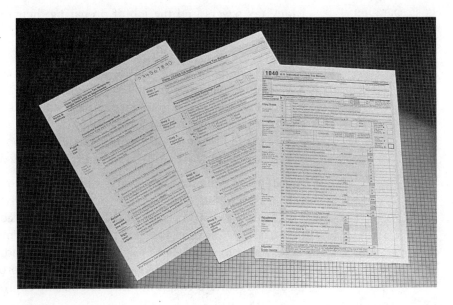

the credit for child care and dependent expenses and the earned income credit.

Form 1040. This form is the most extensive and complex of the three forms. It must be used if income is $50,000 or more, if deductions are itemized, or if an estimated tax return was filed. Tax payers in complicated tax situations (e.g., those claiming moving expenses, those with barter income, those receiving taxable Social Security benefits, and those receiving pension and annuity income) are required to use this form.

The basic 1040 form is supplemented by additional schedules and forms on which various types of income and business activities are reported in detail. The schedules that may be filed include the following:

- Schedule A—Itemized deductions
- Schedule B—Dividend and interest income
- Schedule C—Profit (loss) from a business or profession
- Schedule D—Capital gains and losses
- Schedule E—Supplemental income, rents, royalties, partnerships, estates and trusts
- Schedule F—Farm income and expenses

The forms that may be filed include the following:

- Form 2106—Employee business expenses
- Form 2119—Sale or exchange of principal residence
- Form 2441—Credit for child and dependent care expenses

Tax Preparation Assistance

Many tax payers find the job of preparing their returns too complex or burdensome and turn to others for help. Assistance is particularly appropriate in the following instances :

- When selling or buying a house or other real estate
- When complex investments are involved
- When estate and retirement planning advice is needed
- When incurring moving expenses
- When conducting small business activities
- When getting married or divorced (Strassels & Wool, 1979)

Assistance is available from a variety of sources. However, the services they can provide differ.

Commercial Tax Services. There are many commercial tax services that can provide assistance for preparing tax forms. They include large chain operations, smaller local operations, and individual preparers who work out of their own homes. These services can provide basic advice and fill out tax return forms. They may not be able to provide advice in borderline situations. Some experts believe tax preparers are inclined to be too cautious in taking deductions and that, as a result, tax payers end up paying more than they should.

Most of those working as tax preparers work only seasonally. Even if they are trained in preparing tax forms, they lack the breadth of experience and involvement full-time professionals have. Because of their limited knowledge, tax preparers are not in a position to advise tax payers on tax-reduction

CONSUMER CAPSULE: SOME COMMON MISTAKES ON TAX RETURNS

- Failure to Sign Tax Return

  To be valid, the form must be signed. Two signatures are required if a joint return is filed. IRS sends back unsigned returns for signature, and they may be filed late as a result.

- Failure to Use Peel-Off Label

  Use of the preprinted label that comes with the tax return package sent to taxpayers in the mail will help to minimize errors in handling. Any mistakes in the label should be corrected.

- Use of Incorrect Tax Table

  Taxpayers should be certain they are using the correct tax table. Single people should remember they can use the head-of-household table if they maintain a household for a child or other dependent. These tax rates are lower than the single rates.

- Failure to Write Information on Check

  Taxpayer's Social Security number and purpose of check (e.g., "Form 1040A tax") should be noted on check so it can be credited to appropriate account if it should become separated from return.

- Copying Wrong Numbers from Tax Tables

  Taxpayers should double-check to be certain that correct line of table is used and that numbers are copied correctly.

- Mathematical Errors

  Mathematical calculations should be double-checked. If errors are identified when a return is entered in the IRS computer, taxes are recomputed and the taxpayer is sent a form letter explaining the changes.

strategies. Tax preparers' charges typically are based on the number of forms prepared and usually are moderate.

Accountants. Accountants also can provide assistance in preparing tax returns. Those who specialize in tax matters can provide a fuller range of services, including tax-planning advice designed to reduce tax liability. This group includes both accountants and certified public accountants. Individuals operating as accountants are subject to few controls. Certified public accountants, however, must pass a demanding certification examination.

Certified public accountants, along with tax attorneys, can provide tax payers with advice on tax strategies and guide tax payers in the gray areas of tax law. In selecting an adviser, tax payers should ask for recommendations from friends and respected members of the business community. The most knowledgable adviser will be someone who specializes in taxes on a full-time basis. In selecting a tax adviser, training, experience, and frequency of audits are all considerations. Some experts think a good adviser is one who is audited occasionally because they think this is a sign that deductions are pursued aggressively (Strassels & Wool, 1979). Fees for preparing returns typically are lowest for public accountants, while local CPA firms charge more. Charges from national CPA firms are higher still.

Enrolled Agents. Another group which provides assistance to tax payers, *enrolled agents,* is less familiar to the general public. Enrolled agents must pass a complex Treasury Department examination on taxation. Many are former IRS employees.

Enrolled agents and CPAs are the only two groups allowed to represent tax payers in IRS proceedings. While many commercial preparers promise to accompany a tax payer who is audited, they will only explain how a return was prepared. They cannot serve as a representative for the tax payer or as an advocate. The fees charged by enrolled agents are similar to those charged by accountants.

IRS Assistance. The IRS is also a source of advice on the preparation of tax returns. Tax payers can get advice on specific questions and referrals to relevant publications by stopping in at local IRS offices or by calling IRS' toll-free numbers. IRS also sponsors a volunteer income tax assistance program that provides help in filling out tax forms to the elderly and to low-income, non-English speaking, and handicapped persons.

The IRS provides advice through a number of publications with detailed information on the preparation of tax returns. For the individual tax payer, the most comprehensive and useful of these is *Your Federal Income Tax,* which is also often referred to as Publication 17 (U.S. Department of the Treasury, 1986). It is published annually and offers extensive explanations of typical tax problems along with helpful examples.

Tax payers should note two things about IRS advice:

- IRS disclaims responsibility for erroneous advice given by its personnel or publications.
- IRS publications provide the IRS interpretation of the tax laws. Certain courts may take positions more favorable to tax payers. IRS publications do not reflect these positions until the appeal process is complete.

Dealing With the IRS   The enforcement powers of the IRS arise out of a complex web of laws, regulations, and rulings. The basic authority of the IRS derives from the Internal Revenue Code, which was first passed in 1939, to systematize earlier tax laws. The code has been amended frequently since (Pomerantz, 1984). In addition to covering income taxes, the Code deals with estate and gift taxes and alcohol and tobacco taxes, which also are enforced by the IRS. To implement the tax code, the IRS issues a series of *regulations*. When problems arise in interpreting or clarifying the tax laws, the IRS issues *rulings*. Individuals and corporations may still be uncertain about the tax treatment of a proposed action. They may ask the IRS for a judgment on how the proposed action will be viewed. In such instances the IRS issues a private letter ruling. If the question raised in a request for a private letter ruling appears to be a widespread problem, the IRS often later issues a ruling on the subject.

IRS Compliance Programs. To ensure compliance with the income tax laws, the IRS monitors the accuracy of individual returns. As a first step in checking compliance, the IRS monitors returns when received. One of the checks made is for unallowable items. When such an item is noted, the IRS notifies the tax payer that it is not allowable. Some examples of unallowable items are:

- Personal legal expenses — E.g., the legal cost of drawing a will or a divorce action
- Certain state and local taxes — E.g., hotel taxes, mortgage transfer taxes, sales taxes
- Contributions to a nonqualifying organization — E.g., contributions to lobbying and political action groups
- Educational expenses for individuals other than tax payer or spouse — E.g., college costs for a child (Bernstein, 1985)

The IRS *matching program* compares W-2 information reported by employers on wages and salaries paid and tax withheld. IRS computers match the information forwarded by employers with that reported on a return. The IRS also matches information on stock dividends received and savings interest earned with that declared on the tax return. Individual tax payers receive this information on *1099 forms*. The same information is also sent to IRS by corporations, banks, and brokerage firms. Statements of mortgage interest paid have also been added to the matching program. When an omission is spotted in a tax return, the tax payer is sent a recalculated tax bill.

IRS also seeks out possible violations by detailed computer analysis of individual returns. Individual items on the return are scored, based on the likelihood that an audit will result in an assessment for additional taxes (Bernstein, 1985). The higher the total score, the more likely the return will be audited. While the scoring procedure is kept secret, it is known that both the information included and omitted is scrutinized. Possible sources of questions include:

- Deductions that are high compared to those taken by others at the same income level
- Failure to report dividend earnings even though sale of stock was reported
- Failure to deduct real estate taxes when mortgage interest deduction was claimed

One way to avoid IRS questions is to include documentation to explain any large or unusual claims.

IRS Audits. When the IRS has questions concerning a return, it may make one of three different types of *audits* to examine a return in more detail:

- *Correspondence audit*. When a question appears relatively simple, the IRS requests more information by mail.
- *Office audit*. When a question is more complex, the tax payer is requested to appear at the IRS offce with relevant documents. In some cases, if appropriate documentation is available, photocopies sent in by mail can replace an office visit.
- *Field audit*. When a problem is complex and access to extensive records (such as those of a business or corporation) is required, agents may come to the tax payer's home or office.

The IRS also conducts another type of audit for its tax payer Compliance Measurement Program. These audits are used to obtain statistical information on tax payers at different income levels, to ascertain typical expenses, deductions, and claims.

Tax experts have concluded that fear of the IRS has made many tax payers overcautious. At a result, they fail to take deductions to which they are entitled (Strassels, 1986). A further problem is that too many tax payers, when audited, cave in to an IRS agent's demands too quickly. If tax payers have documentation for a deduction, they have every right to persist in claiming it.

AVOIDING TAXES

No one is either legally or morally obligated to pay more taxes than the law requires. There are, however, some ways in which taxes can be avoided, at least temporarily. None of these methods provides permanent relief from taxes; all merely postpone the day of reckoning. Several of the methods available for postponing taxes are government-sanctioned retirement savings plans.

Individual Retirement Accounts

Individual retirement accounts were discussed earlier as a deduction from gross income in the calculation of income tax liability. The portion of income contributed to the IRA can reduce current tax liability. If it is subtracted in determining adjusted gross income, it is taxed on withdrawal, along with interest or dividends earned.

The following rules govern the tax treatment of IRA contributions:

- Individual workers who do not have an employer-sponsored retirement program may deduct their full IRA contribution up to a maximum of $2,000 ($2,250 for a couple with a nonworking spouse) from their gross income.
- Individuals with adjusted gross incomes under $25,000 (or $40,000 for couples filing jointly) may also fully deduct contributions whether or not they have an employer-sponsored retirement program.
- Individuals with adjusted gross income between $25,000 and $35,000 (couples with incomes between $40,000 and $50,000) are allowed partial deductions.
- Individuals with adjusted gross incomes over $35,000 (couples filing jointly with incomes over $50,000) are allowed no deduction.

IRA contributions must be deposited in a separate account administered by a trustee. Typical trustees include banks, insurance companies, and brokerage firms. Interest, dividends, or other earnings in the account compound tax-free. Earnings and original contributions are taxed at the tax payer's current tax rate when withdrawn.

Withdrawals before the tax payer is age $59\frac{1}{2}$ are subject to a 10 percent penalty. This penalty makes IRAs unsuitable as a short-term investment device. If a particular type of IRA investment proves unsatisfactory, funds can be rolled-over or shifted to another type of investment without taxation as long as the switch is executed promptly.

Employer-Sponsored Retirement Plans

There are several types of employer or company-sponsored plans that permit postponement of taxes. In contrast to IRAs, which are created by the individual tax payer, these plans are created by an employer.

401(k) Plans. These plans, named after the section of the Internal Revenue Code which authorizes them, allow employees to contribute an untaxed portion of their salary to a personal retirement account. In many 401(k) plans, the employer matches all or part of the employee's contributions. Earnings in the account compound tax-free.

The maximum annual contributions to 401(k) plans were reduced by the Tax Reform Act of 1986. The earlier law permitted large contributions and appeared to unduly benefit high-salaried employees. Under the new law, employees may contribute up to $7,000 annually. This amount will be indexed upward annually with inflation beginning in 1988. Total contributions, including the employer's contributions, are limited to $30,000 or 25 percent of earnings, whichever is smaller.

401(k) plans, like IRAs, are subject to a 10 percent withdrawal penalty for withdrawal before age 59½. They are, therefore, unsuitable vehicles for short-term savings. Both earnings and contributions are subject to tax when withdrawn. 401(k) plans are, however, well suited for their intended purpose: building retirement savings.

Another type of company-sponsored plan that permits deferring taxes on wage or salary income is the *SEP* or *simplified employee pension* plan. Employers may create SEPs rather than maintaining a company-sponsored pension plan. Under SEP arrangements, the employer makes a contribution to the IRAs of employees. The employer's contribution and any employee contribution are not included in gross income (Price-Waterhouse, 1986). Employees may not contribute more than $7,000 annually to a SEP. There also is a $7,000 annual limit (indexed to inflation) on total contributions to 401(k), SEP, and union-sponsored pension plans. Employer contributions to SEPs also are limited by law.

Certain employees of public schools, churches, and tax-exempt organizations are eligible to participate in another type of tax-sheltered retirement program. These *403(b) plans* permit contributions by an employer or an employee for a tax-sheltered annuity. 403(b) plans are similar to other tax-sheltered retirement plans in that contributions are not taxed at the time they are made. Instead, contributions and earnings are taxed at the time of withdrawal. Compared to other tax-sheltered retirement plans, 403(b) plans are relatively flexible and are an attractive alternative for those eligible.

Keogh Plans

Keogh plans are separate investment accounts set up by a self-employed person to build retirement savings. The accounts must be administered by a trustee, such as a bank, a brokerage firm, or an insurance company. Keogh (pronounced *key-oh*) plans are available to anyone with self-employment income, including individuals whose principal source of income is wages and salaries.

The limits for contributions depend on whether a defined benefit or a defined contribution plan is chosen. In general, a defined benefit plan permits larger contributions.

Tax Shelters

Before the Tax Reform Act of 1986, tax payers often invested in *tax shelters*. These investments reduced taxable income by producing large losses to offset other income. Real estate investments were a popular tax shelter. Sizable depreciation costs in such projects often created paper losses that could be used to "shelter" income from other sources. The most attractive shelters created losses that were many times the amount actually invested.

The old law tended to encourage investments whose chief merit was their ability to create tax losses, rather than to encourage productive projects with favorable cash flows. One of the major changes of the Tax Reform of 1986 was to limit the use of losses from real estate projects and other passive investments to reduce taxable income. *Passive investments* are ones in which the tax payer does not participate significantly on a continuing basis. Under the new law, losses from passive investments can be used only to reduce income from other passive investments. They cannot be used to offset income from other sources.

Losses from investments made before the new law was passed can be used to offset other income to a limited extent until 1990. After 1990 such losses can be used only to offset income from passive investments. While some forms of tax shelters still exist, most require active (not passive) involvement from the investor. The emphasis now is on projects that produce current income or capital gains rather than losses.

MAJOR CHAPTER CONCEPTS

1. Taxes may be used for a variety of purposes: raising revenues for government operations, promoting economic stability, encouraging economic growth and development, redistributing income, and facilitating social goals.
2. Five evaluative criteria can be applied to tax systems: fairness and equity, ease of calculation, convenience of payment, ease of administration, and minimal economic distortion.
3. Taxes may be classified in various ways—by incidence, progressivity, calculation procedure, and tax base utilized.
4. A value-added tax, national sales tax, or a tax on consumption have been proposed as new sources of federal revenues.
5. Not all income received is subject to tax. In general, wage and salary income and income from investments is taxable, however.

6. Gross income (i.e., income subject to tax) is reduced by certain expenses of producing income to obtain adjusted gross income.

7. Adjustable gross income is reduced by deductions and exemptions to determine taxable income.

8. Taxes are calculated using tax rate tables or schedules. Under the 1986 tax law, the number of brackets was reduced to four.

9. Tax liability is reduced by tax credits to determine tax owed for the tax year.

10. Withholding and estimated tax payments are subtracted from total tax owed to calculate the amount still due.

11. In general, citizens of the United States and Puerto Rico and resident aliens must file a tax return when their income is above a specified amount.

12. Tax payers may use one of three tax forms depending on the amount and types of income received and the complexity of their deductions.

13. Tax payers can get help in filling out a tax return from tax services, accountants, enrolled agents, and the IRS. Certified public accountants and tax lawyers are best qualified to advise on tax reduction strategies.

14. The IRS works to ensure that all tax payers pay their fair share through its compliance and audit programs.

15. Individual tax payers may postpone taxes through the use of IRAs, 401(k) and SEP plans, 403(b), and Keogh plans.

16. Although some tax shelters are available, the Tax Reform Act of 1986 limited their usefulness for tax avoidance.

CONSUMER QUESTIONS

1. U.S. tax laws have been subject to continuing changes. What major changes in federal income tax law have been made in the last two or three years? What were the reasons for these changes?

2. There is a continuing stream of proposals for new types of taxes or modifications in the existing system. Examples include the flat-rate income tax and the value-added tax. Identify a recent proposal for a new type of tax or a modification of an existing tax, and prepare a brief report on it. Evaluate the proposed tax on the five evaluative criteria for taxes identified in this chapter.

3. The IRS compliance and auditing program is a focus of concern for tax payers. What recent changes has IRS instituted in these procedures?

4. What tax deductions and other special tax advantages are available to the following groups: (a) homeowners, (b) salaried professionals, (c) self-employed workers, (d) working parent(s) with young children, (e) single parents heading a household? Use *Your Federal Income Tax* (Publication 17) or another tax guide as a reference.

5. Have you ever prepared a federal income tax return or had one prepared for you? What was your experience in preparing your return?

SUGGESTED READINGS

1. *Consumer Reports,* "Tax Audits: Improving Your Odds" 51, no. 3 (March, 1986): 155-158. This useful article discusses questions that trigger IRS audits, IRS audit procedures, and effective techniques for dealing with an audit.

2. Strassels, Paul N., with Robert Wool. *All You Need to Know About the IRS.* New York: Random House, 1979. Strassels, a tax law specialist, has published this and several other books with advice to tax payers on how to prepare their tax returns and how to deal with the IRS. This book and his more recent ones are full of useful advice based on his five years with IRS and careful IRS-watching in the years since.

3. U.S. Department of the Treasury, Internal Revenue Service, *Your Federal Income Tax.* Publication 17. Washington, D.C.: U.S. Government Printing Office, 1986 and succeeding editions. This sometimes-complicated document is a basic reference for preparing a tax return. It answers the most frequent tax questions in a language that should be comprehensible to anyone who can read carefully.

4. Webber, Carolyn, and Aaron Wildavsky. *A History of Taxation and Expenditure in the Western World.* New York: Simon and Schuster, 1986. This book provides a sweeping examination of the development of governmental budgets and the taxation to support them, from ancient Egypt to today.

REFERENCES

A.M. Best Co. *Best's Insurance Reports: Life/Health — 1985.* 80th ed. Oldwick, N.J.: A.M. Best Co., 1985.

Advisory Commission on Intergovernmental Relations. *1986 Changing Attitudes on Governments and Taxes.* Washington, D.C.: U.S. Government Printing Office, 1986.

Alliance of American Insurers. "Are Mandatory Seat Belt Laws the Answer?" *Journal of American Insurance* 58, no. 3 (Fall 1982): 23-26.

American Automobile Association. *Your Driving Costs, 1984 Edition.* Falls Church, Va.: American Automobile Association, 1984.

American Bar Association. *Buying or Selling Your Home.* Chicago: American Bar Association, 1980.

_____. *Landlords and Tenants: Your Guide to the Law.* Chicago: American Bar Association, 1982.

American Council of Life Insurance. *1984 Life Insurance Fact Book.* Washington, D.C.: American Council of Life Insurance, 1984.

American Council of Life Insurance and Health Insurance Institute. "When Your Children 'Lose' Out." *Family News and Features* (30 April 1979).

Andreasen, Alan. "Consumer Complaints and Redress: What We Know and What We Don't Know." *Research in the Consumer Interest: The Frontier.* Edited by E. Scott Maynes. (forthcoming).

Apple, R.W., Jr. "Swedes Examining Social Cost of Alcohol Abuse." *New York Times* (18 August 1980): 2.

Axelrod, David. "Income Tax, History of U.S." *The Money Encyclopedia.* Edited by Harvey Rachlin. New York: Harper and Row, 1984.

Ballantyne, Harry C. "Actuarial Status of the OASI and DI Trust Funds." *Social Security Bulletin* 49, no. 7 (July 1986): 5-9.

Bank of America. "How to Balance Your Checkbook." *Consumer Information Report 1.* San Francisco: Bank of America, 1975.

_____. "A Guide to Checks and Checking." *Consumer Information Report 10.* San Francisco: Bank of America, 1977.

Beck, Sara, Elizabeth Crosby, and Martha Parris. "Let the Grade Be Your Guide in Buying Food." In *Food — From Farm to Table: 1982 Yearbook of Agriculture,* edited by Jack Hayes, 302-317. Washington, D.C.: U.S. Government Printing Office, 1982.

Belth, Joseph M. *Life Insurance A Consumer's Handbook.* 2d ed. Bloomington: Indiana University Press, 1985.

Bennett, Veronica. "Consumer Demand for Product Deregulation." *Economic Review* (Federal Reserve Bank of Atlanta) 69, no. 5 (May 1984): 28-40.

Bernstein, Allen. *1986 Tax Guide for College Teachers.* Washington, D.C.: Academic Information Service, 1985.

Bernstein, Peter W., ed. *The Arthur Young Tax Guide 1987.* New York: Ballantine Books, 1986.

Best, Arthur. *When Consumers Complain.* New York: Columbia University Press, 1980.

Better Homes and Gardens. *New Decorating Book.* Des Moines: Meredith Corp., 1981.

Biles, B., C. Schramm, and J. Atkinson. "Hospital Cost Inflation Under State Rate-Setting Programs." *New England Journal of Medicine* 303, no. 12 (18 September 1980): 664-668.

Blumberg, Mark. "Health Status and Health Care Use by Type of Private Health Coverage." *Milbank Memorial Fund Quarterly: Health and Society* 58, no. 4 (Fall 1980): 633-655.

Bondar, Joseph. "Effect of the OASDI Benefit Increase, December 1985." *Social Security Bulletin* 49, no. 7 (July 1986): 5-9.

Boschung, Milla D. "Manufacturer's Response to Consumer Complaints on Guaranteed Products." *Journal of Consumer Affairs* 10, no. 1 (Summer 1976): 86-89.

Bowyer, Linda E., A. Frank Thompson, and Venkat Srinivasan. "The Ohio Banking Crisis: A Lesson in Consumer Finance." *Journal of Consumer Affairs* 20, no. 2 (Winter 1986): 290-299.

Christianson, J., and W. McClure. "Competition in the Delivery of Medical Care." *New England Journal of Medicine* 301, no. 15 (11 October 1979): 812-818.

"Cleaner Diesel Engine Rule Postponed for Two Years by EPA." *Washington Post* (18 January 1984): A19.

Congressional Budget Office. *The Effects of PSROs on Health Care Costs: Current Findings and Future Evaluations.* Washington, D.C.: U.S. Government Printing Office, June 1979.

Consumer Reports. "The Other Costs of the Diesel" 45, no. 6 (June 1980): 396.

————. "The HMO Approach to Health Care" 47, no. 5 (May 1982): 246-250.

————. "Blow-Dryers" 49, no. 6 (June 1984a): 312-316.

————. " Medicare-Supplement Insurance" 49, no. 6 (June 1984b): 347-355.

————. "Mid-Priced Stereo Receivers" 49, no. 7 (July 1984): 376-381.

————. "Which Companies Are Best?" 49, no. 9 (September 1984): 506-510.

————. Playing Your Cards Right" 50, no. 1 (January 1985): 47-51.

————. "Auto Receivers/Cassette Players" 50, no. 3 (March 1985): 134-141.

————. "Food, Drugs or Frauds?" 50, no. 5 (May 1985): 282-283.

————. "You and the Banks" 50, no. 9 (September 1985): 508-516.

————. "Shopping Smart for Loans" 50, no. 10 (October, 1985): 581-586.

————. "How to Get the Best Deal" 51, no. 4 (April 1986a): 211-214.

————. "Options: Which to Take, Which to Leave" 51, no. 4 (April 1986b): 224-225.

————. "Clothes Dryers" 51, no. 5 (May 1986): 339-343.

————. "Life Insurance: How to Protect Your Family, Part I—Term Life Insurance" 51, no. 6 (June 1986): 371-402.

————. "Life Insurance: How to Protect Your Family, Part II—Whole Life Insurance" 51, no. 7 (July 1986): 447-470.

————. "The Manufactured Crisis: Product Liability Companies Have Created a Crisis and Dumped It on You" 51, no. 8 (August 1986a): 544-549.

————. "Life Insurance: How to Protect Your Family, Part III—Universal Life Insurance" 51, no. 8 (August 1986b): 515-529.

Corbman, Bernard P. *Textiles: Fiber to Fabric.* 6th ed. New York: Gregg/McGraw-Hill, 1983.

Cordes, Sam. *Public Problem Analysis.* Community Affairs Pamphlet Series No. 1. University Park: The Pennsylvania State University, Cooperative Extension Service, 1976.

————. *The Economics of Health Services.* Health Trustees Leadership Program No. 8. University Park: The Pennsylvania State University, Cooperative Extension Service, 1981.

Cude, Brenda. "The Perfect Information Frontier: A Tool for Teaching the Payoffs to Comparison Shopping." *Journal of Consumer Education* 3 (1985): 7-15.

Cude, Brenda, and Rosemary Walker. "Quantity Surcharges: Are They Important in Choosing a Shopping Strategy?" *Journal of Consumer Affairs* 18, no. 2 (Winter 1984): 287-295

Deacon, Ruth E., and Francille M. Firebaugh. *Home Management: Context and Concepts.* New York: Houghton Mifflin Co., 1975.

Duncan, Greg J. "The Dynamics of Local Markets— A Case Study of Cameras." *Journal of Consumer Affairs* 15, no. 1 (Summer 1981): 64-74.

Duncan, Nancy. "Smart Money." *Sylvia Porter's Personal Finance* 4, no. 10 (December 1986): 16-18.

Eiseman, Leatrice. *Alive with Color: The Total Color System.* Washington, D.C.: Acropolis Books, 1983.

Eisenbeis, Robert A., and Paul R. Schweitzer. *A Study of Tie-Ins Between the Granting of Credit and Sales of Insurance by Bank Holding Companies and Other Lenders.* Staff Economic Study. Washington, D.C.: Federal Reserve Board, 1978.

Eisenberg, Richard. "Real Estate Returns to Basic Economics." *Money* 15, no. 10 (October 1986): 165-175.

Electronic Industries Association. Consumer Electronics Group. *Audio: Your New World of Listening.* Washington, D.C.: Electronic Industries Association, 1984.

Engel, James F., Roger D. Blackwell, and Paul W. Miniard. *Consumer Behavior.* 5th ed. Chicago: Dryden Press, 1986.

Environmental Protection Agency and U.S. Department of Energy. *1986 Gas Mileage Guide: EPA Fuel Economy Estimates.* Washington, D.C.: U.S. Government Printing Office, 1985.

Federal Trade Commission. "Electronic Banking." *Facts For Consumers from the Federal Trade Commission.* Washington, D.C.: Federal Trade Commission, 1980a.

———. *Post-Purchase Remedies: Briefing Book for Policy Review Session.* Washington, D.C.: Federal Trade Commission, 1980b.

———. *What's New About Care Labels.* Washington, D.C.: U.S. Government Printing Office, 1984.

Fornell, Claes. *Consumer Input for Marketing Decisions: A Study of Corporate Departments of Consumer Affairs.* New York: Praeger, 1976.

Friedland, John. "Individual Practice HMOs." *Group and IPA HMOs.* Edited by Dustin L. Mackie and Douglas K. Decker. Rockville, Md.: Aspen Systems Corp., 1981.

Fung, E.E., and William Rathje. "How We Waste $31 Billion a Year." In *Food—From Farm to Table: 1982 Yearbook of Agriculture,* edited by Jack Hayes. Washington, D.C.: U.S. Government Printing Office, 1982.

Gabel, J., and M. Redisch. "Alternative Physician Payment Methods: Incentives, Efficiency, and National Health Insurance." *Milbank Memorial Fund Quarterly: Health and Society* 57, no. 1 (Winter 1979): 38-59.

Geistfeld, Loren V. "The Price-Quality Relationship Revisited." *Journal of Consumer Affairs* 16, no. 2 (Winter 1982): 334-346.

Gerner, Jennifer L., and W. Keith Bryant. "Appliance Warranties as a Market Signal?" *Journal of Consumer Affairs* 15, no. 1 (Summer 1981): 75-86.

Gillis, Jack. *The Car Book.* 1986 ed. New York: Harper and Row, 1986.

Götestam, K. Gunnar, and Ola Röstum. "Alcohol Control Policy in the Nordic Countries (Denmark, Finland, Norway, Sweden, Iceland)." *Prevention of Alcohol Abuse.* Edited by Peter M. Miller and Ted D. Nirenberg. New York: Plenum Press, 1984.

Greenburg, David I., and Thomas H. Stanton. "Business Group, Consumer Problems: The Contradiction of Trade Association Complaint Handling." *No Access to Law: Alternatives to the American Judicial System.* Edited by Laura Nader. New York: Academic Press, 1980.

Greenlaw, Paul S., and John P. Kohl. *Personnel Management: Managing Human Resources.* New York: Harper and Row, 1986.

Griffin, Barbara J. "The Do's and Don'ts of Home Insulation." In *Cutting Energy Costs: 1980 Yearbook of Agriculture,* edited by Jack Hayes. Washington, D.C.: U.S. Government Printing Office, 1980.

Guthrie, Helen. *Introductory Nutrition.* 6th ed. St. Louis: Times Mirror/Mosby, 1986.

Hawkins, Del I., and Gary McCain. "An Investigation of Returns to Different Shopping Strategies." *Journal of Consumer Affairs* 13, no. 1 (Summer 1979): 64-74.

Health Insurance Association of America. *Source Book of Health Insurance Data 1984-1985.* Washington, D.C.: Health Insurance Association of America, 1985.

Hefferan, Colien. "Employee Benefits." *Family Economics Review* (U.S. Department of Agriculture) no. 1 (1985): 6-13.

Henszey, Benjamin N., Barry Lee Myers, and Reed T. Phalan. *Introduction to Basic Legal Principles.* 2d ed. Dubuque, Iowa: Kendall/Hunt Publishing Co., 1977.

Herrmann, Robert. "Families in Bankruptcy." *Journal of Marriage and the Family* 28, no. 3 (August 1966): 324-330.

Hershman, Arlene, and G. Bruce Kneckt. "The Crash in Collectibles." *Dun's Business Month* 119, no. 6 (June 1982): 40-46.

Hirshhorn, Norbert. *Quality By Objectives: A New Way of Thinking About the Assessment and Assurance of the Quality of Health Care.* Health Trustees Leadership Program No. 3. University Park: The Pennsylvania State University, Cooperative Extension Service, 1979.

Hosbach, Howard D. "Standard and Poor's Corporation." *The Money Encyclopedia.* Edited by Harvey Rachlin. New York: Harper and Row, 1984.

Hughs, E., E. Lewit, R. Watkins, and R. Handschin. "Utilization of Surgical Manpower in a Prepaid Group Practice," Working Paper 19. New York: National Bureau of Economic Research, 1973.

Insurance Information Institute. *Sharing the Risk: How the Nation's Business, Homes and Autos Are Insured.* Rev. 2d ed. New York: Insurance Information Institute, 1985.

Insurance Institute for Highway Safety. *The Year's Work: 1983-84.* Washington, D.C.: Insurance Institute for Highway Safety, 1985.

Jackson, Carole. *Color Me Beautiful.* Washington, D.C.: Acropolis Books, 1980.

Jones, Edwin M. "Pension Benefit Guaranty Corporation (PBGC)." *The Money Encyclopedia.* Edited by Harvey Rachlin. New York: Harper and Row, 1984.

Joseph, Marjory L. *Introductory Textile Science.* 3d ed. New York: Holt, Rinehart and Winston, 1977.

Kilborn, Peter T. "Difficulties at Pension Agency." *New York Times* (8 December 1986): D1, D11.

King, B. Frank, and David D. Whitehead. "Introduction: Bank Product Deregulation." *Economic Review* (Federal Reserve Bank of Atlanta) 69, no. 5 (May 1984): 4-5.

Lekachman, Robert. *The Great Tax Debate.* Public Affairs Pamphlet No. 582. New York: Public Affairs Committee, 1980.

Louis Harris and Associates Inc. *Risk in a Complex Society.* New York: Marsh and McLennan Inc., 1980.

Luft, H. "How Do Health Maintenance Organizations Achieve Their 'Savings'?" *New England Journal of Medicine* 298, no. 24 (15 June 1978): 1336-1343.

Mackie, Dustin L. "Financial Planning." *Group and IPA HMOs.* Edited by Dustin L. Mackie and Douglas K. Decker. Rockville, Md.: Aspen Systems Corp., 1981.

Macklin, Gordon S. "National Association of Securities Dealers Automated Quotations (NASDAQ)." *The Money Encyclopedia.* Edited by Harvey Rachlin. New York: Harper and Row, 1984.

Maslow, Abraham H. *Motivation and Personality.* 2d ed. New York: Harper and Row, 1970.

Maynes, E. Scott. *Decision-Making for Consumers: An Introduction to Consumer Economics.* New York: Macmillan Publishing Co., 1976.

Maynes, E. Scott, James N. Morgan, Weston Vivian, and Greg J. Duncan. "The Local Consumer Information System: An Institution-To-Be?" *Journal of Consumer Affairs* 11, no. 1 (Summer 1977): 17-33.

McClure, Walter. "Cost Containment: Choices for Medical Care." *Pennsylvania Medicine* 82, no. 6 (June 1979): 14-23.

McCullough, James, and Roger Best. "Consumer Preferences for Food Label Information: A

Basis for Segmentation." *Journal of Consumer Affairs* 14, no. 1 (Summer 1980): 180-192.

McElroy, Bruce, and David A. Aaker. "Unit Pricing Six Years After Introduction." *Journal of Retailing* 55, no. 3 (Fall 1979): 44-57.

Meeks, Carol B. *Home Ownership: What You Need to Know Before You Buy.* Publication NE 199. Ithaca, N.Y.: Cornell University, Cooperative Extension Service, 1980a.

———. *The Housing Market: A Guide to Sensible Choices.* Publication NE 196. Ithaca, N.Y.: Cornell University, Cooperative Extension Service, 1980b.

Meeks, Carol B., Eleanor Ouderkerk, and Rebecca Bilderback. *Cooperative Housing and Condominiums: Home Ownership with a Difference.* Ithaca, N.Y.: Cornell University, Cooperative Extension Service, 1980.

Merrill Lynch. *The Bond Book.* New York: Merrill Lynch, Pierce, Fenner and Smith Inc., 1981.

———. *Investing in Stocks for Capital Appreciation, Income and Total Return.* New York: Merrill Lynch, Pierce, Fenner and Smith Inc., 1985.

Money. "Making Sense of Annual Reports" 14, no. 3 (March 1985): 201-204.

Morgan, James N., and Greg J. Duncan. *The Economics of Personal Choice.* Ann Arbor: University of Michigan Press, 1980.

Morris, Earl W., and Mary Winter. *Housing, Family and Society.* New York: John Wiley & Sons, 1978.

Morse, Richard L.D. "Making Interest Easy (MITE) with Cents-ible Interest." *Journal of Consumer Education* 4 (1986): 9-11.

Munnell, Alicia H. "Employee Benefits and the Tax Base." *New England Economic Review* (Federal Reserve Bank of Boston). (January/February 1984): 39-55.

Munns, Joyce Matthews. "Consumer Complaints as Pre-Purchase Information: An Evaluation of Better Business Bureau Reports to Consumers." *Journal of Consumer Affairs* 12, no. 1 (Summer 1978): 76-87.

Murphy, Elizabeth W., and Cheryl Garrett. "Better Buymanship—Know Your Labels and Standards.

In *Food—From Farm to Table: 1982 Yearbook of Agriculture,* edited by Jack Hayes, 318-325. Washington, D.C.: U.S. Government Printing Office, 1982.

Nader, Laura. "Alternatives to the American Judicial System." *No Access to Law: Alternatives to the American Judicial System.* Edited by Laura Nader. New York: Academic Press, 1980.

Newman, Jerry O. "High Heating Costs: How to Cut Them." In *Cutting Energy Costs: 1980 Yearbook of Agriculture,* edited by Jack Hayes, 202-211. Washington, D.C.: U.S. Government Printing Office, 1980.

Odland, Dianne D., Ruth S. Vettel, and Carole A. Davis. "Convenience and the Cost of the 'Newer' Frozen Plate Dinners and Entrees." *Family Economics Review,* no. 1, 1986.

Owen, Bonnie L., Carol Culter Riddick, and Sam M. Cordes. *Evaluating Existing and Proposed Health Services.* Health Trustees Leadership Program No. 2. University Park: The Pennsylvaia State University, Cooperative Extension Service, 1979.

Peterson, Cass. "EPA Issues Standards for Diesel Vehicles." *Washington Post* (9 March 1985): A6.

Pomerantz, Alan J. "Internal Revenue Code." *The Money Encyclopedia.* Edited by Harvey Rachlin. New York: Harper and Row, 1984.

Porter, Sylvia. *Sylvia Porter's New Money Book for the 80's.* Garden City, N.Y.: Doubleday and Co., 1979.

Preston, Ivan L. *The Great American Blow-Up: Puffery in Advertising and Selling.* Madison: University of Wisconsin Press, 1975.

Price Waterhouse. *The Price Waterhouse Guide to the New Tax Law.* New York: Bantam Books, 1986.

Rankin, Deborah. "Filling the Gaps in Medicare Coverage." *New York Times* (18 August 1985): F9.

Rathje, William. "The Garbage Decade." *American Behavioral Scientist* 28, no. 1 (September/October 1984): 9-29.

Reader's Digest. *Complete Do-It Yourself Manual.* Pleasantville, N.Y.: Reader's Digest Association, Inc., 1977.

Riesz, Peter C. "Price-Quality Correlations for Packaged Food Products." *Journal of Consumer Affairs* 13, no. 2 (Winter 1979): 236-247.

Roper Organization, Inc. *The 1980 Virgina Slims American Women's Poll*. New York: Phillip Morris U.S.A., 1980.

Rosenberg, Robert, and Dustin L. Mackie. "Physicians and Prepaid Group Practices." *Group and IPA HMOs*. Edited by Dustin L. Mackie and Douglas K. Decker. Rockville, Md.: Aspen Systems Corp., 1981.

Rosenbloom, Joseph. *Consumer Complaint Guide 1981*. 8th ed. New York: Macmillan Publishing Co., 1981.

Rothman, Andrew L. and Roxanne P. Fischetti. "Securities Exchange Commission." *The Money Encyclopedia*. Edited by Harvey Rachlin. New York: Harper and Row, 1984.

Rothschild, Donald P., and David W. Carroll. *Consumer Protection Reporting Service*. Owings Mills, Md.: National Law Publishing Corporation, 1986.

Rubin, Harvey W. "Credit Life Insurance and Its Alternatives." *Journal of Consumer Affairs* 12, no. 1 (Summer 1978): 145-153.

Russo, Louis A. "Pension Plans." *The Money Encyclopedia*. Edited by Harvey Rachlin. New York: Harper and Row, 1984.

Salkever, D. and T. Bice. *Impact of State Certificate-of-Need Laws on Health Care Costs and Utilization*. U.S. Department of Health, Education and Welfare. DHEW Publication No. (HRA)77-3163. 1977.

Serber, David. "Resolution or Rhetoric: Managing Complaints in the California Department of Insurance." *No Access to Law: Alternatives to the American Judicial System*. Edited by Laura Nader. New York: Academic Press, 1980.

Shapiro, Irwin A., and Robert F. Majewski. "Should Dentists Advertise?" *Journal of Advertising Research* 23, no. 3 (June/July 1983): 33-37.

Sherman, Sally R. "Attitudes of the American Public Toward Social Security." *Social Security Bulletin* 48, no. 11 (November 1985): 22-23.

Shimp, Terence A. "Social Psychological (Mis)Representations in Television Advertising." *Journal*

of *Consumer Affairs* 13, no. 1 (Summer 1979): 28-40.

Shuptrine, F. Kelly, and Ellen M. Moore. "Even After the Magnuson-Moss Act of 1975, Warranties Are Not Easy to Understand." *Journal of Consumer Affairs* 14, no. 2 (Winter 1980): 394-404.

Slovic, Paul, Baruch Fischhoff, and Sarah Lichtenstein. "Risky Assumptions." *Psychology Today* 14, no. 1 (June 1980): 44-48.

Smith, Adam. [1776]. *The Wealth of Nations*. Reprint. New York: Modern Library, 1937.

Sproles, George B. "New Evidence on Price and Product Quality." *Journal of Consumer Affairs* 11, no. 1 (Summer, 1977): 63-77.

Stabler, Charles N. "Dow Jones Averages." *The Money Encyclopedia*. Edited by Harvey Rachlin. New York: Harper and Row, 1984.

Staelin, Richard, and Alan G. Weinstein. "Correlates of Consumer Safety Behavior." *Advances in Consumer Research*. Vol. 1. Edited by Scott Ward and Peter Wright. Urbana, Ill.: Association for Consumer Research, 1974.

Stafford, Edward F., Jr., Jack J. Kasulis, and Robert F. Lusch. "Consumer Behavior in Accumulating Household Financial Assets." *Journal of Business Research* 10, no. 4 (1982): 397-417.

Stamper, Anita A., Sue Humphries Sharp, and Linda B. Donnell. *Evaluating Apparel Quality*. New York: Fairchild Publications, 1986.

Stampfl, Ronald W. "The Consumer Life Cycle." *Journal of Consumer Affairs* 12, no. 2 (Winter 1978): 209-219.

————. "Multi-Disciplinary Foundations for a Consumer Code of Ethics." *Proceedings of the 25th Annual Conference of the American Council on Consumer Interests*. Edited by Norleen M. Ackerman. Columbia, Mo.: American Council on Consumer Interests, 1979.

Starr, Paul. *The Social Transformation of American Medicine*. New York: Basic Books, 1982.

Statistics Sweden. *Statistical Abstract of Sweden 1985*. Vol. 71. (Stockholm: Statistics Sweden, 1985).

Stokey, Edith, and Richard Zeckhauser. *A Primer for Policy Analysis.* New York: W.W. Norton and Co., 1978.

Strassels, Paul. *Paul Strassels' Quick and Easy Guide to Tax Management for 1986-1987.* Rev. ed. Homewood, Ill.: Dow-Jones-Irwin, 1986.

Strassels, Paul N., and Robert Wool. *All You Need to Know About the IRS.* New York: Random House, 1979.

TARP Inc. *Consumer Complaint Handling in America: Final Report.* Washington, D.C.: TARP Inc., 1979.

Thompson, Jeffrey L. "Product Safety: Suggestions for Better Use and Purchase Behavior through Consumer Education and Information." *Advances in Consumer Research.* Vol. 1. Edited by Scott Ward and Peter Wright. Urbana, Ill.: Association for Consumer Research, 1974.

Thorelli, Hans B., and Jack L. Engledow. "Information Seekers and Information Systems: A Policy Perspective." *Journal of Marketing* 44, no. 2 (Spring 1980): 9-27.

Tochen, David. *The Product Liability Controversy: A Handbook for Consumers.* Washington, D.C.: Paul H. Douglas Consumer Research Center, Consumer Federation of America, 1979.

Tyndall, Katie. "Doctors Drum Up Business Success." *Insight: The Washington Times* 2, no. 39 (29 September 1986): 60-61.

U.S. Department of Agriculture. "Manmade or Natural? A Question of Energy." *Farm Index* (April 1979): 16-17.

_____. Agricultural Marketing Service. *How to Buy Economically: A Food Buyer's Guide.* Washington, D.C.: U.S. Government Printing Office, 1981.

_____. U.S. Department of Health and Human Services. *Nutrition and Your Health: Dietary Guides for Americans.* 2d ed. Home and Garden Bulletin No. 232. Washington, D.C.: U.S. Government Printing Office, 1985.

_____. Human Nutrition Information Service. *Family Food Budgeting ... Good Meals and Good Nutrition.* Home and Garden Bulletin No. 94.

Washington, D.C.: U.S. Government Printing Office, 1981.

U.S. Department of Commerce. *Statistical Abstract of the United States: 1966.* 106th ed. Washington, D.C.: U.S. Government Printing Office, 1985.

U.S. Department of Health and Human Services. Social Security Administration. *A Brief Explanation of Medicare.* SSA Publ. No. 05-10043. Washington, D.C.: U.S. Department of Health and Human Services, 1986a.

_____. "Social Security Programs in the United States." *Social Security Bulletin* 49, no. 1 (January 1986b): 5-59.

_____. *Thinking About Retiring?* Washington, D.C.: U.S. Department of Health and Human Services, 1986c.

_____. *Your Social Security.* Washington, D.C.: U.S. Department of Health and Human Services, 1986d.

U.S. Department of Health, Education and Welfare. Food and Drug Administration. *State Programs and Services in Food and Drug Control.* Rockville, Md.: Food and Drug Administration, 1978.

U.S. Department of Housing and Urban Development. *Settlement Costs: A HUD Guide.* Rev. ed. Washington, D.C.: U.S. Government Printing Office, 1976.

U.S. Department of the Treasury. Internal Revenue Service. *Your Federal Income Tax.* Publication 17. Washington, D.C.: U.S. Government Printing Office, 1986.

U.S. General Accounting Office. *Rising Hospital Costs Can Be Restrained by Regulating Payments and Improving Management.* Washington, D.C.: U.S. Government Printing Office, 1980.

U.S. News and World Report. "Why Interest Grows in a New Kind of Tax System" 86, no. 6 (12 February 1979): 77-79.

_____. "Playing to Win by the New Tax Rules" 101, no. 9 (1 September 1986): 49-52.

Vaughan, Emmet J. *Fundamentals of Risk and Insurance.* 4th ed. New York: John Wiley & Sons, 1986.

Watkins, A.M. *How to Judge a House.* New York: Hawthorn Books, 1972.

Watters, Elsie M. "Tax." *The Money Encyclopedia.* Edited by Harvey Rachlin. New York: Harper and Row, 1984.

Wayne, Leslie. "Insurance Industry Under Fire: Lower Rates Add to Crisis." *New York Times* (9 June 1986): D1, D5.

Widrick, Stanley M. "Measurement of Incidents of Quantity Surcharge Among Selected Grocery Products." *Journal of Consumer Affairs* 13, no. 1 (Summer 1979): 99-107.

Wiener, Joshua Lyle. "Are Warranties Accurate Signals of Product Reliability?" *Journal of Consumer Research* 12, no. 2 (September 1985): 245-250.

Wilkinson, J.B., and J. Barry Mason. "Unavailability and Mispricing of Advertised Specials: The Food Shopper's Knowledge, Experience and Response." *Journal of Consumer Affairs* 12, no. 2 (Winter 1978): 355-363.

Williams, Elizabeth. *Credit Insurance: A Handbook for Consumers.* Washington, D.C.: Paul H. Douglas Research Center, Consumer Federation of America, 1977.

Williams, Robin M., Jr. *American Society: A Sociological Interpretation.* 2d ed. rev. New York: Alfred A. Knopf, 1967.

Young, James Harvey. *The Medical Messiahs: A Social History of Health Quackery in Twentieth-Century America.* Princeton, N.J.: Princeton University Press, 1967.

Zabriskie, Noel B., and Joe L. Welch. "Retail Cashier Accuracy: Misrings and Some Factors Related to Them." *Journal of Retailing* 54, no. 1 (Spring 1978): 43-50.

Zachowski, Matt. "Commodity-Futures Exchange." *The Money Encyclopedia.* Edited by Harvey Rachlin. New York: Harper and Row, 1984.

558

References

INDEX

Information
    characteristics of, 41-42
    and consumers, 8, 9, 12
    costs of, 130
    and credit, 345, 346-347
    product, 74-75
    sources of, 254
Ingredients, food, 192-193
Injury, personal, 96
Installment credit, 355
Insurability, guaranteed, 455
Insurance, 140, 142, 295, 406-435
    as asset, 303-305, 306, 318
    automobile, 255, 300, 410-411,
        414-424
    and bank accounts, 327, 338
    cost of, 301
    credit life, 362-363
    dental, 478
    disability, 512, 515
    health, 410, 411, 470-494, 498, 515,
        516-517
        national, 483
    home, 252, 410, 411, 424-432
    life, 410, 411, 439-467, 471, 498, 515
    mortgage, 357
    no-fault, 418-419
    policies, keeping, 294, 297
    and product liability, 102
    regulation of, 113
    taxation of, proceeds from, 533
    unemployment, 512-514, 515
Insurance Institute for Highway
    Safety, 223
Interest, 252
    on bonds, 376
    as cost of credit, 345, 352-355
    rates, and consumers, 5
    on savings accounts, 331-335
    tax treatment of, 525, 531, 532,
        533, 535, 540
Internal Revenue Service, 487, 502,
    529, 531, 539-540, 542-543
    audits, 544
    dealing with, 543-544
International Organization of Con-
    sumers Unions, 46-47
Investments, 372-401
    as assets, 304-306, 441
    passive, 547
    planning for, 311-314, 440
    problems with, 307
    records of, 294, 295, 296

Issues, consumer, analyzing, 123-151

J

Japan, 292-293
Jewelry, 425
    as investment, 372, 374, 397-399
Joints, furniture, 269-270
Justice Department, U.S., 493

K

Kennedy, John F., 9
Keogh plans, 304, 546-547

L

Labeling, 69-70, 73-74
    care, 174-175
    of fibers, 163, 165
    of furniture, 271
    nutritional, 187-189, 189-193
Law, consumer, 96-101
Law of large numbers, 409
Lawsuits, 102-104, 118
Leases, 254-255, 256-257
Leave, employee, 515
Legal aid, 118
Leverage, financial, 387
Liability
    doctrine of strict, 101
    insuring against, 407, 414-415, 429
    measuring, 303-304, 306
    product-injury, 102-104
Liberal-reform belief system, 147
Licenses
    professional, 132-133
    state boards of, 113
Life cycle, family, 67
    and housing, 243-244
    and insurance, 440-441
    and investments, 400-401
Lifestyles, changing, 5-6
Liquidity, 336, 373, 374
Loans
    automobile, 360-361
    consumer, 348, 349, 352-355
    against insurance, 456-457
    as liability, 304, 306
    mortgage, 356-360
Location, as criterion for housing,
    240-243

Locks, door, 251
Loopholes, tax, 530-531

M

Magazine Index, The, 53-54
Magazines, and consumer infor-
    mation, 52-53. *See also* Individ-
    ual titles
Magnuson-Moss Warranty—
    Federal Trade Commission Im-
    provement Act of 1975, 77, 101
Mail-order sales, 84, 95
Major Appliance Consumer Action
    Panel, 114, 281
Malpractice suits, and insurance, 487
Management, financial, 291-298
    problems with, 306-307
Managerial belief system, 146-147
Manufacturers, and consumers, 100,
    146
Margin accounts, 387
Market
    and consumer issues, 129, 133, 141
    informationally perfect, 88-91
    segment, new product, 3
    stock, over-the-counter, 384
Marketability of investments, 374, 398
Marketing concept, 146
Marriage
    and credit, 347, 348-349
    and financial problems, 307
Maslow, Abraham, 18
MasterCard, 349, 361, 364
Matrix, decision, 30-31
Maturity, of bonds, 376
Media, popular, 149
    and consumer complaints, 113-114
    and consumer information, 8, 40,
        51-54
Mediation, 108
Medicaid, 491
Medical insurance, major, 478-479
Medical payments, insurance for, 415-
    416, 430
Medicare, 479-480, 491, 492, 500
Menu, quality of, 197
Merchantability, warranty of, 99, 100
Microclimate, housing, 243
Minors, and contract law, 98
Misrings, 86-88
Misuse, product, and consumer
    claims, 103